CW01540056

1 MONTH OF
FREE
READING

at

www.ForgottenBooks.com

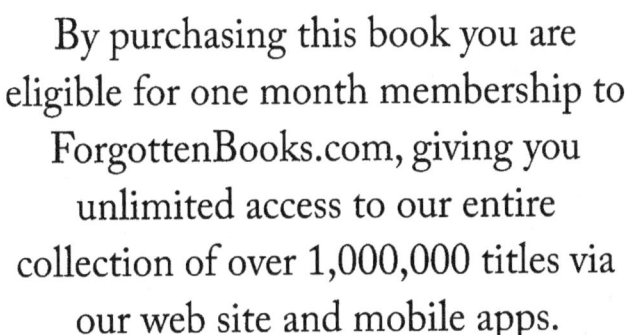

By purchasing this book you are eligible for one month membership to ForgottenBooks.com, giving you unlimited access to our entire collection of over 1,000,000 titles via our web site and mobile apps.

To claim your free month visit: www.forgottenbooks.com/free794547

ISBN 978-0-483-81961-0
PIBN 10794547

Forgotten Books is a registered trademark of FB &c Ltd.
Copyright © 2018 FB &c Ltd.
FB &c Ltd, Dalton House, 60 Windsor Avenue, London, SW19 2RR.
Company number 08720141. Registered in England and Wales.

For support please visit www.forgottenbooks.com

THE

METHODIST REVIEW.

(BIMONTHLY.)

VOLUME LXXXVI.—FIFTH SERIES, VOLUME XX.

WILLIAM V. KELLEY, D.D., Editor.

—————————•·•——————————

NEW YORK: EATON & MAINS.
CINCINNATI: JENNINGS & GRAHAM.

CONTENTS OF THE VOLUME.

JANUARY—FEBRUARY.

MARCH—APRIL.

MAY—JUNE.

JULY—AUGUST.

SEPTEMBER—OCTOBER.

NOVEMBER—DECEMBER.

VOL. LXXXVI, No. 1. | JANUARY--FEBRUARY, 1904. | FIFTH SERIES, VOL. XX
WHOLE No. 462.

METHODIST REVIEW

(BIMONTHLY)

WILLIAM V. KELLEY, L.H.D., Editor

CONTENTS

R.S. Foster

METHODIST REVIEW.

JANUARY, 1904.

Art. I.—BISHOP RANDOLPH S. FOSTER.

In the list of men admitted on trial in the Ohio Annual Conference of 1837 we find the name of Randolph S. Foster. Tradition says that he had already distinguished himself, while a sophomore in Augusta College, as a young preacher of remarkable power. He was full of zeal, very popular in the region round about, extolled by admiring friends, and quite too easily persuaded to leave the college and seek admission into the Annual Conference. Fifty-eight years later, in the sublime and solemn hour of relinquishing his effective ministry, he referred to his first Annual Conference, and said of the first bishop he had ever seen: "I thought of him as a sort of demigod. I felt the impression, when he walked into the room, as if some great being had come from another sphere; and there are a great many people who think of bishops that way now. If they knew them as well as I do they would change their minds. When my name was called—a stripling of seventeen years—I had an inexperienced presiding elder to represent me, and he made this remarkably stupid representation: 'Mr. Bishop, this is a splendid young man.' But David Young, one of the old stagers of the West, arose. He had been presiding elder a long time, and he stretched out his finger and said: 'Mr. Bishop, you have never been in the West before; we call potatoes splendid out here!'" Little did any in that Conference then foresee the truly splendid career of that young man for sixty years thereafter, or imagine that his light would shine

1

more and more until it eclipsed the radiance of many a brilliant eastern star.

EARLY MINISTRY.

The territory of the Ohio Conference in 1837 extended far into Virginia, and young Foster's first appointment was that of junior preacher on the Charleston Circuit, with John G. Bruce as preacher in charge, and Elijah H. Field as his presiding elder. He was changed the next year and sent as junior preacher to the Chester Circuit. In September, 1839, he was admitted into full connection in the Conference, ordained deacon, and appointed to the West Union Circuit, in the Chillicothe District, in Ohio, with John W. Clark as preacher in charge. In the following July he was married to Miss Sarah A. Miley, of Cincinnati, the ceremony being performed by the Rev. W. H. Raper, one of the Methodist pastors of that city. At the next Conference he was stationed at Hillsboro, with William Ellsworth as his senior. It was not until he had traveled four years, and had been ordained elder, that he was made sole preacher in charge, at Portsmouth. Here, however, he remained but one year, when he was changed again to the Hillsboro station, and at the next Conference removed to the Ninth Street Church in Cincinnati. In 1844 he was sent to Lancaster, on the Columbus District, the first appointment in his ministry at which he continued two years in succession. The next two years he was at Springfield, on the Urbana District, and in 1848 and 1849 at Wesley Chapel, Cincinnati, his last appointment in the Ohio Conference.

These thirteen years of his early ministry were a most important period in the life of this young servant of God. They were the preparation and apprenticeship of a great lifework. His power as a preacher grew and strengthened, and his reading and study went far to make up whatever loss he sustained by the ill-advised interruption of his college course. We know not what a full course at Augusta College, Kentucky, might have done for this young man of exceptional capabilities. Perhaps certain qualities of his later voluminous writings which have met adverse criticism would never have appeared had he been more perfectly trained during the plastic years that come before one reaches his twentieth birth-

day. One thing, however, we do know, that, in his later life, he
lost no opportunity to condemn the error of dissuading young men
from the early scholastic discipline which no subsequent labor can
ever fully supply. His colleague in office and his lifelong friend,
Bishop Merrill, writes on this matter as follows: "While no one
can know the extra labor which his early advent into the ministry
caused him, it may be fairly assumed, from experiences of others,
that he felt he was handicapped for years through the unwisdom
of devoted friends who urged him into the Conference while yet
immature in years as well as limited in scholastic training.
Through similar influences," he adds, "my own early ministry
was hampered, and needless burdens, both of work and anxiety,
were borne for many years. Little do our presiding elders realize
the full significance of their mistake, when they insist upon taking
a young man out of school to fill some temporary vacancy, which
would better go unsupplied than to mar the lifetime work of one
whom God has called to make the best possible use of his ministry."

In the rough hill-country of western Virginia our young
itinerant met his full share of the hardships of a Methodist
preacher of that early time. There were long and hard rides, continuous preaching in private houses, barns, public halls, and in the
open grove, poor accommodations and frequent perilous exposure.
But these vigorous exercises and extensive travel had their various
compensations. There was large opportunity for communion with
nature in her varied forms of beauty, and for minute acquaintance
with men and things. And manifold were the blessings of the
young itinerant who enjoyed the confidence and sympathy of an
experienced senior colleague. The first four years of his ministry
Foster was junior preacher, and he was wont to speak in all his
later years with the greatest affection of those elder men of God
who counseled and directed him in his first circuits. The old
itinerant system afforded fine opportunities for a gifted preacher
to magnify his office. On some circuits he could repeat the same
sermon a dozen times in succession without much probability of
its being twice heard by any one person.

Foster's love of nature was absorbing, and his eye and ear
were open to the visions of grandeur and beauty, and to the un-

written music of the world. These were continually speaking to him of the unseen and eternal. He saw God in all, through all, over all. He had his hours of mystic reverie, when "outward forms and inward thoughts teemed with assurances of immortality." In 1878, in one of his Chautauqua lectures on things "beyond the grave," he made a touching allusion to his early days as the memory of them had been awakened one morning by the cooing of a dove: "It came borne on the morning air, and as I listened to its swell it choked me, almost broke my heart; and in a moment I saw a dove on a broken limb of a walnut tree standing by an old crooked lane, down by a worm fence; and I saw its bosom heaving as if its heart would break. I gazed at it. I was a little boy, standing on the yard-fence of my father's house. More than fifty years had elapsed since that event, but it stood out before me that morning as if it had been but yesterday. I lived life over again. I went in and saw my mother, beautiful as she was in her young womanhood. She put her hands on my head, kissed me, and soothed my childish sorrow. I bowed at her knee and recited my infant prayers again. Then came early school days, and old play-mates gathered about me, and old loves and joys were lived over. Creeks, hills, roads, lanes, fields, and woods familiar to childhood looked at me with their old familiar look, each alive and palpitating with precious memories. My cheeks were bedewed with tears, as the thrilling pictures with such strange vividness passed before me. Voices of the long since dead sounded on that still morning air; I seemed to hear them calling over the gulf of half a hundred years, as they greeted me in that long ago. Then I was a young man. My college days were past. The wide world was before me. With anxious and trembling expectation I was looking into the future, all uncertain of what might be its sorrows or successes. My horse was at the gate, my father's blessing sounded in my ears afresh, my mother's tearful farewell was repeated. I hastily mounted my horse and rode away."

In spite of his constant travel and preaching this young itinerant found time for extensive reading, and for continuous and accurate study of what he read. His first published work, written before he was twenty-nine, shows his familiarity with such solid

standards as Calvin's *Institutes*, Dwight's *Theology*, Dick's *Theology*, Ridgley's *Body of Divinity*, and the writings of Jonathan Edwards, to say nothing of the standard works of Arminian authors, and the books required to be studied and read in the Conference course. He began early to collect, and held in high esteem through life, such series of works as the Bridgewater Treatises, the Bampton Lectures, the Hulsean Lectures, and the leading theological reviews. He seems never to have acquired much taste or proficiency in philological and exegetical research, but inclined rather to metaphysical and philosophical discussions, and in his early ministry gave courses of lectures on questions of cosmology, geology, and the origin of life.

Pastor in New York.

During the two years of his work at Wesley Chapel, Cincinnati, he became widely famous as a controversialist in defending the doctrines of Arminian Methodism against the attack of a Presbyterian clergyman of that city. He had already acquired an enviable reputation as a preacher; his letters on Calvinism proved him to be also an accomplished theologian. At the New York Conference of 1850 the Mulberry Street Church, New York city, was left to be supplied, and in September of that year R. S. Foster, then thirty years of age, was transferred to fill the vacancy. Excepting the three years he served as president of the Northwestern University, he continued as a pastor in and about New York until 1868, when he was elected professor of systematic theology in the Drew Theological Seminary. It is interesting to note that he spent two years at Mulberry Street, two at Greene Street, two at Pacific Street in Brooklyn, in the New York East Conference, then again in the New York Conference one year at Trinity, two at Washington Square, one at Sing Sing, three at Eighteenth Street, and two again at Washington Square. During these fifteen years as a pastor in the great metropolis he rose more and more into prominence as a leader among his brethren. He was everywhere recognized as a commanding personality, a man of rich and ripe experience and of many warm and notable friendships. His praise was in all the churches. In the homes of his people ho

was revered and loved. His natural dignity of manner, his genuine urbanity, the purity of his life and conversation, the depth and fervor of his religious experience, all combined to make him distinguished among a thousand. His public prayers were simple, fervid, direct, and at times, when he became deeply moved, his language took on a poetic diction of strange power, carrying all hearts into an element of heavenly flame. Such prayers were memorable as inspired benedictions to many a weary and heavy-laden soul.

During these same years of his New York pastorate his reputation as a theologian and writer added peculiar weight to all he said or did. The Methodist preachers' meetings, held in the early time at 200 Mulberry Street, were often scenes of exciting debate, and Dr. Foster generally appeared in them to great advantage. Subjects involving Christian doctrine, history, philosophy, politics, ethics, and ecclesiastical polity were discussed, sometimes through a series of meetings running on for weeks together. One such occurred in the autumn of 1861, when the moral status of infants and the doctrine of inherited depravity found noteworthy exposition at the hands of R. S. Foster, Daniel Curry, John Miley, John P. Durbin, and Nathan Bangs, then in the eighty-fourth and last year of his life. Another memorable debate took place in 1867 on the best methods for promoting the experience of perfect love, and in this both 'Foster and Curry made memorable addresses. In all such discussions no man commanded greater attention and respect than the subject of this sketch. He was in great demand also for preaching on occasions of note. He was abundant in labors and honors at the dedication of churches, at Conference anniversaries, at college commencements, and at the commemoration of notable events. He was one of the speakers at the reunion service of the New York and the New York East Conferences in the spring of 1868, at St. Paul's Church on Fourth Avenue. Bishops Janes and Clark, Marvin Richardson, Laban Clark, Heman Bangs, David Buck, L. S. Weed, Daniel Curry, and Henry Boehm were also among the speakers that day, and many a touching incident was witnessed or recalled, none more impressive, perhaps, than when Dr. Foster made tender personal allusion to

the death or his eldest daughter, which had occurred but a few
weeks before. His voice trembled with a magnetic pathos as he
spoke of his recent walking so closely to the border of the heavenly
places that he seemed to hear footfalls from within the veil.

THE EDUCATOR.

His three years at Evanston and four at the Drew Seminary
gave Dr. Foster no small practical experience in the work of
higher education. His work at the Northwestern University, however, came at a time when the resources of that institution were
quite insufficient to meet all that its founders and patrons aimed
to accomplish, and the pressing need of funds, together with details
of organization and administration, made him feel that many toilsome years must pass before much fruit could possibly appear in
that field. But those three years were full of delightful labors.
His associations with his colleagues in the faculties were of the
most pleasant character. Both at Evanston and at Madison he
displayed the fine tact to govern without seeming to do so and
without any self-assumptions. He was deferential to the feelings
of those about him. His personal presence was a power in the community. The students and the general public felt the charm of
his superior mind. His talks in the chapel service and on other
like occasions were remembered for years, and there are those now
living who continue to speak of them as full of grace and truth.
His sermons and public addresses commanded remarkable attention and magnified his influence as an educator. His professorship
and presidency at Drew Seminary were more congenial to his
personal taste than the presidency of Northwestern. In the chair
of systematic theology he felt himself perfectly at home, and he
declared many a time that no years of his life were more full of
comfort and satisfaction to himself in the way of work than those
at the theological school. His interest in young men preparing for
the ministry of the Gospel, and his own abundant labors in the
pastorate for nearly thirty years, were no inconsiderable part of
his fitness for this position. Here, too, the peculiar cast of his
mind, his love for theological research, and his personal magnetism
among associates and friends found an inviting field.

BISHOP.

Long before the General Conference of 1872 Dr. Foster had been often mentioned as a suitable man for the episcopal office, but he himself never showed desire or inclination for that position in the Church. His tastes were better satisfied with his professorship at Drew, and he was quite pronounced in his declaration to friends that he preferred the theological chair to the wearying cares of the episcopal office. And possibly his well-known feelings on the subject would have been controlling but for a wonderful prayer which he offered in the Conference the morning of the day set for the election of bishops. A conviction seemed to settle on the minds of the Conference that the pure and lofty spirit who could openly think and speak like that before his God was of all men proper to be intrusted with the highest office in the gift of his brethren. He was elected on the first ballot, and was made to believe, not without some persuasion, that such an election was a manifest call of God to the work.

In this high office and work he spent the last twenty-four years of his effective ministry. The year before this election he was called to part with the wife of his youth and the faithful companion of all his varied intervening years. He entered upon his new work under the spell of a recent bereavement, of tender feeling, and the inspiration of new vows. His duties led him, first and last, to all the Conferences, and to all our mission fields, from Norway .to Italy, through Bulgaria, through Palestine to India, and China, and Japan; to South America and to Mexico. In the earlier part of his episcopal administration he was at times criticised for alleged harshness, and for occasional arbitrary exercise of power. He was known to tell a body of ministers that many of them could never have obtained in other callings or in other kinds of work the social standing and comfort of even the poorest appointments in his power to give them. But whatever these occasional utterances may have been, no one who knew the real spirit of the man and his unswerving purpose to do right, could cherish toward him any bitter feeling. For in the cabinet and out of it he showed the most painstaking care to do his best for every man and for every appointment. His heart overflowed with

tender affection for his brethren. He was incapable of cherishing ill will toward any man. If at times he seemed arbitrary, or ventured upon some line of administration without sufficiently heeding the judgment of others, it was because of deep conviction that his course was one that demanded positive action and a fearless boldness to take upon himself all personal risk of results.

Bishop Foster's personal presence contributed not a little to the efficiency of his episcopal career. How imposing his tall, commanding form! How neat and careful in his dress, dignified in his manner, graceful in his movement! When he stood up before a Conference, or before any assembly, all eyes would turn instinctively to the manly face, the piercing eye, the full head of hair, and the audience would listen expectantly and gaze admiringly, conscious that they were in the presence of a powerful king of men. His manner and speech before the General Conference of 1896, on the occasion of his withdrawal from effective relations, presented a spectacle of saintly grace and moral sublimity never elsewhere seen and never to be forgotten by those who witnessed it. In a sweet and beautiful spirit he accepted the judgment of his brethren, and returned to his home in Boston thanking God for the greater opportunity thus afforded him for completing the literary tasks on which he had toiled for many years.

AUTHOR.

Bishop Foster was a voluminous writer. That which gave him his first distinction as a theologian was a volume entitled *Objections to Calvinism,* published while he was pastor of Wesley Chapel in Cincinnati. The substance of the book first appeared in the *Western Christian Advocate* as a series of letters addressed to Dr. N. L. Rice, a Presbyterian divine and famous controversialist, who bitterly assailed the doctrines of the Methodist Church. At the solicitation of many readers the letters were put in book form and supplied with an appendix in which Dr. Rice's replies were reviewed and effectively answered. Judged by its intrinsic merit as a polemic, and considering the end accomplished by its publication, it may be doubted whether the author ever in any of his later writings surpassed this work of his youth. The subjects

discussed are now comparatively obsolete, but they were burning questions sixty years ago. The early Methodist preachers found the stern tenets of eternal decrees, election, reprobation, effectual calling, and final perseverance serious obstacles in the way of their evangelical ministry. Whitefield and Wesley separated because of the declaration of the latter that his preachers had "leaned too much toward Calvinism." Wesley's sermon on "Free Grace," Fletcher's *Checks to Antinomianism,* Watson's *Institutes,* and Wilbur Fisk's contributions to the Calvinistic controversy, and other Arminian publications, were widely circulated among the Methodist preachers of 1849, and furnished them with strong weapons to resist the persistent attacks of their Calvinistic opponents. It is enough to say that Foster's book against Calvinism is worthy to be placed among the very ablest Arminian contributions to that literature.

The next book to appear from his pen was on the *Nature and Blessedness of Christian Purity,* which was issued in 1851, with an introduction by Bishop Janes. Its main subject-matter was that of a series of sermons given in the Mulberry Street Church, and it has probably been more widely read than any other of his books. It has been recognized as a standard exposition of the privilege and possibilities of Christian believers in their spiritual attainments in this life, and it is a notable fact that it has met general acceptance among all parties and writers in the Methodist Church who are known to differ on sundry questions relating to the doctrine of sanctification. The revised edition of 1869 introduced numerous minor changes, and adopted the title of *Christian Purity; or, The Heritage of Faith;* but in his preface the author says: "It is a pleasant reflection that twenty years of added experience and extended research have not materially changed the views at first expressed. . . . The first writing was undertaken under the inspiration and conducted during the evolution of an exalted experience, and amid the glow of intense zeal. The present writing is the fruit of calm study and mature deliberate judgment."

Among the "Ingham Lectures" delivered at the Ohio Wesleyan University in 1872, on "The Evidences of Natural and Revealed Religion," are three by Dr. R. S. Foster, then president of

the Drew Theological Seminary. These lectures discuss (1) "Personal Cause;" (2) the "Origin of Life: an Examination of Huxley," and (3) "Origin of Species: an Examination of Darwinism." They were all reproduced in substance in his later volume on *Theism*. Another course of lectures at the same university, given "on the Merrick foundation," treats the "Philosophy of Christian Experience," and was subsequently repeated before the Garrett Biblical Institute. These lectures were prepared, he told us, while his "mind was already tense with uncompleted investigations," and he accepted it as a providential relief to turn aside a while and busy himself with the simplest experimental facts and verities of Christianity. Among his minor publications we mention also his *Centenary Thoughts for Pew and Pulpit* and the *Union of Episcopal Methodisms*.

In 1879 he published a little volume entitled *Beyond the Grave: being Three Lectures before Chautauqua Assembly in 1878*. If the treatise on *Christian Purity* has been more widely read and more generally accepted than his other writings, this one, on the subject of man's spiritual nature and immortal existence, has probably been more extensively criticised than any other. He essayed in these lectures to subject the questions of "life beyond the grave" to the processes of reason, examine them in the light of all related facts, and thus secure, as he believed, "the best and most permanent results." No one can fairly find fault with such a method of procedure, and surely no man or company of men can do more than study a subject "in the light of all the facts bearing upon it which lie within the circle of our intelligence." The telling point of some of the adverse criticism upon Bishop Foster's lectures was the charge that he had not fully or clearly dealt with some important relevant facts bearing on the subject as it is presented in the New Testament, nor had he given any adequate interpretation to the scriptural teaching. But the book as a whole was warmly welcomed and has been widely read. Its publication has shown that in the Methodist Episcopal Church "we think and let think." Especially should this be conceded on doctrines of eschatology. So long as one maintains the great facts of a future life, the resurrection of the dead, the coming of Christ

in his kingdom and glory, and judgment after death, we need not and cannot safely insist on a consensus of opinion as to questions of times and seasons and mode.

But the *opus magnum* of Bishop Foster's literary toil is the sumptuous series of octavos which he entitled "Studies in Theology." It was the ambition and persistent purpose of the last fifty years of his life to produce a thorough and comprehensive discussion of the most difficult and most fundamental problems of theological science. His plan contemplated eleven volumes, of which six have been published. He seemed always conscious that he was writing for a "disturbed and earnestly inquisitive age." His sense of personal responsibility was deep with the conviction that he was called to treat questions the most difficult and obscure, the great theological issues of the centuries. "They are perplexing problems," he tells us, "with which we have long wrestled as earnestly as ever ancient athlete wrestled for the victor's wreath. They are the subjects with which the men of the coming age will continue to wrestle. The final result involves the deepest interests of the world." He believed that theology is a progressive science; not that its sources or its principles change, but because the human mind is progressive, and must, with each new period of added light, revise the opinions of the former time. Hence he chose for this series of volumes the running title of "Studies in Theology," rather than a more pretentious name, modestly maintaining that the topics under his discussion are proper subjects of rational inquiry, and must not be handled in a dogmatic tone, as if they were above all contradiction. In his opening volume (p. 6) he expressed his purpose to confine the range of his discussions to "fundamental questions and points which are in dispute between earnest thinkers, and which, from their intrinsic obscurity, need a somewhat more scientific statement, and in some cases a modified expression—the deepest questions which underlie the whole structure of religious and philosophical thought, and, this side of these, questions touching the grounds and some of the more accurate meanings and interpretations of Christian faith."

The first volume of this remarkable series appeared in 1889, and, as its title, *Prolegomena*, implies, investigates the funda-

mental principles and presuppositions which are to govern all
scientific inquiry. We regard this initial volume as intrinsically
the most valuable of the six; for what is here written on the true
spirit of inquiry, the distinctions between idea and concept, knowledge and belief, the conditions of knowledge and the function of
reason, is worthy of long and patient study. It is especially needful to those who go about assuming that all things in theology are
settled, and that modern scientific criticism is a bane. The following paragraph, from page 10, is a most wholesome word of counsel
for all who have a mind to think: "Nothing could be more fatal
to the claims of religion than an attempt to shelter them behind
mere tradition or mere authority, however high or venerable, when
either its facts or the reasonableness of its doctrines are called in
question. We need to keep forever in mind that we can arrogate
to ourselves personally only the position of equals in any controversy. We must not fall into the mistake of supposing that the
divine authority of our sacred books is established merely by our
affirmation or belief of it, or that any such authority attaches to
us or our opinions. This is a common fallacy which we must be
careful to avoid. We need to keep constantly in recollection that
our creed-formularies are only human, and, therefore, always possibly imperfect. However they may contain essential truth, we
cannot assume safely that they will admit of no change. The
fathers were not infallible. There has been advance. There is
room for improvement. There will be modifications. More and
more every increment of Christian teaching will be searched. We
must have the wisdom to discern between the shell and the kernel,
and to avoid the mistake of periling the latter by attempting to
give prominence to the former. The past is full of suggestions on
this line which we may profitably study."

The second volume of the series deals with Theism, and the
fifth with the nature and attributes of God; and the two might
profitably have been condensed into one volume. A large proportion of each is filled with quotations from other writers, and the
entire discussion, while comprehensive and useful, adds scarcely
anything of real value to the literature of the subject. The same
may be fairly said of the treatise on *The Supernatural Book*, a

title not happily chosen or fitting for a book claiming, as this does, to be a comprehensive work on the "Evidences of Christianity." The Bible and Christianity are not synonymous or interchangeable terms, and the contents of the volume show no familiarity with the issues of recent discussions in several departments of biblical research. Over one fourth of the book is given to extracts from writers of three generations ago, whose works are virtually obsolete in the learned world to-day.

The volume on *Creation: God in Time and Space* presents the matured thoughts of the author on a range of topics which engaged his attention for more than half his lifetime. While a pastor in New York, and while at Evanston and at Madison, he would often lecture on the spaces of the universe, the immensity of the Creator's works, the structure of the solar system, the stellar infinitudes beyond, the origin of life and of man, and the progress traceable from inorganic to organic substance and on through sentient to spiritual life. His search was to find as far as possible the "method of the Eternal Cause." The outcome of all his inquiry is that the universe is God's eternal possession. He has been working in it hitherto, and he will work on. "He has an end in view. He will not fail to reach it. The progress will be, as it has been, from glory to glory. Each succeeding generation here standing on the shoulders of its predecessor, and entering into its wealth of inheritances, will advance to improved conditions, and will carry forward an increasingly benignant civilization, made more beautiful by improved knowledge and increase of wealth, and toned and tempered by the presence and power of a divine religion, until the horrors of heathenism and ignorance and wickedness will be driven away, and the earth itself will be radiant and happy" (p. 365).

The last volume published appeared in 1899, just fifty years after the issue of the author's first book, and it is worthy of note that its subject-matter in great part involves not a few of the main points discussed in the earlier production. In this last treatise he inquires into the original state of man, the nature of sin and guilt, and the meaning and momentous significance of the term "punishment." His discussion includes a clear statement of the facts of

free and responsible volition as against all forms of necessitarian-
ism. But in this final volume we trace some signs of a trembling
hand and the infirmities of age. The intellect that deals so vigorously with the sophisms of Dr. Rice is less active here, but there
remains conspicuous the calm confidence of knowledge more fully
ripened, and of faith that abides immovably. And we may say of
the contents of all these elaborate tomes, and of all his other publications, that they are a magnificent witness of the Gospel
according to Randolph S. Foster—the Gospel which he preached
for more than sixty years, preached in love and in power, in the
Holy Spirit and in much assurance, and of which Gospel he
needeth not to be ashamed in the presence of the great God and
our Saviour Jesus Christ.

PREACHER.

The sentiments last expressed prepare the way for saying
that, after all, it is as a preacher of the Gospel that Randolph
S. Foster found his highest place and achieved his noblest fame.
His power as an anointed herald of heavenly truths was above all
that can be said of his work as an author, an educator, or a bishop
in the Church of God. He was great in all these forms of labor,
but his rare and radiant personality shone in its supreme glory
when he stood forth as an inspired prophet of the Highest, with
impassioned heart and soul overflowing with a sense of the gravity
and the vastness of the revelations given him to proclaim. For he
had truly seen the burning bush and heard therefrom the voice
divine. He knew what it is to be high up in the mount of heavenly
vision. It is not extravagant to say that he partook of the spirit
and power of Elijah, the fervor of Isaiah, the mystic depth of
John, and the breadth and dialectic of Paul, whose chapter on
Love was his choice scripture. And when all these gifts were
aglow with the "Power from on high," how majestic his utterance,
how overwhelming his message!

All the great preachers who have been distinguished for extraordinary power with God and with men seem to have possessed a large element of mysticism in their religious life. Like
the child Samuel they hear the voice of the Lord calling them in
the silence of the night, and giving them a message adapted to

make the ears of them that hear it tingle. Or they have impressive visions, like Isaiah, when he saw the seraph fly and touch
his lips with a live coal from Jehovah's altar. Paul also had his
"visions and revelations of the Lord," and when, after his conversion, he "went away into Arabia," we may think of him as
"coming to the mountain of God, even to Horeb," where Moses
saw the burning bush, and Elijah heard the "still small voice."
Perhaps it was then and there that the apostle to the Gentiles was
caught up to the third heaven and heard the words unspeakable.
Time and time again did Bishop Foster evince, in preaching or
in prayer, the mystic depths of such possibilities of heavenly
vision. He walked and talked with God as one familiar with "the
secret place of the Most High."

One might analyze his power as a preacher by noting a variety
of elements. The impressiveness of his personal presence, of
which we have already spoken, was in itself an element of strength.
With intellectual qualities of a high order he combined deep emo-
tionality. He was gifted with a sensitive and poetic temperament,
and a powerful imaginative faculty. His dialectic skill was often
reinforced with telling pictures, so that his hearers were made to
see his thoughts in living forms. The saintly character of the
preacher was also a recognized force in his public ministrations.
The man behind the sermon is always the great potential magnet;
but in his case it was not the man only, but the saint, the theologian, the philosopher, the father, brother, friend. He had a
genius for reasoning, and an absorbing passion for the study of
the deep things of God. He was eloquent in form, and face, and
eye, and thought, and tone. His profound emotion and glowing
imagination kindled a fire in other hearts, and his hearers became
enraptured with the wisdom and power of his thoughts.

The subject-matter of his sermons was characteristically of
a high order. He chose great themes. Even in speaking to a
company of children he would discourse on heaven, and eternal
judgment, and the holiness of God; and he possessed the wisdom
and tact to hold both the young and the old spellbound with his
living pictures of spiritual verities. His own estimate of what a
preacher is under holiest vows to proclaim may be inferred from

his scathing rebuke of the dilettanteism which has disgraced some modern pulpits. In his sermon before the Centennial Conference in Baltimore, in December, 1884, he said, along with many other burning words: "Let the pulpit flame with thought, with earnest Gospel messages, and other truths which illustrate and give force to its teachings. Let the preacher feel the gravity of his great commission, and let him expound the doctrines of faith as if he believed them and felt them. . . . The man who has the effrontery to stand in a Christian pulpit in the nineteenth century, ignorant of its thought and hunger, unconscious of the forces around him, without a sense of the gravity of the situation, to waste the time and abuse the patience of a long-suffering congregation in trashy sentimentalism, or in pompous and hollow rodomontade, deserves to be whipped from the temple as a harlequin. A world swinging in darkness; millions of men perishing for the light of life; continents with signals at half-mast; the cry of distress and despair coming from dying men and women; sin rampant, the wild beast of nameless sin ravening and destroying; death busy mowing down thousands at a swath; eternity in the prospect; everything to stir men with concern, and a puppet in the pulpit of God, with shallow placidity reciting the merest mimicry of thought—a minister of Jesus, the Man of sorrow, sent to save souls; to stand as his ambassador; to tell the pathetic story of his love—a minister of Jesus, able to preach without feeling, without passion, without desire, and then to look into the faces of his fellow-men!"

There are those yet living who remember the annual sermon preached before the New York Conference at Newburgh in 1864 on "Sin and Redemption." Two days thereafter Davis W. Clark offered, and the Conference unanimously adopted, the following resolution: "That the thanks of this Conference are due and are hereby tendered to Rev. R. S. Foster, D.D., for the very able discourse delivered before this body on the first evening of its session; and that a copy of the same be solicited for publication under the direction of the author." Dr. Foster thereupon expressed his keen appreciation of their action, but informed his brethren that the discourse was only an excerpt from a large theological treatise

2

on which he was engaged, and which he expected in due time to publish. One striking passage in that sermon the reader may find on page 245 of the volume on *Sin,* the last one published in the author's "Studies in Theology." We cite a portion of it as a brief specimen of the preacher's characteristic thought and style. Having contrasted the conditions of man under law and under grace, in the first Adam as in paradise, and in the second through redemption, he declared with no little emotion:

"It may be heresy, but for myself, deeply conscious as I am of the plague of a nature utterly sinful in its tendencies, I would rather be in the second head than in the first; rather take my chances with Christ than with the unfallen Adam; rather be born a fallen soul, in a fallen world, under the redemption of Jesus, with all sorrow and suffering brimming my cup of earthly life, than be born of Eve amid the bloom of paradise, with angel brothers around me, under the inevitable exposures and terrible dangers of an economy of unappeasable law; rather take the certainties of sin, with the possibilities of pardon and recovery with a Saviour such as Jesus, than the hopes of fallible immaculateness without a redeemer. If others would choose Adam, I would choose Christ. I am content to enter a fallen world through the gate of suffering if I may feel enfolding me the arms of the pitying, omnipotent Son of Mary, rather than an unfallen world, with the exigencies and perils of fallibility without a rescuer. If others would venture, of choice, on an eternity whose doom hangs in the balance of a single chance under the primeval law, I would cling to the Seed of the woman, who saves to the uttermost of a thousand sins and falls."

These fragments must suffice for this imperfect sketch. The great preacher has ceased from his labors and gone "beyond the grave" to mingle with "the spirits of just men made perfect," and to know what it is to be there. He has left an imperishable heritage of good to all who knew him and heard him preach, and to the thousands who read the printed products of his thought. I cannot better close this paper than by citing the tribute of a fair young spirit who passed into the heavens more than forty years ago, but who felt, when hearing this man preach, that he belonged

to the seraphic natures that stand close by the throne of God. In the diary of Mary E. Willard, which was edited after its author's death by her elder sister Frances, and entitled *Nineteen Beautiful Years,* we find, under date of April 29, 1860, a reference to Dr. Foster's last sermon in Evanston before retiring from the presideney of Northwestern University: "As Dr. F. stood before the large audience—for every seat and even the aisles were full—he looked sad, though very calm. But when, at the close of the discourse, he addressed the students of the university his feelings overcame him. He stopped and covered his face. We all wept together in silence. I seldom cry, but then I could not help it. As Dr. Foster stood before us saying farewell, I thought,

> 'If I should ever win that home in heaven,
> For whose sweet rest I humbly hope and pray,
> In the great company of the forgiven,'

among the radiant faces close by God's throne, I should see that of this great, good man, whom 'none know but to love, and none name but to praise.' "

Milton S. Terry

Art. II.—WESLEY'S RELIGIOUS EXPERIENCE.

It is probable that the things most characteristic of Methodism are to be found in the earliest years of its history, in the work, the plans, and especially in the experience of its earliest representatives. Methodism does not differ in this respect from other great revivals, whether of the national or of the religious life. One may well go to Adams, Jefferson, Washington, and Hamilton for an exposition of the principles which determine our national life. No one has seen the distinctive doctrines of the Reformation more clearly that did Luther. The freshness of their experience, the vividness of their spiritual perceptions, and the ingenuousness of their utterances, make the testimony of the apostles the source of final authority on Christ and Christianity. It is proposed to discuss in this paper the most distinctive thing in early Methodism, which was John Wesley's religious experience; to discover the way in which he was led to this experience, which was by his intercourse with the Moravians, and to raise the question whether we have not lost, or at least obscured, Wesley's point of view. Early Methodism developed novel methods. The class meeting was new, and field preaching was so novel that Wesley could not easily reconcile himself to it. Some of the doctrines he preached were thought to be new, but they were as old as the New Testament. The general doctrinal system had been wrought out by James Arminius, that brave old Dutchman, during the period 1576-1609. As student, pastor, and professor he wrought out nearly all of our great principles, but for some reason they lacked carrying power, and after two and a quarter centuries had scarcely made a ripple in the life of the Christian Church. The primary cause of Methodism is to be found neither in its novel methods nor in its system of doctrine. It is to be found in the fire that came down from heaven and "strangely warmed" John Wesley's soul on that memorable twenty-fourth of May, 1738. He put that new experience *first,* and the Methodist Church of our time very much needs to understand his interpretation of that experience.

There are two utterances of Mr. Wesley that lie very close together in the minds of many Methodists. The first is that declaration concerning his spiritual condition which appears in his Journal on Wednesday, the first of February, 1738. He had just landed at Deal. He writes: "It is now two years and almost four months since I left my native country, in order to teach the Georgian Indians the nature of Christianity: but what have I learned myself in the meantime? Why (what I the least of all suspected), that I who went to America to convert others, was never myself converted to God."* The second utterance is his record of the occurrences of May 24, 1738. He says: "In the evening I went very unwillingly to a society in Aldersgate Street, where one was reading Luther's preface to the Epistle to the Romans. About a quarter before nine, while he was describing the change which God works in the heart through faith in Christ, I felt my heart strangely warmed. I felt I did trust in Christ, Christ alone, for salvation; and an assurance was given me that he had taken away my sins, even mine, and saved me from the law of sin and death."† In order to understand Wesley it is important that we should get his language into the context. Only so shall we get its real meaning, and make its inculcation sane and sound in the spiritual life of the Church. Wesley had a religious experience from the cradle. He was taught to say the Lord's Prayer as soon as he could talk. His consistency of conduct was such "that his father admitted him to the communion table when he was only eight years old. And he himself informs us that until he was about the age of ten he had not sinned away that 'washing of the Holy Ghost' which he received in baptism."‡ He had a religious experience through all the years. He gave himself without stint to Christian works. But with all his saintly devotion, it may be asked was he a converted man?

—The context will show us what he thought of the Moravians, and what they thought of him, and will enable us to understand Wesley's view of his own case. On Friday, the seventeenth of October, 1735, John Wesley first made acquaintance with the

---

* *Journal,* first American edition, vol. III, p. 56.   † *Journal,* vol. III, p. 74.
‡ Tyerman, *Life and Times of John Wesley,* vol. i, p. 19.

Moravians. He was about to sail for America, and had been spending Wednesday and Thursday "partly on board and partly on shore." On Friday, having found twenty-six Germans aboard, he began to learn to speak German. On Monday, the twentieth, he speaks of "David Nitschman, bishop of the Germans." On Tuesday, the twenty-first, he writes: "At seven I joined with the Germans in their public service." He could not know the far-reaching influence of the acquaintance he was making with these humble Christians, and it is certain that the Church has never fully appreciated the extent of its obligations to them. We note a sympathetic interest in them from the day when he went on shipboard. The first pages of his Journal are almost entirely given up to an acount of his intercourse with them. He saw in their bearing and conduct evidences of a spiritual calm which was strangely contrasted with the unrest of his own soul. On Sunday, the twenty-fifth, he writes of a terrible storm and makes it the occasion for a comment on the terror of the English passengers, and on that calm confidence of the Germans which enabled them to sing on through the storm. This contrast impressed him deeply. He gives us an account of his interview on the seventh of February with Mr. Spangenberg, and of the searching questions which Mr. Spangenberg asked him as to his knowledge that Jesus Christ had saved him. He speaks of the ceremony of the election and ordination of one of the Moravian bishops: "The great simplicity as well as solemnity of the whole almost made me forget the seventeen hundred years between, and imagine myself in one of those assemblies where form and state were not; but Paul the tentmaker or Peter the fisherman presided; yet with the demonstration of the Spirit and of power."* Having returned from America, Wesley had been in London only four days when he met Peter Böhler. He cannot keep away from the Germans. He writes that by him he was, "on Sunday, the fifth [of March], clearly convinced of unbelief, of the want of that faith whereby alone we are saved." He proposed to give up preaching faith, but was encouraged to continue to preach faith until he had it; and then because he had it he would preach it. He writes: "Accord-

* *Journal*, vol. III, p. 20.

ingly, Monday, 6, I began preaching this new doctrine, though my soul started back from the work. The first person to whom I offered salvation by faith alone was a prisoner under sentence of death."* The judgment which Wesley records against himself upon his return from Georgia must stand as expressing the belief that, during the years immediately preceding that experience which came to him on the twenty-fourth of May, 1738, in Aldersgate Street, he was not a converted man and was not a Christian.

It may further illuminate the subject to ask what Peter Böhler thought of Wesley and of his religious experience during the months of their intercourse in the spring of 1738. About six years ago, while wandering about in a secondhand bookstore in Leipzig, Germany, the writer had the good fortune to find a history of the United Brethren, and in that history a series of letters from Peter Böhler to Count Zinzendorf, in which he gave a report of the work in London. The following translation of extracts from these letters will show the intimacy that existed between Böhler and the Wesleys, and also Böhler's idea of their spiritual condition:

Oxford, March 2, 1738. On the twenty-eighth of February I traveled with the brothers John and Charles Wesley from Oxford to London. The elder, John, is a benevolent man; he perceives that he does not yet rightly know the Saviour, and acknowledges it. He loves us heartily. His brother, with whom you often spoke, a year ago, in London, is very much disturbed in mind, but does not know how he is to set about learning to know the Saviour. Our art of learning to believe on the Saviour is so very easy for the Englishmen that they are unable to reconcile themselves to it. If it were only a little more artful they would the sooner see their way into it.

March 6. On this night Charles Wesley became very ill. At break of day he therefore sent for me, and asked me if I would pray for him; that God would give him patience in his suffering and give him relief. I prayed with him for the healing both of his soul and of his body. He fell asleep, and his sufferings were somewhat relieved. He knows that his suffering, as well as his relief from the same, comes from God. . . .

At night [the ninth] I watched with Charles Wesley, who is yet sick unto death. The next day I met Pastor Gambold there, who wished to administer the holy communion to him. Wesley desired me to assist in the service, and I did so. There were several present. He was much gratified and said, if he died, he would at least come to the Saviour as a hungry and thirsty soul. . . .

* *Journal,* vol. iii, p. 62.

On this night [the thirteenth] I watched again with Charles Wesley, who is not yet out of danger.

On the evening of the sixteenth I took a walk with the elder Wesley, and asked him about his condition. He said: "Often I am very certain, but often very fearful. I can say nothing more than this: if that is true that stands in the Bible, then I am saved." I spoke very particularly concerning this matter, and besought him earnestly to go to the fountain that had been opened, and not to spoil the matter himself. I also spoke with him concerning the condition of souls in this place, and offered many suggestions as to how, as I thought, one might come nearer to them.

March 21. I traveled from Oxford back to London. The elder Wesley gave me six shillings for my journey. . . .

On the fourth of May I heard John Wesley preach. I then understood all, but it was not as I wished. . . .

I took four of my English brethren, and among them Wolf, of whom I have already spoken, in order that they might relate to him how they were led, and how quickly and deeply the Saviour is moved to compassion and to receive the sinner. They related, one after the other, how they had come to this experience; and Mr. Wolf especially, to whom the experience was quite new, spoke very earnestly and powerfully. . . .

John Wesley and those that were with him were astonished at these testimonies. I asked Wesley what he then thought about it. He answered that four examples did not make out the case and could not convince him. I replied saying I would bring eight others who were here in London. After a little time he arose and said, "We will sing the hymn, 'Here lay I myself before Thee down.' " During the singing he frequently wiped the tears from his eyes, and immediately took me alone into his room, and said that he was then convinced of what I had said of faith, and that he would ask for nothing more; that he saw very clearly that as yet it was not his, but asked how he could help himself, and how come to such a faith. He said that he was not a man who had been guilty of the coarser sins, as other people had. I replied that he had sinned enough in that he had not believed on the Saviour; that he was not to allow the Saviour to depart from the door until he had helped him. I was deeply moved to pray with him. I therefore called upon the Crucified One for mercy upon this sinner. He said to me, "If he will have mercy upon me, I will certainly preach of nothing else than of faith."

May 6. Two Presbyterians who had heard me preach yesterday came to see me early this morning. They spoke with me of the righteousness of Jesus Christ and of faith in him. I must translate for them several hymns from our hymn book, which pleased them very much and which treat of this subject. Immediately thereafter I had a very hearty conversation with John Wesley. He told me of the opposition he had yesterday experienced from certain pious pastors whom he had met, and that because he had taken occasion to explain to them what he now understood and wherein he was yet lacking. He is not concerned about the opposition, but asked me what he should do in this respect, whether he should tell the people just how it was with him or not. I replied saying that I could give

him no rule in this matter, but to do whatever the Saviour should teach him to do. Nevertheless I wished very much that he would not put the grace of the Saviour so far away from him, but would believe that it was very near, that the heart of Jesus stood already open to him, and that his grace toward him was very great. He wept bitterly as I spoke with him of this matter, and I was constrained to pray for him. I can say this of him: he is verily a poor sinner who has a broken heart, and who hungers for a righteousness better than that which he has had hitherto, namely, the righteousness of Jesus Christ.

We come back to the question raised in the earlier part of this paper: Was Wesley a converted man during the years in Georgia and the early months of 1738? According to his own judgment as recorded in his Journal, he was not. Peter Böhler, who was his spiritual mentor during these months, also says he was not. But it is an interesting fact that in later years Wesley modified this judgment concerning his spiritual condition. As a matter of fact, these modified opinions appear in parentheses, in the text of the American edition of Wesley's Journal, published in 1850, but are found in a footnote in the eleventh edition, published in 1856, and are not found at all in the fifth edition, published in London in 1775. He modifies the statement made in the Journal upon his return from Georgia, where he says that he had gone to Georgia to convert the Indians but had learned that he himself had never been converted,* by adding, "I am not sure of this." He explains the statement that Böhler had convinced him "of the want of that faith whereby alone we are saved" by adding, "with the full Christian salvation."† On Friday, the nineteenth of May, he writes: "O, let no one deceive us by vain words as if we had already attained this faith! (that is, the proper Christian faith.)" Here again the modifying sentence found in the American edition is a footnote in the eleventh edition, and is wanting in the fifth edition, published in 1775.‡

Why not permit Mr. Wesley to be a little more human? Allow him to correct himself. He showed very little sense in his judgment of women; he had a tendency to asceticism which discloses another comforting weakness; he believed in a kind of magic use of the Bible, deriving guidance and consolation by opening it

---

* *Journal*, vol. iii, p. 56. † *Ibid.*, vol. iii, p. 62. ‡ *Ibid.*, vol. iii, p. 70.

that unless they *knew* their sins were forgiven they were under the
wrath and curse of God, I marvel they did not stone us. The
Methodists, I hope, know better now. We preach assurance, as we
always did, as a common privilege of the children of God, but we
do not enforce it under pain of damnation denounced on all who
enjoy it not."* Judged by the parable of the vine and the
branches, Wesley's later judgment is correct. Jesus taught, "Ye
are my friends, if ye do whatsoever I command you." The question of conversion is a question of the attitude of one's will.
That loyalty of will which expresses itself in obedience is the test
of conversion. Given a loyal will, however the sensibilities are
affected, and the man is converted. Given a disloyal will, be the
emotions what they may, and the man is not converted. He who
has faith enough to say, "Lord, what wilt thou have me to do?"
has the faith that saves. On the other hand, it is to be said that it
is just the experience that came to John Wesley when he felt his
heart "strangely warmed" that gives to the Gospel carrying power.
The psalmist shows real insight when he prays: "Restore unto me
the joy of thy salvation; and uphold me with thy free spirit. Then
will I teach transgressors thy way, and sinners shall be converted
unto thee." The sensibilities furnish the standard of all values.

* Overton's *John Wesley*, p. 84. I have not been able to verify this quotation.

All motives take their rise in feelings and emotions. Extirpate the sensibilities and neither interest nor motive is possible. It is true that wherever there is volition there is also feeling and emotion. It is also true that the intellectual may be so dominant that the emotional activity is reduced to the minimum. The Gospel appeals to this emotional side of our nature as well as to the intellectual. The peril of sin, the hope of heaven, the forgiveness of sin, the doctrine of regeneration, the promise of the Holy Spirit, the Fatherhood of God—these truths appeal to eternal interests, and appeal directly to the emotional nature. Their bearing upon the emotions is as valid as upon the intellectual. The Holy Spirit is as genuinely present in this as in any other spiritual activity, and if we are to carry the forward movement with power into this century these great truths must be so preached as to awaken interest and kindle emotion. We have been emphasizing the intellectual and critical side of our work for a quarter of a century. It has not been in vain. We have a better basis for a genuine reformation than ever before. We now need to convert the whole intellectual content of the Gospel as we hold it to-day into motive and practical work. We need to make prominent Wesley's viewpoint, and preach Jesus preeminently as Saviour. Only so shall we convince men that religion is not something to be endured, but a joy, triumphant and eternal; that it is a possession so good that we must share it with all men.

B. P. Raymond.

Art. III.—THE LITERATURE OF DEVOTION.

To the thoughtful mood not many things are so impressive as to hear the invitation, "Brother Trueheart, will you lead us in prayer?" Here is a captaincy we have given little heed to in our thoughts of leadership, and yet a captaincy so solemn and sublime as to find no equivalent among the renowned leaderships of men. "Lead us in prayer." Adventure for us and ahead of us out toward God—that is what this invitation urges. But we have forgotten this noble and notable meaning, or, what is perhaps more true, we have never remembered it. He who leads in prayer goes out before us in bold and holy quest of God—climbs the high Sinai as Moses did, unafraid and yet all afraid, to find God and order his cause and our cause before him. In no way can one man render another man a wiser and calmer service than in giving direction to his Godward thoughts—to give, so to say, an initial impulse toward our heavenly Father. Good men and women want to walk out into the divine presence, which is the supreme journey taken by a soul. God is not hard to find, truly; and yet to come to him in the mood of love and devout search both facilitates and enriches our meeting. God is "not far from any one of us," but how to hasten to him with immediacy, with laughing and yet sanctified and sedate approach, is an art to be studied as above all arts made much of among the sons of men. And when some man schooled in the direct route to God sets out, I for one will ask him to let me follow in his steps. I will care to be at the interview. For years I have noted this leadership in prayer with personal and pathetic interest, and seldom have failed in finding as I followed in the wake of prayer to have my spirit helped and sanctified. In prayer meeting the philosophy is not ourselves to pray at our own initiative, but to follow the initiative of another, to go his road to God. I love the road prayer takes, and have with uniformity found how helpful the journey was when taken so. Each heart has its method of access. Each has some subtle undertone of pathos springing from a dead past come to life for a flickering moment, some groping of heart after that hand of pity which

assuages the heartache of the world, some sudden leap of faith strong and bold as if an angel made it, some ingenuous appeal half childish and half grand, some vision of old truths which made old truths new as love; and this is included in the ordinary leadership of prayer.

Devotional literature is such reading as puts the heart in the mood of prayer; for to make life a prayer is to be religious. This is a widely different thing from suggesting that life is to do nothing but pray. Such a life might be essentially undevout. He who sees his brother have need and restricts his helping to prayer would be in every regard irreligious. Doing is as devout as praying. Religion consists not in praying a prayer but in being a prayer; and the devout life, whether in cornfield or kitchen, is on its knees. With such devotion God is well pleased. Prayer is to be understood as the setting of the soul toward God as the tide sets for the shore. Anything this side of that is elocution and not prayer, while anything suffused with this spirit is grandly devout and profoundly religious. To induce this mood, then, is the end of devotion. To make the heart pant for God as the stag for the water brooks when wearied with his running is to render the chiefest service. The devout life is the prayer-charged life. When this is the spirit condition there is no trouble in keeping in tune with heaven and in touch with God. When the devotee may whisper to himself in a whisper's whisper, "I am a prayer," then will he work with least friction, sing not knowing that he sings, pray with his fingers and his feet, toil thinking his work a whole holiday of gladness. This is, as we moderns understand, the Christ theory of devotion. They who say prayers through long nights of vigil and fasting and of cold are not the apostolic succession in such fashion as those who know that the prayers God is most concerned with are those which bleed from fingers worn to the bone with toiling for the saving of the world. The Christian is a working man sweaty with his toil. Yet are we moderns, while clearer-visioned than they who thought to leave the world to get at God, in danger of overworking our work idea. Life is not as the sunflower wholly in the sun, but as the violet partly in shade, partly in sun. Doing is not life's totality. There are midnights just as there are

noons; and every midnight is on the road to noon. We shall not err in reckoning that we are in danger of loss in the sum total of possible effectiveness in working overmuch, in growing breathless, in fumbling our skein when a pause in the toil would be a helper to our effort. The art of pause is a not inconsequential part of the art of music. The rests are in the score. So must there be a pause in the holy life or the music will be sadly marred. One of a pastor's many joys is that as he goes from house to house in the brotherly vocation of pastoral visitation he can take breathing spell by being in a strict privacy with God while he is in transit from one house to another. And so he comes to each parishioner fresh from God. How that privacy washes away the drudgery, so called, from the pastoral office, how filled with calm delight it makes an afternoon so spent, how the Ineffable Presence shines on him as he walks about! It is like a day of summer sunshine in a winter month. The hard-worked man can thus find abundant interval for privacy with God. I have known crowded business men whose times were crammed with many callers and with many business items, and have sometimes asked them how they contrived to get a moment's space with God, and have had as answer, "I seize the moment when it comes to have my word with God." This is the secret of the holy life. We are crowded, but not so crowded as that we may not have quiet in which to make our breathing unto "the God of all comfort." We must make our battle against being crowded. We must have space to catch our breath and calm the unquiet of our turbulent career.

Hence the need of devotional literature, such books as shall help us into the ways of God and shall underscore the weightier thoughts and relations. I have had hours many and happy with such books, and count them among my major joys and helpers. Now, we are all so much ourselves as that no one else can prescribe a devotional literature for us any more than he could a table bill of fare; though for all this we must have noticed how similar the dietary tastes of men are. We eat about the same staples. A salad, a sherbet, and such accompaniments will differ, but the edibles are mainly similar. And it may be so with larger matters more than we are wont to suppose. Some staples of devotion must appeal to

every spirit. All this allowed, room must be left for the individual taste in the devout as in the artistic life. I do not find myself, for instance, helped by the writings of Andrew Murray or F. B. Meyer. This, I hope, is no reflection on me, and assuredly is no reflection on them. To some, even to many, they do make appeal. I chance not to be of that company. They seem to me to write religious platitudes which lack locomotion. They get nöwhere. They lack for me the divine element in such writings, namely, the power to push the soul off into the sea of God as a friend sometimes pushes our boat from the strand when on summer nights we take the neglected oars for a row across waters flushed with the afterglow. The push out into God's sea is what makes a manual of devotion for me. I assume that is what everybody wants and what each must in the end determine for himself. Each must select for his own moral palate. Good talk does not suffice for me to take leadership for my devout life. There must be worthy talk, words that sweat beneath their weight of holy meaning, words which are like initiation into mysteries, greeting with a surprise the soul when it sets eyes upon their face. I demand the quality of the apocalypse. A revelation must be involved. Only where such is do I feel that my life is thrust out into the presence of the mysterious God. In much so-called devotional literature appears to me to be this cardinal defect, of supposing that pious talk is devotional talk. Still speaking for myself, this is an outrageous blunder. Pious platitudes are irreligious when meant for the leadership of others. To indulge in them for one's self may or may not be justifiable, but to inflict them on others in the name of religious reflections is a breach of morals. Goody-goody talk is not devotional, but that talk is devotional which with manly step starts out blithely heavenward, does not saunter but strides, that catches us in its forward goings and we swing out toward Him for whom the soul is hungry. A devotional book is not an argument on religious matters, not in necessity the exposition of certain Scripture texts, not the settled face (as to say, "We shall now be devout"). *The Divine Pursuit* and *In the Hour of Silence*, seem written more or less to defend the author against some charge—I would suppose from the tone, not knowing,

against a charge of heresy. A book of devotion is not a heresy
trial either on one side or the other. Cardinal Bona's *Guide to
Eternity* is open to serious objection: 1. It is more heathen than
Christian. 2. Its views of women are thoroughly those of a priest
and utterly unlike the views of Jesus. 3. The book lacks the impulse Godward. We are weary for deep-sea soundings of the heart.
Some books are good exegeses of given texts but are not winged.
They cannot fly, much less make him who reads them fly. They
tell what a man cannot in sobriety deny, but no electric spark is in
the telling. This is the character of many manuals of devotion
with which I am familiar. I would not say, "I dislike them," but
would say, "I mislike them." They do not tell lies; but they do not
render truths engaging. They are not radiant, heavenly, replete
with longing, glorious with hope, uncontaminate with fear. The
note the poet organist lost and could never reproduce is the note
these writings have lost. I care not for their music. This is not
named as if readers were concerned with my personal predilections,
but as a word of reminder why these suggestions of devotional
literature take the road they do. Nothing dogmatic is here asserted, but simply something personal. As each has his favorite
flower, so each has his spiritual preferences; and these infringe
not upon the rights of anybody else. Give me leave for my posy
for my heart. What, then, from this standpoint, would appear to
be the marks of a devotional book? 1. It should say something.
2. It should say something that breaks across the shore line of
soul as a fifth wave across the sea bar. 3. It should possess depth
as a deep wave, "Too deep for sound and foam." 4. It should
have the power to wake the better part of the heart. 5. It should
have the tang of the unanticipated. 6. It should be big with God.
7. It should prate little, exhort little but say much, and urge the
soul like Christ talking with it face to face. 8. It should cause
the heart to drift into the prayer mood as a quiet wind drifts a
boat. 9. It should serve to give divine matters a stately preeminence which shall belittle every other thing when swung into
the field of vision. 10. It should make God a joy and his service a
holy passion to the soul.

Now, these may or may not be the marks of a devotional frag-

ment, but will in any case serve to help us to a pathway easy to keep. At its best, devotional literature would have all these marks in every instance; but this is not to be anticipated. If a passage or prayer can touch one of these keys we shall be glad to have heard the prayer or passage. Differing times and moods call for differing calls—sometimes the trumpet, sometimes the lute, sometimes the thrush, sometimes the laughter of a child. The soul is so wide of gamut that we must always allow for that. In the list to follow no attempt is made to be exhaustive and give a list of devotional books; but the proclaimed purpose is to name such books or parts of books as have proven devotionally helpful to myself, with the hope that what has given me succor might have leading for others; for it is barely conceivable that in many helpers of one there would not be found some helpers to all. This list is now submitted: St. Augustine's *The City of God* and *Confessions;* Bishop Hall's *Meditations;* Baxter's *The Saint's Everlasting Rest;* Jeremy Taylor's *Holy Living* and *Holy Dying;* Bunyan's three books, *Grace Abounding,* *The Holy War,* and *Pilgrim's Progress;* Spurgeon's *Treasury of David;* Wesley's Journal; à Kempis's *Imitation of Christ;* Luther's *Table Talk; Euchologion;* Rutherford's *Letters;* Phelps's *The Still Hour;* the Book of Common Prayer; *Clarke on the Promises;* William Law's *Serious Call;* Horder's *American Sacred Poetry; The Shadow of the Rock;* Lancelot Andrewes's *Private Devotions;* the Life of George Müller; *The New Acts of the Apostles;* Keble's *Christian Year;* George Herbert's *The Church;* Bishop Wilson's *Sacra Privata;* Armstrong Black's *The Evening and the Morning;* Young's *Helps for the Quiet Hour;* Joseph Parker's *Prayers;* Beecher's *Prayers* and *Sermons;* Pascal's *Pensées;* Bishop How's "For all thy saints who from their labors rest;" Newman's "The Dream of Gerontius;" Jay's *Morning and Evening Exercises;* George Matheson's *Times of Retirement* and *Studies in the Portrait of Christ; The Prayers of the Bible;* Bishop Vincent's *The Church at Home* (a collection of Scripture, hymn, and prayer for each day); Spenser's "Faerie Queene;" Tennyson's "In Memoriam," "The Idyls of the King," "The Vision of Sin," and "The Palace of Art;" Browning's "Instans Tyrannus," "Prospice," "Christmas Eve," "Easter Day,"

3

and "Saul;" Matthew Arnold's "East London;" Bryant's "To a
Waterfowl;" W. H. Channing's "My Symphony;" Henry van
Dyke's *The Source* and *The Other Wise Man;* Longfellow's sonnet
"As a fond mother when the day is o'er;" Rowland Williams's
Psalms and Litanies; Bacon's three essays, "Of Truth," "Of
Atheism," and "On Death;" Milton's sonnets "On His Blindness,"
"This three years day these eyes," and "Written on his reaching
the age of twenty-three;" Lowell's "Sir Launfal," and "The Pres-
ent Crisis;" Wordsworth's "Ode to Duty;" Whittier's "Pictures,"
"Our Master," "The Eternal Goodness," "Questions of Life," and
"At Last;" Annie Trumbull Slosson's "Deacon Phœbe's Selfish
Natur';" Hawthorne's "Earth's Holocaust," and "The Celestial
Railroad;" The Hymnal; The Bible.

The City of God is to me devotional not so much, I think, in
what it is as for the memories it evokes. The name itself sets my
heart singing and hastes me to the hill from which without lifting
up my eyes I can see the eternal city of which I trust myself to be
a citizen. I can see the glinting of the golden street and the
glimmer of the golden towers and catch the blaze of walls of
chrysoprase and sardius and see the peaceful river flow and catch
the splendor of the "sea of glass mingled with fire." Ah me, my
heart, the city of God! And then I am touched to dreams in thinking of that early Christian who saw past all the checkered careers
of falling states the fadeless glory of the things of God. That was
a vision! Augustine wrote the first philosophy of history; and to
compare it with Hegel the similarity is striking. That old lover
of the Lord pulled the far ends of the circle of the ages together
and made them touch. The venture was wild with daring, and he
marches like a captain in the army of our God. And the *Confessions* fairly boil out of a big, hot heart. Augustine was not a
repressed quantity, like Matthew Arnold, but an expressed quantity. The veins in his forehead are swollen to bursting, and you can
hear the drumbeat of his heart—a heart aware of God, and wisely
afraid of him. I like that attitude. We shall do well to go to
school to him. There is something in God to fear; and in our overworked phrase, "the fatherhood of God," many of us have forgotten
the fearfulness of God. He is in a high hill; and they who walk

that way must take great heed. "With godly fear" is a thought worth practicing our lips to pronounce and our hearts to remember. A passion for God, that was St. Augustine. He wanted God; all besides seemed dirt-cheap. He would watch the sun with unwinking eyes and loved the glare of thoughts that burned like fire. He raised all great questions simply because he must who fellowships with God. The gospels are writ in capitals because all things which touch the Christ are rendered illustrious. The sovereignty of God engulfed him as the sea does the random bather. And if he overdrew this side of the divine character, think it not strange. He saw how august God was and tarried there. His mistake in emphasis was natural and laudable. Thought was not yet schooled to get the exact emphasis; but he caught sight of some great meaning foreign to the thoughts of man thus far and blazed it on the pages of his book. God is great, Augustine knew that. God is white light, he knew that too; and so sin was black as summer storm clouds. No book is wholesome devotional reading which does not by affirmation or inference assert the wickedness of sin and so ring the alarum bells of the soul. Sin not a mistake but a curse, that is the tune to which devotion has set its music. All best lives are white with fear of sin, like a scared soldier. Notice that in the books as they pass before our eyes. "O wretched man that I am!" Who is that calling? Paul? No, the centuries of men and women who have caught a full vision of God. Who see Him, fall out of conceit with themselves. Sin is a hard word in the vocabulary of a profound life met with God. That is the crux for Huxley and Darwin and Arnold and Tyndale and the ironers down of the rude wrinkle God calls sin. They think by snubbing sin to iron it out; but their treatment of sin is their doom as moralists. Bunyan and Andrewes and Rutherford and Parker and Browning and Matheson know better. Sin is a *diabolus,* an attacker. This is admirably wrought in *The Holy War;* and for that in particular do I praise that similitude. Sin never wearied, ever renewing its aggressions, subtle, acrimonious, fertile in expedient, indirect, never defeated when defeated—is that not sin? Does it not lie abased in the light of the Eden of the heart always ready, ready to make speedy entrance? Read *The Holy War.*

Bunyan's *Grace Abounding,* for a vivid, that is, a just, sense of sin, has no equal outside the book of God. It is tremendous with the sense of sin, and as tremendous with a sense of grace when men turn from their sins. This book burns like a tank of oil. Compared with such writings as Cardinal Newman's the contrast is visible even to poor eyes in such way as no argument could disclose the defect in Newman's religious writings. Of *Pilgrim's Progress,* to use many words would be "vain repetition." Oliver Wendell Holmes says: *"Pilgrim's Progress,* the *Divina Commedia* of Protestantism, is probably the only religious poem—for it is a poem in all but versification—which is read through like a novel by those who take it up for the first time." In an expression of opinion among prominent Wesleyan ministers some years ago as to those books which had been profoundly influential in their career scarcely one omitted *Pilgrim's Progress.* In our day we read it too little. This book you cannot outgrow. Its fidelity to the experiences of a Christian is so absolute as to make a moving picture of a Christian career. The book is poetry, as Holmes has said. This Bedford tinker when his heart is moved with the Gospel—and a big heart he has—steps into poetry as naturally as a happy child into singing. The Saxon tongue finds the wine pressed from its grapes at the hands of this manly man who thought it joy to suffer for the Christ. I read it repeatedly in a single year. I go and walk alongside Pilgrim and find my heart and lips at prayer as we make journey together toward the Delectable Mountains. When with him I must lift the song. Bishop Hall's *Meditations* have such godly depth, wisdom, research, such gracious piety, such wide goings in search of God, that to hold his hand is strength. You cannot think religion insipid when with him. Baxter's *Saint's Rest*—is it because this book I have belonged to my long-lost mother that its words are become so dear? that she read it with a heart on fire? To untwist these scarlet threads of love is not permissible. We cannot tell; but this *Rest* is dear to me, and its uphill look is full of comfort to my heart. Jeremy Taylor—but why linger? Who does not know the honey-sweet words of this poet divine, and who does not find them full of grace? They mind me of the breath of the heather on the sea cliffs where my

father and mother spent their childhood. Spurgeon's *Treasury of David* I value not so much for what Spurgeon has said, though in such a book he is at his best, but for that quaint multitudinousness of sayings of the saints of God he has gathered into this harvest field of his. The good gather about the psalms as bees about purple asters. Wesley's Journal and à Kempis are to be read together. À Kempis is in the most part too lacking in vigor to suit strength, too like daydreams on holy things, though on occasion, as in his prayer, he becomes the full brother of strength; but to read him, the man of sequestered life, and Wesley, the man of the world parish, the circuit rider whose goings could only be hedged in by death, will afford a wholeness, a help for the antipodes of life. À Kempis, cloistered, introspective; Wesley "shod with the preparation of the Gospel;" for his journeys are so oft that other sandals would wear out. Wesley has dreams, but they lift into action. I know not any books so incitant to action, wakeful, intelligent, and to service cheerful and delightful, as Wesley's Journal. Luther's *Table Talk* must do anybody good. That healthy manliness of his off dress parade, devout, humorous, vigorous, talking out of the deep places of a life which knew only one star—how his talk does put a man in tune with the Infinite! Of Rutherford, say only Adeney's words: "These letters stand in the front rank of devotional works." They glow with a great love and mind us of the love of Christ. *The Still Hour* makes us *think* as well as pray. The Book of Common Prayer has access in it. What more need be affirmed? *Clarke on the Promises* is a book packed full of only what God has promised. They are words sweet, very sweet to hear.

William Law's *Serious Call* is so great and wise and devout a book that Samuel Johnson and John Wesley both found meat for men in it, and Wesley's own hand made an abridgment of it for his Methodists, not as agreeing with the mystical tendency of the author but as being heartened by his profound religiousness. I have found the book very good to know. In Horder and in *The Shadow of the Rock* are poems which can lead the thought and love to God. Andrewes, so loved of Alexander Whyte, is loved of all who know a big heart hungry, wanting God. The Life of George

Müller is faith rendered into modern English. *The New Acts of the Apostles* is a story to put fire in the bones. Keble's *Christian Year* sings us on our way toward heaven. "Quaint George Herbert!" His quaint poetical conceits do but lend emphasis to the man's love of Christ. His poems are incense smoke lifting up to God. *The Evening and the Morning* has the true devotional uplift for my spirit. *Helps for the Quiet Hour,* chosen with that fine literary instinct characteristic of Dr. Young, has words fit to help the traveler along the road to God. Parker's and Beecher's prayers have wings. Of *Sacra Privata* and *Psalms and Litanies,* while many words would not suffice to say the truth concerning books which are crammed with beauty, help, nobility, insight, devoutness, and divine leading, no other word than this is permissible: The books help the faith out a long way toward God. Those good men if they could know this would rejoice and be exceeding glad. How "All Saints" hymn rouses sluggishness into animation, doubt to faith. "The Dream of Gerontius" has vagaries truly Roman Catholic, but a hint of great truths and vision of them, betimes, are good for a soul to have. For me, George Matheson is without a peer among contemporary devotional writers. He says things. He is not given over to ejaculatory piety, but freights his meditations with such heavenly truths that as you read yourself become ejaculatory. That is the side from which ejaculations should proceed. The singer needs not himself applaud; the auditors will do that if the music prove worthy. In Matheson is the moving of deep waters seaward; and his prayers are like your father's when his heart was full. The poems and prose writings here named as devotional, no time is afforded to underscore. But how good they are and full of heavenward look! This remark of Lowell regarding the "Ode to Duty" may touch with a caress these various works: "In the 'Ode to Duty' he [Wordsworth] speaks out of an ampler ether than in any other of his poems, and which may safely "challenge insolent Greece and haughty Rome for a comparison in either kind or degree." From these varied souls may be had a world of help ruddy with the blood of life. I cannot estimate their service to myself, those services have been so real, so varied, so instinct with the generosity learned of Christ, so unthought-out,

so spontaneous, like the lilt of birds. I bless the God who gifted minds to render such a holy help.

The Hymnal! Dwell upon its contribution of help. Who reads Charles Wesley's "Wrestling Jacob," Bernard of Cluny's "Jerusalem the Golden," Thomas Olivers's "The God of Abram Praise," impregnates his soul with odors grown in heaven. 'Tis a book of divine leadings, rich in worthy rendering of love and longing and hope fearless of despair. "Let us all sing."

And God's Book! Read the Psalms for their sense of God and man, and man as interesting to God. How God and man are caught up together in the Psalter! Where man is, there God is and interested in man beyond belief. This it is which makes the Psalms perpetual as the refrain for the heart. This it is which sobs in those tearful tunes where God is seen and man is seen very full of sin. We shall never outgrow the "Sprinkle me with hyssop, and I shall be clean; wash me, and I shall be whiter than snow;" and the "Shepherd Psalm" shall whisper from sleepy lips while mankind endures. We have committed it so to heart that we say it while we fall asleep. Job abashes the soul. Nehemiah makes sloth and indifference to hang head in shame. Lamentations drenches the soul with the grief for a state ruined and a city sin-dethroned. All the prophets wake the life to God. They blow like bugles of tempest. Ecclesiastes declares the insufficiency of the world to satisfy the hunger of man's life. Luke is so human, Matthew so kingly, Mark so martial, John so Christ-filled. Paul's prayers have a celestial summons in them. They take wing when we least anticipate it. And the prayers of Jesus, how they hearten and subdue, how they guide and sustain, how they take the soul into the holiest of all and make such climates have the homelike feeling. He knew how to pray. The cry, the fleeing for succor, the gratitude that laughs while it wipes tears from the eyes, the resignation, the sublime fortitude, all in the prayers of Him who taught us how to pray. Jesus's prayers walk straight into the presence of God. They are not experiment, rather a child walking a well-known path to his father's door. Blessed prayers, blessed access! And the Passion of the Saviour is devotion's self. If ever the heart has dried up like parched ground, if prayers come

slow like words to a wandering intellect, then read the passion chapters of the gospels. The hill they climb leads into heaven. To see Him there! Will that not make the dry heart to be rained upon with tears? I read and cry, "My Christ, my cross!" We are to read each Gospel as it were a journey to a mountain top; for each Gospel narrative climbs to the cross that clouds the mountain summit with its midnight gloom. The august spectacle of God dying for a single human soul, that brings us to our knees, that hushes our poor babblings into expectant silence. The dying God, dying for me! I *must* pray!

I have been impressed that there is room and need for a book of devotion which should be put into twelve vest-pocket booklets, one for each month, thus making the carrying it to the office, on the train, on the street car, possible, and yet make the books of sufficient bulk to contain for each day a prayer, a text, a Scripture passage, a selection in verse or prose from some of those nobler words the hearts of manly and holy men have bubbled up like fountains of water. This would be a book of days. The Anglican devotional books are for the Church year; a deeper Christian philosophy has a book for God's year. The entirety of the year is God's and ours. The secular and the sacred year synchronize. Each day and each season, mine and God's, is the right interpretation of the calendar. And a book conceived from this standpoint and executed with wide knowledge of the literature of life and devotion and a gracious familiarity with the Scriptures of God, with a wise knowledge of the hymns of the ages, with a gift of prayer and a knowledge of the prayers of holy women and men, would not such a volume or volume series (twelve booklets for the months of the year) be a distinct helper for the holy life? All the ages and all the minds might lend their voices to such a book of days. The advantage, as I have found, of a book of devotion has been that it has set the thoughts of the day out with God, and has supplied, so to say, provender for the day's thinking and the day's delight. A scripture looks very different when set out thus alone than when sunk in the context. The average Bible word is too large for the soul to pronounce more than one of them at once; and when they are isolated the real magnitude and meaning light the

landscape of our thought. I appeal to all lovers of God's book whether this be not so. One passage will serve as a staff for the heart all day. The leaning on it for a day of toil makes the staff precious ever after. And a poem holding a radiant thought in solution, to be set out from the book wherein it was housed with many others, becomes thereby personal and visible. The same is true of a thought in noble prose or a prayer which flowed from a heart in which God was consequential. Such a page pushes the boat of life out into the sea of the day, gives it a vigorous thrust which holds to the heart through the livelong day. A book of devotion should be catholic, fetched from afar. The wise souls were never dwellers in a single house. Like families, they live under many roofs. This is the objection to such a book, to select at random, as *For Days and Years,* by Lear. It is an Anglican book and contains that amusing Church egotism which writes Church with a capital "C" and Dissenter with a small "d," and the selections of words from the wise are all but entirely from the Church fathers or Roman Catholics or Anglicans. The obliviousness to the wide Christian world outside of these limits is humorous rather than devotional. Cardinal Newman is scarcely the sanest and most wholesome religious guide, to say the least. What is wanted is the walk through the Churches as Christ among the candlesticks, going everywhere and hearing all and holding the most precious truths as the flower the dew. True Christianity is eclectic in its tastes. What holy moods have meditated and what holy men have done, these are the precious considerations. What cares the good man's heart what Church David Livingstone was of, or Thomas Coke, or Hannington, or Gardiner? For each we thank God and take courage. "There is one God and Father over all, who is rich unto all that call upon him;" and that is the conclusion of the whole matter so far as touches the point of devotion. That heart which hath held God's hand, it is good to touch. Those eyes which for a sublime moment looked into the face of God, it is blessed to look into. The whole family of God is sacred; and the voice of any one of them, no matter what name he wears, is good to hear. Did not our hearts burn while we listened to Him by the way? And there is and can be but one answer.

Let us listen to the words of Brother Standfast as he stands in the river waiting his turn to pass

To where
Beyond these voices there is peace,

recalling Rufus Choate's words, "On the whole, the most eloquent, mellifluous talk that was ever put together in the English language was the speech of Mr. Standfast in the river:" "This River has been a Terror to many, yea, the thoughts of it also have often frightened me. But now methinks I stand easy; my Foot is fixed upon that on which the Feet of the Priests that bare the Ark of the Covenant stood while Israel went over this Jordan. The Waters indeed are to the Palate bitter and to the Stomach cold, yet the thoughts of what I am going to and of the Conduct that waits for me on the other side do lie as a glowing Coal at my Heart. I see myself now at the end of my Journey, my toilsome days are ended. I am going now to see that Head that was crowned with Thorns, and that Face that was spit upon for me. I have formerly lived by Hearsay and Faith, but now I go where I shall live by sight, and shall be with Him in whose company I delight myself. I have loved to hear my Lord spoken of, and wherever I have seen the print of his Shoe in the Earth, there I have coveted to set my Foot too. His name has been to me as a Civet-box, yea, sweeter than all Perfumes. His Voice to me has been most sweet, and his Countenance I have more desired than they that have most desired the Light of the Sun. His Word I did use to gather for my Food, and for Antidotes against my Faintings. He has held me, and I have kept me from mine iniquities, yea, my Steps hath he strengthened in his Way."

W. A. Quayle.

Art. IV.—THE ETHICAL AND THE POSITIVE IN CHRISTIANITY.

CHRISTIANITY is a religion of principles rather than precepts. Its essential principle is love. This practically unfolds into the precepts and prohibitions of the Decalogue. All the law and the prophets are summed up in love to God and men. In examining the duties which arise from our relations to God and men we note a distinction. Some are grounded on reasons we intuitively see, and some on reasons which we do not see. Theologians call the former moral, and the latter positive. Says Bishop Butler in his *Analogy,* that exhaustless seed-bed of Christian apologetics: "Moral duties arise out of the nature of the case itself, prior to external command. Positive duties do not arise out of the nature of the case, but from external command; nor would they be duties at all were it not for such command, received from Him whose creatures and subjects we are." All our duties would be moral, if there were no revelation of God other than that through nature. There can be nothing positive in natural religion, the religion of conscience. It is possible that a collision may occur of a positive with a moral precept where it is impossible to obey both. In such a case no universal rule is laid down in the Scriptures. Should we say the positive must always yield to the moral we would be greatly embarrassed by certain positive commands, as that to Abraham to offer up Isaac and that to exterminate whole tribes of people. There are at least three reasons why generally the moral should override the positive: 1. Because it is written upon our hearts and is interwoven into our very nature. 2. Because positive precepts aim at a moral end, which must have a higher value than the means. 3. When the two are mentioned together in the Scriptures the stress is always laid on the moral. But Bishop Butler remarks that "Mankind have, in all ages, been greatly prone to place their religion in peculiar positive rites by way of equivalent for obedience to moral precepts." They lengthen the creed as a compensation for shortening the Decalogue. Thus many false positive precepts have been foisted upon Christianity. Let us examine

some of these, after we have ascertained the infallible criterion by which they may be tested. We will limit our discussion to the New Testament. We find this essential of every positive institution, that it should be of such a nature as to keep Christ the Son of God in the very center of the system, which collapses if he is removed. A man may become a geometer in utter ignorance of Euclid, who first discovered geometry, but he cannot become a Christian without knowing, loving, and obeying Christ. The positive institute must be Christocentric, like Christianity itself. Of course it must be a direct command, and not an inference merely. It must proceed from the Author of Christianity; for human authority, even that of an inspired apostle, is not sufficient of itself alone to establish a positive precept.

There are only two positive precepts which correspond to these requirements: baptism and the Lord's Supper. These were deliberately instituted by Christ, the latter just before his death, and the former just before his ascension. The central position of Christ in these sacraments is seen by the so-called liberal Christians who deny the supreme divinity of the Son, regarding him as a man only. When they continue to administer these ordinances they are greatly embarrassed by this illogical procedure. The German rationalists baptize their children in the name of the universal brotherhood of man, the only God which Comte, the positivist, teaches his followers to worship. When Ralph Waldo Emerson was a Unitarian preacher in Boston he was asked by his deacons why he had ceased to administer the Lord's Supper; he replied that "it was giving too great prominence to one among many good men." The dilemma in which this incipient pantheist found himself was either an acknowledgment of the Godhood of Jesus Christ, or the total abandonment of that positive institution in which this doctrine was objectively proclaimed. The great purpose of the two positive precepts of Christ was to keep his Gospel from sinking into a mere moral system, by the elimination of his personal authority. Such a tendency has existed in every age, beginning with ancient Ebionitism and ending with modern Unitarianism, whose leaders have gravely discussed the expediency of taking the Bible with its "alleged miracles" and perplexing

doctrines out of their pulpits and of preaching its pure ethics disentangled from its "puerile fables." This would reduce our glorious Gospel to a meager philosophical cult attractive to a few cultured intellects, but bereft of all motive power to lift up the fallen and to save the lost masses submerged in sin. It is instructive to note that the only Christian sect in Church history which neglects and denies the obligation of the two positive precepts of Christ—the Friends—was in 1827 rent asunder by the secession of large portions of six out of ten Yearly Meetings, on the ground of their denial of Christ's true divinity while incarnate. We call the attention of General Booth and his Salvation Army to this hidden rock on which this Christian body may split. We erect a beacon upon it for their benefit.

It should be borne in mind that the Gospel scheme of salvation through faith only, without meritorious works, a faith bearing the fruitage of perfect love and obedience to God and altruistic effort and sacrifice for men, cannot consist with a multitude of positive precepts. Such a number would overload the religion and smother the spiritual life in the legalism of "the letter that killeth." This is demonstrated by the fact, noted by Butler, that "mankind are for placing the stress of their religion anywhere rather than upon virtue." The scribes taught that there are two hundred and forty-eight affirmative and three hundred and sixty-five negative precepts. Hence the necessity of limiting positive precepts to the smallest possible number that will keep Christ in the center of the system. The divinely adjusted balance between the two kinds of precepts must be preserved. The free spirit of Christianity requires us to reject all such positives.

1. *Foot-washing.* We cannot regard this as designed by Christ to be a positive ordinance of perpetual obligation the same as baptism and the holy eucharist. It seems rather an impressive symbol teaching humility, the dignity of service, the necessity of purity of heart, and the duty of every believer to help his fellow-disciples to obtain this great blessing. Paul's requirement of the widow before being enrolled for Christian service, "if she hath washed the saints' feet," must be interpreted as a synonym for altruistic Christian service. This literal act cannot be a positive

precept, for it does not stand our test; it can be performed without mention of Christ's name in the ceremony. When kings, emperors, and popes in a spectacular style observe what Luther calls "hypocritical foot-washing" we think of his advice, "If you wish to wash your neighbor's feet see that your heart is really humble, and help everyone in becoming better."

2. *Confirmation by the imposition of the hands of a bishop for communicating the Holy Spirit to a baptized person.* In some churches it included the chrism as a symbol of the Spirit. The texts adduced in support of this rite are Acts viii, 14-17; xix, 5, 6; Heb. vi, 1. These texts prove that this impartation of the Spirit was a prerogative of the apostles only. As they had no successors clothed with equal authority it ceased at their decease. It was neither instituted by the command of Christ, the Head of the Church, nor does it answer the demands of our criterion. It is out of harmony with the universal atonement and with the proclamation of the Gospel to every creature to grant to a small class of believers a monopoly of the Holy Ghost promised to all believers who will perseveringly ask for him in the name of Christ. In respect to this crowning gift Faber's lines are true:

There's a wideness in God's mercy,
Like the wideness of the sea.

If men are called upon to curse the man who fills his purse by cornering the bread market (Prov. xi, 26), what are they to think of a God who through "the myth of the apostolic succession" (Phillips Brooks) puts a patent-right upon the author and Supporter of spiritual life? It is as evident as the cloudless sun at midday that the Father of mercies and God of all grace has not limited himself to such a narrow channel in the communication of himself to believers in his Son.

3. *Tithing.* The required bestowment of a tenth of our income is alleged by some good people to be a part of Christianity. Giving is a moral obligation, but giving a tenth is not a dictate of our moral sense. If it is a duty it must be positive. We look in vain in the New Testament for such an expression of the divine will. It may be said this is found in Matt. xxiii, 23, "But these ye ought to have done." We will show more fully under our next

topic that our great Teacher did not shock the religious feelings of the Jews by a sudden termination of their rites, but that it was his habit to regulate the manner and spirit in which temporary Hebrew ceremonies should be performed. He found the Jews exercising a disproportionate conscientiousness in trifles, which, according to their traditional conception of duty, they ought to care for; while they were utterly neglecting obligations of overwhelming importance. Moreover, as tithing does not keep Christ in the center of his religion it does not answer to the requirements of a positive precept. While it would be a means of grace to all Christians voluntarily to give at least a tenth of their income to promote the kingdom of Christ and to help the poor whom we always have with us, and to fill to overflowing the various treasuries of his Church, it would in the end be a detriment to bring this to pass by proclaiming the tithe as a positive requirement of Chri_.. It would add to the influence under which too many are drifting into legalism and self-righteousness. The spirituality of those sects which teach that God requires a tenth is, to say the least, not remarkably high; the Irvingites or Catholic Apostolic, the Seventh-day Adventists, the Dowieites or Christian Catholic, the Mormons or Latter-day Saints, and the Sanfordites are of this type. The tithe may enrobe their leaders in gorgeous vestments, fill their purses, and sustain a vigorous propaganda, but it certainly does not produce a deep and intelligent piety.

4. *Fasting or abstinence from food as a religious exercise.* This was not a positive command either in the law or in the Gospel. It is a characteristic of nearly all the paganisms in the world, especially the Asiatic religions with which the Hebrews came in contact. Jehovah appointed a day of atonement for their sins (Lev. xvi, 29-31), a special day in which they should "afflict their souls" by repenting of their sins as a preparation for forgiveness. They found it easier to do as their heathen neighbors did; they fasted from sunset to sunset instead of quitting their evil ways. The prophets at times rebuked this substitution, especially Isaiah, who excoriates the fast which allowed them "to smite with the fist of wickedness." They did not have fasts enough, so during the captivity in Babylon they appointed four more, which Zechariah

afterward turned into "joy and gladness, and cheerful feasts." Neither Moses nor Christ ever appointed a day of abstinence from food. They both called the Israelites to repentance. In examining the New Testament to ascertain whether Jesus Christ gave any positive precept requiring periodical fasting we call attention to several spurious texts dating from about the sixth century, when for the first time fasting ceased to be voluntary and was commanded under the penalty in some instances of the extraction of the teeth. These texts, as the Revision shows, are Matt. xviii, 21, the whole verse being omitted; Mark ix, 29, Acts x, 30, and 1 Cor. vii, 5, where fasting is omitted. These glosses were probably not an intentional corruption of the text. Some monk in his cell when the Church was befogged with a cloud of asceticism penciled on the margin of the manuscript the word νηστεία, where he thought fasting was appropriate. Afterward a copyist, thinking it an omission, innocently copied it into the text. We would also call attention to a mistranslation of "shall" for "will" in Matt. ix, 15, "then will they fast" because of sorrow. The future tense in the third person in Greek does not express obligation. Hence Wesley is careful in his version to change the "shall" to "will" in the sentence, "One of you will betray me." Consistency required the same change in Matt. ix, 15; Mark ii, 20; Luke v, 35. The chief support of the error that periodical fasting is required by Christ is Matt. vi, 16, "Moreover when ye fast, be not as the hypocrites." From its juxtaposition with the verses about prayer, beginning in the same way, "When ye pray," it is alleged that fasting is just as obligatory as praying. The truth is that neither is here commanded. This is conceded by Wesley, a man who, in accordance with the spirit of his generation, was given to rigorous fasting, and in his High Church period fasted twice a week till three o'clock P. M. He says, "Our Lord does not enjoin either fasting, almsdeeds, or prayer; all these being duties which were before fully established in the Church of God." This is a concession that this text is not a positive precept. Here we revert to the idea suggested in reference to tithing, that Christ was in the habit of regulating the spirit and manner of the Jews in their religious customs which he intended his Gospel should supersede, such as

Matt. v, 23, "Therefore if thou bring thy gift to the altar," etc. This does not eternize the obligation to bring material gifts to a material altar, but it does prescribe the spirit in which the Jews should worship God by offerings while under the Levitical law. Again, Matt. xxiii, 2: "The scribes and the Pharisees sit on Moses' seat: all things therefore whatsoever they bid you, these do and observe." Here is evidently a temporary precept. This must be admitted, or we must all go to the synagogue, listen to the rabbis, and obey all their instructions! The fact is, there is not one direct command to fast. So embarrassed was a certain bishop of the Methodist Episcopal Church in an article on "The Duty of Fasting" that he actually invented the following apostolic command, "Give yourselves to fasting and prayer" (1 Cor. vii, 5).* This was done by decapitating a piece of advice to married Christians and erecting the dependent clause of the sentence into a precept. The word "fasting" in this text is pronounced spurious by all the critical editors, because it is lacking in all the uncial manuscripts.

Our most cogent argument against periodical fasting is found in Mark ii, 18-22; Luke v, 33-38, where the question is raised why Jesus and his disciples are supposed to be guilty of the impiety of neglecting this religious exercise so devoutly practiced by John and his followers. His reply was that it was not consonant with the good news which he came to announce to a sad and sinful world. It would be like employing dirge singers at a wedding, while the happy pair are receiving the congratulations of the nuptial guests. It would be like putting a patch of new, stiff, and undressed cloth upon a rent in a garment thin and old. The result would be like the poet Young's baptized infidel, "the worse for mending." He then intimates that when the Bridegroom shall be taken away their sorrow would be so great as naturally to deprive them of an appetite for their daily food. The period of the Bridegroom's absence in the region of the dead was about forty hours. When he returned there was no more any occasion for fasting. "Then were the disciples glad when they saw the Lord." Nor was there any more occasion after his ascension, for just before he mounted the skies, stepping from the footstool to the throne, the Bridegroom of the

* *Methodist Quarterly Review*, New York, 1849, p. 203.

Church said to his bride, "Lo, I am with you always, even unto the end of the world." If she really believes this, how can she put on the apparel of a widow and fast with a sad countenance? Not one of the twelve personally trained by Christ said a word about fasting, except Matthew, who wrote as an historian. It is not named by Peter, James, Jude, or John in his gospel, Apocalypse, and three epistles. It does not occur in the Epistle to the Hebrews, of unknown authorship. The only voluntary fasting by the Christian Church in any place in the New Testament is in connection with two ordinations recorded in Acts xiii, 2, 3, when Paul and Barnabas were ordained and sent away, and Acts xiv, 23, where elders were appointed in every church, a solemnity not required by the Head of the Church, but naturally suggested to Jews who had been accustomed to fast on very important occasions, and especially to Paul, who as a Pharisee was accustomed to frequent fasts. There are also two records of Paul's involuntary fastings to which he was driven by poverty (2 Cor. vi, 5, and xi, 27). If they had been voluntary they would not have been named in both instances in a series of hardships, such as stripes, imprisonments, robbers, and shipwrecks. If he practiced stated fasting, in none of his numerous epistles did he require it, recommend it as a means of spiritual discipline, or even name it except among the sufferings just named. In his pastoral epistles to Timothy and Titus, instructing them respecting the characters which those whom they should ordain as deacons and bishops or elders should sustain, there is not the first hint about asceticism, though this, if a necessary qualification, would most certainly have been specified in company with the caveat, "not given to much wine." We hear nothing about the willingness of the candidates to "recommend fasting by precept and example," and to be diligent in gathering the tithes. We infer indeed that neither of them is divinely required.

The treatment of the subject of fasting by all the Wesleyan theologians is not without interest. Richard Watson, although he lived before the interpolations in the New Testament had been discovered, ignores it entirely, as do Raymond and Miley and Sheldon. Pope speaks of it as "brought from the Old Testament by our Lord, who indirectly enjoined it both by his example and

It remains for me to state the relation of the Methodist Episcopal Church to this subject. In 1784 Wesley sent "General Rules," in which he incorporated fasting among "the ordinances of God," and adds, "All these we know his Spirit writes on truly awakened hearts." It is a good thing that Wesley did not claim infallibility, and that Methodism has no theological *Semper idem*, otherwise we would have no hope of a constitutional change. Legislative changes have been made, and they will continue to be made. When a small boy the writer saw a class book with this inscription in large capitals on the outside covers, "Remember the Quarterly Fast." In 1888 the requirement of the quarterly fast disappeared from the Discipline. Yet the candidate for full membership in the Conference is met at the gate by a bishop propounding this apparently all-important question, implying that an affirmative answer is necessary for his admission: "Will you recommend fasting or abstinence, both by precept and example?" Our contention is that our Church has here created a positive precept not found in the New Testament. Our intelligent young men, who are well aware of that fact, are placed in a painful dilemma. We hope that the Methodist Episcopal Church will erase from her Discipline every sentence expressing or implying the obligation of the ministry to fast, as she has freed the laity by abolishing the quarterly fast. In the meantime I would suggest to clerical candidates for admission the following affirmative answer to the question, "Will you recommend fasting or abstinence, both by precept and example?" Answer: "I will enforce every precept respecting periodical fasting which I find in the New Testament, or which can be inferred from the example of Christ or any of the apostles whom he personally trained, and I myself will set an example of fasting, so far as I can, while obeying the caveat of Christ, that nobody should know that I am fasting."

Daniel Steele

Art. V.—HARNACK'S INTERPRETATION OF CHRISTIANITY.

SOME sixty years ago Strauss published his famous *Life of Jesus,* giving a mythological interpretation to the Gospel. Few theological works have ever created such a profound sensation. All Germany was at once divided into opposing camps, and the shock of battle was felt throughout the Christian world. It was proposed at the time to suppress the book by legal processes, but Neander, then professor of Church history in the University of Berlin, objected, holding wisely that truth only asks an open field. Neander's counsel prevailed, and the theory of Strauss has been so thoroughly exploded that to-day it "leaves not a rack behind." Now, at the beginning of the twentieth century, the successor of Neander publishes a book giving a rationalistic interpretation of the Gospel, which once again divides Germany into hostile camps, and forces a profound discussion over the fundamentals of the Christian faith throughout the world. Harnack's book, *What Is Christianity,* is destined to exert a more subtle, far-reaching, and dangerous influence than Strauss's *Life of Jesus,* for the reason that the work of Strauss was an attack from without, while that of Harnack professes to be a reconstruction from within, along critical, progressive, and sympathetic lines. It will be the purpose of this paper to outline the main positions of Harnack, and touch the nerves of his argument. First of all, let us acquaint ourselves with the man.

Adolph Harnack was born at Dorpat, in the Baltic Provinces, in 1851, where his father was professor of practical theology. The religious atmosphere of that home was simple, ardent, genial. The warmth and glow of Harnack's pietistic inheritance and training lend a charm to all his writings. His curriculum of study began at Dorpat and was completed at Leipsic, where he took his degree in theology and philosophy, and where he began his public work as a teacher. He was called successively to Giessen, to Marburg, and, in 1886, to Berlin, where he still remains as professor of Church history, and rector of the university. Without doubt Harnack is one of the most scholarly and influential living theologians

volume were delivered extemporaneously to great and enthusiastic audiences at the University of Berlin. The fact is, however, that the substance of them all, and in most cases the very form and statement of them, may be found in his carefully labored works. Lowell's epigram on Gladstone will apply quite as well to Harnack:

His greatness not so much in genius lies
As in adroitness as occasions rise,
Lifelong convictions to extemporize.

In truth, the book represents the ripened thought and the matured convictions of a lifetime. It will be helpful here to determine, as far as we may be able, Harnack's philosophical convictions, for the old maxim, "Let me know a man's position in philosophy and I will readily determine his theology," has a great deal of truth in it. Harnack is classed among the Ritschlians, though he has discarded many of Ritschl's peculiarities. Briefly and broadly, Ritschlism and Harnack stand for (1) thorough freedom in the study of the New Testament and Church history, (2) distrust of speculative theology, (3) a profound interest in Christianity as a religious life and not as a system of knowledge. Harnack is the greatest exponent of the so-called historical treatment of dogma. The question, "What is Christianity?" he thus answers: "It is solely in the historical sense that we shall try to answer this question; that is to say, we will employ the method of historical science, and the experience of life gained by studying the actual course of history."* And again he says: "A right and full estimate of the Christian religion is attainable only by a comprehensive induction

* P. 6.

of all the facts of history." Under those words "facts" and "induction" is a Trojan horse of large dimensions; in its vast cavities whole platoons of treacherous and well-armed Greeks are stored away: who shall determine what the facts are, and who make the induction? If the reader will be kind enough to fly a surveyor's flag over this spot we will return to it at a convenient season. The work before us, consisting of sixteen lectures, may be divided into two main divisions, the first treating of the "Essence of Christianity," or the "Gospel in the Gospel," the second treating of the "Development of Christianity," or the "Gospel in History."

1. *The Gospel in the Gospel.* The first four chapters are devoted to the task of determining the essential element in Christianity, discovering the Gospel in the Gospel. We touch the nerve of the argument in these chapters in the following points: the authority of the gospels, the miraculous element in the gospels, and the general conception of the message of the Gospel. Harnack's proposed aim is to distinguish the "husk" from the "kernel," that is, not only to separate the essential meaning from all those alien accretions with which the vicissitudes of nineteen centuries have surrounded and overlaid it, but also to reject inconsistent elements imported by the evangelists, upon whose records we must rely. This he does in the following summary fashion: "Our authorities," to quote his own language, "for the message which Jesus Christ delivered are the first three gospels. The fourth gospel cannot be taken as an historical authority in the ordinary meaning of the word. The author of the fourth gospel acted with sovereign freedom, transposed events and put them in a strange light, drew up the discourses himself, and illustrated great thoughts by imaginary situations. Although his work is not altogether void of a real, if scarcely recognizable, traditional element, it can hardly make any claim to be considered an authority for Jesus's history. Only little of what he says can be accepted, and that little with caution."* Historical science, Harnack tells us, had made a great step in advance by teaching us to pass a more intelligent and benevolent judgment on the synoptic gospels. He thus proceeds to exercise this intelligent and benevolent judgment: "These gos-

* P. 19.

pels," he says, "are, it is true, not historical works any more than the fourth gospel; they were not written for the simple object of giving facts as they were; they are books composed for the work of evangelization." That is the intelligent judgment; now for the benevolent. "Nevertheless," he continues, "they are not altogether useless as sources of history, more especially as the object with which they were written coincides in part with what Jesus intended."* Again he tells us, "Two of the gospels do, it is true, contain an introductory history (the history of Jesus's birth); but we may disregard it, for even if it contained something more trustworthy than it does actually contain, it would be as good as useless for our purpose. We know nothing, therefore, of Jesus's history for the first thirty years of his life."† His position on miracles is clearly and emphatically stated in the following paragraph: "We are firmly convinced that what happens in space and time is subject to the general laws of motion, and that as an interruption of the order of nature there can be no such things as miracles."‡ Accordingly, he rejects the virgin birth of our Lord, his resurrection, and the miracles he is said to have wrought. The Gospel, he claims, is not concerned with the personality of Christ, but has to do with the Father only, and not with the Son. This is the most central, fundamental, dominant, and constructive position in the book. "What is essential in the Gospel," according to Harnack, "may be grouped under our Lord's utterance upon three things: 1. The kingdom of God and its coming. 2. God the Father and the infinite value of the human soul. 3. The higher righteousness and the law of love."§ The three spheres thus distinguished, he says, coalesce. It needs only a few touches to develop this thought into everything that, taking Jesus' sayings as its groundwork, Christianity has known and strives to maintain. In this paragraph we have Harnack's basal principle exposed: the groundwork of Christianity, he holds, is not the personality of Jesus, but the sayings of Jesus.

After epitomizing the Gospel content he discusses the bearing of the Gospel on particular problems: 1. The Gospel and the World, or Asceticism. 2. The Gospel and the Poor, or Socialism.

•P. 20.   †P. 30.   ‡P. 26.   §P. 51.

3. The Gospel and the Law, or Public Order. 4. The Gospel and Work, or Civilization. 5. The Gospel and the Son of God, or the Christological Question. 6. The Gospel and the Creed. The first four of these are forcible and impressive presentations of the teachings of Christianity in relation to subjects with which they deal. They show noble feeling, and a fine discrimination of the Christian spirit in practical affairs. It is difficult to see how exception can be taken to them. The chapter on Christology presents a radical divergence from the traditional and orthodox view. In the first place he declares that Jesus desired no other belief in his person, and no other attachment to it, than is contained in the keeping of his commandments. John's gospel, it will be remembered, is wholly ruled out of evidence, and also such other parts of the synoptics as may be embarrassing. Jesus, he admits, is the Son of God, but not in any exceptional sense, only in a fuller degree of the manner in which every man may become a Son of God. "It is the knowledge of God which makes the sphere of divine Sonship."* He says: "The consciousness which he possessed of being the Son of God is, therefore, nothing but the practical consequence of knowing God as the Father, and as his Father. Rightly understood, the name of Son means nothing but the knowledge of God."* In a word, Harnack rules out Christology as having no essential place in the Christian scheme. He is at one with William Ellery Channing in his estimate of Christ's place in Christianity. "Love of Jesus Christ," Channing says, "depends very little upon our conception of his rank in the scale of being. On no other topic have Christians contended so earnestly, yet it is of secondary importance. To know Jesus Christ is not to know the precise place he occupies in the universe; it is something more, it is to look into his mind; it is to enter into his spirit." Yet Harnack is benevolent enough to recognize a mystery in the Person of Jesus. "How he came," he says, "to this consciousness of the unique character of his relation to God as a son is his secret, and no psychology will ever fathom it."* "We shall never fathom the inward development by which Jesus passed from the assurance that he was the Son of God to the other assurance that he was the Messiah." "How

* P. 128.

Jesus arrived at the consciousness of being the Messiah we can never explain." So he admits, but proceeds to work out a theory that seems perfectly natural and entirely satisfactory to its author.

Harnack's treatment of the resurrection is as feeble a piece of work as we have ever known to come from a thoughtful and scholarly man. To begin with, he assumes that miracles are impossible. Next he sets aside the gospel records as wholly untrustworthy. Then he proceeds to account in a wholly inadequate way, in the most absurd fashion, for the fact which is beyond dispute, that the apostles and Christian Church at Jerusalem did believe that on the third day the tomb of Christ was found empty, that Jesus himself appeared to them, spoke with them, ate with them, taught them; that he visibly ascended before their eyes into the heavens. Paul was specific and clear and emphatic in his testimony to the reality of the resurrection. It is, as he says, the basal truth of Christianity and of Christian hope. It was established in the human heart in the face of the most overwhelming forces. The cross had not then the halo of glory it possesses now. What turned the night of gloom into glorious dawn, if not a risen Lord? Harnack admits the confident belief of the apostles and early Church, but denies its basis in reality. He distinguishes between the Easter message and the Easter faith, and denies this necessary connection. Harnack's theory is that Christ did not literally arise from the dead. He is at one on this matter with Matthew Arnold, as he sings:

Now he is dead; far hence he lies
In the lone Syrian town;
And on his grave with shining eyes
The silent stars look down.

He accounts for the Easter faith in this way. Christ submitted to death as a part of his vocation, and in virtue of his hope and confidence in God gained an inward victory over it that robbed it of its terrors. This is all. Concerning this theory it is to be remarked that this inward victory was gained in the sublime surrender on the cross, and not on Easter Day. Concerning this theory it needs to be explained how this victory is to take its place among historical realities so as to endue men with the conviction of eternal realities, if it remained a secret transaction in the soul

of the Redeemer, and between him and the Father. How could the disciples be certain that Jesus did really triumph over death, unless he returned to assure them? How hard-pressed and illogical Harnack is in treating of the resurrection will appear from this paragraph: "The story of Thomas is told for the exclusive purpose of impressing upon us that we must hold the Easter faith even without the Easter message." "Blessed are they that have not seen, and yet have believed." "The disciples on the way to Emmaus were blamed for not believing, even though the Easter message had not reached them."* Now, as a matter of fact, the record clearly shows that Thomas was reproached for not believing the Easter message, which had been carried to him by living witnesses, and which was to be the basis, not only of his faith, but of the faith of all future generations. The Christian faith commended is never a faith without evidence, but a serene and heroic faith on competent testimony. The same is true of the disciples on the way to Emmaus; the Easter message had reached them, and only their unbelieving hearts kept them from the Easter joy.

II. *The Gospel in History.* Turning now from the Gospel in the Gospel to the Gospel in history, our task is more congenial. Here Harnack is on his own ground, and is almost without a peer. He passes in swift and orderly review the development of Christianity through the Apostolic Age, through Catholicism, through the Greek Church, through Roman Catholicism, through Protestantism. What was said of his interpretation of Christianity in its practical aspects is to be said of this historical review. It is in every way admirable. One rarely reads anything more instructive or refreshing. No pedantry is here, or ponderous learning. The large mass of material is handled with consummate skill, clearness, simplicity, and brevity. His conclusions in this part of his work it would be difficult to successfully challenge. His method, too, is fair, just, and impartial. The characteristics of the Apostolic Age he shows are: 1. Recognition of Jesus as risen Lord. 2. Belief in religion as an actual experience, and involving the consciousness of a living union with God. 3. Leading a holy life in purity and brotherly fellowship. By the year 200 A. D. this primitive Chris-

* P. 160.

tianity gives way to a great ecclesiastical and political community; in other words, to Catholicism. This was brought about by the introduction of the spirit and civilization of the Greco-Roman world, and the struggle with Gnosticism. The prominent features of Greek Catholicism are Traditionalism, Intellectualism (that is, Orthodoxy and Intolerance), and Ritualism. The Greek Church he shows to be in the main Paganism, with a Christian veneer. The characteristics of Roman Catholicism are the Latin spirit, Roman world empire, and Augustinianism. The Gospel says, "Christ's kingdom is not of this world," but the Roman Catholic Church has set up an earthly kingdom. Christ demands that his ministers shall not rule, but serve, but here the priests govern the world. Christ leads his disciples away from political and ceremonious religion, and places every man face to face with God, but here man is bound to an earthly institution with chains that cannot be broken, and he must obey; it is only when he obeys that he approaches God. He shows clearly, however, that in these Churches, Greek and Roman, the true faith still lives by means of the Word and religious orders. Conspicuous examples appear from time to time of men and women who possess a true and rare spiritual insight. Protestantism is at once a revolution and a reformation. Religion is again reduced to its essential factors, the word of God and faith. The Gospel in its simplicity is again rewon. He criticises Protestantism for breaking up Western unity. But that, it may be contended, is not an evil. There is a unity of a watch, and also of the solar system. Green clearly demonstrates that the failure of the Comprehension Bill in England was a distinct gain for civil and religious liberty. Harnack warns us against dogmatism, but dogmatism also, it may be urged, has its side of service. Truth stands best in a form of sound words.

To sum up in brief, while conceding to Harnack's fullness of knowledge, charm of style, and a fine insight into the spirit of the Gospel, yet we believe his interpretation of Christianity fails at these points: 1. He is bound by philosophical preconceptions. He does not approach the subject with an open mind, but prejudges the case, sorting and paring down the evidence to fit his theory. In a word, professing to be a free and impartial inquirer, he carries

his ball and chain. 2. He sets aside Scripture in an utterly unwarranted manner. He edits and emends that which he claims to accept by processes.illogical and absurd. Where a gospel does not suit him he takes a knife to it, or discards it altogether. 3. He unjustly eliminates all Christological elements from his interpretations. He builds his structure, therefore, upon a wholly inadequate basis. The Christianity he presents to us is but "the baseless fabric of a vision." In cutting away the bark he quite kills the tree. He throws out the child with the bath. 4. To go back to the flag we left flying. The historic method has achieved splendid results, but it has its limits. The root principle of Harnack's method, we take it, is false—namely, that doctrine is an historic fact to be accounted for wholly by intellectual activities, Greek, Roman, mediæval, modern, etc. The theory errs (1) in regarding human reason and human causes as the only efficient forces at work in the development of Christian doctrine; (2) in ignoring the divine element in the formation and protection of Christian doctrine; (3) in ignoring the place and service of true dogma. The safe and onward movement of a train may turn on the edge of a rail. It is so in history. Paul, Athanasius, Luther, Calvin, Wesley, were switchmen, who set the moving train of theological conviction, and of spiritual and moral progress on right lines. There is a subtle and necessary relation between root and fruit; cut flowers, even ethical ones, soon wither. Life cannot be kept true and wholesome for many generations without sound doctrine. We venture the prophecy that the world will soon witness the revival of a noble Christian dogmatism.

Harnack opens his book with a reference to Socrates. The reference is apt, for he gives us in his interpretation, not the Christ of the gospels, not the Christ of St. John, of St. Paul, or of the Christian faith, but instead thereof a Hebrew Socrates. And as we close his book we sigh, as Mary sighed in the Garden, "They have taken away my Lord, and I know not where they have laid him."

Naphtali Luccock.

Art. VI.—RELIGIOUS LIFE AT OXFORD.

It is likely that in many American homes the satisfaction that will be produced by the publication of the list of Rhodes scholars will be not unmixed with anxiety. What will be the effect of Oxford upon their Christian faith? In particular, will those who come from the denominations which correspond in America to the "Free Churches" of England be in danger of becoming proselytes to sacerdotalism? It is not long since in England itself many Nonconformist parents were deterred by fear of the "clerical atmosphere" of the university from sending their sons to Oxford, and it is not surprising if it should take even longer to assure observers at this distance that Tractarianism is not the characteristic note of the Oxford of to-day. It is not to be denied, of course, that the Church of England is still the paramount religious influence in undergraduate life, and that the associations of the place give it a rare opportunity of appealing both to the historic sense and to the æsthetic temperament. It is at Oxford, probably, that one sees Anglicanism at its strongest. Its ablest preachers occupy the university pulpit. Both Ritualists and Evangelicals are constantly displaying great activity, and an Episcopalian freshman, of whatever variety, will not lack for sympathy. But to a young Nonconformist who has been rooted and grounded in Free Church principles before leaving home, contact with Oxford Anglicanism is on the whole a healthy and strengthening experience. It tends to liberate him from a certain religious provincialism which he is likely to have brought with him, to show him the significance of aspects of truth and worship that he has undervalued, and at the same time to confirm his belief that the need for the Nonconformist protest and separation is still urgent. For if Anglicanism shows its strongest side at Oxford, it is there that it shows its weakest side also. The acquaintance that such a youth obtains with the motives of many of his contemporaries in their choice of the clerical profession is in itself enough to suggest one particular reason which requires the continuance of the Nonconformist Churches as guardians of the apostolic tradition.

The various academic reforms of the last century have now given complete religious freedom to the undergraduate who is not an adherent of the Established Church. The Anglican is required by his own college to attend so many "morning chapels;" the Nonconformist may substitute an equal number of "roll-calls." This is one of the results of that "disestablishment of religion in Oxford" which was so vehemently opposed by the High Church party, and which was referred to by Bishop King in his lament that it was now possible for a man to pass through his whole course without once praying. Attendance at any of the university services in St. Mary's is quite voluntary, for Anglican and Nonconformist alike. There is no longer any religious test for admission to any examination or degree (except B.D. and D.D.). No modern humorist will have an opportunity of startling the vice chancellor, at matriculation, by Theodore Hook's answer, "Forty, if you like," for no freshman will again be asked whether he is willing to subscribe the Thirty-nine Articles. In proportion to their numbers Nonconformists have taken much more than their fair share of the honors of the university, particularly in theology. A contemporary of my own—a Primitive Methodist layman and now a professor in the theological college of that Church—not only won several of the highest university distinctions in theology, but obtained a college fellowship in the same subject. It is worth noting that last year's chairman of the Congregational Union is a distinguished Oxford man and was formerly fellow of his college, and that a recent president of the United Methodist Free Churches is a D.C.L. of Oxford. Oxford men are to be found to-day in the active ministry of all the leading Nonconformist Churches, some of them in the most difficult places of the mission field at home and abroad. In certain cases the college authorities, though themselves Anglicans, have warmly encouraged the preparation of undergraduates for the Nonconformist ministry, as in the conspicuous instance of the help given by Jowett to T. C. Edwards, the leader of the Welsh Calvinistic Methodists during the last generation. It must be admitted that the Church of England has at various times won a considerable number of members, including recruits for its clergy, from Oxonians of Nonconformist origin; but in nearly

all the cases I have personally known the men who "went over" had already made up their minds to do so before they came up to the university.

So far we have been considering the negative side of the question—the exemption of the present-day undergraduate from religious disabilities. It remains to say something of the provision made for his religious welfare by the churches of the city. In connection with the Evangelical section of the Church of England there are various organizations for Bible study and evangelistic effort in which a Nonconformist may cooperate without any sense of restraint. The undergraduates who so astonished Mr. John Corbin by preaching in the open air at the foot of the Martyrs' Memorial probably belonged to one of these societies. As far as Nonconformists are concerned, I can speak with most intimate knowledge of the Wesleyan Methodists, with whom I was associated during 1882-86 under the successive pastorates of Hugh Price Hughes and George Stringer Rowe. The Methodist undergraduates "met in class" once a week at the minister's house, and formed also a Wesley Guild—partly club, partly essay society, and partly evangelistic committee—which visited the rooms of its members in turn. On one occasion, when our host was a Christ Church man, Mr. Rowe surprised us by the information that, as far as he could discover, this was probably the first Methodist meeting that had been held at Christ Church since the days of John Wesley. We served our apprenticeship by tract distribution, Sunday school teaching, and, in the case of those who went "on the circuit plan," preaching in some of the neighboring villages. Those who shared this experience will remember one village where the service was held in the clubroom of the public house, and another where the only convenient place of worship was a bakehouse, in which the perspiring preacher had to stand just in front of the oven. Two other denominations of Methodists besides the Wesleyans are represented in Oxford and the neighborhood, and give similar opportunities of usefulness.

The position of Congregationalism at Oxford has been entirely altered by the influence of Mansfield College, of which I shall speak presently. The local church in George Street previously

served as the place of worship for Congregational undergraduates. The Baptists have two city churches, but the Presbyterians are not yet represented. There has always been, since the abolition of the tests, a sprinkling of Scotch Presbyterians in the university, but there are so few Presbyterians in the city itself that the formation of a church of that order has been thought impracticable. The probability that several Rhodes scholars will be Presbyterians is, however, raising once more in the councils of the denomination the question of establishing a congregation at Oxford. While it is natural that each of the various churches of English Nonconformity should wish to be represented in the university town, the existence of Mansfield makes such direct representation less necessary than ever before, as far as the interests of the undergraduates themselves are concerned. Mansfield is not, like Balliol, Merton, etc., a constituent college of the university, but a theological school. It accepts no students save those who have already graduated in arts, though not necessarily at Oxford. Accordingly, it does not prepare for the university examinations, with the exception of the honors school in theology. It will thus be seen that the average Nonconformist undergraduate does not become a member of Mansfield, and does not attend its class lectures. At the same time, he receives real benefit from it in many ways. The Sunday morning sermon in Mansfield College Chapel is a kind of Nonconformist parallel to the official university sermon at St. Mary's. The list of preachers includes the names of the leading Congregationalist, Baptist, Presbyterian, and Methodist ministers in the United Kingdom. No less attractive than the Sunday morning sermons are the Sunday evening lectures delivered by Dr. Fairbairn himself. Further, Mansfield often secures the help of some suitable minister as a temporary college pastor. This minister—Dr. Horton, for example, has more than once exercised this function— resides in the college for about a fortnight, during which time he comes into personal touch not only with the men who are preparing for the ministry as members of Mansfield, but with the Nonconformist undergraduates in the colleges of the university. By rendering these services Mansfield has practically made itself the center and rallying point for Nonconformist university men of all

denominations, whether graduates or undergraduates. The freshman who makes himself known to its professors on his arrival at Oxford will be at once admitted to religious opportunities equal to those of his home church. And the cumulative effect of the work done by Mansfield during the last sixteen years has told upon the university itself in such a way that the path of the Nonconformist undergraduate has become far easier than before. Outside the university it has impressed itself upon the churches by the character of the men whom it has prepared for the ministry, some of whom, such as J. H. Jowett and C. S. Horne, are already recognized as leaders. Within the university it has made its mark by the distinction of its professors and the brilliant successes of its students. It has definitely raised the status of Nonconformity in the mind of the Anglican don and undergraduate, to whom it has communicated some suggestion of the importance of the Free Churches to the national life. In Matthew Arnold's university, at least, it has made the Matthew Arnold view of Nonconformity no longer possible. There has thus been removed a certain sense of isolation and eccentricity that was felt by the pioneers of thirty years ago; the student who dissents from the Established Church need no longer disturb himself by the apprehension that he is regarded by his contemporaries as an ecclesiastical freak.

In the history of this change one name will always stand out prominently above all others—that of Dr. Andrew Martin Fairbairn. Much—not too much—has been said of his profound and multifarious learning; but there has been a tendency to overlook his marvelous courage. When he first set up his desk in a hired house in "the High," the *British Weekly* truly said of his invasion of Oxford that there had been nothing like it since the charge of the Light Brigade. There must have been something of the Pauline spirit in a man who could thus risk his reputation on an enterprise which, in the opinion of some who knew Oxford well, seemed doomed to failure. It is difficult to speak without apparent exaggeration of the debt which the Nonconformist Churches of England owe to Principal Fairbairn for his tenacious faith as well as for his rare erudition. He has been assisted by a faculty which has made itself a reputation for scholarship as well as for success

5

in teaching. It included, until his recent resignation to become a candidate for Parliament, Dr. John Massie, who was already favorably known as a theological professor and as a New Testament exegete before Mansfield was founded. There are still on its staff Mr. J. Vernon Bartlet, the leading Nonconformist authority on the history of the early Church; Mr. G. Buchanan Gray, whose book on Old Testament names has given him high rank as a Hebraist; and Mr. G. W. Thatcher, one of the university examiners in the school of Semitic languages. It has to be remembered that a student for the Nonconformist ministry who is in residence at Oxford has also an opportunity of attending the lectures of Dr. W. Sanday, Dr. S. R. Driver, Dr. W. Lock, Dr. D. S. Margoliouth, and other university professors, as well as of receiving instruction from the Mansfield faculty. These advantages are within reach of members of all denominations. The trust deed of Mansfield College requires certain doctrinal subscriptions from its full professors, but imposes no such restriction upon its students. There is no other theological college in England in which students for the ministry are so likely as at Mansfield to be brought into contact with men who are preparing for a similar career in other churches. Mansfield is therefore doing not a little to promote a better understanding between the various Nonconformist Churches, as well as between Nonconformity and Anglicanism.

Herbert W. Horwill

Art. VII.—THE ENIGMATICAL COLERIDGE.

"Who was Coleridge?" is a conundrum nearly a century old. He was somebody, or the question would not have kept running a single year. There have been plenty of hard nuts to crack in the last hundred years; thinking men have little patience to stop and delve into quizzical characters, unless there be something far-reaching in the mystery. Forgotten, Coleridge is not; his spirit will not down. There are only a few great names one hits upon more frequently. The very persistence of his presence in such great fields of thought challenges investigation. Coleridge was a precocious boy, who never won his college degree; he was an affectionate husband, who did not live with his wife; a loving father, who did not support his family; be was a pioneer in German learning, who held it beneath him to translate Goethe's *Faust;* he was a Unitarian preacher, whose clearest work was a philosophical defense of the Trinity; he was a liberal in politics in the days of the French Revolution, who spent his last days buttressing the English throne. He planned a colony for renovating the world, a "pantisocracy," to be established upon the banks of the Susquehanna—because the name was so pretty. His preparation for this new paradise was the marrying a handsome girl, and, when unable to borrow four pounds, abandoning the dream. His fame as a man rests on what he was not; his rank as a poet, on what he might have done; his place as a philosopher, on a system he never so much as outlined; his power as a political writer, on one pamphlet and some editorials in an embryo magazine read by so few that the printer was never paid. His prestige as a religious thinker depends upon some fragments from a notebook. He never gained independence until he had become a twenty-year guest at the house of a friend. His contemporaries spent much time shaking their heads and uttering severe words about his wasted powers; yet several of them are known only as they cling to the skirts of Coleridge—the fact that they stood near him alone rescues them from oblivion. He was the most famous of the brilliant conversers; yet Carlyle, after two hours' listening, wrathfully declared himself

lost in this transcendental moonshine, and defied any mortal to tell what the sage was talking about. Shelley wrote:

> He was a mighty poet, and
> A subtle-souled psychologist;
> All things he seemed to understand
> Of old or new, of sea or land,
> But his own mind, which was a mist.

The *Critic* for March, 1901, brings to light a poem by Aubrey De Vere with penciled notes on its margin by Walter Savage Landor, written in 1843:

> His eye saw all things in the symmetry
> Of true and just proportion,
> Yet dim that eye with gazing upon heaven.

[Landor—The greatest liar that ever did gaze upon it.]

> No loftier, purer soul than his hath ever
> With awe revolved the planetary page
> (From infancy to age)
>   of Knowledge.

[Landor—Alas, were it but so!]

> A-down Lethean streams his spirit drifted
> Under Elysian shades.

[Landor—Drunk with gin and opium.]

> Coleridge farewell!
>   Through life a goodly vein
> Was thine! and time it was thy rest to take.
> Soft be the sound ordained thy sleep to break!
> When thou art waking, wake me, for thy Master's sake.

[Landor—And let me nap on.]

Who was Coleridge? Listen to what may be said: Hazlitt—"The only person I ever knew who answered to the idea of a man of genius." Wordsworth—"I have known men who have done wonderful things, but the most wonderful man I ever knew was Coleridge." De Quincey—"The largest and most spacious intellect, the subtlest and most comprehensive that has yet existed among men." Southey wrote to a friend—"I am grieved that you never met Coleridge; all other men whom I have known are mere children compared to him." J. S. Mill—"The great seminal mind of his generation." Dr. Arnold, Julius Hare, F. D. Maurice, and Newman add words in tribute to the stimulating power of his intellect, as shaping the noblest currents of English thought. Horace Bushnell spoke freely of his own great indebtedness to Coleridge. Lamb declared the neighborhood of such a man exciting as fifty ordinary persons.

Who was Coleridge the poet? A member of a group of epoch-making English singers. His contribution, though, is a thin volume seldom seen, less frequently read—"Genevieve," "Christabel," "Kubla Khan," a few noble odes, and "The Ancient Mariner" are all. "Christabel" is only splendid word-juggling. He tossed the sword in air like an oriental juggler, but the trick was never finished. "The Ancient Mariner" is a nightmare, an allegory, an extravaganza. There are songs without words, this is words and music without a song. It is so weird, its rhymes and similes ever haunt the memory. Now some bold, practical thinker reads between the lines, and tells us what it teaches. Bad luck and wantonly cruel to shoot a goose, is about the practical result that can be squeezed out of it. Others tell us that it is so strange and far-away it is only a curio. It has just one inexplicable thing about it—that one thing is enough—its beauty can never be forgotten. This poet, who stands on a pedestal frail as a Venetian vase, still stands among the mighty men of English song.

Who was Coleridge the talker? At his feet gathered the thinking, eager young literary men of England. Pilgrimages to hear his table talk were reverently made by scores, who listened as to one inspired. Wordsworth—"Like a majestic river the sound or sight of whose course you caught at intervals, which was sometimes concealed by forests, sometimes lost in sand, then came flashing out broad and distinct, and, even when it took a turn which your eye could not follow, you always felt and knew that there was a connection in its parts, that it was the same river." Carlyle's view of this same river of speech was not so clear—"Talk flowing anywhither like a river, but spreading anywhither in inextricable currents and regurgitations like a lake or sea, terribly deficient in definite goal or aim, nay, often in logical intelligibility; what were you to believe or do, on any earthly or heavenly thing obstinately refusing to appear from it? So that most times you felt logically lost, swamped, near to drowning, in this tide of ingenious vocables, boundless as if to submerge the world." Happily, as ever with Coleridge, there is weighty evidence upon the other side—no less than the emphatic judgment of De Quincey: "Coleridge, to many people seemed to wander; and he seemed to

them to wander most when, in fact, his resistance to the wandering instinct was the greatest, namely, when the compass and huge circuit by which his illustrations moved traveled far into remote regions before they began to revolve. Long before his coming around commenced most people had lost him, and naturally enough supposed that he had lost himself. I can assert, upon my long intimate knowledge of Coleridge's mind, that logic, the most severe, was as inalienable from his modes of thinking as grammar from his language."

In literary criticism Coleridge was a creative power. His judgments upon Shakespeare were the first adequate and illumining criticisms upon the great poet; their sanity and penetration remain unchallenged. His work in philosophy was to open the doors of English thought and secure a hospitable place at the British fireside for the *Practical Reason* of Kant. He found a splendid field of action as champion of the practical reason as dominant over the speculative understanding. "There he found an assurance of the ability of man for the immediate contemplation of truth, and that the reasoning powers are not man himself, and that he may rise above their impotence, and have direct faith in unseen realities." Whatever result this contention had in fertilizing the hard and dry field of English philosophy, its most fruitful realm was found in theology. There Coleridge the laggard, the opium-eater, the writer of fragments, the transcendental dreamer, stands the farseeing leader, the prophet of the dispensation of liberal orthodox Christianity. He is the John the Baptist crying in the wilderness of hard theology and mechanical evidences, preparing the way for the doctrine of divine immanence and the evidence of Christian experience. Coleridge came at the time when the battle with deism had been fought and won by the unrivaled logic of Butler and massing of evidence by Paley. If the clumsy and powerful old knights in armor who strove to drive Christianity from the field with lance and mace of deism were routed, a host of weapons of modern warfare was training for the most merciless and insidious and brilliant attacks that religion has ever encountered. The pantheistic movement was ready to advance with its stealthy and subtle methods. It denied the personality of

God, the conscious immortality of the soul; the underlying facts of Christian revelation it would evaporate in poetical mists. Its meaning was hidden, and phraseology reverent. "It came with a Judas kiss." The real strength of its warfare lay rather in its ally, the historical criticism. All supernatural, miraculous events were to be thrown in the line of a perfectly natural development; the beauty and significance of the biblical miracles and the Incarnation were lauded in rapturous phrases, but the fact persistently denied. Legend and myth, poetry and symbol are all allowed, but the reality, the fact, never. The later conflict came from the most candid, powerful, and thoroughgoing foemen Christianity has ever faced—the men of science. The achievements that turned the world upside down gave a new method to all; civilization seemed at first to do away with religion and to drive the very God from the heavens. The smoke of that tremendous duel is now clearing away, and we can see that Christianity was never so well founded in the minds and hearts of believers, but the power of attack and the honest desertion of many earnest seekers after truth have made the onslaught a crisis to be remembered humbly and reverently. Coleridge has done more than any other man to prepare the Christian thinker for this thrice-waged battle. His real power was as an interpreter of spiritual facts, a foremost leader in the "rediscovery of the inner life." What Wesley had done in the practical way of mighty revival in the lives and hearts of millions he interpreted with a philosophy of Christian experience that could be defended in the highest courts of reason and could sing its joy unashamed in the face of the most learned and merciless criticism. He gave a new impulse to all liberal evangelical thinking. He seemed at a sad loss about conducting his own life, yet out of this painful experience as a student of spiritual life he gave a message that quickened and broadened the manliest life of England. The man scathed by his friends for lack of service to men, supposed to be always dreaming, was able to replace reason in religion, whence it had been dethroned, and to give new guidance to Christian feeling, the very years when new dangers were abroad in a restless and stormy era. "I take up this work," he says, "of the inspiration of Scripture with a real purpose to read it as I should any other

work—as far, at least, as I dare. For I neither can nor dare throw off a strong and awful prepossession in its favor—certain as I am that a large part of the life and light by which I see, love, and embrace the truth, and the strength coorganized into a living body of faith and knowledge, has been directly or indirectly derived to me from this sacred volume." "More that finds me than all I have experienced in all other books put together." So his idea of experience, practical reason, gave a basis for his defense of the Bible, and his doctrine of the immanent God got men ready for the scientific attack. Nobody reads Coleridge now. His marvelous contributions to Christian thought at this crisis hour have been absorbed by the eager minds of countless disciples. The gold from the mighty brain, melted in the hot furnace fires of sorrow and temptation in his own life, has passed into the current coin of modern religious thought. Coleridge lived to be an old man, and died at the house of a friend, Dr. Gilliam, near London. He spent the last hours of his life dictating sentences for his great system of philosophy—laying bricks for the first courses of his tower of Babel, upon which his dream-rapt eyes had been for years fondly gazing as it lifted its air-hung turrets before him. The more we look into it, the more perplexing is the paradox of Coleridge's life, the stranger the fate of his influence. His methodical friends never tired of holding him up as a terrible example of wasted powers and paralyzed genius. But they are slowly fading, while the name of Coleridge stands in letters of light. His books are well-nigh forgotten, but he still calls forth the high respect of thinking men. His poor, struggling, half-defeated life is now seen to end in victory. An author without readers, a leader without disciples, a life to be remembered with pity, he is nevertheless sure of a place among the immortals. So we come round to the question with which we began, our circle yet unsquared, and end by still asking, Who was Coleridge?

Franklin McElfresh

Art. VIII.—MORAL EMPHASIS IN EDUCATION.

EDUCATION has to do with mind preeminently. It is the assisted development of mind, and with it the construction of character. The nature of the education determines the character. This is a commonplace. But, like many common truths, it needs more attention as well by the man on the street who wants his child to grow up good and useful, and the metaphysical moralist interested academically in the evolution of the race. The growth of mind is the growth of character. Man has a mind, a subject of the mental life, a spiritual substance back of all mental activity—call it mind, soul, or spirit. By the mind or soul is not meant a mere aggregation of psychical activities. Mind is not matter. Material mind with all its activities accounted for by physical laws is a vanishing theory. With materialists of to-day man has no mental subject, and all activities are accounted·for by physiology. The increased study of the relation of mind to body is a demand in education. But it is far from finding that mental activity can be wholly accounted for by physiology. Man has a soul, affected in multiform ways by the physical body; nevertheless a distinct reality, the ground and agent of his intellectual, volitional, and emotional life. The mind is a unit. It acts always as a whole. While we speak of "faculties of mind," "divisions of mind," and the like, these are only to facilitate expression, and have no existence in actuality.

Now, this mind is character. The mind does not *produce* character. It *is* character. As the mind, so is the man, the woman. As the mind grows, so grows character in kind and degree. *Mind is the man.* Another commonplace; but a significant truth needing emphasis. But while mind is character, what makes mind? What determines the character of mind—the character of character? What gives cast and trend to the mind that is the man? In one word, environment. I use this word in its full content, to include ancestry, heredity, and personal, family, social, racial, national conditions. These all enter into the making of mind. Some of these affect us mediately and some immediately. Some affect us

without our asking or being asked. Some affect us by personal
contact and willing, personal mental activity. Racial, hereditary,
ancestral conditions are beyond our control. But national, family,
social, personal come close to us. We are *in* these; and these are
forming mind—character. The changes in the character of persons and nations produced by changes in environment are as widespread as the race. There is no place where surroundings so
directly and forcefully tell upon the making of character as our
educational institutions. Here active, positive effort is made to
environ and develop the mind. The student is not at school merely
to absorb. Even absorbing would be a powerful factor in his
making. He is there to be molded, changed, developed, characterized. This is the business of the school. It is the duty, the office
of the teacher to create environment by positive effort. And the
student will become what his school is. Let this thought impress
itself on parents, guardians, and intending students. Let them
cease writing for catalogues to compare *expenses* and sending or
going where a paltry dollar can be saved. But let them compare
surroundings—moral, social, intellectual conditions. It is in
these the boys and girls are to be immersed, and they will be
fashioned in character in agreement with these. Here is a third
commonplace, but a tremendous truth. A truth for the times whose
wide preaching is demanded is the education of the mind as a moral
factor. By this is not meant mere teaching of ethics or of psychology; but such instruction as shall bring the student to a
vivid consciousness that he is a moral being, that the cultivation
of the moral is the highest office of education, and that all education should contribute thereto.

Every school of thought regards the moral nature in man the
differentiating one and the highest. And yet it is one of the sur-
prises and anomalies of the education of Christendom that the care
and development of man's highest nature is, in the system, relegated to a subordinate place. There is no plea here for the recognition and teaching in our schools of shibboleths, notions, doxies,
and the sectarian narrownesses with which our blessed Christianity
is overburdened; but for the recognition and teaching of the fact
that the student has a soul, and that this soul must be cultivated

morally and upon the principles of the highest morality known to history and the race. Just as any other institution recognizes the most significant factor in its objects and work, and plies the highest and most effective means for the realization of its ends, so the school must come to recognize the moral in mind as the supreme factor in man, and provide means for its care and culture at least as adequate as those employed in any other department of education. *Now, this study of the moral and its culture must be comparative.* These are the days of comparative study. Ethics, psychology are in the curricula of our schools. They have a large place. Psychology in education is becoming a craze. People are seeking a better knowledge of mind in order to its more perfect cultivation. The mind is divided into faculties, and an attempt made to weigh their relative value in education. But what education? An education where the moral is neither the end nor the chief field of work. The principle is excellent; but it is not applied where it ought to be. People generally emphasize what they regard as of superior importance. It is a significant fact that with all our boasted civilization and educational prominence the moral in man is not practically regarded as the predominantly significant. The study must be *comparative.* We must know what the moral is, what the best moral is, and the best way is to grow the best moral. A man stated recently in public address, "Christianity is the best moral system." Did he *know* this? How did he know this? A man gives his means to send the Gospel to non-Christian peoples, because he says the Christian system is the highest morality. Does he know it, and how? He knows it by comparison, or he does not know it at all—by a comparison intellectual or experimental. People vociferate over our Christianity as the highest morality who actually do not *know* whether their assertions are true or not. It *is* the greatest moral teaching and moral reality, but how do we know this? By comparing it with all other moral systems. The Asiatic is usually intellectually converted before he is evangelically converted—he sees first that what we have is better than he has and accepts the better. Parliaments of religion are useful so far as they result in a just comparison—the moral best of the Orient with the moral best of the Occident.

It is easy now to obtain a knowledge of the ethical systems of the world, past and present. The kernel of each and its differentiating feature can be perceived, and its ability to minister to the moral in mind determined. Why did the Greeks, who claimed and held first place as mental and moral diagnostics, really miss the moral in man, and produce a religion which was mostly comedy? Why did Confucianism, with its "Do not to others as ye would not they should do to you," produce the diverse Chinese and Japanese civilizations, while the same kind of precept in the Christian system produced ours? Why did Taoism, with its "Love your enemies," flinch before Confucianism and collapse before Buddhism? Why did the whole ancient Western philosophy, the creation of the choicest minds, fail to salt and save society? Why did it run the world to moral wreck? Why did the Christian system in the hands of simple fishermen come upon that wreck and deliver it? Why did Hebrewism, the very religion of God, fail upon the very chosen people and produce a moral conjuncture which called forth the anathemas of a Christ and Paul? Comparative study shows all this. This comparison is the educational method. About half the courses of our colleges are only of mediate use in the affairs of life—of little practical value, as we say. A boy does not need Latin to run a steam engine, nor Greek to bind corn, nor natural science to deal in stocks, nor philosophy to cut hair, nor higher mathematics to tan skins. It is astonishing how little of these is immediately needed in what is denominated the practical life of the majority of people. Then why are they in? Why do they persist? Why must they be in? Not merely to help out a liberal education, but because they are essential to the development of mind—because of their relative and comparative value in mind building. Young students say, "We do not need this or that;" "We have no taste for this or that." If some were allowed to choose their own courses they could go to school twenty years and not become educated. They would always select the subjects which follow the line of least resistance, and their will power and application would lie dormant and undeveloped. There is just now a little too much "bent-following" which is not educative, but is the opposite. Away with the humanities if we can find a substitute. The substitute has not thus far appeared.

It is by comparison the student comes to know himself—in the contact and competition with fellow-students. This rubbing and comparing is the great boon of school life.

The method must be *constructive*. It is not enough to posit a soul; not sufficient to recognize the best moral. We must bring the mind and the best moral together in constructive activity. How is this to be done? It can be done only through the religious. To be religious, morality must include God. Atheistic theories are, therefore, defective. They lack the essential religious-moral complement—God. Agnostic theories will not do. No moral character, very strong, can be made up of the "may be" or "may not be" of uncertainty, or any theory of "we cannot know." If we cannot know there is a God how can we construct the religious-moral character? Positivistic theories will not answer. Confucius, six hundred years before Christ, excluded God from his system and made a positivism. The mind must occupy itself alone with the concrete—the human—he taught. And this is the reason that, while his doctrine went as high as the negative golden rule, it produced a Chinese people. The system which excludes the supernatural throws the mind upon itself, or at best upon other human minds, for the material for moral building. Present-day positivism is no better off. It has the Confucian defect. It bars out God and throws the soul upon itself or other souls as the only source of moral supply. Race history amply testifies that man is not sufficient for his own needs. Pantheism will not do. At its best it brings God to his highest consciousness in man. It is again man to satisfy man's moral need. Buddhism will not do. It places the moral in man under necessitated "cause and effect," and makes his only escape from moral evil the annihilation of consciousness; man is morally saved when he is totally extinct. Dualism will not suffice. This virtually lifts the moral conflict out of the hands of men; ulterior beings or principles fight it out to the victory of the good.

The religion of Christianity meets the case, and alone meets it. Its teaching is positive as to God a Spirit. God and man, their natures and mutual relations, are plainly defined. The relations are the most natural. God is a "Power not ourselves that makes

for righteousness." He is a Power, but a Person and Father. He is a Power by whose assistance man can realize himself—can come to the highest moral relation, ability, and activity. It is only man and God conjoined that can work out the true morality ·in man. Christian morality is religion. Christianity is not a written gospel. It is not a posited creed. It is a *power*—"the power of God." It is not a new law. It is not an "old law with new sanctions." It is not a law at all. It is a power, a force. It is a force in the moral realm. Paul said the Gospel is the power or force of God. It is the mode of divine activity in the human mind. Here is what renders it constructive. It builds soul and is built into soul. It is moral power. Moral regeneration is man's reception of this God-power by which he can reach his highest moral ends. The Gospel meant good news of moral help brought to the soul from outside the soul. This moral power makes man altruistic. His highest self is self-fulness, and this is reached not by selfishness, but self-denial. He has a relation and duty to man infinitely higher than the positivist. But more, he is related to God. The denial of self—the subordination of self—gives the power right of way for the morally constructive.

The method must be *objective*. The teacher must possess not merely the theory of the highest moral; *he must be the moral*. Hence, if the religious-moral is to be distinct and dominant in the schools, the kind of instructors must be considered. Our Christian schools can have no place for teachers save those who are unquestionably religious—object lessons, "written epistles." This is the education which demands its rightful place—the making of mind, which is character, on the principles of God in Christ.

John Wier

Art. IX.—SOME ENDURING QUALITIES IN LITERATURE.

It has been pointed out with some show of justice that the comparative method of determining the worth of literature is unscientific and should cease. We are reminded that every great literary production is distinctly *sui generis*. It stands by itself, bearing no paternal or maternal influence. In other words, imitation never stamps itself upon a superlatively great piece of literature, and therefore we have no right to measure the genius of one by the literary yardstick of another. We are told that the matter of greatness is purely a matter of personal opinion, and are cited to a large number of literary men of the greatest eminence whose opinions concerning authors have ranged all the way to antipodal distances. The criticism of literature is conceived to be mainly a matter of caprice, and the inference is that there can be no adequate grounds for determining that which is of permanent value. While the essence of all literary criticism should have for its object the appreciation of literature rather than the measurement of literature, yet it soon becomes evident that there must be some basis of values in literature. The fact that there remains literature which has survived the storm and stress periods of a millennium shows that literature is not left entirely to the caprice of individual judgment. Neither can it be said that literary immortalities are the resultant of a continued and general popularity. Æschylus, Sophocles, and Euripides have been trickling their brain and heart blood through a few college professors and students, but they have always been caviare to the general. Ninety people out of a hundred who read Homer may not like him, and Milton is more admired than read. But no one presumes to say that these men are not entitled to good firm seats on Parnassus. We must acknowledge that there is a subtle process going on that is discriminating between the transient and the permanent in literature, swiftly and quietly at times taking many of the books over which the multitude pursed out its lips and cried, "Live forever," and putting the dust deep on their faces, and taking some of the books which grew in out-of-the-way places, crowned books for the ruling of the world.

We then hold that there is literature which has endured because there are certain qualities found in the productions. Our business now is to inquire concerning these qualities. Recent students—and here we must particularly mention Professor Winchester, of Wesleyan, whose book, *Some Principles of Literary Criticism,* is perhaps the best utterance upon the subject—have informed us that there are four qualities which enter into literature, namely, thought, emotion, imagination, and form. Of these four qualities one above all the others furnishes the distinguishing hall-mark of literature, and that is emotion. The thought element can be transferred easily from one place to another, and the names of various persons may be tacked upon it without doing injustice to any of the writers. No man calls a work on mathematics a piece of literature, unless it has something in it besides a bare discussion of principles. Scientific books which simply seek to unfold the principles of the science, historical works which relate in a cold, impartial way the doing of the past, are not to be included in what is called literature. Hallam and Stubbs, for instance, are looked upon as judicial historians, while Macaulay and Froude are made the targets for sneers from academic quarters. And yet it is frequently ignored that what these judicial historians never attained Macaulay and Froude have attained, and that is making a body of literature. You can transplant Hallam and Stubbs to other soils and give them other names, and you need not justly incur the charge of plagiarism. But the emotional element dies out of its environment. It is a rare thing lightly immeshed in a net of golden words, and the least jar of moving breaks the web and the emotion has effervesced. This is one thing that must be observed concerning the emotional element—it cannot be transplanted, and this must therefore be one of the chief qualities of literature. But emotion must be found in a matrix of other qualities before there can be any effective literature. The thought element must be combined. It is, for instance, psychologically difficult, if not impossible, for a person to be thrown into a high state of emotion with the first sentence of a book. The reader must be coaxed or wheedled along with some thought, some representation of a scene, until his interest has become aroused and he becomes eager to hurry

on to the *dénouement.* But we must ever bear in mind that it is not always the best and deepest and clearest thinking that is literature. Compare Herbert Spencer and Charles Lamb. Spencer wrote a treatise on style which is the classic utterance on the subject. His own style is clear and forceful, while his thought holds in solution some of the weightiest truths expressed during the century. And yet we hardly dare to include the works of Herbert Spencer in what we call literature. The place of Charles Lamb is, however, secure. Although his thought seems but commonplace, and he makes not the slightest excursion into the obscure fields, yet he has pushed his way into the charmed circle of the immortals. We can transplant the thought of Spencer to other pages, and that makes for his immortality, but the soul of Charles Lamb laughs and sings and sighs only in that nervous glancing English of his, and we must go to his pages or never know what contribution he made to the emotional stock of the world, and this makes for his immortality. We shall dwell but a moment on the imaginative element in literature. This element is found frequently conjoined with the emotional element, and words which set forth high images frequently carry emotional effects. But so far as we can conceive the separation of the emotional and the imaginative elements we can see that the latter plays a less important part than the former. Shelley's "Skylark" is a high work of imagination. The emotional element, however, is like a swallow, skimming in and out, but finding no resting place on the rapidly dissolving images of the poet. On the other hand, Keats's "Nightingale" is flooded with the deepest emotion, placed in the most imaginative setting. There is no doubt which is the greater poem. The heart of Keats throbs through his poems, and the English literature can better afford to cast Shelley with all his greatness to the void than lose these delicate breathings of John Keats. In running over some selections from the poets, where poems are classified under different topics, as Love, Friendship, Bereavement, Nature, Description, we are not long in deciding which sections contain the truest and the most abiding poetry. Where the emotions play, there we linger and find our greatest joy, and what we thus do unconsciously we do because we have an innate feeling of what true poetry contains.

G

The formal element in literature is one which the tendency of the age is to ignore. We are thus getting to the farthest remove from the classic period in English literature when Dryden and Pope were the masters. These poets were exact, punctilious to a hair. Rhymes and cæsuras must tick off with the steady measured beat of the pendulum. In poetry we are growing careless of metrical feet, and are not overly sensitive to rhythm. In prose we will tolerate the sesquipedalian antics, nor find fault with the jerky grasshopper style. What we are clamoring for is soul. Give us soul, the critics cry, no matter how you serve it up, give us soul. And soul has been dished out to us pronged through and through with Carlylean brusquerie, while Whitman has struggled through a wilderness of words, and with many contortions and a skillful avoidance of rhythm and music has managed to scare up a covey of thoughts, whereupon the *blasé* literary world has clapped its hands enraptured, as though it had discovered an ichthyosaurus of literature—as it perhaps has. If the decision is between soul and sound our choice shall always be for soul, but there is no need at present of conceiving that great thoughts must perforce come thundering down to us in lumber wains. We are not quite willing to drop out of poetry its music and rhythm because a few soulful pieces have been written without them. William Dean Howells has called our attention to the fact that there are two things which the literary world in general has failed to distinguish, namely, poetry and the materials for poetry. His contention seems just. Emerson furnished the greatest amount of material for poetry of any man of his century, and yet the amount of real poetry which he wrote is small. I have fancied that a considerable portion of the works of Robert Browning might better be classed as materials for poetry rather than true poetry, for there is frequently such a harsh utterance, the verse at times breaking out in such jerky attitudes, and all encompassed about with such obscurity of meaning, that we have felt that some of the chief essentials of verse have been ignored, and we rather choose to classify these pieces as materials for poetry rather than true poetry. Our contention is that the formal element in literature must not be ignored. In all of the highest literature we expect to find clearness, sim-

plicity, and rhythm, and when we fail to find these we infer the coming on of some genius who will take the stock of ideas at hand, as Shakespeare appropriated the ideas of his day, and give to them a setting which the world will cherish.

One of the pleasing signs of our day is the discussion of the theme literature and life. How much Ruskin is entitled to praise for having turned the minds of critics to the relation between life and literature is a matter for discussion. But it is quite evident that since his inspiring pronouncement that art principles articulate with our human nature critics of literature have been more and more taking the cue and have shown that the best literature as well as the best art must articulate with life. I wish to mention several qualities which have common ground in the best literature and the highest living.

First we note the thought of unity. The greatest pieces of literature cannot be patchwork. There must be girders running down from the first word to the last syllable. There is no intrusion of any foreign element. Every word, image, person introduced must be some illustration of the central theme. It avails us nothing to say that there are some great works of literature which violate unity of treatment. Our contention is not that there are no great works in which unity is not apparent, for then we should have to justify ourselves in the presence of Dickens and Thackeray. Keats would slightly suffer in his "Eve of St. Agnes," and even Shakespeare would come perilously near to adverse criticism in his "Merchant of Venice." But despite what exceptions we may find our minds are so constructed as to demand unity. This is the philosopher's search as he perceives the phenomena of the universe, and this is the demand of every soul that appreciates literature. The thought of unity carries with it the thought of climax. That piece of literature is imperfect which has two or more culminating points. "The Merchant of Venice" attains its climax when Shylock has been discomfited. We are interested in the love scene and the pretty escapades which follow, but we feel that the master stroke fell when the cowering, cringing Jew crept out of sight before the Jovian thunderbolts of justice. On the other hand, "Hamlet" is packed together as economically as the kernel in a

nut. Words impinge on words, ideas mingle, souls touch souls, circumstances march on, but all are tending to some predestined goal. We follow Hamlet with no abatement of desire or interest through the agony, the doubt, the trial, the love, until his eyes fail in the glooming night, and, with death a victor coming fast on and voice catching the silentness of the tomb, he whispers, "O God! Horatio, what a wounded name!" And then we pause to hear Horatio, the true man, who never crooked the pregnant hinges of the knee where thrift might follow fawning, "Good night, sweet prince; and flights of angels sing thee to thy rest." And then in our confusion we hear but indistinctly the tramp of the ambassadors and the people, closing with the slow music of the funeral march. This brings a unity of impression, and we have felt the strength of the mind which has brooded over events so dissimilar until they have grown into each other and have carried us with them by gradual steps to the end of a mighty life.

In the second place, we note that all great literature is sincere. It is the transcript of an honest soul. No man ever wrote enduring literature who did not put his heart blood in it. Machiavelian literature is good only for the dung heap after it has been spawned. The subtle aroma of personality pervades the work of the earnest man. We speak of impersonal poets, as Shakespeare, and we sometimes seem to imply that the impersonal is something else besides himself. The fact is that every true man reveals himself, and Shakespeare is not, as we sometimes fancy, the least known of our modern men of literature. He is the best known. It is true that we have not been able to definitely ascertain the color of the sheep he is reported to have stolen, nor the name of the scions of nobility whose horses he held at the London theater. We are in some doubt as to the qualities of his penmanship, and a good many are troubled as to whether Shakespeare was really Shakespeare. But we are not much more concerned about these things than about the clothes he wore. Every man lives two lives. One is where he is the sport of circumstances, caught in the flux of time, and whirled along from cradle to grave, and most of our historians have conceived it to be their chief pleasure to report the places where this bodily entity got washed up on some drift where it became conspicuous

for a breathing moment. This is the life of the body, interesting enough to the man who owns it, but of decreasing importance to the men who coming on see it in a fading perspective. The other life is the life of the mind, or rather of the soul. What the man thought, suffered, loved, enjoyed, how he girded his soul for fight when the enemies came on, how his feet slipped on the perilous paths of temptation and the harpies of remorse preyed on his vitals, what songs he sang when he floated calmly on moonlit summer seas, what aspirations looked out from happy skies and opened long vistas of splendor before him—all these are the life of the soul, and we must hold them to be of vaster importance than the history of eating, drinking, wiving, or dying. We have the history of the soul of Shakespeare, and it has seemed to be a small matter indeed to try to ascertain whether any part of his works, and particularly his sonnets, contain his autobiography. We may hold that everything that he wrote is autobiography. Do we wish to compare Shakespeare and Byron? and say that Byron was personal and Shakespeare impersonal? We simply mean that Byron had but one channel through which he could pour his personality, while Shakespeare had a thousand. The question to ask concerning the creations of Shakespeare is, Are they real? If so, they were a part of him, companions of his, bearing as close relation to him as Ben Jonson, whom he met at the London theater. And that these are real creations the world has long ago conceded. Dickens has told us how his characters would haunt him, and he could not get them from his mind. Nothing was quite so real to him as many of the men and women whom he sought to portray. This sincerity must always enter into the worthiest literature. When a man says, "Go to, I will write a book, so many measures of courage for my hero, so many measures of love, a full-fed stream of incidents to launch him in, and the whole bathed in the moonlight of poetry, and I will have a book," then the world will say, "Nay, nothing but heart blood will satisfy. Tell us what you think and feel and do and suffer and love, and we shall listen, if you tell it well." Even romances to be good must be sincere. He who draws their characters must believe in them. He must hold them as dear to him as flesh and blood. No writer can produce life by compounding a few qualities

with a number of incidents. The great writer is he who sees life, and simply reports what he sees and hears.

In the third place, we note that enduring literature must be chiefly concerned with the things of general human interest. The specialist finds no literary doors open to him. The scientific teacher is tabooed from the field. The philosopher and the metaphysician never enter into the polite circle. The man with the hobby catches but a gleam of the happy lands, and then is swept on with the rushing current of those wrapped round in "the hodden gray of mortality." If we say that Plato was a philosopher and wrote enduring literature, let us not forget that the very part that we call literature in Plato is precisely the part where we note the absence of technical details and find the sentiment taking on the humanity wide sweep. A philosopher and a scientist may have enough of the delicate qualities of style and the finer sentimental perceptions to write enduring literature, but they can never take for their chief and direct object the thought of teaching the truths of their chosen studies. The strictly didactic teacher who seeks to impart special knowledge through the Socratic method of questions and answers has no place with us. Bellamy's "Equality" struck the whirlpool and went down. Young's "Night Thoughts" and Pollok's "Course of Time" are growing dimmer on the horizon with the lapse of time. The true field of literature includes everything that is of general interest. The passions that surge, the loves that twine, the fears that blanch the check, the sorrows that come gray-filleted, the hopes that brighten with the coming dawns, remorse that crouches from baleful fires, peace that nestles down like doves of God—all these are themes for enduring literature, and he who can shadow them forth, the best will find his place the most secure. Literature is not, then, the field for all of human thought, and this at first sight seems an anomaly—that we should hold things to be of enduring value which seem commonplace, and that we should relegate to neglected places the acute projectile utterances which pierce to the very core of things. But our wonder passes when we consider that the most staple and undying product of our globe is human nature. What philosophers think of human nature, what physiological and psychical laws may be deduced, what social adaptation

may be made of the unit to the many, what niche in the body politic the individual should fill—all these are important in their way, but their interests vary much with the climates in which men breathe, and come as juiceless and jejune to the great mass of the human family. The passing of philosophies to their *requiescat* is one of the startling things of history, and should teach us that what we conclude to be the deepest and the most permanent is perhaps then passing on to its rest. But he who has truly caught the varying aspect of the individual human heart, and has wedded his thoughts to the richest surest-footed words, has caught the secret that makes him a companion of the ages. Who was Homer? And the answer comes from many who like to split kindling out of great personalities, "He was seven." And we have no interest in combating that which we may not know, and we have learned a more excellent way than spending time on the question whether Homer was he or they. We have found that the book is human, and if it were written yesterday its face could hardly be more fresh. We have seen the rosy fingered dawn. We have heard the booming of the sea and the sounding of the measured oars. We have seen the long lines of light springing up into the horizon like swaying filaments, until they have laid their tendrils on the clouds and up the gossamer path have gone the chariots of the dawn. There is the smell of fragrance from the asphodel meadows, and the dew is on the world. So far Homer is modern, and we catch the smile of his health. Nature has not outworn her robes of two thousand years ago. And then again we feel the force of the strenuous life, and the blood of the warrior is all about the heart, and we rush upon embattled fields with the fury of the tempest, and in our wanderings we meet strange visions which came to us in our boyhood dreams; but whether we wander or do battle we have said that this is life, our life to-day. And so Homer is with us because he wrote that which he saw and reported that which he heard, and lived his life in what he wrote; and our human nature has not changed in its needs and its loves since those early days in the dawning of the world. Among all the changing things there is one thing we find unchanging, and that is human nature; and he who would write enduringly must express himself in the way that makes the broadest appeal to it.

In the fourth place, we note the quality of indirection as one of the principles of our best literature. This in a measure could be discussed under the avoidance of the didactic, but as it has a phase of meaning somewhat different it calls for special mention. The orator and the writer generally get at the heart by different processes. The orator must have the dogmatic element, and must speak out without undue circumlocution his thoughts. He may exercise skill and tact in the arrangement of his material, but in striving for immediate results he must speak as one who exercises authority. The personal element which shows itself in the earnest manner, the flashing eye, the determined spirit, is so intermingled with the burning words that the convictions of men are at once aroused. This is the strength of the orator. But the strength of the writer is different. True literature catches people with an apostolic guile. It comes with no prospectus of what it intends to accomplish. It does not assume to have any great thoughts. It seems simply to say, "Come, let us go out on the playground a while and be children in the sunlight, by the woods and streams; let us walk a little way down these old paths, and talk of things we used to talk of in other days." And so it invites us with its chatty, breezy face, and we go out to play—for after all play is the highest aspiration man can have for the use of his powers. But we do not mean that all true literature stops here. We simply say that this is its method. It comes with the life of a tripping, laughing child, and takes our hands, and sings us out into the open places, and then grows into our heart and life; and when it has captured us, and we fain would follow it anywhere, it leads us to the haunts of men, and we pry into human hearts and lift up doors that cover human secrets, until we are led to the apex of the hill and greet a large horizon on all sides. Some objection may be raised to this principle of indirection in that it excludes the essay from literature. And it must be acknowledged that the essay in a large measure must be excluded from the realm of the highest literature. But, however large the exclusion may be in this branch through the operation of this principle, there will still remain some essayists who can go in and out through the natural door of literature and need not to climb up some other way as thieves and robbers. The

thought of indirection does not exclude all purpose writing. He who can teach through the natural display of the passions may be an artist of the highest kind, but emphasis must be placed on the naturalness of the method. For instance, in fiction, Marie Corelli carries too much the unbridled dogmatism of a preacher to ever become a great novelist. She always leaves you with the unhappy thought that you have been buttonholed by a not overly pleasant acquaintance, while your ears have been made a sluice for a cataract of words, which you are to take for advice on all matters terrestrial and heavenly. She seems to say, "Listen to me, I am Marie Corelli, and my books sell by the hundreds of thousands, and my business is to take the great salt box of the universe, and salt down this weltering mass of social corruption until it gets some purifying power kneaded into its organism." We have read her *Master Christian* with about the same indignation we should feel toward the man who grabs us by the shoulder, pours a flood of basilisk glances in our face, and dances a protracted hornpipe on our toes. Hall Caine stands on higher grounds than Corelli, but he is a degenerate, and his fall is to be deplored. The earlier works of Caine were strong though tinctured with gloom. *The Bondman* and *The Manxman* carried the stamp of genius and touched the heart like the tears of the lover, but *The Christian* and *The Eternal City* are but the blown bubbles of the moment. They smell of the reformer. The emphasis is placed upon institutions and not men, and hence their fatal defect. Such books violate the deepest underlying principles of literature, and their epitaph is fast coming on. On the other hand, we have read purpose works which were a success. They were the works in which the human interest predominated, and we were more interested in men than in things. The men were artists who knew how to skillfully hide their plans until you felt an irresistible impulse toward their characters. They may have come to you in the guise of humor—that easiest way of gaining admission to the heart—and you thought that there was nothing but merriment and you laughed with them. Then the skies darkened a little, but you said, "This is good company, and I will go on." Then humor turned to tears, and tragedy threw a sable mantle over the scene, but you were now following your

children and could not turn back for storms or tempests, and when
the book closed you knew that you had learned something, but it
came to you with the pain and pleasure of companionship. Dickens
could write a purpose novel that the world will cherish, for he
loved men more than things, and he was a literary man before he
was a reformer. Charles Reade could write a purpose novel that
was a success because of his sanity of treatment and his intense
dramatic spirit. *Uncle Tom's Cabin* is perhaps the greatest purpose novel of the world, and yet the author enters on no disquisitions against slavery. We catch things always through indirection.
How different is the treatment here from that shown in *The
Leopard Spots,* where you seem to be ever confronted by a peda-
gogue who has his finger leveled at you and whose burden of
speech is, "Sweep the negro from this continent into the sea."
William Dean Howells has found fault with Thackeray, and we
think rightly, because he is forever stopping you on the way to
give you a little advice. The best advice that can be given by a
literary man is that which is inferentially drawn from his character, and as readers we resent the hectoring spirit, or even the
complacency of our mildest, easiest-mannered professors. Even
Milton grows tedious as he makes his characters discourse an Arian
philosophy, and we feel rejoiced when the argument is over and
the angels throw down their amaranthine crowns upon the crystal
sea. We care more for the concrete than the abstract in literature,
and he who will teach us the most and find us the most eager
listeners is he who tries the oblique method of teaching through
characters.

The last quality which we shall note in the highest class of
literature is the optimistic spirit. Literature which endures carries
the glow of health. The world has never spared space long for any
morbid or pessimistic work. The eyes of our small writers look
out on what they declare to be an interminable sea of woe, and they
dip their pens in despair to write of lives that fail in living, and
they catch no visions on the heights of the pennons of hope, and
the world tolerates for to-day, but on the morrow has laid by its
sympathy as a worn-out thing. The highest philosophy we may
gain of life may be poor and meager; we may see no light beyond

the clouds, no sun beyond the mountains; life may be to us no more than a blind Titan staggering, falling down to darkness and the grave; but we may rest assured that all enduring literature will rebuke our pessimism.   There is no immortality for sick men or sick philosophies.   *Ships that Pass in the Night, The Gadfly, Jack Raymond, The Story of an African Farm, The Open Question,* some of the books of Mrs. Humphry Ward and of Thomas Hardy—these were on the crest of the popular wave but a short time ago, but we do not care to go back and read them again.   They silently put up monitory hands, and we heed the warning.   Thomas Carlyle in his early days brought a message to the world.   The vigor of health came out with every telling blow at shams.   The world could be a better world, and he saw a shining goal.   This constitutes his claim on immortality.   But soon his vision became obscured, his heart became sour, he lost his inspiration and brutalized his powers.   His work became a menace rather than a tonic, and these have made him of the earth earthy.   Ruskin followed in the same path.   No man held a more polished lance than he, or placed it in a firmer rest as he charged down the lists of error.   But his genius caught the taint of despair, and he became blind to heavenly visions.   And so Carlyle and Ruskin both have given hostages to fame, and if their names get a firm footing in other centuries it is probable that they will go down shorn of that part of their lives nearest the tomb.   Enduring literature has the child's heart, and the child's heart is essentially healthful and hopeful.   It may not talk much of health.   It may never speak of the need of hopefulness.   God and immortality may seldom be upon its lips.   But it has the upward-looking spirit, and claims no fraternity with the morbid and the hopeless.   It holds the world to be a bright world, although tempests lower in the sky, and if pain comes on swift-footed to make its tabernacle with men it has found some medicine of the mind to give it joy.   Some critic has pointed out that Shakespeare is not spiritual in the highest sense, but he is full of virile, worldly health.   We much doubt whether he ever walked to Emmaus and met a Stranger on the way, who spoke some heart-burning things, which if a man once hears his sky will infinitely expand.   There is the music and

the clash and the clangor of love and hate and war, but we listen quite in vain for the trumpeter who stands on far eastern hills to herald the dawning of the perfect day. But this is the segment of the mighty life he failed to fill out. The deep rolling harmonies he heard, the irrefragable laws of justice he announced, the mighty currents of laughter he blew across the world, the loves that meekly walked down moonlit paths and under shining stars, the hates and jealousies that crouched like demons in the darkness—all these come forth so naturally that they betoken unbounded health. Tennyson came in another day, and the spirit of the lyric poet was on him. He heard the rumbling of the scientist delving deep in the caverns of life. Dark and fateful questions flashed through murky skies like fitful gleams of the lightning's wing. Men with spade and mattock were standing at new-made graves and were preaching the funeral of humanity. And then Tennyson's soul took fire, and like Arthur, his beloved knight, he faced the pall and gloom and sin, and preached of hope and the coming out of light, and told men that they were not twinned with death, that there were joys for their pains and skies above their graves, and they must not forget the mighty hopes that make them men. And the words of the singer were set in deathless music, and they came to despairing minds like songs in the night. And this is Tennyson's health and optimism, and his name can be ventured for a large lease on the coming years. And so we conclude that he who would write enduringly must breathe the breath of health, and if he cannot see the path which shiningly runs up great and distant heights he must believe that it is there, for only thus will he gain the ear of the world for good and aye.

W. T. Scott

Art. X.—" WHEN I WAS A BOY."

This is the masculine gender, its feminine counterpart being
"Once upon a time." At least "Once upon a time" suggests a
female voice, and twilight and firelight and childhood and bedtime. "When I was a boy" means a memory. It has a flavor of
sincerity. It carries a tone of authority. It bears an intimation
of the survival of the fittest. In the majority of cases when this
formula is used it is in reference to something good, and not bad,
which happened long ago. In the very nature of things evil is
perishable, the good is permanent. The most vivid recollections
are not the affairs of last week. The sights and sounds and smells
of childhood are indelible. Before me lie some most exquisite
photographs made by my friend during the summer vacation in
the Berkshires. The lines are wonderfully clear, yet the events
of boyhood are even more clean-cut, and they contain color such
as no artist photographer ever produced. Sometimes we wonder
whether personal reminiscences will ever become colonial. Will
people some day search for them as they do for old china and old
books and old mahogany?

The phrase is suggestive of personal responsibility. The
antique is not for the ash barrel. The survival of a moving picture
a half century old does not qualify it for the waste-paper basket.
Much of knowledge is by comparison. Progress is only fully appreciated by looking backward. When your man has had in his
possession for a generation a fact of significance to himself he
should be able to make use of it at the opportune moment. Such
potent memories outweigh any amount of adolescent vaporings.
Every worthy personal experience has its supreme moments, its
turning points, its inspirations. It is in the power of each of us so
to touch the childhood about us that years hence the veteran will
preface his story with "When I was a boy." The peculiar sense
of responsibility which results from being in the presence of a
real boy is unlike any other. It is the exposure that counts; the
development is mechanical, largely. From the divine standpoint
child training is not an experiment or uncertain; the problem is

in the exposure. What is the boy thinking about as he looks and listens? First impressions remain. When I was a boy, to teach me the Bible better, my father sent to Holland for two fine vellum-bound folio volumes containing the Bible history, in Dutch. Upon every alternate page were beautiful copper-plate illustrations. My conception of heaven alone, which came to me through those pictures, will last forever. The sea of glass, the four and twenty Elders, and the Lamb of God and the book and the seals are ever with me, and will be even should heaven be a mistake and a myth. It may be doubted whether childhood's conception of heaven is ever improved upon. Pictorial text-books are wise. The boy learns morals by the use of his eyes quite as much as his ears. When I was a boy I was taken one day by my mother to the home of the Rev. Henry Moore, in London. He was the executor of John Wesley, who burned in the fire Mr. Wesley's valuable notes on Shakespeare. My mother asked him to place his hands upon my head and pronounce a blessing. He did so. The very words he used are lying within my reach now. The words, the face of the man, the closed eyes, the heavy weight of his hands upon my head, his clothing, and every piece of furniture in the room, are indelibly fixed in my mind. But the strongest impression of all was my mother's reverence for old age and her belief that the blessing or the curse of a good man counts. Later on in life I came to believe the same, and have seen the fruits of such benedictions. I can forgive the burning of the notes.

When I was a boy each Sunday afternoon a sermon was preached upon the lawn before my grandfather's house in London. Who the preachers were I never knew; I did not even hear them, but I saw them from the window. Men came and went. Sometimes a hundred stood and listened, and again when I looked there were but twenty. It seemed strange. It was evident that each passer on the street had an errand upon which he was intent, but which he was compelled for the moment to abandon that he might listen, and then go on. This particular feature puzzled and impressed me. Since my boyhood I recognize that street preaching is the severest test of all preaching. When I was a boy a storm at sea almost wrecked the vessel in which the family crossed the

Atlantic. Twice did the captain give up his ship in despair. And well he might, for as a boy I scarcely could tell the floor from the side of the stateroom. Twice the captain descended from the deck to tell his passengers to prepare for the worst. Each time as he approached my mother's stateroom her voice in earnest prayer arrested his attention, and after listening he resolved to go back to his post and try once more to weather the storm. He reported in New York that his ship was saved in answer to prayer. In after years the terrible hazard of that voyage became more apparent, and with it came a double conviction. I learned that sometimes God would have us answer our own prayers, and also that if we are praying for any particular persons it is better that they should know it. These facts are often overlooked. A soul once came to me under very serious religious conviction for which no assignable cause was given. The only explanation attempted was made by the individual himself in the words, "I have come to the conclusion that some one is praying for me." The prayer to God lost nothing because the captain heard it. Jesus asked his disciples to listen to the Lord's Prayer. In church more people listen than pray. We pray, not merely that *God* will save souls, but that *we* may help to save them and that *they* may be willing to be saved.

When I was a boy an elect lady in one of the churches died. A former pastor and an intimate friend of the family was asked to officiate at the obsequies. He could not do so because of important engagements elsewhere. The knowledge that another had been preferred led the regular incumbent so far to forget himself as to hesitate to perform the duty. This led me to resolve that, should I ever become a minister, in the case of any death in the congregation I would immediately ask the family if I might send for any valued friend or any other minister, from no matter where, to minister to them in their sorrow. There are various kinds of ministerial dignity, some manifestly better than others. In the death of Lazarus Jesus saw an invaluable opportunity to teach one of the greatest lessons of his ministry. The appearance of crape upon the doorpost of a member of the congregation is often the supreme moment of the pastor. The Valley of the Shadow of Death seems the only approach to some hearts. One of

the most impressive private funerals in my recollection was that of a poor scrubwoman whose only son, of fourteen years, installed himself as master of ceremonies. The delicacy and courtesy and tact which he exhibited surprised all, for he had long been known as the worst boy in the Sunday school. It was the turning point in his life. We can imagine him in later life referring to the sad occasion and saying, "When I was a boy."

When I was a boy it was a diversion to visit the courthouse of our town at the time of the session of court and listen to the noted lawyers. Two matters impressed me: First, the evident devotion of the advocate to his client's interest and his efforts to save him from punishment. One day a lawyer confessed to friends that he came almost to love a man whom he had put forth all his skill and effort to save, while on the other hand he came to hate a criminal to whom he bore the relation of prosecutor. This was food for thought for a boy. I think the love of Christ did afterward seem larger. I remember once to have heard that great analyst, the Rev. Daniel Curry, D.D., say, "Young man, let people do for you; let them serve you; the more they do for you the more they will love you, depend upon it." Perhaps it is only when we do sometimes for our enemies that it becomes possible for us to love them. The other thing which impressed itself in the lawyer's plea was the emphasis which the advocate placed upon motive. He insisted that if the criminal could be shown to have had no motive for committing the crime with which he was charged the probability was that he did not commit it at all; a course of reasoning which would bring the Ten Commandments and the thirteenth chapter of 1 Corinthians into close proximity—possibly a method also quite as applicable in dealing with men in the church as in the courthouse. Omniscience only is competent to judge of motives, nevertheless the laborious process of tracing human motives to their original sources might diminish the rancor of many a combat.

When I was a boy the eminent pastor of our church was subject to sudden attacks of illness. Such an attack upon one occasion prostrated him at the very commencement of the Sabbath morning hour of worship. In the large congregation there was

seated a very able clergyman of the denomination. An appeal was made to him for a sermon. When the organ ceased to play he was seen to shake his head, signifying his inability to catch the thread of a discourse; he could render no help. The sick man took up the painful burden and bore it manfully, the consciousness of his personal suffering giving him the sympathy of his hearers in an unusual degree. The lesson was impressive to one boy in the congregation. It led to the resolve never to enter a church for participation in the public worship, conducted by whatever denomination of Christians or at whatever time, either at home or abroad, without first formulating at least the outline of a sermon, should an unexpected demand be made. This provision has been tested by actual experience, and mortification and embarrassment prevented, but it was the intuition of the boy nevertheless. It was the recognition of one of those phases of character which is an approach to the divine, namely, the fact of being always ready. The divinely called minister is never off duty. To him even the holiday is a holy day. So soon as the sermon of one Sabbath is ended his eager longing for the next opportunity to preach the Gospel makes surprise impossible.

There is something more, then, than the homely preface to the octogenarian's idle tale in the reference to his boyhood recollections. It is suggestive of a principle the recognition of which may be the making of a new race. In it is discernible the corner stone of human character. It reveals associations which, next to those of a spiritual character, are the most telling known. Nothing is insignificant that can touch the imagination or the conscience of a boy. If he can but create the right vision in his mind the memory will take care of itself and of its message to the future man and the future boy. The sooner the vision of beauty appears to the boy the better. It is a great thing to get the right of way to the heart of the child. Possibly the strongest features of the character of Moses were formed in Jochebed's arms.

Henry M. Simpson

7

Art. XI.—PRE-SEMITIC POPULATIONS IN SEMITIC LANDS.

A USEFUL purpose may perhaps be served by gathering together the few evidences there are of the predecessors of the Semites in their respective countries. In Arabia, which is now generally accepted as the seat of the primitive Semitic race, we have no traces of an earlier population. Nor is it likely that there were such. Arabia has always been, as it is to-day, the preserve of the Semite. The Arab is the truest type of that race, and all the indications point to his having from the beginning enjoyed immunity from the corrupting influences of a foreign environment. In the valley of the Euphrates the Semites displaced the Sumero-Akkadians, a Turanian race. The records of these people are in our hands, and there are traces of them in the literature of their successors. What we know of them and their influence is enough to show us that far beyond the term of their own life as a people they determined the life of the Semites (Babylonians) who had come into their heritage. Cities, kingdoms, and tribes bear names given by this ancient race. Their language and its cuneiform symbols were for a long period the exclusive media of Semitic literature. Before the Semites used their own language, they employed the Sumerian language as well as signs in writing. In fact, we must assume that the Babylonian language had become fixed in its final literary form before it was used to any extent in written documents. The population of the country had by that time become practically homogeneous and their speech was the old tribal tongue of the Semitic nomads, but greatly altered and corrupted through its long contact with the dialect of the older inhabitants. It was at this point, when the Sumerian race and speech were fast disappearing as the new race developed, that Babylonian became a written tongue. The pre-Semitic race in the lower Euphrates region shows its high degree of civilization directly by remains which indicate the possession of many of the arts and some degree of scientific knowledge and indirectly by its influence upon the Semites who came after them. Among these Sumerians commerce and agriculture were diligently followed.

Luxury of living was not unknown. Social life had passed far beyond the primitive forms which obtained in the tribes and clans of the steppe. Religion had reached the stage where a priestly class is developed; where temples are added to the ancient shrine or altar; and where the gods are no longer connected with natural objects but are exalted to abodes in the overarching heaven. Religious meditation had proceeded far in its effort to account for the facts of nature and of human life. Stories of the Creation and the Deluge along with other myths remain enshrined in the literature of their successors to show us at once the development of religious speculation and the successful cultivation of the higher forms of literary effort which prevailed in primitive Babylonia before the Semites became the ruling factor there. We do not, then, marvel at two things in the Semitic civilization of Babylonia: its high development and its marked departure from the primitive forms of typical Semitic life. What the pre-Semitic civilization had already attained is a sufficient explanation.

There is evidence sufficient of a pre-Semitic settlement in Mesopotamia. In the region of the upper Euphrates about the city of Haran there lay the kingdom of Mitâni, or Hanirabbat, whose extension may have reached to the Amanus Mountains westward, and eastward to the Tigris River. Before the famous Amarna letters were written its kings ranked with those of Egypt and Babylonia as the great world-potentates of their time and carried on an extensive commerce with their neighbors. The rise of the Mitânian power and its control of the fords of the upper Euphrates must have greatly hindered the freedom of traffic between Babylonia and the West and have opened up a new market for the merchandise of both East and West. Some have thought that the people of Mitâni were a kindred race to the Hittites, but this is hardly likely. Their center was removed considerably to the east of the point where the Hittites entered Syria, suggesting that their old home lay in a different direction. Moreover, they are clearly distinguished in the Amarna letters from the Hittite tribes, though they are said to have exercised some kind of suzerainty over the latter. Later on, it is true the Hittites did establish themselves on the Euphrates and had as their capital Car-

chemish, which lay within the bounds of the ancient kingdom of Mitâni. This, however, is no support for the hypothesis of a relationship between the two peoples. The decline of Mitâni was due to three causes principally: the advance of the so-called "Aramæan" (really Arab) tribes from the Syrian Desert; the Hittite invasion; and the extension and growing power of Assyria, bringing with it a great tide of genuine Aramæan immigration from Mesopotamia. The incoming "Aramæans," while influenced by their new non-Semitic environment, were so numerous as to gradually overcome the distinctive features of the Mitânians among whom they had settled. In time, the country received a Semitic name—Beth-Eden; and though retaining independent existence until overthrown by Shalmaneser II in 857 B. C., it must have long before ceased to be Mitânian in the original sense of the term. The Aramæan wave of migration from the Euphrates valley, which was changing the character of all the races between the Tigris and the Mediterranean, had carried everything before it in Mitâni or Beth-Eden. The language of the Mitânians is preserved in one of the Amarna letters, but cannot as yet be understood or classified. The letters from this region in the Amarna collection which are composed in the Babylonian language are with us, however, and indicate that a high degree of culture prevailed in the country. That there was a settlement of Semites in the Mitânian territory before the Mitânians came it is fair to suppose, but we are not in possession of data sufficient to give any satisfactory account of its nature.

The Hittites are not to be looked upon as pre-Semitic tenants in the Semitic lands. Their entrance into Syria took place certainly after the Semitic settlement, and the influence they exerted upon the Syrian Semites, in any case not very considerable, was felt for the most part by the Aramæans who came from the region to the east of the Euphrates at a date subsequent to 1300 B. C.

The aborigines of western Syria and Palestine were of other than Semitic race. In the Semitic period there are scores of place names in these parts which can be explained on no known Semitic analogies. Furthermore, in western Syria and Palestine, as elsewhere in western Asia, except in Arabia, the Semites show

a departure from the ethnological type which is due to admixture with the older races among whom they settled. Positive evidence of these races is found in various remains which have been discovered all over the region now under consideration. Sacrificial pillars (menhirs), gravestones or altars (dolmens), ancient shrines of the cromlech pattern, and underground or rock dwellings of artificial construction, belong to an age probably earlier than the differentiation of any of the Semitic races from the original stock. Argument for a pre-Semitic settlement may also be drawn from the names applied by the Old Testament writers to the most ancient inhabitants of the land of Canaan. Such terms as Rephaim (giants), Anakim (long-necked), and Horim (cave-dwellers), being mere epithets, cannot naturally refer to a Semitic race. Other names, as Zuzim, Zamzummim, Emim, and Avvim, seem to be merely artificial creations to designate an extinct people of unknown race. Such names would not be used to denote Semites any more than the epithets just mentioned. The little we know of this old Syro-Palestinian race is enough to show that it was not a people possessed of any high degree of civilization. Its instruments are of rude stone with here and there a token of more advanced culture in the shape of a tool or vessel of bronze.

In the last place, we turn to Ethiopia. The pre-Semitic race in this country was Hamite with some admixture of negro blood. Hamite and Semite were in the beginning of one stock, and Ethiopia was a part of the original home land. That Semites should return thither from Arabia across the narrow strait dividing southern Yemen from Africa was not unnatural. By small groups this return journey had been made from early times and even now is being made by men from Arabia. At definite periods, rather late in the history of the Semitic peoples, larger bodies crossed over to Ethiopia from Yemen carrying with them their south Arabian culture and arts. They were of sufficient numbers and energy of character to determine the development of the country and to assert themselves over the original race. Hence, though Hamite and negro influences have left their deep impression, the people of Ethiopia are to this day in all predominant features a Semitic people.

It is not likely that Egypt penetrated into Palestine and Syria at a period antedating the arrival of the Semites. Her presence in the Bedouin region of Sinai is attested for the third Egyptian dynasty (circa 4000 B. C.), but when she came there she found the Semites already there. Indeed, the very earliest Pharaohs constructed on the northeastern frontier of Egypt a famous defense, known as the "Wall of the Princes," to repel invasion on the part of these ancient Bedouin. A reminiscence of an early Egyptian rule over the Sinai district is found in the application of the name Mutsri to that part as well as to Egypt itself.

In every Semitic land there has been a pre-Semitic race—Arabia alone excepted. In every case this race has largely influenced the development of the Semites by whom it was displaced. In every instance the corruption of the old Semitic type under foreign influences was very rapid, so that everywhere—the Arab again excepted—the Semite when he first becomes known to us has lost much of his original character and taken on many new characteristics. From the moment when the old Semitic herdsmen first left their desert cradle-land, "not knowing whither they went," but always under the unseen hand of the Almighty, they were under a discipline which everywhere and always tended to make them cosmopolites—losing that which made them peculiar and gaining that which brought them nearer to the world they were so powerfully to move.

Walter M. Patton

EDITORIAL DEPARTMENTS.

NOTES AND DISCUSSIONS.

'AVERY 'A. SHAW, discussing the question whether Christianity created Christ or Christ created Christianity, reasons to this conclusion: "Here is our choice—Christianity founded on the Risen and Living Christ, or on fog and rottenness. After all, as one has put it, 'It is better to believe in the supernatural than in the ridiculous.'" Showing that men may know God directly, Carlyle's statement is quoted: "Of final causes, man, in the nature of the case, can prove nothing, knows them (if he knows them at all) not by the glimmering flint-sparks of logic, but by an infinitely higher light of intuition," and also these words from Romanes: "All first principles, even of scientific facts, are known by intuition—not by reason." The necessary conclusion is that, if there be a God, he is knowable by intuition. Faith does not rest on a mere process of reasoning. It is rather the surrender of the whole man to God as seen in Jesus Christ. How it comes about is illustrated by the case of a highly cultured Japanese gentleman. Thoughts came into his mind of a personal Being great and kindly above him. He was anxious to learn if these thoughts were true. Confucius could not help him. At length a Christian gave him a Bible in Chinese. He read until he came to the thirteenth chapter of First Corinthians. These are his words: "I was arrested, fascinated. I had never seen nor heard nor dreamed of a morality like that. I felt that it was above the reach of the human race, that it must have come from Heaven, that the man who wrote that chapter must have received light from God—from God about whose existence I had been speculating. And then I read the Gospel of John, and the words of Christ filled me with wonder. They were not to be resisted. I could not refuse Christ my faith." He saw the divine light in the record itself and became a Christian. The story is also told of a woman of loose moral character who earned a livelihood by posing for a noted artist. She was specially gifted for this work. Her grace of form and her imitative genius made her an admirable model. If she were to pose as Mary Queen of Scots she would gather together all the material of the queen's life, visit her haunts, and after three weeks come to the studio as Mary Queen

of Scots. One day the artist said, "You would make a splendid model for the Magdalene." "And who is that?" she asked, "and where shall I find out about her?" The artist told her, and procured a Testament for her. She went to her home, and for the first time came face to face with herself in Mary Magdalene, and with Him whose words and acts were such as she had never dreamed of. At the end of three weeks she failed to appear. After a further three weeks the artist sought her out, and found a transformed Magdalene, sitting at the feet of her new Master, clothed, and in her right mind, an angel of mercy to those who, like herself, had gone astray.

A PREACHER'S ESSAYIST.*

Among living writers in this year of our Lord one of the essayists for the preacher is Brierley, whose previous volumes were noticed last year. The thirty-six essays of this new volume, *Problems of Living,* are as high in level and as wide in range. They aim to show that the spiritual element in man is not only the one feature that gives distinction to life, but is the only adequate clew to the sphinx riddle of our world; that however this riddle is studied, whether along its physical, historical, or economic sides, or into the inmost depths of Personality, the answer can be found only in the realm of the invisible; that all our problems of living are finally religious problems and look to religion for their solution; that a religion adequate for such solution must be one that allies itself to the nature of things and is at one with the soul's universal affirmations; and that Christianity, properly conceived, is that adequate religion.

As to the intellectual difficulties which some modern minds have with revealed religion, our essayist's opinion is that many of these difficulties arise from antique but remediable forms of statement. And as to all those difficulties, he names two considerations, which are looming more and more in modern thought, and which cast a new and reassuring light in which Faith can make its argument more clear and strong. The first of these considerations is the towering and immense significance of personality. The more personality is considered, the more clearly is it seen that it is only in the Christian doctrine of the Incarnation that the idea of a personal God becomes at all intelligible to us. It is being recognized that on this

* *Problems of Living.* By J. Brierley, B.A. 12mo, pp. 356. New York: Thomas Whittaker. Price, cloth, $1.40.

planet the human personality is the appointed organ of the Eternal Reason, in and through which organ the Divine Voice speaks, and that only along this channel has the Soul of the Universe come to speaking terms with man's consciousness. Admitting that our conception of personality involves limitation, and that the nature of the infinite God may transcend such limits; conceding that the Absolute is beyond our comprehension, and that it is

> The Somewhat which we name, but cannot wholly know,
> Even as we name a star and only see
> His quenchless flashings forth, which ever show
> And ever hide him, and which are not he;

nevertheless man as a person, recognizing, communing with, and receiving revelation from a God who manifests Himself as a person, and who is incarnate, visible, and accessible in Jesus Christ, His Son, our Saviour, not only knows God, but is more and more fashioned into the likeness of the Lord. The second consideration which is prevailing against the intellectual difficulties referred to is that it is growing more and more clear that there is an eternal miraculous and an eternal supernatural in the Gospel. To the question, What is the supernatural? this in substance is the answer given: Man regards as supernatural whatever is above *his* natural. We are supernatural to our dog. We can do things which would be miraculous in him. Byron said that if the dog has a religion, his master is his god. A civilized human being, with firearms, electricity, and all modern arts, is as a god to the savage, and sometimes receives worship from him. When we toss a stone into the air we transcend the laws which belong to the stone. Christ is supernatural to us in His nature and in His powers. Because He is above us He does what we cannot do, and that is miracle to us. First is the stone, held fast to the ground by the grip of something we call gravitation. Then comes man, who defies the power of gravitation, and by exercise of will and a superior power flings the stone up into the air. Next comes a Being of a grade above man, a Being in whom Divine powers are superadded to or blended with the human. As to what this higher Being can and will do when He arrives, we who are below Him in the scale of being are not able to foreknow; we can only wait and see; but that He will speak as never man spake, and that the things which He will naturally do will be supernatural to us and will appear as miraculous wonders, this much is not only credible but sure and inevitable. The supernatural Christ makes all miracles possible. In Him God re-

veals, and man beholds, a new vision of the Eternal. And men look into the face of Jesus Christ, and say with a conviction that transcends all argument that they have seen God.

Of the physiological determinism which declares man's character, mental and moral, to be unchangeably determined and fixed by his physical organism, a fatalism to which a rationalistic philosophy delivers man over, it is made plain that this notion reckons without the spiritual forces which operate effectually upon man, and that the whole reasoning of the physiological determinists is contradicted by plain, notorious, undeniable facts. The savages of Terra del Fuego had sustained no perceptible modifications of physical structure during the period of missionary labors among them, yet even Charles Darwin observed and bore witness to the complete moral transformation which the Gospel had wrought in them. An enormous volume of testimony proves that a central fact of man's nature is its susceptibility to change under the impact and invasion of a higher spiritual Power. Ovid knew no metamorphoses so marvelous as those which Christian history exhibits. Brierley says truly that the effects produced by the Gospel in the labors of the earliest Methodist preachers alone are enough to offset and overturn all the fatalistic physiological theorizings of a Schopenhauer and a Bichat. The final and complete word concerning man cannot be spoken by physiology. Psychology is a higher part of the science of human nature, and a true psychology must take account of man's susceptibility to spiritual influences which work in him the most astonishing and momentous changes.

An interesting essay is one on "Religious Vocabulary," in which it is recalled that Max Müller, in *Chips from a German Workshop*, shows how a study of the language of the primitive Aryans gives a clear idea of the height to which that early civilization had risen. So the language which religion uses, in any place or period, is evidence and index of the height to which man has climbed and exposes to view the richness or the poverty, the simplicity or the complexity of his inner life. The words he coins to express his thought and feeling register the stature and attainment of his soul. Especially does Christianity's language attest its place in the upward and onward progress of humanity. To get a proper sense of the wondrous character and significance of the Christian vocabulary, Brierley says, one needs a course of reading in the classic literature of the old pagan world. When, after a study of the writings of its poets, philosophers, and

moralists, we come to the literature of the Christian centuries, we find something altogether new in the sphere of words. Christianity, in its development, added to the human vocabulary something so startlingly fresh that the grace and beauty of Christian speech rise like a temple above the ground-level of common human expression. A new and higher range of words had to be created to express new and higher facts, and old phrases put into fresh combinations to express new meanings. Apostles and saints, when they talked of conversion, regeneration, baptism, fruits of the Spirit, sanctification, oneness with Christ, divine assurance, and the heavenly life, were compelled to remake or enlarge language in order that it might contain and carry the new treasures of knowledge and experience. The great new vocabulary which Christianity has given to mankind represents the moral and spiritual height to which millions of human beings have risen in all the Christian ages under the Christian revelation and inspiration. An incalculable diffusion of spiritual riches and a consequent visible elevation, refinement, purification, and gentilizing of life, took place in Europe when the great religious vocabulary of the Bible first filtered down and flowed out to the common people through the labors of Wyclif and Luther, whose translations of the Scriptures put the Word of God within general reach and poured the riches of Gospel truth into the public mind; so that the desire of Erasmus moved toward fulfillment. "I wish," said he, of the Epistles and Gospels, "that they were translated into all languages of the people. I wish the husbandman might sing parts of them at his plow and the weaver at his shuttle, and the traveler beguile with them the weariness of his way." And the common people, when these riches were put within their reach, were not slow to grasp them. "After Wyclif's time," says Foxe, "some gave a load of hay for a few chapters of St. James or St. Paul." For us and for all men the religious vocabulary created by Christianity is a magnificent inheritance; it is a ladder by which human souls may "mount from the lowly earth to the lofty skies." Aloft in our spiritual firmament shine those great light-giving New Testament words which stand for Revelation's central truths and the soul's highest possibilities. Apart from the wealth to which they light the way no man can be rich; and no life is blessed upon which they have not shed their mighty meaning. Such, in part, is our essayist's setting forth of the immeasurable worth and clear significance of the new vocabulary which Christ has furnished to men.

Akin to this is what he says of religion's higher energies:

An inspired and prophetic element belongs to the highest kind of religious speech. No true Christian teacher or preacher but in his most uplifted moments finds himself yielding to a kind of inspiration which shapes his utterance for him. He has, in such moments, a tense and awful consciousness that he is in some degree the instrument of a higher Power; that the message he speaks is far more than his own and more authoritative; that even his limitations, weaknesses, defects, and sense of personal nothingness are but factors of a movement in which he, indeed, is taking part, but not as an originator. This was the note of the marvelous preaching of Père Vianney, the apostle of France, preaching which produced its mighty effects with no special preparation except his "constant occupation with God." It was this which Madame Guyon meant when, detailing her Grenoble experiences, she speaks of being "invested with the Apostolic state," and of perceiving and revealing the inmost condition of the souls to whom she spoke or who spoke to her. In order to make connection with the channels of religion's higher energies we need to recover the almost lost art of prayer. That the newer concepts of the universe and of the uniformity of law have affected in any way the reasons for prayer is one of those superstitions which every self-respecting thinker should by this time have seen through. Prayer is one of the functions and forces of the spiritual nature as surely as gravitation is a force of the physical world. It is indeed of itself a gravitation. It is the soul's impulse towards its Center and Source. The author of *Exploratio Evangelica*, who discusses the religious problem in a spirit of the severest science, finds prayer irremovably grounded in the structure of the moral nature. Its practice is its own vindication. Beginning in a semblance of egotism, it ends ever in self-surrender. "Not as I will, but as Thou wilt!" Observing that the higher the tone of his request the more sure it is to be granted, there slowly dawns upon the suppliant the perception of a divine Will which wills what is best. To subject self to It is the ultimate of prayer. And the nature of things decrees a mighty force to self-renunciation. Bishop Westcott said, "A life of absolute and calculated sacrifice is a spring of immeasurable power;" and St. Columba, who knew whereof he spoke, "Whoever overcomes himself treads the world under foot." . . . Sir Walter Scott, in his *Heart of Midlothian*, has a passage which gives but half the truth about prayer: "Without entering into an abstruse point of Divinity, one thing is plain, namely, that the person who lays open his doubts and distresses in prayer, with feeling and sincerity, must necessarily in that act purify his mind from the dross of worldly passions and interests, and bring it into that state where the resolutions adopted are likely to be selected rather from a sense of duty than from any inferior motive." Sir Walter gives here only the under side of the truth. In its higher aspect prayer is the soul's receptivity, the spreading out of its upper surface to receive the rain of that light and beat whose source is beyond the stars. Professor James speaks of it as a voluntary union of man's higher part "with a Move of the same quality which is operative in the universe outside him, and which he can keep in touch with, and in a fashion get on board of." What this union, invited by the Divine Spirit and acquiesced in by the soul, can effect for man's remaking, and that in every department of his nature, is writ large in the history of mankind wherever the Christian religion has gone. In the sense of that union, made vivid in a certain hour, Russell Lowell once wrote: "I never before so clearly felt the Spirit of God in me and around me. The whole room seemed to me full of God. The air seemed to hover to and fro with the presence of Something, I know not what." With or without such a vivid sense of the presence of God prayer is, as Tennyson said, an interflow, between man's spirit and the Father of spirits, of spiritual currents which bring life and power to the moral nature of man. . . . The secret of great revivals is that a single soul filled with and stirred by consciousness of the Divine will communicate its feeling to innumerable other souls, without diminution of its own store of energy. A voice for God charged with intensity of conviction, a personality saturated with sympathy and love, may spread its mystic power over thousands of souls, filling them, while not emptying but rather increasing its own original stock and store. This is proof that while the body has to do with

the finite, the measurable, and the exhaustible, the soul's transactions are, by right of its inherent nature, with the imperishable, the inexhaustible, the infinite. If Churches have lost their hold upon the masses, their only way to regain it is by regaining their hold of the sources and forces of the spiritual life, by prayer, by self-renouncing consecration, by what Brother Lawrence called "the practice of the Presence of God." What is the psychology of a revival? The laws of it are as sure as those of electricity, as the laws of Leyden jars and storage batteries and telephones. Men ought not in this age of the world to be groping about for the right way of winning souls. It is as old as the hills. What is the meaning of the statement that great spiritual revivals have always been preceded by earnest, importunate, believing prayer? It is the formula of the soul's dynamic. It means that a few disciplined spirits, humbled, purified, and incandescent by communion with the Highest, have become recipients and reservoirs of the higher energies; and from them these forces pass out upon their fellows with resistless power. This is the secret and science of revivals. . . . While great awakenings and quickenings, rebirths of faith and feeling are usually traceable to the influence of spiritual leaders whose souls are surcharged with power from above, the unseen genesis of these leaders often lies far back. The natural history of a prophet opens deep questions of heredity, and of the strange interplay of body and spirit, of natural endowments and spiritual gifts. We think of the doctrine he preaches, of his fervor of spirit, of his passion for souls, of his spiritual vision, of his searching and saving power. But the basis and vehicle for all this were preparing by long processes, through generations of ancestors, who developed sturdy qualities, high conscience, spiritual intrepidity, force of will, persistency and power of attack, transmitting to our prophet his red blood, his vibrant and moving voice, his melting sympathy, his endurance, and his flashing eye. God often begins to build, or at least lays the foundations for, His prophet generations before he is born. The ancestors of John Wesley—the fine old non-juring clergyman on the one side and the Puritans who suffered for conscience' sake on the other—were shaping, all unwittingly, the physical, mental, moral, and spiritual constitution of the great evangelist who was to come. Our Christian homes to-day are making, or failing to make, by the qualities they most cultivate and the level upon which they live, the great spiritual leaders who will be needed by the Church in future generations.

In conclusion we gather from this preacher's essayist a few significant quotations. This from Methodius concerning the Cross: "For the Word suffered, being in the flesh affixed to the Cross, that He might bring man, who had been deceived by error, to His supreme and godlike majesty, restoring him to that Divine life from which he had become alienated." This from Hazlitt's description of some Dissenting ministers of his day: "They were true priests. They set up an image in their minds—it was Truth. They worshiped an idol there—it was Justice. They looked on men as their brothers, and only bowed the knee to the Highest. Separating from the world, they walked humbly with their God, and in thought with those who had borne testimony of a good conscience, with the spirits of just men of all ages." This from Huxley's pathetic letter to Charles Kingsley in which, after the death of his firstborn, he says: "*Sartor Resartus* led me to know that a deep sense of religion is compatible with an entire absence of theology." Louis Stevenson's phrase, "the

kindness of the scheme of things and the goodness of our veiled God," recalls Dr. Oliver Wendell Holmes's saying, "I think we have over us a Being infinitely robust and grandly magnanimous." This sentence is fresh from the lips of the young emperor of Germany, "The man whose life is not founded on religion is lost." This British essayist does not attempt to fill the chair of systematic theology or of biblical interpretation; not all his views are to be accepted; but his pages are fresh, illuminating, stimulating, and provocative of further thought.

"A MEMORANDUM OF MODERN PRINCIPLES."*

WE cannot join certain surprisingly incontinent eulogists in ranking the author of *The Religion of Democracy*, who calls his book a Memorandum of Modern Principles, "among the greatest philosophers of the world," nor agree that "he probes as deep as Carlyle and smites with the strength of Ruskin," or that his "splendid literary style suggests the better elements of Emerson, Ruskin, and Hugo," or that "since Emerson nobody has gone so straight to the point in a manner so free from personal prejudice or vanity," or, with Edwin Markham, that this is "a great book of a great epoch." It will probably prove ephemeral and not perceptibly influential. Yet, because of qualities in it which move such readers as Charles H. Parkhurst, T. T. Munger, and Philip Moxom to call it "a stimulating, startling, and, all in all, wonderful book," "a brilliant, searching book that reminds one of *Sartor Resartus*," a book that "clearly belongs to the prophetic literature of the world," it may be admitted to exhibit in these pages something of its essence, spirit, and scope. Although revolutionary in a degree, its audacity is serene and devout. Rhapsody plays some part in its prophetic strains, and while reality is what it is after with tense and strenuous clutch, it is more oracular and paradoxical than convincing. It will not revolutionize anything, nor even "make a profound sensation" among experienced men; but it is passionate, penetrating, and peculiar, as will be seen from extracts here presented. The book opens in this fashion:

The spirit of the age is saying to its children: Have faith. Make yourself at home. This is your own house. The laws were made for you, gravitation and the chemical affinities, not you for them. No one can put you out of the house. Stand up; the ceiling is high. . . . If you should act with simplicity and boldness, do you think that you would have to stand alone and take the consequences? Have you no idea that God would back you up? That is as if you thought this world were mainly bones and the soul a pale prisoner, looking wist-

* *The Religion of Democracy.* By Charles Ferguson. 12mo, pp. 170. New York: Funk & Wagnalls Company. Price, cloth, $1.

fully through the ribs of it. It is as if God were caught in His own body, and could not move otherwise than according to the laws laid down in the books, and as if all the people that pass in the streets had scared, wan souls caught in their bodies like animals in a trap. . . . Are you grieved to see a crowd of people met together to worship God, but not frankly believing in God, and not daring to risk their lives upon the moral law? Do you long to see men simple of heart and honest, believing flatly in the soul, without dodging or subterfuge? Come, then, it shall be so. Stop here and resolve that *you* will not compromise any more. . . . You need not be afraid, any more than a duck is afraid of drowning or a bird of falling. In your inmost soul you are as well suited to the whole cosmical order and every part of it as to your own body. You belong here. Did you suppose that you belonged to some other world than this, or that you belonged nowhere at all— were just a waif on the bosom of the eternities? Is not that unthinkable? Incontestably you belong here. Have not the biologists told you all about it? Nothing is plainer than that God has been at measureless pains that you should suit your surroundings and that your surroundings should suit you with a perfect correspondence at every point. Conceivably He might have flung you into a world that was unrelated to you, and might have left you to be acclimated at your own risk; but you happen to know that this is not the case. This is the ancestral domain. You are at home. . . . The soul is the concrete absolute. Every interest that does not directly relate to it is an abstraction. This is the soul's world clear through, and the inmost law of it is the law of the relation of persons. And to deal with material objects or with ideas without reference to persons is to invert the order of the universe and to take things altogether as they are not. Do you suppose that God cares anything for His performances except as they relate to persons? Do you suppose He is vain of the shimmering sea or the tints of the evening sky? Do you not understand that Life rules here, and that everything exists for Life? The sun does not make signs to the moon, and the stars do not beckon one another; but everything beckons the living soul. It is a shame then to dodge and defer to things or to your own achievements or to any man's. It is a shame to take circuitous courses or to desire social consideration and influence as a means of accomplishing one's ends—as if one were a stranger and an alien here, picking his way fearfully through an enemy's country and compelled to make the most of a scanty equipment. . . . If there is any cosmical ordinance that you do not like, there is something wrong with you. If there is any necessary thing that you shrink from—as death, or labor, or growth and long waiting—then you are not well and sound. To draw back from a fact is to prefer a lie. If you say you do not like the contact of the earth, or the contact of the people, and would withdraw yourself from them, then there is nothing for you but to live in a world of phantoms and shadows. Men can agree to reject death, and labor and love, and to pass their days as if these things did not exist, or were altogether alien; but they are dreamers, and the facts remain to be reckoned with. The cosmos is sound all through, absolutely valid; and it covers the whole ground. There is no room for another universe. If you do not like this one, the door is open into the insane. In the old Hebrew story, Adam would not dress and keep the garden, and so get wise in the divine and vital way by daily contact with real things, but would eat wisdom and ruminate upon it. The original sin was the rejection of the real world and a flight to dreamland; and the healing penalty was a hard necessity that should draw back the man and the woman to the firm, resistant earth—labor, in bread-getting and in child-bearing. All the failures of the world have come out of this flinching from the keen and open air—the attempt to escape into a made-up world within fences and behind doors. The failure of history is in egotism, and this is egotism—to consider oneself as having no essential relationships, no rootage in the real world.

Writing of "The Man of the Modern Spirit," the author tells us that the greatness of the modern spirit is that it keeps close to the

puissant ground and walks in the real world; that because the heart of the age is humble it is only by humility that we can enter into its meaning, utter its longing, or fulfill its faith; that the modern spirit stands at its door expecting to see the Lord of Heaven and Earth pass by in the dusty road and get a message from Him; that it challenges all pleasant lies and vain pretensions, seeking only facts and crying, "Truth, the truth; though it slay me, yet will I trust it." And then follows this unique statement:

The quintessence of the modern spirit is faith in the incarnation. The faith that has gone out from the pulpits and the pews is walking abroad in the streets. Parsons and priests, synods and sacred councils, may not be half so sure that the Son of God must needs be brought up in Nazareth as the workers and fighters are, and the plain people that pass by. Do you know why this name of Jesus pursues you; why you cannot turn and look over your shoulder without seeing Him? It is because He is the man of the modern spirit. He deals with facts; does not talk in abstractions; is concrete, practical, personal; rests on what He is—rests on the facts and their self-vindicating power. He makes no boasts and no excuses. He keeps close to the daily earth, and always has firm ground under His feet. He speaks with authority because He is at home in the world; He rises from the dead because He is on good terms with death. . . . The message of Jesus is moral adventure; go on, take the risk, commit yourself confidently to the eternal currents and the natural order. He takes in the unity of the cosmos, and is tranquilly confident of the validity of its laws. He shrinks from nothing, not from disease nor sweat nor grime. He is sure of the inexhaustible resources of health and of the forgiveness of sins. He never compromises because He keeps close to His facts and they do not compromise. He demonstrates the axiom of the concrete: He does not argue, He illustrates. . . . His is the absolute science. He is the pioneer of a new world. He radiates courage and power, and to believe in Him is to have faith.

Touching the soul's possible supremacy over all things and its greatness as manifest in fearlessness of death, this memorandum of modern principles says:

The man willing to die becomes the master of the world. There can be no freedom or true dignity among men who are afraid to die; and a people to whom success is necessary cannot build a city that is great. The cities of the world, New York, London, Paris, are provincial; we have yet to build a true metropolis —a city of the soul, a capital whose citizens are not afraid of death. The soul is infinite. There is no infinity in mere dying; but to see a man who is willing to die for love, who goes to meet death in the way, who makes light of pain, and, with perfect sweetness and sanity, espouses and celebrates defeat—that is to be witness of the palpable infinite. It is like an arrow passing up into the air and not returning; like the still energy of planets or the resistless growing of the grass; or like the haunting, thrilling murmur of remembered music that faded down the avenue as the soldiers went to war. You are left endlessly expectant; you cannot stop, but must follow that which is beyond, and still beyond. In this immense victory is the soul's greatness; by it the soul comes to its own and finds what is forever good. The sight of it consoles and satisfies you. And it remains. After the money-lord has passed by, clinking his gold, and the war-lord, clanking his steel, this greatness stays and is sufficient. . . . History reports that the world is managed by those who are freest from fear and fullest of faith, by the people who are most deeply rooted in the substratum of things and feel least afraid of accidents. A civilization of refinement, wealth, and culture lies at

the mercy of the barbarians across the border, if the citizens are more afraid of death than the barbarians are. The final test as to which of two things shall remain standing and which shall fall, is which can offer the more martyrs—for which do men in greater numbers stand ready to give their lives. Men say the world is ruled by force, which is true in a way; but it is more especially true that the world is ruled by faith. For the power behind the throne of force is fearlessness—which is bottomed on faith. If the barbarians conquered Rome, it was because there was more fearlessness and faith in Goth and Vandal than there was on the other side; and because the coarsest kind of faith is worth more than the finest kind of skepticism and satire. In the long run the economy of the world is an economy of courage, and the heaviest battalions are heaviest because they are willingest to die. In their origin aristocracies have generally owed their power to their pluck, and they have kept their places as long as they have been more ready than the majority to put their lives in pawn for the sake of worthy interests—but not much longer. Civilization finds its life in losing it. Its organs do their work well in proportion as they take the eternal for granted and are moved by fearlessness of death or of earthly loss. Grandeur of material structure, multiplicity of conveniences, elegance of living—these incidental accessories, it appears, can be commanded not by a soft and sensuous people rapt in the pursuit of happiness, but only by a people of blood and iron, whose happiness does not depend on conveniences and luxuries, and who do not shrink from death. This fearlessness makes the awe and majesty of human life—the mystery and the magnificence; it makes the rituals of all religions, creates the great temples and pictures, writes the great books, and is the master-builder of the City of Justice and of Truth.

The tactics, antics, and pedantics of some one-sided modern scientists provoke comments like these:

Man is not mere eye and brain. He is heart and soul and conscience. Men of science have fancied they could separate their minds from the rest of themselves—that they could set their brains going in the midst of things, while they themselves stand aloof, disengaged and nonchalant. They operate the intellectual apparatus for grinding out knowledge as far as possible from the center of the warm and vital sphere of human feeling. On the remote frontiers of consciousness, where humanity is reduced to its lowest terms—almost is not humanity at all—there they set up their knowledge-threshing machines. They allow only so much of feeling as goes to the perception that things are bulky and that they move. It is not much of a perception; probably worms can perceive as much as that. Starting off there on the far faint outermost circumference of perception, these savants try to work their way back to themselves, taking notes by the way, automatic, mechanical, exact. They try to explain themselves by something external and foreign to themselves—to construe love and aspiration, rage and remorse, in terms of mass and motion. It is prodigious gymnastics, but it will have to be given up. If there were a being whose entire outfit consisted of those instruments of observation; and a mental machine—why then the creature with such a beggarly equipment might be expected to worship the material universe and natural law, rejecting the Gospel and crucifying the Son of Man. But man is not mere eye and brain, capable only of knowing physical facts and natural laws. The haughty high priests of physical science may rend their gaberdines and cry their cold hard gospel of the flinty fatalistic reign of heartless Law; but we will not listen, for by their law we die. . . . But science cannot keep out faith. The wisest science is laying, or uncovering, some deep and firm foundations for faith; and to-day science is itself venturing everything on one enormous act of faith—an immense and comprehensive assumption, to wit, that the cosmos, the whole creation, is constitutionally one with itself; that it is a universe; that it has no irreducible alien elements, no unassimilable facts, no intrinsic contradictions. This assumption is the great adventure of our age, an adventure in which the intellect does not travel alone. To it the modern man

8

commits himself. This distinguishes the present age from all other ages as *par excellence* the age of Faith. Nowhere in Europe or America is any philosophy now accepted which can be called skeptical in the ancient sense. Pyrrhonism has no disciples. Nobody denies to-day the possibility of knowledge, or teaches that the universe is for practical purposes unknowable. It is now held to be reasonable to assume that the whole universe is reasonable, that it hangs together to the minutest detail, and that there are no gaps or crevasses in it to swallow up the mind. Against apparent contradictions, the most irreconcilable, this magnificent modern act of faith ventures on the assumption of the unity of the cosmos, the essential and ultimate congruity of things, and the reasonableness of the creation—which means the reasonableness of the Creator. At bottom it is faith in God, and in ourselves as being made of the same stuff as He is, able to think His thoughts after Him, to trace and follow out and cooperate with His plan, and to understand somewhat of His meaning and messages to us. The scientific faith that the universe is reasonable covers in under its comprehensiveness innumerable particulars. The first comer may tell you that in his opinion death is an incongruity and a disadvantage, and that his interest and yours are at variance. But if death is an incongruity and disadvantage and yet is inevitable, how then can the world be reasonable? And if your interest is opposed to your neighbor's what becomes of the unity and harmony of things? If that is good for him which is bad for you, then there are at least two universes—yours and his; and two gods, or else there is confusion and no God. . . . It is a servile conception—the science of lawyers and pedagogues—that makes God subject to Law. Who then is this God of God? Let us worship *Him!* If the true Deity's name is "Law," let us stop saying "God;" let us go to the Top, whatever the proper name of the All-Mighty is. Is the Deity bound or free? Religion is coming to see the universality of the miraculous. Old miracle theories were aristocratic; they made miracles a privilege and a monopoly, and God a kind of Stuart king breaking the constitution for the pleasure of his courtiers and the confusion of the commons. Their God gets loose once in a while; the rest of the time He is caged inside the bars of Law. If God has only *so* much liberty, then Fate is strong indeed. But modern faith claims the miraculous—it is better to say "God"—on an infinitely larger scale. However anything may seem to us—whether more wonderful or less so—a free and reasonable God is working and counterworking in all things according to His own good pleasure. And one great and happifying persuasion grows and strengthens, rising into a song—the persuasion that the universe is reasonable, that everything has relation to every other thing, that everywhere is rhythm and measure, that the creation answers back to the unity of the mind and is sane. . . . The world waits for the lead of men whose hearts shall be strong with courage, believing in the freedom of God and their own freedom, accepting the world as reasonable and life as improvable and improving, and who shall rejoice in things as they are while all the time laboring hopefully to make them better, hearing the singing in the heart of God and sending back a brave antiphonal across all the deserts and wildernesses of the world.

This "memorandum of modern principles," whose author is described as a Protestant Episcopal minister, a member of the New York bar, a traveler in many lands, a comrade of ranchmen, miners, and Indians, is a difficult book to characterize. It has won admiring commendation from such men as are quoted in praise of it at the beginning of this editorial. Yet one surly critic scornfully suggests that the volume is a section from that original "indefinite, incoherent homogeneity" from which Herbert Spencer saw matter starting on its way to be something or somebody.

THE ARENA.

CAN YE NOT DISCERN THE SIGNS OF THE TIMES?

THE Pharisees and the Sadducees, usually so antagonistic to each other, join hands and come to Jesus with the old request, a sign from heaven. John's question, asked from the dungeon, "Art thou he that should come?" is answered by the statement, "The blind receive their sight, and the lame walk, the lepers are cleansed, and the deaf hear, the dead are raised up, and the poor have the Gospel preached to them." The answer satisfies John and strengthens him for his martyrdom. Certainly the willful unbelievers cannot expect more than the friend faithful unto death receives. Still Jesus was willing to teach if they were only willing to learn. The red sky in the evening, they said, indicated fair weather and the red sky in the morning indicated foul weather. He finds no fault with this reading of the sky, but blames them for not discerning the plainly visible signs of the times. They ask a sign from heaven to prove to them the Messiahship of Christ, but refuse to read the signs of the times which pointed to that fact. Others had read them. The shepherds had, so had Simeon and Anna and the wise men from the Orient. The disciples were slowly learning to discern them. Even Nicodemus and others like him were beginning to understand a little of the great fact which they proclaimed. But the leaders of the people were blind, and their blindness continued till destruction was upon them and their city. The Master's question, "Can ye not discern the signs of the times?" is a pertinent one to-day. Mighty forces are at work and momentous changes are taking place. Everything is moving on a grand scale. What will be the outcome? Some with a pessimistic groan tell us that everything is wrong and getting worse. Some with an optimistic shout proclaim that all is well and getting better. Many are indifferent as to church, nation, and neighbor, and are thinking only of themselves and their selfish hopes. Others, their hearts inspired with the love of the Master, are endeavoring to read the signs of the times aright and are doing their utmost that the individual and society may know Him who alone is able to save.

As at the beginning of the Christian era the signs of the times proclaimed the Redeemer, so in our times they point to him. The great socialistic movement, which demands the attention of every thinking person, points to Jesus. The great truth of the brotherhood of all mankind, which the life and teaching of Jesus so forcibly proclaimed, has especially during the last few centuries been endeavoring to materialize itself. Absolute monarchism and serfdom in Europe had to give way. Then slavery in England and America was overcome, and now it seeks to find a better expression in the social and business life of our day. On the one hand are the immense accumulation of wealth and the formerly unheard-of combination of capital in business enterprises. On the other hand, labor is uniting and making its demands. Everywhere great and successful ef-

forts are being made to educate the people along socialistic lines. Now as always man is inclined to go from one extreme to the other. While socialism and anarchy are far from being identical, the extreme oppression of former times and the injustice often practiced in our own times naturally find their other extreme in the doctrines and acts of anarchy. However much the extremes to which many socialists go are to be condemned, the fact remains that the great truth of the brotherhood of all mankind underlies the movement, and without doubt it will find some expression. Should force be resorted to the results would be terrible, but they would be glorious if the capitalist and the laborer would both sit at the feet of Jesus, learn from him the spirit and life of true brotherly love, and then practice it according to his example. Whether socialism is a menace or a prophecy of better conditions depends upon the relation which it assumes to the Saviour of mankind, and the relation which it will assume depends greatly upon the faithfulness of the Church to the Master.

The material tendency of human efforts is another sign of our times. To become wealthy and do so in a short time is the all-absorbing ambition of the multitude. Not only the individual is bending all his energies in that direction, but the great question which is agitating the nations is the question of market, and that is only another way of saying wealth. This tendency manifests itself in the craze for amusements. Not only are those amusements which most strongly appeal to the senses sought after, but what should be a relaxation from the strenuous strain of business life becomes itself a nervous strain. While some claim that education is being overdone, it is certain that the material and secular lines which are being pursued are an injury to the ideal and spiritual life of the coming generations. As wealth, amusements, and education in themselves cannot satisfy man, greater wealth, more exciting amusements, and more varied education are sought after. All this only increases the discontentment. When will man learn that only Jesus gives contentment, and that in him the greatest wealth, the highest joy, and the deepest wisdom are found? If professing Christians could be induced to use the energy which they now employ for the attainment of material wealth, earthly amusements, and secular wisdom for the upbuilding of the kingdom of Christ the results would be wonderful.

The many false doctrines and half-truths which are being taught to-day and which are finding so many adherents indicate that many unknowingly are seeking the truth as it is in Christ Jesus. The felt need and the expectation of the Messiah caused many of the Jews to accept false Messiahs. So many to-day follow false teachers because they are seeking the truth but do not succeed in finding it. Philips who gladly show Jesus to the people are needed. The Church is so busy with other important and unimportant things that this most important work is too often neglected. Education, Church benevolences, and all other Church enterprises, are only the handmaidens to assist in the real work of the Church, the salvation of immortal souls. While the needs of our times proclaim the necessity of a revival of the religion of Jesus, the desire for and the expectation of a revival are definite promises that it is coming. After years of drought the sign of the Son of God is seen in the spiritual heavens, and

the promise of a rich outpouring of his Spirit is gladdening many hearts. Much is heard about returning to the old methods. This is good as far as it goes, but it is not so much the old methods as the old results which are needed. Not only in Methodism is the revival spirit manifesting itself, but other Churches glory in the fact that they are working in the old Methodistic spirit and warn Methodism lest it lose its old glory of being preeminently the revival Church.   EMIL H. BAAB.
Los Angeles, Cal.

AS TO THE RESURRECTION.

It may not detract from the fact stated in the May, 1903, "Arena," that there is a great deal of freshness, vivacity, and beauty" in the article of Dr. Lance, to express a doubt as to the theory apparently accepted therein, and which was so distinctly asserted by one of our bishops in the statement, that he "had had" in his lifetime of somewhere near seventy years "ten new bodies." For the question at once arises, "How did he, or how can any man, *know* that?" There is a difference between knowledge and belief, the latter, being, therefore, perhaps what the bishop meant. There is, of course, no question but that there is, as to the living body, a constant or periodical influx and efflux going on, and therefore to a certain extent a change in certain parts of the body, but that the entire structure and material of the body is changed may not necessarily follow. If in the course of seventy years a man has had ten *new* bodies, we may pertinently ask why the tenth body is not as good as the sixth or seventh, or as any preceding body. Certainly even the body of the "noblest," excellent as it was for the time of life of this utterance, was not in any sense as good as when we heard from his lips his matchless ante-episcopal prayer. Changes certainly take place, but apparently there must always remain a substratum which is not made new. An illustration of what is meant may be given in the use of a sponge. Dipped in water when new, it readily absorbs and is filled; by pressure the water is discharged. This process may be continued, this influx and efflux, until the sponge ceases to serve the purpose—is, in other words, worn out. Analogously, the human body takes in and throws out, assimilating what it needs and rejecting the residuum, and continues this process in many instances, for all we know, until the substratum is worn out, and death ensues from no other apparent or conclusive reason than from this loss of ability, through use, to absorb, assimilate, or reject. What then remains may credibly be assumed, or at least suggested, to be the subject or object of the anastasis—the upstanding or resurrection—if such there is to be.

The same note in the May "Arena," on "St. Paul on the Spiritual Body," is well deserving of consideration and somewhat extended examination, until that is done it does not seem best to let go without a "caveat" the statement that Paul "affirms unequivocally and unmistakably that only the spiritual part of man shall survive the tomb. 'It is sown a natural body; it is raised a spiritual body.'" Neither is it certain that "no wider contrast exists in the universe than is found between the natural (or material) and the spiritual; they hold no feature or attribute in common."

Nor is it important to determine in this connection whether it is certain or uncertain, since Paul is not writing of the "natural" or the "spiritual" abstractly, but of the "natural *body*" and the "spiritual *body*," and gives no authority for saying that "they hold no feature or attribute in common." "Soma," body, is clearly stated by Paul to be "a feature or attribute" of both. "There is a spiritual body," and as this "spiritual body" is to be "resurrected" it is mere assumption to say that "the material is to be completely eliminated" until it is clearly determined what a spiritual *body* is. There is no evidence whatever that the "material" was "completely eliminated" from the spiritual body of Christ, "the first fruits of them that slept," nor that his eating was not for the need of food, nor that he passed through without opening the door which had been shut for fear of the Jews, and had therefore doubtless been cautiously watched and kept, and opened only when it was safe so to do. In every case of his appearance during the forty days it is distinctly in evidence that the "material" was there, and there is no proof that he was ever divested of it, even when "he ascended to his father and his God." All that is written concerning his resurrection goes to prove that the entire material body came out of the grave, that nothing of that was left in the sepulcher. His "vanishing" or sudden and wholly unexpected disappearance at Emmaus has the same significance, and possibly from these several appearances and departures, and supremely and emphatically from his final ascension, we may reach some definite conclusion as to what in part at least is meant by a "spiritual body," for "body" ($\sigma\tilde{\omega}\mu\alpha$) it is called, and as this word is most uniformly used in the New Testament of "matter" it would seem that it must be here also used and interpreted accordingly. It may help to better understanding of the terms to direct our thought to the characteristics, or what is meant by "natural" in its connection with "body"—a "$\sigma\tilde{\omega}\mu\alpha\ \psi\upsilon\chi\iota\kappa\grave{o}\nu$." This may be, perhaps, correctly partially described as a body organized suitably to the necessities and subject to the laws and forces of the scene or sphere of being in which it may exist or be intended to abide. So, similarly, a "spiritual body" may be understood to be a body organized suitably to the necessities (Jesus ate solid food) and subject only to the laws, forces, etc., existent and active in or on the scene or sphere of being in which it may exist.

Now, it seems to be deducible from the New Testament teaching that both soul and spirit are to be saved for a future life, and the redemption "of our body" is distinctly named as "waited for," presumably by soul as well as spirit, which is expressly named (Rom. viii, 23). It is nowhere taught that the soul and spirit are to exist separately either in the state into which they pass at bodily death, nor yet after the resurrection is it taught that the unity of soul, spirit, and body shall ever be broken up (comp. Thess. v, 23). In this present scene and stage of being both soul and spirit can abide in the "natural body." But the characteristics and phenomena attendant upon Christ during the forty days in which both soul and spirit were existent in the same body indicate clearly that the resurrected body was not so completely subject to the laws, limitations, forces, etc., that were masters or rulers of what was, prior to its resurrection, emphatically a "natural body," and that the body which before death had

been their abode had undergone a change or transformation of some sort, and was now subject rather to the predominating spirit and adapted to the new environments of the spiritual life, and yet by its very constitution was capable of contact and life in a material, physical, or natural world, its body, however, changed, refined, sublimated, its atoms so arranged and combined as to preclude corruption, decay, or the disabilities of its former condition, and so constituted also as to be subject to the rule and forces of the spiritual, the irresistible will of the redeemed soul and spirit. And as such body was the result of the first anastasis, "upstanding," the first fruit in such body shall be the result of the great uprising at the sound of the trump, at the call of Jesus—when the dead shall respond and the changed living join their host, when this stage of being or epochal period shall end, and the stellar orbs of the new heavens and the new and sublimated earth shall renew their solemn rounds, and the undisturbed or reestablished solar system continue its obedient silent worship of the enthroned King Eternal, Jehovah, Jesus, Emanuel.

Pittsburg, Pa. JOSEPH HORNER.

AN EDUCATED MINISTRY.

WE have in view the men whose time and talents are devoted to the work of preaching the Gospel. It is taken for granted that such men are called of God and commissioned by the Church to the office of the ministry. Unless there be a divine call, no amount of education can fit men to edify believers, nor to win sinners for the kingdom. But he who is born from above, and called of God as was Aaron, needs a mental training to fit him for the fields that are white unto the harvest. While the affections of the heart are to be won for God, and the tides of life turned toward holiness, the heart is ofttimes reached through the mind. Strong appeals are made through the mind to the heart. He whose mental powers are educated can express the great truths of the Bible in simple, chaste, and beautiful language. He can thus make the story of the cross more attractive, and his usefulness in the Master's vineyard will be multiplied many fold.

Education means a drawing out of the powers and forces of the mind. Often the mind is asleep; its powers lie dormant, and its forces know not their strength. The mind must be roused from its slumber. It may be awakened by coming into contact with another mind stronger than itself, or by the reading of a good book. In some way the mind is led to look in upon the meagerness of its attainments, and then to look out upon the great storehouse of truth that lies open before it. The spirit of wonder takes possession of the person, the mind is stirred to a diligent search after the truth, and a taste is cultivated for a literature of the highest order. This awakening does not come to all alike; to some it never comes, but to whom it does come it is like a revelation, like the beginning of a new life. The mind until awakened cannot grow; but with the awakening it receives a new impulse that sends it out to use its own powers and to strive after knowledge. The mind of him who has to do with other minds should be awake, with all its forces on the wing, with all its powers tensely strung. An education will give to the minister new views of life, and

show him that it is worth the living. It will give him a breadth of culture the value of which cannot be estimated. It will establish friendships that may prove eternal. It will stock his mind with a store of knowledge from which to draw for all the future. It will impart a delight in knowledge for its own sake. It will bring manifold help to body, mind, and spirit.

It would be foolish in the extreme for a man to build a house which he expected to occupy for some time without using the utmost care in selecting material for the foundation. And it would certainly be a mistake to use inferior material upon which to erect the superstructure. That would not only be a waste of time and a loss of money, but it would also endanger human lives. Of how much more importance, then, it is that the foundation for a lifework be laid in a good education which is sufficient for our plans and for the hopes of our friends! During all his active life the minister works in the realm of thought. To be a good scriptural preacher, which is a holy ambition, a man must have a rich mind as well as a great soul. He who thinks high and holy thoughts will develop that kind of manhood which will fit him for the largest usefulness in this world of work. He will unfold brain power, realize the real worth of humanity, and serve God in his day and generation.

A seed planted in the earth contains all the elements of a fruit-bearing vine. But it can come to perfection and bring fruit to maturity only as it secures a certain amount of sunlight, moisture, temperature, and soil. So a human soul born into the world has in itself all the elements of a perfect life. But there must be a certain amount of brain culture and a right conception of mankind, along with other important elements, before one attains to that perfect life of which Christ was the pattern.

Selma, Ia.   FRANK SEEDS.

THE AMERICAN REVISION OF ROM. V, 1-11.

IN considering the value of the Revision in Rom. v, 1-11, it is important to notice that the American Revision has restored the indicative in verses 1, 2. It is evident that the connection of thought in the passage demands the indicative. The author is stating the consequences of justification by faith; the hortatory portions of the epistle are farther on. Without doubt the manuscripts strongly favor the subjunctive in verse 1. But in verse 2 the form is either indicative or subjunctive. Those who have access to the manuscripts tell us that the interchange of omicron with omega sometimes occurs apparently through a confusion of one vowel with another in pronunciation. Possibly the state of mind of some copyist might lead him unconsciously to substitute the hortative form for the declarative. The word rendered "probation" in the fourth verse means either the *process of trial* or the *result of trial* or a *specimen of tried value.* If the English revisers intended to express the *process of trial* by the word "probation" they are clearly wrong. The process of trial is in the "tribulation which worketh patience." The American Revision is correct: "approvedness;" that is, God's approval.   S. E. QUIMBY.

Milton Mills, N. H.

THE ITINERANTS' CLUB.

PAUL'S ADVICE TO TITUS (Continued)—Titus ii, 7-10.

This epistle does not yield as readily to analysis as some of Paul's other writings, but yet there is an order running through it that is very apparent. He has already instructed Titus as to his duties to aged men, aged women, young women, and young men. He insists that the preacher must be an example as well as an instructor. His language is, "in all things showing thyself a pattern of good works," or, as the Revisers put it, "an ensample of good works." But example is not sufficient. His teaching is to be correct, and so he affirms that in doctrine Titus must show "uncorruptness, gravity, and sincerity." Whence this corruptness comes is not indicated. It may come from the tendency of false teachers to lead astray the people of God. In contrast to this he would urge purity of doctrine, that is, teaching in accordance with the exact truth as revealed by Christ himself and his apostles. The doctrine which he teaches is to be regarded as important, and therefore he places it side by side with his example. Example and teaching are handmaids that must always connect themselves in the faithful minister's thought, and hence he urges it upon Titus. There must be also in connection with uncorruptness gravity, that is, dignity of demeanor, and sincerity. These three elements are followed by a statement that he must be a person of sound speech. This probably refers not so much to the substance of his teaching as to the general healthfulness of it. There is healthy and unhealthy speech; there is wise and unwise speech. His mode of address must be such as "cannot be condemned," that is, will stand the test of gainsayers. He gives further a reason for this, namely, that the person opposed to his doctrine may be ashamed of himself because he is opposing that which must be recognized as healthy in its character and in its influence. The exhortation which was given to Titus was similar to that which Paul gave to Timothy (1 Tim. iv, 12, 13): "Be thou an example of the believers, in word, in conversation, in charity, in spirit, in faith, in purity. Till I come, give attendance to reading, to exhortation, to doctrine." In the Epistle to Timothy the statement is more full, but the general thought is the same.

The apostle now returns to urge upon Titus his duty in regard to a class which must not be overlooked, and which formed a large part of the population, namely, slaves. He here exhorts them "to be obedient unto their own masters, and to please them well in all things; not answering again," or, as the Revisers write it, "not gainsaying." They are not to purloin from their masters, but to be faithful in everything. These are familiar utterances of the apostle, and the reason given is exceedingly beautiful—"that they may adorn the doctrine of God our Saviour in all things." The apostle immediately connects this thought with a reason of great significance in the Gospel, namely, "For the grace of God

which bringeth salvation hath appeared to all men." This includes slaves, and as his grace has appeared to them it is their duty to act in accordance with it, and he makes the application to all men, including himself, "Teaching us that, denying ungodliness and worldly lusts, we should live soberly, righteously, and godly, in this present world; looking for that blessed hope, and the glorious appearing of the great God and our Saviour Jesus Christ."

The homiletic value of this passage of Scripture is alike applicable to Titus as a pastor and the people to whom he was called to minister. He has just instructed Titus as to his duty to young men: "Young men likewise exhort to be sober-minded;" and the apostle follows it at once with an appeal to Titus as to personal example. Youth needs more than precept; it needs practice. Even a pastor may destroy the value of the most truthful words by a life out of harmony with his own teachings. The word here rendered "ensample" is τύπον, which is more than a mere outline. It is intended to express a character corresponding to his own teachings. Here the passage addresses itself with especial emphasis to young preachers. The people are ever disposed to hear with favor a young preacher. There is a vigor, a freshness of thought and style, that arrests attention, but he must be especially careful that his own life be in harmony with his teachings. It is quite common for people to raise the question. Such an example is of great value, especially in young people's societies. The preacher should remember that he is always the pastor, and that his conduct is narrowly watched, though perhaps unconsciously on their part and on his, by the people with whom he mingles. John Summerfield was a remarkable young Methodist evangelist whose name was a familiar one more than a third of a century ago. Another distinguished young minister was Robert Murray McCheyne, of Scotland. They both exerted a powerful influence, but no study of their sermons will account for it. Their influence is to be connected with the power of their example.

The text gives a description of the character of the discourses which are to be delivered, namely, "sound speech, that cannot be condemned." This would involve two elements in the proclamation of the Gospel on the part of the preacher. The first is that it be sound. That word is familiar to our modern thinking and is understood to be truth that is in harmony with the current and accepted thought on the part of the one who proclaims it. Titus is here exhorted that his doctrine shall be in harmony with the general truths of the Gospel such as were taught by Christ and his apostles. He was not to depart from the general tenor of the faith. This would not mean that there was no room for independent thought or expression, but there should be no expression that was out of harmony with the system of truth, called the Gospel, of which he was the expounder. Paul speaks of "my gospel," which afterward he expounded in his various epistles. By sound speech, then, we understand in this case doctrines which were in accordance with that system of truth which Paul taught in his epistles and with which Titus was undoubtedly familiar. Sound speech must also be "so well considered

and judicially applied as to give no undue advantage to opponents." The preacher, therefore, should not speak rashly.

We may further note in this passage a peculiar statement with regard to servants—that they were to avoid doing the things which were wrong in the positions they occupied, "showing all good fidelity," in order that they might adorn the doctrine of God our Saviour in all things." Here we may note two points of much significance. The one that the doctrine of God may be adorned or glorified by his people. God is in the nature of the case the sum of all greatness, of all holiness, and of all truth. It would seem that he was so perfect that nothing could be added to him, but we are here taught that we may adorn the doctrine of God, that is, it is possible to make it so appear as to make it acceptable to others. If this passage refers to choice modes of expression, vivid illuustrations, dignity of language, and everything that may make the truth more acceptable to the hearer, then we may assume that the preacher of the Gospel should not be indifferent either to the graces of rhetoric or the severity of logic. Whatever makes clear and enforces the truth is worthy of adoption by the preacher of the Gospel. If this passage refers to conduct principally, then we may note that by the action of God's people they may adorn the doctrine which they profess. Doctrine in itself is often dry and unpleasant in the view of many, but when it is adorned, that is, expressed in beautiful living and in all the relations of life, whether among those who are Christians or those who are not, then we in a certain sense adorn the doctrine of God.

The doctrinal aspect of this passage may well arrest our attention. The doctrine is that of "our Saviour God." Here we have the source of authority in Christianity. God, who is represented here as the Saviour of all mankind, is the source of all spiritual life as well as of all doctrine. Out of his sacrifice and death comes not only forgiveness of sin, but the power to adorn the doctrine of God. This is well put by Humphrey in his commentary. His language is: "Live your creed, says Saint Paul; adorn your doctrine as indeed you well can. Work from life; let doctrine inspire duty. This is the doctrine of our Saviour God; God the Father Almighty, who made all men and hateth nothing that he made, really did come, as a past fact of history, and manifest his love by sending his only son to redeem all men; that love really does as a present fact of doctrine give us the love of his Son through his Spirit; that love really will as an equally certain fact in the future manifest the glory of his Son as God, and will give us the fullness of divine love."

We see that the eleventh verse enforces the doctrine which has just been given: "For the grace of God that bringeth salvation hath appeared to all men." These great results are the influence of his grace. We have here its marvelous power. The doctrine of salvation by grace is the most fruitful doctrine in the production of works. When men become conscious that they are sinners, that there is no merit growing out of either their characters or works such as shall justify them before God, and accept salvation as a divine gift, then they forsake sin and are enabled to adorn the "doctrine of God our Saviour in all things."

ARCHÆOLOGY AND BIBLICAL RESEARCH.

HAMMURABI AND MOSES.

THE discovery of the Tel-el-Amarna tablets, a few years ago, gave a rude shock to the Kuenen-Wellhausen theory of Old Testament criticism. The very pillars on which this school had built its Pentateuchal structure commenced then to totter. The possibility of the production of the five books of Moses could no longer be denied on purely literary grounds, for the tablets revealed beyond controversy that there was a high degree of culture, religious and secular, over a vast territory extending from the Nile through Syria, portions of Asia Minor, to and beyond the Euphrates. It was clearly demonstrated that Canaan itself was acquainted with writing long before Moses had appeared on the scene of action. The next step of our friends the radical critics was to admit that writing was practiced extensively before the Mosaic age, but to deny the possibility of the codification of laws on a large scale at so early an age. But, alas! the discovery of the Hammurabi Code, which no critic dates later than 2250 B. C., has spiked this particular set of guns. For here is a code, produced nearly a thousand years before the Hebrews left Egypt, which has a wonderful number of laws almost identical with those usually called Mosaic. This necessitates another move, and our friends, with Professor Friedrich Delitzsch at the head of the column, now assure us that no matter who wrote the Pentateuch, or when it was written, most of the lofty ideas therein contained have been derived from the Babylonians. In other words, there is nothing especially supernatural about the Pentateuch. It is in the main of Babylonian origin, whether it be regarded from a religious or legislative standpoint. We shall not, at this time, discuss this particular claim except to say that we are not convinced of the truth of the proposition. Instead of that, we shall call attention to the more striking agreements and differences in the codes of Moses and Hammurabi. This can be done best by parallels. The list is by no means complete, our object being to present the more striking ones. Before proceeding, it should be said that we have carefully read much of the Hammurabi literature of the last two years, and have been especially profited by the *brochures* of Jeremias, Winckler, Oettli, Delitzsch, and others, and that we are indebted to them for many suggestions. We take our citations, in the main, from C. H. W. John's translation, entitled *The Oldest Code of Laws in the World.* The chief defect of this translation is its slavish literalness. But to our parallels:

HAMMURABI.	MOSES.
If a man weave a spell and put a ban upon a man, and has not justified himself, he that wove the spell upon him shall be put to death. 1.	A man also or a woman that hath a familiar spirit, or that is a wizard, shall surely be put to death: they shall stone them with stones. Lev. xx, 27.

If a man accuse anyone of a crime before the elders, and does not prove his accusation, he shall, if that case be a capital suit, be put to death. 3.

If he has offered corn or money to the witnesses, he shall himself bear the sentence of that case. 4.

If a man has stolen an ox, or sheep, or ass, or pig, or boat, whether from the temple or the royal palace, he shall pay thirtyfold. If from a freedman, he shall pay tenfold. If the thief has naught to pay, he shall be put to death. 8.

If a man has stolen the son of a freeman, he shall be put to death. 14.

If a man has harbored in his house a fugitive slave, male or female, of the royal palace, or of a freedman, and has produced them at the demand of the officer, the master of that house shall be put to death. 16.

If a man has broken into a house, one shall kill him before the breach and bury him in it(?). 21.

If a shepherd has caused the sheep to feed on the green corn, has not come to an agreement with the owner of the field, without the consent of the owner of the field has made the sheep feed off the field, the owner shall reap his fields; the shepherd who without consent of the owner of the field has fed off the field with sheep shall give over and above twenty *gur* of corn per *gan* to the owner of the field. 57.

If a man has given a field to a gardener to plant a garden, and the gardener has planted the garden, four years he shall cultivate the garden; in the fifth year the owner of the garden and the gardener shall share equally, the owner of the garden shall cut off his share and take it. 60.

If anyone on a journey intrust silver, gold, precious stones, or treasures of his hand to a man, has caused him to take them for transport, and

If an unrighteous witness rise up against any man to testify against him, . . . and hath testified falsely against his brother; then shall ye do unto him as he had thought to do unto his brother. Deut. xix, 16-19.

And thou shalt take no gift: for a gift blindeth them that have sight, and perverteth the words of the righteous. Exod. xxiii, 8.

If a man shall steal an ox, or a sheep, and kill it, or sell it; he shall pay five oxen for an ox, and four sheep for a sheep. Exod. xxii, 1. (See also verse 9.)

And he that stealeth a man, and selleth him, or if he be found in his hand, he shall surely be put to death. Exod. xxi, 16.

Thou shalt not deliver unto his master a servant which is escaped from his master unto thee: he shall dwell with thee, in the midst of thee, in the place which he shall choose: . . . thou shalt not oppress him. Deut. xxiii, 15, 16.

If the thief be found breaking in, and be smitten that he die, there shall be no bloodguiltiness for him. Exod. xxii, 2. (See, however, the next two verses.)

If a man shall cause a field or vineyard to be eaten, and shall let his beast loose, and it feed in another man's field; of the best of his own field, and of the best of his own vineyard, shall he make restitution. Exod. xxii, 5.

And when ye shall come into the land, and shall have planted all manner of trees for food, then ye shall count the fruit thereof as their uncircumcision: three years shall they be as uncircumcision unto you; it shall not be eaten. But in the fourth year all the fruit thereof shall be holy, for giving praise unto the Lord. And in the fifth year shall ye eat of the fruit thereof. Lev. xix, 23-25.

If a soul sin, and commit a trespass against the Lord, and lie unto his neighbor in that which was delivered to him to keep, . . . or in a

that man whatever was for transport, where he has transported, has not given and has not taken to himself, the owner of the transported object, that man, concerning whatever he had to transport and gave not, shall put him to account, and that man shall give to the owner of the transported object fivefold whatever was given him. 112. (See also 122-125.)

If any be unable to pay a debt, and sell himself, his wife, his daughter for the money, or has given them over to forced labor for the debt, for three years they shall work in the house of him who bought them or their exploiter, in the fourth year he shall fix their liberty. 117.

If any be unable to pay a debt, and he sell the maidservant who has borne him children for money, the money which the trader has paid shall be repaid to him by the owner of the maid, and she shall be freed [or ransomed]. 119.

If the wife of a man has been caught in lying with any male, one shall bind them and throw them into the waters. If the owner of the wife would save her, or the king his slave [he may]. 129.

If a man violate the wife [betrothed] of another man, who has not known a man, and who is still living in the house of her father, this man shall be put to death, but the wife is blameless. 130.

If a wife of a man on account of another male has had the finger pointed at her, and has not been caught sleeping with another male, she shall jump into the river for her husband. 132.

If a man has set his face to put away his concubine, who has borne him children, or his wife who has given him children, to that woman he shall return her marriage portion, ... and she shall bring up her children, ... and she shall marry the husband of her choice. 137.

thing taken away by violence; ... or have found that which was lost, and lieth concerning it, and sweareth falsely: ... then it shall be, because he hath sinned, and is guilty, that he shall restore that which he took violently away, or the thing which he hath deceitfully gotten, or that which was delivered him to keep, or the lost thing which he found; ... he shall even restore it in the principal, and shall add the fifth part more thereto. Lev. vi, 2-5.

If thy brother, an Hebrew man, or an Hebrew woman, be sold unto thee, and serve thee six years; then in the seventh year thou shalt let him go free from thee. And when thou sendest him out free from thee, thou shalt not let him go empty: thou shalt furnish him liberally out of thy flock, and out of thy threshing-floor, and out of thy winepress. Deut. xv, 12-14.

And it shall be, if thou have no delight in her [the captive concubine]. then thou shalt let her go whither she will; but thou shalt not sell her at all for money, thou shalt not deal with her as a slave, because thou hast humbled her. Deut. xxi, 14.

And the man that committeth adultery with another man's wife, even he that committeth adultery with his neighbor's wife, the adulterer and the adulteress shall surely be put to death. Lev. xx, 10.

But if the man find the damsel that is betrothed in the field, and the man force her, and lie with her; then the man only that lay with her shall die: but unto the damsel thou shalt do nothing; there is in the damsel no sin worthy of death. Deut. xxii, 25.

This law of ordeal is given in Num. v, 12-28, which the reader may consult, since it is too long to be inserted here.

When a man taketh a wife, and marrieth her, then it shall be, if she find no favor in his eyes, because he hath found some unseemly thing in her, that he shall write her a bill of divorcement, and give it in her hand, and send her out of his house. And when she is departed out of his house, she may go and be another man's wife. Deut. xxiv, 1, 2.

If a man has betrothed a wife to his son, and his son has known her, and he [the father] afterward defile her and has been caught, then he shall be bound and cast into the waters [that is, drowned]. 155.

According to John the betrothed wife shall also be drowned.

If a man has betrothed a girl to his son, and his son has not known her, and if then he has defiled her, he shall pay her half a mina of silver, and shall pay to her whatever she brought from her father's house, and she may marry the husband of her choice. 156.

If anyone is guilty of incest with his own mother after his father, both shall be burned. 157.

If anyone be caught after his father in the bosom of her that brought him up [stepmother], who has borne children, he shall be driven out of his father's house. 158.

If a man has apportioned to his son, whom he prefers, field, garden, and house, and has given a sealed deed; after the father's death, when the brothers divide [the property], the present his father gave him shall he take, and over and above shall he equally share in the paternal property. 165. (See also 171.)

If he be guilty of a grave crime against his father which cuts him off from sonship, he shall be forgiven for the first time, but if he be found guilty a second time, his father may cut him off from sonship. 169.

If the son of a paramour, or of a vowed woman [prostitute] say to the father and mother that brought him up, "You are not my father or mother," his tongue shall be cut off. 192.

If the son of a paramour or prostitute has known his father's house, and has hated his adoptive father and mother and goes off to his father's house, one shall tear out his eye. 193.

If a man has struck his father, his hands shall be cut off. 195.

If a man has caused the loss of an-

And if a man lie with his daughter-in-law, both of them shall surely be put to death. Lev. xx, 12.

If a man find a damsel that is a virgin, which is not betrothed, and lay hold on her, and lie with her, and they be found; then the man that lay with her shall give unto the damsel's father fifty shekels of silver, and she shall be his wife, because he hath humbled her. Deut. xxii, 28, 29.

The nakedness of thy father, even the nakedness of thy mother, shalt thou not uncover. Lev. xviii, 7. (For the penalty see Lev. xx, 11.)

And the man that lieth with his father's wife hath uncovered his father's nakedness: both of them shall surely be put to death; their blood shall be upon them. Lev. xx, 11.

And Sarah my master's wife bare a son to my master when she was old: and unto him hath he given all that he hath. Gen. xxiv, 36. And Abraham gave all that he had unto Isaac. But unto the sons of the concubines, which Abraham had, Abraham gave gifts. Gen. xxv, 5, 6.

If a man have a stubborn and rebellious son, which will not obey the voice of his father, or the voice of his mother, and though they chasten him, will not hearken unto them: then shall his father and his mother lay hold on him, and bring him out unto the elders of his city. . . . And all the men of his city shall stone him with stones, that he die. Deut. xxi, 18-21.

For every one that curseth his father or his mother shall surely be put to death. Lev. xx, 9.

The following seems to point to the same law: The eye that mocketh at his father, and despiseth to obey his mother, the ravens of the valley shall pick it out, and the young eagles shall eat it. Prov. xxx, 17.

He that smiteth his father, or his mother, shall be surely put to death. Exod. xxi, 15.

Thou shalt give life for life, eye for

other man's eye, his eye shall be put out. 196. If he has broken another man's-limb, his limb shall be broken. 197. (See also 200.)

If he put out the eye of anyone's slave, or break the bone of anyone's slave, he shall pay one half of his value. 199.

If a man, during a quarrel, has struck another and wounded him; then he shall swear, "I did not hurt him willingly," and shall pay the physician. 206.

If he has died of his blows, he shall swear, and if he was a freeborn man, he shall pay half a mina of silver. 207. If he be the son of a poor man, he shall pay one third of a mina of silver. 208.

If a man strike a freeborn woman and cause her to lose her unborn child, he shall pay ten shekels of silver for what was in her womb. 209. If that woman die, his daughter shall be put to death. 210.

If a man has hired an ox or ass [sheep], and a lion has killed it in the field, that loss is for its owner. 244.

If the ox has gored a man, and it is proved that he has been used to gore, and if he [the owner] do not bind his horns, or shut up the ox, and this ox gore a freeborn man, and kill him, the owner shall pay half a mina of silver. 251.

If he [the ox] kill a man's servant, then a fine of one third of a mina in silver must be paid. 252.

eye, tooth for tooth, hand for hand, foot for foot, burning for burning, wound for wound, stripe for stripe. Exod. xxi, 24, 25.

If a man smite the eye of his servant, or the eye of his maid, and destroy it; he shall let him go free for his eye's sake. And if he smite out his manservant's tooth, or his maidservant's tooth; he shall let him go free for his tooth's sake. Exod. xxi, 26, 27.

If men strive together, and one smite another with a stone, or with his fist, and he die not, but keepeth his bed: if he rise again, and walk abroad upon his staff, then shall he that smote him be quit: only he shall pay for the loss of his time, and shall cause him to be thoroughly healed. Exod. xxi, 18, 19.

And if a man smite his servant, or his maid, with a rod, and he die under his hand; he shall surely be punished. Exod. xxi, 20.

'If men strive, and hurt a woman with child, so that her fruit depart *from her*, and yet no mischief follow: he shall be surely punished, according as the woman's husband will lay upon him; and he shall pay as the judges determine. And if any mischief follow, then thou shalt give life for life. Exod. xxi, 22, 23.

If it [any beast] be torn in pieces, let him bring it for witness; he shall not make good that which was torn. Exod. xxii, 13.

But if the ox were wont to gore in time past, and it hath been testified to his owner, and he hath not kept him in, but that he hath killed a man or a woman; the ox shall be stoned, and his owner also shall be put to death. Exod. xxi, 29.

If the ox gore a manservant or a maidservant; he shall give unto their master thirty shekels of silver, and the ox shall be stoned. Exod. xxi, 32.

Finally, we can say with Jeremias: Moses and the law are not empty words. The discovery of the Hammurabi Code has brought Moses back to the glorious company of great lawgivers. His existence is an historical necessity. We may safely say with Von Ranke, "Moses is the most sublime personality of ancient history."

FOREIGN OUTLOOK.

SOME LEADERS OF THOUGHT.

Jean Réville. He has recently assumed the rôle of an apologist of what he calls liberal Protestantism, in the presence of a miscellaneous audience in Geneva where he delivered five lectures on the origin, nature, and mission of liberal Christianity. At the outset we are compelled to praise him for the method of procedure. In opposition to the conservatives, whose standpoint he looks upon as outgrown, he undertakes to show that liberal Protestantism is the true form of Christianity for modern times; and in opposition to those who have broken with religion in general, and who look upon all faith of a religious nature as superstition, he attempts to prove that the Christian not only need not abandon reason, but that religion legitimates itself before both reason and conscience, and that a unitary understanding of the world is possible only in the light of religion. Thus his purpose is not merely to combat the old theology, but rather to sustain the essential elements of religion as he sees them. He says that negation is sterile, and that especially in the domain of religion and morality affirmation alone can produce the energy necessary to life. The genesis of liberal Protestantism is, according to Réville, nothing less than the Reformation itself considered in the light of its fundamental character and consistently and logically carried out. In other words, it is nothing but the Reformation in modern society, and it is neither conservative on the one hand, nor revolutionary on the other, but a progress and an evolution. In general Réville tries to preserve the religious and ethical values even where he feels obliged to sacrifice the substance of orthodoxy, and he is convinced that anyone who will strive to realize all that he maintains as necessary to religion will not think of the religion of liberal Protestantism as poor and inadequate. With this estimate of it we cannot quite agree. There is a "liberality" which is consistent with profound earnestness in religion, even among the masses. But that form of religious faith and practice which seems to delight in calling itself liberal generally has for its effect, except with a very few, a relaxing of all the ordinary expressions of religious zeal. Nor is Réville's contention that liberal Protestantism is the logical outcome of the fundamental principles of the Reformation correct, except in the formal sense that one of the fundamental principles of the Reformation was the right of private judgment in matters of religion. For anyone to say that the ordinarily so-called liberal Protestantism is the logical outcome of the Reformation is to be guilty of the worst kind of logical fallacy. The right of private judgment does not necessarily, nor even generally, lead men to that form of faith which is so dear to the "liberal." Besides, that other fundamental principle of the Reformation, namely, the final authority of the Holy Scriptures in matters of faith, is simply abandoned by those who love to call themselves liberals. There are, indeed, liberals who hold to the authority

9

of the Scripture; but they are not those who parade their liberality. It would be a sufficient refutation of the professed liberals to ask which of their doctrines and practices is an evolution of a doctrine or practice of the principal reformers. For the most part the doctrines of the reformers are so changed by the liberals of to-day as to be contrary to the doctrines of the Reformation. There is something essentially perverse or else essentially dishonest in the reasoning of the so-called liberal Protestant.

Julius Boehmer. He has recently given us an interesting study of the Old Testament basis of the doctrine of the kingdom of God (*Der alttestamentliche Unterbau des Reiches Gottes.* Leipzig, 1902, J. C. Hinrichs'che Buchhandlung). The question in his mind at the beginning of his investigations was whether there was in the minds of the writers of the Old Testament the idea of a kingdom of God and what they meant by the expression. It is Boehmer's purpose to take up in a later work the limits on the same theme given in the apocryphal, pseudepigraphical, and Talmudic literature, so far as this is pre-Christian or contemporary with the beginnings of Christianity. It will thus be his particular merit to have striven to supplement and enlarge the study of the kingdom of God as hitherto conducted. By so doing he will deserve nothing but thanks, even though not all might agree to his conclusions. Boehmer holds that originally Israel not only had the divine name Melech, but that that name meant to Israel what it meant to all other Semites. The gradual development of the religion of Jehovah on the one side, and the establishment of the kingly power on the other, made the name Jehovah as a kingly name impossible. The kingdom itself appeared to the devout Israelites as a blessing sent from Jehovah. But the evil consequences of the kingly rule which gradually became apparent led to a contrary opinion. The pre-exilian estimate of the Davidic kingdom, present and future, became more and more unfavorable. Meantime Jehovah became greater and greater; but, although his position had long been a royal one, after Isaiah, Jeremiah, and Hezekiah, his kingship exhibited itself only in penal judgments on his own people and heathen nations. He could be thought of as Saviour-King only after the Davidic kingdom was past and the idea of the Melech deity had relatively faded out of the consciousness of the prophets. This took place at the end of the exile and appears first in Second Isaiah, who represents King Jehovah as the procurer of salvation for the future Israel. Subsequent to that time two separate series of conceptions of Jehovah as King may be traced. The first connects directly with Jehovah, who is thought of as the bringer of salvation in the near future; the second thinks of King Jehovah as the possessor of all power and might. Boehmer regards the first as the specifically Israelitish conception and as corresponding to the lofty prophetic or revealed religion. The second is more nearly a nature religion, and although it threw off some of the objectionable features of Melechism, and was influenced somewhat by the first conception, so that the power of Jehovah was subservient to the interests of morals, still it was distinctly lower than the first. Here is the distinction between the

God of love and the God of power, and the second was all too triumphant. This is the situation as revealed in the book of Daniel, whose author, pious as he was, failed to reach the depth of the religious conceptions of the great prophets. That Boehmer has done a good service in pointing out the inequalities of the religious development of the Israelites no one can doubt. And he does well when he draws the conclusion that as the kings of Israel were subject to King Jehovah they strove to secure for their people all the blessings Jehovah himself desired them to have. Whether or not he has given too much emphasis to the extra-Israelitish development and influence may well be open to question.

RECENT THEOLOGICAL LITERATURE.

Der Trinitarische Taufbefehl Matth. 28. 19 nach seiner ursprung-lichen Textgestalt und seiner Authentie untersucht (The Trinitarian Baptismal Command in Matthew 28. 19 Investigated with Reference to its Original Text and its Authenticity). By Eduard Riggenbach. Gütersloh, C. Bertelsmann, 1903. It has been for some time a puzzling fact to New Testament scholars that out of the sixteen or seventeen times that Eusebius mentions the command of Christ to baptize all nations he uses the short formula, "in my name," twelve times and the complete formula only four or five times. The testimony for the longer formula in the early Greek Christian literature is very scanty, so that some have supposed that the shorter form was the original, and, as the Latin fathers have the longer most frequently, that the passage in Matthew was enlarged according to Latin ideas; that is to say, that Christ did not give the command as it stands in Matt. xxviii, 19, but only in the short form. Riggenbach takes up this question from two points of view. In the first place, he examines all the early patristic literature to determine, if possible, the date of the appearance of the passage in the text of Matthew. He is obliged to depend upon the fathers rather than upon a comparison of the New Testament manuscripts because these last afford almost no light on the subject. He concludes that inasmuch as Eusebius sometimes uses the longer formula he must have done so not alone because such was the usage of the Church as known to him, but also because his copy of Matthew contained it. This leaves the peculiar fact to be accounted for that for the most part Eusebius employs the shorter form. He explains this by assuming that Eusebius suppressed the Trinitarian formula purposely and in the interest of the secret discipline of the Church. But Origen was earlier than Eusebius, and it becomes important therefore to know Origen's form. Unfortunately, we are confused here by the Latin translation of Origen's works. Strangely enough, Origen's Latin translation gives the Trinitarian form somewhat frequently, while the few Greek remains of his works do not afford satisfactory evidence that Origen knew the Trinitarian formula as belonging to his Matthew. Still he thinks that, in view of all the other testimony, Origen's Matthew must have given the longer form. His investigation leads to the conclusion that Matthew,

as known to the West, certainly contains the Trinitarian formula at least as early as the time of Tertullian. This reasoning does not seem very well to support his conclusion, but the case is worse yet when he comes to the question of the authenticity of the passage, which he next takes up. He begins by calling attention to the arguments against the authenticity, especially that in the second century the short form is very frequent, and in particular that outside of Matt. xxviii, 19 the New Testament gives us no example of the longer formula. He thinks this fact inexplicable either on the ground of accident or on the supposition that it is an abbreviation of a well-known longer form. This would seem to necessitate the denial of its authenticity if it stood alone, but Riggenbach finds other considerations which save him to the Trinitarian form. Chief among these is the early date of Matthew, which he reckons to be not later than A. D. 75. But supposing the gospel to be so early, the real question is, Who wrote it, and on what authority? Here again the critical evidence seems to be against the authenticity, which Riggenbach overlooks. For if Matthew is dependent on Mark for the account of the resurrection Matthew must have been supplied with the ending by some other means. The thing that saves our faith in the Trinitarian form is the want of a motive on the part of the author of Matthew for introducing this form without adequate authority. This too Riggenbach does not seem to recognize.

Études d'histoire et de théologie positive. La Discipline de l'arcane; les origines de la pénitence; la hiérarchie primitive; l'agape (Studies in History and Positive Theology. The Secret Discipline; the Origin of Penitence; the Primitive Hierarchy; the Love Feast). By Pierre Batiffol. Paris, 1902, V. Lecoffre. The four essays of this volume, on the topics named in the sub-title, are all in the interest of the Roman Catholic Church, and yet they are measurably independent studies. The first essay undertakes to prove that the secret discipline of the Church was invented in order to effect more completely the preparation of the catechumens for Church membership. It is interesting to note that while Roman Catholic authorities generally hold that the secret discipline existed from the earliest days of the Church, in order that they may give a certain increased value to rites and doctrines not attested in the earliest literature, Batiffol foregoes this advantage in the interest of the historical testimony, and states that the secret discipline was unknown in the first two centuries. On the other hand, he denies that the secret discipline was developed out of the heathen mysteries. But it will be pretty difficult, if it is allowed that this discipline was unknown until the contact of Christianity with heathenism was so intimate and general, to withstand the evidence which leads to the conclusion that the discipline was at least powerfully influenced by the mysteries. For it is impossible to prove that the secret discipline arose in connection with the catechumenate. Then, how account for the presence of the rites, forms, and formulas of the heathen mysteries in the secret discipline of the Church if they did not come from those mysteries? In the second essay Batiffol strives to justify

the gradual relaxation of the penitential provisions on the ground that the bishops were impelled by a feeling of compassion for the weaknesses of humanity to make the penitence required easier and easier. He shows that in Rome and Constantinople the administrator of the penitential discipline came to pass from the hands of the bishops to those of the presbyters. Coming to the fourth essay, he gives an interesting survey of the oldest witnesses relative to Church government, and asserts that from the very beginning Rome had the monarchical form of episcopacy. But he thinks that the episcopacy, that is, the monarchical, was, generally, an evolution from the plural episcopacy. The early Church organization provided (1) apostles, prophets, and teachers for missionary work; (2) a single order, the presbyterate, which indicated only a more honorable rank; (3) the diaconate, for liturgical and congregational service; (4) the bishops did all that deacons did, and preached besides; and (5) that as soon as the apostles disappeared the monarchical episcopacy with the subordinated priesthood arose. This is so clearly a mixture of historical fact and dogmatic assumption that it is scarcely worth more than a mere mention. In the fourth essay he takes the somewhat astonishing position that there is no evidence of an agape, in the sense of a special meal, during the first three centuries. When the Latins speak of an agape they mean almsgiving, never a feast. In the East there arose during the third century the custom of giving feasts to the poorer members of the congregation and to widows who were supported by the Church. These were called agape and were offered by the wealthy members; but they were by no means a combination of the eucharist and love feast.

RELIGIOUS AND EDUCATIONAL.

Warneck on Missions. Warneck is probably the most highly respected authority on the subject of foreign missions now living, certainly among the Germans. In a recent address he gave expression to some thoughts relative to what we can learn in missionary methods from the spread of Christianity in the first three centuries. He declared that the principal lesson is that the greatest missionary force among heathen peoples is in every case the native congregation itself. From this he says several things follow: (1) That the foreign missionary's work is merely preparatory; (2) that the organization of those converted by preaching is the chief thing; (3) that the results are dependent upon the deepening of the converts in the faith and in the knowledge of the Gospel; (4) along with this must go practical activity; (5) the congregation must be the salt of the earth in the midst of their heathen neighbors; (6) as soon as possible native teachers must be employed; (7) the entire responsibility must not rest upon the foreign missionary; (8) the Christian deportment of the members of the congregation will have its influence in winning others; (9) the missionary energy of the congregation must be made effective, partly by works of mercy and charity, partly by brotherly love, and partly by thorough organization. Warneck says these are commonplaces, but that they are such only in theory; and that they are not put into execution.

GLIMPSES OF REVIEWS AND MAGAZINES.

A SUPERB as well as bulky quarterly is *The International* (Burlington, Vt.), with a brilliant galaxy of contributors in Art, History, Literature, Philosophy, Politics, and the Sciences. Especially noteworthy in its issue for September, 1903, are Kuno Francke's article on "Emerson and German Personality," John Graham Brooks's on "A Socialistic Contention," and N. S. Shaler's on "The Natural History of War." Francke finds in Emerson a sympathetic kinship with the great Germans of the eighteenth and nineteenth centuries, with Kant, and Schelling, and Fichte, with Goethe, and Schiller, and Novalis. In him as in them there is a freedom from mere traditional authority; a supreme interest in the inner life, regarding man as a spiritual being, master of the material world rather than mastered by it, and responsible for his actions to the august tribunal throned in his moral consciousness; and a joyous optimism, a confiding trust in the perfectibility of the race, however slow its advance toward perfection may seem to be. All these men of vision believed that a time must come when the thoughts of the wise and the dreams of high prophetic souls, will be transfused into the lifeblood of the masses and come to actual fulfillment in the ennobling of human life and the betterment of its conditions. These hopeful and confident spirits, the *élite* and exceptionally endowed of human kind, were not like the Neolithic men whose behavior Mrs. Stetson describes. When a far-visioned prophet rose among those primitive men and prophesied a fairer social future

> They all rose up in fury
>   Against their boastful friend;
> For prehistoric patience
>   Cometh quickly to an end.
> Said one: "This is chimerical!
>   Utopian! Absurd!"
> Said another: "What a stupid life!
>   Too dull, upon my word!"
> Cried all: "Before such things can come,
>   You idiotic child,
> You must alter Human Nature."
>   And they all sat back and smiled.
> It was a clinching argument
>   To the Neolithic mind.

Emerson's comprehension of the distinctive quality of the German mind is evidenced to Francke in passages like this:

The German intellect lacks the French sprightliness, the fine practical understanding of the English, and the American adventure; but it has a certain probity, which never rests in a superficial performance but asks steadily, *To what end?* A German public demands a controlling sincerity. Here is activity of thought, it says, but what does the man mean? If he has a meaning, though he cannot rightly express himself to-day, the same things subsist and will open themselves to-morrow. If the burden of a message is on his mind, a burden

of truth to be declared, then his business and calling in the world is to make the fact, the truth, the message known. What signifies that he trips and stammers, or that his voice is harsh and hissing, or that his methods are inadequate? That message will yet find method and imagery, articulation and melody.

Francke thinks there never was an American who was in various respects so closely akin to the German temper as Emerson, of whom he says:

He was, indeed, the Jean Paul of New England. New England country life, the farm, the murmuring pines, the gentle river, the cattle lowing upon the hills, the quiet study, the neighborly talk in the village store or on the common —this was the world in which he felt at home, in which he discovered his own personality. Here he fortified himself against the foolish fashions and silly prejudices of so-called society; here he imbibed his lifelong hatred of vulgar ambition; here there came to him that insight into the value of the unpretentions which he has expressed so well, "I ask not for the great, the remote, the romantic; I embrace the common; I explore and sit at the feet of the familiar, the low;" here he acquired that deep-seated and thoroughly German conviction of the dignity of scholastic seclusion and simplicity which has made his whole life a practical application of his own precept: "The student must embrace solitude as a bride. He must have his glees and his glooms alone. His own estimate must be measure enough, his own praise reward enough for him. . . . How mean to go blazing, a gaudy butterfly, in fashionable or political salons, the fool of society, the fool of notoriety, a topic for newspapers, a piece of the street, and forfeiting the real prerogative of the russet coat, the privacy, and the true and warm heart of the citizen!"

Emerson's description of the ideal American, Francke would apply to Emerson himself: "A reformer not content to slip along through the world like a footman or a spy, escaping by his nimbleness and apologies as many knocks as he can, but a brave and upright man, who must find or cut a straight road to everything excellent in the earth, and not only go honorably himself, but make it easier for all who follow him to go in honor and with benefit." Herman Grimm finds in Emerson a spiritual power, an antidote to the pessimism of Schopenhauer, the cynicism of Nietzsche, the fact-worship of the present day, and the soulless monotony of scientific speculation. In one of his earliest essays Grimm says:

Emerson is a perfect swimmer in the element of modern life. He does not fear the tempests of the future; because he divines the calm which will follow them. He does not hate, contradict, combat; because his understanding of men and their defects is too great, his love for them too strong. I cannot but follow his steps with deep reverence and look at him with wonder, as he divides the chaos of modern life gently and without passion into its several provinces. A long acquaintance has assured me of him; and thinking of this man I feel that in times of old there really could be teachers with whom their disciples were ready to share any fate, because everything appeared to them doubtful and lifeless without the spirit of the man whom they were following.

——John G. Brooks's discussion, "A Socialistic Contention," is over some practical bearings of the question, Environment versus Personal Quality. Its trend may be inferred from the beginning of his essay:

A child's inquiry which is quoted at Hull House raises one of the most troublesome of all difficulties in the theory and practice of the social question. "Who can be good without any back yard?" There is a dignified and very stubborn theory that the back yard has little to do with goodness. Some inherent personal quality, according to this view, determines our destiny.

Whether this quality mature in a rookery or in a palace, it will, after its nature, come to its own. The back yard will neither help nor hinder. I heard long since a lecture by the artist Whistler, called "Ten O'clock." The thesis was that genius in art is independent of all back yards. If the divine sensitiveness to beauty once take possession, it will find avenues to express itself. The dullest age cannot quench it. The meanest upbringing cannot long hold it in check. The artist will thrive in poverty as in luxury. A dreary and commonplace generation cannot defeat him. Whether the childhood is happy or miserable will count for little. Once the talent is here in any age or place, it will mold the unhappiest events and make them tributary to its own destiny. Circumstance is nothing if the careless deities once grant the gift. In Taine's *Philosophy of Art* the reader may find the exact opposite of Mr. Whistler's views put with the learning of an historian as well as with an artist's skill. With Taine, the difference is infinite, whether the man be born here or there, in an age of machine production or in the *cinque cento*. The gloom over the figures of Rembrandt is but the reflection of the somber sky under which the great master painted. The flame on Titian's canvas mirrors the light in which he lived. The splendor of raiment in Van Dyck's pictures would have been impossible but for the condition of Eastern commerce in his time. Give Taine a certain setting of external media, climate, industry, custom, and he returns the result in character, as if character were a product of that into which it happened to be born. The socialist's contention is, Change a man's surroundings and you change his character. His opponents say, Change a man's character and he will change the surroundings. A broad and inclusive wisdom might say, Do all you can to help him change both.

The June (1903) issue of the *International Quarterly* was even richer than the September. In his article, "A Theory of the Comic," W. N. Guthrie exploits genuine laughter as the expressed essence of good cheer and the antidote to melancholy, to spleenful disgust with life, and to a lachrymose or sullen despair of good; as the voice of inveterate and stalwart optimism which is born of a vital, vigorous conviction of the rightness of things or their capacity for righting themselves or for being righted—born of the faith that the universal order will somehow get on quite well even without ourself to superintend it, and that God, after all, is really managing affairs in His heaven and even on His earth. He admits that there is a kind of laughter which is not of faith, a cynical, bitter, devilish laughter, ridiculing faith or gloating over the defeats of goodness, a hideous, sceptical, ironical laugh born of odious unfaith in virtue, nobleness, and sincerity, an insult to truth and goodness and beauty, to man and to God. He thinks faith and goodness need to be defended against the "advocates of an unjoyful, soporiferous gravity and gloom who stalk abroad lugubriously devout in broadcloth or in sackcloth to the shame of the earth and the despair of heaven." He notes the tendency of youth to interrupt its natural excess of happiness with spells of sad solemnity in which it cherishes the doleful domino and hugs the shadowed side of every street; while on the contrary the mature man who has suffered much and survived more, seeing that few hurts are mortal and fewer still immortal, walks out freely into the sunlit open of brave activity, and, knowing both the worst of life and the best, addresses himself courageously to making more of the best and taking a creator's joy in its production. In our teens we affect and cherish grewsome elegies, and in our ripe fifties we renew the exuberant pyrotechnics of the boy.

Good cheer may increase as romance diminishes. Heine was no worse off for awakening to the fact that future ages would scarce be edified to learn that he loved Agnes—some Agnes or other once upon a time—though he should write the story of it across the firmamental blue with a Norway spruce for pen and the fire of Ætna for indelible red ink. We are told of the brave philosophy of one who under the storm and stress of a long experience of misery acquired, as a part of the manly art of self-defense, the habit of instantaneous laughter at every turn of events, laughing at once before he has time to fall a-weeping, and coming out better in the end than if he had allowed his lachrymal ducts to be overworked. The essay tells of Scarron, who, though a tortured bundle of suffering nerves, did not flinch or wail, but expired with a merry jest which filled his friends with soft laughter; and of William Blake, who fell asleep singing in songs of his own improvising the glory of his God, triumphing over the flesh, the world, and the devil. In vindication of our inherent right to laugh the essayist answers some objections made against it. To the assertion that laughter is *irreligious* he replies: "On the contrary, it is religious, since it involves faith. Not necessarily a theological but a religious faith is at the core of it, and faith equal to believing that if I should perish or fail the world will go on nevertheless, and that perhaps my failure may even advantage the world, hard as that is to imagine." To the charge that laughter is *unphilosophical* he answers rather unphilosophically: "Most assuredly. The artist in comedy has reason to hate the philosopher. If Aristophanes pillories Socrates, it is not the fault of Aristophanes but of Socrates. Socrates is after all a sophist. He seeks to further the contemplative life. He would have us stop to think. But he who habitually stops to think will never even start to do anything in this world. You do not want to stop for discussion, you want to go on and do, and discuss when you have done it, provided you are lucky and survive the deed." To the claim that laughter is *immoral* he says: "It is not only *not* immoral, but it is the preservation of morals to cultivate by use a faculty for laughter. It is the hallucination that evil is mighty and will prevail which drives men to despair. Now evil always seems to be prevalent whenever and wherever you scrutinize it, for scrutiny involves confined attention to what lies immediately under the lens in the focused light. Evil existing wherever we see it, we surmise, or even affirm, it to be everywhere. But were it everywhere and dominant, you and I could hardly be here to express such an opinion. Clearly the thing to do is to belittle the evil, to undignify it and so rob it of its horrors that we shall not lose heart in its presence. By laughing at it we get rid of the false impression of its omnipotence; we get a little courage and our despair turns a somersault up into glory from the swinging trapeze of faith." To the objection that laughter is *superficial* the reply, in part, is: "Of course it is superficial. In one sense, however, and not in another. But what objection is there to the surface? Why should people prefer to be driven as a plummet to the bottom of the sea, rather than float as a boat on the surface? The child comes into the world with the art of wailing perfect; the higher art of laughing has to be acquired—it belongs to a later stage

of progress and is a sign of advancement. Some bliss is born of ignorance, but wisdom at its culmination wears a smile. What if the smile
be superficial? There are depths of experience under it." To the charge
that laughter is *unsympathetic*, this is, in part, the answer: "Yes, sometimes it is unsympathetic. But ought one to be always and everywhere
sympathetic? Sympathy sometimes has the effect to increase the sufferer's
estimate of his sufferings, and to make him more helplessly the victim
thereof. Some people say complainingly, 'Laugh and the world laughs with
you; weep and you weep alone.' Why not thank God that when you weep
everybody does not weep, that there is some limit to the sadness and
some brightness in the world outside of your gloom? Sympathy has great
value in life and should be cultivated, but often it has a weakening effect.
It does not help to brace with courage nor incite to effort. An injection
of plain, simple, practical common sense is often better medicine, and
the subtly sweet contagion of a healthy laugh has sometimes brought
salvation to the despondent." The mellow and hopeful faith out of which
genuine laughter is born, and by which it is vindicated, is illustrated in
Professor Herman Grimm as pictured in *The International Quarterly* by
Elizabeth von Heyking, who says:

In his last letter he wrote to me from Berlin, "Everything here is going on
well, which does not exclude that you may find people who will tell you that
everything is going wrong—but there have always been those who would say
that." This shows him as he had grown to be in old age. Harmony and
placidity, his lifelong ideals, surrounded him like a halo. He was, indeed, like
a calm surface of water reflecting heaven above. Goethesque he appeared in
his attitude of Olympian repose. Ever rising higher in his faith, trifles faded
before his gaze and he believed that even the worst and deepest misery must
finally lead to good, that everything is capable of being glorified. He considered
the world as a whole, ignoring its ugly details, turning away from bitterness,
discontent, and evil, not out of want of pity and sympathy, but because these
things seemed to him as a transient phase, sure to change and to be transfigured in that far, far distance where the explanation of the world's riddle
lies. Thither he confidingly toiled on.

THE most valuable articles in *The Bibliotheca Sacra* (Oberlin) for
October, 1903, were by associate editors: "The Samaritan Pentateuch," by
Dr. W. E. Barton; "Metaphysical Needs of Our Time," by Dr. James
Lindsay; "Theodicy," by Dr. Jacob Cooper; and "Park's Theological System," by Dr. F. H. Foster. Dr. Foster thinks that Professor E. A. Park,
of Andover Theological Seminary, surpassed at many points his great
master, Jonathan Edwards. It was in Park, he says, that the Edwardsean
school culminated by attaining perfect symmetry and interior self-consistency; and the Andover professor is glorified as a wiser and abler theologian than his lifelong opponent, the great Presbyterian, Dr. Charles
Hodge, of Princeton, who, says this article, "had no conception of what
proof really is," while Park built up a theological *system* by reasoning
from the known to the unknown and justifying his progress at every step
with logical proof. Park was a stout opponent of Calvinism in its older
form, as taught by Hodge and Shedd. He was far more hospitable to

new ideas than either of those men, saying, "Take the ideas in, and scrutinize them until you know them; and then you can estimate their worth or worthlessness." As to the theory of evolution, which Hodge called "atheism," Park did not adopt it, but felt that, whether true or false, it could not disturb the foundations of theology. We are told that he did not stand in great awe of the Church "Fathers," and the frequent appeals of Anglicans and Catholics to the early Christian "Fathers" as decisive and binding authorities moved him to indignation and scorn. His strong democratic American common sense rebelled against such adulation of mere men, many of them men of so little training and such feeble intellectual grasp that Park once exclaimed, "Fathers indeed! They would better be called the Church *babies*." Park defined God as "the Mind which all other minds are obligated to worship, because they are ultimately dependent upon it." He constructed with great care the arguments of Natural Theology for a Divine creator, preserver, contriver, natural governor, and moral governor. He said:

"Some men believe that all truths in Natural Theology are derived from the Bible; others believe that the Bible is drawn from Natural Theology." His own position is that the Bible is "a part of Natural Theology." Just as we infer a God from the solar system considered as a fact, so we infer God from the perfectness of the biblical description of Christ. The Bible, as a record of assertions, rests upon Natural Theology, and it proves the existence of God not by the assertion that there is a God, *as an assertion*, but by the fact that it *makes* such an assertion, by this *act;* just as Webster proved he was alive not by the *assertion* "I still live," but by the *act* of speaking. The Bible as it is, with all its contents of Natural Theology, demands a cause, and that cause must be God. How happens it that we may find in the writings of Peter a system of Natural Theology more in accordance with later times than in Aristotle or all the ancients? Philosophers grasped only by piecemeal that which fishermen have given in fullness and perfection. All the results of modern investigation can detect no fallacy in the statements of these fishermen who purport to have been divinely inspired. The accord of the Bible with Natural Theology is also seen in the fact that the Bible is explained, in passages otherwise dark, by Natural Theology; and this, as a fact, demands an explanation, which it finds only in the existence of God.

As to miracles, which Hume defined as "a violation of the laws of nature," Park replies that "when we admit the being of a God a miracle is no violation of the laws of nature, for *it is a law of nature that matter obey its Creator*." Inspiration he holds to be a Divine superintendency so exercised over the writers of Holy Scripture as to produce a Bible *perfect for the purpose for which it is intended, communicating religious truth without any error in religious doctrine, and furnishing a perfect guide to a holy life and to heaven.* As to the scientific value of Genesis, Park would not permit anybody to deny it, though he did not affirm it. He contented himself with drawing out its religious teaching, which he embraced under seven heads: "God *made* the universe, by *creation*, in progressive order, for *man;* man himself in the *image* of God, and for God's *worship;* and he added the institution of the *Sabbath. Keep that religious teaching intact,* and you have what Genesis has to give us that is of the greatest importance."

——In the article by H. M. Whitney on "The Study of English Literature as an Instrument of Christian Culture," we cannot agree with the writer that it is wise to turn young people loose without guidance or restraint in the world of literature any more than in the world of life. The following opinion seems to us unwise:

It used to be deemed the dictate of proper parental oversight to hide away the works of Byron, lest the children, not knowing the difference between good and evil, should suffer moral and spiritual damage. He, however, who has not only read but studied Milton's doctrine of this matter in his "Areopagitica" will take the risk of children's being more injured by the reading of Byron than by the consequences of their knowing that the attempt had been made to put Byron out of their reach. The mockery of "Don Juan" is repulsive to a fresh young soul, and those who would read "Don Juan" are sure to get hold of it or of something like it; so that, as the "Areopagitica" says, the effort to keep such books out of children's hands is too much like the nobleman's effort to keep the crows out of his park by shutting the gates. Byron's attitudinizing affectation of pessimism and cynicism and misanthropy, his labored scoffing at a religion that he did not understand, the eating out of his moral purpose by egotism and self-will and voluptuousness, now simply make our young people feel that Byron threw away the opportunities of influence that were opened to him by his rank and by his extraordinary gifts; so the evil of the man serves for warning, while the better self of Byron, that better self which breaks out here and there in his poetry and which, too late for a fuller redemption, enabled him to close his life in an heroic endeavor for struggling Greece—this better self will have at least some distinctive value in the making of a broad, many-sided Christlike man. And, as for those that are bent upon evil, they will find their evil somewhere; and, wherever they find it, they will make it the savor of death unto death.

We do agree, however, that what we want of books is that they shall help us to live rightly:

We want ideals; we want examples, real or imagined, to warn or encourage; we want motives; we want the reason why; we want great thoughts; we want the interpretation of our own hearts to ourselves; we want faith to believe in our fellow-man, in ourselves, in our God. If a book does not do this sort of work, it is not literature; it is only something printed. We can get such help from the voice of a friend; we can get it from the lecture or the sermon; we can get it from the school; we can get it even from some humble clipping from an obscure country newspaper; we get it from the Bible; we get it, without the charm of the voice, but with convenience and permanence and the possibility of review, in a book. It gets home to the heart, it begins to work out into the life, and we straightway begin to be a different kind of men.

Intellectually powerful as Professor Jowett was, he said, "Mere intellect, however keen, is barren apart from the full and just development of feeling, imagination, and, above all, volition." Another has well said, "What this age preeminently needs is not so much light upon the intellect as dew upon the heart." Without the dew which softens and purifies and fructifies the heart, the soul, the character, our education will be like an Arabian desert where the barren sands glitter and sparkle under the blazing sunlight, but no tender greenness adds the beauty and cheer of Life.——A notice of *Old Testament Critics*, a volume by Dr. Thomas Whitelaw, well known for his exegetical work in connection with *The Pulpit Commentary* and *The Preacher's Commentary*, says that Dr. Whitelaw's competence to speak with authority is equal to that of any of the critics, since

he has devoted himself to critical Old Testament study for over a quarter of a century; that his aim in this volume is not so much to establish traditional views as to show that the critics are wrong; that his book shows the flimsiness of the critical superstructure; and that his hale and hearty skepticism toward the disintegrating results of criticism should recall the critics to sanity of mind and sobriety of judgment. Dr. Whitelaw's criticism of the critics represents that conservative wing in the United Free Church of Scotland which is dissatisfied with the teachings of George Adam Smith and others like him.

In the *Hibbert Journal* (London) for October, 1903, the eye is caught by a fine statement from Arnold Pinchard, of Birmingham, as to what the Church teaches concerning human attainment and destiny. It occurs in a criticism and correction of a misrepresentation of that teaching found in a previous article by Mr. Lowes Dickinson on "Optimism and Immortality." Mr. Pinchard's statement is as follows: "The Church upholds before the eyes and hearts of men the highest and most inspiring Ideal of Goodness, wrought out in obedience to the requirements of the Eternal and Immutable Law of Righteousness; diminishes naught from its demands, and proclaims without flinching the penalties of willful moral failure; makes glorious the horizon toward which men may journey with the splendor of an assured hope; sets before men a definite goal of possible ultimate perfection in the achievement of a great destiny; and promises and secures to all alike in their temporal progress such stimulus and help by the cooperation of Almighty God as each may need. At the same time the Church is too true to the facts of life to ignore the possibility of individual failure; too sane not to realize that the loss in such a case must be great and terrible in proportion to the grandeur and glory of the possible success. Yet she will use these dire possibilities of eternal loss to brace and stimulate her children to more strenuous effort rather than to reprobate their seeming failures or to crush their hopes. That no man is altogether and absolutely good or bad; that no man can entirely attain perfection in this life; that final judgment cannot be passed upon any man in the dim twilight of the ignorances of today; that beyond this life there are 'many mansions'—mansions of purification and perfecting—mansions of joy and peace—mansions of progressive Revelation and enlightenment—culminating in the contemplation of the Beatific Vision of the Absolute Good in God Himself, whereunto all men, whatever their inherent weaknesses or hindrances of circumstance, may ultimately attain—these truths she holds for sure, and in her grasp upon them maintains the unfaltering optimism of her steadfast outlook upon life! Yet the Church recognizes as a possibility that there may be found, in that strange and complex mystery which is man, a power of obstinate resistance to Good and of invincible aversion to truth, which may ultimately render the individual inaccessible to every moral influence which, without prejudice or violence to the integrity of his freedom as a morally responsible agent, can be brought to bear upon him; and she sadly acknowledges both the

justice and necessity of the exaction of the penalties and sanctions of that Law which alike gives and demands nothing less than perfection, wherever it has been persistently rejected in the beneficence of its promise, and as obstinately defied in the prerogative of its power. She may hope, she must pray and strive, that there may be but few such losses; she is too sane and too honest, too brave and too true, to deny or ignore the possibility that there may be some. And why should we resent and cavil at this final self-assertion of the Law of Life and Goodness any more than at the operation of the same law in the material universe? We believe that all things move onward toward an Ideal Perfection. But is this Ideal never to be realized? Or can it ever be realized until all that hinders is taken away, and all that mars or tends to mar a single feature of its perfect beauty is eliminated? We believe in this steady upward progress, and we understand somewhat of the Law under which all things thus move together toward a perfect end, which shall be indeed not an end, but the initiation of a new era of unhindered development." Concerning the Universalist notion that all souls must ultimately reach heaven, Mr. Pinchard says: "It is a doctrine calculated to lull conscience to sleep, paralyze all effort, and put a premium on a life spent in playing the concertina beneath umbrageous trees in a languid acquiescence in the assumed ultimate benevolence of all things." Three clergymen who had left Universalist for orthodox pulpits said that what especially drove them from Universalism was the effect of its teachings on the lives and characters of its adherents. It is a powerless and futile faith. Instead of Universalistic teachings, Pinchard presents the following more rational and more moral postulates, as representing the orthodox view:

(1) That the world is not eternally or entirely good, but embodies a real (not merely an apparent) process in time toward an eternally good end. (2) That this end is one in which all individuals may participate if they will; and (3) That individual souls must be at least potentially immortal, and may all of them, if they will, ultimately reach heaven. Here we have three postulates upon which we may base our optimistic outlook upon life. For they are built upon a due consideration of all the facts; they take account of the principle of indefectible morality in the progress of mankind toward a perfect and eternal end; they allow for the claims of Justice, and acknowledge implicitly the Majesty of Eternal and Immutable Law; they provide for the ultimate satisfaction of man's highest aspirations—for the insatiate hunger for eternity —for the passionate though inarticulate demand of humanity for the touch of some perfect thing; they point to a destiny more august than can conceivably be compassed within the short span and narrow limitations of this life; they look to where beyond this darkness there is clearer light, surer knowledge, and an incomparably wider range of opportunity; they take account of man's moral responsibility, and make their appeal to his sense of the greatness of his destiny, to his own personal dignity, honor, and courage; they refuse to ignore or allow him to ignore the possibilities of failure which belong to and are involved in the splendid adventure to which he stands committed; they include within the scope of their optimism every man whose life is honest and characterized by steady loyalty to the truth that he sees and is convinced of in his heart; and if they contemplate the awful alternative of failure, yet they exclude none save the ultimately self-excluded; and they only contemplate it because one dares not so tamper with the elementary principles of morality as to obscure the infinite distinction between Good and Evil, or to ignore the deep and immutable relation in which are bound up with these both Life and Death.

——-In the same issue of the *Hibbard Journal* is an excellent review by F. P. Boys-Smith of *The Life and Letters of Brooke Foss Westcott, Bishop of Durham.* Of Westcott in his Cambridge professorship, this is written: "A mere attendance at the lectures which he gave to candidates for Holy Orders was enough to make one feel the sunny purity of the ethereal soul. What an expressive face his was! Met in the street when hurrying along, the mind withdrawn within, it would look gray, and set, and dried, the broad brow hidden partly by the cap, and the small stature and nervous manner attracting little notice. But during the lecture, in which a verse and a half of St. John's writings would be discussed, unfolded, and illustrated by many another passage, till it became plainly impossible within the hour to reach further than these few words, or to touch upon five sixths of the section which had been intended, there would break from time to time a light over the face and in the deep expressive eyes, which one knew was a reflection of the light of Heaven that was shining upon the lecturer's own soul." Sir W. B. Richmond, the artist to whom Westcott sat for his portrait, says:

It was delightful to watch the ever-moving face, like the seasons, for its variety—how those clear gray eyes flashed, and the brows became almost knotted with the intensity of a thought growing behind them; and then, when the thought was brought to birth, the wrinkles were smoothed out, and, like the cloudless sky of a summer day, his splendid domed forehead exposed a serenity and calm almost godlike. There was no part of his face which did not illustrate emotion: worn with thought, puckered with conflicting struggles, the whole countenance told the history of a temperament wearing itself away with conflict. The spiritual expression was prevented from being sentimental by the virility in the man's nature. One could see under that sweet face the possible presence of a great storm, and under that restrained nature a fire and a passion burning the very life. And it was this sort of perfection of human attributes which gave the charm as well as the force to his character. One felt in the presence of a man that knew the fire, but whose spiritual nature knew how to use it for good.

Westcott's greatest monument of course is the revision of the Greek Text of the New Testament, at which, in company with his friend, Professor Hort, he toiled for twenty-eight years. Preaching at Cambridge, near the end of life he used these impressive words:

"In this chapel, and in these courts, fifty-six years ago, I saw visions, as it is promised that young men shall see them in the last days—visions which in their outward circumstances have been immeasurably more than fulfilled. I have had an unusually long working time, and I think unequaled opportunities of service. When I have failed, as I have failed often and grievously, it has not been because I once saw an ideal, but because I have not looked to it constantly, steadily, faithfully; because I have distrusted myself and distrusted others; because again and again I have lost the help of sympathy, since I was unwilling to claim from those 'who called me friend' the sacrifice which I was myself ready to make. So now an old man I dream dreams of great hope, when I plead with those who will carry forward what my own generation has left unattempted or unaccomplished, to welcome the ideal which breaks in light upon them, the only possible ideal for man, even the fullest realization of self in the completest service of one's fellow-men, in obedience to the Master's command; and to pursue that ideal with quenchless ardor, undiscouraged even if it seems to 'fade forever and forever as we move.'"

BOOK NOTICES.

RELIGION, THEOLOGY, AND BIBLICAL LITERATURE.

Things Fundamental. By CHARLES E. JEFFERSON, D.D. 12mo, pp. 380. New York: Thomas Y. Crowell & Co. Price, cloth, $1.50.

These thirteen discourses in modern apologetics from one of the most influential pulpits of Greater Methodism contain a great deal of good old-fashioned Methodist doctrine, unflinchingly set with sharp edges in the face of current confusion, laxity, and skepticism. Their reasoning is large and strong, firm and faithful, clear and convincing. Their arguments close in on the reason and the conscience irresistibly. Fundamental things are so set forth as to seem inevitable; one might say they are set in battle array to compel surrender. "The Nature and Place of Faith in the Christian Life," "The Nature and Place of Reason in the Christian Life," "The Deity of Jesus," "The Miracles," "Sin and Its Forgiveness," "Sin and Its Punishment," "The Church of the Living God," "The Immortality of the Soul," "The Person and Work of the Holy Spirit," are some of the fundamental things which Dr. Jefferson sets with ancient and mighty force in an array which is strategic in its adaptation to the attitude of the modern mind. That these discourses are both timely and telling cannot be denied. The man who framed them knows his doctrine and knows his time and fits one to the other with tongue-and-groove closeness. It is no exaggeration to call this volume an arsenal of weapons suited to the fields and conflicts of to-day. Dip haphazard into the book and find this: "Our reason is not the whole of us. We have an emotional nature, a nature which has its tastes and affections, its aspirations and hungerings. This part of us is as important as the so-called intellectual. It was at this point that John Fiske parted company with Thomas Huxley. Both were great men, but Fiske had the richer nature. There was more of Fiske than there was of Huxley. The Life of Huxley by his son shows that his mental limitations were serious. His prejudices were numerous and solid. His mind moved within narrow limits. Huxley asserted that there is but one kind of knowledge; which is not so. And he maintained that there is only one kind of evidence; and this also is erroneous. Fiske would not follow him in this. Fiske was inclined to ask him in the words of Tennyson:

> Who forged that other influence,
> That heat of inward evidence,
> That makes one doubt against the sense?"

In arguing for the Deity of Christ from His place and power in history, this is part of what Dr. Jefferson says: "Christianity is not wholly dependent on a book. It is true that Jesus cuts a large figure in the New Testament; but if that were the only place on earth where His figure was

colossal, we should make short work of Him—we should relegate Him to a place among the heroes of fiction. But He cuts a still larger figure in human history. He walks down the centuries with the tread of a conqueror. Nineteen hundred years have passed since He died upon the Cross, and in all these centuries He has been lifting empires off their hinges, and turning the streams of history into new channels. Emerson is right when he says that His name is plowed into the world. Renan is right when he says that His life has been made a corner stone in the building of our race. Lecky is right when he says that the simple record of three short years of Christ's active life has done more to soften and regenerate mankind than all the disquisitions of philosophers and all the exhortations of moralists. Christ in history! There is a fact— face it! Jesus walked along the shores of a little lake known as the Sea of Galilee. And there He called Peter and Andrew and James and John and others to be His followers, and they left all and followed Him. While they followed Him they revered Him, and later on adored and worshiped Him. At last He left them on their faces, each man saying, 'My Lord and my God!' All that is in the New Testament. But put the New Testament away for a while. Time passes; history widens; an unseen Presence walks up and down the shores of a larger sea, called the Mediterranean,—and this unseen Presence calls men to follow Him. Tertullian, Augustine, Anselm, Aquinas, Francis of Assisi, Thomas à Kempis, Savonarola, John Huss, Martin Luther, Philip Melancthon, Ulric Zwingle, John Calvin—another Twelve—and these all followed Him and cast themselves at His feet, saying, in the words of the earlier Twelve, 'My Lord and my God!' Time passes; history advances; humanity lives its life around the circle of a still larger sea—the Atlantic Ocean. An unseen Presence walks up and down the shores calling men to follow Him. He calls John Knox, John Wesley, George Whitefield, Jonathan Edwards, Charles Spurgeon, Henry P. Liddon, Horace Bushnell, Matthew Simpson, Henry Ward Beecher, Richard S. Storrs, Phillips Brooks, and Dwight L. Moody—another Twelve—and these leave all and follow Him. And we find these all on their faces before Him, each one saying, 'My Lord and my God!' Time passes; history is widening; humanity is building its civilization around a still wider sea—the Pacific Ocean. An unseen Presence moves up and down its shores calling men to follow Him, and, at cost of life itself, they are doing it. Other Twelves are forming. And what took place in Palestine nineteen centuries ago is taking place again in our own day, under our own eyes. China becomes like the Holy Land. Only the other day Herod stretched forth his hand and vexed certain of the Church, and he killed James, the brother of John, with the sword. Did you not see it reported in all the papers? Only a year or two ago Stephen, a Christian preacher, was mobbed. Before his persecutors he fell down helpless, and in his dying moments he prayed, 'Lord, lay not this sin to their charge.' It was in all the papers; did you not read it? Very recently Saul of Tarsus, having worked in Asia, in the Chinese Empire, was shoved to the wall by brutal force, and the last thing he said was: 'I have fought a good fight. I have finished my course. I have

10

kept the faith?' Did you not hear it? All these events are notorious. And now what are you going to do with this stream of Christian history flowing down through the centuries, and never so broad and swift and strong as now? How are you going to explain it? It is the great Divine mystery of the ages. The New Testament alone holds the key to unlock this mystery. It alone can explain these nineteen Christian centuries. Christ in history is the explanation." In some strong pages Dr. Jefferson shows how, through nineteen hundred years, that conception of Jesus which stops short of His Deity has been defeated in every fight, has shown its inability to propagate and survive, and has given proof of its practical inferiority to that higher conception which seems to hold within itself the Power of an Endless Life. Coming to the question of Miracles, we read this: "If some one says that the miracles are impossible, the proper reply is that the word 'impossible' is rather a hazardous word to use. This everybody in our generation ought to know. It was once safe, or excusable, to use the word, but modern scientific progress has taken it from our lips. We are not allowed in this age of marvels to be dogmatic as to what is impossible. The meekest men on earth to-day are the great scientists. In a former age scientists dared to say what could happen and what could not. The great Laplace once declared that it is impossible that stones should fall out of the heavens on the earth. Only about sixty years ago Auguste Comte declared it to be impossible for any man by any means to determine the chemical composition of any of the heavenly bodies. The illustrious Stephenson declared it to be impossible for the Mediterranean to be connected by a canal with the Red Sea. A short time ago it was counted impossible to see through an oak plank four inches thick. To-day, the more a man knows the more modest he is about saying what is impossible. And he must have more presumption than wisdom who asserts that the New Testament miracles could not have happened. No man can say that any one of those miracles is a violation of natural law. Many laws of nature have been discovered only recently. More discoveries are to come. Only yesterday Marconi got hold of a law by availing himself of which he turned the 'impossible' into the actual. And if scientists can now touch forces hitherto unknown or unmanageable, by which they work their modern miracles, is it incredible that the Son of God could touch forces unknown to men by which He worked the wonders recorded in the New Testament? The wonders of modern science would be as incredible to the most learned man of A. D. 33, as the miracles of our Lord can possibly seem to the most skeptical denier of A. D. 1903. But some one may ask, How could the course of Nature be changed? Is it likely that once in Palestine the course of Nature was really changed at anybody's bidding? In reply to such a question we say, Why not? I know that I am able to change the course of Nature. In the course of Nature this book lies here on this desk. But I can pick it up and hold it above my head. In doing this I am not violating the Law of Gravitation, nor am I suspending it, for to my certain knowledge the force of gravitation is still at work as powerfully as ever. I am not interfering with the law of gravity in any manner, but am simply working the force of

my will into the force of gravitation in such a way as to get an outcome that would never have been obtained except for the exercise of my will. Now if an ordinary man can work his will into this complex of forces which we call Nature in such a way as to get out of Nature products or results which Nature, left to herself, would never produce, why should not the Son of God be able to work His will into the winds and waves, into blind eyes and shriveled nerves to such an extent as to produce the results recorded as miracles in the New Testament? Here is a piece of land that has never produced a potato since the world was made. The course of Nature has had free course for uncounted ages without ever bringing forth a potato. But I scratch the soil a little and toss into it a few pieces of potato (just enough to give the soil an idea of what a potato is like); and Nature immediately takes the hint and brings forth something never seen on that soil before—a whole big basketful of potatoes. I have changed the course of Nature. God has made it possible for man thus to change Nature's course. To a potato-bug sitting on the fence, I am a worker of miracles. Now, if a man can change the course of Nature and compel Nature to do what she would never have done if left to herself, why should it be deemed a thing incredible for the Son of God to so change the course of Nature as to bring forth such results as the miracles recorded by the four Evangelists? Do we not see that it is wise for us to give up the use of that word 'impossible,' and to say rather that with God all things are possible?" We have no room to show any more of the weapons in Dr. Jefferson's arsenal. Those we have shown are not even his best.

The Table-Talk of Jesus. By Rev. GEORGE JACKSON, B.A. Crown 8vo, pp. 278. Cincinnati: Jennings & Pye. New York: Eaton & Mains. Price, cloth, $1.25.

George Jackson is known by his highly successful ministerial work in Edinburgh, by his addresses last summer at Wesleyan University and elsewhere, and by his volume of addresses to young men entitled, *First Things First*, six thousand copies of which have been sold in two years. The eighteen addresses or sermons now before us are from Mr. Jackson's ordinary ministry. Like those in his previous book, they are forceful and effective, manly in tone and ringing with sincerity. The title of this volume gives no idea of the variety and range of the addresses, it being only the title of one discourse on the text: "He went into the house of one of the rulers of the Pharisees on a Sabbath to eat bread." Nowise remote or irrelevant are these addresses. They have a home-thrusting, business-like directness and practical earnestness. The first one, for example, talks incisively of Sunday golf, and public smoking, and common politeness, while also sounding the evangelic call to come to God *now*. Hear it: "Learning calls, and you say, 'I come;' business calls, and you say, 'I come;' pleasure calls, and you say, 'I come;" and God calls. Have you no answer for Him? Do you know what you are missing? The kingdom of Heaven is a great feast where God Himself is the host. You thought religion meant giving up the sweets of life for dry and tasteless fare, but Christ says it is a feast. And that no man may doubt his welcome, the

King sends this day His servant to you to say to all, 'Come in, for all things are now ready.' But says one, 'I had a seat at the King's table once and tasted His good pleasure, but—fool that I was—I left it; I shut the door upon myself. Will He open to me a second time?' He will, He will; the door is open now; come in, come in! Says another, 'I have had a glimpse sometimes of the light and comfort within, and I have longed— but, ah! I have no right there; look at my garments, mud-splashed and torn—there is no room in there for such as I am.' Man from the highways and hedges, the King bids thee enter; come in, come in! But yet another says, 'And I, too, long to enter, and for years have waited, but, alas! my eyes are dark with doubt, and fear has fast hold upon me.' Sometimes I seem to see, and then the darkness falls again until I wonder if the feast, the proclamation, and the welcome be not all a lie, or if there be any King at all.' Thou art one of His poor blinded ones, and He has given His messengers charge concerning thee that they should be eyes to thee lest at any time thou miss thy way, and that they should bring thee into His presence. Tarry not, but haste and come; the King keeps for thee the seat next Himself." In the address, "What think ye of God?" is this: "How do we name Him? Do we say from the heart, 'Our Father'? A railroad man used to send a message to his wife, saying when he would be home, and often he would put in a word for his little boy, 'Tell Arthur I shall sleep with him to-night.' But a day came when Arthur lay fevered and hot in his mother's arms, sick unto death. 'Don't ky, mother,' he said, 'I shall seep wiv Dod, 'oo know. Send a teledraf to Heaven, and tell Dod I sall seep wiv Him to-night.' I would rather hear my child talk like that about God than know that he had all our catechisms off by heart. What is God to us? Have we learned to call Him Father?" The sermon on "The Missionary Motive" ends thus: "When Paul thinks about the judgment-seat of Christ it is not to remind himself that all men will one day stand there, and to wonder what will befall them, but to remember that he himself will be there, and to pray humbly that at the last he may be found faithful. And if we ask Paul, 'What will God do with the heathen that die in the darkness?' I think Paul will bid each of us rather ask himself this question, 'What will God do with *me* if, when my lamp is lit, I leave my brother man to wander friendless in the night?'" Speaking on "Christ's Love for Man," the preacher says, "A young woman who had spent an evil life lay dying in hospital. Some one had read to her the words, 'He was wounded for our transgressions,' and through them she had caught sight of the mercy of God. Presently she pointed at the palm of one hand with a finger of the other and said, 'There is no wound here; *He* was wounded for my transgressions.' Then she lay silent a while, and then she slowly and feebly put her hands up to her brow and said, 'There are no thorns here; *He* was wounded for my transgressions.' Again she lay still, so that they thought her gone. But a third time she moved, and, placing her hand over her heart, said, 'There is no spear-wound here; *He* was wounded for my transgressions.' And with that plea she passed up to God." Against the dangerous maxim that it is never too late to mend, our preacher gives very solemn warning: "Nature does not en-

courage us to believe such a doctrine. If it is a hundred steps to the edge of a precipice I may take ninety-nine and yet retrace them all; but if I take the hundredth step there is no retracing that. Forgiveness is promised on repentance, but where is any guarantee given that the soul that sinneth will surely repent? 'It is impossible to renew them again to repentance,' says the Epistle to the Hebrews. Coleridge and Shakespeare emphasize this warning. Moreover, the awful facts of life all around us forbid us to say that it is never too late to mend. An habitual drunkard said, 'If a glass of spirits were put before me, and I knew that the bottomless pit was yawning between me and it, I could not keep from taking it.' A physician at the deathbed of a rich man saw that he kept moving his hands about over the counterpane as if he were feeling for something. 'What is the matter?' the physician asked the man's son. And the son answered, 'I know; every night before my father went to sleep he liked to feel and handle some of his banknotes.' So saying, he slipped a banknote into the old man's hands, who then seemed satisfied. And he died fondling the money. So dear to him, to the very end, was the feel of the funds in his fingers. One night a curate in the East End of London was called out in the middle of the night by a woman to see her dying husband. In a rickety house up a squalid court he found a man about forty years old. Bending over the bed, he talked to the dying man as well as he could, while the wife stood by sobbing. The minister dropped on his knees by the bedside to offer a prayer for this poor passing soul, but as he knelt he noticed a sudden eager gleam in the man's eyes. While the minister prayed the man died, and when the curate tried to rise from his knees he found that the dead fingers were clutched tightly through his watch-chain. The man was a hardened thief, a confirmed criminal, and even in dying could not resist the impulse to pick the praying clergyman's pocket. A young man whose eyesight was suffering consulted a London physician. The doctor saw in a moment that it was a case for plain speaking: 'Young man,' he said, 'you are leading an immoral life; if you do not stop you will be blind in three months.' For a moment the young man was silent. Then he moved slowly toward the window, and looking out said in a low, hoarse whisper, 'Good-bye, fair world of light! I cannot give up my sin.' Character tends to become fixed and permanent. 'Sow an act and you reap a habit; sow a habit and you reap a character; sow a character and you reap a destiny.' He who will not repent at last cannot. God damns no man. But the awful fact is that a man may damn himself. His will and choice may become eternally set toward evil." A Brooklyn physician told a man who came to his office for medicine that he must abandon his vicious habits if he expected to be well. The man turned on him almost fiercely and said, "Doctor, do you know what we keep you for? Your business is to enable us to go on indulging in the gratification of our passions, by preventing the consequences. That's what we want of you." The hardened and shameless transgressor will not be warned nor intimidated. His heart is resolutely set to do evil. What he asks is not good advice or saving truth, but to have his path kept from becoming hard. He has gone beyond the point where he could

have any wish to mend. There is forgiveness for penitence, but he will never repent.

An Unpublished Essay of Edwards on the Trinity. With Remarks on Edwards and His Theology, by GEORGE P. FISHER, D.D., LL.D., Emeritus Professor of Ecclesiastical History in Yale University. Crown 8vo, pp. 142. New York: Charles Scribner's Sons. Price, cloth, $1.

October 5, 1903, was the two hundredth anniversary of the birth of Jonathan Edwards. This suggested the present as a suitable time for the publication of an essay of his on The Trinity, the manuscript of which had been mislaid and for a long time lost sight of. The essay was discovered among papers in the possession of Yale University, and is here published with explanatory Preface by Dr. George P. Fisher, who thinks "it will be deemed lucid in its course of thought, and one of the ablest arguments of this species which the History of Doctrine affords in behalf of fundamental positions of the Nicene theology." The late Professor Edwards A. Park did not concur with the philosophical parts of Edwards's expositions of the Trinity, nor with such of his Biblical interpretations as corresponded therewith and aimed to support them. Edwards held to the subordination of Persons in the Divine Being, the eternal generation of the Son being a primary element in his faith—a Nicene doctrine which was discarded by the leaders of New England orthodoxy within the century in which Edwards lived. The intellectual strength and dialectic force of Jonathan Edwards stand out in this argument for the Trinity, but a document written so long ago is like an old flintlock musket, more interesting as a relic than useful as a weapon of warfare for to-day. The same old battle over the doctrine of the Trinity has to be fought to-day, but Hardee's tactics are superseded by Upton's, new weapons are in vogue, and the opposing forces line up along a slope that pitches at a different angle. One who reads this old argument by Edwards, and then reads Dr. George A. Gordon's discussion of the Trinity in *Ultimate Conceptions of Faith,* will see the contrast between theological methods of thought in the eighteenth century and the twentieth, though Dr. Gordon is as positively trinitarian as Edwards. We find, as we expected, the chief interest of this volume in Dr. George P. Fisher's "Remarks on Edwards and His Theology," which occupy, in fact, more pages than Edwards's Essay. Dr. Fisher's seventy pages, it need scarcely be said, are as fresh and pertinent as they are crystalline in style, discriminating, judicious, and mature. For all minds, except the antiquarian and the academically curious, those pages contain the principal value of this book. The course of New England theology is traced through successive modifications from Jonathan Edwards to Horace Bushnell. These modifications, while apparently from within the Calvinistic bodies, were in very large degree due to the prevailing pressure of the more acceptable Arminian teaching from without. Professor Fisher reviews, characterizes, and estimates, in order, the successive writings of Edwards. Of those writings which are most offensive to modern readers Dr. Fisher says that the obnoxious passages are essentially iden-

tical in doctrine with the symbols of the Protestant Churches of Edwards's day—for instance, with the Westminster Confession—and not essentially diverse from the creed of the followers of Augustine in previous
centuries. When Edwards said of infants that, while seeming innocent to
us, "they are in God's sight young vipers" he only expressed in an intense
figure of speech the doctrine of the Augustinian and Calvinistic creeds.
And it is certain that Edwards recognized the all-comprehending benevolence of God toward mankind whatever their guilt, and held the character
of God to consist, at the core, in love to all intelligent beings whether
morally good or morally evil. Dr. Fisher suggests that whoever thinks
of Jonathan Edwards merely as a dry reasoner or an austere preacher
should read his meditations on the beauty and sweetness of Divine things.
In his youth, Edwards tells us, "There sprang up such a sense of Divine
things that the appearance of everything was altered; there seemed to
be, as it were, a calm, sweet appearance of Divine glory in almost everything—in the clouds and blue sky; in the sun, moon, and stars; in the
grass, flowers, trees; in the water and all nature, which used greatly to fix
my mind. I often used to sit and view the moon for a long time; and,
in the day, spent much time time in viewing the clouds and sky, to behold
the sweet glory of God in these things; in the meantime, singing forth
with a low voice my contemplations of the Creator and Redeemer. . . . I
spent most of my time thinking of Divine things year after year; often
walking in the woods and solitary places, for meditation, soliloquy, prayer,
and converse with God. I was almost always in ejaculatory prayer wherever I was." When a very young preacher in New York he frequently
retired to a solitary place on the bank of the Hudson River for contemplation on heavenly things and secret communion with God. Edwards tells
this incident which occurred at Northampton: "Once as I rode out into
the woods for my health, in 1737, having alighted from my horse in a
retired place, as my manner commonly was, to walk for meditation and
prayer, I had a vision, that for me was extraordinary, of the glory of the
Son of God as mediator between God and man, and His wonderful, great,
full, pure, and sweet grace and love, and meek and gentle condescension.
This grace, that appeared so calm and sweet, appeared also great above
the heavens. The person of Christ appeared ineffably excellent, with
an excellency great enough to swallow up all thought and conception
—which continued, as near as I can judge, about half an hour; which kept
me, the greater part of the time, in a flood of tears and weeping aloud. I
felt an ardency of soul to be—what I know not how otherwise to express—
emptied and annihilated, to lie in the dust and be full of Christ alone; to
love Him with a pure and holy love, to trust in Him, to live upon Him, to
serve and follow Him, and to be perfectly sanctified and made pure with
a Divine and heavenly purity. I have, several other times, had views of
much the same nature, and which had the same effects." To these extracts given by Professor Fisher we ourselves will add a sample of the
radiant if not rapturous style sometimes found in Edwards's writings as
seen in his description of the beauty of holiness, part of which is as follows: "Holiness appeared to me to be of a calm, sweet, pleasant, charming,

serene nature, which brought an inexpressible purity, brightness, peaceful-
ness, and ravishment to the soul; in other words, that it made the soul
like a field or garden of God, with all manner of pleasant fruits and
flowers, all delightful and undisturbed, enjoying a sweet calm and the
gentle vivifying beams of the sun." When the trustees of Princeton
College invited Jonathan Edwards to the presidency of that institution he
communicated to them his own defects which, he thought, disqualified
him for that office, naming a constitution which begets a low tide of
spirits, a bashful, retiring manner, and taciturn manner, with a disagree-
able dullness and stiffness which much unfitted him for conversation and
for such business as the government of a college.

Jewish Ceremonial Institutions and Customs. By WILLIAM ROSENAU, Ph.D. (Johns Hopkins
    University). 12mo, pp. 193, with twenty illustrations. Baltimore: The Friedenwald
    Company. Price, cloth, $1.50 net.

Mr. Henry Sonneborn has presented to the Johns Hopkins University
a collection of Jewish ceremonial objects, ninety-two in number, to be
used for the illustrating of the Old Testament and the later Jewish literature in the instruction given by Professor Paul Haupt. The objects are
of considerable diversity, and among them are the following: (1) Cur-
tain for ark in synagogue containing scrolls of the law; (2) Torah
manuscript scrolls of the law on vellum; (3) Band for scrolls of the law;
(4) Covering for scrolls of the law; (5) Silver shield for scrolls of the
law; (6) Silver pointer for scrolls of the law; (7, 8) Silver ornaments
for scrolls of the law; (9) Covering for scrolls; (17) Silver spice box;
(20) Wax taper for concluding Sabbath; (22) Silver circumcision knife;
(30) Mezuzah, amulet for door post; (35) Shofar, ram's horn; (40) Manuscript of a Hebrew bill of divorce; (72) Seven-branched candelabrum;
(73) Charity box, and many more. It would be difficult to overrate the
importance of such a collection, in the ordinary daily routine of Old Testament instruction, and in the skillful hands of one of the most eminent
Semitic scholars and teachers of our time (for such is Professor Haupt
undoubtedly), it is sure to be of increasing importance. Similar collections should be in the theological seminaries of Methodism at Boston,
Madison, and Evanston. At Johns Hopkins it was determined that a
course of lectures be delivered by a man who thoroughly understood
modern Jewish custom and usage, and that the lectures be illustrated
by the collection of objects which Mr. Sonneborn's munificence had
brought together. The lectures were delivered by Dr. William Rosenau,
who had himself been a pupil of Professor Haupt. These lectures in a
more popular form are now published, and are admirably illustrated by
half-tone cuts made directly from the objects in the Sonneborn collection. The book is comprehensive in scope, for its chapters deal with The
Synagogue and its Utensils; The Worshiper and the Week-day Service;
The Sabbath Service; Passover, Pentecost, and the Fasts; the Tishri
Holidays and the Half Holidays; Circumcision and Redemption of the
Firstborn; Marriage; Divorce; Ritualistic Slaughtering, and several
others. It is very clearly and simply written, is interesting enough to

be read through at a sitting, yet is sufficiently detailed to be useful as a
work of reference. Its usefulness in the latter respect would be enhanced
if it were provided with an index. (Ought there not be some way to
compel writers and publishers to provide every book with this prime
necessity?) We commend the book most heartily as a *vade-mecum* for
all teachers and students of the Old Testament or of Judaism, ancient
or modern.

PHILOSOPHY, SCIENCE, AND GENERAL LITERATURE.

Robert Browning. By G. K. CHESTERTON. 12mo, pp. 207. New York: The Macmillan Company. Price, cloth, 75 cents.

This book comes to us with almost as much freshness as if no one had
ever written of Browning before. The author's thought and style are
like those of nobody else, brilliant, paradoxical, vivacious, original, full
of vigor. It is not long since his volume of essays introduced a new
writer to the British public. He is a born and bred Londoner, a staff
writer on the London *Daily News.* Since this volume on Browning in the
"English Men of Letters" series was issued Mr. Chesterton has attracted
still wider notice by entering the lists in behalf of Christianity against
the wholesale assault made upon its very fundamentals by Robert Blatchford, editor of *The Clarion,* a Socialist weekly paper, who has a large following among English workingmen, and who attempts to annihilate the
whole Christian system. It is scarcely too much to say that Chesterton
has been for a time the literary sensation of London. One sharp critic
concedes him "the success of youth, eagerness, cleverness, with endless
novelty and audacity in detail;" while another styles him "a riotous
colt in the literary pasture, rampant with undisciplined spirit." Certainly no one can lounge, indifferent and unaroused, over his book on
Browning. Not one page is "to dull monotony a prey." It is full of
oxygen, full of tingles and fillips, full of darts and sparkles. At the same
time it sees shrewdly into the heart of its subject, Robert Browning, the
man and his poems, the poet "who combines the greatest brain with the
simplest temperament known in modern English literary annals." Browning was a keen artist, a keen scholar, and had "a memory like the British
Museum Library." "Preeminent in him was the spirit of battle; every
line in his stubborn soul and his erect body expressed the fighter." He
never conceived of himself as being what the French call an intellectual,
but rather as being a sanguine and strenuous man. Among his virtues
were boyishness, and absolute fidelity, and a love of plain words and
things. He had no literary egotism. The young poet who wrote "Sordello" was not a young pedant anxious to exaggerate his superiority to
the public, but a hot-headed, strong-minded, inexperienced, and essentially
humble man, who had more ideas than he knew how to disentangle from
each other. If we compare the complexity of Browning with the clarity
of Matthew Arnold, we will realize that Arnold was an intellectual aristo-
crat and Browning an intellectual democrat. Forgetting that other people had not the same exhaustive knowledge of the period of Guelph and

Ghibelline in mediæval Italy which he had, Browning filled "Sordello" with allusions to the persons, struggles, politics, and ideals of that shadowy epoch which made that poem incomprehensible to ordinary readers. This was not because of an ambition to display his own knowledge, but because he overestimated the knowledge and capacity of other people and generally assumed that what was clear to him would be clear to them. Consequently his writing "Sordello" was as if he rushed up to the first person he met and began talking about Ecelo and Taurello Salinguerra, as if that person knew all about them, and with about as much literary egotism as an English baby shows when it talks English to an Italian organ-grinder." As to whether it was right or wrong to give to the world the love-letters of Mr. and Mrs. Browning, as was done by their publication a few years ago—letters which picture "the gradual amalgamation of two spirits of great natural potency and independence"—Mr. Chesterton says: "To my mind the whole question should be tested by one perfectly clear intellectual distinction and comparison. I am not prepared to admit that there is or can be, properly speaking, in the world anything that is too sacred to be known. That spiritual beauty and spiritual truth are in their nature communicable, and that they should be communicated, is a principle which lies at the root of every conceivable religion. Christ was crucified upon a hill and not in a cavern, and the word Gospel itself involves the same idea as the ordinary name of a daily paper. (It is published news.) Whenever, therefore, a poet or any similar type of man can, or conceives that he can, make all men partakers of some splendid secret of his own heart, I can imagine nothing saner and nothing manlier than his course in doing so. Thus it was that Dante made a new heaven and a new hell out of a girl's nod in the streets of Florence. Thus it was that Paul founded a civilization by keeping an ethical diary. But the one essential which exists in all such cases as these is that the man in question believes that he can make the story as stately to the whole world as it is to him, and he chooses his words to that end." Mr. Chesterton thinks that those letters which are of a nature really to convey to the world the love the Brownings felt for each other were justifiably published; but that the others should have been kept unpublished. On one point Browning always maintained an unvarying decision. In the latter part of his life the pessimistic school of poetry was growing up all round him. The decadents with their belief that art was only a counting of autumn leaves were achieving a weary supremacy. Browning could not speak of them without scorn. "Death, death," he exclaimed, "it is this harping on death that I despise so much. In fiction, in poetry, French as well as English and American, in art and literature, the shadow of death, call it what you will, despair, negation, indifference, is upon us. But what fools who talk thus! Why, *amico mio*, you know as well as I that death is life. Without death, which is our church-yardy crapelike word for change, for growth, there could be no prolongation of that which we call life. Never say of me that I am dead." The author says that "The Ring and the Book" is the great epic of the nineteenth century because it is the great epic of the enormous importance of small things,

"The supreme difference that divides it from all the great poems of similar length and largeness of design is precisely the fact that all these are about affairs commonly called important, and 'The Ring and the Book' is about an affair commonly called contemptible. Homer says, 'I will show you the relations between man and heaven as exhibited in a great legend of love and war, which shall contain the mightiest of all mortal warriors and the most beautiful of all mortal women.' The author of the book of Job says, 'I will show you the relations between man and heaven by a story of primeval sorrows and the voice of God out of a whirlwind.' Virgil says, 'I will show you the relations of man to heaven by the tale of the origin of the greatest people and the founding of the most wonderful city in the world.' Dante says, 'I will show you the relations of man to heaven by uncovering the very machinery of the spiritual universe, and letting you hear as I have heard the roaring of the mills of God.' Milton says, 'I will show you the relations of man to heaven by telling you of the very beginning of all things and the first shaping of the thing that is evil in the first twilight of time.' Browning says, 'I will show you the relations of man to heaven by telling you a story out of a dirty and musty Italian book of criminal trials from which I select one of the meanest and most completely forgotten.' In this Browning is the supreme embodiment of his time, the characteristic of which is the apotheosis of the insignificant. The writers of to-day have ceased to believe certain things to be important and the rest to be unimportant. Significance is to them a wild thing that may leap upon them from any hiding place. They have all become terribly impressed with the mysterious powers of small things." The varied byplay of Mr. Chesterton's book suggests that Browning and his poetry must be more or less related to pretty much everything in earth and heaven. It is full of *obiter dicta*, as for example, that, while the roots of the Irish problem lie in the darkness of the age of Strongbow, the branches of it to-day spread out to the remotest commonwealths of the East and the West; that the would-be reformer is frequently troubled with an inordinate conceit of his own superior sagacity, imagining the rest of mankind to be poor blunderers who might enter into rest if they would go his way and forswear forever the right of going their own way; that when a man begins to think that the grass will not grow at night unless he lies awake to watch it, he generally ends in an asylum; that politics in its historic aspect has fascination for the most ardent intellects because it is the one thing in the world that is as intellectual as the *Encyclopædia Britannica* and as rapid as the Derby; that when the author of the book of Job insists upon the huge unmeaning and unmanageable might of Behemoth, the hippopotamus, and says, "Wilt thou play with him as with a bird? or wilt thou bind him for thy maidens?" he is appealing to our sense of the grotesque by his notion of the hippopotamus as a household pet, and is indulging in a kind of humor which is much like Browning's as seen, for example, in Caliban on Setebos; that one of the deepest of human moods is the sudden sense that all things have a meaning which we have missed—such a mood as may strike us in a garden at night, or deep in sloping

meadows, with the feeling that every flower and leaf is uttering something of stupendous importance, which we, by a prodigy of imbecility, fail to understand or hear. What can a man mean by saying that "Browning is a great demagogue with an impediment in his speech"?

The Kinship of Nature. By BLISS CARMAN. Crown 8vo, pp. 298. Boston: L. C. Page & Co. Price, cloth, ornamental, $1.50.

First in the book is a striking and attractive portrait of Bliss Carman. Next, a dedication seven pages long to his former teacher, George R. Parkin, who, he says, was never "one of those aloof and awesome Head Masters who exercise a petty reign of terror over the effervescence of youth;" who was the leader and comrade of his boys in Greek and in football, in tramping for May flowers through the early spring woods, paddling on the river in intoxicating Junes, and snowshoeing across huge white drifts in keen December winds; who taught his boys to be zealous, to be fair, to be happy in their work, to love only what is beautiful and of good report, and to follow the truth. He taught his pupils to look upon the world as their schoolhouse in which they were to go learning life-long; and this scholar, having begun in the early seventies in a Canadian town on the St. John River and having continued until, at the completion of this volume, he finds himself at life's meridian, reflects that life's "school will not keep forever. By the feel of the sun it must be already past noon. Before very long the hour must strike for our dismissal from this pleasant and airy edifice, a summons less welcome than the four o'clock cathedral bell in that leafy Canadian city in old days, and we shall all go scattering forth for the Great Re-creation." Bliss Carman sends out his book as a palpable revelation of himself and his experiences, knowing it will be received only by those in whom it touches a responsive chord. He says: "A book may be a cry in the night, like Carlyle's; or a message from the god of the woods, like Emerson's; or the utterance of a scholar like Newman from the schools of ancient learning; or it may be no more than the smiling salutation of a child on the street. Let him receive it who understands its appeal." Nothing that Carman writes, whether prose or verse, is destitute of delicate grace and exquisite charm, but this volume of Nature essays persuades us that poetry is his native realm in which he is most at home. The essays regard not Nature alone but Life; the first is on "The Art of Life," the second on "Being Strenuous," while others are on "Haste and Waste," "The Luxury of Being Poor," "The Wandering Word," "The Seed of Success," "Concerning Pride," "Play," "The Debauchery of Mood," "Moderation," and "Serenity." Whether the author is pagan or Christian is as difficult to tell from his prose as from his poetry. Perhaps the poet is a bee that sips the sweetness of all sorts of flowers whether of low land or high land, from the slopes of Hymettus or the Ægean plain. When he says, "To keep the Ten Commandments is not the whole business of man, not his whole duty; it is only a beginning, a crude makeshift of conduct; and the law of love by which they were superseded brings us nearer to perfection," he is the pupil of Jesus Christ, though some other word would

be better than "superseded." He quotes with sympathetic approval
Lanier's words: "One has appeared who continually cried love, love, love
—love God, love neighbors; and these 'neighbors' have come to be not only
men-neighbors, but tree-neighbors, river-neighbors, star-neighbors." Writing of "The Crime of Ugliness," he says: "I conclude that joy in one's
work, pleasure in one's emotions, and satisfaction in one's thoughts, go
to make up the sum of happiness. And I am skeptical of the validity of
any theory of conduct which can countenance the cultivation of any one
of these forms of happiness at the expense of the others. We can only
reach happiness by a degree of cultivation of *all* our faculties. We perceive that even piety is by no means a sure bringer of happiness. The
blameless life is sometimes hidden under a mass of woe-begone unloveli-
ness. Our good friends fail of happiness because they have made the mistake of thinking goodness the only aspect of the universe, whereas it is
only one of three. God does not exist as goodness alone; He exists as
beauty and truth also, just as man exists as body and as mind. Certainly
the love of goodness and the love of truth are great virtues; but so also
is the love of beauty." And he goes on talking about beauty in the
worshipful temper of John Ruskin. Carman deplores haste as "the fateful
malady of modern life, the fever of the soul. The great characters of the
earth, in history or in our own day, are those who have been able to hold
themselves undistracted, without haste. They have had that sanity or
balance of mind which could perceive the futility of hurry and the ultimate triumph of serene endeavor. They never allowed themselves to be
flustered, there was nothing in their blood of Kipling's 'fluttered folk and
wild.' He who allows himself to become hurried, and anxious, and fearful is degraded; he deteriorates every minute." Yet the author says to
the man who is compelled to lead the strenuous life: "If circumstances
have placed you in the forefront of the fight where all your splendid life
long you shall never have a minute to call your own, where you shall
never once be able to rest or meditate or sun your spirit in a basking hour
of leisure—complain not. This is the fortune of the captains of humanity;
be glad the good God has done you the honor to lay upon you a work as
great as your powers. The stern struggle and victorious achievement can
never be cramping to the soul; and the cisterns of repose may be opened
to you in another life." And it is declared to be possible for the most
strenuous life to possess within a steadiness of spirit and of purpose like
the undeviating and imperturbable serenity of the wheeling sun. Carman
is long on heart and short on creed; he has more deep feeling than definite faith. Hear him: "If we are compelled from time to time to change
our way of thinking on religious themes, we are not compelled to change
our way of feeling about them. And the essence of religion is the emotion, not the thought—the sure and certain conviction, not the logical conclusion. The foundations of life are still far beyond the reach of scientific
knowledge, but among the realities of life is this trust in continual goodness and abiding love." Bliss Carman once heard a man say to a friend
who was a writer by trade, "Don't you really love a word better than anything else in the world?" The question suggests the power of the word: "In

the Old Book where this story of the creation is told, how the heavens and the earth were made in the beginning, it is written, 'God said.' No other way of promulgating the vast elemental *fiat* could be imagined. By simple word of mouth the revolving firmament was created; and the record is a tribute to the power of the word. . . . And, again, in the New Book, 'In the beginning was the word, and the word was with God, and the word was God.' This is a more illumined way of saying the same thing that the author of Genesis said. If the word was God, and God is unchanging, the word is still Lord of the Earth." Carman does not quite seem to see that Christ is God's Word to men. But he sees how the creatures obey when the Creator sends forth His word to call them: "When the vernal sun is warming the earth and April is spreading resurrection up the sloping world, by what magic is the transformation wrought? In the dim nether glooms of the deep sea all the fin people have received the summons; the unrest has taken hold of them—the fever of migration; and the myriad hosts from the green Floridian waters and azure Carib calms gather and move; surely and swiftly they come, through the soundless, trackless spaces under the broken whitish day, up to the cool fresh rivers and pools of the North. How did they know the date? By instinct? What is that? Somehow the communication came to them, as inexplicably as it comes to us—the unuttered word, the presage, the portent. And their brothers the birds, too; already they are here, hard on the heels of the retreating frost, every tribe with its cohorts full and overflowing; from tree to tree, from state to state, the long unnoted procession comes flying upward swiftly through the night. Why they started, how they guessed the hour of departure, we can only dimly surmise. Their movements are as mysterious as our own, the source of their impulse as undiscoverable. Yet to them, too, the message must have gone abroad. To say that the word went forth among them is to use the simplest and most elemental metaphor of the truth." Carman gives good men warning that a cold, inflexible adherence to duty may make a hard, narrow, and cruel sort of saint. "An unflinching observance of duty, unmodified by mercy, by love, by gentleness, by generosity, may lead to almost inhuman hardness. The devotee of duty may become an unlovely and pestiferous monomaniac, a burden to himself and an infliction to others. We all know how angular and sour and uncomfortable a conscientious fanatic can be. It matters not whether he is a religious or a free-thinking fanatic; his inordinate insistent devotion to his one narrow parochial conception of life may become a nuisance to his neighbors. He is so stiff-necked that he cannot see anything outside of his own pasture. The beautiful flexibility, plasticity, and winsomeness of human nature at its best seem to have been left out of him." Needless to say that Bliss Carman is at his best on the open road in sight of the pageant of Nature. A brave, glad, buoyant, and brilliant essay, indeed, is that on "The Scarlet of the Year." Another volume of his verse, *From the Green Book of the Bards*, lies on our table awaiting notice. Bliss Carman adds a tint and a tone to the literature of our time which none would willingly miss; and he keeps us expectant of something better still.

The Religious Sense in its Scientific Aspect. By GREVILLE MACDONALD, M.D. Crown
8vo, pp. 243. New York: A. C. Armstrong & Son. Price, cloth, $1.50.

In the spirit of Milton, these three lectures, delivered before the students of King's College, London, seek to search what we know not by what
we know. A specially helpful feature of the book is the clear and succinct
"Synopsis" in the opening pages, like a map of the region through which
the reader is to travel under the author's guidance. The aim is to set
forth the true nature of the Religious Sense as seen by the author from
the scientific and the Christian standpoints. He holds that this Sense,
like all other human attributes, is "an inheritance from mighty small beginnings." He thinks he sees this Sense prevailing throughout creation,
evolving from low origins to high ongoings. He sets out to make this
Sense appear to us as real as any other of our senses or emotions, as real
and as trustworthy as any of our intellectual faculties. A sample of his
method and style is this from the first lecture, where he is showing that
the true scientific spirit is in the child's questionings, and that all understanding depends upon simplification, and that the simplification of phenomena consists in relegating or relating them to the law or the Power
responsible for them: "The child who first looks upon an opening daisy
sees in it a revelation of some hitherto unsuspected wonder, and seeks to
find its parallel among his small experiences. Tell such a child that the
daisy unfolds its bud because it cannot help doing so, and he may be
silenced, but he is not enlightened. Tell him rather, as a wise mother
would, that the flower blows because God wished it to do so, and he immediately finds himself confronted with an ethical law which he understands because it is the same bond which connects parental authority and
his own actions; his budding desire for understanding is satisfied because
of this simplification of his facts. And such a reply to the child is truly
scientific in spirit, though the reverential mother, in so speaking, may be
altogether ignorant of the evolution of the flower or of botanical classification. To tell a child that a flower buds because it cannot do otherwise
is an infamous snub to his small philosophic mind; to tell him that God
made both him and the flower to do His will and to justify Him in making them, points out to the child the great truth that there is uniformity
in law between him and the daisy, and that they own a common parentage
in the Power which, from its integral embrace of the universe, we are
warranted in calling Divine." From his scientific standpoint the author
emphasizes the importance of the poet's place in the education of individuals and of the race. He says, "The poet's methods of expressing
thought are the methods of every man, woman, and child, of every race,
cultured or aboriginal, of pope and penitent, prince and pauper. All
language is based upon the system of metaphorical expression. Our
growth in mind is but increasing victory in expression. Human language,
in its words, idioms, and proverbs, is a system of representing abstract
ideas in concrete metaphor. This is Nature's law of thought and speech;
the Poets have made language; they teach us expression, and without the
means of expression there is little chance of learning. Shakespeare succeeds in educating us, where Kant fails. Burns saw deeper into some

laws of Nature than did Plato." Dr. MacDonald broadly defines the Religious Sense as that acknowledgment of the majestic authority of the Law which compels all creatures possessing that Sense to work for and to live for objects or attainments in which the individual has no personal concern; and holds that this Sense plays a great part, indeed the chief part, in the progress of life, and in the development of man's obligation to live in conformity to the Law which is over him and in him. This book is more interesting than convincing. Few, if any, of our readers will think that it succeeds in its attempt to trace the Religious Sense from elementary indications in structureless forms of life up to its lofty manifestation in the exalted nature of Man. It reminds us of Henry Drummond's not entirely successful endeavor to bring the spiritual world under the dominion of natural law. Insisting that the reality of the Religious Sense is as demonstrable scientifically as any other of man's senses, the author answers those who object, first, that this Sense is not real because many do not, or think they do not, possess it; and, second, that this Sense is merely an artificial product of an artificial environment, and is not natural to man. Dividing his subject into the "Religion of Service," the "Religion of Renunciation," and the "Religion of Freedom," our lecturer thinks he traces the development of the Religious Sense from humblest and faintest beginnings up to its supreme and final arrival before the altars of the Christian Faith and in the light of that manifestation of the Divine which is in Christ. Reverently does he say: "It were hardly worth while pursuing our search for truth, whether in Nature or in men's hearts or in the Scriptures, but for one great historic fact which has given us our clearest knowledge of the import of all things. That fact is the coming among us of One whose personal life was inspired by, and perfectly conformed to, Law, and revealed in beauty; whose social life was inspired by love for the children of men and revealed in sorrow because they rejected the Truth; whose oneness with eternal Law, transcending all mundane obligation, was revealed in His sacrifice, and His going from those He loved that they might grow and learn freedom in faith. And now we profess devotion to Him and to the Truth which He revealed to men; yet, spite of this, most of us maintain that we cannot, in the strange necessities of this age, take the injunctions of the Sermon on the Mount quite literally. Yet the study of facts, and the ministrations of pure science will teach us that the Sermon on the Mount proclaims the elemental law of life with its prospective, evolutional possibilities of eternal growth in ever-increasing freedom. Despite the arguments of political economists as to the impractical nature of the Sermon on the Mount, both protestantism and democracy can exist in purity only when their meaning is defined in the words of that great Utterance. Protestantism and democracy, whether judged in the light of Christ's teachings or in the spirit of philosophic freedom, mean but one thing—*the eternal worth of the individual under the cosmic Law.* . . . He who best trusts his religion will least resent its being studied with the scalpel, test-tube, and microscope of scientific methods. By those methods we will best serve the philosophic understanding of the Religious Sense; and if by such

methods we find that all our inexplicable hopes take origin in the depths of an eternal and omnipresent Personality, our gain will not be less real if its proof lies beyond the confines of mere intellect." Professor John Fiske said that evolution predicts the sure coming of a time when the altruism of the Sermon on the Mount will become the normal social principle. Dr. MacDonald closes with this: "As our password into the realms of knowledge, as our beacon amidst the dark paths of conflicting obligations, as our sword in the struggles with material needs and temptations, we may hold in our hearts that saying of Martin Luther through which must come freedom to churches, states, and schools: 'My conscience is a captive to God's word.'"

HISTORY, BIOGRAPHY, AND TOPOGRAPHY.

Reminiscences of the Civil War. By General JOHN B. GORDON, of the Confederate Army. 8vo, pp. 474. New York: Charles Scribner's Sons. Price, cloth, $3.

A brilliant fighter and a brilliant writer is the author of this book, a manly foe and a magnanimous friend. Since Appomattox he has served his reunited country with eminent ability and devotion by doing all in his power to promote mutual understanding and good will in the hearts of all his fellow-countrymen. The soldiers who fought on both sides were brave men; they came to respect each other, and their antagonism ceased with the war. They spent their passion on the battlefield and had none left over. Indeed, they had not enough to last through the war, and before it ended "Yanks" and "Johnnies" often showed more relish for fraternizing than for fighting. Of this, many incidents in General Gordon's book give proof. These *Reminiscences* of a great Confederate commander, who was only thirty-three years old when the war closed, portray American manhood at its strenuous and stalwart best. The story is so told that North and South can take equal pride in the superb record of the tremendous struggle which rocked a continent and almost rent a Nation. European readers of this book will plainly see that ours was a war without parallel, that no such armies were ever mustered in any land as those which here flung themselves against each other for four awful years. The volume is, in ability and spirit, an unspeakable credit to its author; in effect, a just and patriotic glorification of the American people; and in the conflict it portrays, a gigantic spectacle fit to amaze and fascinate the gaze of all the world. The two great military leaders, Lee and Grant, both appear as modest, unassuming, pure-minded, gentle men, without a trace of vanity, ostentation, arrogance, or meanness of any kind. The patriotic story of the heroic endurance of the Confederates during the disheartening years, from that July day when their High Tide ebbed from the bloody heights of Gettysburg until the Lost Cause went down with all on board at Appomattox, is a tale to move the admiring sympathy of friends and foes. General Gordon *thinks* the result at Gettysburg, and, in consequence, perhaps, the result of the war, would have been different if Lee's orders had been exactly and punctually exe-

11

cuted by the generals under him, or if Stonewall Jackson had been there. But as for Gettysburg, we *think* the result would have been different *if* Grant had been there in command instead of Mead, for Lee's army would not have been permitted to get away and recross the Potomac. The summer of 1863 would have made an end of the Confederacy. And as for the possibility of a different conclusion of the war, supposing Lee had conquered at Gettysburg, our conviction is that it was ordained in the purposes of Heaven, for the good of the South and the North and the advantage of all mankind, as well as decreed by earthly conditions, that the mighty struggle, however prolonged, should result in the destruction of slavery and the preservation of the American Union. And with this view we fancy General Gordon would hardly disagree, since he avows "a firm faith in God's providence and in His control over the destinies of this Republic." It is not too much to say that, if no other testimony existed than what General Gordon furnishes, the fame of General Grant as a great military commander, and an honorable, high-minded, and noble man, would be secure. It was in the battles of the Wilderness that Lee first tested the mettle of Grant and felt the force of his indomitable will, tireless persistency, and direct method of delivering constant and heavy blows on his enemy's front instead of seeking advantage by strategical maneuvers. But Lee was not long in learning that Grant's strategical judgment was almost unerring, as General Gordon himself makes plain when he tells us what happened at Confederate headquarters after several days of terrific fighting in the tangled wilderness. Lee's scouts brought him word that Grant's army was preparing to retreat, and Lee's generals believed it. But Lee said, "No, Grant will not retreat;" and ordered the Confederate army to make a hurried night march to Spottsylvania. Being asked the reason for this order, he answered, "Grant will move to Spottsylvania; that is the best strategic move for him; and I am arranging to meet him there." Against contrary information and opinion, he relied on his great antagonist's military sagacity, issuing his orders and setting his army in motion on the certainty that the Union commander would not fail to see and take his best advantage. The sagacious foresight of both commanders appeared when the rushing armies of Lee and Grant met in a head-on collision at Spottsylvania; where was enacted, says General Gordon, a sanguinary drama of three acts. The first act was Hancock's charge; the second, the Confederate counter-charge; and the third, the desperate night-and-day wrestle on the breast-works. This American battle at Spottsylvania is declared to have no parallel in the annals of warfare. For face-to-face fighting, firing muzzle to muzzle; for the longest rattle of incessant, unbroken musketry; for the exhibition of individual heroism and personal daring by large numbers, who, standing in the spilt blood and charging over the heaped bodies of their comrades, for a day and a night faced a wall of flaming rifles at short range—for and because of all this, this general of a hundred battles says, Spottsylvania stands unmatched in our Civil War or in any war of which there is any record among men. Grim and horrible as is the story of merciless war, it is mitigated and lightened in General

Gordon's pages by many a gleam of the humor which not even the direst hardships and most desperate conditions can wholly suppress in men of courage and fortitude. The colored people furnish some of the humor. When Grant's tunnel under the rebel works at Vicksburg was filled with powder and exploded, a Confederate negro was blown through the air and came down unconscious some distance away. When consciousness returned, he saw blue-coated Union soldiers moving about all around him. "How did you get here?" they asked him. "Don't know, Boss. Yistidy I was in de Confed'acy; but, bless de Lawd, last night sumpin busted and blowed me plum into de Union." This colored brother's words might be used to describe what happened to all the Confederates at the end of their four years' fighting. One day General Lee asked a negro, whom he noticed doffing his hat to him, who he was. The black man answered, "One of your soldiers, Gin'ral." "Have you been shot?" inquired Lee. "No, sah." "Well, you can't be one of my soldiers, then; for all my men get shot." "De reason I hasn't got shot is dat I stays back where de ginerals stays." When an old colored man was asked if he was not afraid he would lose his dog, which was running and yelping after every railroad train that went by, he replied that he was not worrying about that, but he was "jist a wonderin' what dat derg gwine to do wid dem kyars when he cotches 'em." Many Southern families were divided on opposite sides in the war. Such was the case with the famous Breckinridge family of Kentucky. One distinguished member, the Rev. Robert J. Breckinridge, was a passionate upholder of the Union cause. From being devoted friends he and Rev. Dr. Stuart Robinson became uncompromising foes because of the latter's being an intense sympathizer with the South. When Dr. Breckinridge lay on his deathbed his family and friends were anxious that he should be reconciled to all men, especially to Dr. Robinson. So somebody at his bedside asked, "Brother Breckinridge, have you forgiven your enemies?" "O yes; certainly, certainly I have." "Well, Brother Breckinridge, have you forgiven *all* your enemies; have you forgiven Dr. Stuart Robinson?" "Certainly I have. Didn't I just tell you I'd forgiven my *enemies?*" "But, Brother Breckinridge, when you meet Brother Robinson in heaven, do you feel that you can greet him as all the redeemed ought to greet one another?" "Don't bother me with such questions. Stuart Robinson will never get to heaven." A Kentucky father whose two sons were killed, one in the Union army and the other in the Confederate, buried them both in the same grave and inscribed on their common tombstone, "God knows which was right." General Robert E. Lee's sister was the wife of a Union officer, and she was loyal to the Northern cause, but she doubted if Robert could ever be whipped. It is remarkable that General Gordon's wife, though but a girl when the war began, decided at once to leave her two little boys in care of her husband's mother, while she went to share with him the hardships and horrors of war; and she accompanied him through the four years of fighting. He says she is not afraid of bullets, but will take fright at a mouse or a big black bug. General Ewell once said, "Women would make a grand brigade, if it wasn't for snakes and spiders."

At Antietam General Gordon received five wounds and was carried out
of the fight unconscious. After the surgeons had bandaged his right
leg, his right arm and shoulder, and his face, and he had rallied somewhat from the shock, his wife was allowed to come to him. As she
approached he saw by her face that he must do something to reassure
her. So he summoned all his strength and said cheerily, "Here's your
handsome (?) husband; been to an Irish wedding." Her answer was a
suppressed scream, whether of anguish or of relief at finding him able
to speak, he did not know. Through weeks and months she nursed him
back to health. General Gordon has written the greatest war book that
has come from the Confederate side. In interest, it divides the primacy
of this season with Morley's *Life of Gladstone.*

Literary Landmarks of Oxford. By LAURENCE HUTTON. Illustrated. 12mo, pp. 274.
New York: Charles Scribner's Sons. Price, cloth, $1.20 net.

This is a pleasant book. It does not pretend to be a tourist's guide. The
casual visitor would better stick to Baedeker and Alden and Goldwin
Smith, for this chatty volume is for him who means to know his Oxford
more intimately. If he loves English letters and is dwelling for a season
at the town upon the Isis, he will enjoy this talkative companion. The
"middle-aged American writer," as Mr. Hutton calls himself, who left
Princeton (the book is dedicated to ex-President Patton) to spend a six
weeks' vacation in Oxford in 1899, wrote these chapters largely in the
Norham Gardens house where Professor Max Müller, in earlier and perhaps more brilliant days, had entertained Emerson and Lowell and
Holmes. The book is not a story of the colleges—indeed, it is only in part
about Oxford at all—but a book of personalities, a scrapbook of odds and
ends concerning famous literary men (mere statesmen or scientists or
artists are passed by) who have studied or taught at the university. Its
value lies in the entertaining anecdotes with which it is liberally
sprinkled, and in the impression it gives of the richness of Oxford history.
What an amazing list it is of the men of letters whom this volume recalls!
Erasmus, Tyndale, and Hooker, Laud, Jeremy Taylor, Sir Thomas Browne,
Heber, Newman, Keble, Thomas Arnold, and Robertson (who was a member of what is now the "sporting college")—they all trod these ancient
halls. Froude, Green, Gibbon, and Freeman; Swift, Addison, Steele, Sam
Johnson (who, on his arrival, decided that his tutor was "no scholar; and
he went to him no more. The next time he met his tutor on the street he
treated his tutor very rudely, an act of which he boasted in his later years.
He cheerfully paid a fine of twopence for nonattendance at a lecture which
he said, openly, was not worth a penny"), Sydney Smith, De Quincey, and
Shelley; Raleigh, Wren, Blackstone, and many another—what a company
is this! Connected with Christ Church alone were Sir Thomas More, Sir
Philip Sidney, Ben Jonson, John Locke, John Ruskin, and William E.
Gladstone, to say nothing of such public men as Lord Rosebery and the
late Lord Salisbury, who do not come within our author's view. And the
roll of Balliol alone includes Wyclif and Roger Bacon, Adam Smith,
Southey, Sir William Hamilton, Cardinal Manning, Dean Stanley, Matthew

Arnold, A. H. Clough, and Benjamin Jowett, (why not also Swinburne and perhaps Browning?) Though the author has no special charm of style, he performs a service in bringing together numberless bits of information about these famous men, even though some items, it must be confessed, are of slight interest. Of past times and pleasant memories the book is full. Here you have a glimpse of that debate at the Union when 90 voted against 33 for the superiority of Shelley over Byron, though "the only Oxonian who spoke in Shelley's favor was a young student of Balliol named Manning, afterward to become a cardinal of the Church of Rome." You see John Richard Green taking part "with rapt enthusiasm, in the May-morning procession of the Magdalen choir boys, to sing 'The Hymn to the Trinity' on the College Tower." You are enlightened as to the ancient modes of hazing and the modern method of making slang, and are treated to many a diverting incident. Robert Burton, the author of *The Anatomy of Melancholy,* was a Christ Church student. He is said to have been, in the intervals of his vapors, "exceeding cheerful; and then he would fall into such a state of despondency that he could only get himself relief by going to the Bridge-foot, at Oxford, and hearing the bargemen swear at one another, at which he would set his hands at his sides, and laugh most profusely." "Many are the stories told of Jowett in Oxford to this day, the generality of them being amusing and apocryphal. One of the most popular, and no doubt the most apocryphal, of these stories is to this effect: A certain irreverent and waggish undergraduate—not probably of Balliol—showing to a group of visiting friends Jowett's college, thus spoke: 'There is the Library; there is the Chapel; there is the Buttery; there is the Master's Lodge; and there'—throwing a stone through the window of the Lodge, at which the surprised and not overpleased Jowett at once appeared—'and there is the Master himself!'" Mr. Hutton complains repeatedly that "Oxford's ignorance of Oxford is phenomenal," yet within six weeks he seems to have gathered enough information to destroy some cherished illusions. None of these traditions which he asserts to be untrustworthy is harder to surrender than that concerning the Wesley rooms at Lincoln College. "Dr. Murray [Merry], the present Rector of Lincoln, knows of no reason, or authority, for ascribing 'Wesley's Rooms' to Wesley. They may, of course, have been Wesley's; they have been so called by more than one generation of Lincolnians, but the Rector fancies them to have been the invention of some clever Hall-porter, who handed them down to his descendants in the Lodge for the sake of the shillings which still pour in from the reverent pilgrims—especially American pilgrims." This is nothing less than cruel. Southey said "he never dreamed at Oxford," and "pronounced the authorities 'men remarkable for great wigs and little wisdom.'" Hogg, Shelley's chum, "says of their life there: 'Oxford is a seat in which learning sits very comfortably, well thrown back, as in an easy-chair, and sleeps so soundly that neither you nor I nor anyone else can waken her.'" This is not true, at least of modern Oxford. A dozen illustrations from charming sketches by Herbert Railton (the most beautiful is that of Oriel "quad") add to the value of the volume, and indices of persons and places make it useful for reference.

The Doctrine of the Church; Outline Notes Based on Luthardt and Krauth. By REVERE FRANKLIN WEIDNER, D.D., LL.D., Professor in Chicago Lutheran Theological Seminary. Crown 8vo, pp. 120. New York: Fleming H. Revell Company. Price, cloth, $1.25.

The author says: "Though professedly based on Dr. Luthardt's *Kompendium der Dogmatik* and Dr. Krauth's *Manuscript Lectures* (some of which have been published), the writer does not seek to intrench himself behind these authorities. These notes are such as a professor of theology would use as the basis of oral lectures. They are the result of twenty years' discussion in the classroom, and have gradually assumed the present form." The book is simply a syllabus of lectures on the doctrine of the Church, printed in small though clear type in brief, numbered paragraphs. A vast deal of information is packed in these pithy sentences, and if one wants to know a moderately High Church Lutheran view of what the Church is and is not, of the ministry, etc., he can do no better than to sit at the feet of Professor Weidner. The most valuable part of the book is the statement and criticism of Roman Catholic views and the setting forth of the views of Luther, Melanchthon, and other Lutheran standards and theologians. In these respects the book is most admirable. But when the author comes to the exposition and criticism of other Protestant Churches he is not so happy. On page 53 he tries to show that the Protestant Churches lack the "one faith," and therefore are not true Churches, and in the course of this he makes several misstatements: (1) "The word of God reveals one system of doctrine." It reveals no *system* of doctrine at all. It reveals doctrinal truths; the construction of these into a system is the work of theologians. (2) The various denominations, he says, "account for the defects in the views of others by the blindness and infirmity of man." That is news to us. In the olden times, when theological rancor ran deep (instance the seventeenth century Lutherans in Germany), the accounting for one's neighbor's heterodoxy by blindness and infirmity, or something much worse, was not uncommon, but that is no longer true. Does Drew call Princeton blind and infirm because her sister seminary is Calvinistic? Heredity, environment, education, inevitable differences of mind, of interpretation—these are the reasons the Churches assign for the others' differences; not blindness and infirmity. (3) "False doctrine, whether regarded as heresy in the sense of a deviation from the faith of the Gospel, or heresy considered as a schismatic division apart from the ground of faith, is treated in Scripture not as a misfortune, but as a crime, a work of the flesh." The inference is that the Protestant Churches, since they do not agree as to the faith, must be heretical, and if so criminal. But what were the New Testament heresies? Were they such differences as divide the Evangelical Churches of modern times? No. They were either far-reaching speculative errors which dissolved the very ground of historic Christianity, like Docetism, Gnosticism, etc., or a compulsory ceremonial Judaism, or thoroughly immoral teachings. Heresy or schism, as applied to the doctrines and divisions of the Evangelical Churches of to-day, was absolutely unknown in the New Testament. The author says again: "The various Protestant denominations do not have a unity of faith, and yet

the Scriptures declare that unity is an essential element of the Church."
How often is this said by Roman Catholics, but—to be wounded in the house
of one's friends! We hope occasionally the author has a larger vision, or
the young Lutheran ministers who issue from the Chicago Seminary will
go forth sadly prejudiced and narrow, besides with a false view of their
sister Churches. For, first, do not the "various Protestant denominations" hold to "the Head, which is Christ" (Eph. iv, 15), and, having
him, have they not a center of faith, a true unity? Besides, have they not
the two sacraments and a valid ministry? Going farther: they have a
"unity of faith" in the Apostles' Creed, in the Nicene Creed, and such a
dogmatic platform underneath them all is not to be despised. Besides all
this, there are other principles of faith which bind them together. In fact,
there is far more unity both of spirit and of doctrine in the "various
Protestant denominations" than in the schools and orders in the Roman
Church before the Council of Trent (1545, ff.), than in the German Lutheran Churches to-day. Second, where do the Scriptures declare that
unity, in the author's sense, "is an essential element of the Church"?
There is a unity that is essential—a unity of the Spirit in the bond of
peace, of love, of purity, of holding to the Head. But it is not a unity
of the Augsburg Confession, or of the Thirty-nine Articles, or the Twenty-
four Articles. Thank God, no! The differences that separated the Jewish
from the Gentile Christians in the Apostolic Church—parties that lived
together in peace—were far greater than those which separate the Protestant Churches. Peter and Paul were farther apart than Hodge and
Whedon, and the differences which separate the Evangelical branch of
Lutheranism and Methodism are child's play beside those of the parties
in the apostolic council of Acts xv. In his historical expositions the
author is sometimes either unfair (Martanism, page 27) or incorrect (Roman view of salvation outside of the Church, pages 29, ff.), and in his
statements of early Church polity he represents an antiquated point of
view. The twelve apostles were *not* at first or at any other time sole direc-
tors in spiritual guidance and business (page 67). But if one wants a concise, clear, and reliable putting of High Church Lutheran ecclesiology,
he can be commended to this meaty little book.

The Story of the Book Concerns. By W. F. WHITLOCK, D.D., LL.D. 16mo, pp. 204. Cincinnati: Jennings & Pye. New York: Eaton & Mains. Price, 25 cents net; by mail,
28 cents.

The Publishing Agents, at whose request this volume was written,
could not have selected a more competent man for the task than Professor
Whitlock. Two eminent qualifications for the work are his possession:
first, thorough familiarity with the facts to be presented; second, the
faculty of condensing and yet presenting in an attractive style the
information, the whole information and nothing but the information
pertaining to the history of the Book Concerns. For twenty years
a member and for ten years the chairman of the Book Committee,
the author is as familiar with our publishing interests as any man in the
connection. The contents begin with "Ante-Book Concern Times," and

end with "Possibilities." Nine intervening chapters packed with facts, classified and arranged in masterly order, comprise the romantic "Story." Further than this, the author, to quote from an appreciative "Introduction" by Dr. H. C. Jennings, "has given us the true philosophy underlying this great enterprise." The range of the "Story" may be gathered from the titles of the chapters: "Ante-Book Concern Times," "Organization," "Location," "History," "Agents," "Book Committee," "Financial System," "Mechanical Evolution," "Periodical Literature," "Books," "Possibilities." In the chapter on "Location" the author, after tracing the evolution of the publishing interests from 1804 to 1893, says: "It is very evident that the great publishing interests which are now the pride of the Church had a very humble beginning. They commanded a very small amount of capital, and that had been borrowed. Embarrassments without number followed. Material and labor had to be paid for promptly. The books were sold on commission to the preachers. . . . The members of the Church were widely scattered. They were poor, and sales to them and collections from them were difficult. The Book Steward's time was necessarily divided between his Church and the Book Concern; he was without clerical help for years; he himself had to perform almost every kind of labor. . . . It almost seemed that the Church expected him to make bricks without straw." The "History," covering sixty-six pages, traces the development of the business from the administration of John Dickins to that of the publishing Agents now in charge thereof. The chapter on "Agents," contains a record of all who have served the Church in this capacity, together with the biographical sketches of those who have gone hence. Under the title of "Book Committee" the author defines the duties and prerogatives of this Board, and gives as complete a list as can be made, beginning with 1792, of the members who have been connected therewith. The capital invested, dividends paid, etc., are fully set forth in the chapters on "Financial Service," while the "printing," "binding," etc," are treated under the title of "Mechanical Evolution." A fund of information concerning the publications of the two concerns is found in the chapters on "Periodicals" and "Books."

MISCELLANEOUS.

The Call of the Wild. By JACK LONDON. 12mo, pp. 231. New York: The Macmillan Company. Price, cloth, $1.50.

A dog story fit to go with *Rab and His Friends*, and *Bob, Son of Battle*. In it semi-human qualities are attributed to "Buck," a cross between a St. Bernard and a Scotch shepherd dog. As interesting as "Buck" himself are the human beings who from time to time belong to him. The deep truth embedded in the narrative is the development of strong good qualities through the stern discipline of infinite hardship; mastership won by a brave nature through suffering and abuse, starvation, fighting, and bitter cold. It is a powerful, exciting, and pathetic story, wholesome for boys or men.

METHODIST REVIEW.

MARCH, 1904.

Art. I.—EPISCOPAL SUPERVISION FOR EASTERN ASIA.

EASTERN ASIA—Japan, Korea, and China—has never had any episcopal supervision save that by General Superintendents. This has been gradually increased—from occasional to yearly visits, then to visits by the same bishop for two successive years, and now to a resident bishop with unbroken administration for a quadrennium. More cannot be secured, under our present constitution, by lengthening the term of service of the resident General Superintendent, for the four-years term stretches its "itinerant general" character almost to the breaking point. If at all, it must be by increasing the number of bishops assigned to this field.

I. The necessity for such increase appears from the following considerations: First, the vastness of the field and the immensity of its population—three great pagan empires, with more than one third of the total population of the earth. Second, the sea-wide separation of these empires from one another and the almost total absence of railways and lines of interior transportation, especially in Korea and China. To illustrate: With steamships for two thousand miles of the round trip, a single satisfactory visitation of our West China work requires, from a bishop resident in Shanghai, four months; an equal period is the minimum for Foochow and Hinghua; work in July and August is virtually prohibited by the tropical heat. Hence the bishop's entire time is gone—if thorough work is to be done—and Central China and North China, with their varied and vast interests, unprovided for, and the entire empires of Korea and Japan untouched!

1²

In his vain endeavor adequately to administer for his entire field, the bishop, ignoring seasons and pestilence and home, constantly afield, reaching Japan from the home-campaign in April, spent the remnant of that month and part of May in Japan and South Japan; crossed over into Korea for a month; crossed over to North China for the remainder of July; spent a week of August in the "Episcopal Residence" writing up correspondence; a fortnight with the Central China Mission; then sped away to Foochow and Hinghua Conferences; then ten days in the "Episcopal Residence;" from November 5 to November 12 in the Central China Conference; since which time, including the date of this writing, he has been *en route* to West China, where he *hopes* to arrive, to open Conference, December 23. Not later than January 5 he must hasten back to Kiukiang to hold the Central China Conference, opening January 20; then visit the "Episcopal Residence" to pick up the threads of his official correspondence; ship for Korea, to hold Conference in Seoul February 17; then off for the island of Kiushiu, to hold the South Japan Conference March 17; organizing the Japan Central Conference, Tokyo, March 29 to April 5; April 5 sailing for General Conference. So far as travel is concerned, one bishop might much more easily supervise all the United States and Mexico than China alone. Is it wonderful that a sense of incompleteness attends his labors, and makes him pray for at least three bishops, instead of one, for Eastern Asia?

Third, the nature of the work. At home the work is established, the flag and the people are Christian, and a great army of well-trained pastors forwards every interest of Methodism. None of this here. The impact of paganism and Christless civilization, the most advanced communicants in the Corinthian period of development, native pastors knowing little of experimental religion and less of Methodist polity, everything in the initial and formative period, constant and close supervision is absolutely necessary as a condition of success. Fourth, the present political situation. Japan's transition is not yet complete, Korea's and China's just beginning. Changes fraught with inestimable results to humanity are pending. In this universal flux the churches

need, as never before and as scarcely elsewhere on earth, the best and ablest men to shape and realize the polity and conserve the spiritual interests of our Methodism. Everywhere our earnest and devoted missionaries should have the presence and inspiration of a bishop equal to the demands of this crisis of the Orient.

Granting, then, that Eastern Asia requires more bishops for the proper development and conservation of our work, a pertinent inquiry is, How many bishops? At least one each for Japan, Korea, and China. The cooperating episcopal bodies of Japan employ the entire time of six bishops. They are scholarly, able, picked men, and take and hold high and commanding rank among the people and missionaries of Japan. With our large membership and multiplied institutions and interests, virtually covering the empire from Hokkaido to Formosa, is Japan's prayer for the entire time of one bishop unreasonable? It belittles her achievements and needs, and crucifies her self-respect, to offer her less. But far more important are the considerations of Japan's influence upon the Orient. It is already dominant, and will so remain. It is not yet Christian. The episcopal factor is essential to the maximum of our influence as a Church in bringing Christ to the spiritual leadership of this mighty nation. That Korea should have a bishop may seem less evident. It will be plainer when we consider her present political unrest and her consequent jealousy of Japan; for in any espiscopal copartnership the firm-name most likely would be Japan and Korea, and such an alliance would irritate the Korean mind by reason of the aggressive attitude of Japan. Further, in the event of war with Russia Korea will in all likelihood be its theater and prize. Hence the need and wisdom of giving her the entire time of a bishop capable of guiding, protecting, and developing our Church in the troublous times almost sure to come. But more important still is the well-nigh unparalleled readiness of the people to accept Christianity. There is nothing equal to it, in extent and sincerity, in the Orient. Our Presbyterian brethren propose to send twenty-five new missionaries the current year to reinforce their already splendid body of workers, having made an astonishingly large per cent in Korea of their total gains in missionary fields. Their success and pros-

pects are no better than our own: everywhere grain-burdened districts white unto the harvest. Give Korea the right man for bishop and no investment will pay larger dividends. This leaves China. The only serious question here is, Will one bishop suffice for China's wide empire and teeming millions? If India, under the English flag, with railroads everywhere, requires the undivided services of three bishops, how many should the larger population of pagan China have, with its almost entire absence of railway communication? Moreover, this is China's birthtime. The throes of a new life are upon her. From one viewpoint China seems helpless, from another a resistless army with banners. Despite the encroachments of the Powers she will persist. Uncounted generations have contributed traditions and history to a race-solidarity that cannot be broken. In industrial, mental, and moral qualities no people surpass hers, nor in variety and abundance of material resources. The Gospel leaven alone can transform her; is transforming her. Christianity is here to win its greatest trophies and to have its noblest development. The genius of no Church is better adapted to the characteristics of the Chinese than that of Methodism. Episcopal Methodism is the most virile type. Could our Church realize this, as well as that other overwhelming fact that our own political welfare is bound up with that of China, she would set her episcopal forces in array and give to every section of China the highest quality of undivided episcopal supervision.

II. Thus far, in this discussion, we have had comparatively fair sailing, but in entering upon the question whether the increase shall be in general or in missionary bishops we navigate rougher seas. It is safe to say that the sentiment at home respecting this is no further from unanimity than on the field. Presumably a majority in Japan and Korea favor the missionary episcopacy. In China, Foochow and North China, our only Annual Conferences, have officially declared for a longer trial of the present plan of resident General Superintendents, and instructed their delegates to General Conference to support the same. Hinghua Mission Conference is unanimous for the missionary episcopacy. Central China Mission has not declared in annual meet-

ing; but a majority of the missionaries favor it. West China has not spoken officially. The quadrennial session of the delegated China Central Conference just held—all missions save West China represented—voted eighteen for a longer trial of the present plan to seven for the missionary episcopacy. All conceded the great advantages in having a bishop's entire influence in the Church used for one field, the bishop for India being a striking example. But it was pointed out that this missionary episcopacy was of comparatively recent origin, and succeeded to the magnificent results of the labors of Butler and the missionary host under General Superintendents, and that as a missionary the influence of Thoburn upon the home Church was well-nigh—if not altogether—as great for India as it now is as missionary bishop; and, far beyond anything besides, it was the Sepoy mutiny and the massacre of Cawnpore that first drew the attention and devotion of the Churches to India. And if the incomparable Thoburn was mitered for successes won as a missionary, and Taylor for his unique and unparalleled career as a missionary at home and abroad, it follows—some earnestly contended—that it is yet to be demonstrated that a wholesale change to the missionary episcopacy is demanded by the interests of the foreign field. Moreover, missionary operations in India have had the immense advantage of being carried on under the protection of the mightiest Protestant flag in Christendom. Such also point out that though our work in Eastern Asia never had a missionary bishop, nor the protection of a foreign flag, yet, notwithstanding it has always been resisted by pagan flags and by pagan civilization of immemorial antiquity, it has won its way into the capital of the empire, and into twelve out of eighteen provinces, with chapels and churches, schools and colleges, dispensaries and hospitals; has hundreds of native pastors and thousands of native members, and multiplied thousands of adherents who have been tried, and not found wanting, in the furnace fires of persecution, matching the martyr hosts of Cawnpore with those who died in and for like precious faith at Peking and Tientsin. And as the Sepoy rebellion focused the eyes of Christendom on India, and aroused the enthusiasm that never has flagged, so now the Boxer outbreak

has set China in the red light of the Church's sympathy and devotion and prepared the way for still greater things. Hence these would say, Let well enough alone.

But the most effective arguments urged against the missionary episcopacy were—upon the supposition that the missionary bishop would be chosen from the field—that he could but favor the mission of which he had been a member, that devotion to the mastery of the language would have deprived him of the ability to preach inspiringly in English, that the coming of a General Superintendent brings a gust of home and Church and newest and best thought—thus lifting the missionaries to nobler heights while binding their cause on the hearts and consciences of the homeland; and, chiefly, that if a mistake be made in selecting a missionary bishop—either from the field or from home—it is for life, while the itinerating feature of the General Superintendency would rectify a similar mistake. Each and all of these, with others not recalled, were heard in conversation or on the floor of the China Central Conference at its recent session, and may be accepted as fairly reflecting the minds of those opposed to the missionary episcopacy. That there is force in the arguments must be admitted; and yet, because of his experience during this quadrennium on the field, the writer has been led to believe that the missionary episcopacy reinforced and supplemented, as the Discipline provides, once in four years by a visit from a General Superintendent is best calculated to promote our cause in Eastern Asia.

There are certain indispensable and universal qualifications which should be found in every bishop wherever he serves: a sound body, a well-trained mind, a positive religious experience, an irresistible call to preach the Gospel, and a capacity for Christian leadership. But for local service in the foreign field, in addition to these, other qualifications are imperatively necessary; three in especial: First, thorough familiarity with the racial peculiarities, the habits and customs, and the social, political, and religious institutions, of the people to be served. He who knows what the people believe, how they may be expected to act under different circumstances, what they regard as proper and improper, right and

wrong, their mental and moral idiosyncrasies, has an immense advantage in approaching, instructing, and influencing them. "A stranger will they not follow." Manifestly this is not to be acquired quickly, and never off the field. Without it the greatest learning, sanctity, and zeal yield comparatively slight and imperfect results. Second, and implied in the foregoing, a thorough knowledge of the language. There is an impassable gulf fixed between the teacher and the people to whom he can speak only through an interpreter. Knowing the laws of their thinking and its verbal expression one enters into their holy of holies, speaks soul to soul; but no man is himself through an interpreter. He might be, could he hypnotize his medium and make him to be his *alter ego,* his very self. This being impossible he is limited to the medium's ability and disposition to catch and convey the exact shade of his meaning, upon which at times everything depends. He is abjectly, pitiably, wretchedly, dependent upon another for what that other's best effort can but poorly perform. Moreover, the bishop is the final arbiter in all cases of misunderstanding between the native pastors and missionaries, and presides in the Conference courts and in the Judicial Conferences, the final court of appeal. If he knows the language he can judge for himself of the cause and the evidence and the pleadings, and the native complainant, defendant, or appellant has confidence that the case will be decided on its merits. But if he is dependent upon an interpreter, who sometimes is the defendant as well, in case of adverse decision it is hardly supposable that the native will be satisfied that he has had a fair chance. Only he who, ignorant of the language, has had to hear charges and preside at trials of native preachers can fully appreciate the absolute necessity of such knowledge to safe and satisfactory administration. Besides, his influence with the officials and with the general missionary body, other things being equal, is in proportion to his knowledge and mastery of the language. It may be suggested that the dialects are many, and that one would require an interpreter in every dialect but the one he speaks. Yet in Japan and Korea there is practically but one dialect. In China there are many dialects, and interpreters are necessary, but the written language is the

same and the Mandarin is the official language everywhere. In our own Chinese work it is spoken by more than three fifths of our members and adherents. The ideal language-qualification would, therefore, be met in China by a knowledge of the Mandarin. Third, that perfect acclimatization is essential is too plain to need amplification. While the foregoing are not exhaustive they form a sufficient basis for answering the question, urged now with greater interest than ever, What episcopal supervision is best adapted to our foreign missions?

The qualifications herein enumerated cannot be found outside the missionary ranks. Other things being equal, or approximately equal, there is no comparison in these respects between the missionaries and all others. Among them alone can be found those who know the habits, customs, laws, institutions, and mental and moral characteristics of the respective heathen fields; who are masters of the language, and able to enjoy all the advantages inhering therein; and who are thoroughly inured to the climate. In so far as these positions are well taken it follows, logically, first, that *pari passu* the best material for bishops for the mission fields is to be found among the missionaries thereof respectively: among those of Japan for Japan, of Korea for Korea, of China for China, and so on. It follows, secondly, that these should be *missionary* bishops; for to be made General Superintendents would, by the change of their jurisdictions thus necessitated, not only destroy the continuity of leadership imperatively necessary in the present formative period of the mission fields, but also the conspicuous qualifications set forth above, and which are particular and not general. It follows, thirdly, that for the best results no man should be made missionary bishop for more than one country. A further support of this position is the patent fact of national jealousy, and that the best representation of a field before the home churches is possible only by an undivided man.

Three collateral considerations will close this paper. First: The spirit of this article is favorable to a decided increase in the number of missionary bishops. If such are to receive the same salary as General Superintendents—and if the missionary bishops are to live in the United States of America they would need it—

then a very momentous increase of expense would follow. But if—as the corresponding bishops of other Churches in heathen lands, and as is contemplated of our own—our missionary bishops live with their brethren on their respective fields the much lower cost of living would make a smaller salary practically equal to the nominally larger home salaries. Indeed, a man of great wisdom and experience as a missionary contends that a missionary bishop should receive exactly the same salary that he would receive as a missionary, the only difference being in the necessarily increased allowance for traveling and office expenses.* This would certainly eliminate the secular element from any contest for the office; the honor itself making the office worthy all proper ambition. But this is wholly in the hands of the Missionary Society, to whom it safely can be left. Whatever it costs, the writer believes it would be cheap at the price. Second: How can the General Conference be sure of selecting the right missionaries for missionary bishops? Where there is, as in India and China, a Central Conference this might be permitted to express its judgment. To this the General Conference could add reliable information from all sources personally conversant with the situation. A

* The following are his exact words: "Among the reasons which favor a missionary episcopacy the question of salary needs consideration. The basis of salary for the bishops in the United States is fixed upon the cost of living in one of the large centers of population and upon the salaries paid to pastors of leading churches of our denomination. The salaries paid by churches to their pastors are determined by the financial ability of the membership, and are often an index of the large responsibility resting upon the recipient. On the mission field, however, the salary for all missionaries is based upon a liberal allowance to furnish the necessities of life, and is uniform. Men of expensive education receive no more or no less than those poorly equipped; those in places of great responsibility and heavy burdens are on the same footing as those who hold subsidiary places. Missionary salary is only support, and is uniform for all. This is the only principle upon which missionary societies can administer their funds and avoid heartbreaking discriminations. It would seem reasonable that the salary of a missionary bishop elected from among his fellow-workers should remain on the same basis as before his election. There can be no good reason assigned for a change of salary from a missionary basis to a home basis, for the missionary bishop is elected for the purpose of continuing his work on the same field and in the same surroundings as when he was an ordinary missionary. If a support was guaranteed him as a missionary he should expect no more as a missionary bishop; for several of his missionaries in places of eminent service receive only their support. Whatever allowance is needed for traveling expenses, secretarial work, or for any other purpose connected with his office, should be allowed to a missionary bishop, so that he should not be placed at any disadvantage, as compared with others, by being obliged to use money for his work which was intended for his support. This allowance for support to the missionary bishop should be paid by the Missionary Society, and not from the Episcopal Fund; as it is important that even in this matter there should be no distinction between a missionary bishop and a missionary worker. The same basis of support, paid from the same source, should be the rule for all on the field as missionary or as missionary bishop."

decision prayerfully based on these would always be reasonably safe. Third: To the incomparable advantages of the missionary episcopacy would be added those resulting from the quadrennial visitation of the General Superintendent, as the Discipline provides. In selecting the visitor let the decision turn solely on ability to advance the work. Then the General Superintendent's coming will be awaited on every field with increasing interest and desire. He will be the final referee in many serious differences of opinion as to men and measures, and to native pastor and missionary bishop alike he will be God's answer to earnest prayer, a mighty inspiration and blessing. Arrange in connection with his visitation a quadrennial Bishops' Conference, over which he shall preside, composed of the missionary bishops of this great field, in which there shall be a careful comparison of methods and views as to policy, administration, etc., and you have the writer's conception of some of the best attainable conditions for the efficient episcopal administration of our work in Eastern Asia.

An Approximation in Tabular Form.

| | MISSIONARY BISHOPS. | | | General Superintend-ents. |
QUALIFICATION.	Chosen from the Field.	Chosen from other Mission Fields.	Chosen from Home.	
Basal—common to all: Health, education, leadership, call, spirituality....................	100	100	100	100
Acclimatization....................	100	75	50	50
Familiarity (knowledge and acquaintance) with country, habits, and peculiarities and religions of the people, and with the general missionary body and work..	95 (practical)	35 (mixed)	20 (theoretical)	20 (theoretical)
Knowledge of language and consequent ability to administer justly to the native Christians and preachers....................	85	25	10	10
Probable ability to administer impartially as between the several missions of his field.............	70	90	90	90
Inspiration of episcopal visits.....	60	65	75	90
Influence upon the home churches for the special field	100	100	100	$\frac{x}{y}$ say 80
Average....................	87.1	70	63.5	68.2

David H. Moore.

Art. II.—THE CRITICAL DOCTRINES OF WORDSWORTH
AND COLERIDGE.

The summer and autumn of 1797 was a rich seed-time for
English literature. It was a happy conjunction, indeed, that set
Wordsworth and Coleridge, each at the full throb of poetic inspiration, side by side in the midst of the lovely Quantock hills,
by the shore of the sea, and ordained for them the companionship
of Dorothy. One loves to picture to oneself these three dedicated
spirits, replete with youth and strength and aglow with inspiration, as they indulged in high converse and noble dreams during
that memorable year at Alfoxden, near Nether Stowey. Dorothy,
no less a poet than her companions, was an attuning medium. Innocent as a child, delicately responsive to the most exquisite spiritual suggestions of nature, and untainted by that "something that
infects the world," she "maintained" as well for Coleridge as for
Wordsworth "a saving intercourse with his true self." We shall
never cease to regret that she failed to record in her charming
journal the conversations that took place between Coleridge and
her brother. What intercourse must that have been! Here, if
ever, were to be found "plain living and high thinking." Unlike
as they were in temper and habits, the two poets found in each
other's company a wholesome stimulus whereby the genius of each
was quickened into unwonted activity. On all deep questions of
thought and life they were of one mind, but their talk ran mostly
on poetry and nature. Both were fresh from creative works of
high order; the imagination of each was teeming with new ideas,
to be shaped later into still more perfect forms of art; and they
were alike in ardent and restless search for first principles upon
which to ground their poetic practice.

What this early intimacy meant between the poets who were
soon to prove themselves the greatest men of their generation, their
contemporaries little guessed. It was hinted by their neighbors
that they were conspirators; and, these hints finding their way
to the government authorities, a spy was sent down into the Quantock hills to search out the mischief. True it was that they were

plotting against the established order, but the conspiracy was such as no flesh-and-blood spy could ever fathom. It was one, rather that the shade of an Addison or a Pope might more fitly have been invoked to ferret out and thwart; for these rebels were in arms against prescription and authority in the realms of poetry, and not against temporal kings and potentates. And indeed the time was ripe for such a revolt. Poetry had temporarily lost its divine and inspired quality. Men had forgotten their birthright, and were feeding upon husks. They had abdicated consciously the high places of passion, and had made themselves aliens from all that is truest in nature and most vital in life. It was as if the nation had become petrified in all but its reasoning faculties. In morals, in manners, in religion, in literature, the desirable thing was conformity, moderation, repression. The emotional nature was held in stern subjection to reason. Common sense fed fat while imagination languished at the outer gate. Above all things men sought accuracy, correctness, urbanity, and polish. Enthusiasm was unpardonable, in however noble or just a cause, while grace, suavity, elegant compliance were deemed adequate to cover a multitude of sins. The appeal was always from the present to the past; from individual taste to social custom; from warm confident impulse to the reasoned prescription of art. Poetry drew its ideals from classical rather than Gothic or romantic models, and, chiefly, from these models as colored and modified by the French temper and treatment. In the year 1800, in connection with the second edition of "Lyrical Ballads," Wordsworth published the now famous Preface in which he set forth—in narrow limits but emphatic manner—his poetic creed. His fundamental thesis is that poetry should give immediate pleasure; and he bases this statement upon the philosophical truth that "we have no sympathy but what is propagated by pleasure." But he, of all poets, invariably wrote with a purpose; that purpose being to teach, to inspire, to suggest moral ideals. Now, how shall we connect and justify two such apparently diverse statements? How is it possible for a poet to assert that pleasure is the legitimate end of poetry, and then straightway invite the reader into the rocky and strenuous paths of didactic and ethical endeavor?

Wordsworth was a philosopher and an optimist. He believed in an ultimate spiritual reality in the constitution of which are imbedded the laws of truth, beauty, and goodness; and he believed that this reality, revealing itself alike in the world of nature and in the heart of man, always seeks beneficent and harmonious expression. Believing, thus, that a great and good spirit is unceasingly at work creating universal forms of beauty, bringing order out of chaos and light out of darkness, and shaping all things, whether cosmic or human, in accordance with eternal laws of truth and righteousness, Wordsworth justly concluded that man ought to rejoice in the spirit of life that is in him. He believed it to be the function of poetry to image man and nature, and he believed that pleasure would inevitably result from doing this truthfully. The poet is one who rejoices in his own volition and passions, who contemplates with delight the exhibition of similar volitions and passions in the ongoings of the universe about him, and who, where he fails to find such expressions of power and beauty, is habitually impelled to create them for himself. By virtue of his finer sensibilities, more ardent enthusiasms, and greater comprehensiveness of soul it becomes his delight to quicken the minds of less gifted men; to suggest to them lofty visions; to solicit them from sordid and vicious emotions to the true sources of feeling within and about them; in short, to apprise them of their spiritual birthright and awake in them "the vision and the faculty divine." But how shall this be done? How shall he proceed rationally to awaken pleasurable emotions of this higher order in the minds of his fellow-men? Certainly not merely or chiefly by recourse to meretricious splendors of diction and style. How then? Wordsworth would reply that the chief pleasure to be imparted by the poet must flow from springs of truth and beauty that take their rise far back in the heart of reality. Men must be led to see that the capabilities of pleasurable excitement inhere in the common and familiar scenes and incidents of daily life. Let the poet cease to gratify the depraved taste of a jaded and besotted generation with extravagant stories dealing with extraordinary incidents and outrageous situations; and let him realize that the simple joys and woes of men, the present and familiar scenes and

actions in which the lowliest habitually engage, are adequate, when presented with truth and vigor, to arouse emotions as profound as life, as high as heaven, and to inspire "thoughts that do often lie too deep for tears." By revealing ordinary and familiar things in new and startling aspects—just as we sometimes see an unattractive landscape transfigured into romantic beauty by a glint of moonlight or by the sudden radiance of the setting sun as it bursts out after a day of gloom—the poet will lead men to revere the divinity that stirs within and about them; will induce them to read their condition in the light of the spirit instead of in the lurid and baleful glare of debased lusts and passions; and will influence taste and morals to substitute for coarse and pernicious stimulants the wholesome and simple delights that, in the nature of things, the world is well adapted to supply and the soul of man richly to enjoy.

But if, on the one hand, legitimate poetic pleasure is to be derived from the portrayal of familiar things under the spiritualizing touch of imagination, it is, on the other hand, to be derived in still higher measure by tracing in the experiences of the lowly the primary laws of human nature, especially "as regards the manner in which we associate ideas in a state of excitement." Wordsworth sought to redeem for poetic treatment what had hitherto been thought the waste places of human experience, and in pursuance of this end he showed in various ways that no soil capable of supporting a primal affection or a universal instinct could be considered as lacking in artistic possibilities or beneath the notice of enlightened minds. "Of genius," says Wordsworth, "the only proof is the act of doing well what is worthy to be done and what was never done before; of genius in the fine arts the only infallible sign is the widening of the sphere of human sensibility for the delight, honor, and benefit of human nature. Genius is the introduction of a new element into the intellectual universe; or, if that be not allowed, it is the application of powers to objects on which they had not before been exercised or the employment of them in such a manner as to produce effects hitherto unknown. What is all this but an advance, or a conquest, made by the soul of the poet?" Was it not just this that Wordsworth himself

achieved when he gave universal and enduring interest to such unpromising incidents and emotions as those depicted in "The Forsaken Indian," "We Are Seven," "Resolution and Independence," "The Brothers," "Michael," "Two April Mornings," "The Fountain," and "Poor Susan's Reverie"? Wordsworth would insist that poetry should draw its subject-matter chiefly from the characters, incidents, and passions of people in humble or rustic life. He believed that in that condition the essential passions of men fix themselves more firmly in the virgin soil of healthy, primal instinct; that, freed from unnatural restraint, they find here their most favorable development, and consequently utter themselves with becoming vigor and freedom; that the elementary feelings reveal themselves in greater simplicity, so that they may be more readily observed as well as more accurately communicated; that the social manners springing from such direct and primary feelings, and coming to perfection amid rural surroundings, are more easily understood and more uniform and enduring; that the sentiments and passions of humanity first drawing the breath of life amid the pure and sublime scenes of nature, and ever mingling with these as they strengthen and mature, becoming like what they feed on, will take to themselves something of the freedom of the winds, the calm of the sky, and the majesty of the hills; and, finally, that such regular and repeated experiences as result from such an environment will give rise to a language more direct and stable than could otherwise be developed, and hence better adapted to reach the heart of man in all ages and in all climes.

As early as 1798, in his brief advertisement to the first edition of "Lyrical Ballads," Wordsworth plainly apprises the public that the majority of the poems are to be considered as experiments; his desire being "to ascertain how far the language of conversation in the middle and lower classes of society is adapted to the purposes of poetic pleasure." He purposed, of course, to free this language from provincialisms, and whatever elements might rationally seem to induce permanent dislike or disgust, but the language of men in rustic life, thus purified, he maintains, ought to be adopted, "because such men hourly communicate with

the best objects from which the best part of language is originally derived, and because, from their rank in society and the sameness and narrow circle of their intercourse, being less under the action of social vanity, they convey their feelings and notions in simple and unelaborated expressions." He could not endure the inane and glittering phraseology—the unreality—of the poetry then in vogue, and in three or four particulars he not only deliberately deviates from but vigorously combats the prevailing practice. He issues notice that, as the personification of abstract ideas is something that never occurs in the flesh-and-blood language of life except when prompted by passion, he will use the figure rarely, and then only because so prompted. What is ordinarily known as "poetic diction" he also repudiates, for the reason that he desires to bring his language as near as possible to the real language of men, and because he proposes to give pleasure of a new kind— that, namely, which ought to arise when such scenes and incidents as come home to men's "business and bosoms" are depicted with vivid truthfulness and reality. He goes a step farther, even, and discards a large class of expressions, in themselves accurate and beautiful, but so degraded by reason of their adoption by inferior poets as to render them irretrievably distasteful on account of their associations, and, finally, he enunciates the extreme and hostile doctrine that "there neither is nor can be any essential difference between the language of prose and metrical composition." How is it possible, he asks, that it should not be so? Is there not the strictest affinity between the language of verse and the language of prose? Do they not draw their lifeblood from the same sources, utter themselves through the same organs, and appeal to the same objects? Will not the passion, if just and noble, indicate the choice of such language as will raise the composition above coarseness and vulgarity, and will not this language, with meter superadded, and with such fresh and lively figures as will spring naturally from the passion, be enough to gratify a rational mind? How is any other distinction possible? Surely we would not have the poet deviate from the natural language of men when speaking through the mouths of his characters, and for him, when writing in his own person under the impulse of high passion, to introduce

any arbitrary splendors of diction would be to quench the light of heaven with rhetorical skyrockets. With respect to meter our feeling is different from what it is toward other artificial devices in poetry. The distinction produced by what is called "poetic diction" is arbitrary and capricious, so that one is never sure what outrage upon taste a poet will commit. But the distinction of meter is regular and uniform, and both reader and author voluntarily accept its spell because the experience of all ages has shown that it heightens the pleasure of its concomitant emotion. Nor is it true that meter affords an insignificant part of the pleasure to be derived from poetry. For, since it is the end of poetry to produce excitement in conjunction with an overbalance of pleasure, and since excitement is an irregular state of mind in which ideas and emotions do not succeed each other in usual order, and since under these circumstances the words and images employed are so deeply saturated with passion as to agitate the mind almost to the degree of pain, the accompaniment of something fixed and habitual with which the mind has previously been acquainted will prove efficacious in restraining and modifying the emotion that might otherwise be too violent or painful. At least, Wordsworth thinks, extremely pathetic and painful sentiments and situations can be more properly rendered in meter, and especially in rhyme, than in prose.

The publication of the famous Preface of 1800 marks a turning point in English literature. Ordained for such a juncture, and with the apostolic fervor of a John the Baptist, Wordsworth appeared among the poets of his generation exhorting them to make straight paths for their feet. To be sure, much contained in the Preface was wide of the mark, much was so self-evident that it had never been disputed, and not a little had been said or implied before. But, granting all this, it is impossible to overlook the fact that it was Wordsworth who set the poets of England once more upon the firm highway of truth and nature, and himself led them to the sunlit summits of song. However self-evident some of the principles for which Wordsworth so vigorously contended, they were almost universally sinned against or ignored; and if in some instances he went

13

too far, in his zeal and indignation, we must not forget what the provocation was. Nor is it true, alone, that he stands, as a matter of history, at the turning of the ways, and that he gave deliberate and energetic utterance to opinions contrary to those almost universally in vogue in his day; he uttered vital and timely truths with such vigor, freshness, and convincing sanity as to set them quite apart from anything of a philosophical character that had hitherto been written upon English verse. In the development of literary criticism he occupies a sure and distinguished place, and his criticism affords an important commentary upon his own poetry. He admits us to his spiritual laboratory and reveals the process by which his poems came to life, and we come to study even the least successful of his productions with keener and more catholic sympathy. Poems that we had hitherto deemed obscure, mean, or trivial, to our surprise assume new dignity and meaning; and if we cannot agree that the poet is right in the estimates he makes concerning some of his most disputed productions we at least learn that he never indulges in idle words or empty thought. One needs but to read his great poems—those that we now consider immortal—to find ample refutation of what was false and mistaken in his doctrine, and surely we are not sorry that his poetic practice sometimes happily belies his critical principles. When he leaves the solid element of criticism, as he often does, to soar with rapturous and unpremeditated art into untraveled and resplendent regions of pure song we rejoice that he has wings as well as feet, and that it is his function to cleave the ether rather than to tread the earth. His poetry speaks a higher language than his creed, and the inconsistencies and limitations of the latter are to be resolved and supplemented by the former. He recognized the essential laws that govern the poet's art—he knew that the subject-matter of a poem must be chosen judiciously, that the language must be selected with reference to the passion to be depicted or the scene to be described, and that the language is to be modified by the "consideration that he describes for a particular purpose, that of giving pleasure"—yet because of a certain inherent harshness and inflexibility of temper he often seemed destitute of taste in the application of these emi-

nently sound and illuminating poetic principles; while on the other hand, as we have seen, when truly inspired he ignores all his favorite rules, and urged by an impulse from within utters sublime and burning truths with a blended ease and dignity as peculiar, as superior, and as distinctive as the Andes or the aurora borealis. No wonder he perplexed his early critics. He was unable to realize that his creed was faulty, and that some of his verse was hopelessly deficient in merit, while they, to their everlasting disgrace, were not able to sift the wheat from the chaff and discern the essential genius of the man who had come with a commission the execution of which was destined to gladden the wilderness and the solitary place and to make the desert blossom as the rose.

Wordsworth's influence upon the development of literary criticism has been incalculable. No mind at once so sane and so inspired, so gifted with spiritual insight and so strong and self-sufficient, had, up to his time, busied itself with the philosophic aspects of literature. In him the poetic and the philosophic temperaments were almost perfectly blended; and while his critical writing is all too meager it is in quality worthy of such a type of genius. Indeed, some of his dicta concerning poetry and the relation of poetry to life are adequate, universal, and final. But we must not forget the part that Coleridge played in this intellectual conflict. Indeed, it is hardly possible that we should be able to do so, since all that is of vital interest in the thought of the two poets was generically as well as historically related. It is true that the opinions of Wordsworth and Coleridge as to a new poetic creed were not so much in unison as we are accustomed to think, nor, for that matter, as they themselves thought up to the time that the Preface of 1800 was published. In a letter addressed to Mr. Sotheby, July 13, 1802, speaking of Wordsworth, Coleridge says: "I must set you right with regard to my perfect coincidence with his poetic creed. It is most certain that the heads of our mutual conversations, etc., and the passages, were indeed partly taken from notes of mine; for it was at first intended that the Preface should be written by me. And it is likewise true that I warmly accord with Words-

worth in his abhorrence of these poetic licenses, as they are called, which are indeed mere tricks of convenience and laziness. . . . In my opinion, every phrase, every metaphor, every personification, should have its justifying cause in some passion either of the poet's mind or of the characters described by the poet. But meter itself implies a passion, that is, a state of excitement in the poet's mind, and is expected, in part, of the reader; and though I stated this to Wordsworth, and he has in some sort stated it in his Preface, yet he has not done justice to it, nor has he, in my opinion, sufficiently answered it. In my opinion, poetry justifies as poetry, independent of any other passion, some new combinations of language and commands the omission of many others allowable in other compositions. Now Wordsworth, *me saltem judice,* has in his system not sufficiently admitted the former, and in his practice has too frequently sinned against the latter. Indeed, we have had lately some little controversy on the subject, and we begin to suspect that there is somewhere or other a radical difference in our opinions." Writing to Southey, July 9, 1802, he alludes to the same subject again as follows: "But I will apprise you of one thing, that although Wordsworth's Preface is half a child of my own brain, and arose out of conversations so frequent that, with few exceptions, we could scarcely either of us, perhaps, positively say which first started any particular thought, . . . I rather suspect that somewhere or other there is a radical difference in our theoretical opinions respecting poetry; this I shall endeavor to go to the bottom of, and, acting the arbitrator between the old school and the new school, hope to lay down some plain and perspicuous, though not superficial, Canons of Criticism respecting poetry." This promise he at last made good in his *Biographia Literaria,* published in 1817, and nowhere, perhaps, does he find fitter play for his critical powers than in this special criticism of Wordsworth's poetry. For keen analysis and just appreciation nothing written on Wordsworth has ever equaled it. It will always remain invaluable. In method and temper alike it is philosophic and satisfying. Wordsworth needed to be saved from himself and his theory, as well as from incompetent critics, and this adventure Coleridge undertook and accomplished with chivalric

competency and address. In the interest of art and truth alike
it was important that the controversy should come to an end, and
Coleridge was correct in his conviction that it remained for him
to strike the last strong and decisive blow. It was he who pointed
out, once for all, that the defects of Wordsworth's poetry are insignificant compared with its beauties; that such blemishes as do
exist are due to the defects of the poet's theory rather than to any
flaw in his genius; and that the essential force and grandeur of
the poet's inspired personality, first or last, illuminates every page
that he wrote with

the gleam,
The light that never was on sea or land,
The consecration and the poet's dream.

The reputation of Coleridge as a critic does not, however,
rest alone upon his special estimates of poets like Shakespeare,
Milton, and Wordsworth, philosophic and suggestive as these estimates are. He enunciated critical principles of absolute value.
There might be set down upon this page a series of brilliant and
profound detached utterances sufficient to furnish out a little critic
for life. At the beginning of the nineteenth century how refreshing must have been such expressions as the following: "Nothing
can permanently please which does not contain in itself the reason
why it is so and not otherwise." "To admire on principle is the
only way to imitate without loss of originality." "Not the poem
which we have read, but that to which we return with the greatest
pleasure, possesses the genuine power and claims the name of
essential poetry." "Poetry is the blossom and the fragrancy of
all human knowledge, human thoughts, human passions, emotions,
language." "The ultimate end of criticism is much more to establish the principles of writing than to furnish rules how to pass
judgment on what has been written by others, if indeed it were
possible that the two should be separated." "He who tells me that
there are defects in a new work tells me nothing that I should not
have taken for granted without his information. But he who
points out and elucidates the beauties of an original work does
indeed give me interesting information, such as experience would
not have authorized me in anticipating." "A poem is that species

of composition which is opposed to works of science by proposing
for its immediate object pleasure, not truth; and from all other
species (having this object in common with it) it is discriminated
by proposing to itself such delight from the whole as is compatible
with a distinct gratification from each component part." Evidently Coleridge in his thinking penetrated to the heart of things.
He could not satisfy himself with their surface aspect or with
unrelated facts. He invariably sought to ground his principles
in nature, and to conform his practice to reality and truth. He
was no less original than Wordsworth; and he not only accepted
the great poetic truths that are characteristic of Wordsworth, and
that must always be associated with his name, but equally with
Wordsworth he deserves the credit of disclosing and propagating
these truths. What now needs to be emphasized still more strongly
is the fact that he rather than Wordsworth gave adequate and philosophical expression to the essential views of poetry which they
held in common, that the poetic creed evolved jointly under their
hands surpassed in philosophic value anything that had appeared
in English literature up to that time, and that it remains a permanent contribution of absolute value in the realm of literary
criticism.

Frank C. Lockwood.

Art. III.—HERDER AND RELIGIOUS THOUGHT.*

GOETHE, writing of recent events in Weimar, mentioned Herder as preaching like a god. Although the greatest of his listeners, the poet was not the only one of them to acknowledge their pastor's extraordinary power to illuminate and to persuade. Herder, however, was always loth to publish his sermons; he knew, like every great preacher, that the printed sermon is only dried foliage from which the life has escaped; and he had no love for the pressed leaves of his own rich mind. The sermons now extant are productions either of an earlier period or of some special occasion, so that we have no means of knowing just what Goethe referred to; whether the preacher's sweep and splendor of thought or his personal charm. Of the latter the poet has given us a vivid and almost startling description in his *Wahrheit und Dichtung;* the former we must construct from Herder's voluminous writings.

All these writings, though, are printed speech. Herder was essentially a talking genius; yet a talker moved more by the necessity of self-expression than by the desire to instruct; more by the disposition to compel his reader than to encourage him to independent thought. And especially in his theological writings does the whole man appear; not only *Geist und Vernunft und Verstand* but *Herz und Gemüth.*† His "Letters to Preachers," for example, were a fiery protest against reducing Christianity to a bare morality and the pastoral office to mere state service. The pastor should be *der Redner Gottes,* whose calling is to nourish faith and hope and love in the hearts of his flock; he is to speak to them, out of a soul transfigured by God's presence, not the formulas of a frozen orthodoxy or the propositions of a frigid rationalism but the latest news from God, the message divinely given to him for them in their time of need and opportunity. This view of the pastor's calling led Herder himself to a study of the Bible according to the law of his own soul. He brought to the

---

* An address delivered at the Herder celebration of the German Department of Northwestern University, Evanston, Ill.

† These five words have no exact equivalents in English, to which fact may be traced much misunderstanding of German thought.

Scriptures a sympathetic mind and a heart unchilled and unperverted; he gave the writers of the Bible a chance, as he had given Homer and Shakespeare a chance, to make their own impression. In this he resembled every great thinker who has shaped the thought of the world touching God's revelation of himself—Paul, Origen, Augustine, Luther, Pascal, Wesley; who never approach the sacred scriptures of mankind as analysts and critics merely, least of all the Christian Scriptures. To Herder the Bible was a great historical product; the fruitage of generations of life. Deeds, events, are the soil from which the teaching springs as God's blessings out of rich ground. This fruitage is, to be sure, the outcome of the narrow national Jewish existence, the history of a fraction only of the human family, but it grows out of that fraction of it from which the Western world has derived its religion. Christianity is here, and it has brought these Scriptures with it; and these have influenced every crisis in its development, and in the development of modern Europe. This life, this history, from which our religion has come, can of course be understood thoroughly only in connection with the large human life of which it is a part. All forms of light are forms of the same radiant energy, diverse though they be. Even so all forms of religion are forms of the same divine energy, diverse though they be. The candle that was quenched by the rising sun, says Shakespeare, shone upon the darkness of a naughty world and only a fool speaks slightingly of its beams. And so with these feebler religions of mankind; not the meanest of them must be disdained. Herder thus led the way, or, to speak more carefully, was the chief of those that led the way to the study of all religions in their essence and in their relations to each other; he grasped, as no one had done since the days of St. Paul, the fact that the whole world, not Israel only, had knowledge of the law of God; the law, to use Paul's beautiful phrase, "the law that is written on man's heart."

The rationalists that followed Descartes had hunted for God in the individual reason; they had failed to find him in the shallow pool; and Kant at last showed why. Reason must remain forever in the phenomenal world. True, so far as conduct is involved we cannot get along without God, and what pure reason

may not do is permitted therefore to the practical reason; the principles of knowledge and the principles of conduct are different things. Now, to Herder, this was splitting up the soul only to glue the parts together again. God must be searched for not merely in the reason of the individual but in the whole man, and not only in man but in humanity; nature must be regarded as something sublimer than a vast coexistence of multitudinous and multifarious phenomena; it must be studied as a glorious procession of appearances; nature and humanity, the chief splendor of it, are in perpetual evolution; in this evolution, if anywhere, we shall touch the hem of God's garment. "The God whom I seek in history," Herder wrote, "must be the same as the God in nature; for man is only a small part of the universe, and his history, like that of the grub, is closely interwoven with the cell in which he lives. In this history all the laws of nature operate; so far from setting them aside, God reveals himself *in them,* in their mighty power, with a beauty unchanging, wise, and beneficent. And as God reveals himself in nature and in history so does he also reveal himself in the impulses of the individual. A beneficent Spirit watches within us, awakening our slumbering powers, saving us from excess and punishing the misuse of our energy. Call it reason, conscience, anything you please; the wise have always recognized it as the voice of God. This impulse has been evoked in many places and in divers manners; in Christianity it is aroused by awakening love." We understand then, according to Herder, both the Bible and Christianity more thoroughly if we penetrate to the significance of the literature of the world and of the religious life of all mankind. Christianity is that to which these all point and in which all the spiritual longings of humanity are realized.

Schiller's famous line, "Nimmer, das glaubt mir, erscheinen die Götter nimmer allein,"* leaps to memory with the thought of Herder and his contemporaries. Lessing was his older and Goethe was his younger brother; and they shared with him this view of history and of revelation. We know also from his own words that he felt himself akin to Wesley, the English preacher, and had he

* "Never, believe me, never appear the gods alone."

lived a few years longer he would have been drawn to Wordsworth, the English poet; to the preacher because of his recognition of the will of God in the deep of the human soul, and to the poet because of his splendid interpretations of the will of God in nature and in human life. Each of these was a mystic, and so was Herder. To him as to Wordsworth there were hours

> When the light of sense
> Goes out, but with a flash that has revealed
> The invisible world.

He too could see a glimpse of God's bright face

> When on some gilded cloud or flower
> His gazing soul would dwell an hour
> And in those weaker glories spy
> Some shadow of eternity.

But Herder went farther than any of these, and in going farther anticipated the thought that has dominated these recent decades, the historical conception of nature, of life, of humanity—the tremendous thought of evolution; and this saved Herder from a purely natural theology. For he saw that nations as well as individuals have their peculiar endowments; that as the Greeks were the more artistic so the Hebrews were the more religious people, and this too by a divine arrangement. His *Archæology of the Hebrews* combined the result of his researches in the early history of poetry and in the origins of religion. In the first chapter of Genesis he detected, so he thought, a national religious poem; to treat it as dogma seemed to him contrary to taste and to reason. The prophet is indeed taught of God; this poem is not human but divine, not an oriental myth, but a revelation from above.

He pursued this subject farther in his famous *Spirit of Hebrew Poesy.* Perhaps no single work has done so much as this one to transform conceptions of the Old Testament. It opened the way to the beauty of these remarkable writings and to the discovery of their sources. Herder, though, was not satisfied to know these things and to write splendidly and discursively about them. He was eager to reconcile culture and Christianity, and especially eager to teach theological students how to unite "Serious Christian thought with genuine humanity, freedom of inquiry with reverence for the Bible, and a fine sense of the value of

antiquity with a clear recognition of the needs of the hour." And
as he sought to reform preaching so he sought also to reform religious teaching and religious song.   Unfortunately, he lacked
serenity; his nature was full of energy and fire and fight; and
Goethe's description of him shows us how physical suffering had
rendered him irritable and moody and mistrustful and capricious.
He lacked too—and this was the greatest misfortune—he lacked
the architectonic faculty; the genius that takes infinite pains,
that works steadily upon a masterpiece until it stands complete for
all time.   He resembled Michael Angelo in the multitude and
sublimity of his plans; he was like him also in the multitude of
his unfinished undertakings.

As he thought more profoundly and studied more widely he
drew closer to Lessing and became enraptured with Spinoza.   The
idea of humanity possessed him and penetrated all his thinking.
The law of spiritual evolution took distinct shape in his mind and
Christianity appeared to him as the revelation of a perfect humanity.   Christ, the Son of man, was at once the flower of antiquity
and the seed of the future; the Bible became in his thought the
archives of the method of the divine revelation.   Four of his
weightiest essays expound this view of Christianity.   They are
astonishing productions; astonishing for their insight and their
eloquence; astonishing even more for their *prolepsis;* that is, for
their anticipation of the main currents of future thought in Germany and in Europe.   The student who masters these, whether he
accepts or rejects their teaching, need never again inquire what
are the essential and permanent elements of Christianity.   Two
of these essays, "The Redeemer of Mankind according to the Three
First Gospels" and "The Son of God the Saviour of the World,"
were the heralds of modern New Testament criticism, and have
been quite properly designated as the beginnings of the vast literature upon the Life of Jesus.   The historian of theology, as he
recognizes the nearness of the Man of Nazareth to the modern
world in its painting, its poetry, its music, in its ethical ideals
and in its religious conceptions, may well stand with bared head
at the grave of this man of sorrows who suffered at Weimar so
keenly while he worked so restlessly to recover for humanity the

Redeemer of mankind and the Saviour of the world. The same historian comparing the Jesus of Herder with the Jesus of Harnack, for instance, sees that the conception of each portrait is essentially the same. Harnack, like Herder a mystic, paints from ampler critical knowledge, and paints more tranquilly; but a hundred years of critical investigation have established only the more firmly Herder's belief that, if Jesus is to be depicted at all, all our knowledge of him must be corrected and transfused with love.

It remains to say a few words touching Herder's famous dialogues about Spinoza; dialogues that he entitled with curt and compelling energy, GOTT. The German people are profoundly religious, not in any narrow but in the most comprehensive sense, and their religious feeling is deeply rooted and continually replenished by their love of nature. Ancient chronicler and modern poet, ancient hero and modern soldier, ancient bard and modern thinker bow their heads and listen awe-struck to the crashing loom upon which are woven the garments of God. Woden, the Storm-god, the leader of souls, who rushed through the air with the spirits of the departed, became, naturally enough, for our German forefathers the god of knowledge and of poesy, the giver of victory and of all good. Wolfram von Eschenbach accords the Holy Grail to Parsifal, the child abandoned by his mother who grew up in the solitude of the forest and who bewailed the birds that fell before his bow. It was amid the trees of Thuringia as they bent before the storm and trembled to the thunderbolt that Martin Luther fell prostrate, crying, "Help me, St. Anna! I promise to become a monk." Schiller in his *Götter Griechenlands*, bemoaned the vanished days:

> Wo jetzt nur, wie unsere Weisen sagen,
> Seelenlos ein Feuerball sich dreht,
> Lenkte damals seinen goldnen Wagen
> Helios in stiller Majestät.
> Diese Höhen füllten Oreaden
> Eine Dryas starb mit jenem Baum;
> Aus den Urnen lieblicher Najaden
> Sprang der Ströme Silberschaum.*

* "Where now, as our sages tell us, only a ball of fire is rolling lifeless on its axis, there of old Helios in quiet majesty drove his golden wagon. These heights were in those days thronged with Oreads; a Dryad died with yonder tree, from the urns of lovely Naiads sprang, silver-foaming, the mountain streams."

And Wordsworth, Saxon that he was, utters the same lament in his daring outcry,

> Great God! I'd rather be
> A pagan suckled on a creed outworn
> So might I, standing on this pleasant lea,
> Have glimpses that would make me less forlorn;
> Have sight of Proteus rising from the sea
> Or hear old Triton blow his wreathed horn.

Now Herder's studies of Hebrew poetry, his intimate acquaintance with the teaching of Jesus and of Paul, united with this primitive German reverence for nature, this primitive and enduring recognition of the seen-unseen, to make the study of Spinoza an epoch in his intellectual life. For in the tranquil mirror of Spinoza's mind he saw an image of God grander and more beautiful than he had found in any modern thinker. His essay enchanted Weimar and intoxicated Goethe. The latter wrote in rapture:

> Was wär ein Gott, der nur von aussen stiesse
> Im Kreis das All am Finger laufen liesse!
> Ihm ziemt's die Welt im Innern zu bewegen
> Sich in Natur, Natur in sich zu hegen,
> So dass, was in Ihm lebt und webt und ist
> Nie seine Kraft, nie seinen Geist vermisst.*

Well, Herder knew that a Soul of the world shaping it from within is just as human a conception as that of an Almighty outsider who keeps it spinning with his finger. He said, rightly enough, "I do not understand your phrase 'outside the world.' Outside the world means nowhere. A God living outside the world lives nowhere." But he said also "God is not the world, and the world is not God; of this there can be no doubt. When we speak of God we must forget our notions of space and time, else our best efforts will be fruitless." Let us, he adds, detect and disclose the laws of nature without bothering ourselves about the place of God's residence or about his particular purposes. "Whoever can show us the laws of nature, how all creation, animate and inanimate—minerals, plants, animals, men—originates necessarily and according to the coworking of forces in such organs as they acquire, would promote a nobler admiration and reverence

---

* "What were a God who could touch the universe from outside only to keep it spinning with his finger? It beseems the Eternal to move the world from within, he abiding in nature and nature abiding in him, so that whatever breathes and weaves and has a being never lacks his force, never lacks his mind and soul."

for God than one who preaches to us God's cabinet secrets, telling us that our feet are to walk with, our eyes to see with, and other such marvelous discoveries."

It is interesting and instructive to compare these words with the utterances of an older contemporary never to my knowledge named in connection with Herder, the great New England theologian Jonathan Edwards. "Absolute sovereignty," he writes, "is what I love to ascribe to God. . . . His excellency, his wisdom, his purity, and love seemed to appear in everything; in the sun, and moon, and stars; in the clouds and blue sky; in the grass, flowers, trees; in the water, and all nature. . . . I often used to sit and view the moon for continuance; and in the day spent much time in viewing the clouds and sky, to behold the sweet glory of God in these things. . . . And scarce anything, among all the works of nature, was so sweet to me as thunder and lightning. . . . I felt God, so to speak, at the first appearance of a thunderstorm; and used . . . to fix myself in order to view the clouds and see the lightnings play, and hear the majestic and awful voice of God's thunder, which oftentimes was exceedingly entertaining, leading me to sweet contemplations of my great and glorious God. . . . It seemed natural to me to sing, or chant forth my meditations; or to speak my thoughts in soliloquies with a singing voice." Alas! for Edwards and for Herder; such ecstasies may not endure in feeble frames. Edwards bemoaned "a low tide of spirits; often occasioning a kind of childish weakness and contemptibleness of speech . . . much unfitting me for conversation," and Herder's sublimity of thought failed to tranquilize his troubled heart and irritated nerves. Mournful indeed is the discontent of his closing years; it warps his feelings and lays waste his powers. The preacher of light dwells in clouds and darkness, the teacher of God's cooperant forces in nature and in history converts the sweets of friendship into tormenting discords that ruin his joy, the prophet of immortality crouches at the feet of Death, imploring just a few more days on earth. Into the causes of this suffering I do not enter; it is not for us to apportion the blame of it between him and his ancestors and his neighbors and the inscrutable forces of nature whose harmony he proclaimed. Enough that he saw

the burning bush which was not consumed, and that, in spite of suffering, he repeated to us the word of the living God that proceeded from the seen-unseen; enough that in intervals of rapture he heard and repeated to us the music of the spheres and the voice of the adorable trinity of Light and Life and Love.

The day before Herder died Ludwig van Beethoven began in a mood of desperate resignation his thirty-fourth year. He was already incurably deaf. Inexorable silence had imprisoned him within the music of his own creative genius; never more to hear the voice of woman, or the song of birds, or the sound of instrument, or the murmur of the tree tops, or the rush of mountain torrents. Was the Ninth Symphony possible without the misery of Beethoven? The visions of Herder without his sorrows? I do not know. What I know is this: They were possible in spite of them!

Charles J. Little

Art. IV.—UNIFORMITY IN NATURE DISPROVES AGNOSTICISM.

If nature be an organized whole, as is a prerequisite to the possibility of a system of science, there must be uniformity of movement between corresponding parts. But in such an extensive and complicated organism there will be many seemingly discordant movements, or such as are incomprehensible by a finite mind at any stage of scientific inquiry. For as we explore the constantly increasing domain of knowledge the periphery of the circle will present an ever-widening field, no matter how limited be the arc examined, and there will be at every step new fields opening out where the movements of natural law and their application to fresh instances will present difficulties which are inseparable from each advancement made into the undiscovered region. This is to be expected; for if the course of science offered no seeming contradictions, and hence no difficulties which could not be resolved at any given time, this would involve infinite knowledge in the investigation at the outset, and dispense with all effort. In that case all would be understood at first, and there would be no room for progress since every man would be as wise before investigation as after. Difficulties and seeming contradictions are therefore to be expected in scientific progress, and present the same sort of conditions as those to which our life is subjected everywhere; for it is our appointed destiny to gain our substance, whether for body or spirit, at the expense of the sweat of our brow, and knowledge must be acquired and character built up by courageously meeting and laboriously overcoming the difficulties which beset our pathway.

Nevertheless there must be uniformity of action as a basis for investigation, and an assurance that we shall obtain a definite result for our labor, else no person would work and no progress would be possible. For if the same means acting under like conditions produced a varying result there could be no inducement for us to put forth any effort. We never could be sure whether the responses to our actions were from the causes we had set in

motion, or from some others unknown to us, or from chance—which is tantamount to none at all. Hence the idea of the Uniformity of Nature must be assumed in every effort that is made in hope for the discovery and confirmation of any new fact.

Such uniformity, being absolutely necessary, is assumed by all systems of knowledge, whether they be theistic, atheistic, or the forlorn hope of doubters and agnostics. Whether the government of the universe be by Mechanical Causation, Immanent Design, or a Personality directing the movement of matter *ab extra,* each and all these theories are compelled to rest on the same fundamental assumption; for when revealed religion points to miracles as a voucher it rests upon the principle of uniformity with, if possible, greater confidence than the mere Naturalist. For in this case *exceptis probat regulam;* since the fixedness of uniformity is so complete that nothing save the action of the Lord of nature can interfere with this, and he does so only for a specific purpose. So, for the purpose we have in view, it makes not the slightest difference which of these theories as to the source of this uniformity be taken; what is asserted is that there is uniformity in the movement of this system which Science tries to expound as the expression of nature. Nor is it incumbent on us to show how this notion of uniformity is gained. Suffice it to say that we believe in it as soon as we arrive at self-consciousness, and find it necessary as a basis for action and thought alike in the affairs of life and in the work of scientific investigation; hence that we are justified in assuming it as an *à priori conception.* All expositions of nature on a materialistic assumption hold that the idea of uniformity is the product of experience. Mill may be taken as the fairest type of those thinkers who hold this view. His contention is that this is gained from the association of ideas. Through repeated experiences of one unvarying result following a combination of causes operating under like conditions we come at length to expect the same in every case. But this does not seem to be an adequate explanation of the facts attested by our consciousness. The first dawnings of intellect make us acquainted with a solid and permanent world. Antedating all well-defined experiment we expect stability in the earth and uniformity of

14

movement in every case as our warrant for acting at all. When
the child attracted by the brightness adventures its hand into the
flames, and suffers, there is no inquisitive second attempt to discover whether like causes—namely, the thrusting of the hand into
the flames—will produce like results. When a substance of a
certain shape, color, and consistency is found, by tasting, to be
sweet and grateful to the palate the hand reaches out for the like
object, expecting a similar grateful experience. This is really an
innate idea, because it is acted upon before there can be any
series of experiences to form an association of ideas. The senses
are believed implicitly from the start, else there would be no inclination to use them. If the child were without any, even the lowest, predilection either way he would never make any effort to test
his organs of sense. Instead we would have for the universal experience of our race in infancy the case of the ass between two
bundles of hay: equal motives operating on him from opposite
directions with no reason, innate or gained through experience,
for eating one way rather than another. There would be the
"freedom of indifference" with a vengeance, and no effort whatever would be made. And if so at the start it must continue; for
until there was an inclination to test the course of nature by
experiment there would be none made. Hence every act would be
indifferent except for the innate assurance that nature is constant.
For if the first result be accidental there would be no reason for a
second or a third trial of the same kind; and hence neither in
childhood nor maturity could there be a beginning made for the
association of ideas. The greatest intellects are sometimes guilty
of a paralogism, and here we have a notable example. It is not
the association of ideas that gives birth to the notion of uniformity
in nature, but the innate conviction of uniformity which renders
it possible that ideas be associated. Unconsciously the principle
is admitted to be innate because it is assumed to exist in order to
account for its own evolution. If the realities of which the ideas
are the symbols were not connected in nature they could not be
joined in an orderly manner by the mind; for what is not joined
in nature cannot be united except arbitrarily, and the mind which
acted on such a principle would find itself in perpetual conflict

with reality. Here again we are compelled to believe that there
is a correspondence, a preestablished harmony, between the constitution of the mind and that of external nature by which the
former is enabled to see things as they are, and proceed upon this
fact as a fundamental truth. This idea, then, of uniformity is one
of the original faculties of the soul; call it innate idea, original
power, or what name soever may please. It is not only operative
as soon as there is sufficient development of personality to enable
it to act independently, it is a precondition of all activity.

But though the testimony of the senses is believed in implicitly, and the outer world on which they act is a constant quantity,
yet there gradually dawns upon the infant mind the fact that he
may be mistaken in his judgment. The first result of such a view
is the suspicion that there may be capriciousness somewhere among
the materials and causes with which he has to deal, for events
wholly unexpected occur. Efforts are made to achieve a specific
result and something totally different happens. So far, then, from
the idea of uniformity being the result of experience, namely, the
association of ideas, there is a spontaneous stage of uncertainty
through which the mind of each person passes. This is like that
superinduced by the deliberate purpose of Descartes when he
sought to establish an unassailable starting point. But at bottom
there is, in both instances, this belief in uniformity. The doubt
arises only from the mistaken judgment which it has founded on
its own experience. Its association of ideas has not corresponded
with the facts of nature of which these are the symbols. And
hence experience leads astray until the reflecting power reasserts
itself and demonstrates, as it were, that there are axioms of intuition which the mind itself possesses as its part of the reasoning
process. It is as absurd to think that the mind can do nothing
of itself as it is true that the body is utterly helpless without the
mind to direct it. And the mind must act independently in the
elaboration of universal truths, since these never can be attained
through experience. It then cooperates with the material instrument by the application of its own native forces. We may call
these axioms, first truths, intuitions, or any other name which
most properly designates its separate part in the processes of intel-

lectual life. Hence, when the mind finds that its experiences and the association of ideas founded upon them are faulty it calls in question not only its own judgments, and those of other men, but the processes by which they have been formed, and learns to rectify them by the aid of the axiomatic principles with which it is furnished. It discovers that the facts of nature are reliable; that her laws are constant; and that the mistakes, which are the wrong associations of ideas acquired through experience, are the result of ignorance of the reality. Thus comes the tendency to doubt, which if not arrested may end in agnosticism. But if this be looked at with the proper spirit it will be found to arise from a narrow and hasty generalization which is discovered to be defective; and this in turn from an indolent temper which will not take the pains to thoroughly test the proof for the facts on which the judgments rest. In the case of Descartes, he was convinced that there is a solid foundation on which the superstructure of knowledge can be erected. But all the mistaken judgments superinduced by the false association of ideas by those who had preceded him must be brushed away, and the mind brought directly in contact with reality. Nature is constant in her operations, and if we can reach her processes and rest implicitly upon them as a foundation we can build an unshaken superstructure of knowledge. But to do this we keep close to her heart, and listen to its constant beats. So far, then, from thinking that nature is not uniform, whether in her material constitution or the laws which are potent, Descartes's method is the true process. This is by yielding everything that doubt can assail to arrive ultimately at those principles which are indubitable and unchangeable. The difficulty has arisen from the attempt to force nature into the molds of our categories, and thus make our associations of ideas the measure of reality.

Now since any fact—if the universe is a system—is connected with every other, there are many forces involved in the production of any result. Those which are positive are counteracted by such as are negative in their influences. But a narrow generalization seizing upon a few, and those which come to hand first, finds that its conclusions do not tally with the truth. For a wider generalization discloses other forces which counteract and render the effect

uncertain. Without the patience. and industry which will not rest content until the last source of information has been exhausted, the indolent doubter, when his hastily assumed hypotheses will not work, jumps at the conclusion that this is a world of chance; or if any uniformity exists it has not and cannot be discovered. This is the legitimate result of making our crude association of ideas the test of uniformity. This temper of impatience, which is too sluggish to expend sufficient energy to arrive at the truth, breeds agnosticism; and transfers to nature herself the blame which properly belongs to the individual. It finds expression among the Know Nothings of every age, from Gorgias* to Lombroso and Clifford, who subvert every possible theory of knowledge. For they propose a specific which is destructive of all thought and action and, if adopted, would leave man in helpless imbecility.

But there is, as we have said, a stage of doubt, through which every earnest inquirer passes, when there seems to be uncertainty attaching to all the processes of nature, and consequently to all her results. The senses are formed to give uncertain information. The phenomenal world appears as a *rudis indigestaque moles.* Instead of what one wishes or expects he gets a disappointing result, and chance seems to be the reigning principle. This temper where persisted in generally grows out of disappointment in some of the cherished purposes of life; where things do not work to suit us and the result does not seem to be commensurate with the means employed. Hence our own temper is projected into the outward world, and the prejudgments of association cause us to see, not what the senses furnish, but what we expect. But those who have courage, perseverance, and industry come through this period of doubt chastened, invigorated, and more trustful. They find that the fault is in themselves, in their methods or lack of system, and their impatience for results too soon after sowing the seed. The senses are not found to be at fault. External nature is constant, and speaks with absolute truthfulness. There has been a wrong interpretation. We have made an association of ideas

---

* Aristot. de Melisso, Xenop., Gorg., cap. v: ὁ Γοργίας οὐκ εἶναί φησιν οὐδέν· εἰ δ' ἔστιν ἄγνωστον εἶναι· εἰ δὲ καὶ ἔστι καὶ γνωστὸν, ἀλλ' οὐ δηλωτὸν ἄλλοις.

which did not have a correlative in reality. Our proof of judgment leads astray because we have not duly weighed the negative as well as the affirmative instances. We find that the uncertainty is due neither to testimony of the senses nor the accuracy of the mental processes, but to our desire to find the truth not for its own sake but for its influence on our interests. Recourse is again had to faith in reality as the first condition of all knowledge. There must be something true, fixed, and reliable, or the framework of nature would fall to wreck and we ourselves could not exist for a moment. And there must be such a correlation of the inner structure of our bodies to the outward environment that the one corresponds with the other and works, so to speak, with its hands, else the functions of life could not be maintained. Still further: unless this correspondence were uniform, having an external reality which is constant, the internal structure and functions, though in themselves constant, would not be in correlation, and therefore could bring about no systematic results. So the very necessity of the case compels us to fall back upon uniformity for our own preservation. We begin again with this cardinal fact, as Descartes did with his *"cogito,"* and start afresh the quest for truth with the assurance that it exists; that it is consistent with itself in order to be truth.* Moreover that which is true and consistent must for that reason be connected in system and can be known, provided it be sought for in the right way.

Relying upon this basis the mind interrogates nature, and when the response does not prove satisfactory the blame is no longer laid at the door of the things in themselves, but in the methods employed for discovery. Mistakes will be made inevitably by a creature that is not perfect at first, but must be developed through his own responsible action. If he could never be mistaken he would know all, and there would be no room for improvement. The prejudices arising from the desire that nature should conform to our preconceived opinions must be abandoned. When she is interrogated she will answer only in her own way; and her

---

* Aristot., Anal. Pri., cap. xxxii: a δεῖ γὰρ πᾶν τὸ ἀληθὲς αὐτὸ ἑαυτῷ ὁμολογούμενον εἶναι πάντῃ. Eth. Nich., i, cap. viii: τῷ μὲν γὰρ ἀληθεῖ πάντα συνᾴδει τὰ ὑπάρχοντα, τῷ δὲ ψευδεῖ ταχὺ διαφωνεῖ ταληθές.

responses must be received with absolute confidence that if we can understand her language she will never deceive. The fact that her extent and variety are illimitable involves the necessity of equally great diversity of forces in carrying out her functions. And if there be a plurality of causes at work there must be also a mixture of effects. Hence it follows that we can know but in part touching any portion of this vast domain. For as no cause operates alone there will be no two effects identical, and we can know any new fact only as it resembles its kindred in the main features. Combining these data we will be prepared to admit the likelihood of failure to reach without carefully weighing positive and negative influences among the causes which lie back of such varied phenomena. But the true causes are somewhere operative in nature, awaiting discovery by him who has the sagacity to separate the essential from the superficial and what seems to be accidental.

The difference between an *à priori* truth or innate idea and one which is axiomatic or self-evident must be noted. There are those truths which commend themselves to our acceptance but which do not admit of demonstration. There are others which involve postulates referring to space and time, and which contain within themselves unassailable proof, being in reality analytic judgments. Wherever the induction is perfect, that is where both the extent and content are manifestly fixed by nature or can be assumed as undeniable definitions, then we have demonstrative truth as the conclusion. There is in such cases an exact correspondence between the content of logic and the content of nature by which knowledge is rendered complete. But this can never be the case with sciences which depend upon observation or experiment to establish their validity. It is clear that we cannot establish the absolute uniformity of nature by this process. For if we could carry it to what we thought to be the nth number of instances, and find them all affirmative, we could not be sure that this enumeration exhausted the list. Nay, rather, we would be certain in advance that the limit of observation could never be reached either subjectively or objectively. Hence the associational school, or such as would establish the uniformity of nature by the

inductive method, are guilty of a paralogism. They attempt to prove that which, from the nature of the case on their assumed theory, is incapable of proof—save by an exhaustive enumeration which would involve the entire extent of nature. Moreover, at each stage of the process there lurks a *petitio principii.* For how could we arrive at one case of uniformity as a basis for comparing any new phenomenon unless the uniformity were already assumed to exist in the part covered by each case? Therefore, if it was claimed to exist in a partial degree, this would be inconclusive, since this degree could not be known to exist unless the whole of which it is a part be admitted. Thus the associational or experimental theory of the origin of our belief in uniformity takes for granted the very truth for which it is contending—and so, while professing to be vigorously exact and to take nothing for granted until proved, starts out with the most glaring fallacy known to logical science!

But when we proceed upon the principle that there is a conformity between the constitution of the mind, in its conception of external nature, and the facts of that nature as they are investigated and reduced to system, there is no fallacy either in the *à priori* conceptions or the endeavor to realize that conception by experiment. The facts are that from the earliest dawn of consciousness the child begins its efforts for knowledge by trusting the veraciousness of nature in her phenomena, and a like veraciousness in our interpretation of the information which our senses give us of the phenomena. And the first efforts of the child, and the results won, are elicited from exactly the same *à priori* truths and through the faith and use of the same methods by the profoundest investigators who have systematized the results of science. Cuvier, Gauss, Lord Kelvin, and Morse have a clearer conception of the First Truths which underlie their methods, as the result of the world's culture, but their faith in the veracity of both is no stronger than that of the little child—though they may be able to give a better reason for their faith. The searcher after truth soon learns that he may be mistaken in his judgments of the individual facts because he is not able to view them in all their connections, and therefore to see which are controlling data. Moreover,

the hidden causes yet beyond the powers of the investigator may be more potent than those on the surface at first sight. The truth must be elicited by a balancing of contrary forces. There is in every case a conflict of causes in the production of each several result; thus realizing the Greek proverb, πόλεμος πατὴρ παντῶν. There is a constant warfare between statics and kinematics wherever there is motion, either material or spiritual. Hence the conclusion as to their interaction may be drawn correctly from the elements apprehended; but it has been by an overhasty generalization, and ought to be revised by the aid of a more thorough investigation of the elements involved. And the distinction must ever be kept before us between the responses which nature gives and our interpretations of them. For while the information actually furnished cannot be deceptive, and our senses by the aid of each other are true in their deliverances, still, the information furnished may be misinterpreted by our reasoning powers. Both sources of knowledge, having parts of nature's processes, are correct when employed in the proper way, but we may fail to use them rightly either because we wish a certain result which is not the true one or are too indolent to employ all the resources within our reach. The bread for body or spirit does not grow automatically; and if it did there would be nothing for us to do. The process of struggling upward through error is unending for such inquirer and will continue to be so while knowledge is fragmentary, coming short, as it necessarily does, of omniscience, and while it is the destiny of man to get discipline of intellect and character by self-directed effort. Hence, this admission of fallibility in the processes by which the instrument works does not call in question the objective certainty of the truth for which inquisition is constantly making. The remark that "Figures cannot lie" is true when applied to their intrinsic power, but the calculator can make them bring out such result as he wishes—albeit his fictitious answer in no wise affects the truth of their plain testimony. Nay, rather, this infallibility in the reality of things is assumed all along; and every search for truth would be futile without it. Investigation on any other principle would be tantamount to a search, not for what was undiscovered or lost, but for what was

believed not to exist; than which nothing could be a more complete fool's errand.

But all knowledge consists in a verification of the facts of nature with reference not to themselves, but to our power to grasp them. There is a system of truth *in rerum Natura* which we must assume every time we think or act. This, while external to and independent of our conceptions thereof, is a necessary basis for our own existence. Nature ,with all her wealth of facts, and the knowledge which is the expression of these facts colligated into a system, may be considered as an analytical judgment. Its parts are the predication of the entire content, the complete range of materials of which the universe is composed. This forms the Middle Term. That is to say: All the predication which can be made of all the subjects in nature may be considered as the Major Premise. If we had omniscience we could see and comprehend this wealth of knowledge. Yet it must exist in reality. For the atoms of which the universe is composed and all their qualities have an essential existence, and if that could be grasped by the mind then the individual elements, if known in their description, would be sure as a Minor Term to come under this Major. The uniformity of nature as a whole must include the uniformity of each constituent part, and both conceptions are equally necessary if the universe be considered as an organized system. In this way we have an *à priori* expression of the innate idea, or First Truth, which is understood by the mind as soon as it is able to comprehend the terms of its enunciation. It is acted upon before the mind can formulate the truth to itself, or even comprehend it when expressed by another. This analytic judgment, embracing all possible truth, offers itself to us for exposition and is the task which in some form or other confronts the mind and awakens the desire for knowledge.

In this method of inquiry we awaken to constantly increasing evidence that the mind assumes this truth on which it is compelled to act if it be a part of that nature which it investigates. "The eye is sunny," says Goethe, because it was made to see and utilize the light of the sun. Because of this correspondence, which proves coordination, the mind assumes in the very first attempt to under-

stand its bearings in the voyage of life the truth which is the compass to steer its entire way; namely, that nature is constant in her processes and that the mind is able to search out and understand them by the use of its own veracious powers. This, the first principle of progress, can never be proved more true than it was at the beginning of the search, but as the application of the doctrine is found to be successful at every step the result obtained by its use is an *à posteriori* confirmation of its truth. Thus it is sustained with equal clearness by the only possible methods by which we can be sure of anything. The discovery of America by Columbus did not create the New World. The establishment of a new fact or the verification of a principle does not create them. For if there were no principle lying back of the forces which have brought it about the fact itself could not have taken place. So the new evidence at each advance of science by which it verifies itself again in some relation new to us is not necessary to the establishment of this uniformity which had to be assumed before there could be a single step forward in knowledge. It is simply a wider generalization of that which had been constant, so far as observed. It is therefore making clearer to ourselves and others that which had already an essential existence but had not been applied in the new discovery. The analytical judgment had not been expanded in all its applications. The knowledge of new facts pushes farther forward the line separating ignorance from knowledge. So the wider application of the same laws does not add to their validity. And while this process goes on continually it shows no more certainty in the application of scientific principles, but brings a wider domain under the control of known and positive law, and instructs the mind how to govern its possessions.

If there could be a single instance shown where nature does not act uniformly the whole principle would be rendered doubtful. But such is the unshaken confidence of all men of science, even if they be agnostics on questions of intellect or morals, that an apparent exception is treated not as contradictory to an established principle but as not yet understood in all its bearings, and hence awaiting explanation and verification. No doubt lurks in the mind of the most obstinate doubter, no misgiving in the language of the

most thoroughgoing agnostic, that there is truth in material nature somewhere; that things have an essential constitution and are regulated by some principle so as to produce a definite result. But our powers are so weak and vacillating that they cannot discover the language that nature speaks, and therefore in many instances her utterances have no meaning for us. The agnostic should best understand his own powers, but if consistent would never open his lips to utter an opinion. The utmost license he should allow himself is to point his finger* to that which he neither has understood nor can ever know, yet by this gesture even he transcends the limits which agnosticism theoretically imposes upon itself. For if he points his finger he either has knowledge or thinks he has. This induces him to call others' attention to that which must have enlisted his own with sufficient force to awaken the desire to impart to some one else that which he possesses. But of course the agnostic must know that he cannot know, and he has to meet the peculiar difficulty of compelling himself to prove a negative.

This process of experiment in enlarging our knowledge of the domain of uniformity must go on without ever ceasing, and each step seems to be, if that were possible, a renewed confirmation. It will go on forever because the work of science, as registering facts and showing their relations both to those hitherto known and those constantly coming to our knowledge, can never end. The proof by experiment is the asymptotic curve. We know that if carried to infinity it will meet the straight line of absolute universality, but in actual practice this can never be effected. The mind at the end of its quest, as at the beginning, must rest upon the *à priori* truth that nature in all her domains is absolutely uniform. This truth must antedate hopeful experiment and support the entire structure of scientific knowledge. Accordingly, as we have a body of scientific truth constantly growing in extent and accuracy, we have a drastic refutation of agnosticism.

* Aristot., Metaph., book iii, cap. v, 1010 a. καὶ οἵαν (δόξαν) Κρατύλος εἶχεν, ὃς τὸ τελευταῖον οὐθὲν ᾤετο δεῖν λέγειν, ἀλλὰ τον δάκτυλον ἐκίνει μόνον· κ.τ.λ.

Jacob Cooper.

Art. V.—PASTOR HOFFMANN, OF HALLE.

HALLE, the seat of a famous university, has been highly favored in the quality of her preachers. Two hundred years ago August Hermann Francke was there in the midst of his great and fruitful labors. Almost one hundred years after his death, in 1727, there came to Halle the young but already distinguished professor of theology, August Tholuck—probably even greater in the pulpit than in the professor's chair. Nor was Tholuck the only notable preacher whom the university could boast in that period. His great colleague, Julius Müller, preached, it is true, rather infrequently, but he preached so well that some—for instance, Albrecht Ritschl, as student in Halle in the early forties—preferred him to Tholuck. And then there was their younger colleague, Beyschlag, a preacher of great elegance and power. But even here the list is not complete, for the university has several men still living whose preaching is very strong and fine. Outside of the university, however, there was in Halle one preacher in the last century who deserved to be ranked with Tholuck. This was Heinrich Hoffmann (died 1899). We must have added another name, that of Ahlfeld, but for the fact that he remained so short a time in Halle. Hoffmann has not yet attained to universal fame in the Church. Whether he ever shall time alone can tell, but there are not wanting distinguished critics who regard him as the greatest German preacher of the last three decades of the nineteenth century. Professor Herrmann, of Marburg, once remarked in conversation: "I believe the impression generally prevails abroad that the preaching in Germany is poor. And if one should judge by the preaching one hears in certain localities I grant the impression is altogether natural. But I always tell the foreign students of theology, 'If you would know German preaching at its best read Hoffmann.'" And some years earlier this same distinguished theologian wrote the following: "If I could preach like F. W. Robertson or Heinrich Hoffmann I should make haste to give the Church as preacher of the Gospel the best that can be given her, and should cease to be an academic

theologian." The significance of this appreciation is the more manifest when we consider how far apart these men stood in their theology. Professor Haupt, of Halle, has unreservedly declared: "Hoffmann is the greatest preacher I have ever heard. We have more famous preachers, for instance Kögel; but I prefer Hoffmann to them all."

Heinrich Hoffmann was born in 1821 in Magdeburg, as son of a bank secretary. His parents were unusually pious and the boy's home life was happy and wholesome. An uncle, too—a man of much wisdom and grace, who had studied theology but because of ill health could not assume a pastor's labors—showed him much affection and exerted a strong influence upon his development. Probably Hoffmann's most marked trait in his boyhood was an excessive shyness, which he never wholly overcame. Until, at the age of eighteen, he left the gymnasium for the university he had had but two intimate friendships. Not that he lacked the susceptibility for friendship; he was simply shy. But he was also sickly. From his thirteenth year on he entertained thoughts of dying. He acquired at that period a cough from which he never afterward was wholly free. This sickliness caused him as a boy to be much alone, and in this way he had opportunity to gratify a strong passion for reading. He also early developed an ardent love for nature, which remained a leading trait of his character throughout life.

When the time came for Hoffmann to leave the gymnasium and go to a university to prepare for some profession he yielded to his father's desire that he should study theology—and herein he manifested a trait of character of which he himself was very conscious. He called it "the lack of initiative." It will be interesting to read his own account of this decisive turning point in his life:

My spontaneity was always very slight; in things that were not directly matters of conscience I have always been much inclined to be controlled from without. I was wont to suffer myself to be led; and so it was in the most decisive turning point of my outward life. . . . Ah, my father did not know what a responsibility he assumed. He had, though, no idea of what the ministry really is, else he had doubtless rather taken the same attitude to the question of the choice of my vocation as my wiser

uncle. Well—I doubt not the Lord had his hand upon it all. For my own part, I was able to judge neither myself nor the ministerial office, which, however, I reverenced. I wonder that my bashfulness did not deter me. Whenever I considered that I should at some time have to appear publicly before a congregation and preach, I shuddered at the thought; this I remember plainly enough. Besides, it was always a puzzle to me how I should be able to bring together so many thoughts that I might continue to speak till the hour had struck. . . . In short, I really do not know how I made bold to resolve to become a clergyman. A man that had not the least inward impulse to exert direct influence upon others, that regarded it as a terrible thing to have to appear in public, a man that was not, indeed, unwilling to work, and to work, too, in the realm of thought, that had also a sense for the ideal and was warm toward the truth of the Gospel, and yet was ever only inclined to grub and dig for myself. On the religious side I had nothing whatever against the ministry of the word of God. The inward connecting point for my subsequent vocation lay absolutely alone in the awakened Christian receptivity of my spirit, conscience, and thinking. At the same time I know only too well that in deciding upon my vocation my attitude was at bottom a passive one. The agony of choosing I did not pass through. . . . When I at Berlin had myself inscribed as student in the theological faculty I subscribed to the renunciation of a good part of the happiness of life, and did not suspect it. If an essential element in one's happiness is a vocation to which one has decided inclination and natural talent—well, to this present day I do not find either the one or the other in me.

And yet he learned more and more to trust that the Lord had led him. Near the close of his ministry he wrote:

Far be it from me to complain of the way in which—with infinite secret sighing, indeed—I have traveled. I believe that the Lord has willed it even as it has come to pass. I believe, too, that herein he designed all for my best good, only—I cannot understand it.

But let us return to the young student. Hoffmann went in October, 1839, to Berlin. The theological faculty was a most distinguished one, yet only one of its professors—Neander—made a notable impression upon him. Hengstenberg's sharp polemics repelled him. In Berlin he remained but two semesters, all the time lonesome and unsatisfied. He longed for closer contact with the charms of landscape and also, though he scarcely suspected it, for some satisfying human friendships. These he chanced not to find in Berlin, and his social instinct was beginning to assert itself. In the autumn of 1840 he went, with his father's consent, to Halle. He had hoped there to find "the world greener." And there indeed

he found what he had missed in Berlin, the satisfaction of a
"tardily developed spirit of youth." The landscape about Halle
is not remarkable, but it afforded what Hoffmann's soul required.
Here, too, he formed several close friendships, which proved to
be both rich and lasting. In Halle, as in Berlin, the professors
made a less powerful impression upon him than one would have
supposed. Even Tholuck, the "students' professor," failed to
draw him closely to his person. This was probably due not simply
to Hoffmann's shyness, but perhaps even more to the unusual independence of his inner life. He was painfully sensitive to any
intentional encroachment upon this sacred privacy; and he mildly
resented what he termed the "inquisitorial" element in Tholuck's
personal relation to his students. Tholuck, however, sincerely
respected Hoffmann's individuality; and when, more than a
decade later, the latter returned to Halle as pastor the two men
sustained the most cordial relations to each other.

In 1843 Hoffmann passed successfully his first theological
examination. About a year later he was seized with an alarming
disease of the chest. Not until the summer of 1846 was he able
to present himself for the final examination for the ministerial
office. In the meantime his mother had died; and now for six
and a half years Hoffmann shared the life of his widowed father.
At the first it was doubtful whether he would ever have strength
for the labors of a pastorate, but as his health gradually improved
the outlook became brighter. These years of retirement, however, were not lost. Hoffmann was an incessant worker. If he
"lacked initiative," he was nevertheless a marvel of perseverance.
During these years he regularly gave a portion of his time to the
tuition of a few private pupils, but the larger number of hours he
could devote to undisturbed study. He was almost thirty-two
years old when at length he accepted a call to become assistant
minister of St. Matthew's Church in Berlin. Somewhat more
than a year later he was called to the pastorate of the Neumarkt
Church in Halle. On the eve of his departure for his new field
of labor he was married to an admirable lady, who became the
faithful helper of his ministry of more than forty-one years. He
worked with wonderful devotion and success until he became

emeritus in 1896. Though always in ill health, he accomplished
a vast amount of work. He increased the number of public services and endeavored by all wholesome means to enrich them all.
He devoted himself in a remarkable degree to pastoral visitation.
He used, vigorously and successfully, many of the various forms
and methods which have been devised for reaching the destitute
and estranged classes, and as the population of his parish grew
with amazing rapidity—in twenty years it increased from 4,000
to 18,000 souls—he had the satisfaction, first, of procuring for
its more adequate service an increase in the clerical force; then
of getting proper limits set to the parish, as it threatened to grow
beyond all control; and, lastly, of seeing built a large and beautiful second church for the parish. This last success alone was a
most extraordinary thing. Hoffmann's new church was the first
that had been built in Halle since the Reformation. The most of
the money was obtained in voluntary gifts from the people of the
parish; and this in Germany, where the Church has been so long
accustomed to look to the State for everything, is something very
extraordinary. In the earlier portion of his pastorate Hoffmann
had much opposition to encounter. It was a period of a good deal
of ecclesiastical agitation, and he was not a politic man. But in
the latter half of his ministry the devotion of his people was
intense and universal.

Hoffmann's most important work, however, was preaching.
Immediately upon the commencement of his pastorate in Halle
the little church was thronged, and this continued to be the case
until the last. Professor Kähler says: "For forty years I was a
regular attendant at the Neumarkt Church, and I count it even
to-day one of God's best gifts to me that I was permitted thus to
attend upon that ministry."

A vivid picture of Hoffmann as he appeared in the pulpit
in later life is drawn by Professor Hering, who as a student heard
him also in the late fifties: "The face framed in long white hair,
the features large, an expression on the countenance now pater-
nally mild, now almost harshly austere, there also the deep fur-
rows graven by age and at last still more by ill health; the eye
closed as if in prayerful meditation, and then again, when intense

15

feeling possessed him, darting forth lightning; the voice unequal, now sinking to a low conversational tone, now swelling to the power of impassioned oratory and accompanied by vehement gesticulation of the stretched-out arm; the delivery often interrupted by considerable pauses and never in any case smoothly flowing; the whole figure bent a little forward and often swaying tremulously. . . . One sought in vain this man of rather uncomely appearance and manner for the attributes with which one habitually conceives 'celebrated pulpit orators' as endowed. He did not possess them, and never strove after them. . . . And yet everyone . . . who was capable of perceiving exceptional merit . . . must have received the impression: the power of God displayed in weakness. . . . What was the secret of this power? . . . It is not easy to give a round answer to this. He knows the human heart, said some; it is because he has wisdom for practical life to offer that I like to hear him, said a famous scholar who was far removed from Hoffmann's 'standpoint;' others called him a psychologist; and each of them might seem to himself to be saying something more to the point than the others. He himself, however, has probably given the best and truest indication of the deepest power of his preaching when, out of the certainty of his faith and his purpose, he gave to the collections of his sermons the titles *Unterm Kreuz; Kreuz und Krone; Eins ist not* ('Under the Cross;' 'Cross and Crown;' 'One Thing is Needful')." To preach the cross of Christ in all its bearings upon life was Hoffmann's object—to know nothing save Jesus Christ, and him as the One who has been crucified for us. Not that he narrowed the scope of his preaching—quite the contrary. Few preachers have had a wider range of subjects or a greater versatility in the treatment of them. But in the cross of Christ he found gathered the light and the grace to dispel all darkness and relieve all weakness. And he understood marvelously how to set human sin and need in the light of the cross.

A marked characteristic of Hoffmann's preaching was the unusual degree in which the person of the preacher seemed lost in the word of his testimony. Hoffmann purposed not to preach himself, but Christ Jesus as Lord; and he would have warned his

hearers, on the peril of their souls, not to consider the person of
the preacher, but only Jesus Christ. And yet, as Professor Kähler
has remarked, "his discourse carried one along so irresistibly even
because it was the utterance of just this person. Where Christian
preaching is concerned the seed of death is laid in its effectiveness
so soon as the speaker stands in the center or comes into the foreground. The secret of genuine effectiveness lies in this, that the
preacher become simply a minister of the word. And just this is
a thing that is apt to find its realization in receptive natures like
Hoffmann's. The word of the Gospel is a seed. Where it falls
into susceptible soil it unfolds itself, and also unfolds, and at the
same time enhances, whatever of natural powers are illumined and
quickened by it. Then afterward . . . the sincerity of the conviction and the agreement of one's walk with one's preaching preach
in conjunction with the spoken word. This, of course, was
emphatically the case with Hoffmann. But over and above this
the whole peculiar way in which in this instance the word acquires
its new individual form has a significance for its effectiveness. To
a great acuteness in the conduct of his thinking was united a
powerful immediateness of his inner nature and of his intuition
in his conception of the facts of salvation. Forgiveness the biting
ointment that burns out the disposition to sin; forgiveness the
soothing balm that heals the despair of the guilty conscience; forgiveness the power of making one ashamed of sin, it brings one
to the point where one utterly falls out with one's sins—this was
the confession of faith that sprang from his innermost experience,
this the keynote of all his preaching. And so the noblest traits
of his soul, which had been ripened in rich and long labor, were
set in motion whenever he laid upon our hearts the old message
with which he had become one. . . . If he had originally no inner
impulse to hand on to others what he himself had acquired he
nevertheless had his joy in doing this very thing when his vocation led him to it."

While Hoffmann's delivery was inartistic, his command of
language was of a very high order. He used the simplest terms
and the most idiomatic constructions. There was often a poetic
grace in his speech, especially where the matter called for the

strong emotions. And there is no trace of conscious embellishment in his style. His expression was precise, but it was the precision of clear and simple and concrete thinking. For terseness and condensation his sermons are probably unsurpassed. In a broad sense his preaching was popular, though hardly the ideal preaching for the uneducated classes. When Adolf Stöcker began his great work, to reach the estranged masses, Hoffmann gave him his warmest approbation, and declared, "If I were still young I should throw away all that I have learned and accomplished if only I might learn the secret of speaking so as to reach the common people." And yet few preachers of his day knew as well as he the way into the universal human heart. His illustrations were apt and luminous, though for the most part thought and figure were so blended in one there was no separating them. Anecdotes he used sparingly, but very effectively. These were drawn largely from his reading of history and from his observations in extensive travel. His soul was open and sympathetic toward all human interests, and he seemed to keep on developing even to his latest years. A rare humor was one of his leading traits. One of his old friends thought him not unworthy to be compared in this regard with the author of the *Pickwick Papers.* And all this had an important bearing on his development as a preacher.

Hoffmann's theology was at the first a pretty strict Lutheran orthodoxy. This was gradually altered into a biblicism of a modern type—an "orthodoxy corrected by the Bible." His preaching was intensely biblical and at the same time in close contact with modern thought and life. It is significant that even a "critical" theologian like Jülicher should entitle an essay on Hoffmann (in the *Christliche Welt*) "A Modern Preacher." In attempting to give a few fragmentary specimens of Hoffmann's preaching one experiences a double embarrassment. The first is, of course, the embarrassment of riches. The second lies in the fact that this preacher's style and method make it specially difficult by brief extracts to convey a fair impression.

We have said that Hoffman was preeminently a preacher of the cross. Let us therefore look first into one of his Good Friday sermons—that on Luke xxiii, 47, 48. A remarkably impressive

introduction leads up to the theme—"The Silent Language of the Cross:" (1) how it preaches repentance, and (2) how it preaches grace. In the first division occurs the following:

Ah, the Lord is not concerned that one should give up his reliance upon one's own honesty and join in the usual talk about oneself as a "poor sinner." If instead of this he can only so impress upon us the picture of his sufferings that it shall be with us wherever we go, this truest heart, this fairest picture, is surely worthy of it! Would we gladly come and stand under the effulgence of his love? Would we walk in this light? Ah, *this* is holy love, that thus for our sake renounced all that the world calls happiness and joy and honor; this is love that never with a single thought sought her own, that thus entered the state of humiliation, thus assailed with the weapons of the truth all that is unrighteous, thus willingly for this cause endured with an invincible meekness, thus recompensed those who did him evil only by doing them good, praying for them and blessing them from his heart, thus plunged into weakness, condemnation, pains of death and agony of hell, in order to pay the ransom for many. This I call the silent language of the cross, when it ever and anon speaks to us and we listen to it, saying, So loves your Lord. And you? and you? Beware how, when men become displeasing to you, your patience, your kindness, instantly deserts you! Beware how your desires fall into wrong grooves! Beware how your soul clings to its half-happinesses and its own honor; how your thoughts have a squint, your heart and your mouth are so sharp in their judgments! O silent language of the cross! Whose heart dost thou now lay bare that he may see its mortal hurt—that is, the power of self-love, which lusts after that which passes away.

Under the second division of the same sermon is the following passage:

But has the cross nothing more to preach than repentance? Nay, rather, it has set in motion also a preaching of grace such as no prophet of the former time could do. . . . It may seem more natural to despair of your soul than to hope in its behalf. But—but, all the more should the word of the cross have its rightful force. On the paling lips of Jesus hovers the word, It is finished. That word should have more credit than the voice of the stricken heart when it says within you, It is all over with you. It is not all over with you! Where you had nothing to pay he has paid for you. You will not allow that the thoughts that *excuse* you are valid, so he wills that the thoughts within you that *accuse* you you shall not hold good. . . . And if, after years of endeavor, the right fulfillment of the good you purposed still is lacking, why would you make your peace of conscience contingent upon your first working yourself so and so far into a good state? Rather let your assurance rest, to the glory of Christ, upon the fact that his finished work has procured peace for you. . . . Your despondent thoughts are traitors! Rest in me! says the silent cross; let your unrest change into good assurance.

With this may be compared another admirable Good Friday sermon, that on Luke xxiii, 39-43, "Christ's Cross our Throne of Grace," with its three simple divisions: (1) Gaze upon it; (2) Draw near to it; (3) Accept the mercy offered there.

Hoffmann's Easter sermons were especially impressive. Particularly noteworthy is the emphasis upon the essential inner connection between Easter and Good Friday. To him .Christ's resurrection is something more than a confirmation of our hope of a future life, and yet he does not fail to do justice to this thought.

> The hopes of our hearts for the future world are like Noah's dove, that flew to and fro over the boundless face of the deep until she found the olive tree from which she brought back the leaf. Thus uncertainly do our hopes fly out over the sea of death until they alight upon the rock that has lifted itself above that surface, even upon Jesus Christ, who is risen from the dead.

But his central Easter thought is that Christ's resurrection is in the first instance the completion of the message of grace which the cross had already uttered. It was in an Easter sermon that Hoffmann declared:

> Whoever is disturbed by his conscience, let him hate his sin, let him look upon and trust his Redeemer, and receive the offered peace with God.

Farther on he says:

> When at last death serves the summons upon life I wish for my dying pillow this: that in sincerity I may be able to say within myself, I have more sins than I can number, but none that is not abhorrent to me, and forgiven; none that I have not died to, none that the Lord has not freed me from.

The Christocentric character of Hoffmann's preaching is especially apparent in his Whitsunday sermons. To him Pentecost is not the substitution of the Holy Spirit for Christ, the Spirit is sent in Christ's name and glorifies him. He restores to us our risen Lord. His Christmas sermons, and particularly his addresses to the children on Christmas Eve, show him in another and a very attractive light. Indeed many admire his Christmas discourses above all the rest. The best of the addresses to the children have been collected and published under the title "Christblumen," and they are classics of their kind—but what-

ever the season or occasion Hoffmann was wonderfully apt both
in the choice of themes and in the treatment of them. While he
was didactic, in the best sense of the term, he was always intensely
practical. He touches upon a multitude of moral questions and
illuminates them with a rare practical wisdom, and yet he never
for a moment sinks to the level of a mere preacher of morals.
Oftentimes his sermons were fearfully searching, and yet sometimes their severity would be relieved by a bit of restrained humor.
In a sermon on "Love's Duty of Sparing Others" occurs this
passage:

> In the afternoon let us visit some coffee circles. What are they doing
> there? Embroidery with their hands, patchwork with their tongues. It
> is, you know, so entertaining to patch up other people. . . . On the doors of
> many an elegant home one might hang the placard, "Warm gossip here
> every day"—as warm rolls at the baker's.

And yet, wonderfully as Hoffmann knew how to lay his finger
upon the sore spot in men's hearts, he was not inquisitorial,
and he seems not to have transgressed the Lord's command,
"Judge not."

The introductions to his sermons were generally very simple,
and always natural, and yet few preachers equaled him in the
quickness and sureness of getting into the heart of the subject
and into the hearts of the hearers. Here is the introduction to a
sermon from John v, 5-14, the account of the healing of the impo-
tent man at the pool Bethesda:

> St. John reports this occurrence because it was this that afforded the
> first occasion for the deadly hatred of the rulers of the people to manifest
> itself. This aspect of the story we pass by; we direct our attention to
> Jesus's behavior toward the sick man. The narrative has two scenes: the
> one at the pool Bethesda, the other in the Temple. Twice Jesus offers
> himself to the man as physician; Jesus the Physician of Body and Soul.
> (1) How he comes to the help of the soul in order to heal the body, and
> (2) uses the sufferings of the body in order to heal the soul.

Very simple, no doubt; and yet it makes one eager to hear what
follows. Here is another example of an introduction both brief
and comprehensive. The text is John ix, 1-7, the story of the
giving of sight to one born blind.

> Thus the long suffering of one unfortunate had such an end that he
> could sing psalms of joy to Him that had caused his sufferings to cease.

The act of Jesus affected directly only this one person. But the accompanying words of the Lord are a great light that shines out over the world and illuminates one of its darkest riddles. I mean the saying: "Neither hath this man sinned, nor his parents: but that the works of God should be made manifest in him." 1. It repudiates the gloomy thoughts concerning a large part of the evils of our life. 2. It shows us gracious purposes of God where we cannot fathom them. 3. It leads us to the sufficient comfort that puts an end to all comfortlessness. It is as Reconciler that the Lord is speaking here, for he is reconciler also in this sense: That he can reconcile us with the unmerited evils of our life.

His style displays great self-restraint and vigor combined. He used adjectives sparingly and he did not exaggerate. Beginning his sermons generally in the simplest manner, he soon rose to the full energy which the subject required. Sometimes, however, as in the Good-Friday sermon on Luke xxiii, 39-43, there is from the first word a full stream of feeling and almost poetic expression:

We are standing upon the holiest place in all the earth, upon Golgotha. He who is the likeness of God is nailed upon the cross, eternal love is consumed in agonies. What shall I say? All that stirs my soul or can stir yours lies in the two words, O Jesus! O Love! So warmly hast thou loved me! O Jesus! O Love! how ill have I loved thee! Yet I would fain learn how to love better. And if by gazing upon thy cross I can learn it a little better I will choose the place that is nearest thee: there where a certain one by beholding thy love found salvation—the place of the thief at thy side. Upon this place the word of Scripture sets us.

And then follows the reading of the text.

Perhaps no sermon of Hoffmann's has been more admired than that on John xii, 24-26: "Through Death to Life." It well illustrates the preacher's easy yet swift rising from the simple to the sublime. In explanation of the words, "Except a corn of wheat fall into the ground and die," etc., he begins:

This is not to be taken as a dead rule in words and letters which the Lord gives his disciples. For he has first of all himself in mind. He sets himself up as a living rule. He portrays, as he so often does, that which is loftiest, that is his very self, before their eyes and ours by means of the simplest image and likeness. The grain of wheat, so long as it lies in the granary, remains as unfruitful as a stone. Planted in the earth, it breaks its hull, dissolution destroys its soft parts, it dies. But within it is a germ of life that had longed for just this planting and dying of the grain of wheat. In the process of dying it unfolds its life, and sends up the stalk and the ear with its hundred grains. Thus the grain by dying attains to

heightened life and multiplies itself. This, written in a little grain of wheat, is the story of the only-begotten Son of the Father who was manifest in the mortal veil of the Son of man. When he, who from eternity was in the Father's bosom, was born man, then it began—then did God plant him as a grain of wheat in the soil of humanity; then at once began his dying. What shall we call such a life as his? For from his childhood up he held the glory of the only-begotten Son of the Father buried in the form of a servant, he humbled himself yet more and more, even unto death, he constantly bore our sicknesses and sorrows, he gave himself up in utter devotion and fell from one anguish of soul into another. This was a constant dying of the grain of wheat. And so it continued up to the point where, in his last hour of need, his soul, troubled unto death and forsaken of God, passed from this life as if it had been consumed by the corruption of the sin of mankind which he bore; and up to the point where his pierced body broke down in death: then it was finished. But as the grain of wheat desires just this, that it fall into the grave of the earth and under the power of dissolution, in order that it may spring up and bring forth fruit—just so with the heart of Jesus, the only heart that knows the sole longing to give its life for the redemption of the many. In no other way could the miracle of love, the love that knows no measure, manifest itself before the eyes of all men than that it should lead him forth to travel all the ways of martyrdom. In no other way could the only power break forth which he designs ever to exert over the hearts of men until the last judgment; that is, the power of the love that takes upon itself our sins in order to atone for them and dies our death in order to put even it to death.

Hoffmann "can begin," writes Hering, "like a catechist and end like a minnesinger of holy love. He can kindle a small light for the obtaining of elementary knowledge of the faith and simple understanding of the Scriptures, but gradually the little flame burns more and more intensely and at last beams with a supernal brilliancy."

An admirable, though brief, account of "the life, the work, and the preaching" of Hoffmann has been written by the distinguished Halle professors, Kähler and Hering. The writer of these pages gratefully acknowledges a large indebtedness to their work.

J. R. Van Pelt.

ART. VI.—THE INTELLECTUAL LIFE OF JESUS.

FRA BEATO ANGELICO, the artist-monk of Fiesole, renowned for the spirituality and mystic charm of the saints and angels he portrayed, always painted the head of Christ and of the Virgin in a prayerful mood, and on his knees. A like reverence will characterize every proper attempt to represent the human aspects of the person of Jesus. Indeed, it is almost impossible to study the humanity of Christ without being so mastered by the sense of his divinity as to be incapable of conducting the inquiry impartially. By the faultlessness of his character Jesus has compelled the homage of men to such an extent that they shrink instinctively from that critical investigation which his human nature invites and challenges, and which may be pursued by his disciples with the utmost propriety. They bow in adoration before the divine presence, and are disinclined to discuss the human figure. When a company of congenial spirits were trying to fancy what their sensations would be if some of the greatest of earth's former inhabitants were to appear among them, and the name of Christ was mentioned, Charles Lamb stammered out, "You see, if Shakespeare entered this room, we should all rise; if Christ appeared, we should all kneel." That is the unquestioned sentiment of every soul that has beheld the divine beauty of our Lord, and it honors him who cherishes it; but it must be recognized as constituting a serious difficulty in the present study. It is always easier for the devout mind to call Jesus the Son of God than to pronounce him Son of man, though this is Christ's favorite designation of himself. Said Lamennais, "When I come to consider his life, his works, his teaching, the marvelous mingling in him of grandeur and simplicity, of sweetness and force, that incomprehensible perfection which never for a moment fails, . . . when I contemplate this grand marvel, which the world has seen only once, and which has renewed the world, I do not ask myself if Christ was divine; I should rather be tempted to ask myself if he were human." This feeling is doubtless shared by many thoughtful Christians. Yet the phraseology which the Church has almost universally adopted

to express her conviction regarding the person of Christ is "very God and very man, of a reasonable soul and human flesh subsisting." Napoleon Bonaparte is reported to have said to General Bertrand, "I know men, and I tell you that Jesus Christ was not a man." Man he could never be in any sense which would exclude the notion of his divinity, but man he must ever be by the fact of his perfect assumption of human nature. Into the profound mystery of the divine-human unity it is futile to peer. But the consummate humanity of Jesus, "without excess or defect," is an indispensable concept and formulary if the Temptation of Jesus and other disciplinary facts of his life, together with the doctrine of the Atonement and the whole New Testament philosophy of life, are to have any significance in the problems of human experience. To accept this position touching the person of Christ is of necessity to impose upon the intellectual life of Jesus such limitations as inhere essentially in humanity. But it must be kept in mind that we are not now concerned with the infinite intelligence of the Absolute, but with the mental phenomena of the man Jesus as observed in the authentic record of his earthly career.

The inspired narrative reveals in Jesus a preternatural intelligence, which seems to necessitate a mind of absolute sanity, as comports with the dignity and distinction of his person. A flawless intellect, no less than a perfect body and a sinless character, would appear to be demanded for the "one mediator between God and men, the man Christ Jesus." Nothing short of this will satisfy our sense of divine fitness. Though we admit that the idea of incarnation inevitably involves the limitation of certain divine prerogatives we cannot believe that the defects and errancies of our corrupted nature were entailed upon the intellectual life of Jesus by the fact of his human birth. "Conceived by the Holy Ghost" is the determining factor in this event. Consequently Jesus must be regarded as possessing a perfect mental equipment. He thus occupies a position of singularity and supremacy in the intellectual history of the race; for it is not contended by those best qualified to judge that we can be sure of such an endowment in any other human being. The greatest minds, it is held, are often affected by abnormalities which under suitable excitement develop

into incipient lunacies, illustrations of which abound with pathetic frequency. But here is one mind which is devoid of the vagaries and illusions, the misgivings and forebodings, the trepidations and superstitions, the passions and vanities, which cloud and enervate many of the noblest minds. Here is a mind which is not dulled by ignorance or stupefied by sin, which never reasons from false premises or makes unwarranted deductions, or defies the principles of logic in any other fashion, but which always thinks with precision and forever moves on to ultimate and impregnable positions; a mind which always sees truth in exact relations; which has no prejudices to efface, no blunders to correct, no fallacies to abandon, no conclusions to reverse; a mind which does not require to be nourished by books or trained by teachers, which knows God and nature and man immediately and intuitively; a mind which is pure and pellucid—like a sky unflecked by a single cloud, in which the sun shines with a brilliancy only modified by the atmosphere; a mind filled with visions of truth transcending the powers of other men to discern and pervaded with the perpetual consciousness of perfect fellowship with God. What a mind is this! Plato defined thinking as "the talking of the soul with itself." What inconceivably sublime self-communion must have filled this mind!

The intellectual life of Jesus as revealed in the Gospels is distinguished by extraordinary acuteness of perception. His apprehension of God and human relations is unparalleled among the sons of men. His insight into the characters, the secret motives, the aspirations of the people he meets is unexampled, and is obviously not the result of shrewd analysis of profound study but springs from his inherent knowledge of the human heart. "He needed not that any should testify of man; for he knew what was in man." He startled Nathanael, the Samaritan woman, Peter, Judas, the scribes and Pharisees and others by the disclosures of his knowledge concerning the inmost recesses of their souls. He probed the minds of his disciples with a word, and laid bare their ignoble thoughts and petty emulations to their evident amazement and confusion. He evinced marvelous powers of argumentation and rejoinder. His enemies not less than his friends were astonished at the authoritative one which he adopted.

"Never man spake like this man" is the confession of those who sought to entrap him. He was in perfect possession of the learning contained in the ancient Scriptures, and he turned his knowledge to great account in refuting the sophistries of his critics. He employed logical processes with merciless precision, and parried the thrusts of his adversaries with such skill that after one encounter it was said, "No man was able to answer him a word; neither durst any man from that day forth ask him any more questions." He rebuked the quibbles of the scribes with sententious utterances which were sharper than needles and with illustrations no mind was obtuse enough to misunderstand. He explained the principles of the kingdom of God by parables which are the most beautiful— as they are the most fundamental—of all the creations of imaginative literature. He convinced the cultured classes of his day that he was an intellectual master, and challenged them to account for his supremacy. "How knoweth this man letters, having never learned?" they ask themselves. He exhibited a wisdom which is greater than any learning, and which may exist independently of formal instruction. It characterized his childhood and it progressed with his developing manhood. He wrote nothing, so far as we know, save the line he traced in the dust in the presence of the sinful woman and her accusers, and that perished with the day; yet he has impressed his wisdom on the thought of all succeeding generations. He looked straight into the face of nature and read therefrom lessons of eternal significance. He peered into the souls of men and interpreted their deathless longings to them in terms which are immortal. He saw God everywhere and explained him in words which quicken faith and intelligence wherever they are spoken. "Nothing," says Francis Peabody, "but the profounder traits in Jesus Christ, of religious vision and moral cogency, could have obscured the intellectual greatness which justifies his message to the scholar." His uninterrupted consciousness of participation in the mind of the Eternal differentiates him from the most godly saints on earth. "O righteous Father, the world hath not known thee; but I have known thee, and these have known that thou hast sent me," he cries out in the sublime prayer which he offers on the night of his betrayal unto death. Truly this is a

mind not illumined by imparted glory but flaming with its own essential brightness. God has not shined upon Jesus: he shines in him.

Despite this transcendent wisdom, however, there is no evidence in the record of this peerless life of any claim on the part of Jesus to possess unconditioned omniscience. On the contrary, there is much to support an opposite view. Nor should this fact occasion surprise when we reflect that this divine attribute, like omnipotence and omnipresence, could not be conceived as expressing itself fully in terms of finite being. If we are unable to understand how God could manifest himself without retaining the complete exercise of his divine prerogatives, no more are we capable of explaining in what manner he could exhibit himself in human form without obscuring or limiting them. The mind finds some relief from perplexity by viewing the incarnation ethically and not metaphysically. The motive of the divine humiliation must be employed to interpret its mystery in so far as it can be apprehended by the intelligence of man. It is God the Son who is described as becoming incarnate in Jesus Christ. This he does in obedience to his own law of love. His consciousness of God is that of eternal Sonship. He becomes man in order that this Sonship may be realized in the sphere of human life, and with a purpose to save mankind. To achieve this he must subject himself to the limitations of a genuine human estate. Says Canon Gore: "The incarnation involves both the self-expression and the self-limitation of God. God can express himself in true manhood because manhood is truly and originally made in God's image; and, on the other hand, God can limit himself by the conditions of manhood because the Godhead contains in itself eternally the prototype of human self-sacrifice and self-limitation, for God is love." It is not ours to discuss here the difficulties which inhere in the acknowledgment of this self-limitation of the Son of God. They constitute the chief battle ground of the never-ending Christological controversy. But we must accept the facts contained in the narrative of Christ's life, and assent to the truths thus objectively presented, though our reason cannot explain them. We are compelled to do this not only by the requirements of the

orthodox faith concerning the person of Christ but by the frank admissions of Jesus himself, who seems to disavow absolute divine omniscience in one instance and to imply as much in others.

The predictive element in the utterances of Jesus doubtless transcends that discoverable in the messages of the prophets who foretold his coming and the apostles who continued his work. Yet in one respect it is similar: his consciousness of future events was limited. He committed no errors of fact, but the extent of his knowledge was restricted. He was infallible in all his teachings, but his vision of the future was not projected to infinity. His omniscience was conditioned by the human nature which he had assumed. Again we must be reminded that it is the man Jesus whom we are considering. He knew that the final judgment impended, that Jerusalem would be overthrown, that he would come again to judge the quick and the dead, but unless Matthew and Mark are unreliable witnesses he assured his hearers that he did not know the time of these events. "Of that day and that hour knoweth no man, no, not the angels which are in heaven, neither the Son, but the Father." Various attempts have been made to explain this declaration in consistency with the theory of Christ's absolute omniscience, but they uniformly cast a shadow on the candor of Jesus. Theodoret's comment is pertinent: "If he knew the day and, wishing to conceal it, said he was ignorant, see what blasphemy is the result. Truth tells a lie." A similar obscuration of omniscience is apparent in the incident of the two disciples' request to be assigned to places of preeminence in the coming kingdom, which Jesus declares are not at his disposal. "From the few utterances of this kind," says Wendt, "we perceive that Jesus, whilst conscious of knowing the divine plan *as a whole*, yet did not therefore claim to possess a foreknowledge of this gracious plan *in its details*." If the future was perfectly clear to him it is difficult to account for the prayer in Gethsemane, "O my Father, if it be possible, let this cup pass from me!" or to explain the agonizing cry upon the cross, "My God, my God, why hast thou forsaken me?" if he saw the uttermost depths of the divine mind. Many illustrations of this subordination of Christ's mental vision to the necessities of his human nature will occur

to every thoughtful reader of the New Testament, and taken in conjunction with the fact that he expresses surprise at some occurrences, that he requests information with evident sincerity, that he has recourse to prayer for guidance and inspiration, that he asserts his dependence on the Father for instruction, that he has not contributed anything to the world's knowledge of material things, though these were constantly employed as symbols of spiritual truth, raise a strong presumption, to say the least, that Jesus did not possess absolute divine omniscience, and afford a singularly impressive interpretation of that inscrutable self-impoverishment and self-emptying of the Son of God which St. Paul describes in 2 Cor. viii, 9, and Phil. ii, 5-11, and which is known to theologians as the *Kenosis.*

But if the intellectual life of Jesus was subject to the limitations which are incident to human nature it is no less true that it also followed the laws of development which are everywhere regnant in human experience. He fulfilled the ideal relations of childhood. His mental equipment was perfect from the beginning, but it was the perfection of the bud and not of the full-blown flower. His mental vision was circumscribed by an horizon which constantly receded as he "increased in wisdom and stature, and in favor with God and man." The training of a pious Jewish home accelerated the development of his understanding. If he enjoyed the doubtful advantages of the conventional religio-ecclesiastical schools of his age at Nazareth, he doubtless felt therein the primary movings of his extraordinary intellectual vigor. "The attempts to bring him into contact with Egyptian wisdom, or the Essenic theosophy, or other sources of learning, are without a shadow of proof," says Dr. Schaff, "and explain nothing after all." Likewise there are no reliable tokens of supernatural intellectual powers in the only authentic record of his early years. Robertson of Brighton fancied that the reason men love to ascribe precocity to great characters in their childhood is that it affords an explanation of their subsequent achievements apart from the patient toil exacted of ordinary persons in winning success. This will perhaps account for the wonders which the Fathers were prone to ascribe to the childhood of Jesus, and for the prodigies

which are soberly set down in the apocryphal gospels. But that he grew up naturally is the testimony of the New Testament, both from what it records and from what it omits. It seems evident that his development was normal from the fact also that in later years his kinsmen thought his fame ridiculous. He progressed in knowledge so naturally that Joseph and his mother had apparently not been encouraged to look for conduct in him which would be regarded as incompatible with childhood. Even if we admit that at this stage of his life he was fully conscious of his divine sonship we are not compelled to consider this any interference with a proper human development. If the scene in the Temple when he was twelve years of age was his first emergence into the consciousness of his true character, if it was the initial evidencing of his wonderful intellectual force, it but serves to emphasize the fact that hitherto his progress had not been unusual enough to awaken surprise. The eighteen years that follow are hidden from view, but they unquestionably matured and compacted his intelligence. Preparation is the chief part of any public man's life, and Jesus offers no exception to this requirement. There was little opportunity for reflection during the crowded years of his ministry. The unknown period of his life, before he broke forth into publicity, gave him this important advantage. He spent his time away from universities, libraries, books, and great men, and busied himself with the common toil of an artisan, but he was making ready for mighty achievements. Thirty years of preparation, three years in which to impart the quintessence of his wisdom—it is a most impressive fact.

This retirement naturally suggests the inquiry, To what extent, if at all, was the intellectual life of Jesus affected by his environment? Did outward circumstance play any part in the development of his mental constitution? Was the cast of his mind in any least degree determined by his surroundings? It is the contention of some that only inferior characters are definitely wrought upon by the attrition of society and the contact of sensible objects. On this supposition the intellectual development of Jesus was a simple and inevitable process of evolution from within. He came to the consummate fruitage of his mind by the

16

inherent energy of his being. It is not less firmly maintained by
others that Jesus was very considerably affected by the material
conditions which encompassed him. It is at least important to
note, as fundamental to this speculation, that he was always oriental in his modes of expression and apparent habits of thought.
The figures of speech he employed were derived from local circumstances. They occasion difficulties of interpretation when
they are communicated to populations whose environment is dissimilar from his. There is a wide realm of illustration available
to an observant man in the natural objects which are common to
all parts of the globe. The sun, the moon, the stars, the sky, the
clouds, the atmosphere, the sea, the lakes, the rivers, the mountains, the storm, the convulsions of nature, life in the air, beneath
the waters, and on the surface of the earth—these are ready for
almost unlimited use among all classes of men to enforce and illuminate public discourse. But these for the most part had merely
incidental treatment at the hands of Jesus. His Gospel was for
all men. The spiritual and ethical truths he enunciated were of
universal application, but the language in which they were couched
was unquestionably determined by the needs of the men nearest to
him and, shall we say, by the peculiar bent of his own mind? It
is the miracle of his speech that truth quickens his parables and
leaps through the disguises of a foreign tongue wherever they
are repeated.

The intellectual life of Jesus was certainly not fostered by
some of the influences which are deemed of chief importance in
modern culture. Travel, literature, art, music, oratory, contact
with scholarship, stirring public events form no part of his training for popular leadership. It must be obvious none the less that
Nazareth with its cosmopolitan population afforded many of the
advantages which are thought to inhere in travel, while the very
unlikeliness and obscurity, not to say insignificance, of the place
supplied the seclusion required for perfecting latent intellectual
energies. For this high purpose Nazareth was unquestionably
superior to Jerusalem. In the capital of Judea, filled with the
baleful influences of traditional religion, rife with discussions of
the bare externals of a devotional life, noisy with the babble of

rabbinical polemics, he could not have enjoyed the calm and repose, indispensable for introspection, which he could secure in the comparatively unruffled peace of Nazareth. No thoughtful person can fail to see the value of such isolation from the arena of controversy for the development of the resources of a great mind. "Conversation enriches the understanding, but solitude is the school of genius," said Gibbon. "Mediocrity can talk, but it is for Genius to observe," said the elder Disraeli. Society undoubtedly is necessary for the development of creative genius, but isolation is imperative for serious preparation. So Descartes thought, and shut himself away from companionship of men in Amsterdam. So Goethe believed, and retired almost within himself at Weimar. The necessity to evolve deep thinking from one's inner consciousness cultivates mental acuteness. Even the deprivation of certain senses seems to assist rather than retard the action of the mental powers. Milton's blindness and Beethoven's deafness were no bar to the exercise of their genius. It is even credible that these infirmities made more quick and pregnant the performances of their minds. In the same manner, being thrown absolutely on one's inner resources by reason of a certain isolation from the world may prove an incomparable blessing. In the matter of pure reasoning the ancients, who had few books, no scientific methods of observation, and an exceedingly contracted horizon, present some of the most remarkable examples we have in the field of ratiocination. It is not without significance, also, as affecting the mental culture of Jesus, that he spent so long a time in association with the peasantry in the actual experience of Jewish artisan life. Men of most humble companionships and occupations in our age have frequently shown extraordinary acumen in matters apparently far outside the range of their wonted pursuits. A list of illustrious shoemakers has recently been compiled from almost every department of human endeavor. A certain concentration of mind incident to the comparative solitariness of this lowly but honorable calling develops, it would seem, unusual powers of thought in persons of serious habits. May it not have been so in the trade which we are led to believe Jesus followed for several critical years of his life? Surely the common toil of a carpenter

would be exceedingly valuable for a proper apprehension of the needs of laboring people. It was a business career to help business men. It was this recognized knowledge of the work of man's hands which gave such significance to his words, "Come unto me, all ye that labor and are heavy laden."

But when, after eighteen obscure years, Jesus stepped forth to execute the great mission intrusted to him, the heated atmosphere, the turbulent conditions of town life would rapidly call forth his intellectual force to its highest possibilities. Jerusalem with its crowded populations and its metropolitan evils would supply this important factor in his mental development. How profoundly he would be moved by the spectacles he witnessed with a keener insight into their meaning than any other man could possess! Charles Lamb told Wordsworth that he often shed tears in the motley Strand from fullness of joy at so much life. What must have been the emotions of Jesus when, gazing upon the hosts of Jerusalem with an eye which looked far beneath the perturbed surface of the multitude, he took up into his thought the problems of life and destiny which were but superficially apprehended by his countrymen—the ambitions, the passions, the poverty, the dreams, the wretchedness of the throng about him! His tears sprang not from excess of joy, but from depths of pity no philosophy has explored. And if the life of men in populous centers influenced the trend of Christ's thoughts, what did the contemplation of nature accomplish for him? If we turn to his public utterances for answer there is little to gratify our curiosity or to enlighten our research. Early he felt the lily of the field discourse to him of the invisible beauty, and the ravens tell him of God his Father. The facts of life about him, the loveliness of the world, the eloquence of river and mountain, of sky and landscape, of the ten thousand enrapturing sights which were visible in that most charming section of Palestine in which he was reared, unquestionably stirred his soul deeply. But it is remarkable that he never drew his illustrations from uncultivated nature; only from fields that were tilled, from the face of nature as it had felt the hand of man. The occupations of his contemporaries were ever at his command to express in a homely but marvelously effect-

ive way the principles of the kingdom he had come to explain. There is little in his words to indicate that Jesus had what we call distinctively the poetic temperament. He was intensely practical. He saw the pulsations of the human heart in all the facts of life and reached forth to them through the whole tumult of things about him. Yet it is impossible to think of him as devoid of a profound feeling for nature which heightened his intellectual sensibilities and imparted a subtle charm to his speech.

But, whatever we may conceive to have been the effect of Christ's environment upon his mental habit, of his perfect adaptation to the requirements of his office there can be no question. It was his function to impart instruction through the medium of extemporaneous address to a thoroughly miscellaneous auditory. For this he was qualified to an extraordinary degree. He was essentially an orator, though it is not usual to think of him in this capacity. He possessed the physical and intellectual qualities requisite for the noble calling, and his forms of speech were the most suitable for the purpose to which he devoted his public ministry. In these suggestions we have a field for study which can only be dimly indicated within the limits of this article. If we add to the elements herein imperfectly sketched the supreme elevation involved in the possession of Christ's mental faculties by the Holy Spirit we have in outline the sufficient explication of his unparalleled intellectual vitality. We see in our day how the humblest men, with paltry endowments, devoid of scholastic training, coming forth from lowly habitations, are lifted by the energy of the Holy Spirit into heights of mental and spiritual illumination truly divine. We behold them through public speech achieving results in the transformations of character which reason fails to explain. Such disclosures of quickened intelligence through fellowship with the Spirit of God help us faintly to realize the possibilities in the intellectual life of Him to whom it is said "God giveth not the Spirit by measure," and whom we recognize as "God manifest in the flesh."

Geo. P. Eckman.

Art. VII.—BROWNING'S "PARACELSUS."

Study of Browning usually begins as a fad and ends as a
fever. The fascination is that of the search for gold: the long
journey, the miles upon miles of soliloquizing solitude—all are
forgotten in finding some golden nugget worth a prince's ransom.
The amateur reader is a literary Klondiker who is just as likely
to starve to death as to find a fortune. Three accusations may be
brought against Browning—prolixity, obscurity, and fondness of
the abnormal. As to the first accusation Browning must have lived
in eternity, for he seems to have no sense of time. "The Ring
and the Book" has twenty-one thousand one hundred and seventy-
one lines—two thousand one hundred and seventy-one more than
Pope's translation of the Iliad. Browning states that when the
inspiration to write this poem came upon him he felt

> A spirit laughs and leaps through every limb
> And lights my eye and lifts me by the hair.

When you open the book to read this poem you know just how the
author felt—at least so far as his hair was concerned. Browning's
obscurity has been attributed to the "panther-like restlessness and
panther-like spring of his intellect." It is claimed that there is a
connection from point to point, but that the panther-poet passes
on so quickly that the ordinary mind cannot follow. On many
a page the thought is well-nigh murdered by a mob of words
—apparently disjointed irresponsible conjunctions, subjectless
verbs, orphaned pronouns, and nondescript phrases—that gather
from time to time and drag the poet's meaning in the dust. And
then Browning really seems to revel in the abnormal. Himself
eminently sane, he evidently delights in the analysis and portrayal
of erratic characters. His masterpiece is an old Roman murder
tale. Not content to tell it once, he repeats it again and again. It
may be urged that his purpose was to portray the whole of life,
but this is disease, not life. The morbid and horrible have no place
in a great and healthful life. John Bright was right in believing
that only high motives and noble characters will be found in the
literary masterpieces of the future.

"Paracelsus" is an example of this morbid tendency. The poem has for its subject a singular and erratic character, a sort of peripatetic doctor and ambulatory theosophist who flourished under this name, with the addition to it of Philippus Aureolus, about three hundred years before. He was born in Einsiedeln in 1493, and his name, Theophrastus Bombastus von Hohenheim. Without a thorough education even for those times, he made his way until he secured a professor's chair at Basle. Here he astonished everybody. He scorned all authorities. In a most dramatic manner he burned the works of Galen before his students and assumed supreme authority in all matters pertaining to medicine. His arrogance was equaled only by his evil habits. To escape well-deserved punishment for a serious outrage against a magistrate he finally fled to Alsatia, and, resuming his wanderings, ultimately reached Salzburg, where he died in 1541. Paracelsus was an exponent of Esoteric Buddhism three hundred years before Madam Blavatsky founded the Theosophical Society. He taught very nearly all the points of Christian Science three hundred years before Mrs. Eddy became afflicted by "mortal mind."* He was an alchemist and charm worker. Hudibras says of him:

> Bumbastus kept a devil's bird
> Shut in the pommel of his sword,
> That taught him all the cunning pranks
> Of past and future mountebanks.

Bombastus Theophrastus being such a worthless fellow, why, you wonder, did Browning select him as a subject for his poem? Not wholly because of the poet's love for the abnormal. Certain qualities in the man and his story were well suited to serve the poet's purpose and enforce the principles he desired to teach: First, with all his grotesque inconsistencies Paracelsus expressed, for his age, the scientific method and spirit. He must be judged by the standards of his time, and so considered he has some claim to scientific credit. He was the first to use laudanum, and practically gave that drug to the world. Professor Furguson says: "His positive services to medicine are summed up in his wide application of chemical ideas to pharmacy and therapeutics; his indirect and possibly greater services to be found in the stimulus,

* G. W. Cooke, *Browning Guide Book*, p. 259.

the revolutionary stimulus, of his ideas about method and general theory." Contradictions did not trouble Paracelsus. He believed in magic and astrology, and held a curious incomprehensible doctrine of signatures, but he was also an emphatic prophet of the scientific method. Kingsley says: "He had one idea to which if he had kept true his life would have been happier—the firm belief that all true science was a revelation from God and was not to be obtained second or third hand, but by going straight to nature . . . and listening to what Bacon calls 'the voice of God revealed in facts.'"

A second reason for this choice of subject was Browning's well-known view that intuition is a source of truth. This was a pronounced personal conviction and teaching of the historic Paracelsus. And the third reason was the fact that the history of Paracelsus illustrated, in a highly dramatic if not tragic way, the failure of the life of the intellect when divorced from the life of the heart. These three elements will furnish an analysis of the poem. Paracelsus is an earnest student intent upon gaining truth. He has a "wolfish hunger for knowledge," and gives up his whole life to intellectual attainment. He devotes himself to this one aim. He says to Festus:

> I am young, . . . happy, and free.
> I can devote myself; I have a life
> To give. . . .
> New hopes should animate the world, new light
> Should dawn from new revealings to a race
> Weighed down so long, forgotten so long.

His motives seem mixed and shifting; at one time he would win fame, and again he would be an oracle for God, but upon one point he was always insistent: he must know. He declares:

> I cannot feed on beauty for the sake
> Of beauty only, nor can drink in balm
> From lovely objects for their loveliness;
> My nature cannot lose her first imprint;
> I still must hoard and heap and class all truths
> With one ulterior purpose: I must know.

It would be difficult to find a better statement of the scientific method than "to hoard and heap and classify all truth," and "I must know" is the exact dictum of the scientific spirit. We shall

see presently that Paracelsus finds that this method standing alone is far from satisfactory. The second teaching of the poem gives a reason for this failure. Browning shows that the deepest knowledge may be attained by a more direct method than scientific induction, and that truth *so* obtained has the most emphatic certitude. Paracelsus at last understands that

> Truth is within ourselves; it takes no rise
> From outward things, whate'er you may believe.
> There is an inmost center in us all
> Where truth abides in fullness; and around,
> Wall upon wall, the gross flesh hems it in,
> This perfect, clear perception which is truth,
> A baffling and perverting carnal mesh
> Binds it, and makes all error; and to KNOW
> Rather consists in opening out a way
> Whence the imprisoned splendor may escape
> Than in effecting entry for a light
> Supposed to be without. Watch narrowly
> The demonstration of a truth, its birth,
> And you trace back the effulgence to its spring
> And source within us; where broods radiance vast,
> To be elicited ray by ray as chance
> Shall favor.

In "The Ring and the Book" the Pope, implying an emphatic affirmative answer, asks,

> Must we deny . . .
> Recognized truths, obedient to some truth
> Unrecognized yet but perceptible?—
> Correct the portrait by the living face,
> Man's God, by God's God in the mind of man?

An eminent critic says: "No more definite description of Browning's attitude toward the religion of his time could be given than is contained in these words. They indicate that he is a transcendentalist, and that he finds the authenticity and proof of religious truth in the soul's intuitions. He would have faith in the thing; that is, faith that God speaks directly to the soul whenever man will listen to that still small voice of the Infinite Truth within, and not faith in the mere report that men once had such a revelation." Our age needs this message. Science needs it for her own enlargement. Science has been of the earth, earthy. There has been an unwillingness to receive all the facts. The apprehensions of reason have been accepted, but facts of the soul have been ruled

out. It may be said that these intuitions are not capable of scientific demonstration, but as elements of consciousness they are more certainly attested than the most unquestioned scientific inductions. Take, for instance, the law of gravitation, declared by science to be universal, and yet it has never had an absolute proof. That proof requires universal observation which, in the nature of the case, cannot be given. It is a stupendous scientific assumption, and yet is so entirely satisfactory that to doubt it would indicate insanity. It will be remembered that no one has insisted with greater force and clearness upon the incompleteness and relativity of scientific knowledge than Herbert Spencer. Too much has been made of scientific certainty. Science as well as religion has her "great Perhaps." Paracelsus holds that the soul's direct discoveries are better assured than its rational inductions. He accepts the witness of reason, he employs the scientific method, he revels in the scientific spirit, but he gives hearty welcome to that larger science, the science of the future, which discards no fact of human consciousness, and so he trusts his soul; for,

> In man's self arise
> August anticipations, symbols, types
> Of a dim splendor ever on before
> In that eternal circle life pursues.

In a sublime passage he declares his confidence in this larger view—this proving of the soul:

> I haste
> To contemplate undazzled some one truth—
> Its bearings and effects alone—at once
> What was a speck expands into a star,
> Asking a life to pass exploring thus,
> Till I near craze. I go to prove my soul!
> I see my way as birds their trackless way.
> I shall arrive! what time, what circuit first,
> I ask not: but—unless God send his hail
> Or blinding fire balls, sleet or stifling snow—
> In some time, his good time, I shall arrive:
> He guides me and the bird. In his good time!

In the third element in the career of its hero the failure of the intellectual life alone to give peace and satisfaction lies the poem's main discussion and chief message. It is not a screed against the pleasures of intellectual attainment. That is not the

poet's position. Indeed such mental delight is eulogized, and
Browning devotes another poem, "The Grammarian's Funeral,"
to showing the joys of the mind. The message is that the intellectual life alone cannot give the deep and lasting peace which
satisfies the soul. At first Paracelsus has the inspiration of high
purpose:

> Make no more giants, God,
> But elevate the race at once! We ask
> To put forth just our strength, our human strength,
> All starting fairly, all equipped alike,
> Gifted alike, all eagle-eyed, true-hearted—
> See if we cannot beat thine angels yet!
> Such is my task. I go to gather this,
> The sacred knowledge, here and there dispersed
> About the world, long lost or never found.

He resolves to put aside everything else, believing,

> My own affections, laid to rest awhile,
> Will waken purified, subdued alone
> By all I have achieved.

Here follows a brief passage full of dramatic fire. He inquires
of his friends, Festus and Michal,

> Do you believe I shall accomplish this?
> *Festus:* I do believe!
> *Michal:*   I ever did believe.
> *Par.:*   Those words shall never fade from out my brain!
> This earnest of the end shall never fade!
> Are there not, Festus, are there not, dear Michal,
> Two points in the adventure of the diver,
> One—when, a beggar, he prepares to plunge,
> One—when, a prince, he rises with his pearl?
> Festus, I plunge.
> *Festus:*   We wait you when you rise!

The next scene opens in Constantinople. Paracelsus has attained,
and now reviews the results of his years of devotion and toil—

> I have dared
> Come to a pause with knowledge; scan for once
> The heights already reached, without regard
> To the extent above; fairly compute
> All I have clearly gained—for once excluding
> A brilliant future to supply and perfect
> All half-gains and conjectures and crude hopes,

and from this point of view he reaches the conclusion that the
reward of all his strivings has been utter failure:

A few blurred characters suffice to note
A stranger wandered long through many lands
And reaped the fruit he coveted in a few
Discoveries, as appended here and there,
The fragmentary produce of much toil
In a dim heap, fact and surmise together
Confusedly massed as when acquired; he was
Intent on gain to come too much to stay
And scrutinize the little gained : the whole
Slipt in the blank space 'twixt an idiot's gibber
And a mad lover's ditty—there it lies.

And yet those blottings chronicle a life—
A whole life, and—my life ! . . .
Spent and decided, wasted past retrieve
Or worthy beyond peer.

An altered brow and eye and gait and speech
Attest that now he knows the adage true,
"Time fleets, youth fades, life is an empty dream."

This soul tragedy, for it is nothing less, is not in the realm of fancy, it is most serious fact. It is an old adage that "Knowledge alone bringeth sorrow," and Paracelsus has allowed his "wolfish hunger after knowledge" to dig out his heart. Darwin's confession shows that he, too, realized this danger. He says: "My mind seems to have become a kind of machine for grinding general laws out of a large collection of facts. Why this should have caused the atrophy of that part of the brain I cannot conceive. If I had my life to live over again I would have made the rule to read some poetry and listen to some music at least once every week." The mind is great, but man is more than mind. When man's thought is filled the problem is but half solved; the heart as well as the head must be satisfied or the riddle of life is not fully read. Along these two parallels, thought and affection, lies the footpath of peace.

In the closing pages of "Paracelsus" we have the record of aspiration and final attainment. He recovers from his disappointment and despair and is cheered into new hope by his friends Festus and Michal, and his poet-friend Aprile. This Italian poet, Aprile, had made his life blunder in pressing to the other extreme and attempting to find life's peace in love alone. The poem does not enter extensively upon his experiences, but at last the two poets meet once more and for the last time. Aprile is dying.

Paracelsus bends over him. Each has a message for the other and in the blended lessons both shall find peace. Paracelsus pleads:

> Love me henceforth, Aprile, while I learn
> To love; and, merciful God, forgive us both!
> We wake at length from weary dreams; but both
> Have slept in fairyland: though dark and drear
> Appears the world before us, we no less
> Wake with our wrists and ankles jeweled still.
> I too have sought to KNOW as thou to LOVE;
> Excluding love as thou refusedst knowledge.
> Still thou hast beauty and I power. We wake:
> What penance canst devise for both of us?
>
> *Aprile:* I hear thee faintly. The thick darkness! Even
> Thine eyes are hid. 'Tis as I knew: I speak,
> And now I die. But I have seen thy face!
> O poet, think of me, and sing of me!
> But to have seen thee and to die so soon!
>
> *Par.:* Die not, Aprile! We must never part.
> Are we not halves of one dissevered world
> Whom this strange chance unites once more? Part? never!
> Till thou, the lover, know; and I, the knower,
> Love—until both are saved.

Aprile dies realizing that "God is the perfect poet, who in his person acts his own creations," and now the scene changes to Basle, where, after twenty years, Paracelsus meets with Festus, his life-long friend, and with him journeys to Colmar in Alsatia. Like Dante's Virgil, Festus becomes the guide of the soul of Paracelsus and leads him into the full realization of the vision of peace which he saw by the bedside of the dying Aprile. They talk of all the past—of childhood's dewy days, of Einsiedeln, whose green hills were once the whole world to them, of the sunny wall at Wurzburg, of Michal's sweet face—alas! Michal is dead. Paracelsus turns comforter:

> Stone dead!—then you have laid her among the flowers
> ere this. Now, do you know,
> I can reveal a secret which shall comfort
> Even you. I have no julep, as men think,
> To cheat the grave; but a far better secret.
> Know, then, you did not ill to trust your love
> To the cold earth. I have thought much of it,
> For I believe we do not wholly die.

This brings us to the final scene—a cell in the hospital of St. Sebastian in Salzburg where Paracelsus makes his final attainment. Inspired by his consciousness of immortality and appre-

hending life's reality in the blending of love and knowledge, holding the hand of Festus and calling the name of his dead poet-friend Aprile, he passes in peace. He has found at last that the loving heart is the lamp of God. Festus presses his hand and as he dies he recognizes Aprile, who years before had passed into the great silence.

Par.: And this is death: I understand it all.
New being waits me; new perceptions must
Be born in me before I plunge therein,
Which last is Death's affair; and while I speak
Minute by minute he is filling me
With power; and . . . my foot is on the threshold
Of boundless life—the doors unopened yet.

  .   .   .   .

                  If I stoop
Into a dark tremendous sea of cloud
It is but for a time; I press God's lamp
Close to my breast; its splendor, soon or late,
Will pierce the gloom: I shall emerge one day.
You understand me? I have said enough.
        Festus, let my hand—
This hand—lie in your own, my own true friend!
Aprile! Hand in hand with you, Aprile!

Festus: And this was Paracelsus.

C. W. Barnes.

ART. VIII.—THE LETTERS OF LIPSIUS.

FROM the library of the late sorely lamented Professor Allen, of Harvard, came into my possession a curious little book which happens to be exactly three hundred years old. It contains eight hundred selected letters in Latin by Justus Lipsius. Printed in Avignon in 1603, it bears on the second blank leaf the name of Martin Boscheron as its owner in 1609; on the third, the name of F. D. Allen, with the date of 1892, to which is added, "Paris, 20 centimes." Here too now stands the record of the appreciation in value which it suffered by being Professor Allen's; for, after subscribing my own name as the present owner, I wrote in the upper right-hand corner "50 cts." It would appear, therefore, that it increased in value more than one thousand per cent in six years! Surely there are some depths that plummets will not sound, some prices that defy all the principles of economics! Justus Lipsius, the celebrated humanist and classical scholar, whose life is nearly coincident with the latter half of the sixteenth century, had an erratic and rather remarkable career, corresponding to his own genius. At different times he was a professor in the universities of Jena, Leyden, and Louvain. For two years he was a Latin secretary in a cardinal's retinue at Rome. He was acquainted with most of the great classical scholars of his time, and long maintained the reputation of being the greatest of them all. To the discriminating critic of to-day it is clear that his classical scholarship was narrow, and in many ways superficial. He knew little Greek, cared nothing for a large part of Latin literature, and published many rash conjectural emendations of Latin texts. For all that, his knowledge of Latin would be astounding to an American youth of to-day. It was he who could repeat the whole of Tacitus by heart, and agreed to do so with a drawn dagger held to his heart, the point to be plunged into him if at any time he failed to go on correctly! His editions of Tacitus and Seneca were really important works; and it is not strange that he left a great body of letters written in the Latin language, which were published in "centuries," or groups of one hundred. The edition

that I have contains eight of these centuries, as the title-page states, of which three are addressed to Frenchmen, Italians, and Spaniards; the fourth, to Germans and Frenchmen; the fifth is addressed to miscellaneous recipients; the last three are to Belgians. Then follows a treatise on the epistolary art, by the same Lipsius. Finally there is an index of "several noteworthy subjects and most elegant similes," supposed to be quite complete, which was inserted, so it is stated, "for the benefit of studious youth!" Each century of the letters, as a rule, is preceded by a separate dedication, and in several cases there is a prefatory appeal "to the reader." In the first of these Lipsius apologizes for publishing a part of his letters at a time, saying that they are a sample, sent forth tentatively, like a scout to test the temper and strength of the enemy. "If there are no enemies, or but few," he concludes, "I will faithfully agree to lead forth into the public gaze of Fame the whole host of my letters. But if pitfalls and snares await me I shall lie quiet, and wisely remain in the camp of trusty silence. My good reader, show kindness and indulgence to one who reciprocates those feelings." In the address to the reader at the beginning of the second century he finds it already necessary to warn others from publishing epistles of his without his knowledge and consent; and sets his imitators an example in the matter by publishing there none of any other writer than himself. It was the custom of Lipsius to date his letters; the first one in this collection is dated 1575, the last one 1601. Of course most of the persons to whom they are addressed are as little known to us as is the barber of Rameses or the hostler of Sennacherib! When we turn the pages, and Gedeon Tserhendrixius, Joannes Drenckvaertus, Petrus Lafaillius, Franciscus Schottus, Augerius Busbequius, and that ilk, pass before us in solemn review, we cannot but ask again and again, "What is fame?" Here and there, however, we find a more familiar name, like that of the classical scholar Gruter, the French statesman Jacques Auguste de Thou, or the genius Joseph Justus Scaliger. In the first address to the reader Lipsius expresses the conviction that a letter should drop hot from the point of one's pen, claiming that his own habit is never to rewrite one, indeed seldom to read one over a second time. Such a method

cannot fail to produce the impression of spontaneity, whatever may be the effect upon style or accuracy. That he was not lacking in the theory of the epistolary art appears from the mere enumeration of the subjects of the chapters of his essay on that topic: "On various names for a letter, and on its form among the ancients;" "What constitutes a letter, and what are its parts;" "Definition and division of the subject-matter, and discussion of the address;" "On the conclusion of a letter and its scaling;" "Variety of subject and its arrangement;" "Invention and order of treatment;" "Style, first, Brevity;" "Clearness, how it is violated, how it is attained;" "Simplicity, which is twofold, and advice how to attain it;" "Beauty and propriety;" "Style in particular to be gained by imitation—what authors should be read for this, and when;" "In what way to quote, and from whom;" "The expression and formation of style by three kinds of imitation."

It would be tedious to attempt any test of the success of Lipsius in carrying out all the principles he lays down. Even a cursory examination of the collection in this volume, however, would enable us to state some of his chief characteristics as a letter writer. The letters are seldom very long—often decidedly short. The Latin is by no means Ciceronian; but that would have been beyond expectation in a scholar trained in the methods of that day; and, besides, Lipsius was no admirer of Cicero. Here, for example, is a letter taken at random, addressed to a certain Lupus Dionysius. Running the eye along the lines I find such expressions as these: *Litteras tuas . . . exosculatus sum; hanc flammam . . . per litteras revelare; ad omnem disciplinam sequaces; militaria vel aulica; eae imbibuntur per lectionem;* etc. But the Latinity is that of one that has read widely and well the treasures of Latin literature from the best classical period down to his own time. Greek quotations occur often; and it is significant that in such cases a parallel Latin rendering is to be found on the margin! Evidently the average reader was not expected to be familiar with Greek. Now and then appear quotations from Latin poetry, but they are not remarkably common. Various forms of address are employed. The stereotyped "S. D." sometimes gives place to *S. dico, S. precor, S. mitto, S. multam precor*, plain *S.*, or to the

17

total omission of everything except the name of the addressee. Even greater freedom may be noticed in the closing sentences of the letters. Such forms as these often take the place of the historic *vale:—deus te servet* ("God save you"); *fata viderint, tu mi—salve* ("The fates see to it that you flourish, my dear friend"); *tibi illam [valetudinem] longam, et hanc bonam . . . posco* ("I beseech for you that your health may long endure and be excellent"); *ergo amare amatum me possum dicere: et ut semper possim, te per Genium tuum Virtuti et Honori sic amicum roga* ("I may say that I reciprocate your affection: pray your Genius, so well-disposed toward Virtue and Honor, that I may always do so as fully"); *nihil liquidi in rebus humanis: in alto hoc erit, quo te meque, mi Veli, Altissimus ille et ὑψίζυγος ducat* ("There is nothing clear in human affairs; that shall be attained on high; and thither, my dear Velius, may He who is above all, throned in the heavens, bring thee and me"); *me, si non ex merito, ex benignitate tua ama* ("Love me—even if I don't deserve it—because of your kindness of heart"); *Deum precor, te ecclesiae suae, magnum et rarum lumen, diu lucere patiatur* ("I pray God that he will long permit you to shine as a powerful and brilliant light of his Church"); and so on in endless mutations. The date regularly follows, last of all. Only an extended study of the letters and a general acquaintance with them can show how successfully he attained to the ideals of brevity, perspicuity, beauty, and propriety which he held. But the curious reader will find a remarkable, often brilliant product in searching for the answers to these questions. The subjects treated are, of course, often mere matters of friendship or details of small business or family and personal interests. But many more important questions are among those discussed. One letter reopens the venerable dispute as to which Alpine pass Hannibal traversed with his elephants and his invincible cavalry. Other interesting subjects are, "Who is the author of evil?" "History of dogs;" "The worship of Cybele;" "The being and providence of God defended against the blasphemies of atheists and Epicureans;" estimates of Homer, Statius, Tacitus, and Tertullian; and emendations to various Latin authors. Among the noteworthy similes employed are those where calumnies are

likened to spiders' webs; grief, to smoke, which is dissipated when it rises aloft; fame, to fire, which does not rise entirely without smoke; life and death, to the sun and moon, which set, not to destruction, but to rise again into more glorious life.

Lipsius is not prone to quote poetry, and seldom himself branches into verse; but occasionally we stumble upon a poetic effusion of some importance. At the end of the eighth letter of the first book, for example, stands a series of glyconic stanzas, with the title, "The Praise and the Prayer of a Happy Life." The poem begins thus:

> Ille est par superis deis,
> Et mortalibus altior,
> Qui fati ambiguum diem
> Non optat levis, aut timet.

The following paraphrase may perhaps serve to reproduce in English its spirit:

> A match for all the gods above is he,
> And far above all other mortals raised,
> Who neither idly dreads, nor thoughtlessly
> Longs for the hidden day of Fate to dawn.
> No foolish wish for what's beyond his grasp,
> Nor craving for base gain disturbs his peace;
> The raging threats of kings affect him not,
> Nor bolt of Jove refusing to be mild;
> But steadfast in his place unmoved he stands,
> And scorns the empty baubles of the crowd.
> For him the day dawns ever free from care,
> Still free from care when sinks the sun to rest.
> If I might pass my life by my desires,
> I would not long for power nor for wealth,
> Nor proudly lead a train of captives on
> Behind the hoofs of glorious snow-white steeds;
> In lonely places I would spend my days,
> Would have my little gardens and my fields,
> And there, beside the murmur of the stream,
> Would cultivate the muses with delight.
> So when the goddess Lachesis has spun
> The last that stubborn Fate allots me here,
> May I in peaceful age depart this life,
> Beloved by all, and kind to every one,
> Like Laugius, my dear friend by my side!

In the fifteenth letter of the second century we may observe him in a different mood. He writes at the close of a letter to Dominicus Lampronius: "My health is poor. I am doing what I can for it by relaxations, little walks, and especially by the pleas-

ures of my little garden. See, here are the rules which I have there. I have inserted them for your amusement." Then follow, after the date, "The Rules of Lipsius's Garden, at the entrance, spoken in the character of a two-faced Janus:"

Good luck! Whoever you may be, stop, read, obey! I, Janus, proclaim here at the threshold: This shall be the rule for enjoying the garden and its master, the former to look at, the latter to talk with. Do not feast, except with the eyes, on anything planted or growing here! Be a Tiro, keep your hands under control. But if you put out your hand to touch or take anything—I put it bluntly—put *yourself* out! Nor may you enjoy my master's society at any and all times. Don't come before six o'clock in the evening, nor stay after seven. At other hours he is otherwise engaged, thinking, writing. Here is his switch—Shoo, fly! Why should he also furnish a feast? Shoo, fly! Also beware of prohibited subjects of conversation. You may jest, tell stories, ask questions; but nothing serious; this is the place for pleasantries. Rather, whatever is especially charming in literary lines, as you walk, discuss, teach, learn; this is a place devoted to the Muses. You who are very serious or very combative, keep out! To you I am the god of closing! Dogs, except one, stay out! Maidservants, save one, keep out! Do you understand? Remember this too, whichever way you go, I see you!

While Lipsius had, evidently, a host of friends with whom he was on most cordial and intimate terms, there are suspicions that his immediate family life was not in all respects an especially happy one. Such suspicions appear to be confirmed by passages like this, addressed to Theodore Leevius:

But you have interested me; particularly by that part of your letter in which you ask my advice about the all-important question in life. You are deliberating between marriage and celibacy. It is a hard matter for me to give you advice about, being myself already almost tied down to prejudice. For you see what I have done in my own case. . . . You do not look for a universal answer, I suppose, whether marriage is a good thing; but rather, whether it is for a wise man, at such a time as this, and for yourself. If you are in pursuit of wisdom and a quiet life, I don't know that you'd better marry. Examples of the ancient philosophers are to be found on each side; but reason points rather toward the negative. For if a mind free before God and oneself is needed for the pursuit of wisdom and tranquillity, I do not see how one can assume that care which is ever present, day and night, which worries and keeps one in a ferment. . . . We steer our own little bark with difficulty; do we then desire to take in tow a ship with all its rigging? . . . If in a horse or a piece of land you have been imposed upon, you can at least expostulate; not so in the case of a wife. . . . Diogenes shrewdly advised against all marriage. For, said he, a young man should not marry yet; an old man, never! . . . These things

can be said on one side; but no fewer on the other. I will add two warnings of Socrates: First, young men are like little fishes playing around the net, wishing to go in; when in, anxious to get out. . . . The other, that the oracle replied to one asking whether to marry or not, "You will be sorry, whichever you do."

In matters of religion Lipsius had the fickle facility of his times and of his race. A devoted Catholic in early life, he finished his career also in the bosom of the mother Church. But the most important period of his scholarly and literary activity was spent at Leyden, where he certainly must, at least in externals, have conformed to his Calvinistic surroundings. That he should have followed in the footsteps of his more illustrious royal master, Henry of Navarre, is not unnatural; but he had no similar excuses to plead for such apostasy. To found a Bourbon dynasty was a temptation almost too great for mortal flesh to resist; and to unite all political and religious factions throughout France in allegiance to a quondam Huguenot was not only a patriotic achievement of the first magnitude, but probably the best thing that could have happened for the Huguenots themselves. The return of Lipsius to Rome, on the other hand, cannot be attributed to patriotism, nor did it even bring any lasting addition to his own glory. Though for the nonce his action aroused enthusiasm in various quarters, he reaped no real advantage. The remaining years of his life were spent in comparative retirement, and his literary activity declined ultimately to the pitiful level of Jesuitical pamphleteering in behalf of minor ecclesiastical hoaxes not dissimilar to that of the Lourdes of to-day. It is not surprising, therefore, if Lipsius was a trimmer in religion, that we likewise fail to discover in these letters any very positive political preferences, or anything that serves especially to illuminate the dark and almost, so to speak, subterranean history of France during this gloomy period of civil wars, with their plots and counterplots and their series of royal assassinations. There are, to be sure, letters to various important personages of the epoch; but such letters deal mostly in flattery and generalities, and particularly in the wares of the scholar—we might almost better say, of the pedant. That Lipsius, however, though no politician, was not dead to the world of affairs about him, and appreciated keenly the drift of events and the unspeak-

able corruptness of the day, the quotation of a single letter will suffice to show. It is dated at Leyden, January 16, 1586. To appreciate it, we must recall the situation at this moment. In France the treaty of Nemours, depriving the Huguenots of their liberties, had just been signed. The "war of the three Henrys" was beginning. The riotous yet effeminate king was as helplessly knocked about between the ultra-Catholic Guise and the Protestant Navarre as was the ball which he himself caught continually in its cup as he languidly paraded the public streets. The treacherous Italian queen mother was still busy with her schemes. Seven different armies took the field this year in various parts of the country. In the Low Countries Philip of Spain was still trying to crush out Protestantism and independence, and his plans for the great Armada which was to humiliate Elizabeth were being matured. In England the affairs of the imprisoned Mary Stuart were approaching the final crisis. The letter is addressed to Lambert Vander-Burch, and reads thus:

I have good reason to be fond of your letters, so full of affection and modesty. For I interpret your praises for me as a proof of love; since it is assuredly rather affection than wise judgment that dictates them. For what am I? I know that I am attempting more than I accomplish, am desirous of doing more for the public weal than I can do. Yet, whatever it does amount to (and I believe you, my faithful friends, when you claim that it is something), in so far it is at least a pleasure to me that it wins me favor in the eyes of such men. Your wisdom is remarkable to me in the reply you make with reference to public affairs. They are indeed in confusion and turmoil, and I would that a catastrophe were not impending! What good man does not join with me in bemoaning the state of things? Indeed, this is all that is left us to do, since to heal the sore is not in our power, nor perhaps in that of any human being. That God, who sends these public disasters upon us, who fosters and nurses the disease, will also bring them to an end when in his Providence we, their cause, shall fall. Our sins do not cease nor diminish, but rather seem to increase and accumulate with our punishment. We daily offend the Divine Will, and, as if there were not already just grounds for punishment, we give new provocation. When were luxury, pride, passion ever more flagrant or unpunished? Religion is on every man's lips, but wickedness is in his heart. While their words sound pious, their deeds are those of ambition and avarice—not merely in now and then an individual, but in every rank and age, and in either sex. Accordingly, I have no hope of peace or tranquillity. "War, dread war," I await, or at any rate a tyranny as undesirable as any war. Those upon whose banners Victory seems about to rest are roused to anger; and it may be doubted if any counselor of mod-

eration would be heeded. In every war the beginnings of peace after victory are crude; but this is especially true in the case of civil war, where hatred and the partisan spirit is most bitter. But God will see to it; and to him, as for me, I commit these my anxieties, as well as my solicitude for my health, which, my good friend, I do not indeed neglect, nor do I voluntarily seek for death; but when I have done what man can do, free from care I await the outcome. My endeavor is, to correct my life, to please my God, to possess a home far above these gloomy clouds, in that heavenly height from which I may look down upon all these human affairs and despise them. Meanwhile, I do not neglect constant study, nor anything public or private by which I think I can profit mankind. This will appear shortly through certain of my writings which I am preparing for a second edition. Your offer of the manuscript of Florus is very gratifying to me. I am indeed discovering many things that were not noticed by Vinetus or Stadius, the previous editors; and I shall find more, I know, if I have the assistance of your copy. And so, if you will send it to me as soon as possible, you will confer a favor on me, and on posterity; and I will not be silent about it. Farewell! Affectionate greetings to your brother Graphiarius, with thanks for the little gift recently sent me.

Unconscious prophet that Lipsius was in so writing, he could hardly have imagined how speedy and terrible a fulfillment of his fears was at hand. It was but a few years before each of the three Henrys had perished by the hand of a murderer; and the seed sown in these days of "luxury, pride, and passion" was destined not to perish without an abundant fruition, a harvest of which the fearful days of the French Revolution after two centuries were but a minor part. God, however, did "see to it," as he always does. Religious and in due time civil liberty came to France. The Spanish Armada proved a colossal failure. The days of the Inquisition passed, and so did the threatening power of Spain. The Dutch achieved their independence. Huguenot and Briton joined with the emigrants from the Low Countries to people the great new western continent with a sturdy race whose mission is to send the Gospel of perfect liberty around the world. God will always "see to it." Asia and Africa, Turkey and Russia are in his hands. He is sending out the message of light and liberty from America to them all; and in his own good time shall dawn the day of divine peace throughout the earth.

Karl P. Harrington.

Art. IX.—OUR LITERARY BIBLE.

Some years ago the question was raised, Shall we teach the Bible as literature. To-day we accept the Bible as essential material for teaching literature. Particularly is this true of academic and collegiate English. Some of our colleges specify portions of the Bible as permissible entrance subjects. But thus far the proper literary method of Bible study has remained a very vague conception, and the importance of some such clear conception is emphasized by recent interest in the biblical element of modern English literature. The study of selections of biblical literature is a very different thing from a systematic examination of the Bible as literature. However clearly we may distinguish the various books and forms of composition, the Bible as a literary monument is essentially one. Any good literary method of study, therefore, must comprehend the whole. But even thus such a method must be more than an examination of the literary forms. These are universal, and such a partial literary study is of immense value. But, while the Bible is as universal and cosmopolitan as these forms, it has taken so unique a position in our English literature and language as to justify a peculiar interest in its growth and form. For as an English book the Bible has had a growth and history coincident with the rise of our literary language. In a very remarkable sense the Bible has been for us a fountain head of literary inspiration, in both material and language. Whether it is such to-day is another question. We are now more properly concerned with its relation to our entire literature. Here opens up a very rich field of study as yet worked only in fragmentary fashion. Our literary Bible is at once the same as the Bibles in other tongues and different from them. Its beginnings are coeval with the beginnings of the language. Its forms of expression have varied with the exigencies of the tongue. Its history is inextricably bound up with the storm and stress of England's political and social growth. Its publication, for centuries only in fragments and finally in many complete forms, has been determined by facilities for production and the spiritual need

of the people. The stories of the Old Testament inspired our earliest native poetry, and Ruskin acknowledged the Bible as the nourisher of his best style. But we are in danger of falling into vain abstraction unless we speedily define our terms. The summary of the preceding paragraph is to be gathered by the most casual student of the subject. We propose a study of the English Bible as an English literary monument. But as such it is the product of an evolution. For the sake of uniformity, and because it has actually been the great authority for three centuries, we should mean to-day the Authorized Version. This has held its place so long, and the revisions have not had time to establish themselves. Indeed, their changes from the old are so slight as to be negligible for our purpose; the essential force of the King James Version in our literature is not affected. However, before the completion of this rendering there were a full thousand years of literary history when the Bible was present in English forms only more or less complete. Indeed, during nine centuries only manuscript copies could be had. The few complete translations were of very limited authority. It appears to have been a very general custom for the clergyman to translate freely from his Latin or other text as occasion required. Still, through all this period biblical word and phrase are constantly cropping out. As a literary force the English Bible was this miscellaneous assortment of renderings chosen for impression on the people's minds and hearts. The particular renderings were for a moment; but the book was lasting as the people's craving for religious truth.

It is evident that the position of the English Bible is thoroughly unique, and therefore requires a peculiar method of examination. Its history is more than a chronicle of versions. The weight of it in our literature cannot depend upon the power of a fixed and definite form for reference. Properly indeed when we speak of the English literary Bible we must mean no particular version. Neither must we infer an abstract literary force. The Bible presented in numerous ways in the early times was a very real thing. Its stories, its songs, its commands, rendered by the clergy in the common tongue, were concrete possessions of the people. The phrases fitting for the ideas entered the daily speech,

and by repetition produced fairly permanent forms. Thus grew up in the tongue of the people prose and metrical versions of various parts of the Bible. And in turn this process of translating deeply affected the language itself. There were ideas in the Hebrew Scriptures not native to the Saxon mind, and when in the restricted pagan vocabulary no sufficient term could be found there was little hesitancy in making the necessary word. In this way the language and the necessities of scriptural expression together determined the version and an enlarged vocabulary. It is important to notice that this process began in the very infancy of the language. The Anglo-Saxon epic "Beowulf" in the earliest form we possess is deeply colored with these new biblical phrases and words. And these were elements not to be subject to surface changes in the tongue. The heaven-kingdom became as much a part of the Saxon's common speech as his own home.

Now, passing over this long period of manuscripts and individual renderings, when we reach the sixteenth century, amid a bewildering array of Bibles and Testaments, again the fact is very clear that for our purpose the term English Bible means no particular translation. The success of Tyndale's New Testament and the editions of the Bible immediately following encouraged a lively speculation in the business, and edition after edition was turned out. We may remark here that the times and authorities and places and reading publics of these various Bibles form an interesting commentary upon the religious history of the time. The Great Bible, "a splendid folio of largest volume," was a fit production for the impressive services of the Church. But the Geneva Bible, printed usually in a readable Roman type instead of the black letter, with the text divided into verses, and marginal notes attached, became the household Bible of two generations. But at the close of the great Elizabethan period the literary language had attained a sufficiently settled form to assure permanence to a new rendering of the Scriptures. It was a most opportune time for the important work which James intrusted to fifty scholarly men. A fine vocabulary—singularly pure it appears when we consider the classical scholarship of the period—had been produced. The capabilities of the English tongue in the entire

range of prose and verse had been tried and assured. A large variety of translations was at hand for comparison, and the long peace had developed adequate scholarship. But our great body of literature was just beginning. No time in the history of the language could be selected better situated to assure to such a version a large influence upon English prose. And yet we must beware of laying too much stress upon what may be termed the purely formal elements of the problem: the times, the language. The book's the thing. At this point as elsewhere a close analysis demonstrates that the essential power lay in the close relation of this book to the English people. We may never divorce the literary Bible from its peculiar spiritual energy. Because of this the Bible became an essential factor in the life of England. And the Bible is of so great weight in English style not primarily because its translators chanced to be masters of our prose, but because the English biblical mode of expression grew up under the stimulus of the Bible's answer to the spiritual needs of a people; because it is the people's book and its language the people's language.

This, then, is the prime significance of biblical quotation in Old and Modern English, not to prove the biblical style good. In the first place, there is no biblical style. Secondly, if there were its fine quality would need no such proof. These quotations and allusions merely serve to emphasize one side of the unique position of the English literary Bible. They demonstrate its intimate relation to the popular life. It is therefore a precise expositor of the essential literary genius of the race. The truth of the matter is that we have had too much of this attempt to demonstrate the literary quality of the Bible by appeal to other literature. In this we cover up the real essential. The Bible is not great because it is great literature; but it is great literature because it is the Bible. And when we lose sight of that fact our perspective is altogether wrong. The Bible is our book of religion, and any worthy study of it must begin with that assumption. As with any book, we determine first, if possible, its purported relation to human life. No piece of literature, no work of art can be adequately appreciated if this foundation is neglected. Students

often fail readily to appreciate the power of Bible English because they do not grasp the significance of its thought. On the other hand, the presence of a skillfully chosen biblical element argues an appreciation of this great fountain of pure English— English all the more pure and strong because of a certain native vigor and rhythm responding readily to the Hebrew spirit. Even the earliest translations were of a remarkable purity of style and diction. Tyndale's work is especially worthy of note. He himself says, "The Greek tongue agreeth more with the English than with the Latin, and the properties of the Hebrew tongue agreeth a thousand times more with the English than with the Latin." He perceived the likeness between the Hebrew and Saxon spirits—a likeness observable in more than one phenomenon of national life.

And here we arrive at another vexed question. We have been told that this literary Bible is passing as did the Vulgate in the Middle Age; that this passing is necessary because a new language and new literary models have been created—that other phrases than those of Holy Writ have become familiar. It is asserted that the narrow literary horizon of our fathers compelled them to seek artistic sustenance in the Bible, but that our present-day writers have discovered new sources and are disregarding the old standards. Now, if these statements are correct, and if there is any truth in the account given above of the influence of the Bible, the situation argues a very decided change in the genius of the peoples who claim the literature of England as a heritage. Certainly this is open to doubt. Some changes, indeed, have taken place in word forms and approved sentence management. But these changes are mostly superficial. They simply bring it about that not all parts of the Bible text sound equally well to the trained modern ear. But this matter of the biblical element in literature is not to be estimated offhand. We may distinguish at least three forms of it: verbatim quotations, allusions, and atmosphere or flavor produced by skillful use of word or turn of phrase. It is clear that all these are not easily to be identified. Moreover, in all essentials of style save the one of archaic word forms the Bible contains all extremes. There is no "biblical style" save as a monotonous reading of the text may produce such an effect. It

would be difficult to find in our literature passages more widely different in style than the fifth chapter of Isaiah and the eighteenth of St. Matthew, yet there is more than a surface likeness in theme. Just as variant also are the uses of the Bible by our writers. True, the manner and method have changed in the last three hundred years. But a casual observation will show to-day a large biblical element in our serious prose and poetry. To determine its precise extent will require finer discrimination. It is true we will not find very many passages *en bloc.* Our skill has gone beyond the primary stage; and the pregnant word, the fine covert allusion, will mean as much now as the literal quotations of a few generations ago. At any rate, this is a question contributory merely to the main interest. Our literary Bible remains. The diction used in its pages is our best illustration of the refining influences of years upon a literature. It is the unique product of our literary history; a type of the ready assimilative power of the English people; at once a product and an active agent in our literary life. It is our most conspicuous example of that backlying power necessary to make a literature. It is not an abstraction. Its nature has been demonstrated many times in the very midst of a nation's life. Over and over the book has been the people's best medium of expression. That alone would stamp it a great literature. Its own utterances assure the title. When we open its covers we enter the very Holy of Holies of that wonderful Spirit of Humanity whose presence must distinguish the temple of a nation's literature.

Charles Addison Dawson

Art. X.—A COMPARATIVE STUDY OF "PARADISE
REGAINED" AND GILES FLETCHER'S "CHRIST'S
VICTORIE AND TRIUMPH."

EARLY in the seventeenth century a young Cambridge student
felt the thrill of a religious emotion such as stirred saintly hearts
in the Middle Ages to paint pictures and see visions and spend
hours of rapt contemplation. Had he lived earlier he might have
betaken himself to some sequestered cloister, there to "welcome
the day with matins and greet with vesper hymns the first couriers
of the starry hosts," or, like some devout Fra Angelico, pour out
the adoration of his soul in the bright colors with which his brush
was familiar. But Giles Fletcher was neither monk nor painter.
He was just a young divinity student of a later age who made
his literary art an expression of his intense devotion. Instead of
pictures he gave to the world in 1610 a poem entitled "The Victorie and Triumph of Christ in Heaven and on Earth," a poem
wrought with the quaint conceits of mediævalism, the simplicity
of an unquestioning faith and the ardor of fervent love. Nearly
fifty years later another poetic genius seized upon the same
theme—a poet as different from Giles Fletcher as Michael Angelo
from Fra Angelico or Isaiah from the Shepherd King; a poet
whose lifework was practically finished, whose powers were full-
summed, whose fame was at its zenith when he undertook this
final tribute of song. It was John Milton; not the dreamy, studious youth, nor the stern, active man of affairs turning aside from
the dear delights of the Muses to serve his country, but John Milton the great Puritan poet and author of "Paradise Lost," the
blind seer who at the suggestion of Ellis sought a sequel to his
great epic and found "Paradise Regained" in the scriptural
account of Christ's temptation and victory. Such was the origin
of the two poems, separated from one another by half a century,
whose likenesses and differences are so striking and interesting.

Before beginning our study it will be necessary to say a few
words about the place of these poems in literature and their reception. The younger poet in fact is so little known except to the

Grosarts and Willmotts that it may even be well to review the few
facts of his life. Giles Fletcher, the younger son of Dr. Giles
Fletcher, was born about 1588, in London. The family is interesting, since his uncle was Bishop of London, his father at one
time Russian ambassador, his cousin John Fletcher the dramatist,
and his brother-poet Phineas the author of "The Purple Island."
Giles took his bachelor's degree at Cambridge in 1606, but stayed
on as divinity student until 1619. He held first a college living,
then the rectory of Alderton, Suffolk. It was a poor parish, but
Fletcher did not live to hold it long. He died in 1623. The only
literary work he has given us is a "Canto upon the Death of Eliza"
written in 1603, the "Victorie and Triumph" in 1610, a prose
tract upon "The Reward of the Faithful," some verse translations
of Boethius and Greek epigrams, and some metrical renderings
of the Lamentations of Jeremiah. No monument or stone at
Alderton marks the place where he sleeps, but, as Willmott says,
"His most lasting memorial exists in his poem, and in it we may
discover the spirit of the author looking mildly and beautifully
forth." What reception his poem met with in 1610 we do not
know, but, whatever its status at that time, we are safe in concluding that it was one of the first long religious poems to leave
its mark on English literature. Such a theme had not been
treated outside of Italy. If we do not quite agree with Grosart
as to its immortality we still may consider it a worthy pioneer
effort which should not die while we care for our minor singers,
and the less conspicuous but truly poetic contributions which have
prepared the way for the masterpieces of literature. Turning
now from the prototype to the perfect artistic creation. "Paradise
Regained" and its origin are too well known to require much in
the way of general comment. Even in early youth Milton had
jotted down scriptural subjects for possible treatment. Some of
these correspond very nearly to the themes of Cantos III and IV
of Fletcher's poem. The subject which he eventually chose to
develop many years later in "Paradise Regained" is exactly identical with the theme of the second canto of "Christ's Victorie and
Triumph." Whether, therefore, the choice of such a theme as
Christ's Temptation was at all due to his early reading of Fletcher,

or whether it emanated only from Ellis's suggestion, must remain conjectural. As a piece of literature the position of "Paradise Regained" is unquestioned. It is not to be ranked as Milton's greatest work, but it takes its place as a masterpiece of poised nobility and perfect workmanship.

Such in brief are the two poems. The exact ground of their resemblance must now be defined. Fletcher deals with the whole triumph of Christ, in heaven and on earth, in a series of four cantos. Only one of these is devoted to the Temptation. We are therefore going to compare the second canto of Fletcher's poem with the entire "Paradise Regained." We are going to compare a section of 533 lines with a poem of over 3,000 lines. To do this it will first be necessary to summarize the contents of each.

"Paradise Regained" is divided into four books. The first is an introduction to the wilderness scene and an account of the first temptation. Milton has expanded the scriptural account by at least eight imaginative additions. They are as follows: Satan is represented as present at the Baptism; his alarm leads to a conference in the world below; there is a scene of rejoicing in heaven; Christ enters the wilderness almost unconsciously, absorbed in a soliloquy; Satan proffers his temptation in the guise of an old man; he gives a long and fawning account of himself; Christ perceives and rebukes the disguise. The Book closes with the ending of the first day. Book II is purely imaginative from beginning to end. It describes very beautifully the sorrow and anxiety of the two disciples, Andrew and Simon, at the inexplicable loss of their Master. This is a beautifully natural touch, and Milton extends it even to the solicitude of Mary. It relieves from the supernatural and gives a sense of warm human reality. Another conclave of evil spirits takes place and Satan's superior subtlety is well shown. The temptation is repeated with different accompaniments, Satan appearing in courtlier guise and spreading a delicious table. The discussion on temperance and indulgence concludes the rejection of his offer. Book III progresses to the second temptation. It culminates in the Specular Mount and the wonderful description of the kingdoms spread before their eyes. This is the completest expansion of scriptural text. Milton's

imagination we have seen to run along two lines: one of pure creation, in harmony with scriptural account but still pure creation, such as the presence of Satan at Christ's baptism or the hellish conclaves; the other an imaginary expansion, often pictorial, of scriptural words. This is what he does here. The evangelist tells us that "the devil taketh him up into a high mountain, and showeth him all the kingdoms of the world." Milton has taken these pregnant words and painted a canvas. In the one case the idea is perfectly original, in the other it is based on a terse statement of fact. It would be hard to say in the presence of such a passage which is the higher type of imagination. The magnificent conception and tremendous power suggest Michael Angelo's paintings. Satan flashes before him all the Eastern powers and argues the policy of overcoming the Parthian and Roman forces. The Book closes with Christ's rejection of Satan's offer to make the kingdoms his. Book IV continues the same temptation. Studious Athens is charmingly described. Satan makes disheartening prophecies and nightfall is heralded with a raging storm. With the dawn comes the last temptation, that on the pinnacle, to which Milton has added only one touch, but it is the artist's: when Christ gives his final answer it is Satan that falls, smitten with amazement. We now see Milton's art in following Luke's order and putting this temptation last instead of second. It forms a fitting climax to crown the complete defeat of evil, fallen as it were like lightning from heaven. Then comes the fanciful description of the angels bearing Christ to earth, the ambrosial feast they spread for him, and the triumph in heaven. This ends Milton's epic. He has kept closely to the scriptural version, and he has developed this by creative additions and imaginative expansion of the material already there. In neither case is there anything to jar with the simplicity and realities of the original. He has expanded his sources by pictorial descriptions, by arguments, by repetition, and by inference. He has added some entirely new features. Both methods are used with greatest care, so that the natural and supernatural are most beautifully combined and the whole narrative unfolds with a lifelike reality and truth.

18

Very different from this is Giles Fletcher's treatment of the same theme. Instead of following a detailed account, as in Matthew or Luke, he has drawn his inspiration from the single verse in which Mark records the fact of the Temptation. This left the poet's imagination a free play, and it is a very different sort of imagination from that of Milton. Instead of realistic creation he has given a series of fanciful images. There is not a hint of probability, not the least attempt to follow the three temptations literally or to present them in a unified whole. Indeed, it is difficult to trace them at all in the labyrinth of personification and allegory, where everything is as remote from life as possible. It is just such a vision as the cloisters would revel in—rich in fancy, utterly unreal, and saturated with the dreamy devoutness of the Middle Ages. The argument is as follows: Mercy, whom we left in heaven in Canto I, "smoothing the wrinkles of her father's brow" and instructing the Graces to unflower their baskets before the Saviour, looks down upon Palestine. There she sees the solitary Figure in the wilderness and immediately descends with all her graces into the person of Christ. Giles calls this describing Christ by his proper attribute, the Mercy of God. The effect of her presence is immediately noted in the wild beasts, who instantly become gentle. Then follows a long description of Christ's personal appearance, taken from Canticles, Psalms, Genesis, and Isaiah. Satan next appears in the guise of a hermit and in a speech of fulsome flattery invites Christ to his abode. As they walk on together he gathers up a stone and remarks on the general desolation, closing with the words, "But thou with corn canst make this stone to ear." One questions if this is meant to be the first temptation; but the matter is dropped there and we find ourselves without further ado at the cave of Despair, which is described in full, with all its occupants. Just what was the temptation offered here is left to vague conjecture. It would seem as if the whole thing might be taken as an allegorical interpretation of the bread temptation; namely the personification of despair of God's providence. Christ prevails, and is now caught up to the pinnacle where the lady Presumption spreads her pavilion. Her character and attendants are fully depicted. She endeavors to make Christ throw

himself down and thus prove worthy of her love, but, failing in
this, is overcome and falls herself.   The Saviour is then borne by
angels to an airy mountain.   The scene changes to one of supernal
beauty.   Everything is lovely and alluring.   Everything appeals
to the sensual side, for this is the bower of Vain Delight, with all
her retinue of luxury, avarice, and ambitious honor.   The sor-
ceress sings him a wooing song, "But he her charms dispersed
into wind."   "A volley of light angels" then prepare our Lord's
repast.   The birds carol their praise; all nature joins in celebrating the victory, and the canto closes with the nightfall and
Christ's return homeward.   We now see the entire difference
between Milton's treatment and Fletcher's.   It would be impossible for us to enumerate the "additions" or "expansions" of the
latter's poem, for it is all fancy, and there is only a word here and
there to guide us in finding a scriptural counterpart for what it
describes.   Instead of dealing with the temptations directly
Fletcher has taken their moral significance and woven an allegory
out of each.   He has personified each one of these would-be sins
and Canto II is the result.   It is noticeable that every temptation
as presented is in striking contrast to Milton's.   Each one appeals
only to the physical side, while Milton's were nearly all of the
intellectual type.   It is again the difference between the recur-
ring mediæval conception and the more matured thought of the
later age.

   In studying the parallel passages and following their variations from an artistic standpoint some very interesting comparisons can be made, but it is hardly fair to contrast the broad stream
with the mountain rivulet which has fed it unless we keep in
mind their relationship.   To begin with, both Milton and Fletcher
have taken pains to describe the effect of Christ's presence on the
wild beasts.   They both stress his power to induce mildness, but
very differently is this rendered by each.   Milton has not changed
the animal nature.   We can easily picture the fiery serpent and
noxious worm fleeing away, and the tiger and lion glaring aloof;
but who can conjure up with gravity a Noah's Ark assemblage
kneeling and dancing about, or lined up with all their eyes fixed
upon him, while to crown the grotesqueness of it all we have such

a circus performance as the goat riding on the lion's back "forgetful of the roughness of the hide." Every vestige of dignity is lost in the absurdity of the conceit. And notice the contrasting conceptions of the wilderness. To Milton it was, "A pathless desert, dusk with horrid shades." To Fletcher's imagination,

> Upon a grassy hillock He was laid,
> With woody primroses befreckl̀ed.
> Over His head the wanton shadows played
> Of a wild olive, that her boughs so spread
> As with her leaves she seemed to crown His head
> And her green arms to embrace the Prince of Peace.

The one is pretty, the other impressive. Milton imparts human reality to his poem by picturing the possible anxiety and distress of the disciples and Mary. Somewhat parallel to this in effect and purpose is Fletcher's portraiture of Christ which now follows. The poet tries to give us an idea of the personal appearance of Christ, but his description is for the most part made up of general comparisons and steeped in the sentiment of Solomon's Song. A painter would only find in it two, or at most three, facts on which to work: the black curling hair, the red and white complexion, and the dress of woolen fleece with the low sandals. But however much has been left to the suggestion some critics would have even more. They would, in fact, efface the description altogether, as fantastic and extremely inappropriate. Grosart, of course, defends it warmly, and thinks the comparison of the raven locks and beaming face of Jesus to the shadows of some light and shining day surpassingly beautiful. The question really seems to be first as to whether the thing should be done at all, and, if so, as to how well it has been done. As to the legitimacy, one can only ask, If we allow the brush to delineate Christ why not the pen? There are certainly some exquisite touches, though all of the description may not be equally pleasing. The lines, "His hair was black and in small curls did twine," may not suggest to everyone beautiful raven locks; but the following, "As though it were the shadow of some light," is truly poetic. The verse which speaks of his eyes and their love-compelling power carries us back again to the mystical mediæval adoration, the feeling of spiritual love and union best typified by the marriage relation. "His cheeks as

snowy apples sopped in wine" and the comparison of the limbs to pillars of a temple are elaborately wrought out, particularly the latter. On the whole, it seems to be a question of personal taste. For those who care for it the elaborate similes and exquisite lines will more than balance the fantastic element; and for those who do not the reverse will be the case.

A singularly parallel idea lies in the presentation by both poets of Satan as an old man. Willmott calls attention to the fact that in several pictures he is so presented. "La Vita et Passione di Christo," published in Venice in 1518, has a wooden cut prefixed to the Temptation in which Satan as an old man offers bread to our Lord. Vischer's cuts to the Bible also portray the tempter as an aged man, and the same conception is found in the painting of the Temptation by Salvator Rosa. The idea was evidently a prevalent one. But the similarity between the two characters ends with the outer semblance. That subtle intellectuality which Milton has created is a fit embodiment of the spirit of evil; not any longer the splendid ruined archangel of "Paradise Lost," but still the prince of the power of the air—wily, seductive, tireless, always in the foreground, the acknowledged head of wickedness, the chosen tempter of Christ. His former majesty has dwindled away and degenerated, but there is an echo of the old magnificence in the defiant ring of the words:

> I would be at the worst; worst is my port,
> My harbor and my ultimate repose,
> The end I would attain, my final good.

In short, Milton's Satan is a veritable personality, a strong undermining force; Fletcher's is a man of straw, or, if we may follow his own phraseology, he is the literal serpent of tradition with fangs barely concealed. There is no art in his fulsome flattery, no wonder in the failure of his clumsy efforts. Instead of being foremost he sinks almost immediately into the background, and after his first effort appears only secondarily, having given place to Despair, Presumption, and Vainglory. These we may roughly compare to Belial, Asmodai, and Incubus. They are not real counterparts, for Milton never intended the latter as personified sins. They are, on the contrary, actual spirits, the fallen angels

of the Hebraic religion, identical with the gods of the heathen mythologies, and tempting, as their names would signify, to lust and indulgence. In thus linking them with history, secular and sacred, Milton has given them as true a reality as that of Christ or Satan. They are not the attributes but the agents of sin. They are not the principals but the subordinates, for their counsel is rejected without a trial. With Fletcher the case is exactly reversed. Despair, Vainglory, and Presumption are not living creatures in the same sense as Milton's spirits. In the world as we know it they could find no place. But they are vital offspring of the wonderland of allegory, and are only slightly inferior to Mercy and Justice of Canto I. They, and not Christ or Satan, are the principal figures of the canto. They are the most completely described, and it is they who offer the allurements. We have no Miltonic Christ refuting the subtleties of the arch intelligence of evil. We have rather a figurehead against which these try their powers. Both poems close with the song of victory, but in Fletcher's it is nature that rejoices, and in Milton's the heavenly host.

An interesting point for consideration is the literary qualities of the two poems with regard to style. Fletcher abounds in the use of figures. Similes long and short crowd his pages; some of them fantastically Vergilian, others truly felicitous. As an example of his admirable mastery of metaphor we have the couplet,

> And through the shady air the fluttering bat
> Did wave her leather sails and blindly float.

Personification, however is his great forte. In this and description he excels, pressing into their service all the wealth of a rich imagination. Mercy, Justice, and Presumption are not colorless figureheads. They throw a brilliance on the page like the bright illuminated manuscripts of the monks. Exactly opposite in effect is "Paradise Regained." There is an entire absence of poetical ornamentation and very little action. Its style is severe and ungarnished. It is the rich eloquence of the speeches, the moral beauty of the sentiment, the impressive style and the smooth elegance of the diction that make it supremely a work of art. Melody, richness, and charm there is, but we carry away with us the roll of

proper names, at least two magnificent canvases, and the high-seriousness of a lofty spirit.

To sum up: the mediæval charm, the fertility of fancy, the happy phrase, and the atmosphere of devoutness with which Fletcher has enveloped his poem are almost on a par with the corresponding qualities where they appear in "Paradise Regained." But what makes the beauty of one is not the distinguishing characteristic of the other. Fletcher's poem is an allegory. It is a series of pictures, not a unified whole. It sees with the outward eye, and sees vividly, but its creatures are of the mediæval stamp. Its cadences are sweet, not deep. Its brilliancy is fragmentary. Its art is roccoco—rich in color, lavish in decoration. Milton's poem is unbroken in its entirety. In power and poise it never flags. Its beauty is the classic simplicity of the Greek. Instead of the soft melody of the rhymed stanzas we have the measured harmonies of blank verse. Instead of allegory we have a great imaginative picture; instead of fleshly conceits, ethical truths. This is not to derogate Fletcher's work. In one sense there can be no comparison between a world-genius and a minor poet. The distance is too great and the superiority must of necessity be all on one side. The effort has been rather to place the two poems side by side in order to appreciate the better the development of thought and the growth of literary art.

Gertrude Andrews.

EDITORIAL DEPARTMENTS.

NOTES AND DISCUSSIONS.

DURING the past year, as during the quadrennium now closing, the circulation of the *Review* has increased; this means also an increase of net receipts. High-water mark in these particulars was reached in 1903. The *Review* is now read by a greater number of ministers than ever before. A large circulation for such a periodical is not easy of achievement. Almost incredible it is how small a list of subscribers our *Review* had in the greatest years of Dr. Whedon, the ablest editor any American religious review ever had.

SOME GERMAN CRITICS.

ONE of the ablest and soundest contributions to historical biblical criticism in the nineteenth century was Bishop Lightfoot's celebrated *Essays on Supernatural Religion,* in which are some justly severe comments on the radical critical literature of Germany that are as fairly pertinent and applicable to-day as when first written. In illustration of the labored, uncalled-for, and preposterous ingenuities of some learned and leading German critics, Lightfoot instances the mass of absurdities nonsensically heaped up by Baur, Schwegler, Volkmar, and Hitzig upon the names of two Christian disciples, Euodias and Syntyche, mentioned in the Epistle to the Philippians. The fantastic, frivolous, and well-nigh idiotic ado made over those two simple names shows what foolishness technical learning can sometimes perpetrate.

First, Baur applied his penetrating intellect to the Philippian epistle, and announced that the pivot of the epistle, which has a conciliatory tendency, is the mention of Clement, whom he thinks a mythical, or almost mythical, person, who, in Baur's opinion, represents the union of the Petrine and Pauline parties in the Church. Then came Schwegler, who carried the theory a step further and declared that the two names, Euodias and Syntyche, actually represent those two parties, while the true yokefellow between them is not Clement but St. Peter himself. Next came Volkmar to show that

the theory that the two names represent the two parties is confirmed by the very meaning of the names, Euodia meaning "Right way" and Syntyche meaning "Consort," denoting respectively the orthodoxy of the one party and the incorporation of the other. Last, came Hitzig, under necessity, if he did anything, to outdo the preceding critics by his inventiveness, saltatory exploits, prodigious learning, supernatural insight, and critical "stunts." Loftily deploring that the interpreters of the New Testament are not more thoroughly acquainted with the Old Testament and more fully imbued with its language and spirit, Hitzig informed his fellow-critics that these names, Euodias and Syntyche, are only reproductions of the patriarchs Asher and Gad— their sex having been accidentally changed in the translation of the names from one language into another—and that they represent the Greek and the Roman elements in the apostolic Church. This theory, as absurd as it is unnecessary, he supported by learned appeals to the Hebrew, Arabic, Syriac, and Armenian languages. And Hitzig added the startling opinion that the whole Epistle to the Philippians is a plagiarism from the Agricola of Tacitus! This Hitzig is naturally enough the knowing critic whose ingenuity suggested that the name of Æsop, the fable-maker, is derived from Solomon's "hyssop that springeth out of the wall." Seized by a momentary ambition to match the shrewd insight of this famous German critic, we venture to inquire why it is not equally clear from the two syllables of Hitzig's name that the first part was intended to indicate his descent from the ancient Hittites; while the last part surely contains a veiled and sarcastic prophetic allusion to the zigzag eccentricities of his overloaded intellect. It is entirely fair to say that the insanely excessive skepticism and the gratuitous imposition of unwarranted and worthless hypotheses, which we have seen practiced by Baur, Schwegler, Volkmar, and Hitzig, also characterize to-day the radical school of critics to which they belonged. All sound-minded and judicious persons must agree with Bishop Lightfoot that it is impossible to have any intellectual respect for men who, upon a subject of such solemn import and supreme dignity as the interpretation of the *Holy Scriptures,* indulge in fancies so irreverent, baseless, and grotesque. It is like the sacrilege of theatrical vaudeville acted in the Holy of Holies. As we were writing these lines, a dispatch from Rome arrived telling us of an Italian sage and seer of remarkable literary and scientific insight, who would, if he turned his attention to biblical interpretation, make a worthy successor to the four acute critics whose exploits we

have just examined. Dr. Francolini, says the message from Rome, has discovered in Pliny and in poets from Virgil to Byron veiled references to radium, together with hints that the place to look for this mysterious metal of portentous qualities is at the source of the Clitumnus, a little river in Umbria which has violet-tinged water. It is evident, as the newspapers say, that anybody who can discover, in the works of the authors mentioned, references to radium, the just-now-discovered metal, must have powers of intellect as wonderful as the powers of radium itself. And it is not strange that on the warrant of so marvelous a genius, men of science should, as the dispatch relates, start for Umbria to search for radium at the head-waters of the river Clitumnus. But what an accession to the ranks of the intuitive radical biblical critics a man of Francolini's piercing penetration and microscopic literary insight would be! In ability to see what isn't there, he is not unworthy of their high society.

A REPLY TO AN AGNOSTIC.

BLATCHFORD, the London socialist editor, has blown such a blast on *The Clarion* as might easily frighten the pusillanimous and the ill-informed. He has sallied gayly forth in vaunting, vicious, and vociferous style, with all his inexperience on his head, to undertake the alluring but oft-abandoned enterprise of demolishing Christianity. His adventure will probably do him good, because he is likely to learn something. In the end he will have some experience and Christianity will have the victory. Against this slashing assailant a swift young swordsman sets himself, with polemic skill, to champion Christianity. Mr. G. K. Chesterton, journalist, essayist, and critic, has made some striking and pungent replies to the Agnostic socialist's attack. No systematic straight-out defense of Christianity is attempted, but dexterous and unlooked-for side-thrusts are delivered in the style of a nimble and versatile journalist apt at asking troublesome questions. One of his suggestions is that, in a controversy with Agnosticism, Christianity has this disadvantage, it really exists and is responsible for things, and so its occasional failures and mistakes can be pointed out. It is an actual power, an active fact, and hence it can be criticised. No such exhibit can be made of Agnosticism's failures and mistakes, for the reason that it is not a power at all; it has not anywhere been intrusted with control, nor has it assumed responsibility

for affairs. It is, out and out, one of the "outs," and for the "outs" to criticise the blunders and shortcomings of the "ins" is always easy. The "ins" are loaded with the responsibility, and have the difficult task of managing obstreperous elements in a perfect way, by the agency of imperfect, even when well-meaning, agents. The "outs" have no responsibility to carry, no task to perform, nothing to do but to sit on the fence and find fault with the management, and jeer the unsuccesses, of the "ins." The business of the opposition is to oppose the government—a very easy job compared with the onerous and complicated work of governing perfectly. Within the borders of civilization Christianity is in office; it is the governing power. Agnosticism is only a critic, not an influential active participant. It is only a negation, a cipher. Among practical realities it has no place, it scarcely exists. For ages there has been a Christian Church, actual and powerful, toiling away at all the world's great problems. It has had to "run" the whole Western World for centuries. Agnosticism is nowhere instituted or established, it is not working out any of the world's urgent problems, nor ministering to humanity's sore need; and it is not "running" anything. It has no solutions to offer. Christian civilization has been and is, and its work stands visible and open to critical examination. There has never been a totally Agnostic civilization. It is true that there have been two civilizations that might be said to represent something resembling Agnosticism. The later Roman Empire was largely Agnostic, and the Chinese Empire is largely Agnostic. The modern Agnostic, however, shows no disposition to boast of those triumphs. This, says Chesterton, is one disadvantage of Christianity in a controversy with Agnosticism: the Christian Church has long been busy doing and making many things; and so its doings are open to comment, and it has made some mistakes. Agnosticism has nowhere instituted itself, has organized nothing, and done nothing, and so its doings cannot be examined. One might say it escapes being criticised by not being at all.

The above is, in part, one of Mr. Chesterton's replies, and he makes another point against the Agnostics as follows:

"The strength of Christianity is a very mysterious thing; it has little to do with the controversial ingenuity either of its supporters or its opponents. Often it has happened that clever men have been on its side; often it has happened that clever men have been on the other side. Its strength lies not in the fact that it is eloquent or successful, or well represented; it lies in the incidental fact that it is indispen-

sable. By indispensable I mean this: It is, to all mortal appearance, impossible for men to attack Christianity without eventually ending up in positions that no sane masses of men have ever held, in positions which would horrify a decent pagan or an unbaptized savage. Schopenhauer attacks Christianity and ends by saying that life itself is a delusion. Nietzsche attacks it and ends by saying that charity itself is a delusion. Others attack it and end by saying that human goodness and badness are delusions. Christianity does not answer: a few of her apologists answer, and generally badly. But she is silent, for she is old, and has seen so many paradoxes. She knows the path you Agnostics and deniers are on, and has seen many on it; she knows that on it are delightful hypotheses and luxurious negations, and that that way madness lies. She knows that as soon as you want any conceivable human reality, if it be only to say 'Thank you' for the mustard, you will be forced to return to her and her hypotheses, where she sits, guarding through the ages the secret of an eternal sanity."

The fact is that in religious circles no weight can be allowed to Agnosticism. There is no force in mere negation, or in confessedly absentee testimony. Learning may properly ask attention to supposed new knowledge, but why should men claim and hold the floor for the purpose of vociferating their ignorance? Huxley spoke of "the absurdity of supposing that we know anything about either spirit or matter;" which amounts to a declaration of comprehensive and all-embracing know-nothingism. Why should a man who claims to know so little talk and write so much as he did about what he doesn't know? We can see no object in all his labor except to try to persuade his fellow-men to confess that they too know nothing. Listening wearily to the volubility of the Agnostics, it is impossible not to wonder why avowed ignorance should wear such learned, important, and pedagogic airs, and be so prolix and repetitious in setting forth by items and in sum the contents of its emptiness. When professed Ignorance assumes to steer the funeral-barge of Faith it were more decorous for it to do so quietly, as when, in Tennyson's idyl, the body of Elaine was floated toward the towers of Camelot,

> The dead, steered by the dumb,
> Went upward with the flood.

After many loquacious years, loud with the vaunt of ignorance, and aggressive with the supercilious arrogance of unfaith, Herbert Spencer, the chief of modern Agnostics, seems to have been visited in

his later years by a sense of propriety which stayed with him long enough to make him confess that silence best becomes the unbeliever; that it is indecent and inhuman for the Agnostic to go about robbing men of the sustaining comfort they derive from their creed, dropping dark and deadly hints to shake their faiths and unsettle their hope; and that the Agnostic is "cruelly thoughtless" of the rights of his fellow-men in so doing, since "nothing but evil can follow" from depriving men of the sacred convictions which enable them to bear the ills they suffer and to carry the exhausting burden of daily duties, often fulfilled without thanks and without sympathy. Agnosticism is an ill-bred creature; to see a momentary sense of decency flit across its boorishness and check its loud volubility is encouraging. Possibly it may yet hear a Voice saying, "Be still and know that I am God: I will be exalted among the heathen." Two classes of heathen there are: the better class, who, though worshiping they know not precisely what, still do worship Some One or Somewhat, and who are worthy in proportion to their reverence and sincerity; and a lower and more hopeless class who worship Nothing, and believe nothing but their own cocksure Ignorance. In war-time there was a sable Agnostic named "Pete," who did the cooking for the Ninth Illinois Regiment. At the battle of Fort Donelson black Pete showed the white feather, ran at the first fire, and "would 'a' runned sooner" if he had "know'd it was a-comin'." Being reproached for not showing more courage, he said: "Dat ain't in my line. Cookin' is my perfeshin." Being asked if he cared nothing for patriotism and honor, he answered: "Dunno nuffin 'bout dem things, sah; I regard 'em as wanities." Is not Pete's insensibility to the reality and power of patriotism in the midst of ranks which it had mustered, and in the hot fire of a fight it was maintaining, very like the agnosticism of some toward religious verities and realities in the midst of a civilization which Christianity has created and is sustaining, and of a variously manifest supernatural Kingdom of God which is making conquests in all parts of the world? And did the agnostic indifference of the colored cook of the Ninth Illinois toward patriotism at all discredit the reality and power of that sentiment which before his very eyes had marshaled a million patriots in arms on fields of death and was fairly rocking the continent with a gigantic conflict?

Speaking roughly, it is fair to say that Christianity proves its reality and power by what it does and what it effects. The fact that Agnosticism, which knows nothing, also consistently does nothing,

builds nothing, and effects nothing, creates a presumption that it is to be classed among nonentities which escape criticism by not existing, as George K. Chesterton suggests.

PRAYING FOR THINGS.

CERTAIN recent discussions of the purpose and value of prayer exhibit a decided tendency to deny specific answers and to eliminate the element of petition, even for spiritual bestowments, except as a somewhat ignorant attempt to institute a personal relation between the soul and God, or to secure the reflex influence of petition. There has been, however, a growing discontent with that view of prayer which finds its chief value in reflex influence. It is increasingly felt by large numbers to be an inadequate formulation of what the praying soul realizes in its devotions, and thoughtful men are gradually abandoning the phrase, and are seeking some other more consonant with all the experienced facts. This is fortunate; for prayer cannot remain a vital factor in the religious life of one who accepts the logical consequences of the doctrine that the only effect of prayer is its reflex influence; for on this supposition prayer becomes a means whose value depends upon a delusion—the delusion that it is a power to move God; and when we discover that we are deluded we will cease to pray. No man will ask God to do a thing which he is perfectly certain God will not do. He will not ask it even for the sake of the beneficial effect the petition might be supposed to have upon his character and conduct. The reflex benefits of prayer are almost inestimable; but the only condition upon which they can be secured is that the petitioner shall believe that God is sometimes moved by prayer, and that he may be moved by it in any given instance. Communion, or the establishment of a personal relation with God, is undoubtedly a truer conception of the purpose of prayer than reflex influence, but the case for it is very little if any stronger on the theory that prayer does not at all move God. The relation of a person with a person must, in the nature of the case, be a mutual relation. There is no true communion with God unless he responds to our approach. Without this we could speak of communion with him only as we speak of communion with nature, fully understanding that by the phrase we mean merely those meditations in which we indulge in the presence of nature. Nor could we be said to commune with God even though to the utmost of our knowledge we brought ourselves into harmony with his laws in

nature and history and to the best of our ability employed them in advancing the interests of his Kingdom. There would be lacking the mutuality which alone constitutes true intercourse between spiritual beings. Communion with God would be a misnomer, and all pretense of such communion would come to a speedy end, were the theory of the immobility of God consistently held. We can move physical nature by physical means, even though we can hold no mutual spiritual communion with her. But God is, by the hypothesis, a Spirit who could be but will not be moved either by any spiritual considerations or by any physical efforts we can bring to bear. He is less accessible to us than the physical world. Because he is a spirit he is qualified to respond to our spirits; but because he is so absolute, so fixed in his purposes and activities, he will not deviate a hair's breadth even to satisfy the heart hunger of his children. If he is thus unresponsive to a creature of his made in his own image, he is, to say the least, a rather unlovely being. If we are not in his image we sink to the level of our thought of the brute. We become, like the brutes, mere recipients of his bounty; we are not coworkers with him. In either case we cease to have any interest in attempting to converse with God.

When one considers what is involved in the assertion of God's immobility by expressed human desire it becomes a serious duty to inquire whether those who affirm it are right. It is easy to understand why thoughtful men should perceive the absurdity of some theories of prayer. And it is easy to comprehend why serious-minded men should fear that praying for things, whether spiritual or material, might lead to certain dangerous moral consequences. Too much dependence upon prayer might naturally seem to render human effort and sacrifice unnecessary. And this has unquestionably too often been the result. Still, it must be said that up to the present date in the world's history those who have been the most distinguished believers in the efficacy of prayer for things have been the most active and self-sacrificing toilers in the effort to benefit mankind. And prayer may have a real value even though some make a highly absurd use of it and though there is some theoretical danger in the doctrine which allows us to pray for things. What reasons are there, then, for thinking that God may do some things in answer to prayer that he would not otherwise do? If we omit the teaching and example of Christ the first and fundamental reason for such an opinion is that the now generally accepted doctrine of the immanence of a personal God implies the possibility of answer. The world is not made, but is

being made. The fixity of things is not in the things, but in the will of the Creator. He is subject to no restrictions except such as he imposes upon himself, and therefore he does freely what he does. If he should see fit to deviate from his usual course of action at the request of a human being there is nothing and no one to hinder him. A second reason for believing in the possibility of answer to prayer is the fact of variety in created things. This indicates that an unnumbered multitude of ways of doing things is open to God, and that he regards any one of these ways as good as any other. The variety in the forms of trees and other vegetable growths is practically infinite. So with human beings; for while there is greater uniformity here, there is still room for extremely wide and almost numberless variations. And in the realm of human history, individual and national, for the development of which the supposed power of prayer has been more freely invoked by Christians than for anything else, there is reason to believe that God has left the largest room for human choices. This suggests the third reason, that is, that God allows men a place in his plans. Unless we are to believe that all man's activities are predetermined by the Creator, we must believe that God regards himself as wise enough to govern the world even when man's free activities are admitted. In other words, if man is really free God must at every moment modify his creation and providence to adapt them to the activities of men. This may give us a world which, instead of being planned in all its details according to an ideal design of God, is planned in part according to exigencies created by man's thought and action; but it is the only kind of a world which is consistent with the doctrine of human freedom and responsibility.

So great is this power of man over the world of nature and history as to suggest that providence is human as well as divine; that is, that God has actually taken man into partnership with himself in that constant adaptation of the world to humanity known as providence. In many departments God seems to do little else than to provide the raw materials, leaving man to prepare them for his own needs according to his own best judgment and skill. What object God may have in thus turning the world over to man we can only surmise; certainly it is not for lack of wisdom on his own part. Whatever may be his reason, he seems thereby to rebuke the doctrine of man's insignificance and to affirm man's great significance. However that may be, it is very certain that he does in numberless instances allow men to dictate by their acts what he shall do. The only question is

whether he will modify his actions at the request of men as he does
in response to the acts of men. To say that he will not is to say that
he refuses all spiritual intercommunion between himself and the being to whom, for some reason, he gives so large a place in the government and development of the world. What he demonstrably allows
to man suggests that he will do more than can be demonstrated, that
is, that he will, at least at times, govern himself in accordance with
human prayer. And this seems to be demanded in order to supplement and complete the cooperation already so prominent a factor in
the relations between himself and man, by adding to cooperation by
independent activities cooperation by mutual consultation. There is
nothing in this belittling to God, but there is much in it that comports
with the dignity of man as revealed by man's place in the world. A
difficulty that stands in the way of many is the fact that it is impossible to demonstrate answer to prayer, while there appear to be so
many cases in which the petitions of human beings are certainly not
granted. It is not trifling to point out that it is vastly more difficult
to prove the granting of a petition than the refusal. We have the
same thing to contend with in the use of remedial agencies for disease.
When these fail we know it with certainty, but it would be almost
impossible to convince the skeptical that the remedy brought about
the recovery of one who became well. Yet we go right on employing
such means as we hope may produce the desired results. Many discriminating individuals have attained to a high degree of certitude
with reference to the effectiveness of certain medicaments; and there
are fully as many of equal powers of discrimination who are thoroughly convinced that prayer has been directly answered, especially for
spiritual ends. In neither case is there proof sufficient to satisfy one
who is disposed to be very exacting in his demands for conclusive
evidence. If this seems to leave the matter of answer to prayer for
things in great uncertainty it must be replied that the only requisite
to the spirit of prayer is the belief, not that God does generally, or
even frequently, modify his activities according to our request, but
merely that he listens to our prayers, takes them into consideration in
the determination of his plans, and that he can, if he sees fit, grant
our desires. Action finds as powerful a spring in hope as in certainty.
So that when the "simple believer," of whom we hear so much, prays
God not to allow her wayward son to go too far in paths of sin she
may have a reasonable assurance that God will give heed to her petition. Or, when another simple believer prays for rain that his crops

19

may not be destroyed by drought he will feel certain that his act is something more than an attempt to establish a personal relationship between himself and God, however blessed such a relationship may be. But it will be said that at least as far as that wayward son is concerned it is inconceivable that God should not do all that he can do to hold him in check without any request from his mother. But it is certainly not inconceivable, nor even improbable. For God has unquestionably thrown upon man a responsibility for the welfare of his fellows. This cannot be explained on the ground that God does not watch with solicitude over the moral and spiritual welfare of men, but it is probably founded on a desire to give the race, for its own good, all the responsibility it can bear. God undoubtedly could, if he saw fit, do all that is needful for each individual without human cooperation; but instead of this he makes man his brother's keeper. That the highest interests of humanity are subserved by this arrangement will be conceded by all. There are, therefore, the best of reasons why God should in some cases and to some extent make his activities dependent upon the request of human beings.

The chief end of prayer is not, as some would have us believe, that we may learn submission to the will of God. We are supposed to have subjected ourselves to him before we pray for things. We say, "Thy will be done," not to indicate that we have no will, but in frank acknowledgment of the superior righteousness and wisdom of God's will. We ask, but we do not dictate; and one of the most frequent and beneficial results of prayer is that by it we ascertain God's will. But over and above this we pray because the world in which we live is seen to be not so definitely planned as to exclude modification from time to time. Much of the world's history—we never know how much —is left to the determination of man. Here, not in those particulars in which constant operations display the fixed purpose of God, is the sphere for effective prayer. Prayer is not designed to change, but to determine, God's plans. For this reason also importunity in prayer is allowable. If God's final plans are to be in some cases fixed in accordance with prayer it is reasonable to suppose that he should wish to secure in those who pray a proper appreciation of the results they ask him to bring about. While not every casual request, therefore, may be granted, certain very much desired favors might be granted. The trite is sometimes, as in this case, the true and the rational. The doctrine of the divine Fatherhood certainly gives us no hint that God shuts his children out from a reasonable share in the mutual deter-

mination of the activities of all the members of the divine family. Rather does it suggest that as the children heed the Father's wish, so the Father, as much as possible, heeds the children's wish. The filial relation, if it is not to be robbed of its very best content, must include the privilege of participation in all planning as well as in the execution of the means and measures by which the common family weal is to be secured. Imagine the effect upon the children's freedom of approach to a father who would give them plainly to understand that their suggestions were not needed, either because he had already divined them or because his superior wisdom made them useless, and that if offered they would under no circumstances affect the father's conduct of the family affairs! So also the idea of the kingdom suggests the value rather than the futility of prayer. The right of petition, direct or indirect, is allowed everywhere except in the absolute monarchy. In proportion as government is in the interest of the governed is the right of petition, or, which is the same thing, the right of initiative on the part of the governed, encouraged. The analogy does not, of course, hold in all respects. Human governments do not have infinitely wise and beneficent heads. But God has in fact vacated his rights and prerogatives to a certain, though by us indeterminable, extent, in favor of man's exercise of his own judgment and powers. So that the situation is, within limits, the same as it is in a human government conducted on the principle of the mutual cooperation of rulers and ruled. And God carries this to the extent of sometimes allowing the beneficent course of events he would doubtless secure if left to himself to be interrupted by the most frightful and disastrous blunders of human judgment and preference. Notwithstanding all this, no thoughtful man would wish that humanity might be excused from its present responsible prerogatives. None would choose the paternal government which gives every determination over to God. In spite of all we suffer by our own mistakes we all prefer the arrangement now in force. And we must believe that God prefers it too, else he would not permit it to be. There must be some high purpose which he can better work out by this method than by the opposite. And since he allows man such extraordinary influence in the work of the kingdom it is incredible that he will not consider man's requests, but will pass them by as though they had not been presented. The supposition that God either cannot or will not answer prayer is out of analogy with all other manifestations of his regard for the preferences of mankind.

THE ARENA.

TITHING A CHRISTIAN DUTY.

DR. DANIEL STEELE contends in the last number of the *Methodist Review* that the giving of a tenth of our income to religious purposes is not "a positive requirement of Christ," and that such requirement cannot be counted "a part of Christianity." He is no doubt technically correct in this, for there is no direct command of the Saviour to this effect, and hence a person does not necessarily and altogether forfeit his claim to be called a Christian when he confines his bestowments within a much smaller amount. But there seems to us considerable danger lest the good doctor's strong emphasis upon this point should unduly relieve the consciences of many who stand in no particular need of such relief and should create a wrong impression of the real condition of the case. He had no space in which to present the other side, it was not in the line of his argument; but there is an argument—which seems to me very strong and greatly to need frequent presentation—to which the attention of Christians who content themselves with giving very much less than one tenth of their income to benevolent or altruistic objects should, in my opinion, be constantly called, that, if possible, they may be led to see more clearly what is the truly Christian attitude in this matter. Surely a thing may be a duty—by force of circumstances, weight of reasonableness, and proved helpfulness in its effect on self and others—when there is no positive enactment of a divine law in so many words, nor yet what might be called exactly an intuition or a "dictate of our moral sense." We rightly say that church membership is a Christian duty, that family prayers is a Christian duty, also attendance on prayer meetings, all of them when practicable. Not that any text of Scripture can be quoted which precisely requires either of these things, but that experience has so far shown them to be immensely beneficial that a plain rule of observance lies in their favor. Expediency, when clearly established, has no less binding authority on the conscience of the Christian than legal enactments; he recognizes it as virtually a command from his higher nature, an indication of the will of God. It is also unquestionably the duty of every Christian to love God with all his heart and soul and mind and strength, and to love his neighbor as himself. Is it conceivable that one with such a love will be anxious to see how little he can do for Christ and his fellow-men, will hide behind the fact that there is no legal enactment absolutely demanding one tenth as a matter of compulsion, and will plead that since he is a Christian, not a Jew, he is at full liberty without qualm of conscience or impairment of his standing to spend nearly, if not quite, all his substance on himself? If we have love enough doing "the things that are pleasing in his sight" becomes fully as important as "keeping his commandments." If we have love enough privileges become duties and duties privileges. The closest possible partnership with the Saviour is to such a one not a

burden to be borne but a delight to be enjoyed. He does not inquire carefully how much he *must* give for extending the kingdom and redeeming the world, but how much he *may* give and not be unjust to other obligations. It is doubtless possible to give too much to God's work. He who simply follows the impulses of a thoroughly loyal, loving heart filled with deep desire that the Master may everywhere be honored, might conceivably forget his duty to his family and his future, might lay himself open to the reproach of not properly providing for his own, might imperil the rights of his children or fail to meet certain claims of justice. He will need to check this tendency by some prudential rule that shall embody the wisdom of the ages in this matter and have the sanction of the best examples.

Is there any other rule that can compare with the tenth? Is there anything that has such a weight of general approval behind it? It comes down from the most ancient times. It was repeatedly insisted upon in the older Scriptures which still remain to us an important source of ascertaining the mind of God. It was grounded, not in the evanescent prescriptions of Mosaism, but in the fundamental needs of human nature. It was so commonly accepted by the early Christian Church as not to call for specific reenactment at the hands of the apostles. It has highly commended itself to vast numbers of the most devoted down through the centuries. It has been continually proved in practice to be attended by the special blessing of God both temporally and spiritually. All this being so, I for one am at a loss to understand how anyone who considers himself a follower of Jesus can justify the crude, careless, slipshod, haphazard habits of giving which so generally prevail, or can really content himself with much, if anything, less, as a rule, than the tithe or tenth. It may be admitted that in extreme poverty a smaller proportion might be accepted of the Lord. It must certainly be held that those who have much wealth should give a good deal more. But that there is any better rule, for the great body of the Church, applicable to nearly all cases, the present writer does not believe. Nor is he willing to admit that there is any special danger of "legalism and self-righteousness" arising from the adoption of this rule as a plain dictate of Christian duty and privilege. The peril of spiritual pride attaches to all high states of grace; this, of course, should make us watchful, but surely need not deter us from setting our mark at the highest level. I greatly deprecate any suggestion or mode of treating this topic that shall seem to give countenance to the vast host of Christian robbers, religious freebooters, who fill our churches and congratulate themselves that since they are not under the law but under grace the burden of devoting one tenth of their income to religious uses does not rest upon them to any degree. So these people feel at perfect liberty to indulge their worldliness and social ambitions, their pride and selfishness and love of personal ease. The follies and luxuries and elegancies of life get their full share, while the pressing claims of the sadly crippled benevolent causes are ignored, and the Church's work is crippled for lack of funds. I firmly believe that systematic proportionate beneficence is an essential part of Christianity, and should be so preached without qualification, for covetousness is so hideous a sin and so heinous

in God's sight that it is not safe to leave ourselves exposed to its attacks without the most ironclad defense. Without some settled rule, some definite system, some fixed proportion, the important principle of Christian stewardship stands no chance of proper recognition. If all is left to impulse and caprice, such is human nature, so mightily is it given to selfish grasping and retaining, that the tendency will be in most cases overwhelmingly strong to put off the religious and charitable schedules of outlay with a very scanty allowance, with not more than will suffice to maintain a decent standing in the community where we live. To prevent this some fixed proportion must be accepted and steadily adhered to, regarded, indeed, as both privilege and duty. And when the inquiry is honestly and carefully made, without selfish bias, as to what should be the proportion, there is very little likelihood, it seems to me, of any other conclusion being reached than that one tenth is that proportion. Let it be remembered that it is wholly a question of distribution, not at all of ownership. All is the Lord's. He has put something into our hands for a season that we may administer upon it. How shall we do it so as best to please him? The setting apart for God's particular work of one tenth of one's property would seem to be placed in the Bible on the same footing as the setting apart of one seventh of time. In neither case was it implied that the portion not thus set aside was to be used selfishly or irreligiously. It would be as fair to charge those who especially observe the Lord's Day with denying that all our time is the Lord's as to charge tithers with denying that all our property is his. Both the prescriptions, as to time and property, antedated the Mosaic law, and both have survived, it is fair to infer, the repeal of that law, being nowhere annulled by Jesus either by the letter or the spirit of his words. That God approved this practice in the days of the past is a very clear indication that he approves it now; for human nature is the same, and it will scarcely be claimed that the needs of religious work are less pressing at present than they were then, or that a less proportion will answer under existing circumstances.   JAMES MUDGE.

Jamaica Plain, Mass.

THE TEMPTATION OF JESUS.

ONE who "was in all points tempted like as we are, yet without sin." This is the testimony. But was Jesus tempted exactly as we are? Did he ever waver as we often do between a right and a wrong act? Did he ever incline to do wrong? A prominent university professor, accustomed to discriminating thought, once said to me, "I think Jesus sometimes felt like doing wrong, like the rest of us." This conception is quite general. I believe it to be wholly wrong. Temptation may be said to exist in three degrees according to the kind of response human nature makes to a stimulus. Temptation implies two factors: object and subject, environment and organism, stimulus and response. The word "temptation" is sometimes applied to the first factor only, with the second factor only conceptually present, as when Dryden writes:

> Dare to be great, without a guilty crown ;
> View it, and lay the bright temptation down.

This lowest degree of temptation exists when the environment or stimulus elicits no response either physical, mental, or moral in the human organism. The only justification for speaking of such a condition as temptation is some property of the object which is capable of causing a person to do wrong. A summer cloud cannot in any way be appropriated by the human organism for wrong purposes. It is no temptation. But a summer apple has properties which are capable of inducing a hungry street urchin to fall from grace. The second stage of temptation exists when an outer solicitation is met by a physical or mental response in the human organism. When the odor of coffee and frying steak strikes the nostrils of an honest hungry man his mouth waters. He forms no intention of stealing a dinner, but he has a lively physical response to the stimulus. All that part of his nature the function of which is to utilize food is powerfully stimulated, but in no immoral way. He is tempted, but without sin. The third and acutest degree of temptation is when the stimulus produces a wavering of the will—when there is a moral response to environment; when the hungry man debates with himself whether he will secure a dinner by illegitimate means; when to steal or not to steal becomes the question. A classic example is Launcelot Gobbo in "Merchant of Venice" debating whether he shall run from the Jew. His conscience says, "Launcelot, budge not." "Budge," says the fiend. "Budge not," says his conscience. A more serious one is Hamlet pondering the question of suicide; and Jean Valjean pacing his room all night torn by a violent conflict within, debating whether he should keep silent and let another suffer from false accusation, or reveal himself and save another by his own sacrifice.

These three degrees of temptation may be best exemplified where the first factor, environment, remains constant. A man who never knew the desire for intoxicants walks by a saloon and smells the fumes of liquor; but he experiences no desire to taste the stuff nor to enter the saloon. In no sense does he respond to that part of his environment. Or, to use a scriptural equivalent, he is dead* to that sin in every sense, physical, mental, moral. Intoxicants to him are only potentially a temptation. Another man, a converted drunkard, passes by the same door and inhales the same fumes. Instantly the old appetite awakes and gnaws at his vitals, clamoring for alcohol. Memory reproduces the experiences of his days of revelry. The old, wild life rushes back like a tide. But not for the fraction of a second does he debate with himself whether he shall go in. With steady step and unwavering purpose he marches by and is more than conqueror. He experiences physical and mental response to the stimulus. Drink to him is a temptation with high potentiality. But in the moral sense he is dead* to the suggested sin. A third man approaches the fatal place. This very morning he promised his wife and perhaps his God that he would not touch the stuff to-day. But he, too,

* Rom. vi, 11.

must meet the same odor from the door of hell. He is seized as by an evil spirit. Appetite and imagination leap in response to the tempter. But that is not all. He stops, starts on, turns back, goes in. Then by an enormous exercise of will he shakes off the spell. Without tasting a drop he goes on to his work and comes home a sober man. He is conqueror; he is without sin; but not without *sinfulness.* His sinful nature, though subdued, is yet alive and strong. His will responds to evil. He is not yet dead to sin. Now is it consistent to think Jesus was tempted in this last degree? Did he suffer this response of will to the tempter? Is there a crumb of evidence that for a single instant his will was not one with the Father's? When Satan suggested making bread out of stones—the gambler's temptation—was there a moment when he wished to do it? Doubtless the suggestion sharpened his pangs of hunger; he gave a powerful bodily response. But not for an instant did his purpose waver. He was tempted also to substitute worldly power and glory for the kingdom of God. Intellectually he grasped all the possibilities of the case. He *saw* the kingdoms of the world and the glory of them. But his purpose not to make the trade was as firm as the mountain on which he stood.

The Garden of Gethsemane is earth's most glorious battlefield. Tours, Waterloo, Gettysburg, great and glorious, are still less glorious than Gethsemane. Here was fought the Battle of the Ages. Here was blood, drawn not by the sword, but by anguish of spirit. Here was conflict not with visible foes, mid booming of cannon and flash of sword and bayonet in the sun of noon—not with heroic comrades at back and shoulder; but with invisible principalities and powers, at night, in silence, alone. But wherein is the glory of the scene? "Father, *if thou be willing,* remove this cup from me: *nevertheless not my will, but thine, be done.*" No vacillation of will, but perfect and unbroken obedience. Jesus shrank from the next day's anguish of soul and body and the horrors of death. To the prospect of an ignominious and painful death he experienced the natural physical and mental response. But who will say there was even a momentary will or desire to run away from the cross? To say that in these recorded temptations he experienced vacillation of purpose between a right and a wrong course is to attribute to the Son of God a weak and sinful nature. Jesus was "dead unto sin but alive unto God." Jesus never had the experience so graphically described in Rom. vii. His will never responded to evil solicitation, but did respond perfectly to the will of God, which was his real environment—his life. "My meat," he said, "is to do the will of him that sent me." He spoke of himself as "the Son of man, who is in heaven." To this heavenly environment he responded without even a moment's interruption. Jesus knew only the second stage of temptation. This is holiness. To be otherwise is to be double-minded men, unstable in all our ways. Jesus was at one with God. He was holy in heart. He knew no divided self. We can be like him. We can be surrounded by inducements to lust, dishonesty, greed, and envy, and be dead to them all, but alive unto God through Jesus Christ our Lord, who knew no sin in act or thought.   WILLARD N. TOBIE.

Urbana, Ill.

EXPOSITORY PREACHING.

THE expository preacher has a rich field to cultivate. Laymen in Sunday school and Bible classes have had the unfortunate effect to drive instruction in the Scriptures, to a large extent, from the pulpit. This result is deplorable, for such teaching in the pulpit is eminently helpful. The expository preacher makes an elaborate explanation of a passage of the Bible, throughout his discourse, while the topical preacher makes a hasty reference to the text and proceeds with his sermon independently of the text. The biblical preacher unfolds the word.

Many thoughtful believers are asking, Can the old faith live with modern research? The true pastor will not go on his way as if scientific methods had not been applied to the sacred volume, but he will show the people the wheat that is left after the threshing of the critics. The early chapters of Genesis, for instance, have been subjected to such a threshing process. The story of the beginning of things is here told from a religious standpoint. Have the accounts any historical character and moral worth; and does their value vanish if scholars can show that the authorship is composite, and, therefore, Moses did not write them all? Thoughtful laymen would be all but a unit in their appreciation of the minister who spoke, from a full mind, on the creation, the fall, and the flood.

But many deny the acceptability of biblical sermons. Mere dogmatic assertion, however, avails nothing. Anyone, to be sure, would grant that the minister that labors under the delusion that an expository sermon consists of an olla-podrida from the commentaries of Whedon, or Alford, or Meyer may well leave for another field of homiletics—in fact, the sooner the better. But will not rhetoric lend its charm to such discourse, and win the ear of the people? The world is to be saved by the foolishness of preaching, not by foolish preaching. The itinerant can keep to the highway despite the darkling bugaboo that declares dogmatically that a biblical sermon must be as dry as chips.

Theological schools are alive to the need of expository preaching. Their professors have been urging the students to plan to deliver regularly discourses expository of the Scriptures. Professor Phelps, of Andover, advised his classes not to let a Lord's Day pass in their ministry without basing one discourse at least, in all its parts, on a passage of Scripture; and a message of much the same tenor comes from Yale and Garrett. Such authority demands attention, but the Church does not have to lean wholly on the word of ecclesiastics. The man without theological training can see the need for himself. Where would the Bible receive adequate attention outside the pulpit? Confessedly, the work of the Sunday school is not usually elaborate and scholarly; and the writings of college and divinity school professors have a scientific character. But the pulpit should be popular and biblical. How solemn is the ordination of the Methodist preacher when he receives authority from the bishop to preach the word! The herald does not tell his entire message unless he becomes an expository preacher, and helps to counteract the sad want of such preaching. Frederick W. Robertson, in fact, lectured on the books

of Corinthians, and William M. Taylor preached on the parables of our Lord; and others less famous, perhaps not infrequently, have done as they did. But a few showers do not break the drought.

The power of sermons explanatory of the Bible arises from the inspiration of the Scriptures. The inspiration does not consist in the perfection of the Bible as a manual of geography and geology, but in its unapproached moral and religious elevation. The prophets were not the mighty men that they were because they reflected a Semitic religious characteristic, as Renan holds, but because Jehovah had vouchsafed to them a special revelation for Israel. The Bible is the Book of Books because it centers in Christ. The beatitude declares that the pure in heart are blessed with a clear vision of God, and the sacred writers make a remarkable appeal to the best in man because they were remarkably pure-minded men. Sermons, therefore, woven into the very warp and woof of the supreme revelation of God must have a part of its spiritual power.

A preacher would not be wise, however, to restrict his sermons to the exposition of Scripture. Such a class makes variety to topical preaching. The bar and the theater do not even now draw such large audiences, week in and week out, as does the pulpit, but complaint is made of its monotony. Many churches fail to have the morning and evening congregations of equal size though most of the attendants live within sound of the church bell. An introduction of a large portion of expository and textual sermons would tend to break the monotony, and give freshness to the jaded spirits of the hearers. For no book bears any comparison with the Bible in rich variety of themes combined with adaptability to the grasp of the people. The picture of the man that received a full day's wages for an hour's work, in the parable of the laborers in the vineyard, is a popular setting of the truth contained in Browning's comforting words, "It's not what we do, but what we would do, that exalts us."

Fox Lake, Wis.   Robert S. Ingraham.

WHAT OF THE REVIVAL?

For reasons all too plain, the question is everywhere asked, "What has become of the old-time revival?" The answer is, the Church has lost conviction. The revival that swept whole communities into the Church did not come without pungent conviction of its necessity, and great power of feeling. The churches are doing their work industriously at the present time, much as a bank teller or a street car conductor does his—without feeling. In fact, we have come to think it unmanly to feel. This is the result of a persistent insistence upon the part of the ministry that feeling is no part of pure religion. That Christians should live well no one should doubt, but a man without profound conviction and great power to feel does not amount to much as a Christian or as a man. He cannot mount up to high spiritual things. Say what you will, it was the power of feeling that characterized the old-time revival. Feeling deeply, the preacher made others feel. Mere thought never did produce in sinners genuine conviction. It is feeling that persuades sinners. "With the

heart," not the head, "man believeth unto righteousness." Every great preacher that Methodism ever produced was distinguished as much for power of feeling as for power of thought. Wesley, Summerfield, Simpson, Marvin, all joined great masterly power to think with great masterly power to feel. They saw things clearly and felt divinely what they saw. It was this which gave them power to make others feel the same. Who that ever heard one of the old-time mighty men of God that does not remember the clear vision of things he had and which he expressed in a voice that had tears in it? There is no shifting the fact, a preacher must have himself a great power to feel. Moreover: What has become of the men and women who once in our revivals agonized and wrestled with God at our altars till a great mountain of feeling pressed upon every unconverted soul in the farthest part of the room. It is high time that clear thinking, good living, and deep feeling go to housekeeping again together. The family has long enough been sad because of so few births and cries in the natal chamber.　　　　　　　　　　C. E. CLINE.

Portland, Ore.

"AN EDUCATED MINISTRY"—A CORRECTION.

IN the *Methodist Review* of January-February, and in the "Arena" department, Rev. Frank Seeds makes the statement that "Education means a drawing out of the powers and forces of the mind." This is a mistake quite too common to pass without correction. In the Latin language, from which our word "education" is derived, there are two verbs whose first person singular, indicative mode, are in the same form, namely, *educo*. These two words are, first, *educare*, a verb of the first conjugation, and its principal parts are *educo, educare, educavi, educatum*, and this is the word used all through Latin literature for expressing the ideas of education, and it means "to teach," "to instruct," "to train up," "to foster," "to impart information," but it never means to lead out or to draw out. The other verb is *"educere"* of the third conjugation, and its principal parts are *educo, educere, eduxi, eductum*. This word means to "lead out," "to draw out," "to raise up," "to build up," "to bring into the world" (said of midwives), but it is never used to mean education anywhere in Latin literature. Its only use there, in connection with schools, is to describe the process of slaves leading Roman children from their homes to the school and back again, but *educare* is never used to describe this leading out of the children. The idea of "lead out the powers of the mind" is neither in the word nor in the process of education, but, rather, the idea of feeding and nurturing the mind that it may grow. Webster's *International Dictionary* is misleading on this word. All who read this are referred to the *Century Dictionary*, all Latin lexicons, and all Latin literature. Corresponding words are used in the Greek language and literature and lead to the same conclusion as is here presented.　　　　　　　　　　J. A. BOATMAN.

West Liberty, Ia.

THE ITINERANTS' CLUB.

THE "Fraternity of Lifelong Educational Endeavor," of which some account was given in the *Methodist Review* for September of last year, hopes to meet in convention sometime the coming summer. Its plan is as simple as its aim, and its members, although busy men, find no difficulty in meeting its requirements. Each member is expected daily to recall its "Ideal," answer one momentous "Question," form a "Resolve," offer a "Prayer," take a broad and comprehensive "Outlook," and follow these simple "morning offices" with "personal reading and study" in lines of one's own selection" from the fields of "Theology," "Psychology," "Sociology," "Ecclesiology," "Biography," and the "English Language and Literature," beginning, of course, with and emphasizing strongly the "English Bible."

The attention of the members of the F. L. E. E. has been called to the admirable volume of A. Morris Stewart on *The Temptation of Jesus;* to *Mankind in the Making*, by H. G. Wells; to *Papal Aims and Papal Claims*, by E. Garnett Man, Barrister-at-Law; to the story of *Mary North*, by Lucy Rider Meyer; to *The Programme of the Jesuits*, by W. Blair Neatby. Other valuable books have been brought to the attention of the members.

One member proposes a special plan for the reading of biography by which a grouping is made, dominating characters placed in centers, and the notable lives they have influenced duly related and adjusted. "I will be an Astronomer. . . . The great lives shall be the suns, each one with its system of stars. . . . When I read the life of Moses I read Hebrew history and literature. When I read the life of Michael Angelo I read the history of art. But where shall I begin? With Moses? Or with the latest autobiography? I shall begin at the center and read both ways. I shall begin with the mighty Alcyone—Jesus Christ. I shall read all lives in the light of his life. I shall read the gospels each year, and every year read some Life of Christ," etc.

Another member reports his use of small blank books—each book about five inches long and two and a half inches wide. One of them he carries in his vest pocket all the time, and keeps it "as a snare to catch and cage casual thoughts that come to the surface of consciousness, challenging attention. Once entertained, they begin to reward one like buds warmed into blossom or birds into song." He says: "I never let a thought go that comes to me in that fashion. I put it down, and with the related thoughts that follow fill one side of a leaf in my little pocket Thought-Snare. The back of that leaf I leave blank. When my book is full I take it apart and classify my leaf-notes in envelopes labeled according to topics. Sometimes I get twenty or thirty distinct thoughts on one subject in the course of a few weeks, and twenty or thirty more later on. And these are *my* thoughts. They came to me. I planted them. I cultivate them. Then I classify and arrange them, and thus sermons and conversations and

newspaper articles grow in my own preserve. The vest-pocket Thought-Snare has been a great gain to me."

An Experience. "I am (let me assume) a Methodist preacher in the first year of my Conference course. Never mind now my antecedents, personal, intellectual, and professional. The Annual Conference has considered these questions and received me as a 'preacher on trial' and I am enrolled as a member of the 'class of the first year.' The studies for this year are announced in the Appendix to the Discipline, ¶ 59, § 2. I have reached my 'appointment.' My first Sunday is over. I have a 'study.' In it are my books—not many, but good. I have a supply of blank paper. Every sheet of it is an exhortation to diligence, fidelity, and originality. And I must begin to study at the very beginning of the Conference year. The temptation is to wait until I know my people, or until I have answered the letters which have accumulated during these weeks of packing and unpacking, or until my library is fully settled and arranged, documents sorted, and all that. But no! No! The first thing to do is to take up my Conference studies. Let me begin with Harman in his *Introduction to the Holy Scriptures.* No, I will begin with Miley in his *Systematic Theology.* All at once I recall a bit of advice from an old friend, and promptly I decide not to begin with Harman, Miley, or any other author, but, as my friend advised, 'study *subjects,* not books!' These books are to aid the examiners at Conference, and not to be the 'all and in all' of the student. I must know all I can of the subjects embraced in the course. I am neither Dr. Harman nor Dr. Miley. I cannot afford to reproach their puttings of the faith. I cannot be their echo. These authors in the first year's course—Harman, Miley, Foster, Hill, Broadus, Wesley, Stevens, Neely, Buckley, Martin, Foss, Dorchester, Cooke, Asbury, and the editor and other contributors to the *Methodist Review*—all of these are my professors. All honor to them! But I am to work my own way as a student, a thinker, and a preacher; and as I study under their guidance the *subjects* (not the books) assigned I shall be helped by them and shall be the better prepared to help the people to whom I am to minister.

"But this is Monday. Let me begin my study to-morrow. No! I don't believe and I won't believe in 'blue Monday.' I rested Saturday. Monday I work—not quite as hard as on Tuesday, to be sure, but fresh from contact with my people and with a new sense of responsibility I can do some things on Monday better than on any other day.

"And now here are my half-sheets of blank paper ready for my memoranda—my Thinking Memoranda. I begin with 'Systematic Theology.' And what is that? What *is* 'Theology'? Here is my Unabridged. No, I won't open it. Here is my Greek lexicon. No, no! Let me first of all put down my own definition of Theology. What *is* Theology? What is *Systematic* Theology? And what other kinds of Theology are there? 'Natural.' Yes. Write down my definition of it. And 'Polemic.' What is Polemic Theology? And '*Biblical* Theology'? And 'Practical Theology'? What other departments of the science are there?—Here comes a caller. Sorry! Ah, good morning, Brother Brooke! 'Tired after Sunday; called

to have a chat.' 'Well, Brooke, I am just puzzling myself over a definition of Theology and trying to make a classification of the different kinds of Theology the scholars talk about. What do *you* think?' 'On Monday?' 'Certainly on Monday! But what *is* Theology? What would you say? What *did* you say when examined? Must go? Sorry! Call again. Call in the afternoons unless you want to study. I must use morning hours for work.' 'Good-bye.' 'Good-bye.' Pencil in hand I think, and try to remember, and ask myself what I should say if I were asked for a definition of Systematic Theology. And I write and revise, erase and rewrite, and think and try again, and put down several questions that my thinking develops: What other words might I use besides 'Theology' to define the field of thought it covers? How does it happen that we have a Greek word instead of English? What is the Latin term? Let me look again at *my* definition. By the way, what is Patristic Theology? How little I know! Now for a talk to my stove and chairs and walls ('walls have ears') about Theology. 'Dear Friends: Theology is a term'—but the bell rings for lunch!

" 'No, my dear,' I say to my wife at the table, 'the morning was not wasted, but it was not fruitful in results. I did start right. That is something. I did work out dear Brooke, who likes to 'rest.' I have stirred my own curiosity into a regular thirst to know how the dictionary and Dr. Miley define Theology. I worked out rather a poor definition of my own. I am anxious to see if it is sound. What do you think Theology is?' And the good soul gave me an answer offhand. She said she supposed that Theology is the result of the thinking men do about God tested and corrected by the teaching of God's own word and illustrated and enriched by personal experience in believing that word and trying to live up to it. Then she looked at me as if she expected me to smile at her. And I believe I did smile with admiration and pride, and I told her that I already saw a sermon in it. Then we talked about doing pastoral work and how we might do it in the best way. And I asked her what were her chief doubts and difficulties in connection with the Bible and religion and the Church. Now if other people have such troubles in connection with these subjects as even my wife confesses to there is room for sermons on Theology and good reason for the careful study of Bible evidences and all that. I believe that these prescribed books of the Conference course will be more entertaining than novels if we find out what our people are thinking about and what they need. To feel the need for one's self and to try one's best to find for himself the way to meet and relieve this need is the way to make books worth something and downright hard study a delight. I see that the way to get ready for Conference examination is to examine and discuss subjects with people of all kinds during the whole year—to study subjects and not books, and to study people while one studies subjects."

———————

Four men, ministers of the Gospel, intent on self-improvement—personal and professional—happening to spend a social evening together, fell into a conversation on pulpit effectiveness. Of the four, Atherton was the

oldest. He had never "gone through college," but was eager to be a cultured man. Benton was a college graduate, a conservative fellow, by the way, and loyal to the old paths. Carter was also college-bred without much "early schooling" and a progressive in—well, in everything, and was not easily "shocked" by some of the modern "statements." He did not accept the "heresies," but he was not afraid of them, and rather liked to look them in the face. He was broad enough and had faith firm enough neither to be alarmed nor exasperated by men who in their search for truth listened to doctrines, entertained hypotheses, and frankly canvassed positions directly opposed to his own. Dalton was the youngest member and by far the best scholar in this country quaternion. He had enjoyed the advantages of a refined home, had been at school from his earliest years, was graduated from one of the best universities in America, had taken a graduate course in Europe, won a high degree, was a man of much personal force and glad to take charge, as a probationer in the Conference, of a humble country circuit. These men lived within ten miles of each other and occasionally met for a social evening. While the wives discussed subjects interesting to them the four young pastors by a blazing fire in the "study" took up one, or more topics relating to their work. This evening Dalton read an excellent paper on "Pulpit Style," and that was followed by a few apt quotations from distinguished authors. And the writer of this article believes that he can render no better service to the readers of this Department than to select a few of these quotations. The comments and conversation of the company must be omitted. The lessons taught by these high authorities are worthy of the thoughtful attention of all ministers of the Gospel—old and young. One golden truth shines in all these gems of literature. Here they are: "In character, in manners, in style, in all things the supreme excellence is simplicity."* "The greatest truths are the simplest, and so are the greatest men."† "Nothing is rarer than the use of a word in its exact meaning."‡ "The words in prose ought to express the intended meaning; if they attract attention to themselves it is a fault; in the very best styles, as Southey's, you read page after page without noticing the medium."§ "If you would be pungent be brief, for it is with words as with sunbeams, the more they are condensed the deeper they burn."‖ "With many readers brilliancy of style passes for affluence of thought; they mistake buttercups in the grass for immeasurable mines of gold under ground."* "When you doubt between words use the plainest, the commonest, the most idiomatic. Eschew fine words as you would rouge."†

The conversation then drifted into the power of monosyllables. Quotations from Abraham Lincoln, Carlyle, Ruskin, and especially from the Bible, were made, and the talk closed with a recitation by Atherton of Professor Joseph Addison Alexander's poem on "The Power of Short Words." It is worth quoting here. Dr. Alexander was a professor in the Theological Seminary at Princeton, a master of seven languages, accomplished in almost every department of learning, and a specialist in oriental literature.

* Longfellow.   † Hare.   ‡ Whipple.   § Coleridge.   ‖ Saxe.

The Power of Short Words.

Think not that strength lies in the big round word,
    Or that the brief and plain must needs be weak.
To whom can this be true who once has heard
    The cry for help, the tongue that all men speak,
When want or woe or fear is in the throat,
    So that each word gasped out is like a shriek
Pressed from the sore heart, or a strange, wild note
    Sung by some fay or fiend? There is a strength
Which dies if stretched too far or spun too fine,
    Which has more height than breadth, more depth than length.
Let but this force of thought and speech be mine,
    And he that will may take the sleek fat phrase,
Which glows and burns not, though it gleam and shine;
    Light but not heat—a flash but not a blaze!

Nor mere strength is it that the short word boasts;
    It serves of more than fight or storm to tell—
The roar of waves that clash on rock-bound coasts,
    The crash of tall trees when the wild winds swell,
The roar of guns, the groans of men that die
    On blood-stained fields. It has a voice as well
For them that far off on their sick beds lie;
    For them that weep, for them that mourn the dead;
For them that laugh and dance and clap the hand:
    To Joy's quick step, as well as Grief's slow tread,
The sweet, plain words we learn at first keep time;
    And though the theme be sad or gay or grand,
With each, with all, these may be made to chime,
    In thought, or speech, or song, in prose or rhyme.

What a great teacher a pastor may be! He has the world of observation, history, and science to draw from in illustration of the world of grace. He may teach while he preaches. He may know and watch the day school which the children of his church attend. He may neutralize the apathy or the silence of secular teachers as to religious teaching, by his Sabbath-day instructions. He may teach in and through his Sunday school by means of superintendent, teachers, chorister, librarians, and platform speakers. He may make his church an institute of theology, of Church history, biblical exposition, and Christian ethics for young and old. He may organize Bible classes for all grades of his adult members, and supplement the most direct and vigorous religious teaching by evening classes, in all branches of learning, for those who want education but who cannot go to the schools to get it. He may organize popular lecture courses in his own church in science and in art, in history and political economy; debating societies; circles for home reading; magazine clubs; recreative evening classes; and any number of useful devices which would help to make his church a school. And in all this supervision of church activities he may devote himself to pulpit preparation and through that agency be the teacher of the multitude as was "the Great Teacher" whom he serves and should try to imitate.

ARCHÆOLOGY AND BIBLICAL RESEARCH.

THE ROMAN CATHOLIC CHURCH AND BIBLICAL CRITICISM.

Of the many false impressions among Protestants regarding the Roman Catholic Church, two might be mentioned as very common: that the Catholic clergy pay no attention to biblical studies, and that the Roman communion throughout the world is a unit on the subject of biblical criticism, and is nowhere troubled by fierce controversies regarding the inspiration, inerrancy, and origin of the several books of the Bible. The allegation of the uninformed Protestant that the Bible is a sealed book to the Catholic clergy is equaled only by the assertion of the Romanist that Protestants alone make shipwreck on the shoals of "higher criticism." At the same time, it is doubtless true that Rome has suffered less from discussions arising from biblical criticism than have some of the less pretentious branches of the Christian Church. The spirit of Rome is ever conservative, especially in countries predominantly Catholic. This is true not only of the more benighted South American republics and Spain, their mother, but also of Italy itself, "the home and headquarters of the papacy." It is scarcely credible, but nevertheless true, that "throughout the length and breadth of Italy there is no sort of society for biblical studies. An academy of this nature which once existed at Rome under the presidency of Cardinal Parocchi at the Propaganda Palace soon languished and died from lack of interest and encouragement, and all the recent efforts of Padre Lepidi, who summoned a conference at the Vatican last May to found another in its stead, were doomed to failure. Can this be wondered at, when in fact there is no chair of biblical criticism in the Roman ecclesiastical schools, and when at the Gregorian and Minerva universities—to cite only two instances—none of the two thousand and odd Church students who flock thither annually are ever examined in biblical knowledge? Nor is any standard of proficiency demanded even from the selecter group, who go forth decorated as Bachelors and Doctors of Theology." This is from the pen of Mr. Austin West (*Contemporary Review*), to whom we are indebted for several suggestions in this article.

The lack of greater interest in biblical study among Catholics is, after all, not hard to explain; for it is well known that Protestants and Catholics stand on very different grounds. The orthodox Protestant plants himself squarely on the Bible, which to him is a sufficient rule of faith and conduct. The Catholic, on the other hand, while fully committed to the doctrine of inspiration, maintains that the pope, and not the Bible, is the final arbiter or court of appeal. For, says he, "the pope cannot, when acting in his official character of supreme pontiff, err in defining a doctrine of Christian faith or rule of morals to be held by the Church." According to the orthodox Romanist the Bible is inspired, but the pope alone can pronounce infallibly upon disputed points and proclaim to men the real

meaning of the inspired word. There are Catholics and Catholics. The United States is not Spain, England is not Peru, and France, even, is not Italy. The controversies which agitated the Protestant Churches of Germany during the past century produced a great impression upon the Catholic Church of the Fatherland. While rationalism was making fearful inroads among the followers of Luther and Calvin, all was not serene among the Romanists. The dead scholasticism which had settled down like a nightmare upon the Catholic clergy, the leaders in philosophy and theology, was vigorously opposed by men like Feneberg and Diepenbrock, brought up at the feet of Bishop von Sailer of Ratisbon, no less than by the learned Baron von Wesenberg, whom Rome refused to make bishop "*ob gravissimas causas.*" The rank and file of the Romish clergy in Germany became more or less saturated with the scientific spirit of the age. No one more so than Von Moehler, of Tübingen, later of Munich. People wonder to this day that his *Symbolik* was not placed upon the Index. The names of Döllinger and Reinikens should not be omitted, for they also cherished advanced views on questions of criticism, though excommunicated on other grounds. Of late years Catholic Germany has been rather quiet as far as biblical criticism is concerned, and yet its sky has not been quite clear. Small clouds have also appeared which have disturbed the Catholics of our own land. Several distinguished scholars, suspected of fostering and propagating too liberal views, have been mysteriously transferred from one college to another, or from one chair to another in the same institution. It is impossible to explain all these changes as being in the line of promotion. The treatment of scholars like Drs. Shields, Bruneau, and Danchy is still openly discussed. But, explain their transfer as we wish, it is certain that the views held by these and others we might name differ very widely from those held by the average Catholic priest or bishop. Articles recently published in Catholic organs in this country and England show which way the wind is blowing, and that there is a strong undercurrent in the apparently placid waters.

In recent years France has been the storm center, and Abbé Loisy the cause of the greatest disturbance. The clouds have gathered fast and thick about the head of this erudite Roman Catholic professor of theology. A few years ago he published a very interesting volume, *L'Evangile et L'Eglise.* Its issue was like a thunderbolt from a clear sky. It at once attracted great attention. As expected, the anathemas of many prominent ecclesiasts were hurled upon the book. The learned abbé saw clearly that he had broken the peace of the faithful and that his book had become a real stumbling-block to many influential prelates in France and elsewhere. He hastened to withdraw it from circulation. The book was intended chiefly as an antidote against Harnack's teachings; as an answer from the standpoint of the learned Roman Catholic biblical critic to the teachings of the more radical and destructive Protestant theologians. Among several other essays published by Dr. Loisy we must mention *La Religion d'Israel: Ses Origines.* This appeared under an assumed name in the *Revue de Clergo Francais,* October, 1900. This again gave great offense, though the friends of Loisy regard it as a complete overthrow of Renan's

utterances on the same subject, which appeared more than fifty years before. This paper, like all that the learned doctor writes, is so permeated with critical ideas, utterly at variance with the traditional beliefs of the Catholic Church, that the editor of the above-named review was warned not to publish any more such articles. Dr. Loisy is a terse writer; "his thought is condensed, his expression concise, he makes no parade of learning, he does not indulge in rhetoric, there is no attempt at effect or edification." His works are mostly exegetical. From reading his *Études Bibliques* one may fairly infer that he holds the following beliefs: The Pentateuch as we have it is not of Mosaic origin; the first eleven chapters of Genesis are not historical; the story of the flood, and probably the fall of man, is of Assyrian origin. The books of Daniel and Ezra are of very late date and apocryphal. Equal inspiration must not be sought for in the entire Bible; this is as true of the New as of the Old Testament. St. John is not the author of the fourth gospel, nor can it be from the pen of an immediate disciple of Jesus or even of an eyewitness. There is much in this gospel, like the resurrection of Lazarus, which is not historical.

After what has been written it is needless to add that such teachings have created great excitement throughout the Catholic Church, reminding one of the Briggs controversy in our own land, or of the Colenso discussion half a century ago. No orthodox communion could be expected to remain quiet under such provocation, least of all the Catholic Church in Europe. His utterances have been valiantly opposed. Among the most influential and distinguished of his opponents we must mention Cardinal Richard, the archbishop of Paris. Dr. Loisy's case, doubtless, after previous personal though fruitless admonition from this high dignitary, was referred to the Holy Office for adjustment. The Holy Office is another name for the Inquisition, or the great ecclesiastical court to examine into matters of heresy and other irregularities, with power to suppress heretical teaching and to punish heretics. Those who have followed the case need not be told that the Holy Office withheld its verdict. No book or essay of Dr. Loisy is on the Index. There is but little doubt that Leo XIII interfered. This diplomatic pope thought it wise at least to defer the matter, and urged that the interests of the Church could be subserved better by appointing a commission to study the questions at issue and to bring in a report on the whole subject of biblical criticism. This is the origin of the "International Pontifical Commission." It was a master stroke on Leo's part. It prevented any hasty decision or rupture in the Church. The commission is composed of twelve members, or, counting Cardinal Parocchi, the president, and his two assessors, fifteen. The majority, as might be expected, are Italians; Germany has two representatives, and the following countries one each: Spain, France, Belgium, Holland, England, Ireland, and the United States. They are without exception scholarly men, several of them specialists in some line of study. Some of them have been persecuted for too liberal views or downright rationalism. The questions on which they are to pass judgment have been more or less defined, but no definite time is assigned within which they must bring in a report. Nor have they any stated time or place of meeting in formal

conference. Indeed, they may never meet. Their work is rather to gain all the light they can upon every phase of biblical criticism and report in writing to each other and to the president of the commission.

Father Loisy—the Harnack of the Catholic Church—is especially learned in the Semitic languages and literatures. He was professor of biblical exegesis in L'Institut Catholique—one of the foremost schools of Paris —for twelve years. He made a great name for himself here, and stood in the front rank of scholars. He was suddenly transferred from his chair to the chaplaincy of a nunnery. Was he forced to resign? Was this change in the line of promotion? Or did his superiors think him safer as a spiritual adviser for a handful of pious nuns and schoolgirls than as a teacher of bright young theologues, the future leaders of the Church in France? The removal of Dr. Loisy was not an unmixed evil, but rather a blessing in disguise, for as with St. Paul in prison, so with this French *savant*, he now had abundant time for his critical studies, and several important essays were the immediate result. These have appeared in the leading Church reviews. A man of Professor Loisy's ability could not long be buried in the seclusion of a convent. The French government, which cares little for creeds, still less for orthodoxy, elected him to a professorship in the *École Pratique des Hautes Etudes*, in Paris. His predecessors in this chair have been great men, some of them distinguished Roman Catholic clergy. Of these we may mention Abbé Quentin and Père Scheil, the eminent archæologist and Assyriologist. The piety and orthodoxy of these two have never been questioned. We must add that Professor Loisy's chair is now under the ban, for certain schools in Paris, for example, L'Institut Catholique, forbid "under pain of expulsion" the attendance of its theological students upon Dr. Loisy's lectures. His lecture room, nevertheless, as formerly that of Renan, is frequented by many young and old Catholic theologians. Loisy has a large following; some claim that the majority of the younger priests are with him on questions of biblical criticism. This is probably an exaggeration; there is, however, a growing number of learned Catholics who advocate more freedom for students of the Bible. Several of the best Catholic reviews have opened their columns to Loisy and his followers, not only in France but elsewhere. Even in Italy, one of the leading organs of the Church—*Studi Religiosi*— has more than once defended his teachings. One need only read the *American Ecclesiastical Review*, an ably edited "monthly *publication for the clergy*," in order to see that some very distinguished American and English Catholics hold views regarding inspiration and kindred topics very like those of Dr. Loisy. An article on Inspiration in this magazine, January, 1901, is more liberal in tone than many organs of evangelical Churches would care to publish on the subject.

The attitude of Leo XIII toward the Loisy controversy had discouraged the enemies of Loisy. The case has been reopened by Cardinal Richard. What will Pius X do?

Since that question was written dispatches have brought from Rome the information that some of Abbé Loisy's works have been condemned and put on the Index. What will Loisy do?

FOREIGN OUTLOOK.

SOME LEADERS OF THOUGHT.

Georg Runze. As professor in Berlin University he has a considerable following among the student body, and he is to be reckoned as an independent and able thinker. In 1901 he published a book under the title *Katechismus der Religionsphilosophie* (A Catechism of Philosophy of Religion), Leipzig, J. J. Weber, in which he sets forth his views on this important subject. According to him the philosophy of religion is chiefly concerned about the origin and nature of religion, though it may not altogether neglect the law of its development. It has practically nothing to do with the defense of any particular form of faith. This belongs in the realm of dogmatic theology. In studying the subject he thinks it is necessary to pursue the ethnological, the pedagogical, and the introspective methods. The first directs attention to the life of those peoples now in existence who are living in a state of nature; the second, to the inner life of the child; and the third, to the religious phenomena observable in the maturer classes among civilized men. The result of such a method of study leads to the conclusion that religion springs from the nature of the entire man, though several factors may be distinguished, as desire and aversion, involuntary constructions of the imagination, the activity of the understanding in attempting to solve the problems of being, the force of the ethical impulse, and the influence of language on the construction of religious ideas. In this connection it is questionable whether he has not given too much weight to the influence of language when he says that religion results from the opaqueness and inadequacy of speech to represent the object sought for with satisfactory clearness. Along with this goes his doctrine that religion is neither exclusively volition nor thinking, but that condition of the life of the soul in which the active will is still the unconscious force and the representative faculty is still sensuous receptivity, or intuition. It is true that the origin of religion might be thus humble and unworthy while religion itself might be so desirable and even necessary as to make us hold on to it. But the conclusion that most men would be likely to draw from Runze's positions is that religion has no place in the life of a truly rational being. The only way to escape such a conclusion would be to say that that which is common to religion is as Runze describes it. Particular forms of religion add so much to the dignity of the origin and nature of religion in general as to lift them above the level of that which is common to all and so to make them worthy of retention by enlightened men. Thus, we might be justified in being Christians when we could not be justified in maintaining a lower form of religion. This makes clear at once the inadequacy of Runze's method. A philosophy of religion should take in all the phenomena of all religions. It is legitimate enough to study the subject from the side of the contribution which the human mind makes to religion, but this is no com-

plete philosophy of the subject. A philosophy of religion which does not consider the validity of religious ideas can but be disappointing. It may indeed be that religion originates in the lower stages of human development, but it does not remain there. It is found in the most enlightened minds of the most enlightened peoples. This finds but inadequate recognition in Runze's discussion of the law of religious development. This conception of religion as a function of art and of art as a function of religion, with the emphasis on the latter, is based on the same inadequate consideration of all the elements which enter into the origin and development of the only religion that can stand examination.

F. Niebergall. To those who are familiar with German devotional literature his name will not be unknown. But in 1902, in Tübingen (J. C. B. Mohr), he published a work of far more than ordinary interest on the subject *Wie predigen wir dem modernen Menschen? Eine Untersuchung über Motive und Quietive* (How shall We Preach to the Modern Man? A Study of Motives and Quietives). Niebergall does not announce any homiletical theory, and he adheres throughout to the most rigid application of modern methods to the study of the Bible. But he rises above all partisan considerations to give us some thoughts eminently worthy of our attention. According to him the purpose of preaching is to offer motives which shall surpass the motives natural to man, and to offer quietives which shall banish the sorrow of the natural man. Preaching should grow out of the knowledge of the Gospel on the one side and of the people to whom it is to be preached on the other. The sources and character of all homiletical material are thus determined. Niebergall believes that the best way to get at the practical teachings of the New Testament is the scientific, objective method. In this respect he is in accord with New Testament theology. But he differs from New Testament theologians in that he makes no attempt to discover a system of truth in the writings of each or of all of the New Testament writers. There may be differences of theories among the New Testament writers, but the purpose is the same in all. He is above all possible inconsistencies and contradictions which trouble the scientific theologian so much. Allowing them all, he still finds the New Testament a rich mine of truth applicable to the needs of mankind. There are, in accordance with these thoughts, three groups of motives and quietives: 1. The reference to the temporal advantages of religion; 2. The reference to the transcendental benefits of religion; and, 3. The appeal to existing religious possessions and forces which should be cherished and employed. It is not necessary alone to exhaust all the resources of the New Testament in preaching, but to know man as he is, and not merely as he has sometimes been conceived of. Niebergall thinks that the feelings are the primary element in man—the foundation of his sane life. Hence the fact that man can be determined in his conduct or volitions by an estimate of values is seen to be the best means of access to human life. In proportion as the preacher can offer the highest good to the contemplation of man will he work effectively for

their elevation. But it is not sufficient to know man in general, the preacher must know man in particular. Niebergall divides men into three classes, in order to discover what motives and quietives will be effective with them: 1. Average people; 2. Church people; and, 3. Educated people who neglect the Church and religion. While Niebergall would find the sources of homiletical material largely in the New Testament, he does not hold that all preaching need be scriptural—that is, drawn from the Scripture. This is impossible, he thinks, simply because, first, there is no complete system of needful truth embodied in the New Testament and, second, because the ideal of life, whether universal or personal, cannot be drawn directly from the New Testament as such. Nevertheless he holds that the New Testament has been most influential in the progress of ethical and religious thought, and that all progress in the understanding of the kingdom of God must be made along the line of the thoughts contained in the New Testament. The New Testament offers not only that which was new in religion, but that which is central, namely, the person of Jesus Christ, who is given us as a supernatural power for our strengthening and comforting, and who can take us children of sin and death and change us into new men in the likeness of Christ. The earthly prosperity and happiness as well as the eternal state of every man depends upon his acceptance or rejection of this Christ who came from God to man.

RECENT THEOLOGICAL LITERATURE.

Die neue Auffassung der israelitischen Religionsgeschichte und der christliche Offenbarungsglaube (The New Conception of the History of the Religion of Israel and the Christian Doctrine of Revelation). By F. Traub, Heilbronn, 1902. Although there has been much discussion of this subject in recent years a new work by a thoughtful man is always welcome. Traub's booklet first of all commits itself to the Wellhausen theory of the religious development of Israel in a brief sketch of its history through its three principal periods—the preprophetic, the prophetic, and the priestly. The question is then raised whether this conception of the history can be made to harmonize with faith in a real revelation from God. He thinks that this must be negatived under two conditions: first, if the doctrine of revelation is so conceived as to affirm the inerrancy of the Scriptures, and, second, if, on the other hand, the assertion is correct that the new theory is inextricably interwoven with a denial of the supernatural. He is of the opinion, however, that neither of these conditions need be assumed. As to the former it is a dogmatic presupposition now almost universally abandoned, while as to the second, the theory of evolution applied to the Old Testament, it is not applied as a principle for the explanation of the world but as a heuristic principle. In the application of this principle of investigation the historian who seeks for causal connections clearly sees that in the realm of history causal explanation can never be asserted without qualification, because the concept of personality forbids it. So that when he thinks himself able to show a development he

thinks of that development not in the causal but in the teleological sense. More positively he makes the well-known point that the question of Old Testament history in no wise affects the Christian faith which has its foundation in the person of Christ. The only way in which a contradiction could arise between the Christian faith and the modern views of the Old Testament would be to hold that the views of Jesus concerning the Old Testament were normative for us. This theory he holds to be an unbearable perversion of the authority of Jesus. As to the further question whether the religious history of Israel in its modern conception can be looked upon as a revelation, he thinks this could be denied only by one who had determined *a priori* that the religious history of Israel would be unworthy of God if it began at a low stage and only gradually rose to the highest point. In answer to the question what there is in the Old Testament history to convince us of a real divine revelation there, he says that historical means and methods will certainly not convince us. These will indeed enable us to show that the belief in revelation was the foundation of the Israelitish religion; but the question whether that belief was justified lies outside of the realm of history. Revelation is not an historical but a religious concept. Hence we cannot deduce the reality of a divine revelation either from the breaks in the causal connection of the historical development or from the self-consciousness of the prophets. Only from the content of the Israelitish religion itself can we discover its revealed character. As the Christian examines that religion in the light of his own he discovers that the same ethical concept of God is characteristic of both, and this it is which assures him of the revealed character of the Old Testament religion. The gradual development of this idea of God in the history of the Israelites produces in us the conviction that that history is at once a record of a revelation and of a process of salvation. Whatever one may think of this argument, it is interesting, and to some it will be consoling to know that the advocates of the most extreme views of the Old Testament believe in divine revelation.

RELIGIOUS AND EDUCATIONAL.

The German Military Requirements and the Clergy. In 1890 a law was passed by the German Parliament practically excusing the Roman Catholic clergy from all military service, even before ordination. Ever since then there has been much discussion as to whether the Protestants should seek to have their clergy excused also. Some favor, others oppose. In a recent meeting of Protestant clergy in Coburg the matter was fully debated, with the result that the following resolutions were passed by a vote of 51 to 29: 1. That the military service should be limited for Protestant clergy to one year; 2. That it should in no case extend beyond ordination. This seems to be about a representative case showing the state of Protestant feeling.

The Social Democrats and Religion. At a recent meeting of the representatives of the Social Democrats in Germany the following de-

mands were made: 1. Separation between State and Church; 2. Cessation of all state support of Church and religion; 3. Abolition of religious instruction from the schools; 4. Substitution therefor of moral instruction independent of all metaphysical basis, and scientific instruction in the history of religions; 5. Prohibition of all teaching of creeds to children under sixteen years of age; 6. Opposition to all superstition by the enlightenment of its adherents; 7. Withdrawal from such religious societies as represent faiths no longer believed. These things are scarcely more radical than those which all Americans take as a matter of course. But the animus of the party is revealed in a different light when the second resolution is read, as follows: Only such persons as belong to no confessional religious organization shall be allowed to be party leaders among the Social Democrats, and only such shall be nominated by the party as candidates for its votes.

Proposed Official Recognition of Woman's Work. The movement for the emancipation of woman in Germany has gone so far as that a respectable author in a well-known religious journal deliberately raises the question whether it is not time to institute an office in the Church adapted to the capabilities of women and to recognize it as fully as the clerical office is now recognized. He proposes that candidates for it shall be thoroughly educated, and that the incumbents shall be provided with regular salaries. He thinks this is all the more necessary since in the large parishes it is impossible for the clergy to perform all the necessary spiritual functions, and these are now in a considerable measure performed by women, but in an unofficial and therefore in an irresponsible way. He thinks the hindrances to such a project are by no means insuperable.

The German Emperor to His Sons. Not long ago two of the sons of Emperor William II were confirmed. At the family table soon after the emperor proposed that those there gathered should drink to the health of the youths. But before doing so he expressed a desire to speak some words of fatherly advice. In so doing he compared the obligations they had just assumed to the oath a soldier takes upon entering the army. In the instructions they had received preparatory to confirmation they had learned of Christ as Lord and Saviour. Many opinions were held concerning Christ, but among all that ever lived on earth he was incomparably the greatest. It was to be their highest duty and privilege to imitate him in industrious service of their fellow-men. This is the brief substance of an excellent address, worthy of any preacher. It would be well if all fathers took as much evident interest in the beliefs and Christian activities of their children.

GLIMPSES OF REVIEWS AND MAGAZINES.

Four of the six contributions in the January issue of the *Princeton Theological Review* (Philadelphia) are addresses: an inaugural on "The Witness of the Gospels," by Professor W. P. Armstrong, at his induction into the Chair of New Testament Literature and Exegesis at Princeton; "Spiritual Culture in the Theological Seminary," delivered at the Fall Opening of Princeton Seminary by Dr. B. B. Warfield; "Jonathan Edwards: A Study," delivered by Dr. John De Witt, at Stockbridge, Mass., at the Edwards bicentennial celebration; and the address of Dr. F. L. Patton on "Theological Encyclopædia" at his inauguration as president of Princeton Theological Seminary. None of these strong addresses is short. Dr. Warfield quotes from Spurgeon these words on meditation:

We ought to muse upon the things of God, because we thus get the real nutriment out of them. Truth is something like the cluster of the vine: if we would have wine from it, we must bruise it; we must press and squeeze it many times. The bruisers' feet must come down joyfully upon the bunches, or else the juice will not flow; and they must well tread the grapes, or else much of the precious liquid will be wasted. So we must by meditation tread the clusters of truth, if we would get the wine of consolation therefrom. Our bodies are not supported merely by taking food into the mouth, but the process which really supplies the muscles and the nerve and the sinew and the bone is the process of digestion. It is by digestion that the outer food becomes assimilated with the inner life. Our souls are not nourished merely by listening a while to this, and then to that, and then to the other part of divine truth. Hearing, reading, marking, and learning all require inwardly digesting to complete their usefulness, and the inward digesting of the truth lies for the most part in meditating upon it. Why is it that some Christians, although they hear many sermons, make but slow advances in the divine life? Because they neglect their closets, and do not thoughtfully meditate on God's word. They love the wheat, but they do not grind it; they would have the corn, but they will not go forth into the fields to gather it; the fruit hangs upon the tree, but they will not pluck it; the water flows at their feet, but they will not stoop to drink it. From such folly deliver us, O Lord, and be this our resolve this day, "I will meditate on thy precepts."

Phillips Brooks, enforcing the lesson that a minister's intense devotion to his studies and careful preparation for his work is a true measure of his faithfulness and fitness, said:

I never shall forget my first experience of a divinity school. I had come from a college where men studied hard but said nothing about faith. I had never been at a prayer meeting in my life. The first place I was taken to at the seminary was the prayer meeting; and never shall I lose the impression of the devoutness with which those men prayed and exhorted one another. Their whole souls seemed exalted and their natures were on fire. I sat bewildered and ashamed and went away depressed. On the next day I met some of these same men at a Greek recitation. It would be little to say of some of the

devoutest of them that they had not learnt their lesson. Their whole way
showed that they had never learnt their lessons; that they had not got hold of
the first principles of hard, faithful, conscientious study. The boiler had no
connection with the engine. The devotion did not touch the work which then
and there was the work, and the only work, for them to do. By and by I
found something of where the steam did escape to. A sort of amateur, pre-
mature preaching was much in vogue among us. We were in haste to be at
what we called "our work!" A feeble twilight of the coming ministry we lived
in. The people in the neighborhood dubbed us "parsonettes." O, my fellow-
students, the special study of theology and all that appertains to it, that is
what the preacher must be doing always; but he can never do it afterward as
he can in the blessed days of quiet in Arabia, after Christ has called him, and
before the apostles lay their hands upon him. In many respects an ignorant
clergy, however pious it may be, is worse than none at all. The more the empty
head glows and burns, the more hollow and thin and dry it grows. "The
knowledge of the priest," said St. Francis de Sales, "is the eighth sacrament
of the Church."

Dr. Warfield asked three men to suggest the five most helpful books of
practical religion, and received the following responses. Dr. James
Stalker named these: Thomas à Kempis's *Imitation of Christ*, Richard
Baxter's *Reformed Pastor*, Jeremy Taylor's *Life of Christ*, John Owen's
Holy Spirit, Adolph Monod's *Saint Paul*. The late Rev. Dr. William M.
Taylor, of New York, named the following five: Dean Goulburn's
Thoughts on Personal Religion, Phelps's *Still Hour*, Tholuck's *Hours of
Christian Devotion*, Alexander's *Thoughts on Religious Experience*, Fa-
ber's *Hymns*. Dr. William M. Paxton recommends: Hodge's *Way of Life*,
Bishop Ryle's *Holiness*, Doddridge's *Rise and Progress of Religion in the
Soul*, Owen's *Spiritual Mindedness*, and Faber's *Thoughts on Great Mys-
teries*. Of religious biographies, Dr. Stalker recommends Augustine's
Confessions, Baxter's *Reliques*, Hanna's *Life of Chalmers*, Blaikie's *Life
of Livingstone*, Witte's *Life of Tholuck*, and Brown's *Life of Rabbi Dun-
can*. Dr. William M. Taylor recommended Bonar's *Memoirs of McCheyne*,
Hanna's *Life of Chalmers*, Arnot's *Memoir of James Hamilton*, Guthrie's
Memoirs, Blaikie's *Life of Livingstone*, J. G. Paton's *Autobiography*, and
Dr. Prentiss's *Life and Letters of Mrs. Prentiss*. Dr. Warfield further
says: "Along with religious biography I venture to mention also religious
fiction. Take the *Chronicles of the Schoenberg-Cotta Family*. Take the
Heir of Redclyffe. Who in the face of the experience of a generation can
doubt the quickening influence of such books? A book that has played a
part such as that played by the *Heir of Redclyffe* in the lives of men like
Dr. A. Kuyper and Mr. William Morris is surely worthy of our serious attention as a religious force in the world." Included in this address is
Augustine's well-known prayer:

Great art Thou, O Lord, and highly to be praised; great is Thy power and
Thy understanding is infinite. Yet Thee would man praise—though but a little
particle of Thy creation: even man, who bears about with him his mortality,
bears about with him the proof of his sin, even the proof that Thou resistest
the proud: yea, Thee still would man praise, this little particle of Thy creation.
'Tis Thou that dost excite us to delight in Thy praise; for Thou didst make us

for Thyself and our heart is restless till it find its rest in Thee. Grant me, Lord, to know whethe.' I should first call upon Thee or praise Thee; whether I should first know Thee or call upon Thee. . . . Alas! Alas! tell me for Thy mercies' sake, O Lord, my God, what Thou art unto me. Say unto my soul, "I am thy salvation." So speak that I may hear. Behold, the ears of my heart are before Thee, O Lord: open Thou them and say to my soul, "I am thy salvation." Make me to run after Thy voice and lay hold on Thee. Hide not Thy face from me. Let me die that I die not: only let me see Thy face. Narrow is my soul's house; enlarge Thou it, that Thou mayest enter in. It is fallen into ruins: repair Thou it. There is that within it which must offend Thine eyes: I confess, I know it. But who shall cleanse it? Or to whom but to Thee shall I cry?

The address of Dr. Patton is marked by his usual positiveness, force, and confident air of mastery. His characteristics appear in the following extracts:

How the profound problems of metaphysics bear upon the philosophy of religion we can see in the Gifford lectures of Ward and Royce. How the distinctive features of Christianity disappear under the touch of the Hegelian dialectic we can see in the writings of the Cairds. We may be thankful, perhaps, that something of supernaturalism is saved from the wreck when we read the brilliant pages of James's *Varieties of Religious Experience;* but then how little it is! And when in despair of a rational basis for religious belief we are left by Höffding and Mallock to console ourselves with value-judgments, we are tempted to ask: Has it come to this? And does our philosophy of religion say for its last word that we keep our religious beliefs simply because we cannot and will not give them up? . . . I do not think we can save our faith by discarding our intellects. The world will not long continue to value a religion which is believed to be irrational, no matter who it is that commends it to our consideration. And whether it be Tertullian or Ritschl, or Hermann or Coleridge, or Isaac Taylor or Balfour, or Kidd or Mallock, or the modern high-potency dilutionists of the Ritschlian School, who in this country are giving us an ethico-sentimental naturalism as the new Gospel for the twentieth century, I make bold to tell them all alike that Christianity will be denied a hearing in the court of feeling once she has been nonsuited at the bar of reason.

Of the importance of the study of Homiletics, Dr. Patton says:

A man who makes a serious study of Homiletics and brings to it a well-furnished mind will need none of the popular homiletical helps and can afford to throw his Dictionary of Illustrations out of the window. I do not feel the difficulty which some experience in settling the boundary lines of plagiarism. A full man, with a fresh mind, after sufficient brooding on his text, will get down to the roots of the text, will see what nobody else will see in the same light; for the thing seen, to use a Kantianism, is not the text-in-itself, but the text-in-itself in relation to the man-in-himself; and this being the case, if the man-in-himself be a man—that is, if he has grown out of his babyhood and rounded into a separate mind—the possibilities are infinite respecting the sermons that may be preached from any text. And so I say to my younger brethren in the ministry, and especially to you young men who have not yet entered it: get powers of expression, get knowledge, get thought-power, get rich Christian experience, get a knowledge of homiletical *technique,* and then

let the sermon be yours—nay, rather, let it be you. Let it be an arrow shot from the tense bowstring of conviction and it will hit the mark every time. But the sermon is not the only thing in the worship of the Church. We belong to the nonliturgical family of Churches, and music does not hold the place in our Church that it occupies in some other branches of Christendom. But that is no reason why we should fail to provide proper instruction in our seminaries in Church music of the better sort or ignore the great devotional formulas which have fed the spiritual life of generations of Christians. I should say that it is the minister of the nonliturgical Church, who is expected to be ready at a moment's notice to express himself in apt, elevated, rhythmical, devotional language, who is likely to be most profited by familiar acquaintance with the liturgical formulas of the Christian Church. For the nurture of his own spiritual life, and for his greater efficiency as a minister of the Word, I commend to every theological student the duty of having an intimate acquaintance with the Word of God in the English tongue; but I would also commend to him the duty of familiarizing himself with the Church's best literature of devotion, and whether it be the *Imitation of Christ*, or *The Christian Year*, or *The Book of Common Prayer* that claims his attention; whether it be the hymns of Watts or Doddridge or Wesley, or Faber or Newman, or Bonar or Heber in which his religious feelings find expression, let him remember that the meditations, the prayers, the hymns of Christian men of all ages are the common heritage of the Christian world.

DR. FRANK H. FOSTER continues his study of "Professor Park's Theological System" in the January *Bibliotheca Sacra* (Oberlin, Ohio). Our chief interest is with the section on the Trinity. It is explained that Park's treatment of this theme was determined by the fact that New England was not yet out of the Unitarian controversy. So it happens that most of the space given to the doctrine of the Trinity is in antithesis to the central part of the Unitarian denial, and is devoted to the divinity of Christ. Dr. Foster says that Park followed Moses Stuart, who had met many of the Unitarian denials by abandoning indefensible positions and concentrating his forces on the central elements of the truth. Instead of using the word "person" to describe each of the three elements of the Trinity, Stuart substituted the word "distinction," thus getting rid of a great mass of pseudo-biblical and philosophically untenable theological barnacles, such as the "eternal generation" of the Son, and the "procession" of the Spirit. And, in general, Stuart had confined himself to the simple results of Nice and Chalcedon—one God in three ontological and eternal distinctions, one Christ in two natures, human and divine. Park also refused to advance beyond this point, affirming our ignorance of many things. "On this doctrine," he says, "we must be careful not to know too much." "The profit of the doctrine of the Trinity is derived in some degree from the fact of its mysteriousness." He thus relieved his pupils of many difficulties which proved highly perplexing to others who had been taught to identify all the forms of this doctrine with its substance. When, in the process of time, the discussions of the new era of criticism and evolution had begun, they had comparatively little to "unload," which was a great advantage. Park begins the Trinity with the doctrine which his-

torically led to it, the nature of Christ; and this he begins at the point nearest to the investigator, the humanity. As to this, comparatively little is said. The ordinary and simple New Testament evidence of a genuine human body and soul are presented, and the conclusion of true humanity drawn without great elaboration. No special controversy existed in New England over this point. Simple facts, like Christ's apparent ignorance of the condition of the fig tree, and the time of the destruction of Jerusalem, are noted without further comment. They serve to help prove that Christ was truly man. When the argument passes to the divinity of Christ, however, the combatant has evidently come forth in his full armor. The sole question is, "What is the *fact?*" and that fact is the biblical fact. Consequently the whole argument consists in a biblico-theological discussion of the New Testament; but it is conducted in the most elaborate manner, with the marshaling of innumerable texts, and under eleven general heads. Christ is God because (1) he is *called* so; (2) said to be equal with God in *condition;* (3) does the *works,* and (4) has the *attributes* of the Supreme Being; (5) receives divine *honors;* (6) has applied to him in the New Testament the *same* passages elsewhere applied to the supreme God; (7) left the *impression* on his contemporaries that he was God; (8) the Scriptures make this *impression* on the masses of men; (9) Christ's divinity commends itself to the *moral nature* of man; (10) the *concurrence* of these proofs is itself a distinct proof; (11) *no other supposition* will reconcile the Scriptures and consciousness. Park summed up his argument in the following definition of the Trinity: "The Father is God; the Son is God; the Holy Spirit is God. Neither is God without the others. Each has a property incommunicable to the others. There is only one God." There is no attempt at a rationale of the doctrine, which is confessedly a mystery resting on revelation, and only partially revealed.——In the same issue of the *Bibliotheca* is Professor Bewer's address, "The Psychological Study of Jesus' Words." Considerably it is a study of the parables as a revelation of Jesus himself, and of the impression made upon his sensitive nature by the outer world. The pictures in the parables are not mere illustrations as the average preacher uses them to-day, but are part and parcel of Jesus's own experience. His world is the world of the working people, of whom he was one. The pictures of domestic life, with its intimate family relations, of industrial and commercial life, of civil and national life—all are painted with delicate grace. Everywhere —in the field and in the town, in the yard and in the market, in the chamber and in the banquet hall, among the farmers and the business men, the fishermen and the slaves, the publicans and Pharisees—he moved, and kept his eyes wide open; saw the actions of the judge and of the physician, of the housekeeper and of the servants, the relations of father and children, of friends and enemies, noticed the growth of the tree and the leavening of the dough, witnessed the joy and the sorrow of men, looked on man and on nature with open eyes and learned, and taught again what he had learned; for he discerned the underlying relations, and brought with clear vision, almost unconsciously, everything into relation to the great central truth which dominated all his thinking and his living—the

kingdom of God. We must, of course, not overlook how clearly Jesus has grasped the fundamental principles, and must be careful not to think that all pictures have taught him new truths. But that they made many a principle clearer to him, will appear as we proceed. He uses illustrations because he is always concrete. He uses no abstract forms of speech, because he is always personal. An abstract, philosophical thinker he has never been, and has never wanted to be; but he has recognized the fundamental principles of true religion with a clearness, and has enunciated them with a simplicity, which evidence unrivaled mastery; so simply and so plainly speaks only he who is a master of thought and expression. And nowhere do we look so deeply into the heart of this simple and yet so great Son of Man as in his parables. He talks here, in the plain language of the people, of those pictures which dwelt in his mind, and out of the inexhaustible fountain of his soul flow those words which reveal his innermost self.——Writing of Church History as an aid to Church Unity, A. D. Severance says: "Intolerance is the spirit that would persecute if it had the chance. We do not have to go back to mediæval history for illustrations. Let the self-satisfied denominationalist read the minutes of the last heresy trial in his own Church, and he will bow his head in shame at the vituperation and bad blood displayed by professed disciples of the Master." Reference is made to the way in which Dr. Augustus Jessopp lectures the Church of England, of which he is a priest, for the unwise treatment the Anglican hierarchy gave to Wesley and his people, in contrast with the wise treatment given the Franciscan Friars by the Church of Rome. "St. Francis was the John Wesley of the thirteenth century, whom the Roman Church was wise enough not to cast out. Rome has always known how to utilize her enthusiasts, fired by a new idea. The Church of England has never known how to deal with a man of genius. From Wyclif to Frederick Robertson, from Bishop Peacock to Dr. Rowland Williams, the clergyman who has been in danger of impressing his personality upon Anglicanism, where he has not been the subject of relentless persecution, has at least been regarded with timid suspicion, has been shunned by the prudent men of low degree, and by those of high degree has been forgotten. In the Church of England there has never been a time when the enthusiast has not been treated as a very *unsafe* man. Rome has found a place for the dreamiest mystic or the noisiest ranter—found a place and found a sphere of useful labor. We, with our insular prejudices, have been sticklers for the narrowest uniformity, and yet we have accepted, as a useful addition to the Creed of Christendom, one article which we have only not formulated because, perhaps, it came to use from a Roman bishop, the great sage Talleyrand—*Surtout pas trop de zèle!* . . . Rome absorbed the Franciscans; they became the Church's great army of volunteers, perfectly disciplined, admirably handled; their very jealousies and rivalries turned into good account. When John Wesley offered to the unwise Church of England precisely their successors, we would have no commerce with them; we did our best to turn them into a hostile and invading force." So says Dr. Jessopp, and the same lesson was administered to the Church of England by the great Macaulay in 1840. Speak-

ing on precisely this point, he says: "The enthusiast, whom the Anglican Church makes an enemy, and, whatever the learned and polite may think, a most dangerous enemy, the Catholic Church makes a champion. . . . Place Ignatius Loyola at Oxford. He is certain to become the head of a formidable secession. Place John Wesley at Rome. He is certain to be the first General of a new society devoted to the interests and honor of the Church. Place Joanna Southcote at Rome. She founds an order of bare footed Carmelites, every one of whom is ready to suffer martyrdom for the Church."

The Expository Times (New York: Charles Scribner's Sons) is a fresh, scholarly, and valuable publication. Noticing, in its November, 1903, issue a sermon on "The Spiritual Vision," by Johnston Ross, of Cambridge, it condenses the gist of the discourse as follows:

Why was it that Paul never had any doubt of the Gospel? Men doubt it to-day after all it has done; in his day it had scarcely done anything. It was because Paul had seen Jesus Christ the Lord ["Have I not seen Jesus Christ the Lord?" 1 Cor. ix, 1]. This was not only Paul's claim to be an apostle; it was also his reason for never doubting the Gospel. He had seen Jesus Christ the Lord. That is his own way of putting the fact on which he staked everything. He meant that he had seen Christ with the bodily eye. This he never doubted nor ceased to affirm. And yet it was not because he had seen him with the bodily eye merely that he believed the Gospel and risked everything on it. It was rather because the vision of the bodily eye had conveyed an impression down into his soul. This is not an inference from the apostle's words; he says so. In the New Testament there are different kinds of "seeing." Our Lord says, "A little while and ye shall not see me, and again a little while and ye shall see me." In reading this sentence we are apt to put the emphasis on the *not* and on the *shall*. But the emphasis is properly on the verb *see*. A little while, says the Master, and you shall no longer see me in the way in which you and all the world see me now (θεωρεῖτε), and again a little while and ye shall see me as the world never can see me (ὄψεσθε), with the vision of the soul. Paul had seen the risen Christ. That certified to him the resurrection from the dead. But what transformed him was the moral majesty of the risen Christ, judging the moral life of man and claiming lordship over his moral life. "I have *seen*," says Paul, "I have seen Jesus as *Lord*." He had had a physical vision, but it was not of that that he made most account. What he made account of was the fact that the vision had opened the gates of his moral life and given Christ entrance. And when Christ appears before us as both the ideal and the realization of moral goodness, we too can say, "I have seen Christ Jesus the Lord, and I cannot doubt the Gospel."

Commenting on a volume of sermons to young men by Rev. Walter A. Mursell, entitled *The Wagon and the Star*, the *Times* says: "It is easier to preach to young men than to any other class. They have lost the intuition by which children detect the least false ring in the offer of the truth, and they have not gained the experience by which old men judge the preacher's very principles. It is so easy to preach to young men that very few preachers can do it. They fail by not being natural. They pass by the

natural, which is the easy; and they strain after imaginative effects. Young men are not imaginative; they are actual, and they are nothing more." Rev. W. R. Webster, writing on Spanish Mysticism, the mysticism of Valdes and Molinos, says: "True mysticism may often be found among the rude and illiterate, who can hardly express their ideas in speech. 'Can you tell me what particular thing led to your conversion?' asked a clergyman of a humble member of his congregation. 'Why, sir, it was hearing Mr. Blank read one morning in church, *As the Lord liveth, before whom I stand.* 'Those are striking words,' replied the minister, 'but I do not quite see how they led to your conversion.' 'Don't you see, sir? *Before whom I stand.* I felt myself standing before my God.' This unlettered man was a far truer mystic than many who have tried to write themselves as such." John A. Hutton, M.A., in his new book, *Guidance from Robert Browning in Matters of Faith*, speaking of this poet's teaching on the conversion of the soul or the soul's discovery of God, says: "I regard Browning's teaching on conversion as his supreme message to our time. It is that teaching, as it seems to me, which ranks him with the prophets. Valuable as is the light which he sheds upon those problems of life and experience which are as old as man, or at least as old as the days of reflection; splendid as is the courage with which he girds his loins, and faces the darkness and the doubt; yet more solitary and distinguished is his teaching on the soul of man, his impassioned confidence that the soul may, in *one grand moment*, leap sheer out of any depth of shame, and leap to the breast of God." The *Times* quotes from Rev. Maclean Watt, of Alloa, these fine lines:

Carry me over the long, last mile,
  Man of Nazareth, Christ for me!
Weary I wait by Death's dark stile,
  In the wild and the waste where the wind blows free:
. . . . . And the shadows and sorrows, come out of my past,
    Look keen through my heart,
    And will not depart,
Now that my poor world has come to its last.

Lord, is it long that my spirit must wait,
  Man of Nazareth, Christ for me!
Deep is the stream, and the night is late,
  And grief blinds my soul that I cannot see . .
    Speak to me, out of the silences, Lord,
    That my spirit may know,
    As forward I go,
That thy pierced hands are lifting me over the ford!

BOOK NOTICES.

RELIGION, THEOLOGY, AND BIBLICAL LITERATURE.

Sunrise. By Rev. G. H. MORRISON, M.A. Crown 8vo, pp. 310. New York: A. C. Armstrong & Son. Price, cloth, $1.50.

These thirty addresses from a Scottish city pulpit are among the freshest and most fertile sermons of the day. Their spirit and temper are indicated in the title given to the volume, and also by the words placed as a motto on the title-leaf, "Unto you that fear My name shall the Sun of Righteousness arise with healing in His wings." In the light of that sunrise these bright, clear addresses are written. The titles like the treatment are unhackneyed: "The Wonder and Bloom of the World," "Mistaken Magnitudes," "The Pagan Duty of Disdain," "Near-Cuts not God's," "Seeming to Have," "After that, the Dark," "When the Child-Spirit Dies," "The Leisure of Faith," "The Glory and the Gate," "A Soul to Let," "The Irksomeness of Religion," "The Note of the Heroic," "The Touchstone of Fact." The sermon on "The Homesickness of the Soul" begins thus: "A delightful American writer, John Burroughs, has given in one of his books a most illuminative paper cn Carlyle. Burroughs visited Carlyle in London and has recorded his impressions in an essay entitled 'A Sunday in Cheyne Row.' One phrase in that essay seemed to me memorable; it was the phrase 'homesickness of the soul.' 'A kind of homesickness of the soul was on Carlyle,' says Burroughs, and it deepened with age. And that is my subject to-night—the soul is homesick. I want to make that thought shed a little light on some dark places: notably two, the unrest of sin and the craving for God. Jesus viewed the unrest of sin as homesickness. The prodigal son was away in a far country. It was not terror and fear of punishment that smote his heart deepest. It was home, home, home, for which his poor soul was crying. He saw the homestead bosomed among the hills, and the cattle coming home at eventide, and the family circle gathered around the fire, and his father crying to Heaven for the poor, foolish, erring boy. He came to himself and he was homesick. By this Jesus would teach us that wickedness is not the homeland of the soul, and that the sinner's unrest is just the craving of his heart for home. We were not meant to feel at home in sin. The soul's native air is obedience and love and purity and joy. . . . Few pages are more enthralling in Charlotte Yonge's history of *The Moors in Spain*, than those in which she tells the story of Abderraman. He was the first Moorish Khalif in Spain. He was an Oriental, bred by the river Euphrates. Superior in beauty as was his Spanish home, nevertheless Abderraman was miserable amid all his groves and gardens, palaces and fountain, of the fair city of Cordova. He longed for his native East, and felt himself an exile. And an Arabian ballad tells us that when he had a palm tree brought from the Euphrates' bank and planted in his Spanish garden, he never could look on it without tears. The sight of it

made the Khalif homesick. And my point is that the soul's unrest and
discontentment, amid all the pleasures of sin and sense, are its hungering
for life in another country, as Abderraman hungered for his native Orient.
It is not facts, it is mysteries, that keep me from materialism. I believe
in the cravings of the human heart, and they overturn a score of demonstrations. If I were a creature of nerves and fibers only I could be happy
in my Cordova, in the pleasure-gardens of fleshly indulgence and ease.
But we were made for higher and purer things; the native air of the
soul is righteousness and love and truth, and the favor and fellowship of
God, and we shall always be dissatisfied and homesick, if we are trying
to live in any other climate or region. . . . And this homesickness of the
soul for God is one of our surest proofs of God. It is an argument more
powerful than any philosophy to convince me that there is a God."
The sermon ends by quoting one of the most pathetic letters in all literature, a letter written by David Gray, the Scottish poet. He was born
eight miles from Glasgow. His father would have made a preacher of
him, but he chose to be a poet. David grew weary of home, and there
came a day when nothing would satisfy him, but he must go to London.
So to London he went, but his health failed there, and he fell into consumption, and after long and great suffering he wrote to his parents:
"I am coming home, homesick. I cannot stay away any longer. What's
the good of me being so far from home when I am weak and ill? O God!
I wish I were home never to leave it more! Tell everybody that I am
coming home—no better; worse, worse. What matters climate—frost or
snow or harsh weather—when one is at home? I wish I had never left
it. . . . I have no money, and I want to get home, home, home. What
shall I do, O God! Father, I shall come back to you because I did not
use you rightly. Will you forgive me? I have come through things that
would make your heart ache for me—things that I shall never tell to
anybody but you, and you must keep them as secret as the grave. Get
my own little room ready quick, quick; have it all clean and tidy and
cozy, against my home-coming. I wish to die there, and nobody shall
ever nurse me again but my own dear mother. O home, home, home!"
And then the preacher says: "I will arise and go to my Father. Thank
God, we need no money for that journey. Is there no one here who has
been far away and who is going to come home, home to God—this very
hour?" Speaking of the Pagan spirit of disdain, Mr. Morrison says:
"The Gospel insists on human brotherhood. Its prayer is to 'Our Father.'
Did the cultured Greek look down on the barbarian? Did the elect and
covenanted Jew despise the Gentile? Did the free man look with an
infinite disdain upon the slave? Clear as a trumpet, strong as the voice
of God, there rang this message on a selfish, proud, and dying world:
There is neither Jew nor Greek, barbarian, Scythian, bond nor free, but
all are one in Christ. Yes, and when that word of command was obeyed,
and the Gospel of Jesus was carried to the heathen, and when the peace
and joy and comfort of it were offered in all their fullness to the slave,
then, like a dark sullen cloud, the contemptuous spirit of paganism broke
away and scattered, and the bright star of brotherhood rose in a clear

sky. It is our kinship in Christ that is abolishing disdain. Brotherhood
forbids arrogance and contempt. God meant us to be like that tiny lass
in Edinburgh who was carrying a strapping infant in her arms, and
when a passing stranger said, 'Why, what a burden for you to carry,' she
answered, 'Please, sir, he's no burden, he's my brother.'" Think of the
splendid brotherliness in the heart of Chalmers of New Guinea, when,
writing of a cannibal chief of that dark island, he refers to him as "that
grand old gentleman." Jesus gave Himself for men because He could see
what was in them. Love, like genius, has eyes to see things which are
hid from ordinary vision.

> The poem hangs on the berry-bush
> Till comes the poet's eye;
> And the whole street is a masquerade
> When Shakespeare passes by.

Side-Lights on Immortality. By LEVI GILBERT, D.D. 12mo, pp. 233. Chicago and New
York: Fleming H. Revell Company. Price, cloth, $1.

The side-lights are from all sides, for Dr. Gilbert's discussion traverses
the entire question of immortality in a general way, as it appears from the
modern standpoint, in an age when, as he says, philosophy and science
have done much to reassure believers and to make clearer the fundamental rationality of their creed. The aim of the book is to strengthen
the convictions, support the hopes, console the hearts, and inspire to
worthy living those who, as followers of Christ, have already accepted
His great apostle's sublime conclusion that this corruptible must put on
incorruption and this mortal must put on immortality. Its argument
avoids theological abstractions and is concise and interesting enough
to attract busy people. From a wide range of reading the author draws
so extensively from prose and poetry relating to the subject that one
reviewer thinks the volume might have been entitled The Witness of
Literature to Immortality. The scope may be inferred from the chapter-
titles: "The Nature of the Proof," "The Question of the Ages," "The
Deeper Definitions," "The Significance of the Belief," "Jesus and the
Resurrection," "The Voice of Science," "The Fallacies of Materialism,"
"Man Made for Immortality," "Eternal Life in the Spirit," "Love's Demand
for a Future," "The Powers of the Age to Come," "Tennyson and Immortality," "Heaven and Hell," and "Some Conclusions." All other evidential
indications are called side-lights, because the one great central proving
light is the Resurrection of Christ, which, for all who believe in Him,
sets immortality among eternal certainties. In relation to that supremely
assuring event, all other evidential tokens are confirmatory. The evidence for immortality is of the same sort as that for God and the
soul; a sort "higher than the testimony of the physical senses, or
solutions by algebraic symbols, or precipitations in a laboratory. We
have no linear measurements for a great ethical principle; we cannot
give the troy-weight of a surging motion of the heart; no quantitative
analysis is applicable to a mother's prayers; the tears of a bereaved one
cannot be put into a scale-pan and so valued; patriotism cannot be esti-

uated in precise monetary equivalents; not by searching with a tele-
scope can we find God; scalpel and microscope have never discovered
the soul." Romanes' words are quoted: "The wise Christian will answer, 'I believe in the resurrection of the dead, partly on grounds of
reason, partly on those of intuition, but chiefly on both combined; so to
speak, it is my whole character which accepts the whole system of which
the doctrine of immortality forms an essential part.'" The new rendering
of the old text in Heb. xi, 1, is quoted: "Faith is confidence in the reali-
sation of one's hopes; it is a conviction regarding things which are not
yet visible." Victor Hugo is quoted: "A better world to come is to me
more real than the chimera which we devour and which we call life. It is
forever before my eyes. It is the supreme certainty of my reason as it is
the supreme consolation of my soul." And again: "Why is my soul the
more luminous when my bodily powers begin to fail? Winter is on my
head and eternal spring is in my heart. The nearer I approach the end, the
plainer I hear around me the immortal symphonies of the worlds which
invite me." Dr. Watkinson, referring to the migratory instinct of birds,
so inexplicable and unerring in its operations, hangs upon it this high
expression of his confidence: "Our instinct of the unknown world and of
the unknown life shall not betray us. Our wing has been fashioned for
a farther flight, and the fact that it has been thus fashioned means everything. The great question is not about the dust of the ground, but about
the Eternal Spirit behind all and working through all. With Him we
have to do. In Him we put our trust. He will keep faith with us.
'Faith in Him is the heroism of the intellect.' Faith is reason consulting with the lessons of time and experience, and then projecting
itself into unknown worlds. It shall not be confounded." Dr. Gilbert
quotes from Harnack: "Christ's grave was the birthplace of an inde-
structible belief that death is vanquished and there is life eternal. It
is useless to cite Plato; it is useless to point to the Persian religion and
the literature of later Judaism. All that would have perished; but the
certainty of a resurrection and of a life eternal which is bound up with
the grave in Joseph's garden has perished, and on the conviction that Jesus lives we still base those hopes of citizenship in an Eternal City which
make our earthly life worth living. 'He delivered them who, through
fear of death, were all their lifetime subject to bondage,' as the writer
of the Epistle to the Hebrews confesses. That is the point, and wherever
there is strong faith in the value of the soul; wherever death has lost its
terrors; wherever the sufferings of the present are measured against a
future of glory, this feeling of life is bound up with the conviction that
Jesus Christ has passed through death, that God has awakened Him and
raised Him to life and glory. It is not by any speculative ideas of philosophy, but by the vision of Jesus's life and death and resurrection, and by the
feeling of His imperishable union with God, that mankind has attained to
that certainty of eternal life for which it was meant—eternal life in time
and beyond time." And from another writer this: "If the Resurrection of
Jesus be not true, Christianity at once shrivels up into a disputable system
of ethics; but if it be true, then Christianity lays its hand upon us and

thrills us, as though with the very hand of God." No stronger chapter in the book than that on "Jesus and the Resurrection"! Dr. Gilbert was not in error in believing that there is room and usefulness for a book like this, presenting with comparative brevity and admirable clearness of style and arrangement the concurrent testimony of revelation and reason upon the most fascinating and momentous subject which can engage and exercise the human mind and heart. Readers will find the volume rich with choicest gleanings from the literature of the faith in immortality. It closes with one from George A. Gordon: "The belief in immortality belongs to human faith and is here to stay. Men are not allowed to rest in the notion that they are children of a day. They are pilgrims of eternity, with thoughts that wander through immensity and affections that raven with immortal hunger. They move upon lines that have no end, and when true to their humanity transcend time. They support their enthusiasms out of the Infinite, and their work, well done, belongs to the universe. Thus faith in immortality lives in the better thought, in the nobler purpose, and in the loftier work of the world; lives on intrenched in the structure of man's being, surviving fear and doubt and open denial, and holding its place in human consciousness against the philosophies that preach the perishableness of the soul as securely as the fortressed Rock of Gibraltar at the Pillars of Hercules." And these noble lines from Paul Hamilton Hayne's "In Harbor:"

> I know it is over, over;
> I know it is over at last.
> Down sail! The sheathed anchor uncover,
> For the stress of the voyage has passed;
> Life, like a tempest of ocean,
> Hath out-breathed its ultimate blast.
> There's but a faint sobbing seaward,
> While the calm of the tide deepens leeward;
> And behold! like the welcoming quiver
> Of heart-pulses throbbed through the river,
> Those lights in the harbor at last,
> The heavenly harbor at last!

We commend Dr. Gilbert's book to the wide reading which its merits invite.

Hebraisms in the Authorized Version of the Bible. By WILLIAM ROSENAU, Ph.D. 12mo, pp. 283. Baltimore: The Friedenwald Company. Price, cloth, $2.

As the preface informs us, this work was suggested to its author by Professor Paul Haupt in 1894, and we have no hesitation in saying at the outset that the book seems to us fully to meet the high standard which Professor Haupt would be certain to set. Never before has the Authorized Version been subjected to a searching analysis to determine exactly how deeply has Hebrew idiom influenced its splendid flow of words and sentences. The influence has indeed been often observed, though never scientifically classified, for the masters of English style have made frequent reference to it. Dr. Roseman is able to begin his work with a full

passage from the *Spectator* (No. 405), in which Addison has beautifully and lightly touched upon the power of the Hebrew idiom, and we may properly borrow it here: "There is a certain Coldness and Indifference in the phrases of our European Languages, when they are compared with the Oriental Forms of Speech; and it happens very luckily that the Hebrew Idioms run into the English Tongue with a particular Grace and Beauty. Our Language has received innumerable Elegancies and Improvements, from that Infusion of Hebraisms which are derived to it out of the Poetical Passages in Holy Writ. They give a Force and Energy to our Expressions, warm and animate our Language, and convey our Thoughts in more ardent and intense Phrases, than any that are to be met with in our own Tongue. . . . If anyone would judge of the Beauties of Poetry that are to be met in the Divine Writings, and examine how kindly the Hebrew Manners of Speech mix and incorporate with the English language, after having perused the Book of Psalms, let him read a literal translation of Horace or Pindar. He will find in these translations such an Absurdity and Confusion of Style with such a Comparative Poverty of Imagination as will make him very sensible of what I have been here advancing." The Hebraisms which Addison *felt*, Dr. Rosenau has elaborately and scientifically analyzed, and has so arranged his results as to make a book much of which may be read with pleasure, while the rest provides an admirable book of reference. The chapters which discuss "Proverbial Biblical Passages in Use," "Biblical Expressions in English Literature," and "Lexicographical Hebraisms" contain a wealth of instructive material in a readily accessible form. Much of it would make totally unnecessary long discussions in Commentaries. Here, for example, is the word "Son," the Hebrew usage of which is thus set forth in tabular form:

   a. male child.

      "And bare a son." Exod. ii, 2. (E.)

   b. boy.

      "My beloved among the sons." Cant. ii, 3.

   c. member of a guild.

      "Sons of the prophets." 2 Kings ii, 15.

   d. descendant.

      "Ordinance to thee and thy sons." Exod. xii, 24. (J.)

   e. train.

      "Arcturus with his sons." Job xxxviii, 32.

The attitude of Dr. Rosenau is distinctly critical, and we are not ready to follow him into all the sinuosities of the Wellhausen theory, nor into some of the bypaths made by more recent investigators. Thus on page 139 we find the words "son of man" followed by this explanation: "This phrase . . . means nothing more than 'man,' and is used for the latter." In support of this contention Bertholet and Kraetzschmar are cited, and no hint is given concerning the importance of the phrase in New Testament literature nor of the theological import of it in still later times. With this hint of caution in its use, we may heartily commend this useful and learned but thoroughly popular book.

PHILOSOPHY, SCIENCE, AND GENERAL LITERATURE.

The Gentle Reader. By SAMUEL MCCHORD CROTHERS. 12mo, pp. 321. Boston and New York: Houghton, Mifflin & Co. Price, cloth, $1.25.

Says the Preface: "When Don Quixote was descanting on the beauty of the peerless Dulcinea, the Duchess interrupted him by expressing a doubt as to that lady's existence. 'Much may be said on that point,' answered Don Quixote. 'God only knows whether there be any Dulcinea or not in the world. These are things the proof of which must not be pushed to extreme lengths.' But this admission does not cool the ardor of his loyalty to Dulcinea; for, after the momentary interruption, he proceeds as if nothing had happened: 'I behold her as she needs must be, a lady who contains within herself all the qualities to make her famous throughout the world: beautiful without blemish; dignified without haughtiness; gracious from courtesy, and courteous from good breeding; and lastly, of illustrious birth.' If, now, following Don Quixote's example, I admit that 'much may be said' in support of the notion that the Gentle Reader no longer exists, let that pass as evidence of my polite tolerance of skeptical contradiction. It remains none the less true that to my mind the Gentle Reader is a reality, the most agreeable of companions, and to make his acquaintance is one of the pleasures of life." In this airy and genial fashion begins a volume of essays on "The Mission of Humor," "The Enjoyment of Poetry," "The Honorable Points of Ignorance," "The Evolution of the Gentleman," "The Hinter-Land of Science," "History Should Be Readable," "Quixotism," and the like. One of the Gentle Reader's characteristics is that he takes a book, just as he takes a friend, for what it is, never minding what it is not. I suppose every one of us has some friend of whom we would confess that as a thinker he is inferior to Plato. But we like him no less for that. We might criticise him if we cared to do so—but we never care. We prefer to take him as he is. It is the flavor of his individuality that we enjoy. So, appreciation of literature is getting at an author so that we like what he is, overlooking all that he is not. . . . Our personal likings rule us as to men and as to books. We admire the acuteness of the critic who reveals the unsuspected excellence of our favorite writer, just as we are pleased when some friend of ours is received into a learned society. We don't know much about his learning, but we know that he is a good fellow, and we are glad he seems to be getting on. We also feel satisfaction in having our personal tastes vindicated and our enjoyment treated as a virtue, just as Mr. Pecksniff was gratified with the reflection that, while he was eating his dinner, he was at the same time obeying a law of the Universe. . . . I asked a little four-year-old critic, whose literary judgments I accept as final, what stories she liked best. She answered, 'I like Joseph, and Aladdin, and The Forty Thieves, and The Probable Son.' Why the parable of 'The Probable Son' delights her, while the preacher's half-hour sermon on that parable makes not the slightest impression on her mind, she does not know. But she knows a good story, just as she knows a good apple. How the flavor got there is a scientific question which she has not considered; but being there, trust the uncloyed palate to find it

day.' Philosophers and all kinds of writers are ordered, nowadays, to cut
it short. This is the age of the telephone and the short story. People
want a literary 'quick lunch.' 'Serve it hot and be mighty quick about it,'
is the demand made on authors and preachers by the impatient temper of
this driven and hurrying age." It is not possible to leave Mr. Crothers's be-
guiling book without listening a moment to what he makes the Gentle
Reader say about the clergy: "There has been a sad falling off in clerical
character. In the old books it is a pleasure to meet a parson. He is so
simple and hearty that you feel at home with him at once. You know just
where to find him, and he always takes himself and his profession for
granted. He may be a trifle narrow, but you make allowance for that, and
as for his charity it has no limits. You expect him to give away everything he can lay hands on. As for his creed it is always the same as that
of the Church he belongs to, which is a great relief and saves no end of
trouble. But the clergyman I meet with in novels nowadays is in a
chronic state of fidgetiness. Nothing is as it seems or as it ought to be.
He is as full of problems as an egg is full of meat. Everything resolves
itself into a conflict of duties, and whichever duty he does he wishes it
had been the other one. When the poor man is not fretting about evil-
doers he begins to fret about the well-doers, who do well in the old fashion
without any proper knowledge of the higher criticism or sanitary drain-
age. What with his creed and his congregation, both of which need mending, he lives a distracted life. Though the author in the first chapter
usually praises his athletic prowess, he seems to have no staying power
and his nerves give out under the least strain. He is one of those trying
characters of whom some one has said that 'we can hear their souls
scrape.' I prefer the old-time parsons. They were much more comfortable
and in more rugged health. I like the phrase, 'Bishops and other clergy.'
The bishops are great personages, whose lives are written like the lives of
the Lord Chancellors; and they are not always very readable. But my
heart goes out to the 'other clergy,' the good sensible men who were
neither great scholars nor reformers nor martyrs, and who therefore did
not get into the Church Histories, but who kept things going." Speaking
of Luther's "Table Talk," it is said that the great reformer had a way of
characterizing a person in a sentence, that was much more effective than
labored vituperation. "Thus, referring to the attitude of Erasmus, he
said, 'Erasmus stands looking at creation like a calf at a new door.' It
was very unjust to Erasmus. Yet it is a perfect characterization of a
kind of mind we are all acquainted with, which looks at the marvels of
creation with the wide-eyed gaze of bovine youthfulness, curious, not to
know how that door came there, but only to know whether it leads to
something to eat." These essays, like Sir William Davenant's poem, have
"shadowings, happy strokes, and sweet graces."

Shakspere and His Forerunners. By SIDNEY LANIER. Two volumes, royal 8vo, pp.
xxiv, 324; xv, 359. New York: Doubleday, Page & Co. Price, cloth, $10.

These are the most elegant and sumptuous volumes in which any of
the writings of Lanier have ever been presented. They are embellished

with one hundred illustrations, and are handsomely as well as durably bound. They contain two sets of Shakespeare lectures delivered by Lanier in Baltimore during the winter of 1879-80, one at Johns Hopkins University, the other to a class of ladies at Peabody Institute. The preface by Henry Wysham Lanier says: "Sidney Lanier came to this study of Shakspere and his forerunners with even more than his usual buoyancy and ardor. The superb exuberance, the daring imagination, the rollicking playful conceits, the sense of unbounded power, which filled the poetry of those years when England's mind was awakening from its long sleep, all appealed to him peculiarly. Arriving at a knowledge of the beginnings of our literature only at maturity, he fairly reveled in the largeness and the freshness of it, in the vigorous expression where the word was still alive and hot with the swing of the deed, and had not become remote, separated, literary. What he set himself to accomplish was to picture Shakspere, the Master Poet, as the culmination of that marvelous Elizabethan Age which came flaming upon a world just beginning to guess at its own true self. In order to show the situation adequately, he selected certain beacon-lights far back—*Beowulf*, *St. Juliana*, *The Address of the Dead Soul to its Body*, and so on—writings which seemed to reveal the mind of Englishmen and their poets during that semi-savage period which is roughly terminated by the Norman Conquest. With his rare facility for bringing together illuminatingly facts apparently diverse, Lanier traced the development in man's attitude toward God, toward Nature, and toward his fellow-man in those early English writings, in the neglected Scotch poets of the fourteenth century, in Chaucer, in Shakspere, and in modern literature. Coming to Shakspere, he made an intimate study of the man and his art, and, gathering together all the facts available, he attempted to reconstruct in these lectures, first, the people and times among which Shakspere lived and wrote; and, second, the order in which the plays were written—leading to his main purpose of depicting Shakspere's own inner personality and his mental and spiritual evolution as shown by the growth of his art." One of Lanier's side-notes left on a scrap of paper was: "What differentiates our day from the antique time is the great growth of individuality. Then a man existed for the state: now the state exists for every man. In religion Christ expresses this prodigious principle; the Sabbath was made for man, not man for the Sabbath. That every man shall be a complete self—that seems to be the aim of things." These lectures survey and analyze the literature of a thousand years. So lofty is the function and so great the power of Literature in Lanier's conception that he declares it has created the ideal world in which we moderns live and move and have our being. Though to us as we drive about our business there may not appear to be much connection between literature and actual life, yet the English-speaking people of this century are practically the creatures of English Literature. Hear Lanier: "Caedmon with his wild Bible-song, and Langley with his Vision of the Plowman, and Chaucer with his Tales, and Shakspere with his awful-beautiful pictures—these literary men molded the very souls of your ancestors. You cannot escape Literature. It has translated your Bible

and interpreted it for you. It has arranged your public constitutions, your social codes, your private morals. It has penetrated your houses; it fills your homes like diffused sunlight; you read your life by it; you see how to eat, how to drink, how to trade, and how to marry by it; you live by it, you die by it. If you attempt to fly from Literature it cries to you in that superb sarcasm with which Emerson's Divinity cries to the skeptic who would fly from God, 'I am the wings wherewith you fly.'" In these lectures we learn not only more of Beowulf and Shakespeare but more of Lanier, from whom no one can withhold admiring love. Speaking of the primitive Norseman's hard struggle against the wild beast for his meat, against the stern earth for his bread, and against the cold that cracks his skin and racks his bones, this Confederate soldier says to his audience: "You know nothing of cold. If your furnace is not giving you sixty-five degrees, Fahrenheit, when you wake in the morning, you shiver and ring to put on more coal. But, thank Heaven, I know what it is to be cold, cold from the crown of the head to the sole of the foot, cold from the cuticle in to the heart. I thank Heaven for it because, knowing this, I have a new revelation of the possibility of suffering, and I am able to find a paradise in a small wood-fire. Knowing this, I declare to you there is not a more pathetic sight in this world than a poor man who is thoroughly cold to the marrow of his bones day and night for weeks at a time. It is dull, heavy, unmitigated torture. I know gnawing hunger, too; but that becomes a sort of insanity which relieves itself. Aching merciless cold is icy torment. I used to see half-frozen men in the army whose silent endurance of cold brought more tears to my eyes than all the hunger and all the wounds." Writing of the sonnet as the form in which poets utter most freely their profoundest personality, Lanier quotes Wordsworth's well-known lines:

> Scorn not the sonnet, Critic. With this key
> Shakspere unlocked his heart; the melody
> Of this small lute gave ease to Petrarch's wound;
> A thousand times this pipe did Tasso sound;
> With it Camoëns soothed an exile's grief;
> The sonnet glittered a gay myrtle leaf
> Amid the cypress with which Dante crowned
> His visionary brow; a glow-worm lamp
> It cheered mild Spenser, called from Fairyland
> To struggle through dark ways; and when a damp
> Fell round the path of Milton, in his hand
> The thing became a trumpet, whence he blew
> Soul-animating strains,—alas, too few.

From old Habington's quaint picture of an ideal wife we take this: "Shee is colleague with her husband in the empire of prosperity; and a safe retyring place when adversity exiles him from the world. Shee can go to Court and return no passionate doater on bravery; and when shee hath seen the gay things muster up themselves there, shee considers them as cobwebs the spider, Vanety, hath spun. Shee so squares her passion to her husband's fortunes that in the countrey she lives without a froward

melancholy, and in the town without a fantastique pride." Lanier says
that studying the hearts of Sir Philip Sidney and William Shakespeare is
like looking into the open skies, "for they were a sort of spiritual heavens,
where stars shine and clouds float, shedding light and giving rain to the
whole race of man." Extracts are given from the seven sermons preached
in 1548 by Hugh Latimer before King Edward VI at Westminster. The
famous preacher, upholding the good of coming to church, says: "I had
rather ye shoulde come of a naughtye mynde, to heare the worde of God
for noveltye, or for curiositie to heare some pastime, than to be awaye.
As the tale is by the Gentel-woman of London: one of her neyghbours
mette her in the streate, and sayed, 'Mestres, whither go ye?' 'Mary,'
sayed she, 'I am goynge to S. Tomas of Acres to the sermon. I coulde
not slepe al thys laste night, and I am now goynge thither; I never fayled
of a good nap there.' And so I had rather ye shoulde be napping to the
sermon than not to go at al. For with what mind so ever ye come, perad-
venture ye may chaunce to be caught before ye go. The preacher may
chaunce to catche you on hys hooke." Preaching about Faith, the renowned Court preacher said: "We must beleve that oure Savioure Christ
hath taken us agayne to hys favoure, that he hath delivered us hys owne
bodye and bloude of hys owne mere liberalitie. This is the fayth we must
come to the Communion with. Fayth is a noble duches; she hath ever her
gentleman usher goyng before her, the confessing of sinnes; she hath a
trayne after her, the frute of good workes, the walking in the commandments of god. He that beleveth wyll not be idle, he wyll walke, he wyll
do his business. Have ever the gentleman usher with you. And if ye wyll
trye fayth, remember this rule, consider whether the trayne be waytinge
upon her. If ye have another fayth than thys, ye are lyke to go to ye
Scalding House, and ther ye shal have two dishes, wepynge and gnashyng
of teeth. Muche good do it you! Ye see your fare! But if ye wyll beleve
and acknowledge your synnes you shall attayne to everlastynge life."
Thus old Hugh Latimer was faithfully delivering to his King the message
of the King of kings, only six years before they burned him at Oxford.
Information of many kinds is given us about other things than literature.
It seems that our word "nicotine" is derived from the name of John
Nicot, a French ambassador in Portugal, who first sent tobacco to France.
When the use of the weed was spreading in England a great war of books
and pamphlets was carried on about it, in which even King James became
a disputant. His *Counterblaste to Tobacco* is a piece of invective as strong
as he could make it. He characterizes the use of tobacco thus: "A custome
loathsome to the eye, hatefull to the Nose, harmefull to the braine, dangerous to the Lungs, and in the blacke stinking fume thereof neerest resembling the horrible Stigian smoke of the pit that is bottomlesse." Lanier
relates an incident illustrating mankind's instinctive belief in a future
life. Being in St. Augustine, Florida, when a party of Indian warriors
arrived from the far West, where they had been disturbers of the peace,
Lanier noticed as the red captives left the cars at the railway station that
one of them seemed very ill and that another Indian was tenderly nursing
the sick one.. The sick man was taken to the hospital, and his faithful

nurse, who was in fact his cousin, was allowed to go with him. When he grew worse and was told that he must die, he managed to secrete a knife, and, watching his chance while his cousin was bending over him, he drove the blade into his tender nurse's breast. Fortunately his strength was so nearly gone that the wound was slight. When asked why he tried to murder his best friend, the dying Indian answered, "I am going to the Happy Hunting Grounds; I wished to take him with me; I love him so that I cannot bear to part with him." In this notice we have quoted mostly from the incidental and digressive parts of Lanier's large work. And we need to reiterate that the well-executed aim of *Shakspere and His Forerunners* is to exhibit Shakespeare as the crowing glory and culmina- tion of the most marvelous literary efflorescence the world has known. Lanier, when referring to a certain famous author, usually says "George Eliot;" but several times he calls her "Mrs. Lewes." By what right or propriety? To that name she never had any title. Her living with George H. Lewes was unlawful, and she was "Mary Ann Evans" all her life until, after Mr. Lewes's death, she became "Mrs. J. W. Cross."

From the Green Book of the Bards. By BLISS CARMAN. 12mo, pp. 137. Boston: L. C. Page & Co. Price, cloth, $1.

This is Number Two of the five volumes of verse making the series entitled "The Pipes of Pan." We have already noticed Number One, *From the Book of Myths.* Few living men are so enamored with the volume of Nature, the green book which the bards love to study, as Bliss Carman. He reads it every morning and ponders it by night, and will, he says, until Death shall bid him cease his reading and put out his light, as his father used to say to him in childhood, "Come, my son, put up your books; it's time to go to bed." Then, says our bard, poring over the green book,

> Then I will leave my volume
>   And willingly obey,—
> Get me a little slumber
>   Against another day.
> Content that he who taught me
>   Shall bid me sleep a while,
> I will expect the morning
>   To bring his gracious smile;
> New verses to decipher,
>   New chapters to explore,
> While loveliness and wisdom
>   Grow ever more and more.

He reads the folklore of the mountains, the drama of the sea, the epic of the thunder, the lyric of the rain, to find some light upon the Author's meaning and the import of man's eternal plight. From studying the Green Book, he says, came the Elizabethan vigor, and the Landorian poise, the sweet Chaucerian temper, the gusty moods of Shelley, and the autumn calms of Keats. The all-pervading theme of this second volume of "The Pipes of Pan" is the response of the world to the call of the Springtime, the universal stir, movement, upburst, outflow, migration, which answer

nurse, who was in fact his cousin, was allowed to go with him. When he grew worse and was told that he must die, he managed to secrete a knife, and, watching his chance while his cousin was bending over him, he drove the blade into his tender nurse's breast. Fortunately his strength was so nearly gone that the wound was slight. When asked why he tried to murder his best friend, the dying Indian answered, "I am going to the Happy Hunting Grounds; I wished to take him with me; I love him so that I cannot bear to part with him." In this notice we have quoted mostly from the incidental and digressive parts of Lanier's large work. And we need to reiterate that the well-executed aim of *Shakspere and His Forerunners* is to exhibit Shakespeare as the crowing glory and culmina-tion of the most marvelous literary efflorescence the world has known. Lanier, when referring to a certain famous author, usually says "George Eliot;" but several times he calls her "Mrs. Lewes." By what right or propriety? To that name she never had any title. Her living with George H. Lewes was unlawful, and she was "Mary Ann Evans" all her life until, after Mr. Lewes's death, she became "Mrs. J. W. Cross."

From the Green Book of the Bards. By BLISS CARMAN. 12mo, pp. 137. Boston: L. C. Page & Co. Price, cloth, $1.

This is Number Two of the five volumes of verse making the series entitled "The Pipes of Pan." We have already noticed Number One, *From the Book of Myths.* Few living men are so enamored with the volume of Nature, the green book which the bards love to study, as Bliss Carman. He reads it every morning and ponders it by night, and will, he says, until Death shall bid him cease his reading and put out his light, as his father used to say to him in childhood, "Come, my son, put up your books; it's time to go to bed." Then, says our bard, poring over the green book,

> Then I will leave my volume
> And willingly obey,—
> Get me a little slumber
> Against another day.
> Content that he who taught me
> Shall bid me sleep a while,
> I will expect the morning
> To bring his gracious smile;
> New verses to decipher,
> New chapters to explore,
> While loveliness and wisdom
> Grow ever more and more.

He reads the folklore of the mountains, the drama of the sea, the epic of the thunder, the lyric of the rain, to find some light upon the Author's meaning and the import of man's eternal plight. From studying the Green Book, he says, came the Elizabethan vigor, and the Landorian poise, the sweet Chaucerian temper, the gusty moods of Shelley, and the autumn calms of Keats. The all-pervading theme of this second volume of "The Pipes of Pan" is the response of the world to the call of the Springtime; the universal stir, movement, upburst, outflow, migration, which answer

Nature's vernal summons to the tribes of the sea, and the tribes of the air, and the tribes of the fields, and the tribes of the forest, and the tribes underground. This theme is played upon with exquisite variations through poem after poem, in verses flushed with ecstasy and musical with liquid intonations that mimic the voices of birds. There is an opening application to April to return, "bringer of sunshine to this old, gray earth, mother of solace with the soft spring rain, restorer of sure health to wounded ones." The disconsolate, the dispirited, and the forlorn cry like children for the coming of the Spring. When April weather and Spring magic reenliven and redress the world, the bard quivers, delirious, under the reviving breath, exults in the rosy maples budding and the willows putting forth, in the blue hepaticas along the waking uplands, in the bubbling marshy whisper seeping up through bog and glade, in the first robin at his vespers calling clear across the twilight, and the piping of the frogs at night blowing up their tiny oboes, in crimson quince-buds and yellow tulips, in the tang of the spicy arbutus and scent of the apple-blow, in the ardor which kindles and blights not, renewing the wondrous world and the hearts of men with joy. His visioned spirit sees the Spring, a mad young beauty, an enchantress, wearing a tattered gown of buds and blossoms and leaves, go glinting through the alder swamp, and loitering by the willow streams, and dancing down the wood-roads dim; "the odorous wild white cherry is her flower, her bird the flame-bright oriole." Amid the wonderful waking of the world's dead-and-buried life at the resurrection-call of the miracle-working Spring, the bard feels the thrill of the season and shouts exultantly:

> The revel of leaves is beginning,
> The riot of sap is astir;
> Dogwood and peach and magnolia
> Have errands they will not defer.
> In the long sweet breath of the rainwind,
> In the warm soft hours of sun,
> They rise at the *Sursum Corda*,
> A thousand uplifted as one.

Reading Bliss Carman's verse-versions of what he reads in Nature's great Green Vernal Book, one recalls a pathetic passage in Herbert Spencer's last book, which shows how tenderly he prized each successive privilege of witnessing the miraculous annual waking of the earth: "For years past, when watching the unfolding buds in the Spring, there has arisen the thought, Shall I ever again see the buds unfold? Shall I ever again be wakened at dawn by the song of the thrush?" Not more than twice thereafter did Spencer behold this Easter of the earth, this resurrection of the dead, this waking of the sleepers. Near the close of this book of verses Mr. Carman tells us what sort of a heretic he is. One day he sat in church and "suffered a long discourse upon sin." Apparently it did not please him. He prefers to listen to what he hears in his own heart, rather than to "the lore the preacher bids us get by rote," or all the loud prosy pulpit "platitudes rethundering from groin and plinth" in stone cathedrals. He 44)e that one whisper of the Holy Ghost to him outweighs a thousand

tomes which repeat what others heard. He will heed God's private wor.1
to him; not Plato's, Swedenborg's, nor Rome's. The Voice which came
to the beloved John, upon his lonely isle, that Voice he will obey, or none.
He waits for the Word that comes from above to the spirit of man and
shakes his soul like a wind-blown flame, till it burns as a light in his eyes.
One wintry day Bliss Carman found a winged insect on the December
window pane, numb and stiff with cold. He stooped down close and
breathed softly on the small creature till his warm breath thawed the
frost and revived the little life, till it began to trim its quick antennæ as
of old, and presently spread its wings and sailed away through the mild
house-air. Then the poet says to this tiny sailor: "Ah, shipmate, there'll
be two of us some night, when the long frost shuts down." And he thinks
that, in that day when he lies numb and motionless, the great Befriender
may bend over him in some unexpected guise, strong, kind, and wise,
and breathe on him with warm, quickening, liberating breath of life, until
he too takes wing. Our bard seems to think that the way to learn the
meaning of life and the secret of the world is to cherish the pliant faith,
the eager mind, and the bright dreams which make the heart of a man to
be as the heart of a little child. The next of "The Pipes of Pan" to be
noticed will be *From the Songs of the Sea Children.*

HISTORY, BIOGRAPHY, AND TOPOGRAPHY.

The American Revolution. Part II. By the Right Hon. Sir GEORGE OTTO TREVELYAN.
	Bart. In two volumes. 8vo. Vol. I, pp. 353; Vol. II, pp. 344. New York: Longmans,
	Green & Co. Price, cloth, $5.

Without doubt this is the most unprejudiced and impartial work on
the American War for Independence ever written by an Englishman. The
two volumes of Part I appeared some years ago. It is from the hand of
the eminent biographer of Lord Macaulay and of Charles James Fox,
who in this vivacious and attractive history returns from politics to
literature, in which sphere he is most at home. That Sir George Trevelyan has the true conception of the art of history-writing is practically
demonstrated by the impressiveness and charm of the work now before
us, and has also recently been argued convincingly in his reply in the
Independent Review to Professor Bury, of Cambridge University, in which
Trevelyan contends that the historian's proper work is not the mere gathering of materials, sifting of evidence, and establishing of facts—all of
which are only the beginning of his task; but that the higher and finer
and larger duty of the historian is to make history teach political wisdom, preserve our heritage in the best ideals and noblest lives of the
past, and cause us to feel the poetry and perceive the Providence in all
human progress. This is the contention of the finer scholarship against
the lifeless, mechanical, analytical, fact-piling methods of the pedants.
Sir George Trevelyan's history represents the American Revolution as in
fact the King's war, and a result of the system of autocratic personal government which George III strove for twenty years to introduce into
England, and which provoked Burke to speak satirically of his majesty

as "the Great Disposer of all things in this lower orb;" while Sir William Anson wrote that British history had hardly known a sovereign less capable of governing an empire. The course pursued toward the American colonies was not approved by the people of England, and the subjugation of the colonists would have been well-nigh as fatal to English liberty as to American aspirations. The mature and judicious view which Trevelyan supports is that our Revolution was an uprising of one part of the British people against governmental oppression, the revolutionists being predominantly of the British race; and that in its inception and warrant the American Revolution was practically identical with the revolutions which deposed Charles I and James II, though in its result it differed from them in depriving the king of a part of his dominions instead of altogether expelling him from his throne. The colonies were lost by the King of England, just as the Methodists were lost by the Church of England, through governmental stupidity and arrogance. In each case, however, the vast and beneficent results of the mistake show how the Almighty can cause the blind wrath and headstrong folly of men to praise him. What we have already said is enough to raise the presumption that we have in Trevelyan's great work a novel and prizable treasure, namely, an Englishman's account of our Revolution which may be satisfactory to Americans. Certain it is that all readers, whether agreeing or disagreeing with his views, will be compelled to acknowledge that these vivacious volumes are the work of a gifted master of his art, and must be classed among the most judicious, interesting, and readable histories written in modern times. For the sake of completeness in any well-selected library they are worthy to stand side by side with the best American history of the great struggle for Independence. No comprehensive review of the work is possible here; only a few bits can be given. Trevelyan says that the Colonial Congress was a practical assembly and selected men for the posts they were best qualified to hold. "It appointed Washington Commander in Chief because he could fight; it sent Franklin to Paris because he had cultivated the art of turning great people round his finger; and it intrusted the Declaration of Independence to Jefferson because, both in style and in substance, his writings betokened the lawyer, the statesman, and the student." Jefferson desired John Adams to draft the Declaration, but Adams refused, replying to Jefferson, "No! You should do it for three reasons: Reason first, You are a Virginian, and a Virginian ought to appear at the head of this business. Reason second, I am obnoxious and unpopular, and you are very much otherwise. Reason third, You can write ten times better than I can." When the American General Charles Lee had been captured by British cavalry, the importance of the event was so greatly overestimated in England that many supposed the war to be about over. The Parish Clerk of Tring in Buckinghamshire posted the following bulletin: "This is to give notice that Thursday night will be held as a day of rejoicin in commemoration of the takin of General Lee, when there will be a sermint preached, and other public demonstrations of joy; after which there will be a nox roasted whole, and every mark of festivity and bell-ringing imaginable, with a ball and cock-fighting at

22

night in the Assembly-room of the Black Lyons." How Benjamin Franklin and John Adams got on as traveling companions appears in the account of their journey from Philadelphia to Staten Island as commissioners to confer with Lord Howe concerning possible terms of peace.
Adams says: "At New Brunswick the tavern was so crowded that Dr
Franklin and I had to occupy the same bed in a chamber not much larger
than the bed, without a chimney, and with one small window. The window was open and I shut it close. 'Oh,' says Dr. Franklin, 'don't shut
the window. We shall be suffocated.' I answered that I was afraid of the
cold night air. Dr. Franklin said, 'Open the window and come to bed, and
I will convince you. I believe you are not acquainted with the theory of
colds.' Opening the window and leaping into bed, I said I had heard of
his theory, but it was inconsistent with my experience; yet I was so curious to hear his reasons that I would run the risk of a cold for once."
Franklin then began to harangue on the theory that catarrhs were usually
produced by overeating and stuffy rooms, and not by cold air or draughts;
but both men were so travel-tired that Franklin's voice soon put himself
and his bedfellow fast asleep. Trevelyan says John Adams never forgot
that night at New Brunswick, and when Franklin died years after, Adams, while regretting the event, could not refrain from calling attention
to the fact that his New Brunswick roommate had fallen a sacrifice to his
own dangerous theory, "having caught the violent cold, which finally
choked him, by sitting at an open window with the chill air blowing on
him." The last chapter of Volume II, Part II, deals with the religious aspects of the Revolution, and is carefully written, but gives undue prominence to the Anglican body and seems ignorant of the greater strength of
the Congregational and Presbyterian Churches, while the Baptists, the
Lutherans, and the Dutch Reformed are ignored. Naturally enough the
Anglicans did not flourish here during, nor for some time after, the Revolution. Its clergy and members were mostly Tories, and many of its ministers returned to England, leaving the Episcopal meetinghouses silent
and deserted. In Virginia only twenty-eight out of a hundred Episcopalian ministers remained in their parishes and saw the war through.
The Methodists on the contrary, as Trevelyan amply shows, were stanch
and enthusiastic supporters of American Independence, were extremely
popular among the colonists, and, "from two thousand, increased during
the years of the Revolutionary struggle to fifteen thousand, while their
preachers were counted by hundreds;" and in the years immediately succeeding the achievement of Independence, Trevelyan says, "The Church
of Coke and Asbury increased in numbers, wealth, and repute with extraordinary rapidity." From which it appears that American Methodism
formed the habit of rapid growth at the very beginning of its existence.
This English historian tells us that some of the Anglican clergy who
abandoned their parishes in this country, instead of going home to England, took refuge in the neighborhood of the British army at New York,
where, says Trevelyan, "Haunting regimental messrooms; collecting and
dispensing scraps of Tory gossip; writing those satires and lampoons
which were the staple political literature of the period; and celebrating

the most recent British military success over a haunch of venison and a dozen of Madeira—they led a desultory and demoralizing life, not becoming to their cloth. Each man of them employed, in furtherance of the Royal cause, such gifts and accomplishments as he individually possessed —from the Virginia parson of the old school who, with a bowl of grog in his hand, drank victory to the British armies, up to Jonathan Odell, the clergyman-poet who had been expelled by the New Jersey Whigs from his rectory at Burlington. That fiery partisan composed with immense elaboration and inordinate length an imaginary poem-picture of the Regions of Torment and peopled his Inferno with prominent members of the American Congress and the Continental army." We read here that Benjamin Franklin, though not much of a churchgoer himself, was always ready to give advice on religious matters. He induced the putting up of lightning-rods on steeples, and the heating of audience rooms. He secured the erection of a nonsectarian meetinghouse in Philadelphia. Concerning the squabbles between Episcopalians and anti-Episcopalians, he wrote to his sister: "The profane and the infidel believe all that each side says against the other, and enjoy the fray." Franklin had "a zeal for curtailing religious ceremonies, and like many reformers he began young; also, he began on his father. When his father was packing a barrel of beef in the cellar one day, the boy Ben suggested that time would be saved at table in the future if his father should now ask, once for all, a wholesale blessing over the whole barrel. In later life Franklin's propensity for abbreviating and for superintending other people's religion showed itself in his assisting in preparing an abridged edition of the Anglican Liturgy." Josiah Quincy was accustomed to New England sermons—long, solid, theological, closely reasoned, and divided into many heads. When he visited South Carolina in 1774 he wrote home that he "listened to a young coxcomb preach flippantly for seventeen and a half minutes" in a Charleston Episcopal pulpit. The religious spirit of many of the colonists who fought in the American army is reflected in the quaint diary kept by Amos Farnsworth, of Massachusetts, extracts from which are given in Trevelyan's history: "May 27, 1775. About ten At night marched to Winnisimit ferry whare thare was A Schooner and Sloop A firing with grate fury on us. But thanks be unto God, that gave us the Victory, for throu his Providence the Schooner ran Aground, and we sot fire to hur and consumed hur thare, and the Sloop receved much dammage. Thanks be to God that so little hurt was Done us when the Balls Sang like Bees Round our heds! ——June 3, 1775. Paraded with the battalion and saw two men whipped for Stealing, and Another drommed out of Camp. O what a pernitious thing It Is for A man to steal and cheat his feller nabors, and how Provocking It Is to God!——August 30, 1775. The Enemy has Bin a Cannonading of us. But do little hurt. I found a young gentleman that I Could Freely convers with on Spcritual Things. I feel God has a Remnant in this Depraved and Degenerated and gloomy time.——Oct. 19, 1775. A Great talk of more troops being Sent to Boston, But our Men aint Scared at trifels. Would that our People had as good courage in the Speritual warfare as they have in the Temporal one.——Dec. 23, 1775. And now O Lord we are

In troble. Boston is a seat whare our Unnatural Enemyes are in Posses. sion. The people of Boston that are our friends have bin forced to leave the town, or be shut up thare among our foes. We have Sinned as a Continent; we have Sinned as a Province; we have Sinned as connected with a town, and as a Famerly, and Privates. But O God do not cast off this thy Land that thou hast Garded so long!——Lord's Day, Feb. 25, 1776. Went to Meeting and heard Rev. Mr. Emerson of Concord. I pray God grant that by the Preaching of this worthy Man I may be stirred up to my duty and to a holy walk with God." On this last entry Trevelyan comments, saying that the gift of imparting healthy and cheerful views on ethical questions seems to have been ancestral in Ralph Waldo Emerson's family. Further reference to this extremely readable and fairminded history may be made hereafter. It makes John Wesley an interested, active, and influential factor in England in connection with the British government's management of the war with the American colonics.

Soldiers True. By JOHN RICHARDS BOYLE, D.D. Large 8vo, pp. 368. New York: Eaton & Mains. Cincinnati: Jennings & Pye. Price, cloth, $2.50.

This is the story of the One Hundred and Eleventh Regiment, Pennsylvania Veteran Volunteers, and of its campaigns in the war for the Union, 1861-65. It is published by authority of the Regimental Association, as a correct record of the experiences and services of one regiment. This it purports to be, but it is really far more than this, for in fact the whole great conflict between North and South is reflected in it, its historic descriptions and judgments covering nearly all the prominent participants on both sides of the contest. It might almost be entitled The Civil War as Seen from One Regiment's Point of View. It is written by the honored pastor of Spring Garden Street Church, Philadelphia, who was second lieutenant of Company H before he was eighteen years old, and afterward captain and assistant quartermaster of the One Hundred and Eleventh Pennsylvania. Told with self-restraint and manifest carefulness, with every appearance of painstaking accuracy and truthfulness, and also with graphic skill, military terseness, and extraordinary picturing power, we do not hesitate to class it among the most interesting books of the War. It is so realistic in its account of actual experiences that whoever reads it will at times come near feeling himself to be a soldier of the One Hundred and Eleventh Pennsylvania, sharing its hardships and heroisms, its successes and defeats, its sorrows and its joys. It is a vivid and absorbing book. Antietam, Chancellorsville, Gettysburg, the Chattanooga and Atlanta campaigns, Sherman's famous march to the sea, and the march through the Carolinas, are among the battles and campaigns here depicted in which the One Hundred and Eleventh Pennsylvania bore an heroic part. A soldier's analysis and portrayal of the qualities of various generals lends especial interest and value. For example, General Hooker receives a setting forth which shows the elements of his strength, but also his marring faults and fatal weaknesses. One of the letters which indicate how great a Commander in Chief our country had in Abraham Lincoln is the one sent to Hooker ordering him to supersede Burnside in command

of the Army of the Potomac. This is part of what Lincoln wrote: "I think that during General Burnside's command of the army you have taken counsel of your ambition and thwarted him as much as you could, in which you did a great wrong to the country and to a most meritorious and honorable brother officer. I have heard in such a way as to believe it of your recently saying that both the army and the government need a dictator. Of course it was not for this, but in spite of it, that I have given you the command. Only those generals who gain success can set up as dictators. What I ask of you now is military success, and I will risk the dictatorship. I fear that the spirit which you have aided to infuse into the army, of criticising their commander and withholding confidence from him, will now turn upon you. Neither you nor Napoleon, were he alive again, could get any good out of an army while such a spirit prevails in it. And now, beware of rashness! Beware of rashness! But with energy and sleepless vigilance go forward and give us victories." And Hooker proceeded to lead his army to disaster and overwhelming defeat at Chancellorsville. The night before that awful battle, Hooker, seated at supper with General Slocum and others, exclaimed with a violent gesture, "The Army of Northern Virginia is the legitimate property of the Army of the Potomac. We will take possession of it to-morrow, and Almighty God himself cannot prevent it." Such was the boastful prelude to a chapter of personal weakness, military blundering, and inexplicable perversity, rarely equaled by the head of an army. The Army of the Potomac found itself in battle without a head. For reasons never fully explained, Hooker was not at Chancellorsville. Having wasted nearly two days of valuable time in hesitation, and having persisted against his chief engineer and ablest corps commanders in putting his army on the most unfavorable ground, he failed to locate his adversary, permitted himself to be fatally deceived regarding the enemy's movements, and then personally collapsed into a condition of incompetence. After the defeat, at a council of war, with Generals Reynolds, Couch, Sickles, Meade, and Howard present, he left the question of continuing the fight to those officers, and retired from the council. The next day Reynolds, Couch, and Meade decided to resume hostilities, and when they sent a staff officer to hunt for Hooker and get from him the necessary orders the commanding general was found on the other side of the Rappahannock River fast asleep! Being wakened, and requested to order the proposed advance, he refused and commanded that the army should retreat. General Francis A. Walker "believed that Hooker's mysterious behavior at Chancellorsville was due partly to that lack of firm moral stamina which often accompanies a spirit of arrogance and boastfulness, but chiefly to a nervous collapse occasioned by the excitement and fatigue of the four preceding days." The judgment of the author of *Soldiers True* is that Hooker's responsibility was too heavy for him; he was unequal to a great independent command. The greatest piece of description in Dr. Boyle's book is of the greatest battle of modern times, if not of all time, the Gettysburg fight. If one wishes a complete account of that gigantic conflict, let him read the one here given from the Union side along with that given by General J. B. Gordon from the Con-

federate side. Dr. Boyle says: "It was in reality a series of five pitched infantry battles and two cavalry encounters. It was fought under a scorching sun, through three oppressive summer days, by an army greatly fatigued by a long and rapid forced march. The enormous loss of life was frightful to contemplate, and the valor and endurance of the troops engaged were almost incredible. Lee's most daring generalship was displayed throughout the struggle. But he had met a new field marshal who, by inerrant foresight, superior skill, and sleepless vigilance, was able to overwhelm him. General Meade within a single week had proved himself a great soldier. He had saved the nation." The appalling aggregate of killed and wounded for both sides at Gettysburg was fifty-one thousand one hundred and twelve. Over fourteen thousand wounded were treated on the field, by six hundred and fifty surgeons working day and night from July 1 to July 6. The First Minnesota Regiment lost eighty-two per cent of its men; and the Twenty-sixth North Carolina Confederate Regiment lost eighty-four per cent. John F. Chase, a private of the Fifth Maine Battery, received forty-eight wounds, and survived them all. The occasional interchange of friendly civilities instead of hostilities between soldiers of the opposing armies appears in *Soldiers True* as in Gordon's *Reminiscences of the Civil War*. When the officers of the guard were out of hearing, a conversation like this would pass between pickets: "Hello, Yank! Are you all over there?" "You bet we're here, Johnnie. Do you want to surrender and come back into the Union?" "I'll surrender you if I get hold of you. But, say, Yank, have you uns got any coffee?" "Dead loads of it, Johnnie Reb. We make it in French pots and serve it with sugar and cream." "Will you trade some of it for tobacco?" "Well, I don't care. But if you try to play Indian on me I'll put you where we put the rest of you at Gettysburg." And then these veteran enemies would stop trying to kill each other long enough to steal out of their rifle-pits and wade into mid-stream to complete their deal like two schoolboys. And not a shot would be heard from either side till both were safely back again. After which it was as dangerous as ever to expose head or hand to the sight of the sharpshooters on the other side. We lay down this book with reluctance.

The Life of Edwin Wallace Parker, D.D., Missionary Bishop of Southern Asia. By J. H. MESSMORE. With an Introduction by Bishop JAMES M. THOBURN. Crown 8vo, pp. 333. New York: Eaton & Mains. Cincinnati: Jennings & Pye. Price, cloth, $1 net.

The lifework of Bishop Parker, who fell at his post in India in the midst of heroic labors undertaken for the Master, furnished his biographer with abundant materials for his task. From 1859 to 1868 and from 1871 to 1901, nearly forty years in all, during the last one of which he occupied the responsible position of Missionary Bishop for Southern Asia, Bishop Parker's tireless energy was devoted to the redemption of India from the thraldom of ignorance, superstition, and darkness in which that portion of the Saviour's inheritance has been fast bound during all the centuries. In the Introduction to the volume before us Bishop Thoburn characterizes his colleague as a strong man; a man possessed of the gift of leadership.

a practical man; a man of broad views and progressive sympathies; a man for the times in which he lived, and, above all, a man "possessed of an almost passionate instinct which led him to give his missionary calling the first place in both his heart and his thoughts." The preparation of the biography was undertaken by Rev. J. H. Messmore in response to a request made at a representative meeting of missionaries of the Methodist Episcopal Church in India. Two objects were had in view in the preparation of the volume: first, to present a connected account of the life and work of Bishop Parker, and, second, to give as much information concerning the missions of the Methodist Episcopal Church in India as could properly be associated with his name. Thus while we have a life sketch of the subject from his birth at St. Johnsbury, Vt., on January 21, 1833, to his decease at Naini Tal, India, on June 3, 1901, the narrative is interwoven with information of great interest and value to students of our mission work. Credit is given in the preface to Rev. J. W. Robinson, of Lucknow, who was Dr. Parker's colleague during the latter's six years of service in Oudh, for a sketch of the Oudh District covering seventeen pages. The volume is illustrated with numerous cuts of a high order.

MISCELLANEOUS.

The Fullness of the Blessing of the Gospel of Christ. By Bishop WILLARD F. MALLALIEU, D.D., LL.D. 16mo, pp. 167. Cincinnati: Jennings & Pye. New York: Eaton & Mains. Price, cloth, 50 cents.

In this earnest little volume Bishop Mallalieu urges afresh, with characteristic fervor and force, the great vital realities for which Methodism has ever stood. In his preface he cries out: "Back to the Wesleys and the Bible! The Bible in its simplicity and power, the Bible as unfolded and illustrated in the prose and poetry of the Wesleys, is really the foundation of the greatest religious movement of the last two most wonderful centuries. Methodism builds on the Word of God. It has no new doctrines, no new and strange theories, no recently invented experiences. Its doctrines, theories, and experiences are those of the Pentecostal Church, and of the earliest centuries of Christianity. Its doctrines are preachable everywhere and always; its theories are reasonable; its experiences are what the immortal souls of men have ever desired and sought." With that statement all Methodism most heartily agrees. Methodism needs no new doctrines. It has no reason for surrendering a single one of its old doctrines. They are all reasonable, scriptural, satisfying. They have spread through other communions which once opposed them. In the region of apologetics those doctrines can be more fully and variously defended now than ever before. The progress of modern thought is in their favor, confirming their validity. To this confirmation philosophy and psychology have made no small contribution. We have more than once pointed out that Methodism's philosophy was at its beginning abreast of the advance line of thought in German universities of that time. Bishop Mallalieu truly says that the hymns and Scripture quotations in his

book, if prayerfully committed to memory, will constitute an intellectual and spiritual treasure of unspeakable value.

The Apocryphal and Legendary Life of Christ. By JAMES DE QUINCEY DONEHOO, M.A. 8vo, pp. lix, 531. New York: The Macmillan Company. Price, cloth, $2.50 net.

Perhaps nothing so enhances the sense of their beauty and verisimilitude as to project the canonical gospels against the background of apocryphal and legendary literature, which, like tares that an enemy thickly sowed, sprang up in the early Christian age to choke the word, and, if possible, bring it to naught. The problem of how the canon was formed soon solves itself when all of its elements are once presented to the mind. Mr. Donehoo admits that this literature presents but few golden grains amid an intolerable deal of chaff, yet he claims that, "weighted down as it is with the dreary verbosity of Gnostic madness and the preposterous if lighter inventions of mediæval legend-mongers, it certainly bears across nearly nineteen centuries a few words of the divine Author of Christianity and a few particulars as to his history upon which the four gospels are silent." Certainly no zeal is misplaced which leads to the discovery of such golden grains, be they never so few, and the irreverent spirits of our time who compass land and ocean in the vain attempt to make void the inspired writings and empty the gospels of Christ of their testimony to his divinity and to his authorship of historical Christianity might well take a lesson from this scholar in the pastorate. As a piece of book-making this work leaves nothing to be desired. It covers the entire subject for the first time in English, and this fact together with its prolegomena, notes, scriptural references, and indices gives it peculiar value and finality.

China's Book of Martyrs. By LUELLA MINER. Crown 8vo, pp. 512. Cincinnati: Jennings & Pye. New York: Eaton & Mains. Price, $1.50 net.

This record of the sufferings of native Christians in China during the Boxer uprising, for their steadfastness in the faith of Christ, reads like a paraphrase of the eleventh chapter of Hebrews. Of whom the world was not worthy is a tribute to thousands of so-called "rice Christians" who astonished their persecutors by suffering martyrdom gladly for Christ's sake, looking unto the recompense of the reward in the world to come. If it be true that the blood of the martyrs is the seed of the Church the fruitage of the dreadful experiences of God's elect in China will be seen in the greater triumphs of the cross in that benighted land for the centuries to come. The experiences recited by the author are taken from the records of ten different denominations operating in mission fields covering hundreds of miles in length and breadth of territory, yet the testimonies given by the martyrs showed the same devotion to the Master, the same abiding trust in the promises of God's word, the same unflinching fortitude in the hour of dissolution. Those who read the volume cannot but be incited to a profounder appreciation and a more generous support of the heroic men and women who against fearful odds are patiently laboring for the redemption of China unto the Lord and his Christ.

John F. Hurst

METHODIST REVIEW.

MAY, 1904.

Art. I.—JOHN FLETCHER HURST.

JOHN FLETCHER HURST was born in or near Salem, Dorchester County, Maryland, August 17, 1834, and died at Bethesda,
Maryland, May 4, 1903. He came from an old Dorchester County
family. His grandfather, Samuel Hurst (1765-1822), served in
the Thirty-ninth Maryland Regiment in the Revolutionary War,
1781-83. His father, Elijah Hurst (1797-1849), who brought up
his children in the fear of the Lord, was a diligent and successful
farmer, of whom the anecdote is related that when the Cambridge
(Md.) Methodist Episcopal church was built and dedicated he
subscribed twenty-five dollars each for his two children, and then
hesitated about his own subscription; then the pastor's eye caught
that of Farmer Thompson, who shouted, "I'll give ten dollars more
than 'Lije Hurst." "Make my subscription two hundred dollars,"
said Hurst. Thompson was thunderstruck, but manfully paid his
two hundred and ten dollars. Elijah was one of the shrewdest
farmers in that whole section, and owned at one time one thousand
acres. It was from him his son inherited his business instincts
and his wonderful administrative talents. The mother, Ann
Colston (1808-41), possessed a beautiful spirit and a fine intellect; from her he inherited his literary gifts and wide
sympathies. Elijah's only other child married Dr. John F. Kurtz,
in the same county, and died in 1886. The famous merchant
millionaire of Baltimore, John E. Hurst (1832-1904), was a
cousin of the bishop, being the second son of his father's brother
Stephen.

23

Our subject, who was a model youth, told the story of his conversion in a most interesting way to the Northwest Indiana Conference in 1889:

I have been trying to serve God now ever since the year 1853; that is about thirty-six years. I had no parents—they were gone home, to heaven—and I was among strangers. My mother died before I was seven years old, so that I don't remember even her face fully—just a mere out-line. I think I will know it; I think I will recognize it when the fight is over and when the happy meetings come, never to separate. My father was a Christian man and died when I was fourteen. I was going home from a little debating society, pretty late at night, and on the other side of the street, as I was going toward my boarding place, I heard them singing in the Methodist church. With me was a young school companion who afterward entered the ministry. We went over into the meeting and crowded well to the front. The minister saw us and came down and spoke to me, and asked me if I didn't want to go to heaven. We both went to the altar, and time after time, meeting after meeting. I was seeking light all the time; trying to do something, trying to per-form some obligation, trying to understand Him, and when I came to see that I could not understand anything He gave me light. One night, going home from church, I remember that a change came over me; a light broke out before me; there was a little river in the distance, and it seemed to shine like silver; I didn't know what it all was; I thought it was some sudden glow of good feeling. I went to my room full of joy, and the Lord revealed to me, "You have a new heart." The Lord had given it to me; there was no consciousness of sin. I felt, like the Pilgrim, that the burden had fallen from my shoulders. I could now lose it be-cause I had gotten to the foot of the cross, and I have been trying to serve the Lord ever since. I have been thankful to him that the change was so sudden, so striking; that I have been able to look back upon it as the hour when God, for Christ's sake, spoke peace to my soul. Now and then a cloud comes. I am not satisfied. I want the sunlight ever here. Our privileges are infinitely greater than we think they are; we can do more for God; religion can be more of a joy, instead of a mere service and hard task beneath the hot sun.

The preacher who led him to Christ was James A. Brindle, who, with Henry Colclazer, was pastor of Cambridge Circuit, Snow-Hill District, Maryland, then the Philadelphia Conference, who were holding meetings at Cambridge in the winter of 1849-50. Brindle died in 1894 after a long, faithful, consecrated, and effi-cient ministry. To him Bishop Hurst pays a glowing tribute in the *Peninsula Methodist* of April 28, 1894. The man who accompanied Hurst to the altar on that eventful night was Benjamin Douglas Dashiell of the Methodist Episcopal Church.

South (cousin to Missionary Secretary Robert L. Dashiell). After a self-sacrificing ministry as pastor and presiding elder in Texas he died in January, 1882, aged about fifty-two years.

Even before this time young Hurst had thoughts of the ministry, and when, in 1843 or 1844, the corner stone of a new church in Cambridge, Maryland, was laid he deposited in it a coin, with his name, and told his schoolmates that he would some day preach in that church—which he did. John Fletcher Hurst was a student from boyhood. After attending school in his own neighborhood he went to the academy at Cambridge, the building of which is still standing on Academy Street. Besides mastering the work at school he would steal away to some quiet nook in the woods or along the shore and pore over books in history. Then came the question of college. The words of Bishop Hurst himself at the funeral of Bishop Peck cannot be quoted too often, as they show how a word spoken at the proper time may mark the turning point of a life:

My mind goes back from this hour many years—over the chasm of a generation, thirty-three years. Away down in the south of Maryland, on the eastern slope of the Chesapeake, when attending a camp meeting I was told that the president of Dickinson College was to preach on a certain day. Such a sermon was seldom heard in that peninsula. Some one had said "college" to me a few times before this, and I had thought of taking a college education, but this seemed well-nigh impossible. I remember a kind preacher brought me to the preacher of the afternoon. I told him something about going to college. Said he: "Don't trouble yourself. Go home and wait until the opening of the term, and then take the stage across by York and come there and I will meet you, and we will live happily together." And for two years I was a student under him. When Dr. Collins succeeded him I remained two years; but no tender heart beat more keenly in sympathy with the student than his. The friend of schools from the Atlantic to the Pacific! So I think of him as a man who took a boy by the hand. And ever since the memories of the man have been precious.

There is nothing to be specially remarked about his college life (1850-54). A fellow-student remarks of him that he was "gentle, quiet, with a certain reserve and dignity. He was an industrious student and came to the recitation room well prepared. In disposition he was cheerful but not hilarious, and while he appreciated fun I never knew him to be in anything which trans-

gressed the rules of the college." The life at the college showed the effects of his home training and the strength of his moral and religious principles. Another classmate (the Rev. D. J. Holmes) says, "I once heard Professor Goodrich say, 'Tell me what a young man is in college and I will tell you what he will be in the world.' This was eminently true of John Hurst." He was a plodder; a diligent, earnest student. He was a member of the Union Philosophical Society (no secret or Greek letter fraternities were allowed in the college at that time), and entered enthusiastically into its literary and debating work. His classmate, General Rusling, says that he read widely outside of his curriculum, being in history and general literature the best read man in his class. "I remember his favorite books were Grote's Greece and Hume's England, and he never wearied of descanting on the excellencies of both. He was especially fond of composition, and took Grote, Hume, and Macaulay as his models, and was the best writer in our class." Rusling adds that in college he was always the quiet scholar and Christian gentleman, the synonym of uprightness and integrity.

After teaching a few months at Greensboro, Maryland, he accepted an invitation to the Hedding Literary Institute, Ashland, Greene County, New York, where he taught languages, literature, and also chemistry.* In 1856 he resolved on theological study abroad and went to Halle and Heidelberg, where his studies were much interrupted by long foot journeys over large parts of Europe, including England. Impressions of some of these years, as well as his later European life, are found in his *Life and Literature of the Fatherland.* Returning to America toward the close of 1857 he applied for a license to preach at Carlisle, Pennsylvania, and served that circuit with Samuel B. Dunlap and Richard Norris. Finding his contemplated marriage would keep him out of the old Baltimore Conference, which seemed to stick to the rigorous old Wesleyan rules, he applied to the new Newark Conference (organized in 1856) at its session at Morristown in 1858. His first appointment was Irvington, New Jersey. Here in May,

* It is singular that the late Dr. A. W. Cummings omits reference to this Institute in his invaluable *Schools of Methodism.*

1859, he married Miss Charlotte Elizabeth Lamont, daughter of Dr. William Lamont, of Charlotteville, New York, one of the most noble and accomplished ladies that ever presided in a Methodist parsonage. Her devotion, her sympathy, her tact, her fine accomplishments, were ever laid on the altar of her home. An artist, a linguist, a woman of literary culture, she yet gave herself freely to the duties of domestic life, and to her devoted helpfulness her husband owed no small measure of his success. A little shelf of inspiring books is the result of her knowledge of foreign languages, literary skill, and sympathetic understanding of Christian life in different ages and countries: *Renata of Este:* A Chapter from the History of the Reformation in France and Italy (translated), 1873; *Queen Louisa of Prussia,* from German sources, 1874; *Elizabeth Christine,* wife of Frederick the Great, from German and other sources, 1880; and others, all published by the Methodist Book Concern. With tragic suddenness this beautiful and gracious spirit was taken from her home in Washington, D. C., March 14, 1890. Of this happy marriage there were born six children: John Lamont, of Denver; Clara, who was laid to rest in the beautiful Friedhof at Frankfort-on-the-Main amid the flowers brought by the loving hands of her little German schoolmates, aged seven years, June 23, 1869; Carl Bailey, recently chief consul at Vienna; the delicate and loving Blanche, who died in Buffalo, 1885, aged eleven years; Helen; and Paul, lieutenant in the Philippine Islands. Bishop Hurst's pastorates in the Newark Conference were as follows: 1858, Irvington, N. J.; 1859-60, Passaic; 1861-62, Elizabeth, Fulton Street; 1863-64, Elizabeth, Water Street; 1865-66, Staten Island, Trinity. On June 6, 1866, he received, and after repeated solicitation accepted, September 20, an appointment as theological tutor in the Mission Institute, Bremen, to succeed William F. Warren, the able theologian and scholar who was to take charge of the educational enterprise which the liberality of Jacob Sleeper and Isaac Rich had set on foot in Boston. The story of the voyage of himself and family over the ocean and their establishment in Bremen is told in the first chapter of his fascinating book already referred to. In 1867-68 Dr. Hurst (he had received the degree of D.D. from

Dickinson in 1866) taught in Bremen, and in 1868 to 1871 did the same service for the young German Methodist preachers at the Martin Mission Institute, Frankfort-on-the-Main—founded by the munificence of John T. Martin, Esq., of Brooklyn, as a part of the centennial movement and formally opened January 17, 1869— during his vacations studying German life and traveling in Europe and in the East; visiting the Holy Land in 1871.

Before he embarked for his work in Bremen the Messrs. Scribner published his *History of Rationalism,* which the Methodist Book Concern also indirectly took up. This book, the only one of scientific importance which he found time to write, made him well known in the learned world, and it has great and permanent value. This was followed by three important books which he translated—"all crowded into three years," said his wife: Professor Hagenbach, *Church History of the Eighteenth and Nineteenth Centuries,* 2 vols. (Scribners, 1869); Professor J. J. Von Oosterzee, *John's Gospel: Apologetical Lectures,* published by T. and T. Clark, Edinburgh, 1869; and Professor Lange, *Commentary on the Epistle to the Romans* (Scribners, 1869). In the Hagenbach he had the assistance of his friend and brother Marylander of the adjoining Talbot County, Professor Bernard Harrison Nadal, who while pastor of Trinity Church, Philadelphia, and later. rendered chapters i-vii, ix, and part of x, Volume I, and parts of xvi, xvii of Volume II. Hurst added (II, 456-479) an excellent chapter on the "Most Recent History and Present State of the Church in Europe." This book was printed in Germany and the stereotyped plates sent to New York. The beautiful and learned work on John's gospel by the Utrecht professor was translated in Bremen and Frankfort, printed in Berlin, and published in Edinburgh. The translator added a few notes, an excellent preface, a valuable list of books on John's gospel, and an index. It remains still one of the best books in defense of the Fourth Gospel, written with fine spiritual insight. The translation of Lange's Romans, a work of great difficulty, won the praise of the general editor, Professor Schaff. Valuable homiletical material was added, drawn from the full sources of English practical theology. When Whedon noticed this book (January, 1870, l'

130) it offended him that the Arminian contribution was confined exclusively to the mechanical part. "Arminian Dr. Hurst is allowed to do the machine work of translation and gathering of homiletical scraps; but he is safely put under keepers, and in the commentary itself no Arminian is allowed to say a word." But that gives Whedon all the better opportunity to say something, and what he does say let those who are so fortunate as to possess a file of the *Review* read for themselves.

The death, in 1870, of Professor Nadal made a vacancy in the chair of historical theology at Drew, for which Hurst urged Charles W. Bennett, recently a student at Berlin and, later, historical professor at Syracuse and at Garrett. The trustees elected Hurst himself, which compelled him to leave his loved Germans at Frankfort-on-the-Main and take up English again as a vehicle of instruction. He came back in 1871, and by the fall of that year was at work in the old northeast room in Mead Hall, where many of those who read these lines will remember his interesting lectures and even more interesting discursions into bypaths of history, biography, and literature. In 1873, when Professor Foster had been elected bishop, Professor Hurst was elected president of the seminary. The first work he published after his return was *Martyrs to the Tract Cause: A* Contribution to the History of the Reformation (Methodist Book Concern, 1872). This small book is really one of the most valuable of those which bear his name. When he was ransacking an old bookshop at Frankfort, in 1870, under the shadow of the house where Goethe was born, he came across the *Martyrer der Traktatsache,* by Otto Thelemann, published on its fiftieth anniversary by the Wupperthal Tract Society, organized at Barmen in 1814. Partly as a translation of this, and partly with additions of his own, he made one of our most interesting brief contributions to church history. This was followed by outlines of Bible and Church History, 1873 and 1874, intended for Bible and normal classes (the Methodist Book Concern). The next contained the rich fruit of his studies, travels, and observations in Germany—*Life and Literature in the Fatherland* (Scribners, 1875). Few books equal it in breadth of view and accuracy; racy, interesting as a novel, full of the keen and genial

observations of one who had the true instincts of a traveler. His next book was *Our Theological Century: A* Contribution to the History of Theology in the United States (Randolph, 1877, 70 pp.). It is a rapid general survey of the ecclesiastical and theological drift of the United States and of its providential position in history, dwelling with special power and pleasure on that divine arrangement which made the United States Protestant, and not Roman Catholic. The pivotal matters of our history are touched on with skill. This was followed by a work compiled mostly by his pupils, notably George Blood Smythe, *Bibliotheca Theologica: A* Bibliography of Theology (Scribners, 1883)—a list of books in English on all the topics in theology, with full titles, notes, publishers, prices, etc., with admirable indices. A complete working over of this useful book was intrusted to the hands of Professor George W. Gilmore, of Bangor Theological Seminary, later of Meadville Theological Seminary, and the result—really a new book (xv, 575)—was *Literature of Theology: A* Classified Bibliography of General Religious Literature (Methodist Book Concern, 1895), and a remarkably full and accurate list of books in English in all departments of theology. It is indispensable to all libraries, bibliographers, and earnest workers in theological fields. An evidence of its completeness is the fact that the Rev. Albert Osborn's admirable index of authors occupies fifty-eight double-columned octavo pages.

Not the least important of Professor Hurst's work at Drew was his recovery of the endowment. When the late Daniel Drew built the seminary at Madison he kept in his own hands the $250,000 of endowment for current expenses, paying interest regularly. This was against his own judgment and wish, as he had more than once proposed to the trustees to pay the money into their hands. The event proved the wisdom of his thought. In 1875 or 1876 his investments were destroyed in the stock exchange by a younger manipulator of consummate skill, and the great and benevolent financier went out in his old age a broken man. The question arose, Shall the seminary be abandoned, or shall its endowment be recovered by an appeal to the Church? Not one of the faculty, though without salaries, had any thought of leaving. They threw

the school on the heart of the Church, and nobly she responded. President Hurst left his library, his lecture room, his family, went here and there all over the Eastern States, visiting churches, preaching, representing the seminary, visiting men and women of wealth, in all of which he was ably seconded by Professor (now President) Buttz, and, thanks to the generous responses of the Church, the lost endowment was more than recovered. What years of work were those, 1876-79! He would come back for a breathing space, take his classes for a little time out of the hands of the ever ready and willing Professor Kidder—*venerabile nomen*—give a great address in the chapel calling the students to a life of utter devotion to the Church, and then off again to his task; perhaps to Europe, as when he attended the Evangelical Alliance at Basel, in 1879, and delivered his able address in German on Christian Union, published in English, revised and enlarged, by the Methodist Book Concern in 1880 (*Christian Union Necessary for Religious Progress and Defense,* 35 pp.); a satisfying paper, illuminated with lights from his wide reading and softened by the catholicity of his large spirit. In connection with his Drew life must be mentioned the launching of an important literary enterprise, the Biblical and Theological Library, in which Methodist scholars should provide books in all departments written with scientific completeness and accuracy. Splendid results have already been attained in the noble volumes of this Crooks and Hurst series, though our view of them is saddened with the thought that some of those who were assigned work were carried off by death—Professor Latimer, of Boston School of Theology; Professor Winchell, of the University of Michigan; Professor Ridgaway, of Garrett, and, finally, Professor Crooks himself, whose *History of Doctrine* is left to another hand.

In 1880 Professor Hurst was made bishop. He entered upon his duties with zest and love. His residences were Des Moines, 1880-84; Buffalo, 1884-88; Washington, 1888-1903. He held the European Conferences in 1884, those in India in 1884-85, and the European again in 1885. As a result of his visit in India we have a most valuable book on that country, richly illustrated, as interesting and with the same wealth of general knowledge as his book

on Germany—*Indika:* The Country and the People of India and Ceylon (Harpers, 1891). In this age of process print illustrations it is refreshing to look upon the wood engravings in this portly volume. All phases of Indian life, civilization, and religion are treated, with notes, tables, maps, etc. For the Chautauqua course he prepared a few little books in Church history: *The Early Church,* 1886; *The Mediæval Church,* 1887; *The Reformation,* 1885; *The Modern Church,* 1888, and *The Church in the United States,* 1890. These were afterward published in one volume with the title, *Short History of the Christian Church* (Harpers, 1893). Bishop Hurst took great interest in the Ecumenical Conference of 1891, where his address of welcome was a notable and never-to-be-forgotten feature; parts of it spoken in the different languages represented by the Conference—English, French, Italian, German, etc. At the Conference in London, in 1901, his health was beginning to fail, and especially the news concerning President McKinley prostrated him, but parts of his addresses there display the old-time beauty, breadth of view, and pertinency of thought and language. It had been his almost lifelong aim to write a history of the Church, and while professor at Drew he had prepared it up to the time of Charles the Great; but the absorbing work and dissipating details of the espiscopate made impossible its completion by himself. He had also planned an elaborate and richly illustrated *History of Methodism,* to be completed in about ten volumes, each country to be written by some one acquainted with its history, and the whole illustrated lavishly from all available sources.

And now we come to his last work: the founding of the American University. A national university had been proposed at Washington—thought of by Simpson, urged by William Arthur —but it was left to Hurst to realize the dream. That a man of sixty should plan this vast scheme, buy ninety-one acres of land, raise the $100,000 to pay for it, and, in the midst of multitudinous affairs that took up all of mind and heart as well as bodily strength, carry the scheme through to the extent of having one building finished, another under way, about $1,150,000 endowment and other resources pledged, of which $500,000 has been paid in, see

the university indorsed by the General Conferences of the two churches in the United States—where has a picture like that been seen in the history of the world! What courage, what faith, what vision, what endurance! The land was bought in 1890, paid for by 1895, the university incorporated in 1891, the Hall of History built in 1896-98, and the corner stone of the Hall of Government laid May 14, 1902. The university is to be purely post-graduate, intended to cap the educational structure of our Church. The Roman Catholic prelates, with their usual sagacity, had already seen the immense importance of Washington as an educational center, and in 1889 opened there a great university. With the vast resources of the capital thrown open free to students—its archives, its museums, its libraries—the American University could perhaps shortly open its halls to our young men in a few courses—say history and political economy—leading to the degrees of M.A. and Ph.D. Will the Church prove true to this great trust?

At the bishops' meeting in Trenton, in 1901, Hurst was the guest of General Rusling, his college classmate. He writes thus to Registrar Osborn:

What a charming week that was! How delightful and suggestive along every human line! We talked and gossiped much each day, and . . . of course we talked much about the American University. It was then heavy on his heart, but clear in his mind, and he felt sure that it would "come to pass" duly. It had come to him, he said, as a "heavenly vision," and he had only "been obedient to it," and he felt sure God would yet carry it through; if not in his lifetime, then afterward. He longed to see it opened, and its halls thronged with young men and women—the best in America—and he confidently believed that God would order it all right, whatever happened to him. He was then feeble in health but strong in soul and purpose, and looked and talked as Moses or Elijah might have done in their last years.

It is the pathos of death that one must leave his work undone. What fields of knowledge to explore, what books to write, what good influences to start, what institutions of love or light to help or to found—but death touches the arm of the sculptor! So it was with our friend. Browning says:

There shall never be one lost good! What was shall live as before;
The evil is null, is naught, is silence implying sound:
What was good shall be good, with, for evil, so much good more;
On the earth the broken arcs; in the heaven a perfect round!

What is the historical significance of the life we have been considering? 1. He, with McClintock, Crooks, and a few others, was among the first to make known American Methodist scholarship to the English-speaking world: by the works which he wrote; by the Library of Biblical and Theological Literature edited by him and Dr. Crooks; indirectly by the presidency of the American Society of Church History, and—thanks to the earnest scholars whom he called to his aid—he permanently enlarged and deepened the range, the volume, and the quality of Methodist scholarship. 2. By his work in and for our schools he wrought himself into the intellectual fiber of our Church in a unique way. By his work in the saving of Drew he placed the Church under unending obligations. By his founding of a post-graduate university at Washington he marked out both the place where and the plan upon which the Church must inevitably take the next step in its educational progress if she is ever given the courage and self-sacrifice to follow the path of her farsighted leader.

Many will echo the greeting of his college and lifelong friend, General Rusling: "And so, John F. Hurst—good friend, brave heart, generous soul—hail and farewell! Surely in the hereafter —sometime, somewhere, somehow, as God wills—we shall meet and greet each other again, and part no more forever!"

ART. II.—THE CLIMAX OF HUMAN HISTORY.

Accent the human. We seek to know what greatest things men have achieved unaided by a divine revelation and providential help. This will inevitably be associated with the meanest things. If the Creator and Upholder of the universe directly aids nations in matters of sanitary science, civil institutions, revelation of ideas undiscernible by themselves unaided, by expansion of mind, and by the more abundant spiritual life, there is no limit yet reached of things possible to men so aided. But up to the present there have been great national developments over continents and through centuries without what is understood as divine revelation and providential help. Where have they been the greatest? We would naturally say that greatness is indicated by possession of fertile soil, by the utilization of the forces of nature, by armies raised and wielded, by the arts of life, architecture, painting; also by the outgoing of mind in poetry and metaphysics, and the natural feeling after God in their human religions.

In asking where is the climax of human history we propose to pass by Babylon, Nineveh, Egypt, Greece, and even Rome, and present the claims of India for that distinction. In regard to a fitting field for vast empire it certainly has no rival. It is a triangle about fifteen hundred miles on a side, all inhabitable. The great Gangetic valley certainly has no equal in the world. One can go one thousand miles and never come to a hill. The vast range of the Himalayas at the north pours down a perpetual flood of fertile silt that is not approximated by the Mississippi or the Nile. Except for occasional drouths and consequent famines, about ten in a century in some parts of it, there is no place where the fecund earth offers to provide for such an abundant population. This desirable India has been coveted by all the great conquerors of the world. Nearly every student of Greek remembers how he entrancedly read of the wars of Darius five hundred years before Christ. Two centuries later came Alexander the Great, defeating King Porus and his vast hordes of men, horses, and elephants. How well we remember that the captured Porus

answered Alexander's question of how he wished to be treated, "A a king." Here Alexander heard of the kingdom of Magabda on the Ganges, whose sovereign, Sandrocottus, could bring into the field an army of six hundred thousand men, three hundred thousand horses, and nine thousand elephants. Mohammedan prowess sought to possess itself of India through Persia, which had been previously conquered. The sacking of cities and the slaughters of men and women were incredibly savage through the centuries, till Mahmoud of Shizni came in 1024. It was at Somnath, in the Guzerat, that he refused to be bribed to spare the great idol fifteen feet high (probably a pious laudatory fiction of Firishta) but smote it with his iron mace and found its huge body filled with pearls, rubies, gold, and diamonds. Incredible amounts of booty flowed for centuries back to the Tartar tribes. Then came the great Tamerlane in 1398 for more incredible slaughters. He is said to have massacred on one occasion one hundred thousand prisoners. It is during the rule of his descendants that we look for the climax of human history. Omitting even the names of emperors many and great, we come to Baber, A. D. 1526, descended on his father's side from the great Tamerlane and on his mother's from Genghis Khan, two of the greatest Tartar conquerors that ever lived. The spirit of the man is seen in this: On one occasion in extreme peril of utter defeat he writes in his memoirs that he repented of his sins and implored pardon of God, solemnly resolved to drink no more wine, which he acknowledged that he had sometimes used to excess, he caused his drinking vessels of gold and silver to be melted up and distributed to the poor; he vowed to remit the stamp tax on all Mohammedans if it should please God to give him the victory over his enemies. He then assembled his officers, made a frank and fiery address, which closed as follows: "The voice of glory is loud in my ear and forbids me to disgrace my name by giving up what my arms have with so great difficulty acquired. But as death is at last unavoidable, let us rather meet him with honor, face to face, than shrink back to gain a few years of a miserable and ignominious existence. For what can we inherit but fame beyond the limits of the grave?" The whole assembly, inspired as by one soul, cried out, "W

War!" (Firishta, vol. ii, page 119.) That he was not conquering a weak, effeminate people is evident from a single incident that might be duplicated many times. When the garrison of the besieged Chanderi saw that they could defend themselves no longer, "they, according to their dreadful customs, murdered their wives and children in the following manner: They placed a sword in the hands of one of their chiefs, and he slew the unhappy victims, who bent of their own accord before him, even contending among themselves for the honor of being first slain. The soldiers then issued forth with swords and shields and sought death, which they all obtained. Not one was found alive in the fort when it was taken." Firishta says that Baber was "a master in the arts of poetry, writing, and music." He was constantly employed in making plans for aqueducts, reservoirs, canals, caravansaries; for introducing foreign fruits and other edibles, for the improvement of the country. His Memoirs, written by himself, are exceeded by few works ancient or modern. In his old age his son Húmáyun, his designed successor, was very sick. According to the custom of his country, he believed that he could offer himself as a substitute and save his son. After long devotion he believed his substitution was accepted, and exclaimed, "I have borne it away, I have borne it away." The son recovered, the father soon after died. He was succeeded by Húmáyun, 1531; by Akbar the Great, 1556, who was doubtless the most powerful monarch on earth at the time; by Jehángir, 1605; by Shah Jéhán, 1627; and by Aurung-Zeb, 1657. This is the period that we call the climax of human history. What were its achievements?

One of the objects of human endeavor has been the accumulation of wealth. The wealth of Ormus and of Ind is famed throughout the world. Where the gorgeous East pours on her kings barbaric pearls and gold is equally the theme of poetry. Cafoor plundered a capital in the Deccan in 1306, and brought away a recorded weight of gold worth five hundred million dollars. Even the common soldiers had so much gold they had to leave the mere silver behind them. The amount of booty brought to Delhi under Allah ud Dín gave the city the appearance of great wealth and prosperity. "Palaces, mosques, universities, baths, forts, and all

manner of public and private buildings seemed to rise by power of enchantment, neither did there in any age appear a greater concourse of learned men from all parts of the world; forty-five men skilled in the sciences were professors in the university. There were distinguished professors and teachers of poetry, philosophy, medicine, divinity, astrology, music, morality, languages, and in all the fine arts then known in the world." (Firishta.) Everyone has heard of the begemmed peacock throne at Delhi, the plunderer of which, Nadir, carried away jewels, gold, the peacock throne, and the famous diamond Koh-i-nur, variously valued. Perhaps a fair average would be about two hundred and fifty million dollars. The greatest displays of Akbar's grandeur were at the festival of the vernal equinox and on his birthday. At least two acres were spread with silk and gold carpets and hangings as rich as velvet embroidered with gold, pearls, and precious stones could make them. The emperor was weighed in golden scales against gold, silver, perfumes, and other rich substances in succession, which were then distributed among the spectators. Shah Jéhán thus celebrated one festival, the expense of which was, according to Khafi Khan, seven million five hundred thousand dollars. I have seen two silver cannon and two gold cannon weighing two hundred and eighty pounds each; and a small rug eight feet by six made of pearls, diamonds, and other precious stones, of one hundred and twenty-five thousand dollars in value. All did not, however, choose to live in such wasteful extravagance. Nasr-ed-Dín defrayed his personal expenses by making copies of the Koran and selling them. He had but one wife, and she cooked all his food. When she asked for an assistant he refused, saying he was "only a trustee for the state," and that he was determined not to burden it with needless expenses. But what did these people build? Every period of India's history has been distinguished by the building of magnificent temples, palaces, forts, columns of victory, and mausoleums. Sir Thomas Roe, an English ambassador, came to India in September, 1615. He passed Chittoor on his way to Ajmir, and said: "Above one hundred temples, many lofty towers, and houses innumerable were seen crowning the lofty rock on which it stands, but it was at this time entirely deserted.

The principal glory of some dynasties was the number of temples they destroyed. Mohammedanism was essentially iconoclastic. They ruined temples for the glory of God. No general description of buildings can be attempted. Two instances of building shall suffice. The Diwan-i-khás, or Hall of Private Audience, at Delhi has not, and never had, a rival for magnificent splendor and minute adornment. The Taj Mahal at Agra is the world's wonder. Bishop Heber says, "The Moguls designed like Titans and finished like jewelers." It took twenty thousand men seventeen years to build this poem in marble, and the cost, if all the materials and labor were paid for, is estimated at from fifteen to thirty millions of dollars. It was so built that now, after two hundred and seventy years, one finds nowhere a corner chipped, a crack in the elaborate lacework of pierced marble screens, nor a bit of uneven floor. It is fit to be immortal. It is not only architecture but poetry, and the result of most delicate and tender emotion, being built to the memory of an immortal love. Mumtaza Mahal, "the Pride of the Palace," to whose precious memory it was built, had borne Shah Jéhán seven sons and died in childbed with the eighth while with him on a campaign in the Deccan. All the city constantly flows out to the park in which it stands to gaze for the hundredth time on its entrancing beauty. The birds hover over it for hours, certainly not looking for food but attracted by its splendor. One wants to believe in the transmigration of souls, and that the one who built this marvel and the one to whom it was built can come back and poise on airy wing over the one building in the world most fit to be immortal. I watched two birds a long time in pleasant fancy that this dream might be true.

The position of woman is a measure of a civilization. While the position of woman in India has never been what it should have been, any more than it was in Egypt, Greece, or Rome, yet as there have been Cleopatras, Aspasias, and Cornelias in them all, so there have been numerous Rezias and Jéhángirs in India. Sultana Rezia was among the most famous of India rulers. "The princess was adorned with every qualification required in the ablest kings, and the strictest scrutineers could find in her no fault but that she was a woman." (Firishta.) Jéhángir married Núr Mahál.

24

"He took no step without consulting her, and on every affair in which she took an interest her will was law." She was a veritable Joan of Arc in battle, a Josephine in refinement, an Elizabeth in council. The burning of widows on the funeral pile of their husbands resulted, at first at least, from the unappeasable grief and devotion of the wife. And just before it was finally prohibited in 1829 by English law, when commissioners had been appointed to see that it never took place except by the voluntary act of the widow, there was no lack of victims. The fact that the finest monument ever erected to one greatly beloved was erected to a woman is significant of the place she held in one mind at least. The whole force of the Vedic writings was for the exaltation of woman. The maiden of the Vedic times would be an exquisite charm to-day or any day. They could make their own choice of husbands. There was no child marriage nor enforced widowhood. Human history presents no higher devotion than that of Damayanti for King Nala, and Rukmini for Krishna. Edwin Arnold's exquisite idyls of love had foundation in fact. He himself writes: "The native Indian chronicles are full of the mention of famous, beautiful, accomplished, and influential women. It would be easy to enumerate five or six score of such, from the lovely queen of Shah Jéhán, whose tomb is the Taj Mahal, and Aholinga Bai, the noble Mahratta queen, to native ladies royal or otherwise now living, whose characters for generosity, loyalty, or strength of nature maintain the ancient traditions." The old Mahabharata says: "A wife is half the man, his truest friend. A loving wife is a perpetual spring of virtue, pleasure, wealth; a faithful wife is his best aid in seeking heavenly bliss."

Such wealth could not be gathered and accumulated again and again after being plundered, nor such structures reared, without some regard to the welfare of the common people. Allah-ud-Dín published an edict against the use of wine and strong liquors under pain of death. That was a prohibitory law that prohibited. He emptied his own wine into the streets; the people followed his example to such an extent that for days the common sewers of Delhi flowed with wine. The whole force of the vigorous Mohammedism of the period was against any use of spiritous liquors

Mohammed Tughlak spent the revenues on public works. He made fifty canals to promote agriculture by irrigation, forty mosques, thirty colleges, one hundred caravansaries, thirty reservoirs for irrigation, one hundred hospitals, one hundred public baths, and one hundred and fifty bridges. For the permanent support of these he assigned endowments of land. This was five centuries ago. Shere Shah, who held the throne of Delhi for five years in Húmáyun's exile, made a highroad extending for a four-months' journey from Bengal to the Indus, with caravansaries at every stage, with provisions for the poor at every one, and with wells every mile and a half. The road was planted with rows of trees for shade. Akbar systemized the revenue of the empire, abolishing a great variety of taxes and collecting taxes from the product of the land in proportion to its productiveness. These elaborate state papers have been translated into English by Mr. W. Gladwin under the title of *Ayeeni Aknari,* and constitute a system worthy of the most enlightened sovereigns of to-day. Works on diseases and their cure show that much attention was given to medicine. Some of these works were translated into Arabic, and the indebtedness of that people is freely acknowledged by the Arabians. Vaccination for smallpox was practiced in India long before it was known in Europe. Venesection, lithotomy, and couching for cataract were understood and practiced. Doubtless charms and gross superstitions abounded, but knowledge was sought and to some extent attained. Astronomy received such attention that eclipses were accurately predicted and are to this day by tables then made, but which are not now understood by those making the predictions. The ruins of three observatories are gigantic, and clearly indicate that right ascension, time of rising of the stars, etc., were clearly noted. Akbar used to assemble learned men from all countries every Friday to discuss philosophy and religion. Three times he sent to Goa requesting Christian missionaries to come to these discussions, to which Brahmans, Mohammedans, Jews, Christians, philosophers, and disciples of Zoroaster were invited. He usually closed these Chautauqua assemblies himself, reviewing the arguments of all. This liberality gave some offense to the more bigoted Mohammedans. I followed

Bishop Heber's example and went with real reverence to what Heber calls his "magnificent" tomb. It stands in a park of forty acres. It is four stories high. The block of marble above the body is most delicately carved. On one end are the words, "God is great;" on the other, "Let his glory shine." Close by stands a marble pillar that once held the Koh-i-nur diamond as a subsidiary ornament of the place. In regard to philosophy India went to the extreme limits of thought in all directions. I think it was Gladstone who said metaphysics had exhausted its possibilities in India two thousand years ago. Philosophy asks, "Whence came evil?" Against this cold, rocky shore human thought has dashed itself for ages. It has been flung back without breaking the rock or softening its terrible realities. It first said, "No God." No Creator at first and no Providence afterward, or there would be no evil. But atheism was unthinkable. Universal mankind rejected this preposterous glacial theory. Then India proposed transmigration of souls and evil in every life the result of sin in a previous one. This doctrine was not in the four Vedas. They took a cheerful view of life, while this is utterly pessimistic. All the six systems of philosophy that rose after the Upanishads or commentaries on the Vedas regarded life as a curse. Hence life of all kinds, physical, mental, or that of the desires, was to be reduced to the lowest possible limit. Their efforts in this direction are altogether too efficient. The metaphysics of Kabir in the sixteenth century and of Nanak soon after ran all things back to monism; but whether it was conscious or pantheistic they could not decide. Their discussions whether the me or not me could be distinguished were long and the result never settled. The people are as acute concerning questions of no profit to-day as ever.

What of religion? "An unbiased consideration forces us to conclude that religion, everywhere present, as a weft in a warp running through human history, expresses some eternal fact." (Herbert Spencer.) "The soul of man is naturally Christian." (Tertullian, seventeen hundred years ago.) India has originated at least two great religions. It has furnished religions for hundreds of millions of others and never borrowed one for itself. Islamism was forced on India by the sword, but never adopted.

The voluminous Vedas were written over thirteen hundred years before Christ. The Upanishads contain extracts and commentaries on the theological doctrines of the Vedas. There are fifty-two volumes. There are six works called Durshans, each containing a system of theological philosophy. There are eighteen works called Purans, and eighteen supplementary works called Upo Purans. The amount of matter contained in these works is prodigious beyond belief. The Vedas say repeatedly: "There is in truth but one deity, the supreme spirit, the Lord of the Universe and whose work is the universe." A summary of their teaching concerning God is thus given by one learned in them: "Perfect truth, perfect happiness, without equal, immortal, absolute unity; whom neither speech can describe nor mind comprehend; all-pervading, all-transcending, delighted with his own boundless intelligence, not limited by time nor space; without feet moving swiftly, without hands grasping all worlds, without eyes all-surveying, without ears all-hearing; without any intelligent guide understanding all; without cause the first of all causes; all-ruling, all-powerful, the creator, the preserver, and the transformer of all things; such is the Great One." It is degeneracy from this ideal that gives India three hundred and thirty million gods, mostly abominable beyond expression. It will be remembered that India perfected the Sanskrit language, of which Sir William Jones says, "It is a language of wonderful structure, more perfect than the Greek, more copious than the Latin, and more exquisitely refined than either." Such encomiums have been passed upon it by many men learned in its perfectness. The sacred books of the Hindus are written in Sanskrit. The amount of its literature is enormous. Buddhism was the next form of religion. It had power enough to become the religion of the millions of people, and India had power enough to cast it off. Mohammedism with its primal tenet of monotheism came next. It is a religion that still commands a degree of devotion hardly equaled by any other. I have seen an assembly that was calculated to contain ninety thousand people, almost entirely men, in absorbing devotion and prayers at an ordinary weekly meeting.

Just here has been enacted in our times the most signal

triumph of discipline over disorder, of loyalty over treachery, of right over wrong, and I might say of Christianity over heathenism, the world ever saw. Three thousand Englishmen outside the fortified city of Delhi set themselves against forty thousand men that they themselves had drilled and armed, who were inside the elaborate fortifications, and won. As a result, good order, adequate protection, even-handed justice to all, relief from famine, suppression of virulent diseases, large opportunities for education, and consequently a higher range of employment, the breaking down of the most iniquitous system of caste and the swiftly coming acceptance of the one only divine religion, have come to these hundreds of millions with a speed never known before. A nation has been born in a day. Is it not clear that in India was the climax of human history? We must still accent the human. It has man's most horrible characteristics. All of human weakness, wickedness, and passion run rampant has been scattered over every page. There have been limitless slaughters and cruelties beyond expression. The Black Hole of Calcutta, eighteen feet square, into which the Sirāj-ud-Daulā thrust one hundred and forty-six men on a hot June night, and out of which only twenty-three living persons could be dragged the next morning, and they delirious and scarcely conscious—that is a fair sample of the dreadfully human side. The builder of the famous Taj Mahal slew all his brothers and their sons to be rid of all danger from them as successors to the throne. He in turn had a tenfold composite of Absalom and Ananias for a son, named Aurung-Zeb, who sought to follow his father's example and exceeded it by imprisoning his father for the last seven years of his life. His daughter, Jehanara, preferred to share imprisonment with him to liberty without him. But we are compelled to remember the rest of the world. It was the general era when Charles I of England was beheaded in 1649; when the Inquisition, established by Gregory IX in 1235, was still doing its terrible work in Spain, Portugal, Italy, and Peru; and when numberless murders followed the revocation of the edict of Nantes in France. The human tendency of one man to say, "I am holier than thou, stand on a lower level," was frightfully accentuated in the establishment and maintenance of castes. It was slavery

without civil law or physical force. It laid manacles on mind, and held in subjection by chains stronger than iron. In other lands one might be punished for teaching a slave to read, but the slave himself would be unharmed. He is too valuable. But in India it was the slave himself who was punished. He had no value for anyone. "If a sudra gets by heart any part of the Vedas or the Shastras the magistrates shall put him to death. If a sudra shall presume to read any part of the Vedas or Shastras or Purans to a Brahman, or Kshatriya, or a Vaisya, the magistrates shall heat some bitter oil and pour it into the sudra's mouth; and if a sudra listens to the Vedas or the Shastras, then the oil heated as before shall be poured into his ears, anseez shall be melted together and the orifices of his ears shall be stopped therewith." (Halhed's Gentoo Code.) "Let the same punishment be visited on him who kills a sudra (lowest caste man), as on him who kills a cat, owl, or lizard." (Laws of Manu, page 937.) Janab Khan struck copper coins and ordained that they should pass as silver. But when the taxes were paid into his treasury in this coin he had the same experience as those who issue paper money without gold for its redemption. The Hindus say that the wild lust of Mohammedans, whose very heaven was to be made up of joys the most debauchingly sensual, compelled their women to go veiled, resulting in the zenana system of seclusion in vogue to-day. In a harem of multitudinous wives, seldom visited, it would be human to err. I saw in the grand and gorgeous palace at Delhi a too human provision for them. It consisted of four very small rooms; first a place to leave their elegant palace robes; next a bath for purification of the body; then a mosque for the soul, to fit it for the passage; then an utterly dark cell, the only furniture of which was a crossbeam for suspension. Being cut down from this, the naked body dropped into a well one hundred and twenty-five feet to the level of the river. The euphemistic answer to the inquiry where such a lady of the court might be was, "She has taken a trip down the Jumna River." The men were not sent on that voyage. This, too, is very decidedly human.

The hobbles and clogs on the feet of progress in India have been many. This great empire has always been divided into many

separate, warring kingdoms. The asserted sovereignty of individual states was the ruin of the splendid republic of Greece, and was attempted to be of the more splendid republic of America. The degradation of any one man or class of men is so much subtracted from the sum total of greatness. In India the degradation touched the greatest number and was of the deepest character. In religion men sought out many inventions. As Paul says, they became vain in their reasonings, and their senseless heart was darkened. Professing themselves wise, they became fools. The divine remedy for all in the time of Christ was to give the Roman eagles free flight over three continents and to offer to make every man a free man, a child of God. The victory of the first gave free course for the second to run and be glorified. God duplicates his ways of working because they are the best and perfect ways. The cross of St. George flies from the perpetually radiant Himalayan peaks on flagstaffs, and streams in victory from sea to sea. This gives safety to any men or women missionaries to the Himalaya Mountains to-day and will protect them in Tibet to-morrow. Happy the missionary individual or Church that can go forward when the pillar of cloud and of fire so obviously moves on. There is much land to be possessed.

Henry W. Warren

Art. III.—THE NEW EMPHASIS ON RELIGIOUS EXPERIENCE.

WHAT are the constituent elements of religious experience? Most Protestant Christians, and especially Methodist Christians, are open to the charge of having unduly emphasized the emotional elements. It is the reaction from that emphasis which makes the old-time revival methods ineffectual in most churches. Men no longer believe that emotional depression plus emotional exhilaration are the normal or necessary states of a soul making the acquaintance of God. Many affirm that glooms and raptures are not only unnecessary but positively unwholesome, and even irrational. But that is the extreme of reaction. Tumultuous emotion, while doubtless unwholesome when mistaken for the deeper verities of the religious life, may prove "the finest of the wheat" when grown in the good soil of holy purpose. The emotional is a permanent element in human nature. It is irrational to say we may look for the transports of human love, the fine flashing joys which come from sweet human intercourse, but must not dream of such results in connection with God. Much of the revelation of the Bible has its essence in the transforming experience of the mighty men of the Bible—by which we do not mean a dry chronicle of events in their lives, nor a catalogue of their opinions nor a record of their actions, but vision, glory, rapture, joyous conviction about God. And when we, as did they, brood upon God's truth and reverently and intently gaze upon his work, and by a visitation of his Spirit the splendor of them breaks in upon us and the soul spreads its wings for eagle flights, the glory is not a bit of hysterics, nor a delusion, but a valid and highly rational spiritual enthusiasm.

> Oh, we're sunk enough here, God knows!
> But not quite so sunk that moments,
> Sure though seldom, are denied us,
> When the Spirit's true endowments
> Stand out plainly from its false ones.
>
> .   .   .   .
>
> There are flashes struck from midnights,
> There are fire-flames noondays kindle,

and the flames of religious ecstasy may be the "authentic fire" of God.

But the glories of religious feeling have doubtless been over-emphasized. Religious rapture is not open to all. That a soul may cultivate its sensitiveness to things divine is not to be doubted. If it will maintain the conditions of humility, purity, and loyalty which the Gospel lays down any soul may have acquaintance with God, but all have not in the same degree of development the power to see the invisible and to estimate the wealth of the treasury to which faith is the key. To insist, therefore, upon any standard of spiritual vision or spiritual emotion as a condition of fellowship with those who believe would be illiteral and absurd. To "become certain of God," to use a phrase of Harnack's, may stand not as a description of certain moods of the soul as a statement of the result of all the experiences of the soul. And we must not be so unwise as to believe that feeling is the only route into the certainty. Clear vision is a most satisfying religious experience. Intellectual emancipations and satisfactions such as Browning hinted at when he said,

> The acknowledgment of God in Christ
> Accepted by thy reason solves for thee
> All questions in the earth and out of it;

the "Vision of Sin" which Dante had, and Tennyson, not because they were acquainted with the sins described but because they could *see;* that clear perception of sin's nature and results, conviction of its danger, horror at its tragic work, were not these visions religious experience—made possible by knowledge of God ? And when quietly we review our conduct, look our tempers in the face, search our motives, even though the process be unemotional is it not religious experience ? Or when in the presence of great truth its inner meanings break upon us and the soul exults in clear vision, "This Vision—is it not He ?" When thought is disciplined, checked in its riots, brought under control, made the interpreter and courier of the King, is the ordered thought of the mind captive to Christ no part of experience ? Emotion may help to give insight, and we need the hours of insight to give us material to fill the hours of patient, sturdy, indomitable purpose. But

we must not confuse the emotion with the vision, nor fancy that
the one equals the other.

Nor must we forget purpose as an exceedingly precious bit
of experience.

> The things in hours of insight willed
> May be in hours of gloom fulfilled.

Those choices by which the soul is irrevocably committed to what
it sees in its moment of insight are among the richly vital things.
In Professor Coe's analysis of answers received from college students to the query "What is permanent in religious experience?"
it is shown that seventy-seven per cent found permanent religious
experience in things volitional as against seventy-one per cent
finding them in things emotional. From which the lesson is plain
that "states of the will as well as of the sensibility are included
in religious experience." When one makes a holy choice, adopts
a lofty ideal, sacrifices self for others, holds persistently to duty
though the decisions involve pain in the making and patience in
the keeping, such surrenders of the life to righteousness, even
though quite unemotional, are veritable glories of experience. The
appeal of Jesus to our hearts is not alone as a patient sufferer
but as an heroic leader. His life does not merely melt us to tears;
it stirs us like a bugle blast. We think not only of the meek
humility with which he endured the scorn of men but of the splendid purpose with which he faced the devil and death. The perfect submission of the garden was no more religious than the
indomitable will which won the battle in the wilderness and made
his face like flint as he looked from Hermon to Calvary. And his
cross shows not only meek submission but heroic resolve. To use
Dr. Parkhurst's words, "It is at once the tenderest and the sternest
thing in all history. It is pathos, but it is flint. It stands for the
weeping obstinacy of our God." And when we choose a course
which means impoverishment, pain, unsatisfied hungers, as sometimes we must; or a course which provokes misunderstanding, loss
of sympathy, and perhaps defamation, and quietly accept the consequences in obedience to our vision of duty, our resolute tread in
the chosen path is surely religious experience. There may or

may not be gladness in our step; there surely *is* the power of genuine religious life.

And to our vision and purpose we must add our aspirations. When unutterable longing for what we have not yet attained surges within us these profound, unspoken pleas are important throbs of the soul's life.

> All instincts immature,
> All purposes unsure,
>
> .   .   .   .   .   .
>
> Thoughts hardly to be packed
> Into a narrow act,
> Fancies that broke through language and escaped;
> All I could never be,
> All men ignored in me,
> This, I was worth to God.

When our "reach is greater than our grasp" as it must be if we are thoroughly alive, we find cause not for discouragement but for gratitude—bits of valuable experience, touches of God, assurances of heaven.

> The high that proved too high, the heroic for earth too hard,
> The passion that left the ground to lose itself in the sky,
> Are music sent up to God by the lover and the bard;
> Enough that he heard it once: we shall hear it by and by.

Does God report himself in our experience? If he transcends all possible human experience, then of course, we can find in our experience, however divine it seems, no proof of his existence and no syllable of interpretation of his life. Religious belief and religious form in such case may be of use in developing man, but of no use in revealing God. But that he is in human history is hardly called in question by present-day thought, and that he touches us can hardly be denied. If he is to be found in natural forces as certainly as in exceptional manifestations then his touch is a constant thing. If science and philosophy are suggesting that cosmic force in the last analysis is "as clear an expression of will as is spiritual love" then we may reason ourselves into the belief that God, in the manifold forces which operate about us, is deliberately ministering to us. But the question we are especially concerned with is not "Does he touch us?" but "Are we conscious of his touch?" Is there a sense of the spiritual

world—an immediate perception of God which makes one imper-
vious to denial and independent of argument? Take Tennyson's
exaltation of man:

> In moments when he feels he cannot die,
> And knows himself no vision to himself,
> Nor the High God a vision;

and his comment on his own poem, when he passionately declared
to his family, "Depend upon it the spiritual *is* the real. You may
tell me that my hand and foot are only imaginary symbols of my
existence, I could believe you; but you never, never can convince
me that the *I* is not an eternal reality, and that the spiritual is
not the true and real part of me." Take Browning's rapturous
certainty of God, or Lowell denying the need of argument or of
religious form to sustain faith:

> My soul shall not be taken in their snare,
> To change her inward surety for their doubt
> Muffled from sight in formal robes of proof:
> While she can only feel herself through Thee,
> I fear not Thy withdrawal.

Are we to say that these clear-sighted souls and the multitudes
who, less lofty in stature, may nevertheless claim likeness in experience are deluded in their beliefs? Professor James does not
think so. "We and God have business with each other; and in
opening ourselves to his influence our deepest destiny is fulfilled."
It is quite safe to say that deep spiritual experience is an argument for God. And it is the argument which most needs development and is the most convincing, for it is "invulnerable to the
assaults of logic."

Given the experience, to deduce God therefrom is a simple
logical process. God is the only adequate cause of spiritual life.
To be content with any other explanation is to make the highest,
most splendid life of which we are capable untrustworthy, unreal.
As Brierley says, "The inward life of a saint points as certainly
to an actually existent spiritual world as the coloring of a flower
to the existence and potencies of light." No analysis of experience
weakens the argument. Our psychologists may point out all the
constituent elements of religious vision and passion, may discover the stages of intellectual development which are most favor-

able to religious impressions, may seem to make the whole spiritual history of a man a purely psychical affair which can be explained scientifically by means of nerves and temperament and emotionally exciting events, but they have not weakened the argument for God. To point out the processes of life is quite different from explaining its mystery. When men offer a materialistic basis for spiritual life they invert the pyramid, perpetrate a logical absurdity, make a joke of the holiest facts with which we are acquainted. New knowledge of methods has more than once made us fear for the foundations, but it need not. When science bade us believe that this material universe did not spring into being full grown, but by "continuous progressive change, according to certain laws, by means of resident forces," we feared that God was omitted both from the origin and movement of things. But he was not. As John Fiske says, "We are still perfectly free to maintain the direct action of Deity. We may have learned something new concerning the manner of divine action; we certainly have not substituted any other kind of action for it." "At no imaginable future time can science even attempt to substitute the action of any other power for the direct action of Deity." And the same truth holds in regard to the scientific study of religious life. When psychological science scrutinizes the spiritual phenomena of a soul, sets them in order, determines their laws, describes their accompanying conditions, she is not casting God out of them. She is learning his methods. If our experiences be traced to psychical origins and made the result of organic conditions or nervous conditions, in fact a natural product of temperament under certain exciting causes, even if our psychological experts have made out a case, it still remains open for us to say that God is the cause of the experience. God has not been driven from the material universe because we have outgrown the old mechanical notions of his action and think of him working patiently, persistently, through resident forces. Nor is he driven from human life if we say he has used events and the senses and the vital organs and the nerves to bring visions of his face. By what argument can men decide that he is expelled from his temple because they point out that he has used its furniture? The God whose movements may

be known in "every beat of the mighty rhythmic life of the universe" works upon and in the human soul.

"Ye shall be witnesses unto me" said Christ. But we cannot get adequate material for testimony without contact with him. To form a clear mental picture of the Christ of Galilee and Judea from the record furnished in the gospels will not be enough. It is perfectly clear that the attitude of the New Testament writers toward Jesus Christ is that of souls who have looked upon a transcendent marvel. Nothing recorded of him in the gospels is too great to be associated with the Christ of the epistles. His greatness is beyond portrayal. The estimate of those first lovers of his depended not wholly nor chiefly upon their knowledge of his earthly ministry, but upon the spiritual vision they had of him and the moral transformations he had wrought in them. That assuredly was true of Paul, who had not known his Master in the flesh; and as true, we believe, of John, who had known him with the intimacy of tender love. Their exaltations of their Lord cannot be explained apart from their constant spiritual communion with him. Nor will we get adequate conception of him nor be able to give inspired reports concerning him without vital contact. "Back to Christ" must mean not merely back to the customs and thought of his time, back to the history and traits of his nation, back to the actions and words of his three public years, but back to the transcendent, transforming divine Christ who is back of and is flashed upon us by the entire New Testament.

Experience is needed as a satisfying basis for faith. We need to keep constantly in mind the truth so finely stated by Dr. George A. Gordon: "The believer who is despondent over the signs of the times must remember that the Christian truth of the Holy Spirit is a truth for the intellect no less than for the heart. . . . Truths are anchored off shore; the shallows do not allow them to come in. A new use of the grace of the Spirit, a fresh experience under him, is essential to the incoming of these excluded truths. The flood tide of the Spirit is the only hope of the believer." Just as

> Life's bases rest
> Beyond the probe of chemic test,

so faith's bases rest beneath the reach of a merely intellectual test. The things of the Spirit are spiritually discerned. The Master manifests himself to his lovers. John P. Coyle said that in determining to love and follow the Christ whom he knew he broke the thralldom of intellectual skepticism. Of course belief must not be determined wholly by experience. The soul that does not travel outside the limits of its own consciousness for materials to build into the body of its creed may have an intense faith but a meager one. "The individual tends to identify his own experience with the whole of the religious life, and to judge others by their agreement or disagreement with his subjective standard." Such a tendency is to be resisted. The truth of God is vastly larger than can be accommodated by a human soul. No soul is large enough to contain the doings of God. We must attend to universal experience. Much of our spiritual wealth is by inheritance, not by achievement. We do not separate ourselves from Christian history. We are helped to know that which is vital in us by reference to the historic consciousness of the saints. We will be kept sane by remembering that the Christ to whom we bow is known to us not only by the effects he produces in us, but by the genuine portrait of him bequeathed by the historians of his earthly ministry. The spiritual standards against which we measure ourselves are historical as well as ideal. Experience does not fix the area of our faith, it is our map of that part of it already surveyed and so becomes our guarantee of the reality of its outlying unexplored portions.

Experience should be the inspiration and goal of service. We would not be justified in saying that experience is to be sought because of its possible usefulness. Such a motive would probably make impossible the experience desired. There must be perfect simplicity in dealings with God. Perfect obedience to his call will forbid any ulterior motive, even though it be as lofty as the wish to serve. But service, though not the purpose of experience, is the result of it. Fervent love is one of the notes by which the genuineness of Christian experience may be known; love which leads the soul away from the contemplation of its own attainments or its own needs and makes it glow in self-forgetting service. Thi-

receives special emphasis in our day. Service rather than cloistered virtue or spiritual rapture is the demand of the hour. "It is not only he that would be great, as Jesus said, but it is every philosophical formula or economic scheme or social institution that would be permanent which must prove itself the servant of all." But there is danger that the forms of love be mistaken for its substance; the service of man be made a religion in itself; charity regarded as the only sanctity; the love of man substituted for the love of God. We have no struggle to decide whether we will stay with the blessed vision or go to the hungry poor. The service is more attractive than the vision and in the intervals of the service we do not return to the vision. Yet service is no substitute for immediate knowledge of God. It is rather the result and, in turn, a fresh cause of such knowledge. To decry philanthropy would be ungracious. The beneficent streams of social service are broader and more fertilizing than ever before; and the Church of the living God must engage in such service and be the inspiration of it. But we must see to it that the service is Christian in its spirit and motive and spiritual in its aim. Service is not to be welcomed as a substitute for experience nor regarded as a supplement to it, but as its consummation.

Experience has its value to theology and a value greater than is often admitted. It is a guide to God and a revealer of his truth. Cautious intellect has denied its value in the realms of truth: its apparent disclosures are not to be trusted, its suggestions are to be received with a good deal of reserve. But that is a denial of a vital Christian principle. "The things of the Spirit are spiritually discerned." "He that loveth me, I will manifest myself to him." There is no guarantee of satisfying knowledge of God apart from the passion which Christ inspires and the vision which the Spirit gives. Said Martineau, "To say, as some strangely do, that religious people cannot judge about religion is like saying that the humane cannot understand suffering, or genius appreciate poetry; that for truth in art you must avoid consulting Raphael, and in music you must keep clear of Beethoven. In contradiction to all such pedantry I venture to maintain that only through love and trust can God be known."

25

It is a principle which has been too little used in the construction of our theologies. They have often been too merely intellectual, too little devotional. They have been built too exclusively of the materials furnished by a dry-eyed, critical observation of the facts of history and Scripture, and have rejected as flimsy the materials offered by flaming experience. Yet how can any soul really know, much less state, the power of Scripture or the meaning of Providence without having, in its own right, a deep-lodged experience of God's leadership? The theologian who does not find his interpreting principle in the glowing spiritual life which is in his own and in other souls is unbiblical in his method. Back of the biblical portraits of God lie the experiences of men. The Psalms are vital with the longings and satisfactions of passionate souls. Isaiah's vision lay back not only of his ministry, but back of his perception of God's character which determined the methods of his government, and back of his understanding of God's purposes as suggested and demanded by the traits and policies of the nations. Paul's vision and acceptance of Christ may be found underlying those mighty expansions of his lordship in Ephesians and Colossians. This is the principle to which we should always hold as we peer into nature in our search for God. Henry Drummond, who loved and served the sacrificing Son of God, found love as well as selfishness in the long story of life's development, and in chapters which are full of the discerning poetry of science has shown us the self-sacrifice which has marked much of the weary struggle of life up from its lowest forms. He has been criticised as being unreliable in his interpretation and charged with reading Christian truth into the natural order. Well, why not? Has Christian experience no part to play in nature study? Which is truer to God as we know him in Jesus Christ—to make the gospel of his love a supplement to nature or to make it nature's innermost and ultimate truth? Which gives us the best hint as to method in nature study—"The strength for the life of others" in *The Ascent of Man* or the sketch of nature's moods and history given by Romanes in his *Candid Examination of Theism?* Personal interest in the outcome may doubtless tempt a student to suppress some facts and exaggerate others, but it is a temptation

is not enough. Reason cannot throw its rays for enough. To read clearly "the increasing purpose which through the ages runs" we must have our eyes blessed with the vision of God. What he does in us is suggestive of what he is doing in the wider fields of general human history. The principle of historical interpretation in Bossuet's *Discourse on Universal History* is vastly truer and more profound than the soil and climate theory of Buckle. And that which should make us sure of Providence, and be the death of any pessimistic tendency in our reading of current events, is experience. God's dealing with the soul illustrates his purpose for the race. The individual acquaintance is the prophecy of the universal friendship with him toward which the world is moving. This vision is given and kept bright by him who saw so clearly the kingdom's destiny. We are not greatly forcing a precious text if we say "He that hath seen me can see the Father." Jesus is the "Light of the world," and we may put into our analysis of that word both the processes of nature and the life of history.

In the formulation of Christian doctrine experience should be given more prominence. We can establish the place and power of prayer from modern Christian life. To our studies of the Atonement we should bring as legitimate materials the pain, the rapture, the freedom, the power which come to the souls who really see the Cross. "The Atonement comes to us in the moral world and deals with us there; it is concerned with conscience and the law of God, with sin and grace, with alienation and peace, with death to sin and life to holiness; it has its being and its efficacy in a world where we can find our footing and be assured that we are dealing with realities." If this be true; if the Atonement is an actually operating force, a verifiable fact so far as character results are

concerned, then the souls who have tested its power, brought to it their sin, and received from it spiritual glory, are available illustrations of its divine purpose in human life. If the revelations of God are not over, why neglect the discoveries of his grace made by souls who know the redeeming power of his Son and confine ourselves to his ancient manifestations? Martineau mourned the fact that we have dropped the "Lives of the saints" from our curricula and reminds us that "the only knowledge that can really make us better is not of things and their laws, but of persons and their thoughts." We need the study of rich human lives not only for personal culture but for the discernment of God's way and for vivid understanding of the power of his redeeming grace. In other branches of science the authorities are those who make original study of facts, not those who are wise with book knowledge. And the wider the field of research the surer is the induction. The same necessity is upon the theologian. He must study not only the vital facts of Scripture days but also those of our own days. He should collate varied human experiences not to illustrate psychical laws but to discover the habits of God. Above all, that his conclusions may be not only true but inspiring, his own consciousness should be throbbing with God's life. Theological judgment may be damaged by theological partisanship, but not by religious fervor. Says Dr. Brown, "One of the serious obstacles to Christian progress is the fact that our technical statements of belief so imperfectly represent living issues." "The theology of the future . . .will have its roots deep in life. It will find evidence of God's presence in the movements of the time, and will take up into its catalogue of sanctities the familiar experiences and duties now too frequently relegated to a lower sphere."

More than all, our inner spiritual experience must make character. In the various histories of Christianity we have the record of heresies and orthodoxies; of councils and decrees; of divisions and strife; of creeds and customs and policies; of persecutions and toleration, of church order and worship and activity. But the truest history would be of that which cannot be written: the lives of Christlike people who reach back in solid phalanx through the centuries, humbly and earnestly, though not with her

fect accuracy, revealing the beautiful character of their adored Master. Our moments of vision, our perceptions of truth, our thrills of rapture, our days of peace, our brave decisions, our eager yearnings must bring, if they would be certified as genuine, patience, gentleness, kindness, energy, honesty, fidelity to truth and duty. In the introduction to Julian Hawthorne's recent book about his father is recorded a touching incident concerning a cabin in the heart of the Colorado mountains. In traveling the son entered this humble home for rest. In the corner of the room was an old miner who had been paralyzed for years. When this help-less paralytic heard the name of the stranger, and learned that he was the son of the great Hawthorne, new life came to him. The old eyes beamed with delight and burned with eager questioning. Nathaniel Hawthorne had been the old man's literary idol. For fifteen years he had read the books of no other author. In the face of the son the dying man searched for suggestions of the dead author's spirit. And the son records his wish that he had for one hour the face of an archangel that he might sustain that search-ing scrutiny and worthily bear the responsibility which had been made his by the possession of an honored name. Whatever other value is to be found in the conscious possession of the life of God this must not be lacking: our union with him must make us able to meet the questioning eyes of men and give them hints at least of his own holy, loving life.

What is the mission of our religion? One student in a recent answer finds the distinctive element of Christianity in the absence of any specialty, in the balance of its truths, the harmonious con-crete manifestation of the elements of the one religion of which all historic religious faiths are partial statements. Another finds its essence in Jesus himself, who is the revelation of the divine ideal for man and also, through his transforming influence, the most powerful means of realizing that ideal among men. And still another declares that the great distinctive thing in Christianity is the gift of the Holy Spirit to men; in this resides the power of salvation and everything in Christ leads up to and culminates in this divine gift. Perhaps between these last two there is no con-flict, the one being the statement of the method and energy of

the revealing, transforming Christ of the other. It would seem, if we attend to the teaching of the New Testament and of Christian history, that these latter conclusions are near the truth. Christ was no mere exhibition of God, nor authoritative teacher of the truth concerning him, nor sage with wise reflections upon the beauty of virtue and the danger of sin. His was a dynamic mission. By all declaration, manifestation, and ministry he toiled to get this uncovered, illustrated, divine life lodged in human souls to cure their sin and make their character. And it is this life, this abundant life, redeeming, transforming, gloriously and eternally satisfying, of which our nerves are scant. And this must be the treasure we keep in view for ourselves and for those to whom we minister. By personal example, by church life and worship, by social service, by theological thought and speech, by beautiful character to make common man's experience of God, until the treasure shall be so valued and the search for it such a fixed habit that in all our varied human activities, industrial and political as well as social and religious, he shall be known and declared.

Wallace MacMullen

Art. IV.—A MODERN THEORY OF MIND.

PRESIDENT STARR JORDAN, of Leland Stanford University, in an article published two or three years ago in a leading scientific magazine, defines mind as "the collective function of the sensorium or brain of men and animals," "the sum total of all psychic changes, actions, and reactions," psychic changes being understood to "include all operations of the nervous system." "The study of the development of mind in animals and men," he continues, "gives no support to the mediæval idea of the mind as an entity apart from the organ through which it operates. . . . There is no ego except that which arises from the coordination of the nerve cells. All consciousness is colonial consciousness, the product of cooperation. . . . The 'I' in man is the expression of the coworking of the processes and impulses of the brain." This quotation is given somewhat at length because it lucidly states the theory, held by many of our leading scientific men, that our mental states are compounds, and the ego is the sum of the resultants of certain nervous processes. When we investigate the grounds of this theory we find that they pretty much reduce to three, namely, the desire of evolutionists to preserve universally the continuity of their law in its application to every domain of thought, the widely observed dependence of mind upon its physical organism, and the revolt which is felt against dualism, with the desire to find a consistent monistic basis. Let us turn to consider whether these grounds are adequate and can be consistently held.

Advocates of the theory of evolution feel that it is necessary to pass without break from inorganic matter to organic and from organic to its highest manifestation, mind. Consciousness must therefore be transformed energy, or attendant phenomena of matter, and since the basis of matter is atoms, the synthesis that we find in thought must be "the coworking of the processes and impulses of the brain, which is made up of individual cells," as "England is made up of individual men." But the necessities of a theory do not establish its truth; and while it suits the imagination well to think of each atom as having a little endowment of

mind, and the more highly organized structure as being accompanied by corresponding increase of mental development, there are
objections to the scheme which have so far proved insurmountable.
Not the least of these is to see how an atom can possess such contrary qualities as mind and extension, how these qualities are
related to each other, and how they can work alongside of each
other in the development of more complex forms. But, waiving
this difficulty for the present, we have the task presented to us of
seeing how these little bits of consciousness with which atoms are
supposed to be endowed can fuse together to produce such a larger
and fuller consciousness as we find in the higher organic beings,
and especially in man. It is easy to use the word blend, or fuse,
but by waving the magical wand of a word over a difficulty we
cannot logically solve it. The "I" we have in consciousness is
something more than a sum of elements, it is a unity; but the
heaping of elements together can never make a true unity. It can
give us an aggregate, but an aggregate or sum is a unity only to
the mind that thinks it, and never in itself. The realities are
always the elements. Even the thought of forces fusing does not
help us, for force properly conceived is only a static condition of
an atom. It is nothing that can pass out of the atom and exist
apart from it, helping make up a·new thing. The activities of the
molecules of the brain can exist only in the molecules, and the
mind in the molecule, if it has it, can exist likewise only in the
molecule, and cannot get out of it to come and joint itself to other
bits of mind which have also left their molecules to fuse together
and make a new product, the consciousness of the particular ego.
When we use the word "sum" in the sense Mr. Jordan does when
he says the mind is "the sum of all psychic changes" we commit
the fallacy of the universal, and give to a concept objective reality
as much as when we give to triangle or horse a real existence.
Class words have their reality in thought, the only ontological
existences being the individuals which compose them; and this is
true when applied to the statement that mind is the sum of the
bits of consciousness with which the molecules of the brain are
supposed to be endowed. We claim, therefore, that there is no
way of conceiving how the atoms can so unite the mental element

claimed for them by the theory before us as to make the unity we feel in consciousness when we say, "I feel," "I think."

If we turn to the second consideration which has led to the theory of a "collective" or "colonial mind," we shall find that many facts at first seem to sustain it. Nothing is more apparent than that our mental condition is affected by our physical states. If the activities of the brain are paralyzed by chloroform a cessation of consciousness ensues. If the brain is disordered there is a corresponding disorder in mental action. A stimulant will quicken thought and a narcotic depress it. The illustrations are innumerable and have been observed from the time men began to ponder psychic phenomena. But to conclude, from this dependence of mind on brain, that thought is a product of molecular activity is to make a hasty and unwarranted inference. In the first place, it is to be noted that we have here an argument from observation and experience; but experience also teaches us that mind can affect brain. Says Dr. Strong: "If the facts of sensation indicate an action of the physical on the mental, then those of volition with equal clearness indicate an action of the mental on the physical, and the latter is as much an ascertained fact as the former. . . . The case of volition is the exact converse of sensation, and by as much as the one set of facts proves the dependence of mind on the body the other set proves the dependence of body on mind. If, on the other hand, the facts of volition do not prove that the mental state sets up the neural process, then those of sensation do not prove that the neural process sets up the mental state. To admit the evidence for causation in the one case but reject it in the other is to have two weights and two measures." We have few experiences which come to us more positively than our ability to control our physical activities to a certain extent, and also our mental states. We can both will and do. If a thought comes to us which we think is not profitable we can refuse to consider it and give our attention to other things. We can also set before us ends to achieve, and start a train of physical movements which will accomplish what we have in view. This fact of observation and experience makes the question of dependence at best a drawn battle. Nor does it by any means follow, as Shadworth Hodgson would

try to convince us, that the dependence of mind upon body is equivalent to causality; for it may be otherwise explained. We must remember what Hume has taught us about not seeing causes, and that a concurrence of events does not necessarily prove cause and effect. Things may be in relations of interdependence without one being caused by the other. It may be that the phenomena of mental and cerebral action are to be regarded "as conjugate of an unknown cause which has coupled them together for a time," as Mr. Richmond suggests. This is much easier to think than that consciousness is produced by the molecular activities of the brain, a conception which Professor Tyndall has truly said "eludes all mental presentation." Concomitant relations would give us exactly the same phenomena as if the relations were causal. Theories of interaction, or parallelism, or mediation, each of which has strong advocates, would quite as well account for the observed dependence of mind on brain activity as the theory we have under consideration.

Let us now turn to consider whether a "mind stuff" theory can furnish us with a consistent monistic basis for our thinking. Writers of this school tell us we have thought too poorly of matter and have failed to appreciate the higher qualities with which it is endowed. Matter is not simply the old matter with which physics has made us familiar; but, as one phrases it, is a "double-faced somewhat," or, in the words of Bain, "a double-faced unity;" a substance with two sides—on the one side matter and on the other side mind. In all organic forms there is the psychic element; and as organisms become more complex this appears in higher manifestations until it reaches its climax in man. Thus we are informed that, besides being material, atoms have a mental endowment, and occasionally, when the conditions are ripe, run a side line and do a little business in mentality besides doing their ordinary work. Our first objection to this new conception of matter is that it is incapable of being thought. The imagination can picture it, but no one can form an intelligent conception of it. A double-faced somewhat, on the one side matter and on the other mind, is as unintelligible to clear thinking as a round square or a black white. When we posit such a substance we try to solve

difficulty by running into the fog banks of mysticism. To explain anything we must first of all have a clear conception of terms, and the appeal must be not to fancy but to definition. An hypothesis like the one before us, suggesting what no one can conceive, can give us no explanation. It is as if when a strange object passes the window a mother should answer her child's inquiry, "What is it?" by saying, "It is a centaur." This answer might arouse the imagination of the child, might stir its curiosity, but it would bring the child no knowledge, for it has never seen a centaur, does not know how it looks, acts, or what it is or can do. The answer simply refers the child to an object beyond its experience and hence is no answer at all. The same is true when in explaining facts of consciousness we are referred to a new kind of substance— a double-faced somewhat, on the one side matter and on the other mind. We have here a philosophical centaur, a construction of the imagination, not a matter which experience has verified. We might as well speak of the length of a thought, or the color of a volition, as of "a mind atom," or matter with a double side. We are playing with words, taking them out of their known meanings and putting into them qualities and meanings at will, stuffing them with hypothetical values. If this is permissible we can prove anything—that the moon is made of green cheese, or the reality of Santa Claus and the bogy man. A second objection is that, in this theory of monism, the relation of the mind side and the matter side of the atom, or in man of the brain series and the thought series, is not satisfactorily defined. There are three possible hypotheses, each of which we shall show is inadequate—namely, thought and feeling are effects of brain action, or they attend brain activity, or they are aspects or phenomena of brain substance. To the hypothesis that thought and feeling are effects of brain activity we have, first, the objection that it is in contradiction to the scientific doctrine of the conservation of energy. It is a law of physics that energy can only pass into terms of itself; that is, into some other form of physical energy. Hence, if thought is produced by the specific grouping of molecules of the brain, it follows that thought must be assimilated to causation in the physical world, which means that thought must be material or the law of

the correlation and conservation of energy is broken. For thought cannot be produced by the brain molecules without the expenditure of energy, and each mental effect must represent a certain loss of nervous force. The energy which has thus been used must disappear from the physical realm, must be lost to the physical series. It cannot be returned since, by hypothesis, thought is an effect and not a cause—that is, it cannot enter the chain of effects and be a cause to what follows it. The series stops with the production of thought; for, if thought can react on the physical series, then the physical series is not independent, and we have as much evidence that the mental can affect the physical as that the physical can affect the mental, which is the very point the materialist's theory is framed to deny. It cannot admit, without committing suicide, that thought, feeling, and volition can count in the course of events as well as physical forces. The energy therefore which goes to produce mental effects is lost and cannot be returned to the physical series; which, as we have said, is to sacrifice the principle of the conservation of energy in the interest of a new and hypothetical theory of matter for which we have no other proof than that we hope it will help us solve a difficult problem. But besides this objection we have another equally serious: the qualities of matter and mind are entirely different, and the passage from one to the other is unthinkable. Between the sentient and the nonsentient, between thought and motion, there is a great gulf fixed and no man has yet been able to bridge it. Matter has form, solidity, position, but thoughts and feelings have none of these. The one order of facts is quantitative and the other is qualitative. Modern science is to-day no nearer making matter and mind commensurable than was Democritus twenty-four hundred years ago. We can explain sound, light, and heat on the physical plane, but not the sensations of sound and light and heat. In the words of Professor Tyndall: "Here, however, the methods pursued in mechanical science come to an end; and if asked to deduce from the physical interaction of the brain molecules the least of the phenomena of sensation, or thought, we must acknowledge our helplessness. Between molecular mechanics and consciousness is interposed a fissure over which the ladder of physical reasoning

incompetent to carry us." Dr. Maudsley, who has striven with all
his power to break down the fence which separates the physical
from the mental, has been forced to give up the task and admit
that the observation of physical objects and the more careful study
of nerves and brain cannot give us the least direct information
about "feelings, desires, volitions, and ideas." Even Herbert
Spencer in one place frankly admits: "That a unit of feeling has
nothing in common with a unit of motion becomes more and more
manifest when we bring the two into juxtaposition."

With these difficulties in the way it is plain that we cannot
hold that consciousness is an effect of brain activity, and in explaining the relation between the two we must seek some other
way out. This way is found by some in claiming that thought is
not caused by brain movement, but attends it. "The physical
series is self-contained and independent. It suffers no loss and no
irruption." The mental series is "the subjective shadow which
attends the physical series." "Physical energy is not expended in
producing thought, but in producing physical combinations which
have a thought face." In the words of Professor Huxley: "Our
mental conditions are simply the symbols in consciousness of the
changes which take place automatically in the organism." Herbert
Spencer says that mental phenomena are the "inner side of
molecular motion in the brain;" they are the shadows cast by
certain combinations of molecular activities. It does not take
much pondering of this explanation to see that, while it is easy to
state, it is exceedingly hard to understand. We know what a
shadow is, for we have seen it many a time, but a subjective
shadow of molecular activities of brain is something of which only
a great imagination can get any conception. The same is true of
physical combinations having a thought face, or consciousness
being a symbol of organic processes. Mr. Spencer might say that
the terms are figurative; certainly figures, especially when used in
defining theories, should contain some meaning, but we are confident that these figures do not represent any idea which comes to
us in thinking of the implications involved in brain molecules and
their movements. They are simply magic terms with which
Spencer, Huxley, and their class conjure with difficulties. They

give no clear idea of the relation which exists between the thought series and the physical series, but only obscure the problem. They do not explain why one combination of molecular activities is attended by thought and feeling and another is not; why there is any order in the mental series, and thought is not chaotic; why some movements have, as their subjective side, ideas, others feelings, and others volitions; or how, if the two faces of matter, the mind face and the force face, do not affect each other, it comes about that the mind face side is shadowed forth by physical movements of the brain; nor do they show how the unity of the atom can be retained if it is endowed with a thought side and a thing side. There must be something in certain molecular movements which elicits and makes manifest the thought series, and this makes thought an effect of matter, or puts the cause back in some hidden ground of mystery in matter itself, which is equivalent to abandoning the problem; or at best it is giving "a double movement to matter, a physical and a thought movement," which "leaves it doubtful whether matter as moving or matter as thinking is the true reality, or whether there may be something deeper than both," either alternative of which is "fatal to the assumed self-sufficiency of the physical series."

But may we not state the relation of the thought series and the physical series differently, and affirm that thought is an aspect or phenomenon of matter? Professor B. P. Bowne, in a lecture before the American Institute of Christian Philosophy, has replied to this hypothesis as follows:

This suggestion does seem to help us a little until we remember that the phenomenon imply not only something which appears but a subject to which it appears. When, then, the thought side of matter is said to be phenomenal the question at once emerges, What is the subject and where the consciousness for which the phenomena exist? For the materialist there is no such subject. Yet so natural is the thought of self that we never divest ourselves of it even when denying it. When the materialist views the brain as a thinking machine he always tacitly assumes himself as a reading machine which reads off the result. When we are told that nerve motions have thoughts for their inner face, a self is always supplied for whom the thought exists. Materialistic statements tacitly assume by the side of the organism which conducts the neural process a looker-on who tells of the processes and interprets their meaning. Thus thought is said to be a sign of nervous process; but for whom does the sign exist? The

tiser could not see the thought, but only the nerve movements. For whom, then, is the thought a sign? ·For the thinking self, of course. Thus the self which the materialist labors to destroy peers complacently through the very arguments which are framed for its destruction.

Having examined the grounds on which the theory of mind in question rests, we wish to append a few arguments of a more positive nature showing why consistent thinking must reject it.

1. All knowledge we have, both of the outer and the inner world, is through consciousness, and in its analysis we find a subject as much an element of its existence as an object, or, to use Professor James's expression, the "I" is as real as the "me." Hume affirmed the contrary, and said: "For my part, when I enter most intimately into what I call myself I always stumble on some particular perception or theory of heat or cold, light or shade, love or hate, pain or pleasure. I never catch myself at any time without a perception, and can never observe anything but a perception." With this idea President Jordan and all who represent the "sum" idea of mind must agree. But let us look at Hume's statement somewhat carefully and see if he does not affirm what he denies. What does he mean when he says "I," and "catch myself," and "for my part," and "I stumble," and "I call"? When he declares, "I never catch myself without a perception," his words clearly imply that he catches himself *in* a perception; for he tells us plainly he observes the perception, and how can an observation be made unless there be some one to do the observing? If we can affirm we never find ourselves without a perception, we may also say a perception never exists without our finding it. The fact is, self-consciousness is a factor in all consciousness, and the principal thing we have to explain is not a thought or a feeling, but the fact that *I* think and *I* feel. Whoever takes the ego out of consciousness destroys it; for it exists only in the antithesis of subject and object. When we study any facts we study them not as abstracts, but as the self knows them. Thoughts, feelings, and desires are not mere successive effects but experiences; and an experience is only a word we use to express a state of self. An experience is not something which occurs *in vacuo*, but only in the existing self, or, in other words, there is no

experience of anything unless there is some one to experience it. The materialist's theory of mind cannot be accepted, for it denies the ego, the element of self-consciousness, in consciousness, which is a part of all our mental states and experiences. It does not give us a subject to detect the meaning and realize the value of the symbols which constitute the series of mental states.

2. We think it can be clearly shown that the two words the materialist most frequently uses to describe our mental life, namely, "series" and "sum of mental states," both imply the reality of the self. I have previously shown that the term "sum" is a mental word and its only reality is to mind. The same is true of all synonymous words used in like connection, as "collective," "aggregate," "colonial," all meaning the total mass of mental states. There is no such thing as a sum, or collection, or aggregate, except to a mind that gathers the factors in a single conception and classifies them into groups by class words. One may put elements together, but they always remain elements and the wholes are of the mind. Indeed, the word "sum" could never have come into existence if there were not an ego to do the summing. And so when we speak of a series of mental states; for the very idea of a series requires the reality of an abiding subject. A series indicates a quantity of flowing or passing states; but how can the idea of the passing be known except there be a subject that abides and realizes the successive character of its states? If there be a stream of consciousness it is only because there is a factor which does not float away with the stream. Such ideas as change and succession can only come as contrary conceptions to identity; and identity can only be thought by that which abides. Hence when Hume says, "The mind is a kind of theater, where several perceptions successively make their appearance, pose, repass, glide away, and mingle in an infinite variety of posture and situation," we ask, Who sees the show? Each successive perception passes and is over as it passes; how can it know anything of what has gone before or comes after? To perceive the progressive unfolding of the play Hume talks about we contend there must be some spectator who occupies the seats and sees the play go through. We conclude, then, to have a series or succession of states of consciousness that we

must be a self who abides and is conscious of the states so. as to know that they constitute a flow.

3. We maintain that we arrive at the idea of mind in the same way that we arrive at the idea of matter, and have, therefore, as much reason to believe in the reality of the one as of the other. What we have with which to begin our thinking is experience. We do not have things as thoughts except as states of consciousness. Now, when we analyze a state of consciousness we find some factors which are permanent and others which are transitory. Thus in the perception of a thing we have a complex, consisting of extension, color, form, resistance, and other qualities. Of these qualities extension and resistance are permanent, and found in every perception of a thing, but other qualities, such as shape and color, vary indefinitely. We therefore abstract the permanent qualities from the percept and regard them as essential, and as revealing nature. Hence we say that matter and force are realities, manifesting the basal qualities or essence of things. We thus come to think that there is a physical substance which grounds all forms and qualities, and settle down to believe in the objective reality of the physical and go on to reason learnedly about matter. But this matter, let us note, is but an abstraction from our experience of certain permanent factors in our perceptions. Now, when we come to consider mind we find an analogous process and experience. A state of consciousness is a complex in which there are some factors which are permanent and others which are transient. Thus we have ever present the distinction between subject and object, or, to use James's phrase again, the "I" and the "me." The "I" is permanent. There is no state of consciousness without it, for consciousness is the realizing of something. But the factors of the object, the "me," are various and innumerable. They change with every new state of consciousness. Now, as in the conception of a physical thing we abstract extension and resistance as permanent qualities which reveal the essential nature of physical reality, so we abstract the constant factors in a psychosis and think of the abiding and permanent "I" as the psychic reality. As this abides and the thoughts and feelings come and go, we say the "I" has these thoughts and feelings, just

20

as we say matter has shape and color. And as we cannot think of color as being alone, as not being the color of a substance, so we cannot think of a thought or a feeling as existing by itself, but only as the thought or feeling of a self whose states they are. To those who say we have no consciousness of a self apart from the complex involved in every state of consciousness, we reply that, even if we admit this, we likewise have no idea of extension and force apart from a complex in which there are a variety of factors. In both cases the reality is obtained by abstracting the abiding and permanent elements in a state of experience. We have therefore exactly the same ground for believing in the reality of the ego as that which grounds thought and feeling as we have to believe in the reality of a matter which grounds extension and force. But as a matter of fact we have more reasons to believe in the reality of the ego than in the reality of matter, for the "I," the knower, is necessarily and immediately experienced, while the "me," the known, is always a thought known and not a thing known, and the reality is by hypothesis—namely, the hypothesis that there is an objective reality corresponding to the percept which we have in consciousness. The thing, therefore, matter, has not so direct evidence in its support as the "I," the psychical reality.

4. Materialism in none of its forms can give an adequate account of the constructive and synthetic powers of the mind. The ancient definition of man was that he is a thinking animal, and Pascal has told us that it is his thinking which constitutes his greatness; but on the theory that the mind is only the sum of our conscious states, these states themselves being but symbols of molecular processes, there can be no thought, no reasoning, no rational life. To think there must be not only a series of states of consciousness, but "a consciousness of states." There must be a subject that recognizes the things which come up in consciousness as the same or as different from those that have been experienced before. There must be a synthetic mind which can compare states of consciousness, distinguish between them, and unite them into wholes. There is no way that a successive series can hold together the factors of experience, can so grasp them in the unity of a single act as to compare them and form judgments, or elaborate them

into reasons and conclusions. Nor could there be any forming of ideals, or acting to accomplish ends. But nothing is more constant and certain in experience than what I may call teleological activities. We are ever engaged in the work of developing plans and forming hypotheses, applying rules and formulas, and carrying out ends to their conclusion. The entire history of our mental processes is, therefore, a contradiction to the "sum" theory of mind.

5. The bearing of the theory on the problem of knowledge deserves extended discussion, but can only receive mention. Since the mental series is only the shadow cast by the physical series, since thoughts, feelings, and volitions are only symbols of brain states, all mental movements are absolutely determined by brain activities and conditions. When a conclusion has been reached we have simply the shadow cast by a certain combination of molecular activities. This being the case, we reduce truth to results, direct or indirect, of nervous action, or in other words we cancel truth; for truth means that we compare ideas with some standard that experience has given us and pronounce judgment. Conclusions are not justified by reasons, but "coerced by psychological antecedents." As Professor B. P. Bowne says in his *Philosophy of Theism:*

> Nothing, then, depends on reason, but only on the physical and mental states; and these, for all we know, might become anything whatever with the result of changing the conclusion to anything whatever. But this is the extreme of skepticism. Beliefs sink into effects; and one is as good as another while it lasts. The coming or going of a belief does not depend on its rationality, but only on the relative strength of its corresponding antecedents. But this strength is a fact and not a truth. . . . On the plane of cause and effect truth and error are meaningless distinctions.

Nor is there any way to prove on the theory that our thoughts of things correspond to reality. To say that thought is the inner face of the physical process, and must therefore correctly symbolize it, would be a way out if we could hold the position; but no one would care to say that when we see a house or tree the molecular activities in the brain are in the form of a house or tree. In fact, in no case do we see in the symbol the massing of molecules or the brain movements which are supposed to occasion them. What is re-

ported is things and activities that are going on outside and not inside the cranium. Now, then, if thought is the symbol of certain brain movements, or a phenomenon which attends such movements, do we know that there is in reality anything corresponding to what the senses report to us? To believe this we must hold to a parallelism between the symbols and external things that the theory in no way explains or accounts for; or, as another has expressed it, on purely arbitrary grounds we must "affirm an opaque harmony between matter and thought."

Without going into the practical consequences which would follow the theory under discussion, or bringing forward additional criticisms, it seems plain that we cannot follow the "mind stuff" theorists in affirming, in the words of President Starr Jordan, that the mind "is the sum total of all psychic changes," that "all consciousness is colonial consciousness," and that "the study of mind in animals and men gives no support to the mediæval idea of the mind as an entity apart from the organ through which it operates." It would seem, if thought is but the symbol of molecular movements, that there is but little value in Mr. Stanford having given millions of dollars to found a university and place President Jordan at the head of it; but then we remember that this may have been due to the peculiar working of the molecules of Mr. Stanford's brain, and that Mr. Stanford, the ego, did not really exist and have any part in it. It was not, therefore, a result of rational purpose, but a psychological occurrence, due to a certain state of Mr. Stanford's brain molecules. It is needless to add that some of us who have charge of educational institutions would like to see the molecules in the brains of other rich men chance to make similar combinations.

Samuel Plantz

Art. V.—THE PASSING OF A GENERATION.

For a year or two past it has been known that in the city of Brighton, on the southern coast of England, a sight was to be witnessed of pathetic interest to the literary world. There from day to day an aged man, long past his prime but with his faculties intact, would sit musing in his chair, brooding the time away. Seaward his gaze would always wander, the calm blue eyes fixed on the channel waves, as though to typify the steady scrutiny with which for nearly two generations he had sought to penetrate the mysteries of the world about him. A lonely old man he was, with none of kith and kin to cheer him by their sympathy as the shadows lengthened on life's dial, and strength slowly ebbed away, like the tide receding across the sands before his feet. Lonely too he was, and always had been, because of a certain aloofness of circumstance and character which raised a barrier between him and the world in which he lived. For though Herbert Spencer had done much to lead his age, as to control its thinking, he had never gained a warmth of personal affection commensurate with his intellectual renown.

Spencer, moreover, had outlived his chief associates, the mental giants of his time. Darwin, who called him "our philosopher," had died in 1882, after a life of richest mental fruitage. Tyndall had died in 1893. In 1895 Huxley, the most brilliant of the group, perhaps, if not the greatest, had also passed, doubting to the end—yet also hoping, as the pathetic verses show which he had chosen to be inscribed on the stone beneath which his ashes lie. Of the Metaphysical Society, founded in 1869 by Tennyson and others for the discussion of the burning questions of the day, Spencer was not a member, though often subjects suggested by his writings formed the topics for debate. At the first meeting of the society Tennyson's "Higher Pantheism" was read by the secretary, in the author's absence, and Mr. R. H. Hutton gave a paper on Spencer's evolutionary theory of conscience. Now of that brilliant galaxy of thinkers—poets, artists, men of letters, rulers, as well as men of science, philosophers, theologians—but a

scanty few remain. Mr. Balfour, the latest of all to be elected to the society, mingles literature and statecraft still, following the greater Gladstone, who, as Mr. Morley, another member of the society, tells us, once closed a letter on public business with the statement that he must hasten to a discussion with Huxley concerning the immortality of the soul. But James Martineau, who steadfastly maintained the cause of positive truth against the negative giants, has gone to his rest. Frederick Denison Maurice was early taken home. Tennyson is gone. Ruskin is gone. Dean Stanley, at whose home the first meeting was held, and Manning, who with others of his later faith, defended spiritual things from the standpoint of the Church of Rome, and Henry Sidgwick, than whom there has been no sweeter spirit among the thinkers of our age—all passed from mortal ken. With truth was it remarked in the London *Spectator,* when Mr. Spencer followed in December of the closing year, that in him "almost the last of the great figures of the Victorian age had departed." His well-grounded and enduring reputation lasts still, and may be expected to continue while men lay stress upon the thought expressed in our mother-tongue. But the zenith of his renown was passed before he left us, so far as contemporary thought is to be considered and the higher measure of control which his system had exercised over the mind of his own age. Some consciousness of this fact, it is reported, clouded, even embittered, the latter days of him who in so many respects had exemplified the qualities of the sage. One would like to believe otherwise as one thinks of that lonely shrunken figure seated in his chair in the Brighton sunshine, or gazing channel-ward under the soft gray skies of an English winter, waiting for the end to come. But inflexible as he was in his devotion to that which to him seemed truth, unbending, almost fanatical, in his refusal to compromise concerning naked fact or law as he discerned them, Spencer would have been the last to ask that aught but the fullest truth should be told; and so the critic has to record that, though Mr. Spencer's philosophy remains one of the great monuments of the thinking of our time, his influence, alike in its extent and in its intensity, had considerably diminished before his own departure.

In general the fame of the Spencerian thinking and its successes were always of a remarkable kind. Its acceptance has been
much greater in the United States than in Great Britain, the home
of its author, while on the continent of Europe it has been for the
most part less known and less influential than an English-speaking
critic would consider deserved. Everywhere it has gained relatively little favor with philosophers by profession—a singular fate
for the foremost philosophical venture of the time. Discussed it,
philosophical students have always, from the appearance of its
earliest parts, now more than forty years ago, to the final revision
of the *First Principles* by their aged framer in April, 1900. It
has been discussed by philosophers and debated by them. Parts
of it they have even accepted, as in much larger measure it has
made its way into the general spirit of the age, but among those
whose lifework it is to ponder the ultimate problems of thought
you will find but few who can be counted members of the Spencerian school. With men of general education the case is different.
Physicians, lawyers, men of letters or of business, with a taste for
speculation or inclined thereto by the perplexities of the age—
many such have found in Mr. Spencer's work a type of thinking
which has satisfied at once their intellectual and—strange as it
will seem to most readers of this *Review*—their spiritual need.
How fully the Synthetic Philosophy has appealed to men of
science the writer finds himself at a loss to decide. Concerning his
work in special fields it is almost trite to say that each expert in
turn admires it in the department of investigation with which he
himself is not best acquainted. But whether its use of scientific
material, its claims to exemplify scientific methods, its accentuation of scientific conclusions, notably the theory of evolution, and
its self-styled reconciliation of religion and science—whether these
features may not have proved attractive to scientific thinkers it is
difficult to say. If I were compelled to give an estimate, I should
be inclined to conclude that the case with men of scientific leanings
has been much the same as with thinkers at large: the suffrages of
the deepest minds have not often been gained by Mr. Spencer; men
of lesser caliber, especially such as with comparatively imperfect
preparation have been impelled to face the problems of our day,

have in greater numbers become disciples of his doctrine. The word "doctrine" in application to the Spencerian thinking is deliberately chosen; "dogma" might even be substituted for the broader term without any violation of accurate statement. In fact, the dogmatic tendency was characteristic of the man as well as of his system. In a recent communication to the London *Times*, reprinted in the New York *Tribune* of January 12, 1904, Mr. G. W. Smalley gives an excellent illustration of the trait. Mr. Spencer, to his lasting credit, was one of that small number of distinguished Englishmen who during our own civil war steadfastly sympathized with the cause of freedom. Unlike Gladstone, even, he had never to express regret, as Gladstone so nobly did, for errors of opinion or of speech which in the dark days of 1860-65 helped to turn the minds of our English kinsmen against the North. But Spencer, though he saw clearly in the matter of the larger issue, labored under the delusion that his view was shared by the mass of his people, and, more, he burned to prove it. His private secretary—one cannot refuse *him* sympathy—was sent to the British Museum to gather data to support the thesis that "England had, at the outset, shown more sympathy for the Northern States than she had ever shown to any other people—had exhibited a unanimity of feeling unparalleled in respect of any political matter, domestic or foreign." The argument in proof was at length prepared, but for the time suppressed, on the advice of Mr. Spencer's American friend and follower, Professor Youmans. Much later Mr. Smalley obtained it and secured its publication in the *Tribune*, of which he was then the foreign correspondent. The result is best described in the philosopher's own words: "There was an accompanying leading article referring in a slighting way to the evidence it contained, and, as I gathered, though some small effect was produced, it was but small. Demonstration fails to change established beliefs."

His own established beliefs at least were proof against variation. In great things as in small he always had his opinions, and to them he stoutly adhered. In the preface to the definitive edition of his *First Principles*, written, as has been said, in April, 1900, nearly four years before his death, and introducing the last important work which he accomplished, there are passages which

give well-nigh formal expression to this element in his intellectual character. "In ten days more forty years will have passed since the first lines of this work were written," he begins. Then, after noting the revisions of 1867 and 1875:

Since then there have been introduced no alterations worth mention-ing. Of course the advances of knowledge in many directions during intervening years, have made needful sundry corrections in the illustra-tive passages. Criticisms, too, have prompted a few modifications of statement. Add to this that further developments of my own thoughts have suggested certain improvements in the exposition. . . . Meanwhile neither the objections made by others nor further considerations of my own, have caused me to recede from the general principles set forth. Con-trariwise, while writing the succeeding works on Biology, Psychology, Sociology, and Ethics, the multiplied illustrations of these principles furnished by the facts dealt with, and the guidance afforded by them in seeking interpretations, have tended continually to strengthen the belief that they rightly formulate the facts.

And the man who wrote these words at eighty years of age was a man conspicuous for candor though deficient in some of the gentler qualities which adorn, when they accompany, the unswerving love of truth. And think of the years which Spencer's life had spanned, or more pertinently of the years elapsed and the changes in them wrought since the publication of the prospectus of the system in March, 1860: changes in science, from Darwinism to the germ theory of disease; in philosophy, from the mid-century materialism in Germany to the neo-Idealism of the latest English schools; in theology, from debates about Colenso to assertions, roundly made, that the higher criticism is the bulwark of Christian faith; in politics, from the Italian campaign of Napoleon III to the assaults of the French republic on the Church, and the war between Boer and Briton for supremacy in South Africa; in ethics, from the argument that slavery is divinely sanctioned to the longing of civilized man for brotherhood and universal peace. And yet, after four decades of such development, the creator of a system which professedly is based upon facts—of a system, moreover, which was planned and announced when nearly every one of these movements was still to come—could calmly finish his work, "Neither the objections made by others nor further considerations of my own have caused me to recede from the principles set forth."

In order to the production of such a result other qualities were necessary, and higher, than mere dogmatic bias. Foremost among these should be named a noble tenacity of purpose: forty years of ill-rewarded labor—for Mr. Spencer at first drew largely on his rather scanty means to defray the cost of publishing his system; forty years of steady intellectual effort on the part of a man of feeble constitution, and often irritably suffering—for Spencer, like Darwin, was hampered by his lack of health in the execution of his lifelong task. It is said that we live in a money-seeking age, that the things of the mind are now neglected in the rush of the market and the store. Here at least is an exception to the asserted rule. Mr. Spencer's thinking may be true or false, or both at once in parts—it may shortly perish, or it may contribute elements of value to the ultimate theory of the world. But in his devotion to noble aims, persistently pursued in face of difficulty through a long period of years, he is surely worthy to be ranked with the greatest thinkers of all time. A second quality contributory to the fulfillment of Mr. Spencer's great enterprise was a marvelous breadth of view. Four full years before Darwin published the *Origin of Species* (November, 1859) Spencer had interpreted mental phenomena from the evolution point of view in the first edition of his *Principles of Psychology.* Two years later, but still prior to Darwin's announcement of his discovery to the Linnæan Society, he had printed in essay form the views which he embodied in certain of the most important chapters of his own *First Principles.* Within six months after Darwin's masterpiece appeared he distributed the program of his entire system. Thus, just after the mid-century was passed, and with little aid or none from the great biological discovery which marked its culmination, he had thought out in outline an evolutionary theory of things—beginning with the star-dust from which our worlds are formed and ending with the highest manifestations of mind and social life. And this tremendous plan he continued to work at until he reached his goal as the century was passing over into the age which was to come. Such an example of intellectual foresight, of anticipation of work remaining to be done, or organizing genius, it would be hard to parallel in the history of the world.

This said, however, it is needful to consider less pleasing questions; to ask whether in an appreciable degree this marvelous achievement was facilitated by the limitations of its author as well as by his transcendent gifts. Universal knowledge is at this stage of the world's history a more than doubtful thing. Leibnitz knew all that the seventeenth century had to show, or nearly all; for Alexander von Humboldt, three generations ago, something similar might also plausibly be claimed; but has there been any other thinker since the author of the *Kosmos* died of whom the same estimate could accurately be made? Perhaps the issue had better be left in an interrogative form: Was Spencer's systematic activity furthered, or was it hindered, by that impossibility of knowing all things created by the progress of knowledge itself? Would he so tenaciously have carried his theory through to the end, had he been fully aware of the difficulties to be encountered in the special departments of thought, with all of which no finite mind can now possibly be acquainted? Certain other doubtful points are more easily determined. It has been sometimes hinted, or even gravely argued, that Spencer's philosophy is false because in early years he lacked the advantage of a university education. But the criticism is hardly of moment; although it might be an interesting speculation to inquire whether the sweep of his thinking would have been more narrowed or directed, had his early flights been confined within the limits of a university environment. That our scientific philosopher, however, was lacking in imagination and in humor, that his mentality was marked by a certain pedantic rigidity, can scarcely be denied. Now, such tendencies of character cut deeper than the surface view of things. There is fair ground in them for surmising that Spencer's lack of imaginative insight seriously influenced the nature of his intellectual conclusions. This is especially true of his agnostic views. For the present purpose these need be stated only in briefest outline: That knowledge—interpreted, a student of philosophy would want to add, in the crude empirical fashion—that knowledge yields man acquaintance merely with finite facts and laws, yet that in some indefinite, and quite indefinable, way man has a notion of an infinite Being on which the world depends; that the existence of

this Infinite is the common postulate of science and religion when they are rightly understood, and that it so may be made the basis for their peaceful reconciliation; that the reality of the finite itself. *eo ipso* is the phrase the author uses, implies the reality of the Infinite, but that beyond its bare reality nothing further can be known; that, nevertheless, it may be spoken of as Cause, and Force, as the Unknowable Force, as the Incomprehensible Power, as the Eternal Cause, which forms the ground of the relative world. Such is Mr. Spencer's agnostic doctrine—and such doctrine, as it has been often shown, stands in a position of unstable equilibrium. For to say that the Absolute is unknowable, and to say that an Absolute surely exists, that it is one, that it is a Power, that it stands under and back of the finite forces which constitute the phenomenal world—these, as most men judge, are opposing and contradictory principles; or, to be exact, most men judge so who are not agnostics, who are unwilling to confess that they know absolutely nothing at all.

But an objection may here be suggested, based on the relation of Mr. Spencer to his age. Does not, it may be pertinently asked, this unstable theory fairly represent the position of many earnest thinkers of recent years? Unquestionably the answer must be given in the affirmative; as it must be also said that for many Mr. Spencer's doctrine has helped to save some remnant of religious faith and comfort amid the stress and struggle of our perplexing time. Nay, more; this belief in an Infinite Ground of all things, though in truth it falls far short of complete theism, may furnish a world view of real religious value. At this point the mind of the student of philosophy inevitably turns to the vision of another lonely thinker, who lived and wrought in an earlier century of the modern era. Not a Briton now, but an Iberian Jew, his family driven by persecution from Portugal or Spain to settle in Holland, then the home of toleration. This man works at his trade as a grinder of optical glasses to secure a meager living. When freed from labor he thinks out his system, which so shocks his world that his own people read him out of the synagogue with the major excommunication. But still he pursues his way undaunted, yielding to no temptation. He loves truth so

supremely that he will not accept a university chair, even with a guarantee of freedom, lest in some way he should be diverted from pure devotion to truth's service. And Spinoza too is filled with a sense of the majesty of the oneness of creation, as his thinking and his living together culminate in what he calls the *amor Dei intellec-(aalis,* "the intellectual love of God." But there are two notable differences between the Spinozistic and the Spencerian views. The first is logical and has already been suggested. Spinoza argues pantheism on the basis of positive intelligence, maintaining that reason shows his own system the only possible solution of the world. Spencer argues a sort of pantheism from an impotency of reason, and thinks he can defend it by a negation of thought. The second difference concerns the content and value of the doctrine considered as a religious force. Many historians have discovered in Spinoza a mystical element which, if you will, raises the man above the limitations of his creed. In Spencer's doctrine there is an absence of passion; there is little glow and ardor, little burning flame of devotion to the Supreme. Passion of other kinds, indeed, Spencer sometimes shows. His ethical feeling, for instance, is broad and deep, pervading in a noble way very much that he wrote. But religious sentiment, at least in the form of great currents of exalted feeling, is mostly lacking—just as we have discovered a certain lack of imagination and ideal thinking in his mind at large. And this deprives his religious conclusions, even when they are constructive, of their full worth. Specifically, it explains in part his failure to advance from his doctrine of the Absolute to belief in a living God. Never was this defect more cruelly brought out than in the debate between Spencer and Frederic Harrison, on the nature of religion, in the *Nineteenth Century Review* and the *Popular Science Monthly.* Cruelly, even grotesquely, ran the controversy, so that, while faith might profit by the general ruin of the arguments on either side, it is always with a certain sense of shame that one draws lessons from the conflict. Mr. Spencer mocks Mr. Harrison as he defends the religion of humanity. Mr. Harrison represents Mr. Spencer's followers as making supplication to an unmeaning symbol:

And in the hour of pain, or danger, or death, can anyone think of the Unknowable, or find consolation therein? . . . Schools, academies, temples of the Unknowable, there cannot be. But where two or three are gathered together to worship the Unknowable, there the algebraic formula may suffice to give form to their emotions; they may be heard to profess their unwearying belief in (x^n), even if no weak brother with ritualistic tendencies be heard to cry, "O x^n, love us, help us, make us one with thee!"

But, after all, Mr. Spencer's agnosticism was merely the preamble to his system; an introduction, moreover, as he came himself to recognize, which is relatively unimportant for the remainder of his work. The substantive and enduring significance of the Synthetic Philosophy, the contribution to thought which is most likely to give its author permanent renown, are rather to be found in his evolutionary theory. The Spencerian evolution represents a distinct and characteristic type. It is not the biological evolution of Mr. Darwin, which explains the genesis of species by reference to organic law. Nor is it the evolution of the pure metaphysician, as for instance, Hegel, which interprets the world-process in terms of absolute symbols. It is more inclusive than the first, since it starts, or professes to, from primitive chaos, and ends with the most complex forms of moral life. But it neither delves so deep nor flies so high as the second, for it confines itself, again at least professedly, to that which may be directly and positively known. More positively and technically stated, it is cosmical evolution of a phenomenalistic type. The principal defect of this evolutionary theory is its materialistic stamp. The law of evolution* is framed in terms of mechanism only; the world to be explained includes mind, and purposive activity, and the varied forms of man's social and ethical life. It is for this reason, as well as because of its vagueness, that the fundamental formula proves inadequate for the purpose for which it was intended, and progressively retreats into the background as Mr. Spencer proceeds from the simpler to the more complex portions of his task. For inorganic science, though with gaps and breaks

---

* "The law of the continuous redistribution of matter and motion." Fully stated: 'Evolution is an integration of matter and concomitant dissipation of motion; during which the matter passes from a relatively indefinite, incoherent homogeneity to a relatively definite, coherent heterogeneity; and during which the retained motion undergoes a parallel change.' —*First Principles*, 6th ed., §§ 92, 145.

of grave extent, he makes shift to make it do. At least he so
entangles the untechnical reader that it seems to hold. In his
biology it is not so prominent. In psychology it begins to break
down definitely, holding directly of the evolving brain alone and
but indirectly of the mind. In sociology it becomes still more
figurative, while in the *Principles of Ethics* it has often to be
looked for, tucked away in preambles or dragged into concluding
statements, before or after the real work of the discussion is
accomplished.

It is true, of course, that Mr. Spencer rejected any
materialistic interpretation of his positions. In reply to the charge
of materialism his argument always ran that he was an agnostic,
not a dogmatist of either school. Not professing to know what
the universe might be in its ultimate analysis, *a fortiori* he could
not be held responsible for any given view of the world which men
might juggle into his system or extract from it. And undoubtedly
his contention has its force. Full and avowed materialism the
Spencerian philosophy is not, nor materialism in its crass and
cruder forms. There is even distinction drawn at times between
mind and brain, or consciousness and motion; and some have even
thought to find in certain passages from his later writings a
tendency more hospitable to the hypothesis that the world-ground
is a Conscious Being. But when all this has been said it remains
true that, although it is not out-and-out materialism, the Synthetic
Philosophy is at least materialistic. A system which starts from
the intention to explain the whole phenomenal universe on the
basis of matter and motion, which includes in its fundamental
formula naught but mechanical change, for which in strictness
there are no distinctions but those of less and greater integration,
definiteness, and coherence of movements or positions in space,
which conceives the Absolute as Force, and force after the analogy
of the activities which the physical sciences reveal—such a system
may file an agnostic caveat at its beginning or reassert one at its
close. But its whole momentum, its influence, its world-view, are
of a materialistic kind. In the enforcement of the general idea
and principle of evolution, on the contrary, Mr. Spencer's efforts
met with great success. Three men in particular, in the century

just ended, have done most to give to later thinking its evolutionary cast: Hegel, Darwin, Spencer. In the first the German tradition culminated. Arguing from idealistic premises, Hegel so wrought the genetic view of things into the thought of the nineteenth century that it is safe to say that, had neither Darwin nor Spencer been born, the world in this age would have been considered from a developmental standpoint. Twenty-eight years after Hegel's death Darwin's *Origin of Species* burst upon the notice of a startled world. The legitimation of a very ancient hypothesis, transformed by the genius of a master, Darwin's work succeeded because it was a product of the rarest union of the observational and the rational faculties of mind. Spencer is often praised as a great reasoner. But the commendation were better bestowed upon the patient, when need was, silent, observer of nature who carefully worked out his principles until they were so firmly grounded that they were fitted to withstand the folly of adherents and the attacks of bitterest foes. Above, some of the data have been given which show that the idea of universal development was maturing in Spencer's thought, or even inchoately promulgated, before he was at all acquainted with Darwin's views. But there need be no controversy concerning the question of independence or the extent of influence. Each man had his tremendous work to do. As the one established a first principle of biology which in its expansion developed into a masterful theory of the world, the second, joining speculation and the principles of general science, sweeping also the results of psychology and sociology into one comprehensive survey, successfully labored to impress the doctrine upon the later modern mind.

A. C. Armstrong.

Ar. VI.—THE LEVEL OF PROPHETISM IN BABYLONIA AND IN PALESTINE.

The historical books of ancient Israel have not claimed that the ancestors or the descendants of Abraham and Jacob had continuously, and as an entire people, had the same religion. The ancient Hebrew historians have, on the contrary, candidly admitted that the ancestors of Abraham had at one time served other gods (Josh. xxiv, 2), and they are equally explicit in mentioning the fact that ofttimes larger or smaller companies of people in Israel had either worshiped other gods or had violated the spirituality of God by worshiping images, etc. Such conduct of the Old Testament historians must be emphasized, because it belongs to the many characteristics of the Old Testament historical writings not customarily made prominent in our day, but recently collected by me in the small work, *Glaubwuerdigkeitsspuren des Alten Testaments* (published by Edward Runge, Gross-Lichterfelde-Berlin, N. O. 75).

Nor have the historical books of Israel been especially silent concerning the fact that many forms of divination were harbored among the people; for example, the practice of *'ōnēn* (or *ghōnēn*) is lamented, which verb may have designated the observance of certain formations of clouds, or this *'ōnēn,* as Hubert Grimme has recently surmised,[*] may have been a kind of *"oshinn* magic" (*csinn* a pretended demon). Again, we find the practice of *nichchash* mentioned, which reminds one of the Assyrio-Babylonian *luchchushu,* "whisper of charms."[†] We also hear the complaint: "My people ask counsel at their stocks, and their staff declareth unto them" (Hos. iv, 12). Here, then, rhabdomancy is spoken of, which is mentioned by Herodotus (iv, 67) and Tacitus (*Germania.* chap. 10) as a custom of the Scythians and ancient Germans. And Isaiah laments that a portion of his people takes part in the divinations of the East and the West (ii, 5, f.). Thus we might continue to unfold the picture drawn by the historians of Israel

---

[*] Hubert Grimme, *Unbewiesenes im Babel-Bibel-Streit* (1903), p. 79.
[†] Muss-Arnoldt, in *The American Journal of Semitic Languages* (1900), p. 221.

27

of the relation of many among their people to divination. These few strokes will suffice, however, to reveal the character of this painting. All we ask further is that the reader observe closely the inscription flashing on the border of the picture: "There is no divination in Israel" (Num. xxiii, 23); that is, in that part of Israel that was faithful to God. This part of the people of Israel was conscious of possessing the prophesyings of speakers or prophets of the Eternal (= Jahwe). Hence the historic sources of Israel very clearly place prophecy (*nebûa*) over against divination (*kèsem*); indeed they distinguish various grades and tendencies even among the representatives of prophecy. In the first place, they speak of members of associations of prophets, prominent especially in the day of Samuel, of Elijah, and of Elisha; but alongside these mention is chiefly made of those prophets who claimed to speak by authority of the Eternal but who represented the tendencies of kings and parties who had erred from the legitimate religion of Israel. One need only bear in mind the unique scene that transpired before King Ahab when he purposed opening a campaign against the Syrians. A whole host of prophets vouchsafed victory, but there was one man who would not make common cause with these. It was Micah, the son of Jemla, who chose imprisonment rather than to deny his prophetic certainty of the unsuccessful issue of such a campaign (1 Kings xxii, 6, ff.). This prophet Micah in the ninth century was a shining contemporary of Elijah. Their successors were, for example, Isaiah, who mentions prophets five times (iii, 2, ff.), whom the people called "their prophets and prudent," and Jeremiah, who had that remarkable contention with Hananiah at the gate of the temple (xxviii, 1, ff.). But to gain a conception of the height of consciousness attained by Isaiah we must consider the words: "Woe unto them that call evil good, and good evil; that put darkness for light, and light for darkness; that put bitter for sweet, and sweet for bitter! Woe unto them that are wise in their own eyes, and prudent in their own sight" (v, 20, ff.). Behold how this man discerned all sophistical perversion of ideas and illusionary fancies, and how he dared to brand them, and then judge whether he can be accused of just these errors!

What, now, was Babylonia's and Assyria's position toward divination and prophecy? The answer to this question must naturally be gained primarily from the most recent and most copious source that has been found concerning the culture of the countries of the Euphrates and the Tigris and their relation to the spiritual conditions of Israel. This chief source at present is the new edition of the work *Die Keilinschriften und das Alte Testament* (1903), the first 342 pages of which are by Hugo Winckler (Berlin), and pages 343 to 653 by Zimmern (Leipzig).

What a detailed portrayal we have here of the relations of the Babylonians and Assyrians to divination! Here we are informed that "Shamash (the sun) was considered the god of the priests of the oracle, or the diviners, who trace their science back to him and look upon him as their guardian patron" (p. 368). "The rôle of Rammân, as the god of the oracle, is unique, and not yet clearly understood as to its origin" (p. 449). But is this rôle of the "weather-god" Rammân not entirely conceivable, since Assyrio-Babylonian divination takes its signs chiefly from the outlines of the clouds and their resemblance to animals or ships, and from the direction in which the clouds move, as has been shown principally by Carl Bezold in his work *Nineve und Babylon?* (1903.) *Keilinschriften und das Alte Testament* informs us further that diviners traced their origin to Enmeduranki, a king of Sippar, the favorite of Anu and other gods. For, as it is recorded in cuneiform writings (p. 533, f.), "these gods called him to commune with them. . . . To view oil on water, the mystery of Anu, the tablet of the gods, the omen tablet(?), the cedar staff, they committed unto him." The latter was likely a cylindrical implement of cedar by means of which the questions addressed to the oracle were spoken into the ear of the sacrificial animal, from the liver of which the answer was divined. Viewing livers is also ascribed to the Babylonian king in Ezek. xxi, 21. Moreover, "the sources from which the divining priest gained his information concerning future things were quite varied." The following are prominent: divination from the course of the stars, from the configurations and coloring of the clouds, from the entrails of sacrificial animals, especially from the livers of

sacrificial sheep, and hydromancy. It was also quite natural that divination from the flight of birds and interpretation of dreams were extensively practiced in Babylonia, and that prophecies were based upon all kinds of other phenomena of nature, especially upon unnatural phenomena such as monstrosities, etc. (p. 605). What an interesting result! In general the relation of the Babylonians and Assyrians to divination was the same as that of the common superstitions of Israel to divination, excepting that, for example, there is no mention made in ancient Hebrew literature of tracing a "guild of diviners" back to a personality of antiquity like King Enmeduranki, mentioned above. The great difference, however, is this: in Babylonia and Assyria divination, with all its means and organs, was not only tolerated but it was an official institution. Likewise in Egypt the horoscopers were a special class of the higher priesthood,* and were known in processions by the palm leaf, the symbol of time, which they carried. Among the Hellenes, who in many respects ranked high, even Plato declared the stars to be gods (*Timaios,* 38 E), and Aristotle bowed his head in the presence of the stars as in the presence of animated beings (*Ueber den Himmel,* ii, 12). But the representatives of the legitimate religion of Israel were above interrogating the stars, to say nothing of worshiping them. Ancient Hebrew Scriptures repeatedly praise the God "that maketh the seven stars and Orion" (Amos v, 8), the cult of the stars is expressly opposed (verse 26), worship of the sun, the moon, and the twelve signs is prohibited (2 Kings xxiii, 5, ff.). The prophet cried: "Lift up your eyes on high, and behold who hath created these things" (Isa. xl, 26), and the poet causes Job to ask: "Did I behold the sun when it shined?" (xxxi, 26, f.). Indeed the same heaven shone above Babylonia and Palestine, but in the former man looked only to heaven in order to search out in its external mutations the decrees of the gods, and in the latter man looked beyond the heavens into "the heaven of heavens" (1 Kings viii, 27), that is, into yonder innermost sphere of the universe, where in the flight of phenomena God is the fixed pole and the innermost fountain of all life (Psa. civ, 29, f.). Hence

* Georg Ebers, *Egypten und die Buecher Mosis,* p. 343.

Babylonia and Nineveh possessed an abundance of striking parallels to divination as it appears and is prohibited in the Old Testament. But did they also have the prophecy the proclamations of which are preserved in the Old Testament?

Who that hears this question does not at once think of Hammurabi, the old king of Babylonia so much spoken of in our day? It is widely known that in regard to the religious hegemony of Old Testament literature Delitzsch, in his second lecture on *Babel und Bibel,* has called attention to this ancient Babylonian king, since he too has claimed to have received his laws from the sun-god. But by the words used to introduce the inscription of his laws Hammurabi simply places himself in the line of rulers. It is natural that the position of a ruler would be looked upon as a gift of divine guidance of history, although in historic events human freedom also constitutes a factor. Hence it easily came to pass that even more important acts of government were traced back to an incitement on the part of a deity, or the manifestations of God may even be thought of as mediated by the viewing of sacrificial animals or other omens, as is possibly the case of the Moabite king Mesa in his inscription (pp. 14, 32). Moreover, in the plastic representation which shows him above his inscription standing before the sun-god, Hammurabi, according to the most probable interpretation, is supposed to be the companion of the sun.* For in the lines written beneath the representation it is said: "Anu [the god of the upper world] and Bel have called by name me, Hammurabi, the high prince, who fears God, in order that I, like Shamash [the sun-god] should rise above the black-headed, and enlighten the land;" and the close of said inscription also makes Hammurabi, no less than Shamash, the originator of laws. For the close begins with the words: "Laws which Hammurabi, the wise king, has established," and we read further: "My words have been well considered, my wisdom is unequaled."† Would such a sentence ever have come to the mind of Moses, if we

---

* In *Unbeweiesencs im Babel-Bibel-Streit* Hubert Grimme has expressed the opinion that Hammurabi is here intended to be represented as a *worshiper* of the sun-god. But this is less certain.

† Not until *after* this do we read: "By order of Shamash, the great judge of heaven and earth, justice shall arise in the land." Thereupon we read again: "The law of the land, which *I* have given."

consider the entire tradition concerning him? The discourses of the later prophets of the Old Testament often contain the exact opposite. Isaiah would have nothing to do with those who were wise in their own sight (v, 21), and who were called "their prudent" by the then ruling party (xxix, 14). And how loudly Jeremiah protested against the thought of his having received his proclamations from his own heart, that is, from the workshop of his own thought (xiv, 14, f.; xxiii, 26, f. etc.).* Where in Assyrio-Babylonian literature are there any parallels to the discourses of the Old Testament prophets and their sublime words concerning the deepest principles and loftiest goals of the world's history? In the Omina collections, which have been found in the library of Assurbanipal (at Rujimdshik), and one of which begins with the words: "If the Bel-star, etc."? Or in the other large collection of Omina, which is devoted chiefly to lunar phenomena, and which contains, for example, the following sentence: "If an eclipse occur between the first and the thirteenth day of Siwan [which answers essentially to our June], growth will be retarded in the land"? See here thy competitors, O book of Isaiah!

Has it really been acknowledged in the most recent treatises on the relative status of Babylonian and biblical culture that the countries of the Euphrates and Tigris offer no parallel to that Old Testament prophecy by which the true religion of Israel is mediated? Indeed not! One speaker formulates the sum total of his opinion in the sentence: "How thoroughly homogeneous everything in Babel and Bible is" (Delitzsch, Second Lecture, p. 16), and another writer even claims to be able to prove the parity of Assyrio-Babylonian prophecy with the true prophecy of the Bible. Must it not be interesting to follow this demonstration? Come, then, let us accompany him step by step. In the new edition of *Die Keilinschriften und das Alte Testament* we read (p. 170, f.): "At that time (the time of Jeremiah) Judah was a vassal state to Babylonia. Hence [why "hence"?] the Grand King kept his overseers in Jerusalem, who had access to the king, and together

---

* Jeremiah also censures the prophets who were wont to cry out: "I have dreamed! I have dreamed!" (xxiii, 25.) Delitzsch overlooked this fact when in his second lecture (p.) he remarks: "Here [in Babel], as there [in the Bible], the same world of continuous revelation, *chiefly in dreams.*"

with the strong Chaldæan party were commissioned to work for the interests of their lord, and against the incitements of the opposing party." "If in the capital city the leaders of the party were themselves able to represent the interests of the Grand King in the sense stated, there were professional agitators [nebi'im, speakers]* for the surrounding country, whom the opposing party naturally had to employ in entirely the same manner." H. Winckler graciously adds: "Of course, among these, too, there were men differing in endowment; men of independence, and with ideas of their own, or mere speaking tubes of their employers. As the called political spokesmen of the people, however, all nebi'im play their part, and hence answer in their relations to what in our day we call politicians." But why does the author take pains to construct the differences that are said to have existed among the "professional agitators" in the country towns of Judæa? Either the prophets, like Jeremiah in the country town of Anathoth (about an hour's walk north of Jerusalem), were "overseers" of the Babylonian king, who had to preserve "the interests of their lord," or they were not. Are we to suppose that they were even traitorous overseers of their pretended employers? What does Jeremiah say to this? What was his consciousness, testified to tenfold by him? With whom did he make common cause? With "agitators" of the "Grand King"? Yea, verily, of *the* Grand King; namely, of the heavenly world-king. For thus he *says* in the name of *his* employer: "Since the day that your fathers came forth out of the land of Egypt unto this day I have even sent unto you all my servants the prophets" (vii, 25). Hence Jeremiah was conscious of being a member in a succession of men who, from the fundamental deliverance of Israel out of Egypt until his own day, had stood in the service of the Deity; and whoever supposes that Jeremiah and the teachers of Israel related to him would represent the interests of any other lord heaps insult upon them. Was there a parallel in Babylonia or Assyria to these prophets?

In the new edition of *Die Keilinschriften und das Alte Testament* mentioned above we do not read in answer to this question: "No," or "not in reality," or "only in the sense in which

---

* *Nebi'im* is the Hebrew word for prophet!

Hammurabi—perhaps—considered himself to be, yet did not call himself, a speaker of the sun-god." No, in answer to this question said book contains nothing but the following note to the expression "politician" (p. 171), quoted above: "On such 'prophets' in Assyria see Peiser in *Mitteilungen der Vorderasiatischen Gesellschaft* (1899, p. 260)." Now what will the reader find in the work referred to? In these *Mitteilungen,* in the volume of 1898 (not 1899), the Assyriologist Peiser (in Koenigsberg, Editor of *Orientalische Literaturzeitung*) produces the following fragment from the literature of cuneiform writings of the seventh century as a sample of "courtly poetry" ("*hoefische Poesie*") (p. 257): "I, the servant, the prophet of the king, his* lord, proclaim these prophecies for the king, my† lord. The gods whose names I have enumerated shall receive and hear these prophecies for the king, my lord. But may I, the prophet of the king, my lord, stand before the king, my lord, and pray with all my heart on my side (? *ina a-hi-ia*). If my sides grow weak, may I by the power of my word (?) put my strength to the highest possible tension. Who shall not love a good lord? (For it is written) in the song of the Babylonians: On account of thy gracious mouth, my shepherd, all men look up to thee" (pp. 258, f, 260, f.). On this Peiser remarks: "The prophets, of course, could not labor without remuneration.‡ In case they received no fixed salary, concerning which we know nothing, they, as members of a free calling, were dependent upon the favor and mercy of the ruler or the notables" (p. 260). This, then, is the material on Assyrio-Babylonian prophecy to which H. Winckler has called the attention of his readers in the new edition of *Die Keilinschriften und das Alte Testament.* In these expressions he thinks he has shown his readers Assyrio-Babylonian parallels to those Israelitish prophets whom he had just characterized (p. 170). But what does the reader of these words from cuneiform writings really find? He hears an Assyrian prophet speak who stands "before the king,"‖ and who never tires of calling the king "his lord."

---

* *Bi-li-su,* "*of his* lord," is what we really read.
† Here the correct reading is *bi-li-ia,* "of my lord."
‡ By the way, by whom was Socrates paid?
‖ That means "in his service" (comp. 1 Kings xvii, 1, etc.).

This Assyrian prophet, referred to by H. Winckler, is said to resemble those prophets of Jahwe with whom we meet in the presence of King Ahab (1 Kings xxii, 6). But those are the prophets whom the ruling party in the days of Isaiah called "its prophets and its prudent" (xxix, 14). They are the prophets of the people, like, for example, Hananiah (Jer. xxviii, 1, ff.). But the men who were the mediators of Old Testament religion separated themselves from these prophets. Micah ben Jemla felt himself so completely separated from the prophets of Ahab's court that he alone disturbed their unison, and chose to be imprisoned rather than to speak according to the mouth of Ahab (1 Kings xxii, 9, ff.). The prophets mentioned in the portion of cuneiform writings quoted above resemble the men of whom Isaiah's contemporary Micah said: "They bite with their teeth," that is, they like to take part in feasts, and "they divine for money" (Mic. iii, 5, 11), that is, they are in the service of material interests. Prophets like those described in the words quoted above from the cuneiform writings, and like some, alas, even in Israel, were considered by Isaiah (iii, 1; xxix, 14; xxx, 1) and Jeremiah (xxiii, 1, ff.; xxviii, 1, ff.) as their complete antipodes; and when the last named prophet especially is branded "the politician Jeremiah," and is accused of conspiring with the Babylonians,[*] we ask the representative of this accusation to bear in mind the following words. It was none other than the well-known Karl Heinrich Graf who, in his excellent commentary on the book of Jeremiah, remarked: "No reproach heaped upon Jeremiah can have less foundation than that of a lack of national consciousness. . . . All his words and deeds were permeated by the most intimate love for his people. . . . He exposed himself to all kinds of danger and suffering in order to save his people from destruction, toward which he saw it rushing. . . . He was certain that an extended subjection of Judah under the supremacy of Chaldæa was the will of God," etc. (p. xxix, f.). This last thought must be expressed more pointedly thus: In Nebuchadnezzar Jeremiah saw the executor of the judgment that had to be visited upon the godless majority of the people by the Ruler of the world's history. In the

---

[*] *Die Keilinschriften und das Alte Testament* (1903), p. 170.

name of his employer, therefore, he had to warn against opposing —without avail—the then executor of the will of the Judge of the world. Thus do we understand Jeremiah.

If an analogy to the utterances of the Assyrian prophet, to which Winckler has referred, should be sought in ancient Hebrew literature, a somewhat similar statement might be found in the words of the writer of Psa. xlv, where we read: "My heart is inditing a good matter: I speak of the things which I have made touching the king: my tongue is the pen of a ready writer" (v. 1). But the words of the Assyrian prophet quoted above have no parallel in the discourses of the prophets with whom Jeremiah identified himself. A double operation is necessary in order to find Assyrio-Babylonian prophecy in the prophets whose writings are contained in the Old Testament. In the first place, the two lines of Jahwe prophets distinguished in ancient Hebrew literature—the false and the true—must be confounded, and, in the second place, the level of the line of men with whom Jeremiah identified himself in the words quoted above (vii, 25) *must be lowered.* But T. K. Cheyne, a recognized representative of "advanced criticism," has said of the latter line of prophets: "This at least we may say without fear of contradiction, that a *succession* of men so absorbed in the 'living God,' and at the same time so intensely practical in their aims—so earnestly bent on promoting the highest national interests—cannot be found in antiquity elsewhere than in Israel."* In fact, the specific position belonging to the true prophets of Jahwe in the history of the religions of mankind can be defended on grounds so sure that it will never be shaken. These grounds of proof are pointed out by me, for example, in a pamphlet, entitled *Alttestamentliche Kritik und Offenbarungsglaube,* which is now in the press. Hence only one point will be elucidated here that is not touched upon there. It is the relation of Assyrio-Babylonian and Israelitish prophecy, as regards their content. On this point we read nothing in the new edition of *Die Keilinschriften und das Alte Testament,* except the following sentence: "It is the same view,† the same world-system,

---

* *Encyclopædia Biblica*, vol. iii (1902), col. 3854.
† A few lines back we read "ancient oriental world-view."

which is the foundation of the narrations in Israelitish, as well as Roman and Arabic (Islâmitic) primitive stories, and which in its essentials is found everywhere in the wider sphere of mankind. It appears again in the calculations of a new age, in reckonings bearing on the time of the advent of a Messiah in Jewish and Christian apocalyptic writings, and of an *imâm* in the Islâm, and forms the foundation of the doctrine of the connection of things, which Kabbalistic Astrology had preserved till the founding of modern astronomy" (p. 2, f.). The opinion of several modern scholars, that "the ancient oriental world-view" forms the background of biblical historic writings, has been answered in my little book, *Babylonisierungsversuche betreffs der Patriarchen und Koenige Israels* (second edition). For the rest, however, the sentences of the new edition of *Die Keilinschriften,* etc., quoted above, contain nothing that could be considered a parallel to the content of the prophecies of the Old Testament. Or does F. Hommel, the well-known orientalist, offer a tenable complement?

Partly in the new periodical *Glauben und Wissen* (1903, p. 9, f.), partly in his book *Die altorientalischen Denkmaeler und das Alte Testament* (second edition), this Assyriologist has voiced a peculiar opinion on Adapa. This name appears in a myth, *Adapa and the Southwind,* contained in cuneiform writings found on the tablets of Tell-el-Amarna and published in the library of cuneiform writings, vol. vi, 1, p. 92. There we read: "[1]Prudence a wise man g . . . [2]His command like the command of Anu. [3]He completed for him an open ear for revealing the configurations of the land. [4]To the same he gave wisdom, eternal life he gave him not. [5]At the same time, in the same year, the all-wise son of Iridu,[*] like one among men Ia[†] created him. [12]May Adapa hear, the seed of man, [13]who with his . . . victoriously broke the wing of the Southwind, [14]ascended to heaven," etc. Now, is this Adapa supposed to be primitive man? The fact that he appears as a priest in the sanctuary of Ea in Eridu, and goes a-fishing to secure the necessaries for the sanctuary, is an adequately certain contradiction of such a view; for it is naturally presupposed that he was not the only inhabitant of the city of Eridu. The view

* The usual pronunciation of the name is *Eridu.*   † Other Assyriologists read *Ea.*

that Adapa is the first human being is quite certainly refuted by the fact that besides him "bakers of Eridu" are mentioned (line 10, f.). And the expression "seed of man"[*] does not prove the contrary,[†] since said expression can also mean "scion of man." Indeed, in his notes to the above text of the Adapa-myth (p. 100, line 12) P. Jensen remarks: "Even according to this line Adapa is not 'primitive man'" (p. 413). And H. Zimmern considers it "natural to identify the name and person of Adapa with the second Babylonian primitive king of Berosos, Alaporos (to whom Alaparos would apply equally well),[‡] even though this identification cannot yet be considered certain" (*Die Keilinschriften,* etc., 1903, p. 522). Said scholar of Munich sees "a synonym of Adapa in Mirri-Mullu-dugga, or in Mirri alone, without the addition of Mullu-dugga, which latter suffix means 'good man' (or also 'man of the good,' that is, of the good God)," and he adds: "In the course of time the Babylonians simply identified this god 'Mirri, man of the good,' with their god Marduk (or, Hebraized, Merodach)."[§] But a priest in the sanctuary of Ea in the city of Eridu, hence a man, is again simply said to have been a god. Besides we read in *Die Keilinschriften,* etc. (1903), p. 446: "A name Bir, Bur, Mir, Mur, of the weather god, presumably suggested in cuneiform writings, especially in Aramaic words, is not well founded, and had better be left out of consideration entirely, especially as an explanation of the element ר2 in Aramaic names," and the author of these sentences adds expressly that he had directed this opinion against the assertions of Hommel (*Aufsaetze und Abhandlungen,* p. 219, ff.). Consequently the further opinion of Hommel is unsafe,[‖] that Adapa had been the god who was beheaded in order that men might be made from his blood. He says that on the sixth of the seven creation tablets published by L. W. King, of London, in 1902, Marduk is spoken of, "and not the old Bel-Marduk, the world-creator proper of cantos i-v, but Mirri-Gullu-dugga,[¶] who, however, is Adapa again.

[*] *Zêr* or *Zîr amêlûti* in line 12.
[†] This must be emphasized against Joh. Nikel, *Genesis und Keilschriftforschung* (1903), p. 129. [‡] This is particularly easy in a text of Greek uncial letters.
[§] Monthly *Glauben und Wissen* (1903), p. 9.
[‖] *Die altorientalischen Denkmaeler und das Alte Test.,* second edition.
[¶] Here Hommel no longer reads " Mullu," but " Gullu."

as is shown by the beginning of canto vii, and also by the mention
of Ea in canto vi.

According to Hommel the seventh of these tablets reads:

> When Marduk heard the word of the gods,
> His heart impelled him, and he conceived a plan.
> He opened his mouth and spoke to Ea,
> What he had planned in his heart, he imparted to him: -
> My blood will I take, and will (form) bones,
> I will produce a man, a man shall . . .
> I will create man, that he shall inhabit (the earth),
> That the service of the gods be instituted . . .
> And I will change the paths of the gods, and will transform
>   (their ways)
> May they all be honored, may they all be (fortified) against evil.

Therefore Hommel thinks he is justified in considering
Adapa, or the god Mirri, etc., to be the *demiurge,* or *logos,* who is
supposed to have stood between God and the first man. He also
sees the same Adapa, or god Mirri, etc., appear in the scene that
is wont to be spoken of as the dialogue between Ea and Marduk,
and is often met with in adjurations. According to Hommel lines
1-9 of this dialogue read:

> The god Mirri-Mullu-dugga looked upon him (sick man)
> And approaches his father Ea in his house and says:
> "O my father, sickness has befallen man,
> I know not wherewith he shall be healed."
> Then Ea gave his son Mirri-Mullu-dugga answer:
> "O my son, what dost thou not know? What new thing shall I teach?
> What I know, thou knowest also,
> And what thou knowest, know also I;
> Go, my son, and free him (the sick) from his ban,"

and then follow instructions for adjuring disease. The same
scholar also calls attention to the following. He has observed that
where among the Chaldæans Mirri-Mullu-dugga appears, which is
always written with the characters "dwelling place" and "eye," we
meet with Osiris even in the pyramid texts. Hommel further
emphasizes that this name, like its Chaldæan double, Mirri, is
written with the two characters "dwelling place" (*os*) and "eye"
(*iri*). Another parallel between Mirri and Osiris is found by
Hommel in the fact that this Egyptian god also had the surname
Won-nofer—"good being," or also "being of the good (god)." In
harmony with this is the other fact that Osiris is always repre-

sented as a human being, whereas the Egyptian deities were pictured with the heads of animals as their emblems.

But even granted that all these opinions could be verified,
they would prove anew only the following: Certain portions of
ancient mankind recognized man's likeness to God in the myth
that the blood of the "god" Adapa-Marduk had been used in producing man, and the healing, or in general redeeming, tendency
of God. But this latter knowledge, manifest in the introduction
to Assyrio-Babylonian adjuration of disease quoted above, and in
the Egyptian myth of Osiris, plays only in the sphere of the
physical. Is all that till now, according to the above survey, could
be cited as Assyrio-Babylonian analogy to Old Testament prophetic
discourses really prophecy—that is, declaration concerning the
future? True, there is such a declaration contained in another
cuneiform text which has recently been cited as an analogy to the
Old Testament prophecies. In the *Encyclopædia Biblica*, vol. iii
(1902), col. 3063, T. K. Cheyne quotes the following passage as
"a Babylonian parallel" to "faith in the Messiah:" "Seacoast
against seacoast, Elamite against Elamite, Cassite against Cassite,
Kuthæan against Kuthæan, country against country, house against
house, man against man. Brother is to show no mercy toward
brother; they shall kill one another," and he adds: The countries
mentioned are those nearest to Babylonia, which are to be a prey
to war and anarchy until "after a time the Akkadian will come,
overthrow all, and conquer all of them." He thinks the triumph
of Hammurabi, the king of Babylonia, is foretold in this part of
"poesy or prophecy." But all these are very inadequate elements
($\sigma\tau o\iota\chi\epsilon\tilde{\iota}a$) compared with the rich and sublime structure of
prophecy that we behold in the literature of the ancient Hebrews.

But the content of the prophecy of Israel is to be esteemed
sublime, because it has its sphere proper in the domain of the religious and moral, inasmuch as it gives promise of the restoration
of the natural harmony between God and the human heart as the
final goal of God's course in history. This information shines
forth for the first time in the profound passage bearing on the final
subjection of the power hostile to God (Gen. iii, 15), and there-
forward star after star appears on the dark firmament of antiq-

religiosity. This sublimity was not lessened by the fact that the divine Spirit striding through history chose a single nation to be the nursery of true religion and morality, for together with the light of knowledge sent this nation its duties were augmented, and how often it groaned beneath the burden of its historic responsibility! Nor could the nobility of Old Testament prophecy suffer through the further fact, that the flames to which its finger pointed were alike the judgment fire for impiety and immorality and the rosy dawn of a more beautiful day for humility and moral purity. And, finally, the sublimity of Old Testament prophecy could not vanish when it was surpassed by the work of Him who proved himself a sovereign even in comparison with the prophets. No; meditation on Old Testament prophecy and New Testament reality only puts into our mouth the words with which I closed *The Exile's Book of Consolation:* "Prophecy is like the rosy dawn which ushers in the day. The prophetic word is 'a light which shineth in a dark place, until the day dawn, and the day-star arise in your hearts' (2 Pet. i, 19). Prophecy is as trustworthy as the dawn certainly kisses the hem of the sun's robe. Moreover, were there no dawn there would be no day, and the soft glow of the morning red prepares the eye for the brighter light and cheers the heart that yearns for the day. But the rosy hue of morning is not the blazing day-star itself. Aurora pales when the monarch Sun assumes his radiant sway."

But if from this point we cast a summary view upon the subject discussed we can but say: It will not occur to any sensible person to decry the effort of the Babylonians in behalf of human culture. Nowhere has this been more willingly recognized than in my book *Bibel und Babel,* tenth edition, p. 20-22. But if anyone exclaims: "How thoroughly homogeneous everything in *Babel and Bible* is!" and when there is silence concerning the difference of the level of Assyrio-Babylonian prophecy and that of Israelitish prophecy, then we must feel ourselves constrained to protest in the name of historic reality.

Ed. König.

Art. VII.—THE VALUE OF THE STUDY OF SCIENCE FOR MINISTERS.

THE minister, by virtue of his profession, is expected to be master of all realms of knowledge that throw any light upon man's origin, duty, or destiny. In common with all men he may gratify intellectual curiosity, develop mental power, and enrich his general equipment by excursions into many fields of thought, but his professional duties require of him the mastery of all that helps in the understanding of man or in the apprehension of God. He is not at liberty to say of anything God has made, done, or permitted to be done, "I do not know," till he has used all diligence in the effort to know. Self-respect forbids that he should have so little energy as to live in a house without going into the cellar and garret, as well as into the kitchen and parlor, that he may know what provision infinite love and wisdom have made for the happiness of the race; gratitude and love to the giver, as well as duty to his fellow-occupants, certainly require him to explore and find out what kind of a world the Lord has fitted up for his abode, and what use may be made of its resources to further his purposes. It is of the nature of disloyalty for him to leave the friends of unrighteousness to discover these treasures and turn them against the designs of their Maker. As "stewards of the mysteries of God" it is our first duty to know all that may be known about them, that we may expound them to others and defend them from the attacks of enemies. To live in God's world without being able to lead the inquiring young through its various apartments with intelligent explanations of its structure, apartments, and adaptations is worthy only of an intellectual and moral sluggard. It lies in the very nature of the ministerial office, and is involved in loyalty to God as his ambassador, that the minister should be able to expound the words and works of God and give a fairly comprehensive view of the divine procedure in this world. We might therefore go beyond the question of value, and show that the study of science belongs to the very essence and integrity of ministerial

character and function. It is a one-sided equipment and service that deals only with the written word of God. His works as truly as his word are from him, and they are the best comment on his word. The word has passed through many human hands, through hands of transcribers and translators: but the works of God stand to-day as they left his hand, original and uncorrupted.

The study of science enables the minister to vitalize the material universe as the creature and habitation of God. The intellectual and spiritual power to bring God near, to make all visible things throb with his life, to be able to point to his footprint on stone, leaf, and flower, and to read the records of his doing in the heavens and in the hidden places of the earth till all things seem to constitute one great temple of the Lord Almighty, is very important for the preacher. The deepest philosophy, as well as the finest poetic and moral feeling, stands reverent before the spectacle of nature's ceaseless activities, certain of an invisible worker there that must be God, or one so like to him as to differ only in name. The impiety of the world has crowded God out of the material, out of the business, and out of the social world, and has relegated him to a little corner called the Church; it is the duty of the minister to bring him back into the temple that belongs to him and enthrone him in the midst of his works as "Lord of all." To do this he must himself be thrilled and inspired by such an apprehension of God, in and over all things, as comes from the thorough, reverent study of his works; he must have his mind filled and thrilled with the facts of nature and of the Gospel, and in his own deep conviction and reverent feeling fuse them into one living message of truth to men. Since the study of science by itself tends toward skepticism, it is imperative to unite these two lines of study, that Gospel truth may sanctify science and science broaden and vitalize Gospel truth and the minister become a living example of the possible union of the two in one person. We shall counteract the skeptical tendencies by studying, understanding, and spiritualizing the field, not by anathematizing it. The Master constantly appealed to nature, and wove into incomparable parables the scientific knowledge of the times; he used the visible and the palpable to help the understanding in grasping the in-

28

visible and the spiritual. He kept close to nature, held it close to God, and made it vocal with the declaration of spiritual truth. For wisdom of method and energy of force he is the model teacher for all who have minds large enough and hearts warm enough to translate into human speech the message of truth that lies locked up in nature. The immanence of God in all his work must be seen and felt by the preacher, as well as believed, if he is to deliver to the world the full message he was sent to give. And the study of science will aid the minister in developing a well-balanced mind. Nothing adds more to the weight and influence of a preacher than the conviction that he has a well-balanced mind, that he has looked on all sides of the subject he is treating and of all related subjects, and that, having mastered the whole field, he is presenting well-considered conclusions. If he become the mere hawker of second-hand phrases on well-worn themes; if he is one-idead, if he treats of only one segment of truth and is unable to connect it with the whole circle of human knowledge, he is discredited with intelligent listeners and loses influence with all classes. Study on one theme or on one class of subjects tends to produce a lop-sided, one-idead mind, a thinker that may not be safely followed. Hence come our theological and denominational bigots, our specialists, ranting advocates of a single idea—a pestiferous brood that has done the truth much damage.

It is important to distinguish between studying science and preaching science. The one is a question of intellectual balance, discipline, and furnishing; the other is a question of professional fidelity and stands related to character. An honest man will do that for which he is employed, the thing he engages to do; if it is to preach the Gospel he may use science or politics to illustrate it, but not as a substitute for it. It is half-educated and imperfectly developed minds, minds that do not know the real or relative greatness of themes, that substitute science for the Gospel; a real scholar, a deep thinker, must forever see the superiority of Gospel truths to the facts or theories of science. The thorough mastery of science, if it is not attended with the neglect of Bible study, will only throw additional light on the greatness of the Gospel and make its superiority the more manifest. The study of language, of mathe-

matics, or of history may be helpful in the same direction, but they do not bring us so close to God nor occupy the mind with truths so directly helpful to the minister, nor do they present facts so definite, fundamental, and authoritative as those of science. Not so much by showing that we are masters of one subject as by showing that we are masters of all truth in support of one subject do we gain the confidence of men. We should indeed be "men of one book," but men with ability to bring the stores of all knowledge to the illustration and support of that one book.

The study of science will aid in saving the minister from dullness and dryness, the great vices of the pulpit. The most common complaint about sermons is that they are dry and dull. This is due to the intellectual life of the preacher. The themes are the most varied, interesting, and stirring that may possibly engage the mind, and when they fail to interest it must be due to defective presentation. If the minister falls back on the dignity and importance of his message, or the authority by which he is sent, or the sacredness of his office, he will learn by sad experience that the prophet must win his way by the effective putting of truth and by his power over the minds of men. One of the greatest preachers of the last generation, the late Bishop Janes, used to say, "It is a sin to be dull in the pulpit." The character of his mission, the greatness of his themes, the interests at stake, and the resources at command make dullness in the minister unpardonable. Yet the cause is not always moral or spiritual, for as matter of fact many most godly men are miserably dry and dull as preachers. The sprightliness, liveliness, vigor, and earnestness of a vital intellect are necessary in addition to spiritual fervor; and these qualities will be aided by scientific studies that will break up the monotony of intellectual life that results from dwelling continually on one class of subjects and naturally leads to dullness. The mind needs to be freshened, waked up, and turned about by change of scenery, variety of food, and shock of transition from one subject to another. This is a law of intellectual life that applies to all thinkers and to all professions as well as to the ministry. The man who shuts himself up to law, to medicine, or to science alone becomes a dry and humdrum hack

that no one wishes to hear. To preserve intellectual freshness and vigor is one of the first duties of the minister, and even if it requires prolonged excursions into side studies, extended travel, or laborious discipline it will pay large returns for the effort expended. The glowing fervors of a true piety need the sprightliness, vigor, and versatility of a thoroughly equipped mind to translate them into speech that will adequately express them to the thought of the world. Much of the best life of the world perishes for want of such adequate expression.

Truth acts on the mind very much as water does on the wheel—sets all the machinery of the mind in motion and wakes up its slumbering and latent energies, thus adding to while calling out the powers of the mind. A hard fact of science thrown into the stagnant pool of thought may agitate and disturb its quiet till the very ripples flash brightness and beauty to the beholder, investing old themes with a new charm. So vast and varied is the field of science that it seems impossible to pass from theology to science and from science to theology without developing a robust intellectual life. The primary question is this of intellectual life, for the truth lies everywhere in rich abundance; but will man find it, feel it, and have muscle to hurl it forth with effective force? Henry Ward Beecher used to go down to the docks and watch the great horses and the mighty ships to get the suggestion of power, to rouse and stimulate his mind to action. It may be even better to dive into the depths of the ocean, climb the mountains, travel among the stars, or come into touch with the mighty forces of heat and electricity; or one may find enough in the torrent that is forever surging and murmuring along his own arteries and veins to keep thought and imagination alive. Insects, birds, flowers, and all things about us are embodiments and expressions of truth so wonderful that a little attention to them must preserve the mind from dullness. Give to the mind this trinity of forces— science, revealed truth, and spiritual life—and they will drive dryness and dullness from the pulpit. The study of science by the minister will promote adherence to fact and to its accurate statement. One of the vices of the pulpit is extravagant and inaccurate speech; that is, speech that does not accurately expre

the fact. An effort to be impressive, to avoid commonplace and dullness, to arouse attention, and to give just effect to important truths, leads many honest minds into this extravagance, while others attempt to cover up shallowness by high-sounding words and to atone for the lack of honest hard study by volubility and excess of statement. If the themes themselves on which ministers speak do not invite to this extravagance their nature gives special opportunity. They are transcendental, they appeal to the imagination, to the feelings, to the sentiment of reverence and devotion where limits are not clearly defined, and there is manifest difficulty in speaking with exactness and propriety. Exhortation, expostulation, warning, and entreating tempt the mind to reckless, extravagant speech. And there is always a large contingent of hearers who are ready to applaud extravagance for strength, rashness for courage, and volubility for eloquence; and when it is found that such cheap stuff passes for real coin the temptation to use it may be very great, especially if the supply of the genuine has been exhausted. The study of science cultivates exactness of thought and language. Expression here must, by the nature of the subject, be as accurate as the measurements of a building or the die of the mint—if for no other reason, because any inaccuracy becomes at once manifest and can be pointed out. Measurements, weights, forces, and proportions are exact and invariable. If we go into the laboratory for experimentation, sincerity, honesty, and good intentions do not count; exactness is the only way of salvation. Acids will burn you, gases will spit in your face, and explosions will blow your brains out if you are not exact. Ignorance is worthy of damnation, carelessness is a deadly sin, trifling is scourged with whipcords of flame, and no prayer is heard, nor is mercy shown to the bungler. Or if we enter the wider field of observation and study all progress is along the line of facts clearly proven and accurately stated. I do not now speak of hypothesis, speculation, or theory, but of actual science. Here all search is for fact, and all expression an effort to define it accurately. The material and tangible character of the subjects dealt with makes this a necessity, not only for intelligent progress but also for defense in case of attack. The discipline of such studies is in-

valuable for the minister as a corrective of the tendencies in the sacred office to which I have alluded. Who has not heard from the pulpit assertions about the teachings of other churches, or of prominent writers or educators, that could not be placed by the side of the ninth commandment? Sometimes a grace or duty, good in itself, is presented so out of place and out of proportion that the whole body of truth is distorted, the minds of honest people confused, and evil rather than good is done. Sometimes a lawless sentimentality is allowed to foam, fume, sputter, and pour out a seething mass of extravagance that only hurts and disgusts sensible people. The facts of the Gospel are great, stirring, melting, moving, and saving, if only we know how to state them and are willing to trust them. The task of the minister is to keep his fervor, his passion, and enthusiasm within the limits of Gospel truth and good sense; and as a discipline for acquiring power to do this the study of science is invaluable, for the very inner soul of the true scientific spirit is strict adherence to fact.

The study of science will be of great value to the minister in developing intellectual strength. This does not imply that theological study and sermonic work will not develop intellectual power, but that the mind will acquire greater strength by adding another kind and a wider range of studies. The mind held too long to one subject loses interest and enthusiasm in it, and gives itself over to humdrum and routine. Healthy growth and development are then arrested, and the mind waits the incoming of new material and the opening of new realms of thought to quicken its energies and arouse its enthusiasm. As the body requires variety of food for its health and strength, so does the mind. One article of food alone, though it be the best, will produce dyspepsia or anæmia. Do not many sermons show signs of one or the other of these diseases, and in their very structure and spirit give evidence of having sprung from a too meager intellectual diet? It is a law of intellectual life, for the preacher and all brain workers alike, that there must be variety of studies in order to intellectual health and strength. Heresies, vagaries, and false theories of science and theology result from the neglect of this rule. Mr. Darwin, the great scientist to whose vast learning and invaluable labors the

world is so great a debtor, is himself an illustration of how devotion to one study alone may pervert the action of the mind, and dwarf, if it does not destroy, some of its noblest powers. In 1836-39, in the beginning of his career, he could say: "I took much delight in Wordsworth's and Coleridge's poetry, and can boast that I read the 'Excursion' twice through. In my excursions during the voyage of the *Beagle,* when I could take only a single volume, I always chose Milton." Toward the close of his career he gives a very different account of his mental state, showing a complete metamorphosis as the result of the exclusive study of science. He says: "But now for many years I cannot endure to read a line of poetry; I have tried recently to read Shakespeare and found it so intolerably dull that it nauseated me. I have almost lost my taste for painting and music." This confession indicates a lamentable decay, from neglect and devotion to one line of study, of some of the noblest tastes and powers of the mind. It is of first importance to the preacher to keep up genuine intellectual strength and true humanness of feeling, instinct, taste, and aspiration by a wide range and variety of studies, and thus save himself from falling off into soft sentimentalism, lazy verbosity, one-idead fanaticism, driveling and whining sanctimoniousness, and a foolish attempt to atone for the absence of real strength by ranting. The strength of the personality, like the strength of the body, depends upon the symmetry, the balance and harmony, of powers. If a man has strong limbs and a weak heart he is a weak man; if he has a splendid frame and a wasting consumption he is little better than a dead man. We plead for strong, round, well-developed, symmetrical minds; and there is no better method of securing this for the minister than by the study of science. And this knowledge will make the minister instructive. By statement of fact as a basis for argument or for illustration the minister may impart a vast amount of information that will stimulate and direct the minds of the young of his congregation and win them to him. His work lies on a higher plane than this, but often the attention, respect, and confidence of the listener is gained by the discovery that the preacher is a man of large intelligence, and thus the way is opened for his message of saving truth. The man who has

learned a new truth from a minister always entertains a special regard for him and is peculiarly accessible to him. There are many young people looking and listening for the newest and best facts, eager to enlarge the area of their knowledge, and ready to follow anyone who proves himself a capable leader. The minister will greatly strengthen his influence with such persons if he occasionally drops a new fact into their hungry minds, thus acquiring a leadership that he can use for his highest aims. To save from sin is not the only mission of the pulpit, but to build up character in righteousness and knowledge and by such building aid the primary work of salvation. It is within the proper scope of the ministerial function, and according to the example of the great divine Teacher, to use the works of God to illustrate and expound his word. Any act of God in creation or in providence may engage the minister's attention and find a place in his message. It is his business to teach the people the mind of God, and this he finds revealed in two volumes—in his word and in his works.

The study of science will help to keep the minister out of ruts. The processes of thinking, like the rolling wheels of a vehicle on soft earth, cut a track for themselves, that grows even deeper as they are repeated along the same line, that holds them to it and renders it difficult to get into a new and independent course. Many ministers have a few well-worn paths of thought and set phrases of expression, and whatever the text or the occasion they are quite sure to fall into these—to the weariness of their hearers. It is the result of sluggishness, and the want of real energy in pushing out into new fields of truth for something with which to instruct and build up the people. It becomes very monotonous and uninteresting to the preacher, as well as to his congregation, to find that he is in a deep rut that holds him to the same round of topics and phrases. What he needs is something to free him from the old bondage and set him upon a new course, or give him wing to fly instead of plod. Nothing can be more helpful to this end than the study of science. It will hopelessly explode the old narrowness, wrench and twist the mind out of its old grooves, whirl it about in the sweep of great forces, and, like the young eagle flung out of its nest, compel it to fly in the trackless heavens, free, and able

to make its way wherever it will. Intellectual narrowness is to
be broken up by broader fields of study that widen the horizon
of the soul. Every preacher knows how jaded the mind becomes
in an unvarying round of theological studies; commentaries,
lexicons, and books of divinity become very dry, and his soul
hungers for something fresh and invigorating—and so do the
audiences. The study of science will also help the preacher in
preventing or breaking up an offensive professionalism. He
should speak as a man to men; when he assumes a professional
manner or cast of thought he loses power. When manliness, freshness, vigor, and spontaneity are crushed out by a superincumbent
ecclesiasticism or theological system, "which neither we nor our
fathers could bear," ministerial usefulness is greatly impaired.
A man who has been crammed, theologized, dehumanized, made
artificial, and thrown out of touch with the world, must get back
to naturalness before he can accomplish anything worthy of his
calling. It is not walking bodies of divinity or systems of theology
that the world needs, but renewed, natural, radiant, forceful men,
full of the Holy Ghost and of power. This abnormal professionalism will scarcely be possible to a man who walks among the flowers,
listens to the singing of birds, comes into sympathy with insects
and creeping things, studies life in its multiform manifestations,
digs among the rocks, floats in the air, rides upon the sunbeam
from star to star, and in roaming through the vast fields of nature
keeps himself natural, reverent, and devout. The study of science
will enable him to make the hemisphere of theology a complete
globe of truth, and that which was partial and unsatisfying by
itself will become complete and satisfying. The world wants the
Gospel, but it wants it with the accessories and adjuncts that
naturally belong to it. No one has a right to take it out of its
beautiful setting in the system of nature and present it in the hard,
cold, bald way in which it is sometimes given to men. The world
needs the Gospel; not some new thing, but the same old bread and
butter on which the saints have lived the ages through. But it
must be confessed that much depends on how the bread and butter
are made and served. Dry, sour bread and rancid butter have
been known to have great power in thinning out a congregation.

The old soul hunger in men is as sharp and quick as ever to respond to that which really satisfies. The Gospel is old, as sunlight is old, as roses are old, as love is old—old but ever new. This is the minister's task, the field for his sanctified genius: to make the Gospel new; to put life into it; to adapt it to the new conditions that arise, and to coordinate it with all knowledge and with all phases of the world's ever-changing life.

But there are those to whom this study of science seems attended with many dangers. That there are dangers I freely grant, but that they are such as to justify the neglect of such studies I deny. There is no good that has not its perils. Our first parents could not walk through Eden without encountering danger, and there has never been a garden since that has not had its dangers, nor an earthly paradise that has not had its lying serpent and tempting devil. There is the alleged danger of a tendency to skepticism; but the proper study of science must ever tend to the strengthening of faith. Many of the most devout men see danger in the temptation that will come to ministers to make a show of their learning in the pulpit. It must be granted that Greek roots and Hebrew stems have often been flourished about before gaping congregations in a manner out of all proportion to their real value; but this is not a valid objection to the work done by the great Greek and Hebrew scholars who have interpreted the Scriptures to us. Others fear it will lead to the substitution of science for the Gospel. This can never be in a well-balanced mind that is permeated by the spirit of Christ. The truths of the Gospel are so much greater and more vital than those of science that a really capable mind will be in little danger at this point. The greater danger for the pulpit is that of becoming dull, prosy, dry, or heavy; these are the vices that are eating out its substance and destroying its power. The path of safety and highest efficiency certainly lies in a wise use of all sources of knowledge, so blending them as to give truth its due proportions and proper colorings.

S. M. Vernon

Art. VIII.—EPISCOPAL SUPERVISION FOR MISSIONS.

WHAT is the best form of episcopal supervision for the work of the Church in foreign fields? There has been a great deal of legislation to meet the requirements of this question, and a number of plans are being tried, but they all seem to be of a tentative nature. Nothing is settled. That the state of things is not satisfactory is evinced by the fact that the plans are frequently changed, and by a lack of unanimity among those most concerned as to the efficiency of the methods now in operation. At least four plans are now being employed. A brief outline of these may help one to understand the situation.

The first plan for episcopal supervision of the foreign work of our Church is that of sending out periodically, at least twice in a quadrennium, a general superintendent, to visit and inspect the work, hold the Conferences, and perform any other necessary episcopal functions in some particular mission field, who, upon his return, makes a report of his work and gives his impressions, gathered while in the field, to the Missionary Society and to the Church at large. The second plan is that known as missionary episcopacy—an authorized form of ecclesiastical supervision exercised by bishops set apart for certain mission fields within which alone they have jurisdiction. The third and most recent plan is that of assigning a general superintendent to a certain foreign field, or fields, within which has been fixed an episcopal residence where he is supposed to reside during the quadrennium and supervise the work of his field. The fourth plan is a combination of the first and second, requiring "that once in every quadrennium every Mission over which a missionary bishop has jurisdiction shall be administered conjointly by the general superintendents and the missionary bishop," they being coordinate while in the field, but in case of disagreement the general superintendents having the supremacy. All four of these plans are now in operation in the various mission fields of the Methodist Episcopal Church: the first in South America and Mexico, the second in Southern Asia and Africa, the third in China and

Europe, and the fourth, in connection with the second, in Southern Asia. These miscellaneous and disjointed forms of episcopal supervision in the great mission fields of the Church indicate a weakness in administration and are out of harmony with an otherwise compact and uniform ecclesiastical government. Moreover, no one of the various plans enumerated above is adequate to meet the needs and requirements of the Church either at home or abroad. It may be a guide to more harmonious legislation if some of the virtues and a few of the more glaring defects of each of these heterogeneous plans for ecclesiastical administration be pointed out, and what might prove to be a better method, combining the virtues of each and excluding most of the defects, briefly outlined.

Concerning the first method, that of sending out from time to time general superintendents to inspect and administer the work in specified foreign fields, it may be said that this plan may keep the Mission in closer touch with the home Church and the source of supplies, and may provide the Missionary Society and the General Committee with an official means of communication and administration in foreign parts and tend to conserve harmony and uniformity in ecclesiastical government throughout the connection. Yet such visits must of necessity be intermittent, and the visitor, at best, only a visitor; precluding, in the short time he can give to the field, much familiarity with the peculiar methods essential to success or thorough acquaintance with the needs of the work or with the strange people among whom he briefly sojourns—their language, their customs, their habits, their religion—and enabling him only to do the routine work of the Conferences and attend to the more urgent matters which present themselves at the time. Moreover, in the interim between his visit and the visit of his successor grave emergencies sometimes arise, requiring immediate attention, with no one on the field having authority to meet them. Add to this the fact that but rarely the bishop visits and administers the same work twice—thus giving a changeable and sometimes conflicting administration—and it may be seen how unsatisfactory this plan is, especially to the missionaries on the field.

There is much to be said in favor of missionary episcopacy. It has been tried in Africa since 1858, during which time three good men have exercised its functions, and in Southern Asia since 1888, represented, likewise, by three men of exceptional ability. It has succeeded so far as its limitations will allow. This plan provides a leader who may also be a missionary. It requires continuous residence on the field. It insures continuity of administration. In the opinion of the Central Conference in the large mission field where the plan has been tried for the past fifteen years, "None can dispute the fact that the system which now operates in our wide and expanding field has made many advances possible that would not otherwise have been contemplated, and besides administering nearly all the field in detail has left its impress upon every institution connected with our Church. Best of all, it has made feasible frequent personal counsel and advice for every responsible worker from one intimately acquainted with the genesis and growth of the enterprises each represents." And the senior missionary bishop has affirmed that "The presence of a superintending leader is of the utmost importance. The isolation of the workers, the inexperience of most of the convert preachers, the pioneer character of the work, the necessity of devising new measures, the constant care to make organization keep pace with progress, the liability of dissension—these, and a score of other reasons, might be named as indicating the urgent need of a superintending leader on the field." But missionary episcopacy, as a policy, is but a tentative measure. At best it is only a makeshift. It has inherent weaknesses which may become more fully manifest at any time. A quadrennial episcopal candidature on the mission field does not conduce to harmony. The selection of a missionary bishop is not restricted to a choice from among missionaries of long residence on the field. The one chosen may not be a missionary at all. If taken from the nonmissionary ranks the result might be the opposite of those claimed for the system. The choice from among missionaries is limited; a misfit would be a calamity difficult to recover from. Furthermore, missionary episcopacy is limited episcopacy. A missionary bishop is not a general superintendent, and cannot become one except by

distinct election to that office. He is not a bishop at all out of his
own field. He cannot perform any of the special functions of the
regular bishops beyond the limits of his diocese. His field must
be inspected at least once in every quadrennium by a general
superintendent. It may not have been so intended, but this is a
degradation of the man and of the Mission. As some one has said,
"The missionary episcopacy must struggle hard to ennoble itself.
The office humiliates the officer." And hence a great man submit-
ting to it for the work's sake was yet clear-minded enough to see
that "the restrictions imposed on missionary bishops are a trifle
absurd." It "forbids a man who has authority to ordain in Lucknow and Bombay to perform the same duty after he passes Aden,
at the mouth of the Red Sea, even though requested to do so by
sixteen bishops." Missionary episcopacy takes the mission field,
in a measure, out of touch with the home Church. The field loses
some sympathy by having its own special advocate, and yet when
he is on his field he is away from the source of supplies, and
when he is away from his field he is not a bishop. The absurdity
of this disjointed and limited episcopacy renders it objectionable,
especially as all its many undoubted advantages would still be
retained after a simple and just act of legislation, inaugurating a
better plan, had done away with it.

Fixing episcopal residences in foreign fields for general
superintendents is an advance upon all previous legislation, for it
insures, what is essential to the success of the work, "the continuous personal superintendence of a responsible leader," and
gives a definite field of labor to a general superintendent. This is
much better than "a series of annual visits from an ever-changing
number of bishops." It is even better, in some ways, than missionary episcopacy, for it is not limited. But still it is liable to
some serious weaknesses. The person sent may not go from choice.
He is simply assigned to the field. He may not have any special
interest in missions. He will, usually, be the latest addition to
the Board of Bishops. If he has no particular liking for the field
to which he has been assigned he may not remain on it continuously. The quadrennial inspection of a Mission under the
jurisdiction of a missionary bishop by a general superintendent

has occurred twice, and has been successful as far as the limitations of the plan will allow. It corrects one of the defects of missionary episcopacy by bringing the field into closer touch with the Missionary Society, in whose interests the visitation is made; but it also appears to point out and emphasize the defects and limitations of missionary episcopacy and tends to minify and degrade the office. Moreover, it seems like a useless expense, and, in fact, would never have been thought of had the bishop in the foreign field been a general superintendent. It would be rendered entirely unnecessary if the changes herein advocated were adopted.

We come, therefore, to the conclusion that no plan for the episcopal government of foreign missions has yet been devised which has not in its practical workings shown inherent weaknesses. These weaknesses are all in the policy; for no one can find fault with the administration of the incumbents, whether general superintendents or missionary bishops. There never will be that harmony which is desirable until a plan is devised which will conserve the strength and unity of episcopacy and at the same time meet all the requirements of the work on the field. The kind of episcopacy that is needed is that which provides a leader who thoroughly knows both the foreign mission and the home Church, and who is not only once a bishop but always a bishop, a bishop everywhere and all the time. He should be familiar with the particular field over which he has supervision, and, if possible, know the language, history, literature, religions, customs, habits, feelings, and heart life of the people among whom he lives. He should know the men and women working in his field and their ability and adaptability in and for the work to which he appoints them. At the same time he should be a man of the largest influence at home. He should be able to exercise full episcopal powers in all lands and in all climes. He should feel, and be able to make others feel, that the Church is one, and has but one form of episcopal administration, and that there is no territorial limit to episcopal functions and powers, and that in the Methodist Episcopal Church, from Boston to Borneo and from Bareilly to Berlin, there is but one kind of bishop; and that there is no administrative need to have one bishop sent to inspect another's work

or to have the work spasmodically administered by an unfamiliar official of the Church. There are but three easy steps to the accomplishment of the much-needed plan proposed. Each of the plans now in operation can contribute something toward the success of the desirable plan, which, when in operation, will at once eliminate the main defects of the methods now being tried. The first step is to so group the Conferences and mission fields as to allow a bishop to exercise his episcopal functions in a certain district during a quadrennium, the same bishop being eligible for reappointment. This is practicable, for it has already been done for China and Europe. The next step will be to delete from the Book of Discipline all reference to missionary episcopacy, whether in the Third Restrictive Rule or in Part Third. This can be done in the Disciplinary way provided for in the Constitution of the General Conference. And the last step will be to elect to the general superintendency the three noble men—the peers of any bishops on the Board—now serving as missionary bishops in Africa and Southern Asia, and assign them, as general superintendents, to their present respective fields. To provide for succession in office let well-tried men on the various fields, or men familiar with those fields and who have the missionary spirit, be elected, as required, to the office, and assigned, as they naturally would be, to the fields which they are best fitted to administer. This plan would do away with the present grades in the episcopal office, would bring the Missions into closer touch with the mother Church, and, by having able men, who have power to administer anywhere, preside over them, would give the Missions a more efficient administration, would remove that unrest and friction among the missionaries on the field over the ever-recurring and never-settled question of administration and succession, and, lastly, would tend to bring about that unity and harmony throughout the whole Church so essential to its success.

J. E. Scott.

ART. IX.—THE ENGLISH MAY MEETINGS.

LONDON is not England any more than New York is America, but an observer who wished to gauge the sentiment of the English Churches or to estimate the style of English religious eloquence might gather all the necessary material by spending two or three weeks in the English metropolis—provided they were the right weeks. At one particular time of year there may be found within two or three London halls representatives of all the Churches from all parts of the kingdom, and the speakers who address these assemblies are equally varied in ecclesiastical connection and local habitation. The area covered by the unique institution of the May Meeting is surprisingly large. Originally every May Meeting was held in May, but the program has become so enlarged that four additional months have been pressed into service. Last year the first entry on the official list was the meeting in behalf of the Children's Hospital for Hip Disease, on March 25, and the last the anniversary of the Pentecostal League on July 21. But in spite of this expansion May still retains the most important place, as of the twenty-two pages in the guidebook twelve are devoted to that month. The range of organizations represented is of corresponding extent. All the Protestant Churches—Anglican, Methodist, Congregationalist, Baptist, Presbyterian, Moravian, etc.— have their own denominational meetings, mainly in connection with their home and foreign missions. The great undenominational religious societies, such as the British and Foreign Bible Society, the Religious Tract Society, and the Young Men's Christian Association, appear on the list, as well as Protestant associations, temperance societies, and peace and arbitration societies of various shades. One notable feature is the number of organizations for the promotion of the religious life among members of specific professions and occupations; for example, the Medical Prayer Union, the Lawyers' Prayer Union, the Law Clerks' Christian Association, the Civil Service Prayer Union, the Commercial Travelers' Christian Union, the Soldiers' Christian Association, the Christian Police Association, the Railway Mission,

29

and the Mission to Coalies and Carmen. Benevolent societies bulk largely, for we find many such items as the Reformatory and Refuge Union, the Children's Fresh Air Mission, the Governesses' Benevolent Institution, and the Cabdrivers' Benevolent Society. The ingenuity of modern evangelism is suggested by the announcement of the Tram and Bus Text Mission, while the advertisements of the Prophecy Investigation Society and the British Ephraim Society provoke reflections upon the waste of misdirected zeal.

Amid all changes, Exeter Hall remains *par excellence* the home of the May Meeting, for eighty-five per cent of the meetings appearing on the complete program are held within its walls. In addition to the large hall, which accommodates five thousand persons, it possesses several smaller assembly rooms, so it is not at all unusual, in the thick of the season, for two or three meetings to be set down simultaneously for this one building. Exeter Hall has the advantage of an accessible situation, being only a few yards from Charing Cross, and—what is worth far more—of a great evangelistic and philanthropic tradition. Quiet and decorous as are most of the people who compose its gatherings, it has been the headquarters of agitations that have turned many things upside down—and big things too. That it has made itself felt is evident from the sneers of its critics no less than from the eulogies of its admirers. Dickens had his fling at it when, in *Nicholas Nickleby,* he made Miss La Creevy, the miniature painter, looking out of her window for ideas of noses, declare that "there are flats of all sorts and sizes when there's a meeting at Exeter Hall," and Macaulay's gibe at "the bray of Exeter Hall" has become proverbial. Macaulay never had the reputation of being a good judge of musical sounds, and it may be that his ear was at fault in this instance; but, if he was correct in his appreciation of the characteristic vocal expression of Exeter Hall feeling, it is at any rate a bray that has been heard round the world, and that has penetrated some distinguished craniums that have been deaf to parliamentary speeches. Mr. Moncure Conway—a man certainly not prejudiced in favor of evangelical religion—scarcely exaggerated when he declared some years ago, in a lecture on the prose and poetry of London, that "the anniversaries of Exeter Hall determine peace

or tribulation for the tribes of Africa, India, China, and other regions." When visiting Hongkong I came across an interesting illustration of the influence of this much-abused center of philanthropic effort. I was talking to a government official, and happened to refer to the licensed gambling houses from which the neighboring Portuguese colony of Macao derives most of its revenue. "Yes," said he; "we used to have the same system here, and we derived a large income from it, but we had to give it up, as Exeter Hall was too strong for us." A much newer and more attractive building is the Queen's Hall, which is used for concerts all the year round and is growing in popularity with the promoters of May Meetings. Its name is a reminder that it was opened in the year of Queen Victoria's jubilee. St. James's Hall, in Piccadilly, well known as the home of the late Mr. Hugh Price Hughes's mission, is also in considerable request, but its usefulness in this respect will soon be at an end, as it is about to be torn down. The Albert Hall, which will hold an audience of ten thousand, is engaged when what is mainly required is a "demonstration" of numbers, but its size makes it unsuitable for anniversaries of the ordinary kind. Speaking is rarely effective there, even with a full house, and an assembly of only two or three thousand scattered about so huge a building is a pitiful spectacle. A few societies are fortunate enough to secure the cooperation of the lord mayor, and consequently enjoy the privilege of using the Mansion House or the Guildhall. It seems, perhaps, incongruous that May Meetings should be held in hotels, but year by year the Cannon Street Hotel, the Hotel Metropole, and the Holborn Restaurant figure on the list. These, however, are rarely utilized for meetings of the usual type, but are generally pressed into service for breakfasts, dinners, and receptions in aid of various charitable societies. But the May Meetings are not limited to "neutral" ground. Churches which rent Exeter Hall for their larger missionary meetings often turn their own buildings to account for other gatherings. Thus, there is often something going on at Lambeth Palace, Sion College, and the Church House (Anglican), City Road Chapel (Wesleyan Methodist), the City Temple and the Memorial Hall (Congregationalist), and the Metropolitan

Tabernacle and Bloomsbury Chapel (Baptist). And as some anniversary celebrations include a sermon as well as a public meeting, we may even find St. Paul's Cathedral appearing several times in the handbook.

Every now and then some one laments that the May Meetings do not arouse the interest they once did, but there is no actual reason for any doleful outlook. The meetings are certainly increasing in number and in size, and there is no evidence of any decay in enthusiasm, particularly in the case of missionary anniversaries. And on the whole they make a powerful contribution to the religious life of England. Many a country pastor, who has been toiling for twelve lonely months in some out-of-the-way village, makes his pilgrimage to Exeter Hall, and is brought so closely into touch with the great movement of Christian progress that he goes back with a new spirit of cheerful zeal. His visit, though it may be only from Monday to Saturday, is a spiritual tonic. It means something to have had an opportunity of hearing the distinguished preachers and speakers of whom he has read so much; it means much more to have had a quickening of his faith, hope, and love. For it is on this trinity of virtues that Exeter Hall is built. Once remove faith, hope, and love out of the Christian experience, and you might take your pen and run it through every line in the May Meeting program.

Whatever may be said of the "otherworldliness" of the Christian believer, there is nothing in all London more practical than the ministry to the suffering and the fallen which gives an account of its stewardship at these gatherings. And when we ask the laborers themselves what inspires them to this service they have nothing to say but "We love, because He first loved us." So, after all, we must put Exeter Hall on our list of Evidences of Christianity; for Mr. Spurgeon spoke for the universal conscience when he declared, "The God that answereth by orphanages, let him be God."

Herbert W. Horwill

ART. X.—THE CORONATION OF THE COMMON PEOPLE.

THE vanishing from the world's stage during the past fifty
years of so many gifted and brilliant men has frequently been the
subject of special remark and regret. The disappearance of such
a constellation of extraordinary characters from the heavens of our
poor human world has by some been regarded as a sore calamity,
and many are the lamentations which have found expression,
especially in the realms to which those supreme spirits belonged.
The sadness of the bereavement is all the keener and deeper from
the fact that few of all the splendid lights gone out have found any
worthy successors to fill the vast spaces they have left behind. The
mantles dropped by the great orators, musicians, painters, poets,
epoch-making scientists, singers, preachers, and by the men of
royal imagination whose creations rouse and hold us as if by some
magic and masterly charm, lie here and there unclaimed, and it is
certain that the world has passed through the portals of the new
century with a singular absence of men of commanding genius in
any of the spheres so richly illuminated in the different periods
of the past. The regrets that reach us through many voices on
the removal of so many of earth's favored sons may be well
founded, but while we respect the convictions of men who bemoan
the disappearance of the magnificent we do not in any great
measure share them. For special reasons we gladly welcome this
distinct parenthesis in the annals of the great and the sublime.

The closing of the gates through which processions of brilliant
personalities have passed has been the occasion for the opening of
wide doors of opportunity for the middling man to show that in
this dull dress of commonplace qualifications there is enshrined a
man, a mighty factor, an unheralded sovereign, with mandates,
authorities, empires all his own. The average man at last has
made his advent, and from the present outlook he has come to
stay. Too long he has been kept in the shade by the dazzling
brightness of a few royally gifted men. Unappreciated, unhonored,
the brother of the ordinary talents marches to the front and no
command of any proud Cæsar can force him back to the bitter

humiliations of former days. Socially, politically, mentally, religiously, the average or middling man has risen, as if by some grand instinct of the new age, to a throne of power. This enfranchisement of the commonplace mortal which enables him to stand up in God's world in his full independent individuality, taking a full, unfettered breath, every time, is an achievement in the development of humanity which ought to inspire our deepest gratitude. But why should the disappearance of so many splendid figures from the active forces of the world furnish a subject rather for quiet congratulation than for moaning regrets? For the simple reason that the middling man may demonstrate the merits and powers that are his and that in due time he may secure his proper place in the direction and government of the world. The average individual is by far the most numerous type in the world's population of this and every age. The genius, the magnificently endowed, and the rank which falls below the ordinary are the extremes and exceptions of mankind. They constitute the outskirts, the capes and promontories of the race, but the great continent of human existence lies between and is made up of the men of ordinary powers. The true strength and real life of the planet is not found in the exceptional climes, the arctic frost or torrid heat, but in temperate lands we find the realm where the grape ripens and the wheat turns yellow in the constant sun. So in the temperate zone of mankind we find the most productive and most reliable source of those forces upon which the world depends for the actualization of its highest aims.

It is also a fact more apparent now than in any other time that by far the largest amount of work, both in the Church and in the world, is being done by the middling or the average man. Goethe has said that God chose the Jew above all others for his toughness, and it would appear that this quality of endurance is possessed by the commonplace mortal in a larger degree than in the other extremes of human life, and this power for holding on to purpose and immense undertakings is a great factor in all the achievements which are pushing the race onward and upward. And what a splendid faculty for common interest and coöperation

is enjoyed by the type of man which sums up such a vast majority of earth's population to-day! The richly gifted, by the very nature of things, are isolated from their fellows. So mighty has the average man become that he possesses a power which means panic or progress in all the great realms which make up the age in which we live. And it is evident that this rising force is the real sovereign which is to rule the twentieth century- as commander and dictator of the future destinies of mankind. Carlyle concludes his *Past and Present* with ringing words as he sees the great army of industry, and the gradual lifting of the vast central mass of mankind into power. With sturdy eloquence he exclaims: "This enormous, all-conquering, flame-crowned host is marching to subdue chaos and make this old world worthier of God and more fit for man."

William Harrison

EDITORIAL DEPARTMENTS.

NOTES AND DISCUSSIONS.

PROFESSOR DUGALD MACFADYEN, editor of the Temple Biographies Series, in his introduction to Dr. Edward Dowden's new life of Robert Browning, published by E. P. Dutton & Co., which is "a biography of the Poet's mind," writes:

Browning has become to many, in a measure which he could hardly have conceived possible himself, one of the authoritative interpreters of the spiritual factors in human life. His tonic optimism dissipates the gray atmosphere of materialism, which has obscured the sun-clad heights of life as effectively as a fog. To see life through Browning's eyes is to see it shot through and through with spiritual issues, with a background of eternal destiny, and to come appreciably nearer than the general consciousness of our time to seeing it steadily and seeing it whole. Those who prize his influence know how to value everything which throws light on the path by which he reached his resolute and confident outlook.

Because that statement is entirely true of Browning, as of no other modern poet, we have for years conceived it to be a high duty to assist in giving vogue to his robust and peremptory faith, his resolute and confident gospel, in comparison with the priceless value of which all criticisms of his eccentricities of style are so academic and trivial as not to concern mankind.

AN INCORRIGIBLE BLUNDER IN GRAMMAR.

FOURTEEN years ago the following appeared in a New York city newspaper:

MISUSE OF THE PRONOUN "WHOM."

To the Editor of the Tribune.

SIR: How do you explain the fact that one of the most obvious violations of grammar is so frequently found in high quarters, even in stately reviews and newspapers that pride themselves on their correct English? Here are specimens:

In an article on marriage and divorce in a religious review a man "denies that he ever intended to marry the woman whom lawyers endeavored to prove was his first wife." Whom was. Her was not.

In the report of an accident a man is described as "searching for his daughter whom he thought might have been saved." Whom might. Her was not saved, you see.

In the investigation of a case of arson a man testifies that the house "had been purchased by Harry Baker, a man whom the State says has no existence." Him may have been dead.

A Long Branch report speaks of a clergyman "whom Christian scientists claim has shown a leaning toward their beliefs." Whom showed.

A letter from the revered object of a certain cult runs thus: "Dear Sir: I have not in my possession a picture such as you desire, but I will send your letter to a photographer in Washington whom I presume will furnish it to you." Whom will. But perhaps him did not write this sentence just as printed. If so let him look to the proofreader whom did it. So plain and inexcusable a mistake ought not to be so common. Will *The Tribune* help to correct it?

St. John's Church, Brooklyn, July 4, 1890.

WILLIAM V. KELLEY.

(*The Tribune* will, cheerfully.—ED.)

A few days later the editor of the *Tribune* replied to a counter-critic and objector thus:

"W. A. L." writes to take exception to one of the several admirably selected examples of the misuse of the pronoun "whom," selected by Dr. Kelley and pointed out in a letter to *The Tribune*, recently published. "W. A. L." says: "In the first case, we think he is mistaken. Will the doctor please reconsider his statement, and look at another word in the sentence?" No, Dr. Kelley was not "mistaken." Why should he reconsider his statement? The sentence which he quotes reads: "The man denies that he ever intended to marry the woman whom lawyers endeavored to prove was his first wife." Whom could never be the subject of "was," if it lived till the blast of Gabriel's trumpet was sounded. Just punctuate after "woman" and "prove." Read it this way: "The man denies that he ever intended to marry the woman whom (lawyers endeavored to prove) was his first wife." Pretty bad, isn't it?

In spite of all corrections and protests this gross and glaring blunder in grammar mysteriously persists, undaunted and undiminished by criticism. It seems utterly incorrigible. Intelligence appears to be no protection against it, and the most finical purists often walk straight into its snare. Nobody is surprised when the *New York Journal* reports that "the man *whom* the police believe *sent* the blackmail letters to a wealthy druggist has been arraigned," for bad grammar may be expected of yellow journalism. Nor does any sense of wonder overcome us when the manager of the football team in an Eastern college sends out to principals of preparatory schools a request for "the names and data of any good athletes *whom* you know *will be ready* to enter college next September." We can even bear it, if not excuse it, when the business manager of a great review asks us to send him the names of a few of our friends *whom* we feel *would be interested* in his review. It might seem unfeeling to criticise a request so feelingly expressed. But it gives us a shock to find a stern reformer of abuses, a merciless censor of human

errors, infirmities, and infelicities, an icily proper pink of perfection, like the *Springfield Republican,* printing on August 24, 1903, the editorial paragraph:

> The Humberts, the greatest swindlers of a century, get five years in a French prison; yet madame goes down with colors flying, repeating to the last that the Crawford millions do exist. M. Labori has furnished the only other feature of interest in the trial by showing that, as a lawyer, he could defend a supreme scoundrel, *whom* he knew to be guilty, with as much eloquence and zest as he could a Dreyfus, *whom* he had every reason to believe *was innocent.*

Perhaps the dog-days did it. Even the loftiest critic is liable to nod in mid-August. And one does not expect to find in stately and scholarly reviews sentences resembling the invitations sent out by Chuck Connors, the "King of the Bowery Boys," the "Mayor of Chinatown," asking his unwashed friends to his annual ball at Tammany Hall; invitations which are fairly described as being "couched in carefully ungrammatical English." Yet in so brilliant a review as the *International Quarterly,* on page 251 of the issue of September, 1903, an article on Herman Grimm quotes Professor Grimm as saying of Goethe, "Without abdicating our intellectual independence, we may yet devote ourselves to him *whom* we feel *has* a legitimate right to our services." (Whom has a right! Why not write and punctuate it properly? *Who,* we feel, *has* a right.) Again, in the same great review, on page 234, December, 1903, Louis Lucipia, in an article on "The Paris Commune of 1871," quotes Jules Favre as saying, "I have heard men *whom* I thought *were* sane and intelligent declare that the best thing to do was to take their wives and children and let them all be killed." (Whom were!) We are reminded of a notice which a friend saw on the summit of the Rigi above Lake Lucerne, posted in the corridor of a hotel which always wakes its guests in time to see the sun rise, the literal translation of which is: "Messieurs and venerable voyagers are hereby advertised that when the sun him do rise a horn will be blowed." This is an exact rendering of French idiom, but is intolerable English. We wish "a horn" might "be blowed" announcing the rising of a day in the light of which a blunder which any schoolboy in the first grammar class should be able to avoid may disappear at least from the higher circles of literature and culture, and never be heard from any presumably educated pulpit. The misuse of "whom" for "who" is due partly to lack of clear thinking and careful attention, partly to a failure to punctuate properly. A notable correction of this misuse is seen in Mark viii, verses 27 and 29 (as also in the corresponding passage in

Luke ix, verses 18 and 20) as printed in the Revised Version of the Bible. The King James Version has it, *"Whom* do men say that I am?" and *"Whom* say ye that I am?" It is impossible to parse "whom" in these verses. There is no rule of grammar which can be stretched or twisted so as to justify or permit its use. There is no verb of which "whom" can be the object, nor any infinitive to which it can stand as subject. And the translators of the Revised Version did not need to be expert grammarians in order to be able to make the grammar respectable by rendering the verses, *"Who* do men say that I am?" and *"Who* say ye that I am?" Any graduate from a public school ought to be able to make so simple and necessary a correction. The "split infinitive," as it is called, which consists in inserting an adverb into the infinitive form where it does not belong, as in saying "to kindly request" instead of "kindly to request" or "to request kindly," is a far less grievous mistake, being only a question of the proper location and order of the words in a sentence, and not of rendering the sentence utterly unparsable.

While upon this subject we may admit a communication referring to another very common mistake:

SIR: The symposium of grammarians in *The Tribune* has been entertaining and instructive. I did not feel willing to intrude among the banqueters, but now that the symposium is at an end you might let me in, under the pretense of bringing in the apollinaris on a waiter.

Can anyone explain the universal practice of mislocating in a sentence the word "only"?—"I only paid a dollar," "He only slept an hour," "They only heard it once." The *Saturday Globe* before me says: "Dead! and you and I were only talking of him last night!"—apparently intimating that their mere talk could not possibly have killed him. In another paper this catches my eye: "One site which cost $10,000 was only purchased last June;" that it was not paid for, or possessed, but merely purchased. Any number of similar sentences can be clipped from a pile of newspapers. In current literature the error is very common. Frederick Anstey says in *Tariah,* which I am reading at the moment, "She only came back last night," and so anyone who asserts that she went away again is mistaken. In fact, this queer mode of expression has imbedded itself firmly in our common speech. Very few persons on the platform or in conversation put the word "only" where it properly belongs. Why? How came the language by this bad sprain?   S. H. MEAD.

Eustis, Fla.

(Undoubtedly this long-suffering word is often misplaced. It should be as near as possible to the word or words it qualifies. In the first example given the word is so placed as to indicate that the speaker alone paid a dollar; but if the meaning be, as it doubtless is, that only a dollar was paid, the sentence should read, "I paid only a dollar." The same remarks apply to the second, which should read, "They heard it only once;" the third should read, "Only last night;" the fourth, "Was purchased only last June;" and Mr. Anstey should have said that "She came back only last night," unless he meant that she came alone, or that she did nothing else besides coming.—ED.)

We also transcribe a letter which protests against overfastidiousness and finical purism:

SIR: I have myself been called a purist, and I certainly detest corruptions of English speech; but I must say that I am made very weary by the finicky criticisms of some who, while using without question numerous current barbarisms, object with hair-splitting logic to such well-established and expressive idioms as "higher up," "lower down," "further on," "gather together," and the like. The translators of our English Bible were pretty good masters of English speech, and they did not hesitate to say, "Friend, go up higher," just as St. Jerome, in the Vulgate, had said before them, "Amice, ascende superius." Milton, too, in *Paradise Lost*, wrote, "Ascend up to our native seat." The biblical translators again wrote, "When He had gathered together," and Burton, in his *Anatomy of Melancholy*, gave us the proverbial saying, "Birds of a feather will gather together"—which is almost invariably misquoted "flock together." It would be far better for would-be language reformers to quit such "egregious folly of purism," and pay attention to suppressing real evils, such as "sending a wireless," "electrocuting," and "making a combine." Yet I know people who habitually use these latter expressions but regard "higher up" with holy horror.   W. F. J.

New York, February 2, 1904.

Whatever force be conceded to this protesting letter, no one can accuse us of purism or fastidiousness in our protest against the misuse of "whom" for "who," which is a most flagrant mistake as indefensible as it seems incurable. Strange that so elementary a matter should ever need to be expounded and emphasized in educated circles!

THE BIBLE SOCIETY CENTENNIAL.

ONE of the most important events in the religious annals of the present year is the centennial of the British and Foreign Bible Society. The founding of this society just one hundred years ago marked the inauguration of what has been fitly called the greatest literary enterprise of the Christian era. What grander, nobler undertaking can be imagined than to give the pure word of God without note or comment, the source of unspeakable temporal and spiritual blessings, to all the millions of mankind? It is no wonder that the project once started speedily fired the hearts of multitudes, and enlisted the hearty cooperation of men of all creeds. The only marvel is that it was not entered upon before. The story of the origin has been often told, yet it deserves a brief rehearsal here. A venerable clergyman and a little girl seem to have been the prime factors in initiating the movement. The Rev. Thomas Charles, of Bala, a town in Merionethshire, Wales, a man fully given to good works, fertile in expedients for God, saintly, indefatigable, apostolic, was the main instrumentality. There

is no question concerning the world's indebtedness to him. Nor is the nature of the little girl's part doubtful, although her precise personality is not altogether clear. In fact, there would appear to have been at least two girls who figure quite significantly in the narrative that has come down to us. Possibly when the mysterious processes of higher criticism have been sufficiently exercised upon the incident the two may resolve themselves into one, and the part which tradition has played with fact may be brought plainly to view. But at present it is not plain. According to one account—given in *The Book and Its Story*, put forth at the Jubilee of the Bible Society—as Mr. Charles was walking the streets of Bala he met a child who attended his ministry. He inquired if she could recite the text from which he had preached on the previous Sunday; she was silent, and the inquiry was repeated. At length she answered, "The weather has been so bad that I could not get to read the Bible." The reason of this was soon ascertained: there was no copy to which she could gain access, either at her own home or among her friends; and she was accustomed to walk seven miles over the hills every week to a place where she could obtain a Welsh Bible, for the purpose of reading the chapter from which the minister took his text. According to another account, which may be the same in a slightly different dress, and which is the more usually told, the girl, Mary Jones by name, being without a Bible—as were most of the people at that time, for there was a veritable famine of the word—and longing to possess one, set herself in right good earnest honestly to earn it. For six years she toiled and prayed and saved, and then with a brave heart full of hope, but with bare brown feet, she walked twenty-five miles from her home to Bala to buy the sacred book from Mr. Charles. But, alas! the good pastor had to tell her that the only unsold copy in his possession was already promised to another, and she had to walk back those weary twenty-five miles almost broken-hearted. It is also told us that twelve Welsh peasants subscribed together to purchase a copy of the Bible which was to circulate among the hills. Each family was to keep it a month and then pass it on. When it arrived among them an old man, who had been the last subscriber, finding his name at the end of the list, wept bitterly, saying, "Alas, it will be twelve months before it comes to me, and I dare say I shall be gone before that time into another world." From these and other incidents, which might be related, it is evident that the destitution of Bibles was appalling, such as might well give rise to energetic efforts for an improved situation.

The Society for Promoting Christian Knowledge, established in 1698, was at this time the main source of Bible supply, although there were a few other associations of similar character which did a little in the same line. And this society in 1799 printed ten thousand Welsh Bibles, but they were no sooner published than sold, and not a fourth part of the country was furnished. No more from that quarter was to be hoped for, and there was urgent need that something be done. Societies of one kind and another were just then decidedly in the air. The Religious Tract Society had just been started; also, in the few previous years, the Baptist Missionary Society, the London Missionary Society, and the Church Missionary Society. And it occurred to Mr. Charles one morning, as he lay wakeful upon his bed, thinking upon the hard necessities of Wales, Why not a society solely for Bible distribution? He hurried to London and laid it before the next meeting of the Tract Society. Whereupon the Rev. Joseph Hughes, one of the secretaries, after expressing his approval of the idea, said, "And if for Wales, why not for the empire and the world?" The meeting cordially agreed, and instructed its secretary to follow up the suggestion. A letter was prepared which called together about three hundred persons of many denominations at the London Tavern, March 7, 1804, and they speedily effected the establishment of the Bible Society, "the first institution," as Mr. Hughes said, "that ever emanated from one of the nations of Europe for the express purpose of doing good to all the rest." Seven hundred pounds was subscribed upon the spot. In Wales, which rejoiced exceedingly at the good news, and which was soon abundantly furnished with Scriptures, nineteen hundred pounds was contributed the first year, mainly, it is noted, "from the lower orders of people." The noble and the good rallied round this inspiring banner, especially "the men of Clapham." William Wilberforce, Zachary Macaulay, Granville Sharp, and the rest of that illustrious band. An Executive Committee of thirty-six laymen was constituted, the membership fee was fixed at one guinea, and Lord Teignmouth was chosen president. The society, it may be remarked, has been most happy in its presidents. They have been only five in number. Lord Teignmouth, a former governor-general of India, devoted his best energies to this cause for thirty years. His successor was Lord Bexley, who served for seventeen years, followed by the Earl of Shaftesbury in 1851, who highly prized the honor of the position and filled it conspicuously well for thirty-five years; then came the Earl of Harrowby, who gave the society fourteen years' dis-

tinguished services, closed by his death in 1900. The Marquis of
Northampton now worthily fills out this illustrious succession of most
honorable names. What hath God wrought through this agency and
the similar ones which have since been set in motion mainly by its
example! Figures but faintly indicate it. Yet they are eloquent. In
its hundred years the British and Foreign Bible Society has circulated
in round numbers 187,000,000 Bibles, Testaments, and Scripture portions; the American Bible Society, in its eighty-eight years, over
74,000,000; the Scotch, in its forty-four years, about 24,000,000—
making 285,000,000 for these three alone. For the many other minor
societies which act independently of these we have not the precise
figures at hand, but it would be perfectly safe to set them down at
15,000,000 more, thus making the grand total of 300,000,000 copies
of some vital part of the word of the living God sent out during the
century by this means alone, to say nothing of what has been done by
private firms. The British Society now distributes about six million
copies a year—one million Bibles, one and a half million Testaments,
three and a half million portions—the American about two millions,
and the Scotch about one million. But there is, of course, also an
enormous sale from private publishing houses, like that of the Bag-
sters, the Cambridge and Oxford University Presses, and a vast number of others, many of whom do nothing but issue Bibles. Twelve
million copies a year is probably not too large an estimate for the
total output at the present time, when so many revised versions are
thronging the market. And when it is remembered that there were
not more than five or six million copies of the Bible in existence at
the beginning of the last century the progress can be readily discerned,
and may well call forth heartiest praise. At the beginning of the
last century the Bible was current in about forty different languages.
Fifty translations are said to have been in existence, but only thirty-
five were in living languages, and the entire Bible was by no means
in all of these. The long, slow struggle of eighteen hundred years
had led to this meager result. There had been gradually added to
the original Hebrew and Greek, to the Septuagint and the Samaritan
Pentateuch, the ancient Syriac, the old Latin and the Vulgate. Then,
after a time, it became credible that the sacred writers could be made
to speak in the modern tongues. The Bible was the first of Russian
books, as it had been the first of Gothic, and the first of Armenian.
Germany in 1466 obtained its earliest Scriptures in the vernacular;
Italy soon followed, in 1471; France in 1474; Bohemia in 1488. The

printing press started its wonderful career with the Mazarin Bible 1450. Twenty editions of the Latin Bible had been printed in Germany alone before Luther was born; and in 1517 the fourteenth known issue of a German Bible took place—these fourteen issues being not mere reprints, but various translations from the Vulgate. In 1516 Erasmus's Greek Testament appeared. Luther grounded his great Reformation in the marvelously effective version of the Scriptures which he wrought, in 1522, which is still standard. The English Wyclife (his new Testament appeared in 1378) and his successors, culminating in Tyndale, gained this great boon of the Gospel story in their mother tongue. But it was seventy-five years after the first printed Latin Bible before the English had even a printed New Testament in their own language, and that was imported from the Continent. In 1536 the English clergy were ordered to put an English Bible and a Latin Bible in the choir of every parish church, that every man who chose might read therein; but not until some years later did any Englishman or Scotchman hear the Bible read in his own tongue as part of the public service.

How different the state of things now! Dr. Dennis, in his *Centennial Survey of Foreign Missions,* gives as the total of all living versions (including transliterations) in use at present by people of all languages and dialects, 452. His figures, in some respects the fullest yet gathered, show a total of 478 missionary translations, only ten of them issued before the nineteenth century. He reckons also six principal ancient versions, and sixteen standard modern versions, thus giving 478 ancient and modern, living and obsolete, Bible translations. Taking out 46 as obsolete, and adding the 20 transliterated versions now in use would give the 452 mentioned above. But since these figures were collected some three years ago they are subject to quite a little addition; for no less than eight new versions—Fioti, Kikuyu, Shambala, Karanga, Nogogu, Laevo, Baffins Land Eskimo, and Madurese—have been added during the past year by the British Society alone. No year passes without some additions; and the list of versions issued by the British Society now includes the names of three hundred and seventy distinct forms of speech. Its first volume, singularly enough, was for the Indians of the Mohawk River. It sent them two thousand copies of the Gospel of St. John bound in calf. Its final volume will not be issued until the judgment angel shall proclaim that all activities in this probationary world must cease. Nor will there be, until a period now apparently very remote, any

printing press started its wonderful career with the Mazarin Bible 1450. Twenty editions of the Latin Bible had been printed in Germany alone before Luther was born; and in 1517 the fourteenth known issue of a German Bible took place—these fourteen issues being not mere reprints, but various translations from the Vulgate. In 1516 Erasmus's Greek Testament appeared. Luther grounded his great Reformation in the marvelously effective version of the Scriptures which he wrought, in 1522, which is still standard. The English Wyclife (his new Testament appeared in 1378) and his successors, culminating in Tyndale, gained this great boon of the Gospel story in their mother tongue. But it was seventy-five years after the first printed Latin Bible before the English had even a printed New Testament in their own language, and that was imported from the Continent. In 1536 the English clergy were ordered to put an English Bible and a Latin Bible in the choir of every parish church, that every man who chose might read therein; but not until some years later did any Englishman or Scotchman hear the Bible read in his own tongue as part of the public service.

How different the state of things now! Dr. Dennis, in his *Centennial Survey of Foreign Missions,* gives as the total of all living versions (including transliterations) in use at present by people of all languages and dialects, 452. His figures, in some respects the fullest yet gathered, show a total of 478 missionary translations, only ten of them issued before the nineteenth century. He reckons also six principal ancient versions, and sixteen standard modern versions, thus giving 478 ancient and modern, living and obsolete, Bible translations. Taking out 46 as obsolete, and adding the 20 transliterated versions now in use would give the 452 mentioned above. But since these figures were collected some three years ago they are subject to quite a little addition; for no less than eight new versions—Fioti, Kikuyu, Shambala, Karanga, Nogogu, Laevo, Baffins Land Eskimo, and Madurese—have been added during the past year by the British Society alone. No year passes without some additions; and the list of versions issued by the British Society now includes the names of three hundred and seventy distinct forms of speech. Its first volume, singularly enough, was for the Indians of the Mohawk River. It sent them two thousand copies of the Gospel of St. John bound in calf. Its final volume will not be issued until the judgment angel shall proclaim that all activities in this probationary world must cease. Nor will there be, until a period now apparently very remote, any

cessation in the strenuous effort to overtake the very large number of tongues and dialects as yet unsupplied with the word. The need is still very great. Within the borders of the Indian empire alone no versions of Scripture exist in one hundred and eight languages used by seventy-four million souls. In the islands of Polynesia and Malaysia and on the upper waters of the Amazon there are hundreds of dialects in which the Scriptures have never spoken. If there are, as Dr. Cust estimates, two thousand languages in the world, then at least one thousand five hundred of them have not been honored by the word of inspiration; and probably half of these are sufficiently important to merit it. Out of the translations of the Scriptures now existent in living tongues no fewer than two hundred and nineteen have been made in languages which have been reduced to writing for the purpose within the present century. The missionaries of the American Board alone have taken twenty-nine unwritten languages and reduced them to writing to put the Bible into them, in part or in whole. Scores of tribes in Africa use languages the very names of which are scarce known to us. The Lolo is spoken by ten millions of people on the equatorial tributaries of the Congo. There are vast tracts where different dialects are met every ten or fifteen miles. In some lands by no means wholly barbarous the diversity of tongues is enormous and amazing. The Bible Society agents sold Scriptures last year in 53 languages of the Russian empire, 20 of the Austrian empire, 28 in Burma, 30 in South Malaysia, 53 in the Egyptian agency stretching from Antioch to Uganda, and 14 in Cape Town alone. It can from these facts be at least somewhat understood what an unending and Herculean task is assigned to the translation and revision departments supervised and financed by the Bible Society; also to the colportage and distribution department. This latter maintained last year a total colportage staff of 870, who sold 1,830,000 copies, a gain of 90,000 over the highest previous record. The society also supports 685 native Christian Bible women, who minister to their neglected and secluded sisters in Eastern lands. Controlled by the translation department about one thousand representative missionaries and native assistants are at work in different countries under the society's auspices, and largely at its expense. It lays out some five thousand pounds a year on this work, and has from the beginning spent in it about five hundred thousand pounds. Translation work is now being carried on in one hundred and thirty-seven languages. And so the word of God goes flying all abroad.

The connection of the Bible Society and the Missionary Society, as will readily be inferred, is of the most intimate character. What could either do without the other? Their mutual relations are of the closest kind. The Bible Society relies upon the missionaries to translate and circulate its multiplied versions. The missionaries depend upon the Bible Society for supplies of that which is of the highest importance in their work. And the Bible Society deals with them in the most liberal manner. It sends out the books that are needed free of cost and carriage paid; in return, the missionaries remit to the Bible House any proceeds arising from the copies which they sell, after deducting the expenses of circulation. At best only a small fraction of what the Bible Society expends on the preparation and delivery of these missionary versions can ever come back to it as the result of such sales, while the missionaries obtain all the Scriptures they require without any cost whatever to their own societies. In ten years the grants from the Bible Society to one missionary organization amounted to not less than one thousand eight hundred pounds, while the missionaries returned to the society only about fifty pounds. To the London Missionary Society the Bible Society furnishes the Scriptures in over fifty different languages, to the Wesleyans in over forty, the Presbyterians use about sixty different versions, while the Church Missionary Society, which uses more than a hundred translations, gets full ninety of them from the Bible Society. Where the missionary himself, for special reasons, cannot go, the colporteur and the Bible are often allowed, and the Bible alone has frequently penetrated, with most beneficial effect, to otherwise inaccessible regions. Grants of Scriptures are also made freely to the home lands, through auxiliaries and branches, which in England number 5,875. Especial attention is paid to providing Scriptures for the blind, and soldiers are particularly looked after. In the Russo-Turkish struggle 478,000 copies were sent to the seat of hostilities, and in the South African war 133,000 to the belligerents on both sides. It can well be seen, perhaps, even from this hurried presentation, that every Bible Society stands in urgent need of funds. As a business undertaking it cannot be supported without a wide departure from usual financial principles. It is deliberately run at a loss. And the greater the demand for the Scriptures the greater the outlay necessitated. Since the foundation of the British Society it has disbursed over £11,000,000. Its total net payments last year were £254,204, while its net receipts from all sources were £233,138. During the last five years it has expended

£60,000 more than it has received. And a fund of 250,000 guineas is imperatively demanded (and it is hoped may be raised before the month or the year shall close) to prevent any curtailing of the society's beneficent operations.

It is earnestly to be hoped also that the American Bible Society, only twelve years younger than its British sister, and every way worthy to stand beside her in all respects, may reap substantial profit from this year's renewed interest in the noble cause she represents. The resources of this society have been seriously diminished of late from a variety of reasons. Its former income has been largely depleted by the increasing appeals for denominational causes and for local charities. Its work is easily forgotten because done so quietly and out of sight. A false impression that the society is rich has hurt it not a little. Its entire income from investments and rents is only enough to carry on its work for six weeks. It needs at least two hundred and fifty thousand dollars a year from the Christian churches, and it is by no means getting it. The benevolent receipts for the last year fell about fifty thousand dollars below the average for the last ten years. Unless large special gifts are received at once the work will be greatly damaged by the cessation of agencies, the dismissal of tried workers, and the stopping of the presses. Surely this cannot be allowed. It would be a disgrace to American Christianity with its large and constantly increasing wealth. This society has employed during the past year in foreign lands 447 persons to distribute Scriptures. Some have been remarkably successful. In the Philippine agency the circulation has nearly doubled over the previous year, reaching a total of 91,260. In Porto Rico the circulation has been 10,000 copies as against 3,000 the year before. The total issues in foreign fields were 1,258,909, with 731,649 in the United States. It works in 100 languages, including 28 European, 39 Asiatic, 9 African, and 12 American. The total receipts for 1903 were $412,406, of which only $98,085 were gifts from the living, and $53,926 were in legacies. Each of these important sources of income, especially the first, should be at once doubled.

The history of Bible work in America has peculiar interest for us, and deserves more than the page we can give it. So long as the colonists were subject to Great Britain all their supplies of Scriptures were imported. During the Revolutionary War such was the scarcity of Bibles that Congress in 1777 voted to print thirty thousand copies; and when it was found impracticable, from want of type and paper,

it directed the Committee on Commerce to import twenty thousand from Europe, giving as a reason that "its use was so universal and its importance so great." When this too, in consequence of the embargo, was found impracticable Congress passed a resolution (1782) in favor of an edition of the Bible published by the private enterprise of Mr. Robert Aitken, of Philadelphia, which it pronounced "a pious and laudable undertaking subservient to the interests of religion." But in spite of such high congressional indorsement this first English Bible printed in America—a small 18mo, a book so rare that a copy has been sold in modern days for six hundred and fifty dollars—was produced by its publisher at a loss of three thousand dollars in specie. From 1790 onward many editions were brought out by publishers in Philadelphia, New York, Boston, Trenton, Worcester, and elsewhere. They were, however, inadequate for the wants of the growing republic, besides being sold at prices beyond the reach of the poor. After the starting of the British Society in 1804, kindred associations were soon organized in different parts of this country, but they were local, independent bodies, having no connection nor intercommunication. The Philadelphia Bible Society was established in 1808, and the London Committee at once voted it a donation of one thousand dollars and sent it consignments of Scriptures at cost price. Six years later the number of Bible societies and kindred associations in the States had increased to sixty-nine. In 1815 the Bible Society of New Jersey, prompted by the venerable Elias Boudinot, its president (formerly president of the Congress of the United States), issued a circular to the several Bible societies in the country inviting them to send delegates to meet in the city of New York the ensuing year. The New York and Philadelphia societies entered cordially into the measure. A convention was held in New York in May, 1816, composed of sixty delegates representing thirty-five Bible societies in ten States. Dr. Boudinot was chosen president, and a full organization readily effected. The receipts of the society the first year were $37,779, and its issues 6,410 volumes. For the first period of twenty-five years it issued 2,798,366 volumes; for the second period, 18,987,210; for the third 32,478,138; for the fourth period, if the present rate be continued, the total will reach 50,000,000. Again and again the society has carried out the colossal undertaking of canvassing the entire country, with the aim of visiting every family. As the result of two of these costly and protracted efforts the entire number of families reported to be visited was 11,764,416, and out of 1,299,150 of these

that were found destitute of the Bible 850,061 were supplied by sale or gift, and 598,924 persons besides. More than one half of its annual issues go into the hands of pagan, Mohammedan, or nominally Christian people outside of the United States. Last year 561,040 were sold in China alone, and more than 8,000,000 volumes in the various dialects of that empire have been printed during the last fifty years. It is supposed that at least 2,000,000 were sold there last year by the British Society alone and at least 3,000,000 by all agencies, so unprecedented is the demand. In the neighboring empire of Japan, where the three great societies have for the last ten years been united in their operations, over one million copies have been distributed. These are but instances of how the world is opening more and more to the word of God. It is not now a crime to circulate the Bible anywhere. Religious liberty increasingly prevails. In 1886 a ton of Bibles was condemned to be publicly burned in the capital of Ecuador. Now the colporteurs are welcomed in all parts of South America. Even the Roman Catholic Church is reversing as rapidly as could fairly be expected its age-long policy of denying the Scriptures to the common people. Popes send out encyclicals urging the universal study of the word of the Lord. Most significant is it that the Society of St. Jerome, composed of Roman Catholics, is, with the pope's approval and with Bible society methods, putting the Scriptures into the hands of the common people of Italy. One hundred and seventy thousand copies of the Gospels and Acts in one volume, at four cents in paper covers and eight cents in cloth, have rapidly been sold. This is a new, scholarly, and simple translation from the original Greek.

The twentieth century starts out magnificently well as a patron and promoter of the blessed book. It inherits from the nineteenth a vast accumulation of material and a wonderfully improved apparatus for work patiently procured at large expense. It takes over also a profound and abiding conviction that the Bible is a mighty force which God has appointed for the use of his Church in the discharge of its duty to the world, a potent factor in the world's deepest, highest life, and the mightiest of helps to the evangelization of the nations. It cannot be questioned that in Christian lands the Scriptures are more carefully studied than ever before in the world's history. It is true that they are studied sometimes in a way that troubles timid souls. But the studies and conclusions of scholars concerning authorship, dates, and species of composition, or literary

forms, relate simply to the settings of the truth, not to the truth itself. They do not affect the eternal, the essential, the experimental. Prime Minister Balfour said last year at the inaugural centennial meeting of the Bible Society at the Mansion House, London, "The researches of critics have made the Bible far more a living record of the revelation of God to mankind than it ever was or ever could be to those who, from the nature of the case, had no adequate conception of the circumstances under which the revelation occurred, or the peoples to whom it was revealed. And I most truly think that not only is the Bible now what it has always been to the unlearned, a source of consolation, of hope, of instruction, but it is to those who are more learned augmented in interest and not diminished, a more valuable source of spiritual life now than it could ever have been in the precritical days." With this most modern scholars agree.

The Bible is indeed the book above every book, in whose pages God is met as he is met nowhere else. It has a vitality which nothing can touch. Twenty years ago the circulation of the Scriptures in Germany amounted to ten copies per thousand of the population. Last year it amounted to eighteen copies per thousand. While learned men have discussed and doubted and even denied, the German people have doubled their purchases of the precious volume. It is the book of all saints, in whose revelations men have found, and are still finding, the best discipline for Christian character. It is the book of converts, making them in most marvelous ways out of raw heathen, and then still further training them into righteousness and true holiness. It is the book of the progressive nations, of those which have the largest colonizing and civilizing energies, of those which are certain more and more to dominate the earth. It is the reconciler of differences, the healer of breaches, the promoter of union among Christians above any other instrumentality, breaking down the middle walls of partition and bringing about spiritual intercommunion of the churches. It is the only universal book, the book of unvarying victories, the book of most magnificent achievements. Through centuries it has withstood countless storms, it has survived countless foes, and remains the only book wherein God speaks the eternal message which satisfies the needs and aspirations of the human soul.

> Captains and conquerors leave a little dust,
> And kings a dubious legend of their reign;
> The swords of Cæsar, they are less than dust;
> The Bible doth remain.

THE ARENA.

MAN GREATER THAN NATURE.

How insignificant is man! It is only as we think of human insignificance and frailty that we get a startling conception of man's superiority and power.

There is a disposition in some minds to belittle man, and reduce him to such absurd insignificance in the universe as to nullify the importance of human conduct and destiny, and to escape the notice of the Creator. Think of man, therefore, in his physical structure. The body comprises but thirteen of the seventy-two simple substances. A French chemist tells us the average man is composed of a few pounds of oxygen, hydrogen, carbon, nitrogen, a few ounces of phosphorus, calcium, chlorine, and salt, a few pinches of silica, sulphur, potassium, magnesia, and iron. How closely akin is man to the clods in the field! Stop and reflect. What do a few pounds of earthy substances amount to in comparison with the mighty volume of the earth, or the huge frame of the shining sun? What is one human being among all the multiplied billions of beings on the numberless planets of space? In a universe of fathomless spaces, of immeasurable forces, of worlds without number, what is man? What are human achievements? What is man's destiny? A "mere mote of dust in the sunbeam of time." A mere ripple in the ocean of immensity. A dream—and a forgetting.

How insignificant is man! Weak and puny is his arm compared with the elastic strength of the greater brutes, or with the power of the tempest, or the might of the earthquake. How frail is man! His body, composed of a few simple substances, endures perhaps for threescore years and ten, and then crumbles into dust, but the giant fir and the lordly redwood tower aloft for a thousand years; and the snow-capped peak stands a mute sentinel while continents endure; and the stars shine on while men and mountains pass away. The mind of man, how frail! So subject to hope and fear, to truth and error, and so limited in its powers that it knows but little of the infinite kingdom of knowledge. The skeptic thus muses upon man, and reduces him to a vanishing infinitesimal, and laughs moral responsibility out of existence, as such an exceedingly small matter. Some take a flippant view of human existence, but while man in a sense is insignificant, we should take a more reverent view even of his insignificance. When we consider the size of the human body, the brevity of its earthly life, the limitations of its powers, in comparison with sizes, and durations, and forces in the universe around us, well may we be overwhelmed with the thought of human littleness—but in the very insignificance of man do we find hidden his most startling superiority. Stop and reflect. The revolving earth is a mere pygmy in comparison with man, as the earth belongs to the kingdom of matter, but man belongs in the kingdom of mind. Mere earth, whether at rest or in motion, is inert; it must continue in its

state of rest or motion until acted upon by some external force. But consider man. He has life, consciousness, and volition. He is able to origi-
nate motion. Man is, in this, far superior to the material world. The
giant forces of nature, gravity, steam, electricity, are but dwarfs when
compared with man. These natural forces operate from the laws of necessity, but man is free to act or not to act. Nature's forces, then, are subject
to necessity, while man has freedom. Moreover, these gods of the materialist fall before man, for in his superiority he makes them his servants to do his bidding. Man, "the mote of dust in the sunbeam of time,"
is mightier than the earth upon which he treads, or the sun which shines
upon him, or the skies which bend over his head. These belong to the
realm of the inert, lifeless, unconscious, unthinking, and are ruled by
necessity, while man dwells in the nobler kingdom of mind and is endowed
with life, volition, intelligence, moral consciousness, and has freedom.
Even the earthworm is mightier than the planet in which it grovels, for it
possesses the physical qualities of inert matter, but it possesses something
more. It possesses life and volition and knowledge. Although the materialistic thinker laughs man into nothingness, from the intellectual standpoint man holds dominion over the earth, its treasures and forces.

How insignificant is man—yet how superior! Man's superiority over
the kingdom of nature appears in three great facts: In physical structure
he stands at the head of earthly creatures. He is provided with feet, enabling him to move from place to place, but with hands free to perform
the many tasks and inventions of daily life. In his mental powers man is
far superior to all his contemporaries. He is able to do for himself many
things nature has left undone. Nature teaches the brute by instinct, but
man lives and triumphs by the powers of reason. He adapts himself to
the various conditions of climate, the diversity of natural productions,
and makes his home in every land from the regions of perpetual summer
to the shores of the frozen ocean. He conquers the forest and plain and
ocean, and wrings from them the comforts and luxuries of life. Talk
about the insignificance of man! The supremacy of man's mind and the
skill of his hand are seen in the march of science and the riches of art.
But the crowning superiority of man over the material universe lies in his
moral consciousness, and likeness unto his Creator. We conceive of the
Creator on high, beholding the circling worlds, which are obedient to the
behests of law. We think of him peering into the kingdom of living
things, and observing their thrift and their enjoyment. We imagine him
contemplating man. It is not too much to think the Supreme Mind rejoices in the mathematical movements of the starry universe and in the
prosperity of the lower kingdoms of life. It is fair to presume God rejoices as he contemplates man, a being able to think God's thoughts, to
apprehend the glory of virtue, and to commune with the Creator and reciprocate his love. The creature that responds to the attraction of virtue
and of love is vastly superior to the creature that can respond only to the
attraction of gravitation. Right here we plainly see the towering superiority of man over the material world and the hosts of the stellar spaces.

Roseburg, Ore.   GEORGE H. BENNETT.

THE REVIVAL IN CHURCH AND COLLEGE.

A good pastor and able preacher writes: "The work done in revivals of religion is not to be compared in quality with the work done by churches in their ordinary methods. Hand-picked fruit keeps the best." Abstractly, the statement concerning the careful picking of fruit, for good keeping, is true, but the analogy is not so good when applied to saving men. Experience has not always confirmed the theory that men brought into the church through the ordinary routine work are better than those who have been brought in through a genuine spiritual awakening. It is the glory of Methodism that the old-time revival of religion, attended ordinarily with deep feeling, rooted the people, where it occurred, out of old soil into new. Excitement there was, to be sure, but what of that? There must needs be excitement where children are born—travail, labor, great excitement indeed, and agony, ending in much joy. These strenuous things seem inseparable from life; and is it not better so? Can anything be worse than chronic barrenness; or the going on of a church from year to year in a condition of dead propriety, with all the fountains of feeling smothered and drying up? It may come to pass some day, possibly, that piety itself shall be carried to a level so high, so systematized, purified, and understood, as to become less fitful, less disposed to moods, but that time has certainly not yet arrived. As things now are, there is no time and no condition under which wicked men, living habitually in low sensual moods, feel or see so keenly, and truly, as when under the stimulus of a genuine revival of religion. Such men are so dense they have to be slugged into a spiritual fact, before they can see it, and if they ever get to the brink of a decision, they have to be shoved over, or else they draw back. This is the only way left. Many eminent saints have thus entered the Christian way.

Nor is this all: It is believed that the experience of every Christian teacher in our earlier Methodist colleges, like old Augusta College, Kentucky, the first Methodist Episcopal college in the United States, where John P. Durbin, Martin Ruter, Bascom, and other able men gave instruction, turning out such men as Peter Akers (afterward president of McKendree College), Randolph S. Foster, John W. Locke (likewise one of the presidents of McKendree), John Miley, Colonel Hatch, and others of but little less note, and the Ohio Wesleyan, which is Augusta College transferred across the Ohio River into free soil, retaining all the virtues of the old plant and adding many excellencies thereto. In these schools the annual revival was, and is still, considered practically to be a part of the regular curriculum, in order that the ideals set forth may be reduced to practical life.

In fact, it seems to be well understood by the men in charge of our Church schools, both East and West, that the college student passes through a certain transitional state, of a speculative tendency, liable to unsettle him in matters of Christian faith, the antidote for which is the Spirit of God working coordinately with human reason in the study of the sciences and philosophy. Nothing short of this anchors the young man during college life. Aaron Burr, the young grandson of Jonathan Edwards, just

at this stage of student life was spiritually and morally wrecked by the counsel of an infidel physician of the town, to whom young Burr went while under conviction in a college awakening. At such times the revival, deep and pungent, opens the mind and heart of the young man as the plow opens the field ready for things to be planted. This the common-place methods of church work do not always accomplish.

Portland, Ore. C. E. CLINE.

"AN EDUCATED MINISTRY" AGAIN.

ONE who has pondered considerably the very thought presented in the *Methodist Review* of January-February, in the "Arena" department, by Rev. Frank Seeds, on the subject, "An Educated Ministry," and the so-called "correction" of Rev. J. A. Boatman in the March-April *Review*, cannot help but think that often a "correction" is merely stating another phase of the subject and, in this case, is considering the letter but missing the spirit. It may seem assumption to say this, but looking carefully at the former article we read such expressions as "mental training," "taste cultivated," "mind until awakened cannot grow," "unfold brain power," "brain culture," etc. These expressions surely show a broad conception of the meaning of education. But directly considering the expression in apparent dispute, namely, "Education means a drawing out of the powers and forces of the mind," nowhere therein does the author declare that this is the primary meaning or sense of the word "education," neither does he say that this is all there is to it. In fact, his article makes it clear that he does not exclude the thought of training, much less does he deny that it is derived from the Latin *educo, educare, educavi, educatum,* as set forth in the criticism. And granting that the primary meaning was "to teach," "to instruct," "to train up," "to foster," etc., it does not follow that this Latin word is not etymologically one with *e-duco, educere, eductum,* which means to lead forth, to draw out. As Dr. C. B. Hulbert, ex-president of Middlebury College, declares, "This makes the distinctive idea in education to be eduction. It implies the existence in man of latent germs, properties, capacities—call them by what term you please—which in a process of disciplinary training need to be developed." When the author of the second article adds, "to impart information," he misses the better meaning somewhat, for it is not the imparting, but the informing process, that makes the desired change in the mind. Education in its better sense is not what is done on the *outside* and *for* us, but what is done on the *in-side* and *by* us. And, as Dr. Hulbert again says, "the distinctive idea of an education is not to increase what a man knows, *but to augment what a man is.*" A teacher who imparts rather than draws out—imparts facts instead of developing inlaid powers—is a dismal failure. Neither is the one who retains the most the best educated, necessarily. "Feeding and nurturing" is not so much educating as the growing of the inlaid, God-given powers of mind. Parents make a mistake who try to induce a child to enter a profession which is antagonized by the inlaid bent of mind. According to the *Century Dictionary,* to educate meant to bring up a

child physically as well as mentally, and while *educere* was usually used with reference to bodily nurture and *educare* more frequently referred to the mind, these distinctions were not strictly observed, so that there is no authority for the statement that the *primary* sense of educate is to "draw out or unfold the powers of the *mind,*" but of the *body* as well. Both articles are right as far as they go and do not conflict. The criticism was uncalled for. Education comprehends all this and more—God does much not mentioned.   B. F. EBERHART.

Orleans, Neb.

"SAINT PAUL ON THE SPIRITUAL BODY."—A REJOINDER.

IN the *Methodist Review* for January-February is a critique on an article bearing the above caption and published in the "Arena" of the *Review* for May, 1903. The article is not annihilated by the critic, but may be strengthened by a reply to his criticism. Does the critic intend to affirm that spiritual is not diametrically opposed to material, or that they are alike? If so, his argument requires that he should give some instance proving their similarity, or some particulars in which they are the same. This he has not done unless in the sentence " 'Soma,' body, is clearly stated by Paul to be 'a feature or attribute' of both." A fair parallel to this statement is this one: Light and darkness are alike, for they are both concepts of the mind, or describe the conditions of a locality. To my mind the statement is a begging of the question at issue. The only definition found in the *Standard Dictionary* which can fairly be applied to a body is this: "Spiritual—Of or pertaining to spirit, as distinguished from matter; . . . incorporeal, opposed to physical." Spirit is defined, "The form of being or substance characterized by self-consciousness, self-activity, and personality, and by the absence of the properties that distinctively belong to matter, as extension, inertia," etc. Now, if this is to be accepted as authoritative we shall look in vain for a more complete distinction or difference, in the width of the universe. Our critic affirms further: "Nor is it important to determine in this connection whether it is certain or uncertain, since Paul is not writing of the 'natural' or the 'spiritual' abstractly, but of the 'natural *body*' and the 'spiritual *body*,' and gives no authority for saying that 'they hold no feature or attribute in common.' " Now, this would reduce Paul's statement, "There is a spiritual body," to a string of words without meaning. If an adjective is used legitimately the attribute described by it is by its use declared to belong to the noun in relation to which the adjective is used. For example, in the phrase, "a white dove," the dove is affirmed to possess the attribute which the adjective "white" describes. Now as fully as the dove is declared to be white, so the affirmation of Paul, "There is a spiritual body," declares the body of which Paul is speaking to be spiritual, or entirely destitute of matter, or any attribute which belongs to matter. To say less is to affirm that Paul did not realize what his words meant, or did not know the truth regarding that of which he was speaking.

One of the statements of the critic, logically interpreted, to my con-

ception concedes the exclusion from the resurrection body of all matter: "A 'spiritual body' may be understood to be a body organized suitably to the necessities . . . in or on the scene or sphere of being in which it may exist." Well, now, the resurrection body is to be "with Christ" and the angels "in glory." Surely in such a "sphere of being" it would be reasonable to conclude it to have no need of matter, but to be like the other inhabitants of that "sphere," spiritual. "Are they not *all* . . . spirits?" Our critic seems practically, if not formally, to affirm that the resurrected body of Christ was material, and needed food, or at least that he ate for purposes other than identification. Perhaps it would be perfectly legitimate, if not indeed conclusive, to state that, the critic having the floor and the affirmative, we would wait for the exhibition of his proof. But it may safely be affirmed that, on the contrary, no evidence can be adduced from the Gospel narratives that Christ either manifested any of the attributes of matter, or ate save for the purposes of identification during his post-resurrection appearances. His single occasion of eating, or the instances wherein his body appeared to consist of matter, are fully paralleled by the behavior of the angels (whom we know to be pure spirit) during their visitations to the saints of old; while, on the other hand, it is altogether inexplicable, if his body was material, why his disciples met him but ten times, and at such times for merely a brief interview, and why they were not comforted by his continued presence during the forty days. The entire duration of all ten appearances may be fairly presumed to be less than twenty hours out of the nine hundred and sixty hours of the forty days: ten minutes each for the interview with Mary, the women, Peter, James, and Paul; two hours each for those on the Emmaus journey, each of the two evening appearances in the upper room and the journey to Bethany and the ascension; six hours each for the gathering at the Sea of Galilee, and that of the "five hundred brethren"—in all eighteen hours and fifty minutes. Again: Had Christ entered the door in the manner our critic suggests, there would have been neither ground nor reason for the fear of the disciples that a ghost was in their presence; for ghosts do not knock to obtain entrance, neither are they admitted by doorkeepers. Lastly: Would our critic affirm that the spiritual body named by Paul and defined by the article would meet with a cooler welcome in the day of resurrection, from the "soul as well as spirit" of the disembodied saint, than the material body which he so hazily defines? If not, what is the purpose of this digression?   HENRY G. BILDIE.

Owatonna, Minn.

MINISTERIAL SWEARING.

Is there such a thing as ministerial swearing? It does seem that some phrases and words, such as, "*In God's name*, let us," etc., and "I want to say that such things are *damnable*," need to be condemned not only as rude but as actually sinful. And it is truly disgusting to hear the "(hic)-er-(hic)-old-fellow-(hic)" of the drunken man imitated.

Morris Heights, New York City.   EDWIN H. CARR.

THE ITINERANTS' CLUB.

PAUL'S ADVICE TO TITUS—Titus ii, 11-15.

THE practical advice which Paul has thus far given to Titus, outlining the things which he should communicate to the different classes of people to whom he was called to minister and urging them to abstain from that which is evil, is followed immediately by a reason. This is shown in the eleventh verse, which reads, "For the grace of God hath appeared, bringing salvation to all men." This is the Revised Version. The margin, however, puts it more in harmony with the previous context, "hath appeared to all men, bringing salvation." This marginal reading seems to be a justification of the breadth of the counsel which the apostle has urged upon Titus. He has referred to them by classes, and to each class has offered special counsel. What more fitting, then, than that the apostle should say that "the grace of God hath appeared to all men, bringing salvation," that is, there is no exception; all classes, slaves included, are the subjects of the grace of God? Verses 11 to 14 express with great brevity and force some of the fundamental truths of Christianity. It is interesting to notice that even in the most practical advices of the apostle Paul he introduces the central teaching of his theological system as though there was a close relation between the doctrine and the practice which he enjoins. It is his constant teaching, on the foundations of which all true ethical life must rest. A study of these verses will bring out this more fully.

The grace of God is the source from which the great stream of blessings for mankind flows. The word "grace" is a standard word in the New Testament and a central word in Christian theology. Salvation by grace is the watchword of Christianity. Paul frequently uses "grace" and "peace" together, showing how closely the one is related to the other. We find this in his doxology (2 Cor. xiii, 14), "The grace of the Lord Jesus Christ, and the love of God, and the communion of the Holy Ghost, be with you all," and also in his salutations. *Saved by grace* is the constant phrase with which the Christian expresses his thankfulness for his salvation. Hence, the use of the word "grace" for the expression of a gracious act. In 2 Cor. viii, 19, a collection for the poor churches in Jerusalem is called a grace. It means kindliness, favor, a gracious condition, a contribution. It is a broad word, but in the passage before us applies to the favor which comes to the world through Jesus Christ. "For the grace of God hath appeared" refers to the incarnation of the Son of God undoubtedly, but also refers to every manifestation of Christ when he has appeared to bless the world. The churches ever recognized this epiphany of the Son of God as the central point whence grace for the world emanates.

Further, we are informed that the grace of God is an educational

force in the world, "teaching us." This word, which in the King James Version is rendered "teaching" and in the Revised Version "instructing," may also be fitly rendered "educating" us. The grace of God which brings salvation is represented as an education for the world. This grace of God has been most effective in the training of humanity. The very fact that God has been gracious to all the world is itself an uplifting fact. Then, too, the incarnation of the Son of God has been a great educational factor in the world. It has exhibited to men the greatness of the divine love, God condescending to visit the earth in the person of his own Son. Then grace is itself a discipline. All gracious acts have been educating factors. That grace may be exercised toward others there must be a discipline of our nature: a self-denial of the thing which we often desire. This discipline comes through the means of grace, prayer, the sacraments, and the training in the Scriptures, all of which are God's gracious gifts.

We may further note the blessed results of God's grace in the personal life. This grace of God so works on the heart that a person in whom it manifests itself refuses to indulge in those things which are opposed to God's grace: "denying ungodliness and worldly lust." The word "ungodliness" may well be rendered "impiety," a failure to worship God, and this ungodliness is expressed by the apostle elsewhere as "without God in the world." Those whom grace has educated recognize God as their Father, and the Father of all men. But they refuse worldly lusts, that is, things that are of the earth earthy. Worldly lusts often are mental as well as physical. They are things of the mind and the soul. They are elsewhere described as the "lust of the flesh, and the lust of the eyes, and the pride of life." The one on whom the grace of God has come has been educated to refuse these things. This involves mental choice. God's grace in the heart leads to a choice; negatively, to refuse; positively, to live. They are exhorted here to "live soberly, righteously, and godly." Bishop Ellicott makes the remark: "The Christian duty under three aspects, to ourselves, to others, and to God."

"We should live soberly." This is that which relates to one's inner life. It is to live wisely according to proper judgment of things, a looking at everything in its proper light. To live righteously is the relation to which one stands to other lives, and to God. All these represent the kind of lives which the grace of God brings into the world. It is further said of the effects of this grace that this righteous living is in the present world. It does not indicate that we are not to live for the next world. This is shown in the following verse, but we are to see to it that our desire is to live righteously in the age of which we form a part. We have a similar passage in Gal. i, 4, "And our Lord Jesus Christ, who gave himself for our sins, that he might deliver us out of the present evil world, according to the will of our God and Father." The present age is characterized as an age of evil in which Christians are sent forth as lights in the world and the kind of living they represent is urged in contrast to the regular living of the world. This passage is peculiarly appropriate to the age in which we live, an age of pleasure, too often an age of ungodliness, and an age of carelessness as well. All these things are corrected

when mankind are educated by the grace of God which brings salvation to all men.

This living which the apostle urges upon Titus is stimulated by the blessed vision which is ever opening before his view and which is found in the thirteenth verse: "Looking for the blessed hope and appearing of the glory of our great God and Saviour Jesus Christ." It is the chief characteristic of our Christianity that it is a religion of hope. This word "hope" is a favorite word with the apostle Paul. It appears about thirty-five times in his epistles, not always with the same reference. Sometimes it expresses a hope to be enjoyed in the soul, sometimes an objective manifestation of the hope such as we find in this text, namely, "the glorious appearing of the great God and our Saviour Jesus Christ" (King James Version). This passage has been an embarrassment to the translators. The revision of 1881 translates it, "looking for the blessed hope and appearing of the glory of our great God and Saviour Jesus Christ." As a marginal reading we have "of the glory of the great God and our Saviour." Another form of rendering is, "our great God and Saviour Jesus Christ." Spence, in his Commentary, remarks: "In this sublime passage the glory of the only begotten Son alone finds mention. Taken thus it is a clear declaration of the divinity of the Eternal Son, who is here styled our great God and Saviour." Reasoning merely on grammatical principles either translation would be possible, only even then there is a presumption in favor of the translation we have adopted. But other considerations are by no means so nearly equally balanced. The word manifest (epiphany), the central thought of the counsel, is employed by St. Paul in his epistles five times, in every one of them to describe the Christ and in four of them to designate the future manifestations of his coming in glory, as here. The term epiphany is never applied to the Father. Theodoret says, "St. Paul calls Christ the great God, and thus rebukes the heretical blasphemy which denies his Godhead." Chrysostom remarks: "What can those persons say who allege that the Son is inferior to the Father?" Thus the blessed hope to which St. Paul looks forward is ever in his mind; the hope of that glory which comes to men through Christ.

This passage further presents to us another of the great fundamentals of our Christianity, namely, the redemption through the atonement of Jesus Christ, "who gave himself for us." Here is a Pauline doctrine in Pauline language. The statement that he gave himself is similar to Gal. i, 3, where the whole passage is strikingly similar to this. It is part of the apostle's salutation to the Galatian people, "Grace to you and peace from God the Father, and our Lord Jesus Christ, who gave himself for our sins." Here is the doctrine of redemption; the deliverance of men by a ransom, the purpose of which was "to deliver men from all iniquity and to purify unto himself a people for his own possession, zealous of good works." Deliverance and purification through Christ are fundamental elements of the apostle's teaching. They are set forth so frequently and so clearly that any discussion of Pauline theology that should omit them from consideration would be at once recognized as a misrepresentation

of the teachings of the apostle. They seem to fall from his lips as commonplaces of his system without which he could not conceive of Christianity.

Lest there should be fearfulness on the part of Titus to communicate these truths to the perverse people whom he is appointed to serve, Paul closes this part of his admonition with a strong exhortation: "These things speak and exhort and reprove with all authority." It is well to note that this admonition is in the present tense. Titus is not to rest content with one sermon or with one exhortation, but he is to persevere until he accomplishes the purpose for which he speaks. "These things," he says, "speak" and bring them to their remembrance. Paul urges him with all the intensity of his nature. He adds a final word on the subject, "with all authority." This word may be rendered "with all commandment." He was not to speak hesitatingly or doubtfully; he was not to apologize for the utterances which he was to make, but to speak by way of command. He was an authoritative preacher, and should speak with the authority of one sent of God.

His final admonition in this part of his letter is, "Let no man despise thee." It is supposed that this passage means that his voice should be positive. It indicates that he should have a character which must be respected and a message to which people must listen. It is the setting forth of his message as a minister of the Church of Christ—the assurance of his right to speak—and it implies that it is the duty of the people to hear. But there is another meaning which may naturally grow out of this passage. In this view Titus is exhorted to conduct himself so that no man can despise him. There are some ministers that cannot be despised. They may be disliked, but never despised. This is not merely because they speak with a voice of authority, but because the life which they exhibit before men makes their utterances authoritative. It is the duty of the minister to live so closely with God, to be so thoroughly in love with his people and the truths which he is called to speak, and so useful in his life among men, that they cannot fail to respect him. Such ministers are everywhere respected, even by those who do not sit under their ministry or heed their voice. This closing verse of the second chapter of this epistle is very suggestive to ministers of the Gospel. They are reminded of the great fundamental principle of Christianity, namely, the grace of God. As was said in the opening of this paper, "grace" is one of the great words of the New Testament. It is one of the great central points of Christianity. Without it the Church is destitute of power, with it she is able to bestow manifold blessings upon the world. The apostle does not hesitate to combine practical exhortation with fundamental Christian truth in his exhortation to Titus, whom he had appointed as the pastor of the church in Crete.

ARCHÆOLOGY AND BIBLICAL RESEARCH.

DELITZSCH AND HIS CRITICS.

OUR readers are familiar with the origin of the Babel and Bible controversy, which, though on the wane, has not yet spent its force. St. James's apothegm: "Behold, how great a matter a little fire kindleth!" was never better illustrated than in this discussion. Delitzsch's first *brochure* contained only thirty pages, his second, one less, and both together, not more than thirty thousand words, or about sixty such pages as this. He is out with another pamphlet of seventy-five pages, entitled *Babel und Bibel, Ein Rueckblick und Ausblick* (Retrospect and Prospect).

The first two *brochures* were unmercifully attacked by critics of all schools and shades of opinion—Christians and Jews, Protestants and Catholics, orthodox and liberal theologians, and several expert Assyriologists. It seems that everybody had something to say. We knew this apart from the new *brochure*, from which we learn that the learned Assyriologist, having completed his duties for the summer semester at the university, and having placed his own museum in order, retired for rest (?) to the British Museum, so rich in Assyriological treasures and cuneiform inscriptions. Before leaving Berlin he selected from a wilderness of criticism which had been sent him no less than 28 pamphlets, 300 long articles, and about 1,350 shorter ones, most of which were adverse to his pamphlets. The criticisms which he regarded as of no value, as well as those written in foreign languages, were left in Berlin. He further adds—what he told the writer last July—that criticisms still pour in incessantly, and that literally from every part of the globe, "from Calcutta to the remotest farm on the California prairies, and from Norway to Cape Town. They come from all classes, high and low; many of them from women, and most all of them anonymous and unfriendly in tone."

The popularity of the booklets is well known. Edition after edition has been published, not only in German, but also in English, Danish, Swedish, Hungarian, Italian, and Czech. We can readily believe the professor when he says that nothing is more distasteful to him than publicity, and that the charge of "nothing new" is not unwelcome, though an injured air pervades the entire new pamphlet. Those who know Professor Delitzsch know him only to love him. He is fully as amiable as his late beloved father, so well known to a large number of our older American theologians. He stands in the front rank of Assyriologists, and may properly be called their corypheus. He is a charming man, most unassuming and approachable, and never happier than when surrounded by a few pupils, desirous of delving into the mysteries of archæology.

Notwithstanding the great success of his pamphlets, nobody is satisfied. Delitzsch chafes under the imputation that they lack originality. He says with some feeling: "My Christian and Jewish friends monotonous-

31

ly assure me, till I am exhausted with their repetitions, that my booklets contain nothing new, nor even present the old in an especially intellectual [*geistvoll*] form. Then, why all this stir, if, as theologians, professors, and pastors, and cuneiform experts in the bargain, aver, my lectures contain absolutely nothing new?"

Delitzsch is not convinced of the justice of this charge. He instances, in proof, the following: the Sargur documents, with their teachings regarding paradise and sheol—not known till 1901; the *Javc-ilum* or *Ja'um-ilum* tablets, known only to experts, and not published by the British Museum till 1898 and 1899, and the parallels between the codes of Moses and Hammurabi, which cannot be called old, since his second lecture was delivered in January, 1903, and the code of Hammurabi was not given to the public till October, 1902.

But why this stir, demands Delitzsch, if nothing new has been said? The real answer is that both lectures were delivered before the emperor. Now, his majesty had always been regarded not only as very religious, but also as quite conservative in his theological beliefs. The fact that Delitzsch was invited to deliver a second lecture in the castle was interpreted by many as a proof that Wilhelm II had been converted to the professor's views. Nothing was farther from the truth, for the emperor has since defined his position in most unequivocal language. Harnack puts the whole matter in a nutshell thus: "The opinion was likely to become widespread, had indeed become widespread, that the emperor occupied the same theological standpoint as Professor Delitzsch. Not wishing to permit this misunderstanding, the emperor wrote as the public read." The fact that the emperor was present at the two lectures, and that Delitzsch was asked to repeat them at the palace, added to the fact that his majesty wrote as he did to Admiral Hollman on the subject, explains to a great extent the great sensation produced, though Delitzsch does not seem to accept this view of the case. He attributes the extensive circulation and discussion of his booklets to entirely other causes, namely, the great chasm between the professional theologian and the layman in the Church. The latter, he claims, has been kept in ignorance of the great advances in biblical criticism and recent archæological discoveries. The public schools, the pulpit, and the theological professors are responsible for this gap, which should be bridged over at any cost. The indifference of the teacher and clergy to these modern views he attributes, in the words of Harnack, to "indolence and fear of disturbing existing conditions." The truth must be boldly proclaimed, since "it is the truth, the unveiled truth, the whole truth, that makes us free." Cornill, representing the theologians, protests, saying that German scholars have no esoteric doctrines, but that their views are publicly proclaimed from their chairs, and all have the privilege of procuring their books. If the public does not avail itself, the scholars must not be held responsible. He naïvely adds, there are matters in theological "science concerning which discretion is the lesser evil." Delitzsch resents the imputation of Gunkel—that he has been actuated by a desire for *sensation.* Gunkel published, September 3, 1903, in *Der Rundschau,* a Berlin daily, a sharp animadversion, entitled

"Funeral Oration over Babel and Bible," in which occur the following words: "May our science [theology] be spared from such another sensation for centuries." Such a remark is at least ungracious.

He also protests against the charge of superficiality, explaining that the pamphlets were first delivered as lectures before an audience, made up, it is true, of cultured people, yet chiefly of nonspecialists, embracing every shade of religious belief. Besides, his time was limited, and the subject "had to be treated so as to interest and charm, and not to bore or lull his audience to sleep."

Another charge against Delitzsch is that he overstepped the boundaries of his profession. This point was, we believe, first made by the emperor. Our readers will remember that on Delitzsch's second visit to the palace he became entangled in some religious or theological discussion with the empress, who is ultra-orthodox, and with Dr. Dryander, the court preacher, also very conservative. The emperor was there too, but, strange to say, he simply "listened and remained passive." Delitzsch, to use the emperor's own words, "unfortunately abandoned the standpoints of the strict historian and Assyriologist, going into religious and theological conclusions which were quite nebulous and bold." The emperor characterizes his attack upon some of the Christian doctrines as "a deed for which the study of Assyriology did not justify him." This sentiment is shared by the theologians and Assyriologists alike, for one of the latter, Dr. Bezold, says: "In questions pertaining to revelation, Assyriology has no voice whatever."

Delitzsch admits that he might have given the mere facts without any comment, but says that would have been cowardly, for had he not, on taking his degree (Ph.D., the only title he has, and this he never parades), solemnly sworn that "he would voluntarily represent the cause of truth and defend the same bravely as long as he lived"? He believed what he said and therefore had to say it. He further believes that he is qualified for such discussion and possesses sufficient knowledge of the Old Testament to be entitled to an independent judgment. He reminds his critics that he has studied the Bible from his youth, that he devoted six years to the religions of India, that from his twenty-second year, then, under the guidance of some of the most celebrated Old Testament scholars, he has incessantly continued his investigations in the religio-historical, extending them to the Koran and to the Babylonian-Assyrian cuneiform literatures. It is folly therefore to charge one who has done all this with ignorance of which no intelligent theological student at the close of his first semester at a German university should be guilty. We are inclined to think that Delitzsch has the right in this *ne sutor ultra crepidam* argument.

The charge against which Delitzsch protests most strongly is that wherein he is accused of teaching that Israel's monotheism is derived from Babylonian sources. He accuses König of great unfairness in reiterating this charge, in later editions of *Babel und Bibel*. He is still more severe on Gunkel. He finds it passing strange that his colleague could have published a "really false statement," namely, that "he [Delitzsch] had proclaimed Babylonian monotheism in a loud voice." Then he pays

his respects, without deigning to name him, to one of his old pupils, our Professor Hilprecht, thus: "It is deplorable that even Assyriologists who understand all the circumstances should imitate such jugglery, and that *one of these* should declare in different German cities that Israel did not derive its monotheistic conception from that immense graveyard, Babylon; worse still, when another declares that there is not a trace of monotheism to be found in Babylon."

He cites several passages from his lectures or *brochures* to show that he is not guilty of saying that Israel derived its monotheism from the Babylonians. Let the reader decide whether he makes a case:

"And now may I be allowed a final word regarding that which invests the Bible with a general historical significance—its monotheism?"— *Babel und Bibel*, i, p. 44.

"The religion of the Canaanitic tribes who had immigrated into Babylonia soon disappeared before the polytheism of many centuries, which had been practiced by the ancient inhabitants."—P. 47.

"In spite of all this, polytheism, crass polytheism, remained for three thousand years the state religion of Babylonia."—P. 49.

"I have never ceased to emphasize the crass polytheism of the Babylonians, and feel under no obligation to palliate it."—ii, p. 32.

The term "ancient inhabitants" is a little ambiguous, and we should call attention to the fact that it is often applied to the allophylian, or primitive, pre-Semitic inhabitants of Babylonia, often called Sumerians. These dwelt in the fertile plains of the Euphrates and Tigris, and very naturally their territory was invaded by outsiders from less fertile countries. There was a constant going and coming, war followed conquest and conquest war. These invaders, without doubt, brought in many new ideas, religious and otherwise. This explains the second reference above to "the religion of the Canaanites," who invaded Babylon about 2500 B. C. Then came the Cassites about 2000, and the Chaldeans about 1000 B. C.

It was from these regions that Abraham went to Canaan. He must have carried some Babylonian ideas with him. This does not say that Israel derived its monotheism from the Babylonians as a people, but simply that the progenitors of Israel were acquainted with Babylonian customs, language, and religion. This fact is further shown by the study of many proper names of the period, especially those compounded with *Jave* or *El*. Delitzsch promises a discussion of the name Moses, which he conjectures to be of Babylonian origin and not Egyptian, as has been commonly supposed. Now, if Abraham came from southern Babylonia, it is not wonderful that the supreme being was known there under the name Jave.

Delitzsch emphasizes the high state of morals in Babylonia, in some regards higher than those of the Israelites; at any rate, not any less humane, nor more cruel, as has been generally supposed. He also takes pleasure in explaining that the theophanies of the Hebrew Scriptures are not to be taken literally any more than those of the cuneiform texts. Indeed, most of the former are paralleled in the latter. Both are symbolical and not historical. Thus the angelic visions and the giving of the law on Sinai are not to be believed as historical facts, but religious symbols,

This, he adds, is the more probable, since now many of the leading Protestant clergy teach that even the ascension of Christ has no historical basis, but is symbolical only.

Now, what are Delitzsch's views of inspiration or revelation? Lest we may misrepresent him, we shall answer this question in his own words. He says: "I hold the view that in the Old Testament we have to deal with a development effected or permitted by God, like any other product of this world, but, for the rest, of a purely human and historical character, in which God has not intervened through a special supernatural revelation." He says again: "The modification of the original conception of revelation, deeply rooted in ancient orientalism, by a surrender of the verbal inspiration, made by both evangelical and Catholic theology, and even by the Church, irretrievably divests the Old Testament of its character as the 'Word of God.'" He believes in a revelation, of gradual growth and historical development. He comes out flat-footed against some of the modern critics, who seem to straddle the fence; he says that the term "divine revelation," as held by the Church, and historical or human development are irreconcilable contradictions." One or the other must be accepted. *Tertium non datur.* Then again, speaking of the Torah, or Law of Moses, he says: "The divine character of the Torah will have to be excluded from scientific discussion."

The only doctrine of revelation to which Delitzsch will subscribe is a general one, common to all men and times, where God speaks to the head and conscience of men, as he does in nature and history. Alexander the Great, for instance, appears with special clearness as the instrument of such a divine agency (*Walten*). God's fatherly love embraces all mankind, he speaks to all nations alike. He quotes Gunkel with approval, who says, "Far be it from us to limit revelation to Israel," and then as a parting shot taunts "the theologian" with the glaring contradiction, for saying in the same pamphlet, "Israel is and will remain the people of revelation." He then sarcastically adds, "Only theologians by profession should speak on the subject of revelation."

In conclusion, we must thank Professor Delitzsch for his third pamphlet, not that it contains a single new idea, but for its freshness and frankness. His language is generally perspicuous and unambiguous, especially when he speaks of inspiration and revelation. The Old Testament is no more inspired than other religious books. Indeed, the songs of Arndt are worthier of a place in our religious education "or to be carried by our boys every day to school," than are the war songs of the Old Testament. It would be a good thing for some of our American modern critics, who are sadly "on the fence," if they also could speak with more clearness and less ambiguity on the question of inspiration and the nature of revelation.

FOREIGN OUTLOOK.

SOME LEADERS OF THOUGHT.

Bernhard Weiss. It is interesting to find a man so old engaged in literary work with as much zest as he had in youth. But such is apparently the case with Weiss. During 1903 he not only published the seventh edition of his Biblical Theology of the New Testament, but also an entirely new work on The Religion of the New Testament (*Die Religion des Neuen Testaments.* Stuttgart, J. G. Cotta'sche Buchhandlung, Nachf.). This book differs from the same author's Biblical Theology of the New Testament in that it attempts to set forth, not the various types of Christian thought of the different individuals whose writings we have in the New Testament, but to show that those types are capable of being proved unitary. Not only are they not contradictory, they are not even divergent in such a sense as to suggest different growths from the same root. They are parts of a whole, in accord with each other, and all of them necessary to the whole. The multiplicity of ideas in the New Testament can be reduced to a unity—this is with Weiss axiomatic. The New Testament can be understood only when considered in the light of Christ as the revelation of a manifested salvation. The religious life of the New Testament kindles a similar life in the reader of the New Testament, and the personal experience thus arising is the proof of the unity of the New Testament through which that life flows. Under such circumstances it would be impossible that the various parts of the New Testament should contradict each other. If any New Testament document contradicted or hindered the development of the effect of the whole that document could not be a part of the revelation and would have to be excluded from the canon. The only elements constitutive of the New Testament not directly contributing to the whole unitary effect are a few ideas which are not fully assimilated to Christianity. The motive of Weiss in attempting to harmonize the details of New Testament teaching into a unit is that thereby the place of the cross in the Christian system is more clearly brought out. To Weiss the message of Jesus was the Fatherhood of God and the Brotherhood of Man. But taking the New Testament as a whole, not this teaching of Jesus, but the death of Jesus, is the fact that is emphasized; and it was the fact of the death that overcame the world, while the world overcame Christ as the teacher of his great truths. Such are the guiding principles in Weiss's conception of the religion of the New Testament. We must confess it does not seem to us that Weiss has succeeded very well. The attempt to harmonize all the different ideas of the New Testament depends upon arbitrary methods of reconciliation as truly as the old-fashioned harmonies of the four gospels did, and it is therefore as unsatisfactory. As to the argument from personal experience to the effect that since the New Testament as a whole produces that experience the New Testament must therefore be unitary, it overlooks the fact that it is not

the details which produce the experience, but the unitary fundamental principle running through the whole. If Weiss had spent his strength in showing that there are certain great principles constitutive of the religion of the New Testament, and that they are each and all direct or implicit teachings of Jesus, he could have made out a good case. It is not necessary to the unity of the Christian religion that the conception of it held or emphasized by all the New Testament writers should be identical. Such a unity would not necessarily reach deeper than to mere externals. A unity in principle is entirely consistent with many divergences of individual application. And it is just the glory of the religion of the New Testament that it admits of such varied application. It seems to us also that Weiss erred grievously in making the message of Jesus one thing and the message of the apostles another. By so doing he destroyed the unity of the New Testament religion, and mutilated the teachings of Christ, who certainly did include in his message the fact and significance of his approaching death.

Alfred Seeberg. In a recent work on The Catechism of Primitive Christianity (*Der Katechismus Urchristenheit*, Leipzig, 1903, A. Deichert, Nachf.) Seeberg has attempted to turn all the "modern" critical conceptions of the origin of doctrinal and ethical formulas topsy-turvy. His claim is, in brief, that within a very few years after the crucifixion of Jesus there was extant among the Christians a well-formulated system of doctrine and of ethics, that this formed the substance of the teaching of all the apostles, and that this was accompanied by a practically uniform method of administering baptism and the Lord's Supper. This kind of theory is a severe blow to those who hold that practically everything we regard as peculiarly ecclesiastical is the product of an age considerably later than the apostles. Seeberg certainly has found coincidences between some expressions and teachings of Paul and such later documents as "The Teaching of the Twelve Apostles," which are, to say the least, striking. The "ways" of the "Teaching of the Twelve" have, Seeberg thinks, their origin in the "ways" Paul refers to in 1 Cor. iv, 17, where Paul's "ways" are not to be understood as his ways of doing things, but as the ways of life described by him. That such an ethical norm existed and was known to the Roman Christians from the first existence of the church in Rome is clear, thinks Seeberg, from Rom. vi, 17, where the "form of teaching" must, according to the context, have referred to questions of conduct rather than of opinion. According to Seeberg, therefore, when Paul speaks of his "ways" he uses the term "ways" as a technical designation of a tolerably well-fixed series of utterances on moral themes—a warning against certain sins and a recommendation of certain virtues. And he thinks that Matt. xv, 19, and Mark vii, 21, give us hints that there was essentially such a teaching among the Jews and that it was known and adopted by Jesus. So much for his opinion concerning the fixed ethical formulas of the earliest apostolic age. As to the doctrinal formula Seeberg is equally certain. He thinks Paul makes clear use of it in 1 Cor.

xv, 3-5, as also in Rom. vi, 1-7, and Col. ii, 11-13. But he thinks that Paul
did not use the whole of this doctrinal formula in 1 Cor. xv, 3-5, but that
he omitted there both the opening and the closing portions of it. The
opening words of the formula must, according to Gal. iv, 4, and Rom. viii,
3, have declared that the living God, the Creator of the world, sent his
Son, Jesus Christ (2 Cor. i, 19), who was of the seed of David (Rom. i, 3).
The formula must have concluded, according to Rom. viii, 34; Col. iii, 1,
and Eph. i, 20, with the reminder that Jesus Christ now sits at the right
hand of God; that the evil spirits are subject to him (Eph. i, 21; Col. ii,
10-15), and that he will come to judge the world (Rom. ii, 16; 1 Thess.
i, 10). This same formula, with slight modification, Seeberg sees in 1 Pet.
iii, 18-22; iv, 5; and in 1 Tim. vi, 13, f., and 2 Tim. ii, 8; iv, 1. He thinks
also that it was the basis of the speeches in the Acts, chapters ii, iii, v, x,
xiii, and of the words of Jesus as reported in Luke xxiv, 44-47. Further, it
is referred to in Heb. iii, 1; iv, 14; x, 23. What, now, shall we think of
these extraordinary ideas? In the first place, it must be said that it is
truly refreshing to find one who undertakes to determine what was apostolic and what post-apostolic by a study of the New Testament. This the
great majority have not done; but have simply assumed that post-apostolic
in time meant post-apostolic in thought; and that, as a consequence, if any
ways of looking at things were found in post-apostolic literature they were
not in existence during apostolic times. A careful study of Paul's "ways"
as referred to above lends color to Seeberg's theory concerning an early
ethical formula; and that there were doctrinal formulas in apostolic times
Seeberg has once more made clear. But there is no sufficient reason to
think that the ethical and doctrinal teachings of the earliest apostles or of
Paul were in fixed form as early as Seeberg thinks they were. The great
outlines of later ethics and doctrine were held from the first; their development into fixed formulas was the work of a later age.

RECENT THEOLOGICAL LITERATURE.

War Jesus Ekstatiker? Eine Untersuchung zum Leben Jesu
(Was Jesus an Ecstatic? A Study in the Life of Jesus). By Oscar Holtzmann,
Tübingen, 1903, J. C. B. Mohr. Before any estimate can be made of the
worth or worthlessness of this book it will be necessary to ascertain the
sense in which the author uses the word ecstatic. Unfortunately he employs the term in such a variety of meanings which are so diverse and
unconnected that it is difficult to determine just what he does mean.
Among other things that he says of the ecstatic are the following: The
ecstatic is the instrument or medium of a spirit foreign to himself, and
acts when impelled by this spirit. Manifestations of ecstasy are seen in
acts of an unaccountable, sudden, or passionate kind. The ecstatic speaks
what is dictated or designated by the spirit, and his speech is as unaccountable and unexpected as his deeds. Holtzmann adds to these accounts
of the ways of the ecstatic certain definitions that tend to confuse us,
though in some ways they give dignity to ecstasy. For example, ecstasy
is sometimes identified with enthusiasm (apparently in a good sense),

sometimes with fanaticism, sometimes with excitement, sometimes with revelation, or inspiration. Everything in the thought or deed of anyone is ecstatic which lies far beyond the circle of the ordinary human, or which transcends the common way of looking at things. Holtzmann is sure that Jesus was at times an ecstatic; and he thinks that the recognition of this makes our thought of Jesus clearer and more vivid. He thinks that John the Baptist was also an ecstatic, and that in this respect Jesus was a follower of John. Without this ecstasy Jesus never could have come to think of himself as the Messiah. This ecstatic state began with his baptism, and the Spirit which controlled him was the Spirit of God. From that time on Jesus knew that he was under the influence of a Spirit hitherto foreign to him. These preliminaries being settled, Holtzmann proceeds to decide which of the words and acts of Jesus were or were not ecstatic. Among the speeches of Jesus those in Luke x, 18-24, and Matt. xii, 28, and xix, 28, are ecstatic; while the eschatological speech of Jesus in Mark xiii is not ecstatic. This belief in the immediate end of the world, and that he himself was destined by God to be the Lord of the future, was ecstatic, and out of this belief flowed the idea that the kingdom of God was not wholly in the future, but was actually effective then and there. The eight woes of Matt. xxiii were in some degree ecstatic. The ecstatic in Jesus sometimes manifested itself in his miracles, as, for example, in the cursing of the barren fig tree and the stilling of the storm, but not in the multiplication of the loaves and fishes. Jesus's prophecy of his suffering and death betray ecstasy, without which the worth of his self-denial could not have been recognized by him. The word of Jesus concerning his burial in connection with the anointing at Bethany was not, but his words and actions in connection with the Last Supper were ecstatic. According to Holtzmann there were instances in which Jesus was a vigorous opponent of the ecstatic state, and his book contains a lengthy section on the nonecstatic activities of Jesus. This is a strange book. Its chief value is, perhaps, in the fact that it gives us a new grouping of the words and deeds of Jesus, and thus helps us to see them apart from the traditional connections. The book is also an honest attempt to recognize the influence of the Spirit of God in the work of Jesus—the Holy Spirit is the foreign Spirit which, sometimes at least, wrought through Jesus. But just here is also the weakness of the book. It assumes that the Spirit of God is essentially foreign to Jesus, whereas the assumption of the New Testament writers is that the Spirit of God is, so to speak, native to him. Holtzmann's attempt to classify the words and deeds of Jesus as ecstatic and nonecstatic will appear to most readers as arbitrary and unsuccessful.

Jesus, was er uns heute ist (What Jesus Is to the Man of To-day). By Alfred König, Freiburg i. B., 1903, P. Waetzel. This book is an attempt to show what Christ, apart from any elaborate doctrine concerning his person, is, religiously, to the modern world. The book is in two principal parts, the first treating of the rejection of Christ by the modern man, the second of the grounds upon which Christians affirm his worth

for our time. In the first part König takes up several types of rejecters of Jesus. First, the materialist and practical atheist, who, while not a new phenomenon, represents a tendency quite strong in modern times. König makes the strong point as against materialism when reduced to practice, that it is just the dark background against which the facts of Christ's life shine out with the greater beauty; so that practical materialism is compelled against its own will to give its testimony in favor of Jesus. As a second type of those who reject Jesus König names the man of the modern view of the world, who is not only not a materialist but perchance an idealist—the man who finds in the teachings of Jesus presuppositions which conflict with modern ideas. To such a man König points out that a distinction must be made between the essential teachings of Jesus, which have permanent worth, and those features of his teaching which had but temporary significance, but which were necessary to the impartation to the then world of the divine truth. As a third type he considers at length the cultivated man of the world, to whom the somewhat austere requirements of Jesus are offensive. He makes the point that the teachings of Christ do not pretend to give a direct answer to every question that can be asked, but that Jesus did set up the true goal and ideal of morality, toward which we must strive as individuals and as a social whole. The approaching end of the world in which Jesus believed influenced his teaching and that of his disciples in their ethical views. But the spirit which pervades Christian thought is more powerful than any particular form in which Christian thinking betrays itself in any age, and this spirit is the corrective of all that is temporary or transient in Christian history. This all-pervading spirit teaches not the forsaking of the world, but the overcoming of the world, its subjugation to the ethical ends of life. Thus the teachings of Christ appear of permanent value to all earnest men, and a source of inspiration to earnest endeavor to others. As a fourth type he names the man who is struggling for existence, to whom Jesus offers himself as a Saviour and true Helper in the struggles of life. In the second part of the book König points out that Jesus is to-day, as ever, our helper in attaining to a true relation to God. He does this not alone by teaching that religion is a filial relation to God, but by living out and embodying all the virtues of that relation. Furthermore, he helps us to a true relationship to ourselves and to the material world in teaching, as he does in Matt. xvi, 26, that our life is worth more than all that this world has to offer. Third, he helps us to a true relationship to the world of mankind by making his religion the saving power for social renewal and health. König believes that the harmony between the Gospel of Jesus and the human soul is such that it is as necessary to all men to-day as ever it was. König believes that the real significance of the life of Jesus was that he strove to make the sons of men one with God the Father as he was one with him. And in this also consists the abiding significance of his personality, that it works to-day as ever in the same direction. The book reminds one of Harnack's *What is Christianity?* Both books may be recommended as likely to do their readers good.

GLIMPSES OF REVIEWS AND MAGAZINES.

WITH wide variety and ample scope fourteen distinguished contributors from Europe and America write in the December-March number of the *International Quarterly* (Burlington, Vermont) on such subjects as "The Paris Commune of 1871," "Early Teutonic Society," "The Consciousness of Animals," "Modern Orchestral Conductors," "Alexander the Great and Universal Monarchy," "Porfirio Diaz: Soldier and Statesman," "Trade Agreements," "The Economic Value of Advertising," "Japan and the United States." Rollo Ogden, writing of "Political Satire," says: "Too strong a satirical bent is as fatal to a public man as is a reputation for levity. The late Thomas B. Reed had great political ambitions, as well as great powers. But his native talent for satire often ran away with him. He answered fools according to their folly. He flung out biting epigrams. He lashed and girded right and left with his sharp tongue. Thus he made resentful enemies of men who might have been his admiring supporters. He gibed at President McKinley as "the Emperor of Expediency," and hurled at the expansionists after the Spanish War the epigram that he already had more country than he could really love. But he did not rise to the height of great events in a crisis. He was not the man to front a great emergency, or to go to his countrymen with words of weighty remonstrance and passionate appeal. In Speaker Reed the satirist killed the statesman. He could set off squibs, and made a reputation as a man of smart sayings but not of large, serious, and lofty utterance." Some allege that Edward R. Ames made too free and frequent use of his native gift of satire, and that his cutting sarcasms, sometimes mercilessly flung out, detracted from his usefulness, his influence, and his dignity as a bishop. As to the justice of that allegation we record here no opinion, but remark in general that the man who can wantonly or recklessly wound his brother's feelings is not fit to be trusted with power over his brethren. And sarcasm is a weapon the use of which is seldom justifiable. Professor W. M. Payne writes nobly of the present position, opportunities, and responsibilities of the American scholar. He says that "all the encroachments of materialism upon American life cannot conceal the fact that this nation was founded upon idealism, political, ethical, and religious, and that America still believes in the sunlit peaks, however they may be obscured by the sullen vapors of these lower slopes on which much of our life gropes to-day." He gives great credit to Emerson for keeping idealism alive and making it victorious, and being a helper of all who would live in the spirit. Referring to the war against slavery, he quotes John Morley's saying that "Emerson's teaching was one of the forces which nourished the heroism of the North in its immortal battle." Emphasizing the need of intellectual honesty, he quotes Carlyle's familiar prayer: "May the Lord deliver us from all cant. May the Lord, whatever else

he do or forbear, teach us to look facts honestly in the face, and to beware (with a kind of shudder) of smearing them all over with our despicable and damnable palaver, into unrecognizability, and so falsifying the Lord's own gospels to his unhappy blockheads of children, all struggling down to Gehenna and the everlasting swine's-trough for want of gospels." Professor Payne points out that the great inspirers and leaders of mankind have been men who had that fortitude of soul which is based on an assured faith in the future, on an unwavering confidence in the ultimate triumph of right over wrong and of light over darkness; a faith not so much in a particular creed or body of defined doctrine, but in the validity of every fine, noble, altruistic impulse, every generous motion of the spirit; a faith in the perfectibility of mankind, which can turn from the disheartening spectacle of man as he now is to the vision of man as he is to be when he escapes from "the passions of the primal clan" and the eons "touch him into shape:"

> All about him shadow still, but, while the races flower and fade,
> Prophet-eyes may catch a glory slowly gaining on the shade,
>   Till the peoples all are one, and all their voices blend in choric
> Hallelujah to the Maker, "It is finished. Man is made!"

It is faith of this fervent and invincible sort, at bottom a faith in God, which sustains the leaders and helpers of men in the darkest hours of human history. Such was Mazzini's sublime faith in the future of his dear Italy, uttered most eloquently at a time when Italian liberty seemed well-nigh extinct, and when to prophesy its rebirth was like preaching the resurrection to an unbelieving generation. Such was James Darmesteter's faith in a better future for France, eloquently spoken at a time when she was following blind guides along strange paths of defeat and disaster. This faith in a nobler future for mankind fills the familiar passage from Condorcet's *Progrès de l'Esprit Humain.* "How this picture of the human race freed from all its fetters, withdrawn from the empire of chance, as from that of the enemies of progress, and walking with firm and assured step in the way of truth, of virtue, and happiness, presents to the philosopher a sight that consoles him for the errors, the crimes, the injustice, with which the earth is yet stained, and of which he is not seldom the victim! It is in the contemplation of this picture that he receives the reward of his efforts for the progress of reason, for the defense of liberty. He ventures to link them with the eternal chain of the destinies of man. It is there that he finds the true recompense of virtue, the pleasure of having done a lasting good. Fate can no longer undo it by any disastrous compensation that shall restore prejudice and bondage. This contemplation is for him a refuge, into which the recollection of his persecutors can never follow him; in which, living in thought with man reinstated in the rights and the dignity of his nature, he forgets man tormented and corrupted by greed, by base fear, by envy; it is here that he truly abides with his fellows, in an elysium that his reason has known how to create for itself, and that his love for humanity adorns with all purest delights." Especially Professor Payne insists that

it is the highest duty of the American scholar in our new century to uphold, not merely faith in humanity and in progress, but also the special faith that to our own nation has been given the mission to lead the world toward a true conception of the fellowship of man, that the new world has, indeed, been divinely appointed "to redress the balance of the old." That democracy must in the end prevail in the societies of human beings who are worthy to be called men, was held to be truth unquestionable by the Fathers of the Republic, and whatever strength has hitherto nerved us in the great crises of our national life has been born of that belief—our splendid heritage from those who have gone before us and whose example we are fain to emulate. In our own day, that belief has found no lack of advocators, and among them we hold in most grateful remembrance that fine flower of American scholarship and American manhood whose Birmingham address on "Democracy" offers the most persuasive and convincing modern exposition of our political gospel. James Russell Lowell seems, indeed, to have been the ideal American scholar of Emerson's prophecy. Singularly receptive to the benign ministries of nature, he was also at home in the world of books, yet he never allowed books to usurp for him the claims of life. And when the pressure of events called upon him to act, he stepped buoyantly into the arena, and bore his share of the brunt of the conflict. He held, moreover, that the duties of scholarship were paramount to its privileges, and shirked no task that was set him to perform, cast aside no burden that was laid upon his shoulders. And to all his life-activity he brought the moral fervor that had come down to him from the generations of his Puritan ancestry, and nursed the fire of his indignation until it became a devouring flame upon all those who sought selfish aims at the expense of the commonwealth. Indicating the measure of the American scholar's duty to his country there is quoted the inscription which occurs in a painting of the last judgment which adorns the great hall of the Ducal Palace in Venice: "Those are to be accounted wise who, by their own, avert their country's perils, for they render to the republic the honor which is its due, and would rather perish for, than with, many. For it is desperately wicked that we should treasure for ourselves the life which nature bestowed for our country's service; to surrender it at nature's demand, but refuse it when our country asks it. Wise, too, must they be accounted who shun no danger in their country's service. This is the price we are bound to pay for the dignity we enjoy in the republic, this the foundation of our liberty, this the wellspring of justice." In such stately terms was wisdom defined by the little island republic of the Adriatic; our own continental republic, its shores washed by two oceans, will hardly be able to better that instruction, or improve upon that ideal of devotion to the commonwealth. In an article on "Modern Orchestral Conductors" is related an incident somewhat interesting to any minister who has had a conflict with his choir as to whose authority is supreme in arranging the order of service. Theodore Thomas was conducting the performance of an oratorio, the soprano part of which was taken by Adelina Patti. At the rehearsal a dispute arose regarding the pace at which a certain air should be taken. Madame Patti claimed

that her opinion ought to prevail, because she was the prima donna; whereupon Mr. Thomas retorted, "I beg your pardon, Madame, but here I am prima donna." This confused the genders but ended the dispute. In the same article we are told of the masterly power of Liszt as conductor of an orchestra in filling his players and singers with the spirit of the composition they were interpreting. Anton Seidl thus described him: "His Jovian countenance filled everybody with a sort of holy awe; his colaborers were lifted to the top of a lofty pedestal; all were profoundly, majestically moved, inspired, and made conscious of a high mission. Liszt radiated an exalted magic on singers as well as instrumentalists. . . . He compelled all to love and believe in the composition he brought forward." A similar power may radiate from the inspired preacher, the enkindled enthusiast, in the pulpit, compelling men to love and believe in the divine message he brings them.

AMONG the art publications of the Macmillan Company are *The Artist Engraver*, a quarterly magazine of original work for persons who are interested in engraving on copper, steel, or wood, in lithographs, or in etchings; and *The Burlington Magazine* (New York and London) issued monthly at twelve dollars a year for connoisseurs in all branches of the Fine Arts, edited by C. J. Holmes and Robert Dell with the advice of a consultation committee of forty eminent art experts, European and American. The March number which closed the fourth volume contained fourteen articles, including one by Cyril Davenport, F.S.A., on "Embroidered Bindings of Bibles in the Possession of the British and Foreign Bible Society;" the articles being explanatory of, or illustrated by, more than thirty finely executed plates. This one issue deals with pottery, tapestries, mosaics, jewels, porcelains, embroideries, paintings, woodcuts, armor, inlaid pavements, vases, colored glass, ancient weapons, carved furniture, bronzes, shrines, candelabra, and terra-cotta ornaments. This expensive magazine is manifestly not for ordinary taste or purses; but is one of the refined luxuries of wealth and æsthetic culture. What it aims to do for the development, culture, and sensitizing of the sense-faculties, it is our business to do with still greater effort, devotion, enthusiasm, delicacy, and power for the nobler spirit-faculties which apprehend Realities that do not perish or pass away. Among the articles the one most nearly adjacent to the interests and sympathies of our readers is that on "Three Pictures in Tempera by William Blake." The pictures which are reproduced, full-page, have biblical subjects, The Flight into Egypt, David and Bath-sheba, and The Nativity. William Blake, the poetic genius, author of the Book of Thel, Songs of Innocence, The Marriage of Heaven and Hell, The First Book of Urizen, Europe, and Songs of Experience, was also an artist who left numerous woodcuts, wash-drawings, engravings, and some elaborately finished pictures of which the three here reproduced are samples. Considering Blake's position as a painter Roger E. Fry writes: "A singular, an inexplicable phenomenon was the intrusion, as though by direct intervention of

Providence, of this essentially Assyrian spirit into the vapidly polite circles of eighteenth-century London. Puritanism had for a century and a half blocked every inlet and outlet of poetic feeling and imaginative expression save one; and it was the devotion of Puritan England to the Bible, to the Old Testament especially, that fed the spirit of William Blake directly. from the inspired sources of the most primeval, the vastest, and the most abstract imagery which mankind possess. Brooding on the vague and tremendous images of Hebrew and Chaldean poetry, he arrived at such indifference to the actual material world, at such a vivid perception of the elemental forces which sway the spirit with immortal hopes and infinite terrors that what was given to his internal vision became incomparably more definite, more precisely and clearly articulated, than anything presented to his senses. The forms he uses are the visible counterparts to such words as *the deep, the firmament, many waters, the foundation of the earth, the pit, the host,* and others like them, whose resonant overtones blur and enrich the sense of the Old Testament. Blake's art moves us by a similar evocation of vast elemental realities and forces. The obsession of his nature by great spiritual ideas and *sensations,* if one may so use that word, was complete; he was entirely without curiosity about such trivial and ephemeral things as the earth produced. His temperament was anti-Hellenic; he had no concern, either gay or serious, with sense phenomena: they were too flimsy and transparent to arrest his eye. His great difficulty was that the appropriate forms for conveying his highly spiritual ideas were not supplied by the art resources of his day. Tintoretto, who had a similar temperament and felt a similar need of conveying directly the revelations of his internal vision, was more fortunate, inasmuch as, although he was by comparison a trivial and vulgar seer, he was able to achieve a more effective expression by using the richly expressive forms which lay ready to his hand in the art of Titian and Michelangelo. . . . Blake declared that the Byzantine style of art-expression was directly revealed to him, and he certainly did succeed in recovering for a moment that pristine directness and grandeur of expression which puts him beside the great Byzantine designers as a fit interpreter of Hebrew tradition and literature. The Byzantine artists were masters of the expression of imaginative truths; and Blake was an eloquent and persuasive master of the language of symbolic form by which the spirit communicates its most secret and subtle impulses. He boldly made the plea for art that it is a language for conveying impassioned thought and feeling which takes up the objects of sense only as a means to this end, owing them no allegiance and accepting from them only the service they can render for this purpose. He says, 'Poetry consists in bold, daring, and masterly conceptions; and shall painting be confined to the sordid drudgery of realistic facsimile representations of merely mortal and perishing substances, and not be, as poetry and music are, elevated into its own proper sphere of imagination, invention, and visionary conception?' Into the figures of The Flight Into Egypt Blake puts a supernatural dignity, hieratic solemnity, and superhuman purposefulness. The Virgin sits on the ass as though enthroned in monumental state, her limbs

fixed in the rigid symmetry which oriental art has used to express complete withdrawal from the world of sense. And the same exalted mood is upon the figures of Joseph and the guiding angel. William Blake gave visible form to profound spiritual conceptions and emotions, and lent to Hebrew and Christian history and tradition a new significance and elevation."

The Forum (New York) for April-June contains articles on politics, finance, foreign affairs, applied science, music, and education. A paper of special interest is on "Literature: Popular Criticism," by Herbert W. Horwill, one of the editors of *The Forum* and an occasional contributor to the *Methodist Review.* From A. C. Benson's biography of Alfred Tennyson Mr. Horwill quotes the following illuminating comment on the complication and obscurity of "The Princess:" "It is strange that the charge of obscurity so frequently launched against Robert Browning has never been hinted against Tennyson; and yet I declare that the speeches, both in 'The Princess' and the 'Idylls,' are some of the most obscure reading that it is possible to discover in modern poetry—a strong desire for compression, for ornateness, for coagulating a clause into an epithet, for epigrammatic and proverbial touches, making the language like a labyrinth of sonorous walls, even when the thought to be expressed is neither abstruse nor complicated." Benson agrees with Fitz Gerald that the quality of Tennyson's writings declined when he became popular, that he was drawn aside from his natural path by social influences, the pressure of public expectation, and the desire to modify and direct public thought. The gist of the criticism is in this paragraph: "I suspect that he was overshadowed by a fictitious conscience; he was human, though a very large and simple character; and the atmosphere in which he lived was unreal and enervating. If he had not been a man of overpowering genius and childlike simplicity, the effect upon him would have been disastrous. He would have become pontifical, self-conscious, elaborate. As it was, his position only acted upon him with an uneasy pressure to write and think in ways that were not entirely consonant with the best (? bent) of his genius." "Maud" is instanced as showing the beginning of this decadence—as marking "the period at which the purely poetical impulse began to flag, and required to be roused by a violent situation, a tragic interest." Mr. Benson doubts if the bard is in his proper place, when pacing up and down the platform and indulging in strident tirades against the general moral slothfulness of the world. The biographer of Bret Harte says that Harte never could make himself a writer of distinction because "his style lacks firmness and consistency, much as his life lacked these qualities; it lacks refinement, precisely as his nature lacked refinement. With all his particularity in the choice of words he could only use them as counters. He had no sense of language as an organism, and his diction is consequently often conventional, inflated, or coarse." Ferris Greenslet says of Walter Pater's writings that "while one may fail to agree with this or that opinion, or may tire of the subtle, intensive style, he who will approach

him sympathetically may sweeten the day by the reading, and be sure of taking from his pages a lively sense of the fullness and color of the world, and a fresh impulse to a gracefully ordered, thoughtful life." In the same number of *The Forum* Grant Allen gives some personal reminiscences of Herbert Spencer. Spencer used to say that you cannot find a better gauge of a man's intelligence than to observe the proportion which personalities bear to generalities in his conversation. Spencer rarely spoke of any person except for some practical purpose, or else to illustrate some general principle. He generalized incessantly. If you remarked it was a fine day, he would answer: "Yes, anticyclonic conditions like those of yesterday seldom break up without warning of the advent of a depression from westward." If you observed that Mrs. Jones is a pretty woman, Spencer would reply: "Her father was a West Highlander, and her mother was Irish; and intermarriage between Highlanders and Irish almost always produces physically handsome but intellectually inferior children." Once at Marian Evans's house, the talk turned on fly-fishing, and she asked Spencer what sort of fly he preferred to fish with. "Oh," said he, "I lay little stress on the particular kind of fly; I make my own; and all I aim at is to give what the fish expects— the vague representation of an insect fluttering about over the surface of the water." "I see," said Marian Evans (so he always called her), "You're so fond of generalizing that you fish with a generalization." Grant Allen who was no exacting moralist, admits serious moral defects in Spencer's character as well as serious errors and lapses in his intellect. Herbert Spencer's father was a Wesleyan Methodist. But young Spencer was a rebel in many ways; he *wouldn't* go to school, he *wouldn't* study languages. He finally consented to learn mathematics and sciences, and later civil engineering. Grant Allen says unfairly, as we think, that "the faculty for linguistics is most developed in the lowest order of minds, being most common in children and in the inferior races." Early in life Spencer gave himself up to the work of systematizing the evolutionary idea. He determined to become a monk of study, a poor friar of philosophy. A lifelong bachelor he shut himself up to this work, living frugally on the small patrimony left by his father, until that was exhausted and he was so destitute that friends like Stuart Mill and E. L. Youmans felt constrained to offer financial aid. He lived in a boarding house and did all his work in a bare little room over a milk-shop. Grant Allen admits that Spencer was so dogmatic in his conclusions and assertions that he was irritated when others opposed their convictions to his and that he sometimes fell upon opponents with bulldog ferocity. Allen thinks Herbert Spencer "*knew* he had the largest brain of his time, he *knew* posterity would put him above Aristotle, Bacon, Newton, and Kant,—though he never said so." Did Spencer really *know* this? How could he or anybody else know it? Is this the sort of certainty men of science mean when they say "I *know*"? A homely sage has said that it is better not to *know* so much than to be cocksure of so many things that *are not so.* If Grant Allen is right as to Herbert Spencer's estimate of himself, what a modest gentleman the author of *The Synthetic Philosophy* was! But is not consciousness the universally revered authority to-day?

32

And if a man is *conscious* of being the greatest man alive, who can dispute it? Is not that the end of all controversy? As to Herbert Spencer's appearance Mr. Allen says: "A tall thin man, very springy of step, whose looks were at first distinctly disappointing. Some men look their greatness the moment you see them—for example, George Meredith. Spencer did not. At a cursory glance you might think him the confidential clerk of some old business house. His face though disappointing was serene and placid. The lower half was poor and ill-developed. If you screened the lower part so as to see only the forehead and eyes, you would say, What a glorious head! But if you screened the upper part and saw only the chin and mouth, you would say, What a feebly endowed emotional nature! The one great charm in Spencer was a clear and silvery voice, surpassed only by Edmund Gosse's and Sarah Bernhardt's. His enunciation had a beautiful distinctness. In later life when pessimism soured him, the silvery tone was lost in querulousness. Once when somebody beat him at a game of skill in which he thought himself an expert, he declined to play any more and withdrew saying solemnly: 'Some acquaintance with games of skill becomes a cultivated mind, but mastery such as yours bespeaks a wasted youth. I wish you good morning!' "

THE first number of the *Baptist Review and Expositor* (Louisville, Kentucky) is before us. It is edited by the faculty of the Southern Baptist Theological Seminary, with President E. Y. Mullins as editor-in-chief. The editors "believe there is both need and opportunity for a Baptist quarterly in North America. They are not unaware of the disappointing results of similar efforts in the past, nor insensible to the perils which lurk along the way of all such publications. They think there is need of such a review in their Church, because many minds are in need of guidance and help. The *Review and Expositor* accepts evangelical Christianity as commonly held by the Baptists of to-day. Its sympathies are with truth from any and all sources. To 'prove all things' and to 'hold fast that which is good' will be its aim. All important contributions will be signed by the writers. The editors are responsible only for their own views. It will be neither possible nor desirable to maintain a rigid doctrinal uniformity. Neither Northern, Southern, nor Canadian Baptists are wholly agreed among themselves on all doctrinal matters. It is inevitable, therefore, that considerable diversity of opinion will appear." The April issue contains eight solid articles on such topics as "Symbolism in the New Testament," "The Virgin Birth," "An Analysis of the Sermon on the Mount," "The Twentieth Century Sunday School," "The Code of Hammurabi," and "Is God's Moral Government Out of Order?" A notice of Professor W. N. Rice's *Christian Faith in an Age of Science* says that he has done good service in showing that Christian faith can live side by side with scientific convictions. We welcome this lastest-born to the family of Reviews, and hope for it a large circulation in its denomination.

BOOK NOTICES.

RELIGION, THEOLOGY, AND BIBLICAL LITERATURE.

The Teaching of Jesus. By Rev. GEORGE JACKSON, B.A. Crown 8vo, pp. 252. New York: A. C. Armstrong & Son. Price, cloth, $1.25.

Undeniably worth reading by the men of to-day are the writings of George Jackson, author of *The Table-talk of Jesus*, *A Young Man's Religion*, and *The Old Methodism and the New*. He dedicates this latest volume to his children, whom he calls "My wisest teachers in the things of God." These Sunday evening discourses delivered to mixed congregations are proof that "a man may preach freely on the great themes of the Gospel and yet be sure that the common people will hear him gladly, if only he will state his message at once seriously and simply, and with the glow that comes of personal conviction." Mr. Jackson acknowledges his indebtedness to Professor George B. Stevens's *Theology of the New Testament*, commended here by us some time ago, and calls it "a work of which it is impossible to speak too highly." He also mentions gratefully Selby's *Ministry of the Lord Jesus*, Robertson's *Our Lord's Teaching*, and Hastings's *Dictionary of the Bible*. Speaking from the British point of view, he says: "Now that Dr. Dale has gone from us, there is no one to whom we may more confidently look for a reasonable evangelical theology which can be both verified and preached, than Dr. James Denney, of Glasgow," whose great book, *The Death of Christ*, published by our Book Concern, we recently noticed. The author wisely says that however a minister may follow in his studies the critical discussions of debatable questions, when he has passed from his study into his pulpit his sole business is with the *Certainties*, of which there are enough to occupy a lifetime of preaching. Harnack is here spoken of as "a critic who is ready to give to the winds with both hands many things which are as dear to us as life itself." Touching the attempt of some to show opposition between the teaching of Paul and the teaching of Jesus, we have the following: "The doctrines of Paul are not so much theological baggage of which the Church would do well straightway to disencumber itself. After all that the young science of Biblical Theology has done to reveal the manifold variety of New Testament doctrine, the book still remains a unity, and the effort to play off one part of it against another—the Gospels against the Epistles or the Epistles against the Gospels—is to be sternly resented and resisted. To Paul himself any such rivalry would have been impossible and unthinkable. There was no claim which he made with more passionate vehemence than that the message he delivered was not his but Christ's. 'As touching the gospel which was preached by me,' he says, 'neither did I receive it from man, nor was I taught it, but it came to me through revelation of Jesus Christ.' 'We have the mind of Christ,' said Paul, and both in the Epistles and the Gospels we may seek

and find the teaching of Jesus. The words of Paul and his brother apostles are, in a very true sense, 'the final testimony of Jesus to himself.'" It is pointed out that one reason for the stability and irremovableness of Christ's teachings is their winnowedness, their freedom from any chaff which the winds of time and change can drive away. The keen mind of George J. Romanes noticed that while Plato was the greatest of human thinkers in the direction of spirituality, yet the Greek seer teaches errors which are absurd to the reason and shocking to the moral sense. His words cannot stand. Vastly different are the words of Christ; there is in literal truth no reason why any one of his words should ever become obsolete. He has no doctrines which the subsequent growth of human knowledge—whether in natural science, ethics, political economy, or elsewhere—has had to discount or modify. This fact seemed to Romanes one of the strongest evidences for Christianity. Mr. Jackson's sixteen chapters set forth the teaching of Jesus concerning God, concerning Himself, concerning His own Death, concerning the Holy Spirit, the Kingdom of God, Man, Sin, Righteousness, Prayer, the Forgiveness of Injuries, Care, Money, the Second Advent, the Judgment, and the Future Life. Speaking of Christ's word concerning himself, "The Son of man came to give his life a ransom for many," our preacher says: "There is in Edinburgh a Unitarian church on the front of which is carved these words of Paul, 'There is one God, and one mediator between God and man, the man Christ Jesus.' Why did not the Unitarians finish the quotation? Paul only put a comma where they have put a full stop. The next words are, '*Who gave himself a ransom for all.*' But could he do that if he was *only* 'the *man* Christ Jesus'? 'No *man* can save his brother's soul, nor pay his brother's debt.' And Christ's life could be no ransom for our forfeited lives if he were only one like unto ourselves. The only explanation that can explain what Christ taught concerning himself is the one given by his first disciples and reechoed by every succeeding generation of Christians: 'Thou art the King of Glory, O Christ; Thou art the Everlasting Son of the Father.'" Similar to the Edinburgh Unitarians' misuse of an incomplete quotation in support of heretical doctrine is a quotation on the front of "All Souls' Universalist Church" in Brooklyn, New York. The passer-by looks up and reads on the stone these words of the Lord, "ALL SOULS ARE MINE" (EZEK. XVIII, 4). There is no need to ask why the All Souls' Universalists did not go on to quote also the troublesome words which the Bible puts so uncomfortably near in the last clause of that very same fourth verse: "*The soul that sinneth, it shall die.*" From Dora Greenwell the author quotes part of a pitman's story of how, when he was in his sins, this word of fire got into his heart and would not let him be: "The Son of God, who loved me and gave himself for me."

> It was for me that Jesus died! for me and a world of men
> Just as sinful and just as slow to give back His love again;
> And He didn't wait till I came to Him, but He loved me at my worst;
> He needn't ever have died for me if I could have loved Him first.
> And could'st Thou love such a man as me, my Saviour? Then I'll take
> More heed to this wandering soul of mine, if it's only for Thy sake.

From Thomas Hardy's most powerful story this is quoted: "Did you say the stars were worlds, Tess?" "Yes." "All like ours?" "I don't know; but I think so. They sometimes seem to me like the apples on our tree. Most of them splendid and sound—a few blighted." "Which do we live on—a splendid one or a blighted one?" "On a blighted one." The passing of Dr. William MacLure in Ian Maclaren's touching idyl is also reprinted here. "A'm gettin' drowsy; read a bit tae me," said the doctor to Drumsheugh. Then Drumsheugh put on his spectacles, and searched for some comfortable Scripture. Presently he began to read: "In my Father's house are many mansions;" but MacLure stopped him. "It's a bonnie word," he said, "but it's no for the like o' me. It's ower guid; I daurna tak' it." Then he bid Drumsheugh shut the Book and let it open of itself at the place where he had been reading every night. Drumsheugh did as he was bidden and the book opened at where the Master tells what God thinks of a Pharisee and a penitent sinner. And he read, and when he came to the words, "And the publican, standing afar off, would not so much as lift up his eyes to heaven, but smote upon his breast, saying, God be merciful to me, a sinner," once more the dying man stopped him: "That micht hae been written for me, Paitrick, or ony ither auld sinner that hes feenished his life, an' hes naething tae say for himsel'." Nothing to say for ourselves—that is what it comes to, when we see and know the truth about ourselves. "Not by works done in righteousness, which we did ourselves, but according to His mercy He saved us." Commenting on the words, "Watch and pray, that ye enter not into temptation," Mr. Jackson quotes from Charles Kingsley's *Yeast* these words of Colonel Bracebridge: "I am no saint, and God only knows how much less of one I may become; but mark my words—if you are ever tempted by passion and vanity and fine ladies to form liaisons, as the jezebels call them, snares, and nets and labyrinths of blind ditches to keep you down through life, stumbling and groveling, hating yourself and hating the chain that binds you—in that hour of temptation pray—pray as if the devil had you by the throat—cry to Almighty God to help you out of that cursed slough! There is nothing else for it. Pray, I tell you; pray!" Those are words for every young man, in the ministry or out of it, to lay to heart. And in every crisis hour of need, distress, danger, what else can a man do but, as Browning says, catch at God's skirts and pray?

Advent and Ascension; or, How Jesus Came and How He Left Us. By D. W. FAUNCE, D.D., author of *A Young Man's Difficulties with His Bible, Prayer as a Theory and as a Fact, Shall We Believe in a Divine Providence?* etc. 12mo, pp. 215. New York: Eaton & Mains. Cincinnati: Jennings & Pye. Price, 75 cents.

Doing what we have never done before, we adopt as our own the notice given by another review to this volume issued by our own Book Concern. We adopt it because we approve it. The *Bibliotheca Sacra* says: This defense of the miraculous character of Christ's advent and ascension is one of the best which we have ever seen. But the subject is much more inclusive than it seems. It is practically a presentation of the whole supernatural element running through the life of our Lord, involving the entire range of distinctively Christian doctrines. Christ's work

depended upon the exaltation of his nature. His work was what no mere man could do. The blending of the supernatural with the natural is continuous from beginning to end of his career. That it is mysterious is beyond question. But mystery envelops all truth; and that of the blending of the natural with the supernatural in the life of Christ is no more a bar to our believing in it than is the union of the mental and the physical in our own constitution a bar to our believing that our personality involves the union of mind and matter. The author's statement of the relations of Christ's two natures to each other is peculiarly happy. After summarizing the impressions made upon the Virgin Mother, upon the general public, upon his own disciples, and upon successive generations of believers, and after considering the import of Christ's own statements concerning himself, the author condenses his views as follows: "Only four inferences are possible: If we shall say, looking on one class of facts, that he is only divine, there remains a large class of facts of which no account can be given. If we shall say, on the other hand, that he is only human, one equally large class of facts remains not included in the theory. If we shall say he was superhuman only, neither human nor divine, but in some way superior to man and inferior to God, then what becomes of both classes of facts, neither of which is accounted for in this hypothesis? These three theories of Christ's nature set aside, as not covering the facts, one more remains: that the Person whom we know as Jesus Christ was the God-man; the Son of God becoming the Son of man, 'God manifested in the flesh.' And this conclusion reconciles and combines both classes of texts—those which speak of him as God and those which speak of him as man. The question is not whether this is or is not explicable. We bow before it as the divine mystery. But we must not so hold the revealed fact as to make the divinity absorb the humanity, or the humanity the divinity, nor yet so as to claim a double consciousness in the one Person, our Lord Jesus Christ; nor need we hold to two natures separately existing side by side, now one acting and now the other. Yet the whole mode in which this incarnation was accomplished must always baffle us. Human reason has no plummet that can sound the depths of God. There were those who felt that the impassibility of God forbade any words about the divine nature as suffering. There were those who held that there could be no self-deprivation of the divine attributes, no self-renunciation of any divine perfection; not even a voluntary self-limitation. But all this was to limit God's power to limit himself, and so it actually affirmed in one direction what it denied in another. Whether it is necessary to call in the idea of self-limitation or not, some have questioned. The phrase frequently used about 'the limitations of humanity' as applied to our Lord needs to be employed with great caution. God self-limited—limited by himself in the exercise of his attributes—is a widely different conception from God limited by humanity—God limited by man. Indeed, what has been claimed as limitation in the case of Christ is really extension to the conditions of men. He was able to extend his being so as to become babe, child, man. He reached out and came into every variety of human experience. It may be considered as an expansion rather than a contraction, an enlargement rather than a reduction. It is the condescension of Divinity to care

for the lowliest. Infinite greatness is shown in the greatness of care for minutest objects. Jesus was able to die, showing thereby his power; God was seen in self-sacrifice at the cross; and these were not limitations but divine extensions toward our human needs" (pp. 128-130).

Primitive Semitic Religion To-day. A *Record of Researches, Discoveries, and Studies in Syria, Palestine, and the Sinaitic Peninsula.* By SAMUEL IVES CURTISS, Professor of Old Testament Literature and Interpretation, Chicago Theological Seminary. 8vo, pp. 288. Chicago and New York: Fleming H. Revell Company. Price, cloth, $2.50.
Ursemitische Religion im Volksleben des heutigen Orients, Forschungen und Funde aus Syrien und Palästina. Von SAMUEL IVES CURTISS. Deutsche Ausgabe, nebst einem Vorwort von WOLF WILHELM GRAFEN BAUDISSIN. Crown 8vo, pp. xxx and 375. Leipzig, J. C. Hinrichs'sche Buchhandlung. Price, paper, M. 9; cloth, M. 10.

The works of American scholars rarely appear in German editions. German scholars read American books in reasonable measure, though not to the extent in which German books are read by us. But they do not seem to wish them translated into German, and in a recent instance they have sharply attacked an American scholar whose book is appearing in German. It may have required some courage for Professor Curtiss to put his book forth in Germany, but we are glad that he has done it. The form in which it appears is a compliment to the Germans, as the scientific leaders of the world, for the German edition greatly exceeds the English in size and contains a number of chapters which do not appear in the English edition at all. It is introduced by a preface written by the distinguished scholar, Professor Baudissin, of the University of Berlin, which is a perfect model of what such introductions should be, but rarely are. Professor Baudissin is not only an Old Testament scholar of the highest rank, he is also one of the first living authorities in comparative religion of the Semitic peoples. He praises Professor Curtiss's work, and praises it with dignity and generosity. He shows how Professor Curtiss has sought to explain, in part, the religion of Israel by the religion of the Semites who still inhabit the ancient territory of the Hebrews, and in this investigation has followed in a measure the example set years ago by the great German Arabist, J. G. Wetzstein. But while thus recognizing in the fullest degree the importance of the work and commending its methods and results, Professor Baudissin expresses his dissent on a few points and upon others emphasizes the need of caution. The frankness and the soberness of this introduction are characteristic of its author, and will raise the book in the estimation of scholars the world over. Professor Curtiss has written a book which plainly grew slowly and naturally, and is therefore totally different from the hastily conceived and quickly executed works with which the market is flooded. In the autumn of 1898 he made his first trip in Palestine, and perhaps few men are better prepared for the journey than he. He had then been Professor of Old Testament Literature and Interpretation in Chicago Theological Seminary for twenty years, and before that time had the incomparable enrichment of four years' study at the University of Leipzig under Professor Franz, who counted him a favorite pupil. His first tour in the East began July 9, 1898, and concluded August 17, 1899. The second extended from June 11, 1900, to August 23, 1900; the third began June 5, 1901, and ended August

24, 1901; while the fourth comprised the weeks between May 26 and the month of August, 1902. During these periods Professor Curtiss covered practically the whole of Syria and Palestine, visited Sinai and Petra, and made a long tour in Egypt. His object was to seek out every evidence of the primitive forms of Semitic worship which have survived to the present day. He found sacred stones, sacrificial altars, and many another evidence of ancient forms of worship. He questioned large numbers of persons, and from them secured illustrations of the present-day observance of religious rites and ceremonies, which presumably go back to primitive times. The investigation has been carried on with immense care, with every effort to eliminate possible errors, and is a model piece of entirely original research. It would be a pity to spoil the reader's interest by making extracts, and we forbear. Students of comparative religion will need no urging to read the book. To others it will be sufficient to say that the investigation pours a flood of light upon the Old Testament, that it is all couched in simple and attractive style and will well repay even the ordinary reader. All who can use German easily will find the German edition valuable, in addition to the English. Others may content themselves happily with the English.

PHILOSOPHY, SCIENCE, AND GENERAL LITERATURE.

Vocal and Literary Interpretation of the Bible. By S. S. CURRY, Ph.D. 12mo, pp. 384. New York: The Macmillan Company. Price, cloth, $1.50.

Dr. Curry has been teacher of Elocution and Oratory in Boston University, in Newton Theological Institution, in Yale and Harvard Divinity Schools. This volume contains the wisdom of many years of experience, and brings to the preacher sensible and valuable instruction, suggestion, warning, and encouragement. It is for serious study, not for entertainment. The author says his book has had no predecessor, and Professor F. G. Peabody agrees that both in its method and its spirit it is without precedent. Its purpose is to teach the minister to read the Scriptures in public so intelligently, impressively, and effectively as to convey the sense. Not only are principles given, but numerous specific passages of Scripture are here interpreted and rendered so as to illustrate the principles; and this we think to be the book's most definite value. Every minister who has any sense of responsibility for making his message and the word of God effective will welcome Dr. Curry's book with eagerness, and study it with gratitude. No part of public worship is so often perfunctory, careless, and uninspiring as the preacher's reading of the Scripture lessons, although nothing else is more susceptible of being made vivid and powerful. A clergyman asked a humble member of his church what led to his conversion, and the answer was, "Why, sir, it was hearing the minister read one morning in church, 'As the Lord of hosts liveth, before whom I stand.'" "How did those words lead to your conversion?" said the clergyman. "Don't you see, sir? 'Before whom I stand:' *I felt myself standing before God.*" The Scripture lesson must have been feelingly and impressively read that morning. How to interpret, by his

reading of them, the various messages of the Bible with sympathy, yet without artificiality or extravagance, is surely one of the minister's most serious duties. The wonder is that, with our poor, careless, unintelligent reading of the word, men listen so patiently; and that, with our frequent mispresentation of Christ, so many believe on him. The contents of this very helpful book are arranged in four divisions, "The Problem," "The Message," "The Technique," and "Preparation and the Service." Some wise suggestions are made concerning public prayer. "An elaborate prayer giving information to the Deity is irreverent, and a prayer containing the news of the week or a long catalogue of petitions for things which are not expected is blasphemous." As we said, many of the most striking passages of both the Old and New Testaments are here analyzed and explained, sentence by sentence, clause by clause, to show how they require to be read in order to their proper powerful effect. We wish we had room to transcribe the ten pages in which the author shows how the story of the Prodigal Son ought to be read, that parable so full of dramatic elements; or the Sermon on the Mount; or the story of Naaman; or Paul's great addresses; or others of the numerous passages so impressively rendered with vocal modulations and movements. All extremes and shades of feeling are in the words of Scripture. The words of Christ himself contain a wide range of differing emotions. What variations of expression in voice, tone, look, and gesture must have accompanied his varied utterances! What regret is in his words, "How often would I have gathered your children together as a hen gathers her brood under her wings"! What approval in "Go in peace"! What sorrow in "O Jerusalem, Jerusalem"! What sarcasm in "Go tell that fox"! What indignation in "Ye offspring of vipers"! What tender sympathy in "Woman, behold thy son"! What sorrow and pity in "The cock shall not crow before thou shalt deny me thrice"! What supreme confidence in "I, if I be lifted up, will draw all men unto me"! What persuasion in his "Come unto me, all ye that labor and are heavy laden"! What admiration in "I have not found so great faith, no, not in Israel"! What infinite love and compassion in "Father, forgive them, they know not what they do"! To give, in our public reading, such variations of voice modulation as their meaning requires and as the Master doubtless gave them is a worthy object of ambition and endeavor. One of the important matters in reading is the placing of the emphasis. This may be seen in Matt. xxvii, 11: "Art thou the King of the Jews?" The word "thou" has a peculiar value in the meaning which must be indicated in the vocal accentuation. Canon Farrar gives the meaning thus: "There, amid those voluptuous splendors, Pilate, already interested, already feeling in this prisoner before him some nobleness which touched his Roman nature, asks him in pitying wonder, 'Art thou the King of the Jews?'—thou poor, worn, tear-stained outcast—thou pale, lonely, friendless, wasted man, in thy coarse peasant garments, with thy tied hands and the foul traces of the insults of thine enemies on thy face and on thy robes—thou, so unlike the fierce, magnificent, truculent Herod, whom this bloodthirsty multitude acknowledged as their sovereign—art *thou* the

King of the Jews?" Such a rendering of the meaning is exegesis, not rhetoric. Another important matter in reading is the intelligent use of pause, which properly managed may add vastly to the impressiveness. This is fully set forth and illustrated by specific Scripture passages in Dr. Curry's book. On page 322 we find this quotation from Delsarte: "Accentuate the fundamentals, and you will have power; accentuate accidentals, and you develop mediocrity and show weakness." The thing which strikes us in that saying is the wide range and many realms in which it is true. Delsarte applied the statement to the actions of the body, an application relatively unimportant. But how momentously true in most important things is the saying, "Accentuate fundamentals, and you both manifest and produce power; accentuate incidentals, and you both show and promote weakness"! It is as true in theology, in biblical study, in character, and in life as it is in public reading of the Scriptures. The strong wise man is he who knows what the fundamentals are and puts mighty stress on them; the weak foolish man is he who does not know the difference between the important and the unimportant, but spends himself equally on both and often makes a great ado and a fierce fight over the nonessential—an error out of which comes the blurring of distinctions, the undue prominence of little men and cranks, clamorous and strident about some detail, and a wide welter of confusion, wherefrom in Church and State we do often suffer. Delsarte's dictum is a text to carry in the vest pocket of one's memory, for frequent application. Dr. Curry's book raises all kinds of questions. Should the minister reading the Scripture lesson comment as he goes along? Spurgeon did nearly always, and Beecher sometimes. There are dangers in the practice. All depends on the audience, the occasion, the particular passage, and the man himself. Shall the minister make gestures in reading the Bible? Seldom, if ever. Dr. Curry's aim and spirit are revealed in such words as these: "This book aims to awaken higher ideals regarding the conducting of public worship. It endeavors to open all eyes to a neglected function, to an overlooked means of power, and especially to impress the importance of reading the Bible better. What is more needful than the true vocal interpretation of the Holy Scriptures? Nothing is so likely to strike home. The wildest and most reckless man in your congregation may have heard at his mother's knee the words you read. If rightly read they will fix his attention. They may awaken tender memories, renew spiritual aspirations, strengthen the weak and wavering will. Without debate, without arousing antagonism, the sublime words appeal straight to the intuitions of men's hearts, and make them feel themselves spoken to by the Eternal. What is the preacher's final appeal in struggling with a soul at some crisis? To some sentence from the Bible. When he faces a young man wavering at some turning point what does he give him? Some words of the Master. When he stands up at a funeral service and looks around on the broken-hearted, what can he do but read those divine words which have ministered to the sorrow-stricken for thousands of years? In the Bible are the most simple, heart-searching, touching, and potent words ever spoken. Their spell is mighty wherever they touch hu-

man nature. Well may a man tremble at the thought of presenting or misrepresenting the meaning of these words to his fellow-men. Who can dare deliver them coldly or carelessly?" A great biblicist has said, "The heretic is he who does not study his Bible, or does not study it reverently and thoroughly, with the best aids available." And surely that minister is a culprit who does not take studious and persevering pains to read the Scriptures impressively and movingly.

The Faith of Robert Louis Stevenson. By JOHN KELMAN, JR., M.A. 8vo, pp. 302. New York and Chicago: Fleming H. Revell Company. Price, cloth, $1.50.

Mr. Kelman is a notable and magnetic Edinburgh preacher who has especially a strong hold upon students and young people generally. More than any other man he succeeds to the place and the work of Professor Drummond. He finds in the writings of Louis Stevenson a faith which is precious to him and vitally helpful. The expression of this faith is largely in Stevenson's own words. The man is made to reveal himself. To many the amount of religious matter in Stevenson's writings for making a book like this is a surprise. It is not claimed that Stevenson was a saint; in some early years he was wild enough and often rudely and daringly irreligious; but it is shown that religion was an increasing force in him as the years advanced. He speaks of himself as having been "pestered with a damnatory creed," against which he revolted in youth. He was one "whose God no house of words that men have builded can contain." His final conception is probably explicit in his address to the Samoan students: "The meaning of religion is a rule of life; it is an obligation to do well; if that rule, that obligation, is not seen, your thousand texts will be to you like the thousand lanterns to the blind man." When some Sisters of Charity arrive at Molokai to minister to the poor lepers, Stevenson greets them with, "Ladies, God himself is here to give you welcome." In Samoa he became a church attendant, a Sunday school teacher, an enthusiast for foreign missions and missionaries, a leader in family worship for which he wrote prayers that are memorable and almost classic. Mr. Kelman shows that religion always had a vital interest for Stevenson, even in the early years of revolt, and at last it took complete command of him. Always, God was the overshadowing fact; God, of whom Joubert said, "It is not hard to know him, provided we do not force ourselves to define him." In Stevenson's morning prayers were expressions like these: "Let not our beloved have cause to blush for us, nor we for them. Accept us, correct us, guide us, thy guilty innocents." Also: "Help us to look back on the long way that thou hast brought us, on the long days in which we have been served not according to our deserts but our desires; on the pit and the miry clay, the blackness of despair, the horror of misconduct, from which our feet have been plucked out. For our sins forgiven or prevented, for our shame unpublished, we bless and thank thee, O God!" Also: "Lord, defend me from idle conformity aimed to please the face of man, and from all display designed to catch applause." His mother tells us that when he was four years old he said, "You can never be good unless you pray;" and when asked how he knew,

he replied, with great emphasis, "Because I've tried it." Stevenson always kept the feeling and spirit of a child. From California he wrote in depressing illness: "But death is no bad friend. A few aches and gasps and we are done. Like the truant child, I am beginning to grow weary and timid in this big jostling city, and could run to my nurse, even though she had to whip me for my truancy before putting me to bed." Eight months before his death he wrote: "As I go on in life, day by day, I become more of a bewildered child; I cannot get used to this world." Bunyan's *Pilgrim's Progress*, which charmed Stevenson's childhood, lived in his mind forever, and he even gave thanks for the pictures illustrating it, which made him feel as if he knew "every turn and town along the road to the Celestial City, and that bright place itself, seen as to a stave of music, shining afar off upon the hilltop, the candle of the world." We read that, from Stevenson's point of view, Edinburgh was a place chiefly notable for "conscious rectitude, eminent respectability, and freezing formality," which description reminds us of some saints and churches. He writes of the "clockwork virtues" of a prim pattern woman, with her "irritating deliberation and correctness," and says, "If she would only write bad grammar, or forget to finish a sentence, or do something or other that looks fallible, it would be a relief." He criticises the average sermon because it "flees the point, disporting itself in that Eternity of which we know, and need to know, so little, and avoiding the bright, crowded, and momentous fields of actual life where destiny instantly awaits us." One of his phrases is "the commanding immediacy of life." He insists that there is "a manifest God for those who choose to look for him." And he says: "If you believe in God, where is there any more room for terror? If you are sure that God, in the long run, means kindness by you, you should be happy." Facing those conflicting aspects of Nature which sometimes darken our vision of the divine goodness, he says:

> And methought that beauty and terror are only one, not two;
> And the world has room for love, and death, and thunder, and dew;
> And all the sinews of hell slumber in summer air;
> And the face of God is a rock, but the face of the rock is fair.

One of Stevenson's favorite doctrines is that eternal dissatisfaction with one's self and one's attainments is the condition of progress. "The artist who says *It will do* is on the downward path." "To have many aspirations is to be spiritually rich." "To travel hopefully is better than to arrive, and the true success is to labor." "Happiness, temporal or eternal, is not the reward a man seeks. Happinesses are but his wayside campings; his soul is in the journey." "Our business in the world is not to succeed, but to continue to fail in good spirits; and when the end comes to be content with this epitaph, Here lies one who meant well, tried a little, and failed much; or, There goes another faithful failure." But Mr. Kelman properly remarks that such a doctrine is safe only for the strenuous: most of us are only too willing to accept it and consent to fail. Stevenson himself is one who *never consents to fail*, but ever gallantly struggles to achieve "the glory of going on." Near the end of life he wrote a friend:

"For fourteen years I have not had a day's real health. I have written in bed, written in hemorrhages, written torn by coughing, written when my head swam for weakness; and thus far it seems to me I have won. The battle still goes on—ill or well is a trifle, so as it goes. I was made for a contest, and the Powers have so willed that my battlefield should be this dingy inglorious one of the bed and the physic bottle." He welcomed "the harsh voice of duty" and "the bright face of danger." Duty was a lifelong summons. The call he heard was, *"Wanted, Volunteers to do their best for twoscore years!"* The Parable of the Talents was his favorite Scripture. He said: "The man who has only been pious and not useful will stand with a long face on that great day when Christ puts to him His questions." He holds that God delights in those who "sow gladness on the peopled lands, and spin the great wheel of earth about with laughter, song, and shout." Deploring duly the excesses of appetite and passion, he finds the truly diabolic rather in "envy, malice, the mean lie, the mean silence, the calumnious truth, the backbiter, the petty domestic tyrant, the peevish and selfish poisoner of family life." "It is our business," he said, "to make excuses for others, but none for ourselves." He hates "those who have an eye for faults and failures, taking pleasure in finding and publishing them, and who forget the overveiling virtues and the real success." He also says, "There is no more sure sign of a shallow mind than the habit of seeing always the humorous side of things." He resents Thoreau's mean saying that we are always disappointed in our friends, and contends that "We are ninety-nine times disappointed in our beggarly selves for once that we are disappointed in our friend." His is an appreciative soul, believing enthusiastically in man in general and in many individual men in particular; and, while in Samoa, especially in some missionaries. "The best specimen of the Christian hero I ever met was one of the native missionaries." "The excellent Clarke was here almost all day yesterday, a man I esteem and like to the soles of his boots; I prefer him to anyone in Samoa, and to most people in the world; a real good missionary." Of another missionary he says: "A hero, a man who fairly took me by storm, the most attractive, simple, brave, and interesting man in the whole Pacific." Of his friend, James Chalmers, the New Guinea missionary, he writes: "You can't weary me of that fellow; he is as big as a house and far bigger than any church." One of his convictions is that "the world must return to the word Duty, and be done with the word Reward. There are no rewards, but plenty of duties. And the sooner a man sees that and acts upon it like a gentleman, the better for him and for the world." He bids "never to set up to be soft, only to be square and hearty, and a man all round." He likes strong, healthy, high-strung, generous natures, honorable, simple, and righteous. After praying that we may clearly see and deeply feel our failures and offenses, he adds: "Help us at the same time, Lord, with the grace of courage, that we be not utterly cast down when we sit lamenting amid the ruins of our happiness or our integrity; touch us with fire from the altar, that we may be up and doing to rebuild our city." He tells the story of one who made shipwreck through folly, and who in the bitterness of loss and shame came to him-

self and began a nobler life. "In his youth he took thought for no one but himself, and he voyaged away; when he came ashore again, his whole armada lost, he seemed to think only of others. He had gone to ruin with a kind of kingly *abandon*, like one who condescended; but once ruined, with the lights all out, he fought as for a kingdom." Stevenson, suffering, battling, dying, wrote near the last, "Sick or well, I have had a splendid time of it; I grudge nothing, regret very little." Enduring ills which might make some men pessimists, he said: "In the harsh face of life faith can read a bracing gospel;" and again: "Whether on the first of January or the thirty-first of December, faith is a good word to end on." When he was fighting with death and losing he wrote Professor Colvin: "The tragedy of things works itself out blacker and blacker. Does it shake my cast-iron faith? I cannot say that it does. I believe in an ulti- mate decency of things; aye, and if I woke in hell, should still believe it." That is the faith of one who can

> Feel, in the ink of the slough
> And the sink of the mire,
> Veins of glory and fire
> Run through and transpierce and transpire,
> And a secret purpose of glory in every part,
> And the answering glory of battle fill his heart.

Mr. Kelman believes that the first necessity of the present day is for an encouraging and heartening type of faith, lest we sink to that dejection in which an age "goes dispiritedly, glad to finish." And Louis Stevenson administers as antidote and prophylactic the spirit of buoyant and ex- hilarating hopefulness. This is the true *Zeitgeist.* Blind-deaf-dumb Helen Keller says of Stevenson, "I can never again be disheartened since that sturdy preacher gave me my lesson of 'the fashion of the smiling face.'"

The Diversions of a Book-Lover. By ADRIAN H. JOLINE. 8vo, pp. 323. New York: Harper & Brothers. Price, cloth, $3.

The author of *Meditations of an Autograph Collector* tells us that these discursive papers must not be regarded too seriously, but regarded as diversions to draw the mind from care, business, or study, and thus rest and amuse. They are the free and easy confidences of one who loves books for their own sake, and are meant to be taken up and laid aside at odd moments. It is a book which only a book-lover seeking light diver- sion will care much about—miscellaneous odds and ends. A Scotchman, revising the old lines, spoke of preachers who "find stones in the run- ning brooks, sermons in books, and good in everything." John Burroughs said of Thoreau, "He is almost as local as a woodchuck." Milton wrote: "Many a man is a burden to the earth, but a good book is the precious life- blood of a master spirit, embalmed and treasured up on purpose to a life beyond life." In *Lawyers and Literature* Irving Browne says: "To call a clergyman a hypocrite, a physician a murderer, and a lawyer a liar, has long been one of the favorite amusements of a part of mankind." Bret Harte, in one of his *Condensed Novels,* burlesqued the style of Cooper's

novels by making "the judge" say to his daughter: "Ginevra, the logs which compose yonder fire seem to have been incautiously chosen. The sibilation produced by the sap, which exudes copiously therefrom, is not conducive to composition." And the fair Ginevra replies: "I see, father, but I thought it would be preferable to the constant crepitation which is apt to attend the combustion of more seasoned ligneous fragments." But our author says truly that a page of Cooper is worth volumes of such triflers as Le Gallienne, Oscar Wilde, and others of that ilk. Cooper has the stalwart vigor of the pure open air, and they have the sickly debility of a stuffy artificial modernity. Cooper's account of the Battle of Bunker Hill in *Lionel Lincoln* is brilliant, and *The Deerslayer*, with all its imperfections, appeals to the lover of robust adventure and of the beautiful in nature, to every healthy sound-minded man who has rich, good blood in his veins. Thackeray said Montaigne's *Essays* were one of his bedside books: "I read them in the dozy hours and only half remember them." Macaulay said, "Some books which I would never dream of opening at dinner please me at breakfast, and *vice versa*." Our author prefers "Elia at bedtime, Thackeray in the afternoon, with an installment of Dickens in the bright, clear morning, and perhaps De Quincey, Holmes, or Lowell at noon." He does not know when he would appropriate time for Henry James or Mrs. Humphry Ward, but thinks they might be of some value in a period of insomnia. Edmond Scherer said: "A cult once established, a dogma once accepted—then no more freedom of analysis, no more independent criticism, no more permissible dissent; nothing but to admire like a dumb beast." Critics and reviewers catch it frequently from authors. This author credits them with usually meaning to be just and fair, but thinks they often miss the mark. Disraeli said critics are men who have failed in literature and art. Coleridge said: "Reviewers are usually people who would have been poets, historians, biographers if they could." Shelley said: "Reviewers, with rare exceptions, are a stupid and malignant race." Southey once enticed Shelley into his study and read his (Southey's) own verses to him till the listener fell asleep under the table. Tennyson once read aloud to Charles Sumner the whole of "The Princess" at one sitting; and Sumner never dared visit the laureate again for fear of a similar infliction, though the Massachusetts senator was sometimes an egotistic bore himself. Of Wagner's "Tannhäuser" Prosper Mérimée said: "It is a prodigious, a colossal bore. I am convinced that I could compose something similar if inspired by the scampering of my cat over the piano keys." Mr. Joline says he has had a strange affection for Carlyle since reading how his wife scolded him for feeding the cat at the table. He says Charles Dickens was a born actor, whose daily life always suggested the footlights. When Horace Walpole was suffering from the gout Gray, of the "Elegy," wrote him: "The pain in your feet I can bear." Such heartlessness saddens the souls of those who wish to believe in the brotherhood of man. Bill Nye said of the *Century Dictionary:* "I like it immensely. It is quite thrilling in places, and although somewhat jerky in style and verbose, perhaps, its word-painting is accurate and delightful." Our author refuses to abase himself before Louis Stevenson or

Walter Pater as models or authorities in literary style. Pater lacks simplicity and freshness, loses the natural in devotion to the formal, and is a dispenser of literary millinery. Pater says: "Racy Saxon monosyllables, close to us as touch and sight, intermix readily with those long savorsome Latin words rich in 'second intention.'" But Mr. Joline says that when a writer pauses to bethink himself of his Saxon monosyllables and savorsome Latin words he loses spontaneity, becomes a specimen of affectation, devoid of soul and animation. The secret of forcible style is to write simply, clearly, directly, after the straight fashion in which men talk to their fellows. Flaubert is a master of form, but lacks strength, heartiness, and vitality. Even Pater insists that a man's style should be his own and not borrowed. Thus he says: "Style in all its varieties, reserved or opulent, terse, abundant, musical, stimulant, or academic, finds justification so long as it is really characteristic; the sumptuous good taste of Cicero being as truly the man himself as would have been his portrait by Raffaelle in full consular splendor, in his ivory chair." Mr. Gosse says of Pater: "He exhausted himself in the research after absolute perfection of expression, noting with extreme refinement delicate shades of feeling and exquisite distinctions of thought and sentiment. His fault was to overburden his sentences, to annex to them too many parenthetical clauses and adjectival glosses. He was the most studied of all the English prose writers of his time." Mr. Joline regards Pater as a melancholy monument of mistaken mannerism, who has no hold upon men. It may be so. Doubtless there is an over-preciseness in Pater's style, an excess of polish; nevertheless we cannot help admiring and revering the man who aims at perfection and toils hard to attain it. Whatever his misconceptions or practical mistakes, his nature is noble, the blood-royal is in his veins, he is worthy of a crown. Our author speaks of Andrew Lang as "the eminent Panjandrum of literature." Coleridge accused Gibbon of having reduced history to a mere collection of splendid anecdotes. Dean Stanley said to J. R. Green, the historian: "I see you are in danger of becoming picturesque. Beware of it. I have suffered from it." Goethe said of Byron: "There is no padding in his poetry." There is no padding in Green's historical work. He is more valuable than Stubbs or Freeman. His *Short History of the English People* created such a furor that fashionable ladies carried it about with them on their visits to country houses. With these and similar desultory and diverting bits of quotation, anecdote, opinion, and reminiscence, the author of *Meditations of an Autograph Collector*, previously noticed here, has filled over three hundred mildly interesting pages.

HISTORY, BIOGRAPHY, AND TOPOGRAPHY.

Representative Modern Preachers. By LEWIS O. BRASTOW, D.D., Professor of Practical Theology in Yale University. 12mo, pp. 423. New York: The Macmillan Company. Price, cloth, $1.50.

A difficult and delicate task in preparing a work on Representative Modern Preachers is the selection for consideration of a few out of a

great multitude who belong to this class. In turning the pages of this work we miss the names of colossal preachers who have stood in the modern pulpit conspicuous types of their class. It is remarkable that the Methodist pulpit, which has been distinguished for its eloquence and effectiveness, has not a single name in this "Hall of Fame." Surely Bishop Simpson merits a place in that goodly company. The book is a portraiture of nine representative preachers: Schleiermacher, Robertson, Beecher, Bushnell, Phillips Brooks, Cardinal Newman, Mozley, Guthrie, and Spurgeon. The author discusses these nine with critical discrimination. Unlike many biographers who read themselves into the characters they study, he has the rare gift of subtle intuition by which he penetrates the most diverse natures, thinking their thoughts, participating in their motives, feeling all, living all. So they move before us as living beings with no suggestion of mechanism worked by the professor's hand. We do not object to the evident sympathy with the persons he portrays; for we believe that love rather than passionless criticism is the truer interpreter of character; excepting where love becomes an enchantment, a sort of hypnotic spell, in which black appears white, and deformity is grace itself. In only a single instance do these studies awaken a suspicion of any obscuration of facts by the glare of love; they rather impress us that they were written with the calm impartiality of a loving though disenchanted critic. The single exception is that of Cardinal Newman. The author discounts about every charge that critics such as Kingsley, Rigg, and Newman's own brother have made against him. "Whatever may be the final verdict as to the value of Newman's work, and whatever our estimate of the rationality of his principles and the sanity of his methods, . . . that his motives were at bottom other than sincerely religious will not be readily credited by any man who has ever felt the power of his passionately earnest soul." That certainly seems to be the general judgment of this singularly fascinating personality. And there is probably no true man who would take any pleasure in pointing out a single defect in the venerable figure whom all classes of whatever sect love to honor. He was unquestionably a man of brilliant genius; a poet born and original whose songs will make music through the ages; an exquisite writer of English prose; a preacher of marvelous insight into character and extraordinary power of persuasion; a man of stupendous achievements and high ecclesiastical rank; and one who could win, not only those who knew him at a distance, but also those who were near to him, to a reverence which is hardly distinguishable from worship. Nor was his "spell" in any appreciable measure weakened by his removal from the English Church to that of Rome. We stand too near the sepulcher of this great man to enter any demurrer at this time to the general hero-worship. But we do think that in a critical estimate of Newman as a preacher the fact ought to be specially noted that his ablest sermons were preached while he was in the Anglican pulpit. That at least is the judgment of many who have studied them. There was indeed "a sudden freedom and spontaneity of movement which characterized his discourses immediately after his entering Rome," which did not appear in his earlier

33

sermons; but as Gladstone suggests, whom our author quotes, that was probably due to the fact that he was "unmuzzled." In other respects the earlier sermons were the stronger. His admiring biographer Hutton presents at length his ministry at St. Mary's as superior in every quality of a preacher to his later ministry at Birmingham. Another fact ought to be strongly emphasized in order to explain Newman's career; namely, his want of historic insight. Hutton says: "The ultimate basis of Newman's theology was feeling; that of Döllinger was history. For this reason he and Döllinger could not get on together. The cardinal said, It was like a dog and a fish trying to make friends." Professor Brastow does indeed recognize this fact and says that Newman was afraid of the free application of the methods of historic criticism in dogma. But it is our impression that it was something more than fear that led him to such utter perversion of history at times, as when he defends the Roman Church from the charge of persecution in such language as this: "Rome has been a never-failing fount of humanity, equity, forbearance, and compassion. We find in all parts of Europe scaffolds prepared to punish crimes against religion; scenes which sadden the soul were everywhere witnessed; Rome is the one exception to the rule. The popes, armed with the tribunal of intolerance, have scarce spilt a drop of blood; Protestants and philosophers have shed it in torrents!" History indeed! It is well for us not to allow the splendor of genius and charming personality to blind us to serious defects. One of the most powerfully drawn pictures in this gallery and one that must satisfy the most critical observer is that of Schleiermacher. While no one man can be said to have occasioned and directed the rebound of the German heart from the deadening rationalism of the eighteenth century, it is certain that the reactionary movement toward a new spiritual life in dogma and experience found in Schleiermacher its most conspicuous and influential representative. In the judgment of our author, Neander, McClintock, and others he received from his early Moravian training "a spirit of tender subjective religiousness which ever lingered like a heavenly aroma over everything which he wrote and spoke." He, like all true prophets, saw that behind all creeds, all ecclesiastical pageantries, all ethical rules, and all philosophies there was an eternal True, a spirit divine, whose breath would awaken life in the individual, the Church, the school, the nation. To preach that was the work of his life. His was a voice in the wilderness which startled the torpid conscience of German university and pulpit. It is to Schleiermacher more than to any one man of the century that we owe the popular distinction between religion and doctrine which is so mightily affecting the modern pulpit. Doctrine is the result of the effort to formulate in thought that which is deeper and wider than all human thinking. Taking his dictum that "religion is feeling," then the basal facts of all religion are those revealed in Christian consciousness: not that of one man, but "the collective Christian consciousness is the ultimate test of Christian truth." Hence the value of creeds, ecclesiastical symbols, and even the apostolic testimony is not that they are an absolute objective authority, but only in the fact that they express the facts of Christian consciousness

at a given time. We can readily see how that this principle, when pursued to its logical end, will not only exclude all speculations on religious life, but also all authoritative statements of it; a position which the life of the Church has demonstrated as untenable. It is certain that as piety fruits in truth, so truth feeds piety. His conception of religion as natural, belonging as it does to the constitution of the human soul, and as supernatural in having its inspiring source in God who is revealed in Christ, is also influencing the modern pulpit. It helps to bridge the gulf between the natural and the supernatural. The supernatural itself has an element of naturalness. Furthermore Schleiermacher's spirituality so unlike the ascetic type of Rome, and the merely emotional type of certain evangelistic schools, demands a practical thorough moral life. "His system has developed the ethical side of Christian life more fully than it had ever been developed before and has made to it the most important contribution of the last century." Of the other preachers presented in this volume, Robertson, "the most gifted preacher of his century," and Beecher, "the most brilliant of American preachers," are both "path-breakers in the work of the Christian pulpit, and may be classed as epoch-making men in modern preaching." Guthrie and Spurgeon "have contributed little or nothing to the thought of the Church, and the up-to-date man is interested in neither, yet it would be a mistake to minimize their significance for the practical life of the Church." Bushnell, with "homiletical genius," personality, and doctrine, and Phillips Brooks, "the great humanist of his generation," have already won and "will continue to win the moral and spiritual allegiance of men."

History of the Christian Church. By GEORGE H. DRYER, D.D. 12mo. Vol. I, Beginning of the Kingdom, pp. 415; Vol. II, The Preparation for Modern Times, 600-1517 A. D., pp. 642; Vol. III, The Reformation, 1517-1648 A. D., pp. 653; Vol. IV, The Puritan Reform and the Evangelical Revival, 1648-1800 A. D., pp. 605; Vol. V, The Advance of Christendom, 1800-1901 A. D., pp. 730. Cincinnati: Jennings & Pye. New York: Eaton & Mains. Price, cloth, $7.50.

With the author's estimate as to the value of Christian history all readers of these volumes will at the outset agree. A just confidence in the authority of the Church and an enthusiastic belief in its glorious destiny are without doubt conditioned upon a knowledge of its origin. With this conviction as a starting point—and it must be the inspiring conviction of every historian who is worthy of the name and who does work that survives—Dr. Dryer has written the volumes which are now before us. The mention of several evident characteristics of his work, as they impress the reviewer, will perhaps give a sufficient understanding of his methods and his purpose. It goes without the saying, for instance, that his plan is elaborately comprehensive. It is a far step from the times of the flourishing, but pagan and decadent, Roman empire to the opening of the twentieth century. The long ages that intervene are not those of inactivity. They ring with the hymns of early worshipers in the catacombs, the voices of disputants in the great councils, the tread of armies enlisted in religious wars, the anathemas of popes and the defiance of reformers, the impassioned words of evangelists and the cry of the multitudes for salvation.

Only a patient and brave historian would essay the task of sweeping so
large a field. We cannot wonder at the statement which is made by Dr.
Dryer that he has spent years in the preparation of his volumes. Inci-
dentally to turn his pages is to realize his herculean labor. Nor has he
written in the narrow spirit of a mere compiler of historic data. But,
with the synthetic instinct of the true philosopher, he relates the secular
to the religious and finds a close and vital connection between the first
and the second. So it is that, intermixed with the events directly relating
to the growth of the Church, we sometimes find the description of the
existing social and governmental conditions which have prevailed in the
successive ages; or, sometimes, the enumeration of those movements in
literature, in the arts and sciences, and in discovery which have enriched
human life; or, sometimes, the names of the great world leaders whose
deeds are immortal. Choosing at random, the reader discovers the mention of the social fabric of Rome, with its aristocracy and its slaves; the
portrayal of the fascinating Elizabethan reign; the thrilling story of the
Puritans; and the last "political and social progress of Great Britain."
Here is told at length the story of the Renaissance, with references to
Angelo, Dante, Petrarch, and more. Here the caravels of Columbus move
across the sea; here Copernicus and Galileo sweep the heavens; here great
inventions are catalogued, from that of printing, in the fifteenth century,
to that of the telephone, at the close of the nineteenth. And here such
literary lights as Chaucer, Shakespeare, and Bacon, with many others,
shed their luster on the scene. So that we forget, for a moment, that we
are turning volumes of Church history, and seem rather to be wandering
in the enchanting fields of history general. And yet these digressions
are the means to an important end; and by them the settings of the
great religious movements Dr. Dryer describes are made more distinct.
A third characteristic of these volumes is therefore their vivid quality.
"To read history," the author in one instance says among his advices,
"read it first as you would a novel." In this spirit he has made his pages
interesting for his readers. None of them are dull, while at times he
has vitalized the scene and caused the past to throb with life. In his
chapter entitled "Pictures from Mediæval Life," for instance, he draws
this sketch of the English peasant on a beautiful morning in June: "He
looks toward the parish church as the bell strikes the hour of prayer, and
he vaguely feels all Christians pray together then. He feels that the
church is his; about it lie buried his kindred of the generations gone;
its service and festivals break the narrow round of his daily life; it brings
thoughts of a better life beyond this, if also of terror for his sins and
dread of purgatory. In the great hours of his family life, in marriage
and baptism, in sickness and death, at any time of distress, he feels he
has the right to the service and sympathy of the priest, who can bring
something of the infinite power of God and comfort of Holy Mother
Church to his heart and life." And so it is that the narrative is always
attractive, and sometimes takes on the character of the enchanting. It
is important to state that the last three volumes are devoted to the discussion of the modern Church. With the fifth, which opens with the

tragedies of the French Revolution, we begin to breathe the air of recent times. A mention of some of the chapters in this closing volume will show its important character. They include "The Evangelical Church in Germany," in which Dr. Dryer traces the work of many conspicuous scholars of that land and describes the work of Higher Criticism; "The Evangelical Church in Great Britain and Ireland;" "The Christian Church in the United States," covering its development in the last fifty years of the nineteenth century, and including matter that is encyclopædic; "Eastern Christendom;" "Outer Christendom," or the present mission fields of the Church; and "Characteristics and Tendencies." Among the last, he holds, are the movement toward organic union—as seen in the Presbyterian Churches of the United States and the Methodist bodies of Canada and Australia—and that for "the Christian conquest of the world." On this he writes: "Compare the position of the Christian Church at the beginning of Napoleon's consulate and at the death of Queen Victoria, and there is no other contrast in the history of the century so striking and so significant. To the high service of this purpose have come all revision of creeds and liturgies, and searching criticism of the Bible text and authorship. Christians bring a better Bible, a more united and better Church, than ever before to the non-Christian millions of the world. What will not serve this purpose must soon drop away. Our Lord shall see of the travail of his soul and be satisfied." And so this volume closes in that spirit of Christian optimism which expects nothing less than the universal dominion of the Church of Christ, and which prays, "Thy kingdom come." Of other general characteristics of these books it is not now possible to speak—including the generally impartial spirit in which Dr. Dryer has discussed all phases of his theme; or the voluminous citations of "Literature" found in each work and evidencing the wide research of the author in different languages and lands. To write a "popular history of the Christian Church"—in harmony with a long conviction of its need—has been the author's purpose. A purpose fully accomplished.

A Short History of Ancient Peoples. By ROBINSON SOUTTAR, M.A., D.C.L. With an Introduction by the Rev. A. H. SAYCE, M.A., D.D., Professor of Assyriology at Oxford. Large 8vo, pp. xxi, 728. London: Hodder & Stoughton. Imported by Charles Scribner's Sons, New York. Price, cloth, $3.

The wide range of this volume may be indicated by a summary list of the peoples whose history is comprised within it. In the order in which they stand in the book they are as follows: Egypt, Babylonia, Assyria, Medes and Persians, Hebrews, Phœnicia, Carthage, Greece, Rome. The history begins with the early kings of Egypt who are apparently (the author is not very definite) dated about 4000 B. C., and it concludes with the Emperor Augustus at A. D. 14, and with these words: "We have now carried the history of Rome over a period of eight centuries. We have seen the hamlet develop into a village, the village into a town, the town into a great city, the city into a mighty empire. We have watched also the process of political development, the patriarchal community, the monarchy, the republic, and now the rule of the one man, autocrat in all but name. The scheme of the present work renders it impossible to

carry the narrative farther here. The Roman empire continued to influence the world, and to be of high importance for centuries. It even extended its boundaries in certain directions before it began to decline, and
at last to fall. But the interesting story of its grandeur and decay must
be left for another volume." The book is admirably written, the style is
dignified and worthy, and betokens the man of fine culture and wide reading. It is interesting withal, nay, even entertaining, and many would find
it a very useful introduction to that wonderful ancient world, of which
even the fairly well educated know so sadly little. The only safe guide
for the future is the past, and if our break with the past be sharp we shall
readily become the prey of the demagogue. How few are the allusions
to the great leaders and great historic movements of other ages and climes
found in current American newspapers! And who shall deny that the
editors are right in the judgment that few of their readers would comprehend them? For the many who need to learn the simplest facts about
the general movements of the past we may commend this work, but with
the keen regret that we can give it no higher praise. At the very first
glance the book awakens suspicion of the author's acquaintance with the
literature of his subject. The List of Authorities is printed on pages
xxiii and xxiv, and a sorry list it is. The first surprising lack to be
observed is that not one single book in French or German is mentioned.
It puzzles us to comprehend how any man could possibly assume to guide
others who did not himself know the leaders in his subject. It is idle to
dispute that some of the greatest historical work of modern times has
been done in Germany. We have no right to ask Dr. Souttar to produce
an historical work based on original sources. He was not planning to do
that, and there is always room for the skillful and learned popularizer.
But we may rightly insist that the popularizer shall command at least the
literature of his subject in German and French. Dr. Souttar ought to
have had by him Eduard Meyer's *Geschichte des Alterthums,* Maspero's
Contes populaires de l'Egypte ancienne, W. Max Müller's *Die Liebes
Poesie der alten Ægypten,* Meyer's *Geschichte des alten Ægypten,* W. Max
Müller's *Asien und Europa,* Erman's *Ægypten,* Hommel's, Tiele's, and
Winckler's *Babylonisch-Assyrische Geschichten,* and so on through scores
of volumes dealing not only with the Orient but with Greece and Rome.
But to make the case much worse, Dr. Souttar does not use the latest ma-
terial in English. Where is Holm's *History of Greece,* Rogers's *Baby-
lonia and Assyria,* Kent's and Ottley's *Histories of the Hebrews,* Petrie's
History of Egypt (Budge's *History of Egypt* probably appeared too recently), Winckler's *El-Amarna Letters,* Wellhausen's *History of Israel,*
Smith's *Historical Geography of the Holy Land,* and so on indefinitely?
The English-speaking peoples are long-suffering indeed, but their patience
ought long since to have been exhausted by the appearance of books written
by men who had made no pretense to know the latest word of exact
scholarship. This lack of acquaintance with recent literature has vitiated
what might otherwise have been an admirable book. The author has the
skill of a ready writer, he has imagination, and he has a persuasive manner. But the book has errors and careless statements a-plenty. Here are

a few specimens: "When Callisthenes visited Babylon in the train of Alexander the Great, he found and sent home to Aristotle copies of astronomical observations and calculations dating from B. C. 2000" (p. 80). Now Simplicius asserts that Callisthenes found observations extending back 31,000 years! Lehmann tries to show that they really go back only to 2233 B. C., but this rests on a supposed error in a translation and we have no proof of it. This is a fair specimen of many loose and inaccurate statements in the book. Karrak (p. 85), according to modern reading, ought to be Isin. Ramman-nirari III (p. 89) is now called Adad-nirari III. "The Sabbath was observed by both Assyrians and Babylonians as a day of rest, on the seventh, fourteenth, twenty-first, and twenty-eighth days of the lunar month" (p. 111). Perhaps there is some truth in this, but it is not yet proved. We have the "Sabbath" Calendar for only two months in the year, namely, Elul and Marcheshwan, and in that calendar the nineteenth day is also included. We do not know whether this *Sabbatu* ran through the year or not, and if Dr. Souttar were an accurate and painstaking student he would never have spoken in such cheerful carelessness. On page 115 there is mentioned a King Tiglath-Bir I. This is the king who is called in all recent books Tukulti-Ninib; the former reading is used apparently by nobody but Professor Sayce, and if Dr. Souttar chose to follow his reading he ought at least to have given the alternate reading used by all other modern scholars. The name Rimmon occurs frequently in Dr. Souttar's pages, and this also is due to Professor Sayce, for other scholars have used the form Ramman until quite recent times, when they have all abandoned it for Adad, and Professor Sayce now uses Hadad (see his Gifford Lectures). "Ethbaal was king of Tyre when Phœnicia came into conflict with Assyria" (p. 288), but the Old Testament quite clearly calls him the king of Sidon (1 Kings xvi, 31), and there is no reason to doubt the accuracy of this statement. He became ruler practically of all Phœnicia, and from Menander Dr. Souttar must have derived the word "Tyre." "The date of the founding of Carthage is generally placed a century before that of Rome [i. e., 853 B. C.], and this is probably as good an approximation as we need desire in a matter so indefinite" (p. 307). But Timæus and Menander place the founding of Carthage in 814-3, during the reign of Pygmalion, and this ought to have been stated, instead of the loose mention which we have quoted. Such inaccurate, indefinite, or erroneous statements might be multiplied indefinitely, and a book thus written can hardly be commended without much misgiving. The book was printed at the Aberdeen University Press, which is the same thing as saying that it is exceedingly well printed, and though bulky it is light and not inconvenient to handle.

MISCELLANEOUS.

Sunday Talks on Nature Topics. By D. A. JORDAN, D.D. 12mo, pp. 133. New York: Eaton & Mains. Cincinnati: Jennings & Pye. Price, cloth, 75 cents.

These are short talks from the pulpit to children and youth. They are adapted to awaken and hold the interested attention of the young, to

instruct in many of the facts and processes of nature, using those facts in a way to suggest various valuable moral lessons. The *Talks* tell the story of how the world came to be, and how the soil was made, and what sort of workmen God employed to crush the rocks into soil and pulverize it and plow it and get it ready to bring forth crops of all kinds. They tell of seeds and how they are scattered and planted by winds and birds and squirrels and rabbits; of the wonders of growth, its power and its conditions; of harvest, enforcing the lesson that we will reap what we sow; of frost and snow and the beauty of snow-crystals and the use of snow and glaciers and icebergs; of clouds and fogs and vapors and rain; and of quaint Easter customs, with the meaning of Easter. All these wonders of Nature, described in terms intelligible to children, are made to fix spiritual lessons in young minds. The simple picture-illustrations serve to make the *Talks* still plainer. Dr. Jordan believes with Horace Bushnell that it is our privilege and duty, as preachers of Christ, to do more preaching to children. For years he has practiced on this conviction with eminent success. In this little book he presents some of the pulpit talks which have made his ministry attractive and edifying to the young. The progress of child-study in our day renders it probable that we shall have an increase of this sort of preaching in the near future. To have no children in our pews is wrong. To have them there, but understanding nothing of what the preacher says, is not ideal. To make them like to be there is a triumph. Often the children listen to us with the feeling expressed by a seven-year-old girl who went across the street one morning to look at an Annual Conference which was in session in her church. She soon returned home, explaining to her mother, "They all talked great big grown-up things, so I comed away." That little girl is now a missionary in India.

The Illustrative Lesson Notes for 1904. By Thomas B. Neely, D.D., LL.D., assisted by Robert R. Doherty, Ph.D., and Rev. Henry H. Meyer, A.M. 8vo. New York: Eaton & Mains. Cincinnati: Jennings & Pye. Price, cloth, $1.25.

In the preparation of this standard annual unusual care has been taken. For a quarter of a century the "Illustrative Notes" have enriched the libraries of Sunday school workers with their treasures of knowledge. While no amount of aid can render less imperative the necessity of studying God's word "without note or comment," yet such helps as this volume affords are of inestimable value to the most diligent students of the Scriptures. The treasures of the standard commentaries, exegetical, homiletical, and practical, in condensed form are here presented. In addition thereto hundreds of maps, pictorial illustrations, and blackboard diagrams render the exposition of the lessons by both teachers and reviewers at once easy and interesting. The volume is indispensable not only to teachers, but likewise to advanced students of the word in Bible classes. Privileged indeed are these workers, since concerning them it may be affirmed, "Other men labored, and ye are entered into their labors."

CPSIA information can be obtained
at www.ICGtesting.com
Printed in the USA
BVHW04*1753190818
524841BV00015B/400/P